"Car dealers take advantage of their knowledge and the customer's lack of knowledge... Edmund's New Car Prices... provides standard costs for cars and optional items."

—Steve Ross, **Successful Car Buying**
(Harrisburg, PA: Stackpole Books, 1990)

"Never pay retail. Buy only at wholesale or below. When buying a car, it is imperative that you know the dealer's cost. Refer to Edmund's ...price guides for current dealer cost information. Armed with this information, you can determine the price that provides the dealer with a minimum 'win' profit."

—Lisa Murr Chapman, **The Savvy Woman's Guide to Cars**
(New York, NY: Bantam Books, 1995)

"How much should you pay for a new car?... Your goal is to buy the car for the lowest price at which the dealer will sell it... To be accurate about profit margins, you should use the most recent edition of Edmund's New Car Prices."

—Dr. Leslie R. Sachs, **How to Buy Your Next Car For a Rock Bottom Price** (New York: Signet, 1986)

"Edmund's publishes a variety of useful guides... buy the guide that deals specifically with the type of car you need.

Wouldn't it be nice if you could know beforehand the dealer's cost for the new vehicle you just fell in love with? Wouldn't it be even nicer if you knew how much to offer him over his costs, a price he would just barely be able to accept?

Well you are in luck. You can find out exactly what the car cost the dealership ...in Edmund's auto books."

—Burke Leon, **The Insider's Guide to Buying A New or Used Car** (Cincinnati, OH: Betterway Books, 1993)

Most people have three things in common when they buy a car.

Edmund's Perfect Partners

USED CARS: PRICES & RATINGS

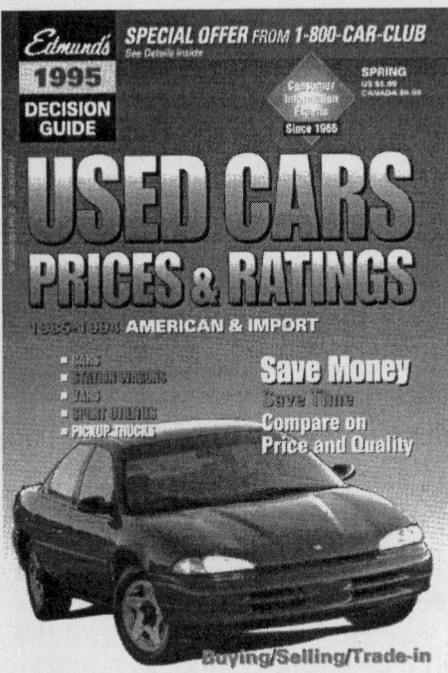

For 30 years, Edmund's has guided smart consumers through the complex used car marketplace. By providing you with the latest wholesale and retail pricing, you are able to determine fair market value before negotiations begin.

Whether buying, selling, or trading, Edmund's *Used Cars: Prices & Ratings* gives all the information you need to get your very best deal.

√ Prices All American and Imported Used Cars, Pickup Trucks, Vans, and Sport Utilities

√ Shows Summary Ratings Graphs for Most Used Vehicles

√ Listings Cover Models Over Last 10 Years

√ Price any Vehicle Quickly and Accurately

√ Adjust Value for Optional Equipment and Mileage

Edmund's *Used Cars: Prices & Ratings* takes on a completely new organization and format, designed for your ease of use...

***For information on all Edmund's Automotive Books, call* 914-962-6297**

1995

Edmund's

NEW CAR PRICES

BUYER'S GUIDE

"THE ORIGINAL CONSUMER PRICE AUTHORITY"

Publisher: Peter Steinlauf

Cover photo:
1995 Dodge Stratus ES

Published by:
Edmund Publications Corp.
300 N. Sepulveda, Ste. 2050
El Segundo, CA 90245

ISBN: 0-87759-474-0
ISSN: 1047-0751
Library of Congress Catalog
Card No: 71-80100

Editor-in-Chief
Michael G. Samet, Ph. D.

Automotive Editors:
William Badnow
Christian Wardlaw

Creative Design:
Debra Katzir

Cover Design:
David Allen

Information Specialists:
Victor Friedman
Alexander Friedman

Advertising Manager:
Brenda Davis

Printed in the United States

NEW CAR BUYER'S GUIDE

TABLE OF CONTENTS

SUMMER/FALL 1995 **VOL N2902-9512**

Look for Edmund's NEW Audio Tape offer on page 437

SPECIAL OFFER from 1-800-CAR-CLUB details on page 3

INTRODUCTION 1

Since 1966, Edmund's has been providing consumers with the ammunition they need to get the best price on a new car. This edition of *New Car Prices* continues the tradition of listing most of the cars available on the market today, including pricing data for dealer invoice cost and Manufacturer's Suggested Retail Price (MSRP) on the vehicles and their available accessories. We also include detailed descriptions of the standard equipment available on each car across all trim levels, specifications for each model, and helpful articles that will allow you to make an educated decision about your purchase.

New for 1995 is our easy-to-use format, which combines all American and imported vehicles in one guide, allowing our readers to compare alternative automobiles regardless of their country of origin. Please note that *New Car Prices* includes only cars; all pickup trucks, minivans and sport utilities can be found in Edmund's *New Pickup, Van & Sport Utility Prices*. For the convenience of our readers, we include station wagon models in both books.

The format of this guide is patterned after the familiar dictionary model, with the automobiles listed alphabetically according to make, and then to model; you may use the tabs on the sides of the pages of the book to easily locate a make, or glance at the top corner of the page to find the model that you want.

Each listing offers a representative photograph of the model, followed by the base dealer invoice cost and base MSRP. The destination charge is also listed, and don't forget to add it to the base price of the vehicle when making your calculations. Following the base price information is a listing of the vehicle's standard equipment. The first standard equipment paragraph pertains to the base model of the vehicle listed. If more than one trim level is available on the vehicle, successive paragraphs explain what additional features the higher trim levels include over the base model.

Following the standard equipment descriptions, you can find listings of the accessories, or options, that are available on the vehicle. For most of these accessories, a factory code is provided in the column bordering the left margin. Each accessory has the dealer invoice cost and MSRP listed. Additionally, some of the options have short descriptions that tell you, for example, what might be included in a particular option package, or that you must purchase the power lock group to get the power sunroof.

Some imports do not have an options listing. This is because the automaker includes the most popular accessories as the standard equipment on a particular trim level, and any additional items you might like to add to the vehicle will have to be purchased separately from the dealer or are installed on the vehicle at the port of entry. For example, the Honda Civic EX Coupe comes with power door locks, power windows, a power sunroof, upgraded engine and six-speaker stereo standard from the factory. Air Conditioning is a dealer add-on, and each dealer may price the item differently. Generally, you can haggle about 15% off the price of most dealer accessories.

In using this guide, it might be necessary for you to copy the information from the window sticker on the vehicle you are considering, and then refer to the listings herein to find out the dealer's cost (see our article regarding dealer holdbacks for help in calculating a 'fair' price). However, car sales have been hot, and new models like the Dodge Stratus are in high demand, so don't expect big price discounts from dealers. In fact, until the supply of these models satisfies demand, you might find dealers adding an additional profit surcharge to the MSRP, and expecting to get it.

Speaking of hot new models, by the time you read this, Acura and Infiniti will have introduced the new 1996 TL-Series and I30, respectively, and BMW will be offering a hatchback version of the popular 3-Series. Unfortunately, at the time we went to press on this issue, the prices for these cars had not been made available. They should be now, and you can obtain them by calling 1-900-AUTOPRO ($2.00 per minute). Please see the ad on the inside back cover of this book for details.

At the back of the book, we have grouped specifications of all the vehicles listed within, so that you can easily compare dimensions, capacities and other such data between different models and trim levels.

New Car Prices has even more to offer, from step-by-step costing forms that you can use right at the dealership, to articles that provide you with the information you need to make an informed decision about a new vehicle. Edmund's strives to give you precise, accurate data so that you can make your very best deal, and we'd love to hear your comments and suggestions regarding this book. Please send correspondence to:

Edmund Publications Corporation
300 N. Sepulveda Blvd., Suite 2050
El Segundo, CA 90245
Attn: Automotive Editor

We wish you luck in your hunt for a new vehicle, and in your use of the information provided here to your advantage!

Traction Control: Do you need it? Yes!

We just spent several hundred miles behind the wheel of a Ford Thunderbird LX, equipped with Ford's magnificent 4.6-liter V-8 engine and traction control. The V-8 T-Bird is powerful, fast, and is driven by the rear wheels. This combination is fine for dry, fair weather climates and for conducting adolescent experiments that focus on the effects of heat and friction on rubber, but in the rain and snow a drivetrain such as the one in our Thunderbird makes for nightmarish driving conditions.

Not so in the Thunderbird with traction control. The system cuts power to the rear wheels as they slip, and gives the hefty T-Bird good grip in a variety of conditions. Fortunately, a button that shuts the system off resides in the center console for those times when wheelspin is a good thing, like rocking yourself out of the snowdrift the plow left at the foot of your driveway, or terrorizing the neighbors with smoky 4,000 rpm burnouts at the stop sign... not that we condone that sort of thing.

Traction control is becoming as important a safety feature on modern cars as anti-lock brake systems (ABS) have, but like ABS, they require a shift in traditional driving styles to take advantage of their benefits. If you buy a car equipped with traction control, find a deserted and safe place to test out some of the characteristics of the particular system you have. Often, manufacturers will provide detailed instructions inside the owner's manual, which is that silly little book you got for free when you bought the car. It usually sits in the glovebox. Read it.

There are three types of traction control, and we'll briefly outline each system.

1) Limited-slip differential. This system transfers engine torque to the wheel that has the best traction in any given situation. It is not an electronic system, and generally doesn't perform as well as newer types of traction control. Modern limited-slip differentials are able to transfer power to the good wheel before slippage occurs, however, if both wheels are on a slippery surface, this system will leave you just as stuck as a car without it.

2) Brake System Traction Control. Working just like ABS in reverse, this type of system uses the same sensors and hardware that ABS does to apply the brakes and keep a wheel from spinning. Each wheel is individually controlled, making this setup a perfect match for a variety of slippery surfaces. Generally inexpensive and highly effective, this system is designed for low speed slippage. Because the braking components are used, higher speed slip control would generate too much friction and heat, damaging the braking components.

3) Drivetrain Traction Control. Our Thunderbird was equipped with this system, which retards power delivery to the slipping wheel or wheels at any speed. Using the same ABS-type sensors as the brake system traction control setup, this one employs a processor that will do one of four things: (a) close the throttle, which is how the cheapest of these systems works; (b) cut the fuel supply; (c) retard spark timing; or (d) shut down cylinders. The most advanced drivetrain traction control systems will do all of these things, plus push the accelerator against your foot to tell you it's working. Because this system cuts power in all slippery situations, a button is almost always provided to turn the system off for situations where slippage is desired.

Our experience with traction control has convinced us that it is one more in a series of important automotive safety breakthroughs. We highly recommend it, especially for people who commonly drive in adverse weather conditions.

Understanding the Language of Auto Buying

Many consumers are justifiably confused by the language and terms used by automobile manufacturers and dealers. To assist you, here are some basic definitions:

MSRP — Manufacturer's Suggested Retail Price The manufacturer's recommended selling price for a vehicle and each of its optional accessories.

Dealer Invoice The amount that dealers are invoiced or billed by the manufacturer for a vehicle and each of its optional accessories.

Dealer Holdback Many manufacturers provide dealers with a *holdback allowance* (usually between 2 and 3% of MSRP) which is eventually credited to the dealer's account. That way, the dealer can end up paying the manufacturer less than the invoiced amount — meaning that they could sell you the vehicle at cost and still make a small profit. Holdback is also known as a 'pack.'

Destination Charge The fee charged for shipping, freight, or delivery of the vehicle to the dealer from the manufacturer or Port of Entry. This charge is passed on to the buyer without any mark-up.

Preparation Charges These are dealer-imposed charges for getting the new car ready to drive away including a full tank of gas, checking and filling the fluid levels, making sure the interior and exterior is clean, etc.

Dealer Charges These are highly profitable extras that dealers try to sell in addition to the vehicle itself. Items such as rustproofing, undercoating and extended warranties fall into this category. Most consumer experts do not recommend the purchase of these extras.

Advertising Fee The amount you are charged to cover the cost of national and local advertising. This fee should be no more than 1-1½% of the MSRP.

Manufacturer's Rebate/Dealer Incentives Programs offered by the manufacturers to increase the sales of slow-selling models or to reduce excess inventories. While manufacturer's rebates are passed directly on to the buyer, dealer incentives are passed on only to the dealer — who may or may not elect to pass the savings on to the customer.

Trade-in Value The amount that the dealership will give you for the vehicle you trade in. Generally, this amount will be about 5% below wholesale value of the vehicle. The trade-in value will be deducted from the price of the new vehicle.

Upside-down When you owe more on your car loan than your trade-in is worth, you are *upside-down* on your trade. When this happens, the dealer will add the difference between the trade-in value and what you owe to the price of the new vehicle.

Note: Occasionally there will appear in the "Dealer Invoice" and "MSRP" columns, prices enclosed in parenthesis, example: (90), which indicate a credit or refunded amount is involved.

ABBREVIATIONS

16V	16 Valve Engine
2WD	Two Wheel Drive
3A/4A	3-Speed/4-Speed Automatic
4M/5M/6M	4-Speed/5-Speed/ 6-Speed Manual
4SP	4 Speed Transmission
4SPD	4 Speed Transmission
4WD	Four Wheel Drive
4WS	Four Wheel Steering
5SP	5 Speed Transmission
5SPD	5 Speed Transmission
5SPD/AT	5 Speed, Automatic Transmission
6SP	6 Speed Transmission
6SPD	6 Speed Transmission
ABS	Anti-Lock Braking System
AC	Air Conditioning
ADJ	Adjustable, Aduster
AIR COND	Air Conditioning
ALT	Alternator
ALUM	Aluminum
AMP	Amperes
ANT	Antenna
AT	Automatic Transmission
AUTO	Automatic
AUX	Auxiliary
AVAIL	Available
AWD	All Wheel Drive
BLK	Black
BSW, BW	Black Sidewall (tires)
CAP	Capacity
CASS	Cassette
CD	Compact Disc
CFC	Chloroflorocarbon
CNTRY	Country
COL	Column
CONV	Convertible
CPE	Coupe
CRS	Cruise
CTRL	Control
CUST	Custom
CU IN	Cubic Inches
CVRS	Covers
CYL	Cylinder
DFRS	Dual Facing Rear Seats
DLX	Deluxe
DOHC	Dual Overhead Camshaft
DR	Door
DRW	Dual Rear Wheels
EFI	Electronic Fuel Injection
ELEC	Electronic, Electronically
ENG	Engine
EQUIP	Equipment
ETR	Electronically Tuned Radio
EXT	Extended, Exterior
F&R	Front & Rear
FBK	Fastback
FI	Fuel Injection
FRT	Front
FS	Flareside
F/S	Fleetside
FWD	Front Wheel Drive
GAL	Gallon
GRP	Group
GVW	Gross Vehicle Weight
GVWR	Gross Vehicle Weight Rating
HBK	Hatchback
HD	Heavy Duty
HO	High Output
HP	Horsepower
HUD	Heads Up Display
HVAC	Heating/Ventilation/Air Conditioning
HVY	Heavy
HT	Hardtop
ILLUM	Illuminated, Illumination
INCLS	Includes
INCLD	Included
INJ	Injection
INT	Interior
L	Liter
LB	Longbed
LBK	Liftback
LBS	Pounds
LD	Light Duty
LH	Left Hand
LKS	Locks
LR	Left Rear
LTD	Limited

LTHR	Leather
LUGRK	Luggage Rack
LUX	Luxury
LWB	Long Wheelbase
LWR	Lower
MAN	Manual
MAX	Maximum
MED	Medium
MIN	Minimum
MLDGS	Moldings
MPI, MPFI	Multi-Port Fuel Injection
MPG	Miles Per Gallon
MPH	Miles Per Hour
MT	Manual Transmission
NA, N/A	Not Available, Not Applicable
NBK	Notchback
NC	No Charge
OD	Overdrive
OHC	Overhead Camshaft
OHV	Overhead Valves
OPT	Optional
OS	Outside
OZ	Ounce
P/U	Pickup Truck
PASS	Passenger
PDL	Power Door Locks
PEG	Preferred Equipment Group
PEP	Preferred Equipment Package
PERF	Performance
PGM FI	Programmed Fuel Injection
PKG	Package
PKUP	Pickup Truck
PNT	Paint
PREM	Premium
PS	Power Steering
PW	Power Windows
PWR	Power
QTR	Quarter
RDSTR	Roadster
REQ	Requires
RH	Right Hand
R, RR	Rear
RPM	Revolutions Per Minute
RWD	Rear Wheel Drive
RWL (Tires)	Raised White Letters
SB	Shortbed
SBR (Tires)	Steel Belted Radial
SDN	Sedan
SEFI, SFI	Sequential Fuel Injection
SFTTP	Soft Top
SNRF, S/R	Sunroof
SOHC	Single Overhead Camshaft
SP, SPD	Speed
SPFI	Sequential Port Fuel Injection
SPKRS	Speakers
SPT	Sport
SRS	Supplemental Restraint System (Airbag)
SRW	Single Rear Wheels
ST	Seat(s)
STD	Standard
STS	Seats
SU	Sport Utility
SW	Station Wagon
SWB	Short Wheelbase
SYNC	Synchromesh, Synchronized
SYS	System
TACH	Tachometer
TBI	Throttle Body Injection
TEMP	Temperature
TP	Tape
TPI	Tuned Port Injection
TRANS	Transmission
TRBO	Turbo
TURB	Turbo
VOL	Volume
W/	With
W/O	Without
W/T	Work Truck
WB	Wheelbase
WGN	Wagon
WHL(S)	Wheel(s)
WS	Wideside
WSW, WW	White Sidewall (tires)

How to Buy Your Next New Automobile

Every new automobile buyer has but one thought in mind - to save money by getting a good deal. Your goal should be to pay 2-5% over the dealer invoice, not the 8-10% the dealer wants you to pay. To select a dealer who will appreciate your Edmund's-supplied knowledge of dealer costs, check the Automobile Dealer Directory at the back of this book. Use the following guide to help you plan your new vehicle purchase:

Step 1 Study alternatives carefully and choose the make, model and accessories you want.

Step 2 Visit a local dealership to test drive the model you intend to buy. Pay special attention to safety features, performance factors, design and comfort, visibility, handling, acceleration and braking, ride quality, etc.

Step 3 Once you've decided on a particular model, check with your insurance company to make sure the cost of insuring the vehicle falls within your budget.

Step 4 Contact your bank or credit union to obtain loan-rate information. Later on, you can compare their arrangement with the dealer's financing plan.

Step 5 Use the information in this book to determine the dealer's actual cost. Then...

a) Total the dealer invoice column for the model and equipment you want using the costing form on the opposite page.

b) To this total, add destination and preparation charges, dealer extras and the advertising fee.

c) Add to the dealer's cost what you think is a reasonable dealer profit (on most vehicles, a reasonable amount is 2-3% over invoice — this excludes hot selling models which will command a higher dealer profit). *Remember the dealer also makes an additional profit because of the dealer holdback..*

Step 6 Bargain for the best price — visit several dealerships. The dealer who comes closest to your "target price" should get your business. Be sure that the dealer's price quote will be your final cost. Beware of extra dealer charges! Don't buy items such as rustproofing, undercoating, extended warranties, etc., unless you really want them.

Step 7 Deduct any manufacturer's rebates or dealer incentives from your final cost.

Step 8 If your present vehicle will be used as a trade-in, negotiate the highest possible value for it. Try to accept an amount that is not less than 3% below the trade-in vehicle's wholesale value. (Consult Edmund's *Used Car Prices & Ratings* book). If you trade-in your old vehicle, deduct its agreed-upon value from the cost of the new vehicle. If you owe more on your trade-in than the dealer will give you for it, you are *upside-down* on your trade and must add your *trade-in deficit* at this point.

Step 9 Add applicable state and/or local taxes and registration fees.

Step 10 Enjoy your new vehicle, knowing that you did everything to get the best possible deal.

Alternatively, if you want to save lots of time and effort, call 1-800-CAR-CLUB (1-800-227-2582). Their expert buyers will find the exact vehicle you want at a dealer near you, and they will negotiate the best and final price, which could be less than 2% over the total invoice amount. They will even arrange competitive financing or an attractive lease for you in many markets.

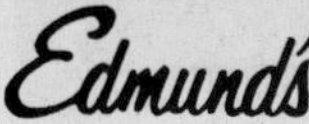

STEP-BY-STEP COSTING FORM

MAKE: EXTERIOR COLOR:

MODEL: INTERIOR COLOR:

BODY STYLE: ENGINE SIZE/TYPE:

ITEMS	MSRP	INVOICE	BEST DEAL
Basic Model Price Only			
Optional Equipment/Accessories			
1.			
2.			
3.			
4.			
5.			
6.			
7.			
8.			
9.			
10.			
11.			
12.			
13.			
14.			
TOTAL			
SUBTRACT Rebate Amount			
ADD Destination Charge			
ADD Preparation Charge			
ADD Dealer Charges ("Extras")			
ADD Advertising Fee			
ADD Dealer Profit			
SUBTRACT "Trade-In" Amount or ADD "Trade-In" Deficit			
FINAL PRICE			
ADD Sales Taxes and Fees			
TOTAL COST			

DEALER HOLDBACKS 1

Look in last Sunday's newspaper, and you will likely find a car dealer advertising inventory at one dollar below dealer invoice. Many people discount proclamations such as these, thinking that there's gotta be a catch. Yes, there is. The dealer is most likely receiving some factory incentives to move the merchandise, and will be keeping any rebates currently available on the car. Additionally, the dealer probably has profit built into every vehicle they sell. That built in profit is called a holdback, or *pack.*

You should take dealer holdback into consideration when bargaining the price of a new car or truck. Since dealer holdbacks are usually about 3% of the MSRP amount, you ought negotiate the price of the car down to about 2% above the dealer invoice amounts listed in this guide, after subtracting dealer incentives and rebates. You get a sweet deal, and the dealer makes approximately 5% profit on the car.

For example, take a Ford Probe GT with package 263A, anti-lock brakes and leather seats. Retail price of such a vehicle would be $21,480 including destination charges. Dealer invoice would be $19,366, which includes a holdback of 3% of the MSRP, amounting to $644 of built-in profit to the dealer. The price you should shoot for in negotiations is $19,753 (2% above dealer invoice of $19,366), which would still give the dealer a profit of $1,031 or about 5% of his actual cost.

Now assume that this particular Probe qualifies for a $500 rebate. Deduct the $500 from the dealer invoice price of $19,366, **before** adding the 2% profit. Ask if the dealer qualifies for any factory incentives, and deduct that amount from the invoice price as well. To get the latest information on rebates and incentives, go to your local library and consult the lastest issue of *Automotive News,* or, call the dealer anonymously and inquire about them. Good luck!

DEALER HOLDBACKS 2

Make	Holdback
Acura	No holdbacks
Alfa Romeo	Unknown
Audi	No holdbacks
BMW	2% of the MSRP
Buick	3% of the MSRP
Cadillac	3% of the MSRP
Chevrolet	3% of the MSRP
Chrysler	3% of the MSRP
Dodge	3% of the MSRP
Eagle	3% of the MSRP
Ford	3% of the MSRP
Geo	3% of the MSRP
GMC	3% of the MSRP
Honda	Unknown
Hyundai	No holdbacks
Infiniti	No holdbacks
Isuzu	3% of the MSRP
Jaguar	2% of the MSRP
Jeep	3% of the MSRP
Kia	Unknown
Land Rover	Unknown
Lexus	No holdbacks
Mazda	No holdbacks
Mercedes-Benz	No holdbacks
Mercury	3% of the MSRP
Mitsubishi	2% of dealer invoice
Nissan	3% of MSRP
Oldsmobile	3% of MSRP
Plymouth	3% of the MSRP
Pontiac	3% of the MSRP
Porsche	No holdbacks
Saab	3% of the MSRP
Saturn	Unknown
Subaru	3% of the MSRP
Suzuki	No holdbacks
Toyota	2% of MSRP in Alabama, Georgia, Florida, South Carolina & North Carolina only
Volkswagen	2% of the MSRP
Volvo	$700 on the 850; $900 on the 940 & 960

WARRANTIES & ROADSIDE ASSISTANCE

All new vehicles sold in America come with at least two warranties, and many include roadside assistance. Described below are the major types of warranties and assistance provided to consumers.

Basic. Your basic warranty covers everything except items subject to wear and tear, such as oil filters, wiper blades, and the like. Tires and batteries often have their own warranty coverages, which will be outlined in your owner's manual. Emission equipment is required to be covered for five years or 50,000 miles by the federal government.

Drivetrain. Drivetrain coverage takes care of most of the parts that make the car move, like the engine, transmission, drive axles and driveshaft. Like the basic warranty, parts subject to wear and tear like hoses and belts are not covered. However, most of the internal parts of the engine, such as the pistons and bearings, which are subject to wear and tear are covered by the drivetrain warranty. See your owner's manual or local dealer for specific coverages.

Rust. This warranty protects you from rust-through problems with the sheetmetal. Surface rust doesn't count. The rust must make a hole to be covered by the warranty. Keep your car washed and waxed, and rust shouldn't be a problem.

Roadside Assistance. Most manufacturers provide a service that will rescue you if your car leaves you stranded, even if it's your fault. Lock yourself out of the car ? Somebody will come and open it up. Run out of gas ? Somebody will deliver some fuel. Flat tire ? Somebody will change it for you. See your owner's manual for details, or ask the dealer about the specifics, and don't pay for extended coverage if your insurance company already provides this type of assistance.

WARRANTIES & ROADSIDE ASSISTANCE

Make	Basic (yrs/mi)	Drivetrain (yrs/mi)	Rust (yrs/mi)	Roadside Assistance (yrs/mi)
Acura	4/50,000	4/50,000	4/Unlimited	4/50,000
Alfa Romeo	3/36,000	3/36,000	6/60,000	3/36,000
Audi	3/50,000	3/50,000	10/Unlimited	3/Unlimited
BMW	4/50,000	4/50,000	6/Unlimited	4/50,000
Buick	3/36,000	3/36,000	6/100,000	3/36,000
Cadillac	4/50,000	4/50,000	6/100,000	4/50,000
Chevrolet	3/36,000	3/36,000	6/100,000	3/36,000
Chrysler	3/36,000	3/36,000	7/100,000	3/36,000
Dodge	3/36,000	3/36,000	7/100,000	3/36,000
Eagle	3/36,000	3/36,000	7/100,000	3/36,000
Ford	3/36,000	3/36,000	6/100,000	3/36,000
Geo	3/36,000	3/36,000	6/100,00	3/36,000
GMC	3/36,000	3/36,000	6/100,000	3/36,000
Honda	3/36,000	3/36,000	3/Unlimited	N/A
Hyundai	3/36,000	5/60,000	5/100,000	3/36,000
Infiniti	4/60,000	5/70,000	7/Unlimited	4/60,000
Isuzu	3/50,000	5/60,000	6/100,00	5/60,000
Jaguar	4/50,000	4/50,000	6/Unlimited	4/50,000
Jeep	3/36,000	3/36,000	7/100,000	3/36,000
Kia	3/36,000	5/60,000	5/100,00	3/36,000
Land Rover	3/42,000	3/42,000	6/Unlimited	3/42,000
Lexus	4/50,000	6/70,000	6/Unlimited	4/Unlimited
Lincoln	4/50,000	4/50,000	6/100,000	4/50,000
Mazda	3/50,000	3/50,000	5/Unlimited	3/50,000 (929,Millenia,RX-7only)
Mercedes	4/50,000	4/50,000	4/50,000	Unlimited
Mercury	3/36,000	3/36,000	6/100,000	3/36,000 (Towing only)
Mitsubishi	3/36,000	5/60,000	5/Unlimited	5/60,000
Nissan	3/36,000	5/60,000	5/Unlimited	None Available
Oldsmobile	3/36,000	3/36,000	6/100,000	3/36,000
Plymouth	3/36,000	3/36,000	7/100,000	3/36,000
Pontiac	3/36,000	3/36,000	6/100,000	3/36,000
Porsche	2/Unlimited	2/Unlimited	10/Unlimited	2/Unlimited
Saab	4/50,000	N/A	6/Unlimited	4/50,000
Saturn	3/36,000	3/36,000	6/100,000	3/36,000
Subaru	3/36,000	5/60,000	5/Unlimited	3/36,000 (SVX only)
Suzuki	3/36,000	3/36,000	3/Unlimited	None
Toyota	3/36,000	5/60,000	5/Unlimited	None Available
Volkswagen	2/24,000	10/100,000	6/Unlimited	2/24,000
Volvo	4/50,000	4/50,000	8/Unlimited	4/Unlimited

ACURA

INTEGRA *(1995)*

CODE	DESCRIPTION	INVOICE	MSRP
DC434S	RS 3-Dr Sport Coupe (5-spd)	13581	15460
DC444S	RS 3-Dr Sport Coupe (auto)	14240	16210
DB754S	RS 4-Dr Sedan (5-spd)	14249	16220
DB764S	RS 4-Dr Sedan (auto)	14908	16970
DC435S	LS 3-Dr Sport Coupe (5-spd)	15936	18140
DC445S	LS 3-Dr Sport Coupe (auto)	16595	18890
DB755S	LS 4-Dr Sedan (5-spd)	16639	18940
DB765S	LS 4-Dr Sedan (auto)	17298	19690
DC238S	GS-R 3-Dr Sport Coupe w/Cloth Interior (5-spd)	17877	20350
DC239S	GS-R 3-Dr Sport Coupe w/Leather Interior (5-spd)	18580	21150
DB858S	GS-R 4-Dr Sedan w/Cloth Interior (5-spd)	18168	20680
DB859S	GS-R 4-Dr Sedan w/Leather Interior (5-spd)	18871	21480
DC436S	Special Edition 3-Dr Sport Coupe (5-spd)	17474	19890
DC446S	Special Edition 3-Dr Sport Coupe (auto)	18132	20640
DB756S	Special Edition 4-Dr Sedan (5-spd)	17957	20440
DB766S	Special Edition 4-Dr Sedan (auto)	18616	21190
Destination Charge:		390	390

Standard Equipment

INTEGRA COUPE - RS: 1.8 liter 16-valve DOHC inline 4 cylinder engine, programmed fuel injection (PGM-FI), 5-speed manual transmission, 4-wheel independent double-wishbone suspension, front and rear stabilizer bars, variable power assisted rotary valve rack and pinion steering, 4-wheel disc brakes with ventilated front discs, P195/60R14 85H M+S tires, driver and front passenger air bag SRS, side-impact door beams, side-intrusion hip pads, 3-point outboard seat belts, front and rear 5-mph bumpers, front and rear crumple zones, projector beam headlights, body color front/rear bumpers, dual power operated door mirrors, protective bodyside moldings, rear window defroster with timer, rear window wiper/washer, body color door handles, galvanized body panels, 3-coat

3-bake paint, driver's seat lumbar adjustment, passenger side walk-in seat, center console with armrest, 50/50 fold-down rear seatback, rear seat divider, rear seat headrests, tilt steering wheel, power windows, AM/FM stereo/cassette with 4 speakers, power antenna, intermittent front wipers with mist, remote trunk/fuel filler door releases.

LS (in addition to or instead of RS equipment): Michelin XGT-H4 P195/60R14 85H M+S tires, anti-lock braking system (ABS), air conditioning, cruise control, power door locks, power moonroof, map lights.

SPECIAL EDITION (in addition to or instead of LS equipment): Cast aluminum alloy wheels, Michelin XGT-V4 P195/55R15 84V M+S tires, Special Edition emblem, leather seating and trim, rear spoiler.

GS-R (in addition to or instead of LS equipment): 1.8 liter 16-valve DOHC inline 4 cylinder engine with VTEC, 5-speed manual transmission with close ratios, cast aluminum alloy wheels, Michelin XGT-V4 P195/55R15 84V M+S tires, rear spoiler with integral brake light, AM/FM stereo cassette with 6 speakers.

INTEGRA SEDAN - RS: 1.8 liter 16-valve DOHC inline 4 cylinder engine, programmed fuel injection (PGM-FI), 5-speed manual transmission, 4-wheel independent double-wishbone suspension, front and rear stabilizer bars, variable power assisted rotary-valve rack and pinion steering, 4-wheel disc brakes with ventilated front discs, P195/60R14 85H M+S tires, driver and front passenger air bag SRS, side-impact door beams, side-intrusion hip pads, side intrusion shoulder pads, 3-point outboard seat belts, front and rear 5-mph bumpers, front and rear crumple zones, child-proof rear door locks, projector beam headlights, body color front and rear bumpers, dual power-operated door mirrors, protective bodyside moldings, rear window defroster with timer, body color door handles, sashless door glass, galvanized body panels, 3-coat 3-bake paint, driver seat lumbar adjustment, center console with armrest, one-piece fold-down rear seatback, rear seat headrests, seat belt height adjustment, tilt steering wheel, power windows, power door locks, AM/FM stereo/cassette with 4 speakers, power antenna, intermittent front wipers with mist, remote trunk/fuel filler door releases.

LS (in addition to or instead of RS equipment): Michelin XGT-H4 P195/60R14 85H M+S tires, anti-lock braking system (ABS), air conditioning, cruise control, power moonroof, map lights.

SPECIAL EDITION (in addition to or instead of LS equipment): Cast aluminum alloy wheels, Michelin XGT-V4 P195/55R15 84V M+S tires, Special Edition emblem, leather seating and trim, simulated wood console.

GS-R (in addition to or instead of LS equipment): 1.8 liter 16-valve DOHC inline 4 cylinder engine with VTEC, 5-speed manual transmission with close ratios, cast aluminum alloy wheels, Michelin XGT-V4 P195/55R15 84V M+S tires, AM/FM stereo/cassette with 6 speakers.

Accessories

NOTE: Acura accessories are dealer installed. Contact an Acura dealer for accessory availability.

See the Automobile Dealer Directory on page 448 for a Dealer near you!

ACURA

LEGEND COUPE (1995)

Code	Description	Invoice	MSRP
KA816S	L 2-Dr Coupe (6-spd)	33817	39400
KA826S	L 2-Dr Coupe (auto)	33817	39400
KA17S	LS 2-Dr Coupe (6-spd)	37079	43200
KA27S	LS 2-Dr Coupe (auto)	37079	43200
Destination Charge:		420	420

Standard Equipment

LEGEND COUPE - L: 3.2 liter 24-valve SOHC V6, programmed fuel injection with variable induction system, 6-speed manual transmission, 4-wheel independent double-wishbone suspension, variable power assisted rack and pinion steering, anti-lock brakes, dual airbags, front seat belts with automatic tensioners, variable diameter door beams, 3-point outboard seat belts, 5-mph bumpers, impact-absorption zones, flush-mounted dual lens halogen headlights, tinted glass, dual power heated body color mirrors, protective bodyside body color moldings, rear window defroster with timer, galvanized body panels, 4-coat 4-bake paint, leather-trimmed interior and steering wheel, simulated wood trimmed console and power window controls, driver's 8-way power seat with adjustable lumbar support and memory, fold-down rear center armrest, height and tilt adjustable front headrests, air conditioning, Acura/Bose Music System, steering wheel mounted remote control audio system, pre-wiring for CD changer, power-operated moonroof with sliding shade, power windows with key-off feature, power door locks with driver's side dual unlocking feature, theft-deterrent system, electronic tilt/telescopic steering column with automatic tilt-up, steering wheel memory system, center console with armrest/covered storage compartment/beverage holder.

LS (in addition to or instead of L equipment): Traction control system (TCS), burled walnut-trimmed console and power window controls, front passenger 4-way power seat, heated front seats, automatic climate control, Acura/Bose Premium Music System with 8 speakers (incls AM/FM stereo/cassette, Dolby, Dynamic Noise Reduction [DNR], FM diversity antenna system, anti-theft feature), illuminated entry system.

Accessories

NOTE: Acura accessories are dealer installed. Contact an Acura dealer for accessory availability.

CODE DESCRIPTION INVOICE MSRP

ACURA

LEGEND SEDAN *(1995)*

CODE	DESCRIPTION	INVOICE	MSRP
KA755S	L 4-Dr Sedan w/Cloth Interior (5-spd)	30470	35500
KA765S	L 4-Dr Sedan w/Cloth Interior (auto)	31156	36300
KA756S	L 4-Dr Sedan w/Leather Interior (5-spd)	31757	37000
KA766S	L 4-Dr Sedan w/Leather Interior (auto)	32444	37800
KA769S	Special Edition 4-Dr Sedan (auto)	33388	38900
KA767S	LS 4-Dr Sedan (auto)	34075	39700
KA758S	GS 4-Dr Sedan (6-spd)	36049	42000
KA768S	GS 4-Dr Sedan (auto)	36049	42000
KA769S	Special Edition 4-Dr Sedan (auto)	33388	38900
Destination Charge:		420	420

Standard Equipment

LEGEND SEDAN - L: 3.2 liter 24-valve SOHC 90-degree V6 longitudinally-mounted engine, programmed fuel injection (PGM-FI) with variable induction system, 5-speed manual transmission, 4-wheel independent double wishbone suspension, variable power assisted rack and pinion steering, anti-lock braking system (ABS), driver and front passenger air bag SRS, front seat belts with automatic tensioners, variable-diameter door beams, 3-point outboard seat belts, front and rear 5-mph bumpers, front and rear impact-absorption zones, flush-mounted high efficiency dual-lens halogen headlights, tinted glass, dual power-operated body color door mirrors, protective bodyside body color moldings, rear window defroster with timer, heated door mirrors, anti-soiling bottom door guards, galvanized body panels, 4-coat 4-bake paint, leather-trimmed interior and steering wheel, simulated wood-trimmed console and power window controls, driver's 8-way power seat with adjustable lumbar support and memory, fold-down rear center armrest, height/tilt adjustable front and rear headrests, air conditioning, Acura/Bose Music System, steering wheel mounted remote control audio system, pre-wiring for CD changer, power operated moonroof with sliding shade, power windows with key-off feature, power door locks with driver's side dual unlocking feature, theft-deterrent system, electronic tilt and telescopic steering column with automatic tilt-up, seat and steering wheel memory system, center console (with armrest, covered storage compartment, cupholder).

LS (in addition to or instead of L equipment): Electronically controlled 4-speed automatic transmission, burled walnut-trimmed console and power window controls, front passenger 4-way power seat, heated front seats, automatic climate control, Acura/Bose Premium Music System, illuminated entry system.

GS (in addition to or instead of LS equipment): 6-speed manual transmission, traction control.

Special Edition (in addition to or instead of L equipment): Leather seats, unique alloy wheels, keyless entry system, custom floor mats, CD-changer.

Accessories

NOTE: Acura accessories are dealer installed. Contact an Acura dealer for accessory availability.

NSX-T *(1995)*

Code	Description	Invoice	MSRP
NA118S	2-Dr Coupe (5-spd)	69522	81000
NA128S	2-Dr Coupe (auto)	72526	84500
Destination Charge:		725	725

Standard Equipment

NSX-T: 3.0 liter 24-valve PFI V-6 Engine, 5-speed manual transmission, variable assist power steering, power 4-wheel disc anti-lock brakes, air conditioning, driver and passenger airbags, rear window defroster, speed control, tilt and telescoping steering wheel, power windows, rear spoiler, power door locks, leather bucket seats with dual 4-way power control, Acura/Bose AM/FM stereo radio with cassette, power antenna, dual power OS mirrors, traction control, fog lights, remote control fuel filter door release, tachometer, remote control trunk release, variable intermittent windshield wipers, front and rear stabilizer bars, alarm system, P215/45ZR16 tires (front), P245/40ZR17 tires (rear), aluminum alloy wheels.

Accessories

NOTE: Acura accessories are dealer installed. Contact an Acura dealer for accessory availability.

164 *(1995)*

CODE	DESCRIPTION	INVOICE	MSRP
—	LS 4-Dr Sedan (5-spd)	29635	36140
—	Quadrifoglio 4-Dr Sedan (5-spd)	31930	38940
Destination Charge:		460	460

Standard Equipment

164 - LS: 3.0 liter MPI 24-valve V6 DOHC engine, 5-speed manual transmission with overdrive, power 4-wheel disc brakes with anti-lock braking system, air conditioning with auto climate control, front wheel drive, cruise control, power sunroof, power windows, front and rear fog lights, power assist rack and pinion steering, power door locks, 15" cast alloy wheels, P195/65ZR15 SBR BSW tires, rear window defroster, AM/FM stereo radio with cassette, power antenna, power outside heated folding mirrors, dual air bag supplemental restraint system, rear window sunshades, heated 8-way power leather sport seats, tachometer, automatic dimming interior mirror, illuminated passenger visor vanity mirror, power fuel filler door release, power trunk release, anti-theft security system, headlight washers, intermittent windshield wipers, front suspension (MacPherson struts with lower wishbones, coil springs, anti-roll bar), rear suspension (struts, double transverse links and single trailing link per side, coil springs, anti-roll bar), digital clock, center front and rear armrests, center console, 3.35:1 axle ratio, rear seat reading lamps, ski boot, leather-wrapped telescoping steering wheel.

QUADRIFOGLIO (in addition to or instead of LS equipment): Front air dam, rear decklid spoiler, ground effects package, aerodynamic rocker panel moldings, unique bodyside cladding, electronic sport suspension, 3.41:1 axle ratio, sport alloy wheels.

Accessories

CODE	DESCRIPTION	INVOICE	MSRP
—	**Automatic Transmission** — 4-speed - LS *incls 4.20:1 axle ratio*	740	900
—	**Metallic Paint** — LS	345	420
—	**California Emissions**	48	48
—	**Compact Disc Player** — LS	520	625

90 *(1995)*

CODE	DESCRIPTION	INVOICE	MSRP
8C24U4	90 4-Dr Sedan (5-spd)	22578	25670
8C26U4	90 Sport 4-Dr Sedan (5-spd)	22926	26070
Destination Charge:		445	445

Standard Equipment

90/SPORT 90: 2.8 liter 172 HP V6 engine (incls variable intake path geometry and fully electronic engine control system, knock sensors, electronic idle control, hydraulic valve lifters), hydraulic engine mounts, engine/automatic transmission oil coolers, front-wheel drive, 5-speed manual transmission, long-life exhaust system, power rack and pinion steering, front coil spring/shock absorbers (gas charged) struts with wishbone lower control arm, rear torsion beam linked trailing arms, lowered sport suspension with sport springs and shock absorbers (Sport 90), front and rear stabilizer bars, 7J x 15 10-spoke alloy wheels (90), 7J x 15 5-spoke alloy wheels (Sport 90), 195/65HR15 all-weather tires, power assisted 4-wheel disc brakes (vented front with load-sensitive pressure proportioning), anti-lock braking system (ABS), asbestos-free brake and clutch linings, 4-door sedan body style, unit body using fully galvanized sheet steel (all panels, both sides), multi-step factory rust protection, body color front and rear bumper aprons, body color outside mirrors and door handles, protective bodyside moldings, flush-mounted glass/door handles, aerodynamic halogen headlights, front fog lights integrated in lower bumper apron, rear fog lights integrated in left rear light cluster, high pressure headlight washer system, full-width rear reflective light panel, fuel cap hanger feature, foldable windshield wipers, 5-mph bumpers, right outside convex mirror, flared fenders, clearcoat metallic paint (90), sport uni-color paint: white, red, black (Sport 90); comfort seats with Chenille velour seat upholstery (90), sport seats with Jacquard sport cloth seat upholstery (Sport 90), burled walnut wood inlays (incls instrument panel, center console, door panels), reclining front seats with seat height adjustment, folding front center armrest with height adjustment (90), fold-down rear center armrest, full center console with storage bin (90), beverage holders, front and rear "open" head restraints (foldable rear), driver and front passenger air bags with knee bar (SRS), front 3-point safety belts with height adjustment and automatic tensioners, rear outboard 3-point safety belts, leather-wrapped steering wheel, leather shift knob and boot (Sport 90 manual trans), folding overhead assist handles, individual passenger reading lamps, front seatback storage pockets (90), red backlit instrumentation (incls tachometer, 160-mph electric speedometer, coolant temperature gauge, fuel gauge, digital clock, trip odometer), sports gauge package in lower center console (incls voltmeter, engine oil pressure gauge, oil temperature gauge) (Sport 90), outside temperature gauge (manual trans), driver

CODE	DESCRIPTION	INVOICE	MSRP

and passenger illuminated vanity mirrors, illuminated glove box/trunk/lighter/ashtrays, lockable glove box, retained accessory power for windows and optional sunroof, interior lighting with courtesy delay feature, ignition key with integrated light, front and rear color-coordinated carpet floor mats, full-width trunk lid liner, anti-theft vehicle alarm system (incls horn and lights), CFC-free air conditioning, heat and AC vents to rear footwell, tinted glass, windshield with tint band, rear window defogger with automatic timed shut-off feature, electronic cruise control with resume and speed-up features, power windows with child safety lock, driver's window with one-touch down feature, dual power outside mirrors with defog feature, power central locking system (incls trunk and fuel filler door), child safety rear door locks, electronically tuned AM/FM stereo cassette radio with anti-theft coding, 6-speaker sound system with dual diversity antenna system, 2-speed intermittent wipers, gas strut supports for hood and trunk lid, 60/40 split folding rear seatback.

Accessories

CODE	DESCRIPTION	INVOICE	MSRP
—	**Paint** — pearlescent metallic	461	530
	90 req's Comfort and Convenience Pkg, Quattro permanent all-wheel drive system		
PCC	**Comfort and Convenience Pkg**	1549	1780
	incls automatic air conditioning, 8-way power driver seat, power steel tilt/slide sunroof, infrared remote locking system; Sport req's Quattro permanent all-wheel drive system		
3X1	**Ski Sack** — expandable	135	155
—	**Upholstery** — Kodiak leather	1079	1240
	Sport req's Quattro permanent all-wheel drive system, Comfort and Convenience Pkg		
OLM	**California Emissions**	NC	NC
OLS	**Massachusetts Emissions**	NC	NC
3FD	**Sunroof** — power tilt/slide	835	960
QTR	**Quattro Permanent All-Wheel Drive System**	1500	1500
PAX	**All-Weather Pkg #1**	296	340
	incls heated windshield washer nozzles, heated front seats with individual temperature controls; req's Comfort and Convenience Pkg; Sport also req's Quattro permanent all-wheel drive system		
—	**Transmission** — 4-spd ECT automatic	850	900
	incls transmission oil cooler		
PAW	**All-Weather Pkg #2**	383	440
	incls heated front door locks, heated front seats with individual temperature controls, heated windshield washer nozzles		

What's New for *Audi* in 1995?

90: All-wheel drive is now available across the line as a separate option. Next year the 90 is replaced by the A4, which will spawn coupe, convertible and wagon versions

A6: A new name and minor styling tweaks turn the 100 into the A6.

Cabriolet: New colors and an optional blue top are the only changes to this pricey convertible.

S6: Transformed into the S6 from the S4 for 1995, Audi's studly sport sedan receives minor styling revisions this year.

A6 (1995)

CODE	DESCRIPTION	INVOICE	MSRP
4A23X4	4-Dr Sedan (5-spd)	26867	30600
4A53U8	4-Dr Wagon (auto)	29170	33170
Destination Charge:		445	445

Standard Equipment

A6 SEDAN/WAGON: 2.8 liter 172 HP V6 engine (incls variable intake path geometry, fully electronic engine control system, knock sensors, electronic idle control and hydraulic valve lifters), hydraulic engine mounts, engine/automatic transmission oil coolers, front-wheel drive, 5-speed manual transmission (Sedan), 4-speed automatic transmission with adaptive shift program and automatic shift lock (Wagon), long-life exhaust system, vehicle speed-sensitive power rack and pinion steering, front coil spring/shock absorber (gas charged), struts with lower control arms, torsion beam axle rear suspension, front stabilizer bar, 7J x 15 8-spoke alloy wheels, 195/65HR15 all-weather tires, power assisted 4-wheel disc brakes (vented front with load-sensitive pressure regulator), anti-lock braking system (ABS), asbestos-free brake and clutch linings, 4-door sedan/wagon body style, unit body using fully galvanized sheet steel (all panels, both sides), multi-step factory rust protection, integrated body color front/rear bumpers, body color outside mirrors and door handles, body color protective bodyside moldings, flush-mounted glass/door handles, aerodynamic halogen headlights, projector beam headlights with integrated front fog lights, rear integrated fog lights, fuel cap hanger feature, foldable windshield wipers, 5-mph bumpers, right outside convex mirror, roof rails (Wagon), clearcoat metallic paint, automatic climate control system, comfort seats with Chenille velour upholstery, wraparound dash/door panel design, burled walnut wood inlays for instrument panel/center console/door panels, color-coordinated lower dashboard trim, 8-way power driver's seat, manual front passenger seat with height adjustment, manual front seat lumbar adjustment, height adjustable folding front center armrest with storage compartment, fold-down rear center armrest with expandable ski/storage sack, full center console with storage bins and beverage holders, front/rear "open" head restraints (Wagon), front/rear "Full cushion" head restraints (Sedan), driver and front passenger air bags with knee bar (supplemental restraint system), front/rear 3-point safety belts, ratcheting mechanism for securing child seat, leather-wrapped steering wheel, leather shift knob and boot (Sedan - manual trans), folding overhead passenger assist handles, individual passenger reading lamps, front seatback storage pockets, red backlit instrumentation (incls tachometer, 160-mph electric speedometer, coolant temperature gauge, analog clock, fuel/oil temperature gauge, oil pressure gauge, trip odometer), outside temperature gauge, active

CODE	DESCRIPTION	INVOICE	MSRP

auto check system, low fuel warning light, driver and passenger illuminated vanity mirrors, illuminated glove box/trunk/lighter/ashtray, lockable glove box, retained accessory power for windows and sunroof, interior lighting with courtesy delay feature, ignition key with integrated light, front/rear color-coordinated carpet floor mats, fully carpeted trunk, tilt and telescopic adjustable steering column, anti-theft vehicle alarm system (incls horn and lights), CFC-free air conditioner, rear seat heat and air conditioning vents, tinted glass, windshield with tint band, electric rear window defogger with automatic timed shut-off feature, electronic cruise control with resume and speed-up features, power windows with driver's one-touch down feature, dual power outside mirrors with defog feature, right outside mirror with reverse tilt feature, power central locking system (incls trunk and fuel filler door), child safety rear door locks/rear window lock-outs, 2-way power tilt-slide steel sunroof with convenience close feature and automatic pre-select function, electronically-tuned AM/FM stereo cassette radio with anti-theft coding and 8-speaker sound system, dual diversity antenna system with signal boosters (Sedan), tri-band roof-mounted antenna with signal booster (Wagon), 2-speed intermittent wipers, rear window wiper/washer (Wagon), electric remote trunk lid release (Sedan), rear inside tailgate release (Wagon), gas strut supports for hood and trunk, 60/40 split folding rear seatbacks (Wagon), cargo area luggage cover (Wagon), rear window retractable sunshade (Wagon), cargo area folding 2-child seat (Wagon), cellular telephone prep.

Accessories

CODE	DESCRIPTION	INVOICE	MSRP
7A1	**Radio** — Audi/Bose music system	539	620
PCC	**Comfort and Convenience Pkg** *incls infrared remote locking system, power front passenger seat, 2-way power tilt/slide glass moonroof with sunshade, 4-position memory for driver seat and outside mirrors*	870	1000
OLM	**California Emissions**	NC	NC
OLS	**Massachusetts Emissions**	NC	NC
—	**Transmission** — 4-spd ECT automatic - Sedan *incls transmission oil cooler*	850	900
—	**Paint** — pearlescent metallic	461	530
—	**Upholstery** — Kodiak leather seats	1270	1460
9W1	**Cellular Telephone**	861	990
PAW	**All-Weather Pkg** *incls heated windshield washer nozzles, heated front door locks, retractable high-pressure headlight washer system, heated front seats with individual temperature controls*	426	490
QTR	**Quattro Permanent All-Wheel Drive System** *incls automatic disengage of rear differential lock, Torsen center differential*	1500	1500
CD2	**Compact Disc Changer** — 10 disc *req's Audi/Bose music system*	687	790

CABRIOLET *(1995)*

CODE	DESCRIPTION	INVOICE	MSRP
8G74Y8	2-Dr Convertible (auto)	31545	35900
Destination Charge:		445	445

Standard Equipment

CABRIOLET: 2.8 liter 172 HP V6 cylinder engine w/fully electronic engine control system, knock sensors, electronic idle control and hydraulic valve lifters; hydraulic engine mounts, engine and transmission oil coolers, front-wheel drive, 4-speed auto trans w/auto shift lock, long-life exhaust system, rack and pinion power steering, coil spring/shock absorber (gas charged) struts, front /rear; lower wishbones, front; torsion crank axle with panhard rod, rear; front and rear stabilizer bars, 7J x 15 5-spoke alloy wheels, 195/65HR15 all-weather tires, power assisted 4-wheel disc brakes (vented front with load-sensitive pressure proportioning), anti-lock braking system (ABS), asbestos-free brake linings, unit body using fully galvanized sheet steel (all panels, both sides), multi-step factory rust protection, body-color front and rear bumpers, outside mirrors and door handles; body-color protective side moldings, flush-mounted door handles, aerodynamic halogen headlights, front fog lights integrated in lower bumper apron, rear fog light integrated in left side lamp cluster, full-width rear reflective/light panel, headlight washer system, fuel cap retention feature, foldable windshield wipers, 5-mph bumpers, convex right outside mirror, flared fenders, clearcoat metallic paint, Kodiak leather seat upholstery, burled walnut wood inlays for center console and door panels, reclining front seats with seat height adjustment, expandable ski/storage sack, full center console with storage bins and beverage holders, "open" front head rests, airbags with knee bar (driver and front passenger sides), front 3-point seat belts with automatic tensioners, rear 3-point seat belts, leather-wrapped steering wheel, wood shift knob, reading material pockets for rear seat passengers located on front seatback, low glare red backlit instrumentation, tachometer, electric speedometer (160 mph), coolant temperature gauge, digital clock and fuel gauge, trip odometer, illuminated vanity mirrors (driver and passenger sides), illuminated glove box, trunk, lighter and ashtray; lockable glove box, retained accessory power for windows, interior lighting with courtesy delay feature, ignition key with integrated light, front and rear color-coordinated carpet floor mats, full-width trunk lid liner, power top and boot system including insulated soft top with headliner, flexible plastic rear window and fully covered storage; anti-theft vehicle alarm system including horn and lights, CFC-free air conditioning, heat and A/C vents to rear footwell, tinted glass windshield and side windows (windshield with tint band), rear window fan defogger, electronic cruise control with resume and speed-up features, power windows with child safety lock (driver's window with one-touch down feature), central switch for simultaneous operation

CODE	DESCRIPTION	INVOICE	MSRP

of all windows, dual power sideview mirrors with defog feature, power central locking system including trunk and fuel filler door (operable from driver and passenger front doors and trunk), electronically-tuned AM/FM stereo cassette radio with anti-theft coding, 4-speaker sound system with power mast antenna, 2-speed wipers with intermittent mode, gas strut supports for hood and trunk lid, safety reflectors on all doors.

Accessories

CODE	DESCRIPTION	INVOICE	MSRP
—	**Pearlescent Metallic Paint**	461	530
7S1	**Windscreen**	331	380
PAW	**All Weather Pkg** *incls heated frt seats, heated windshield washer nozzles & heated dr locks*	383	440

S6 (1995)

CODE	DESCRIPTION	INVOICE	MSRP
4A2555	4-Dr Sedan (5-spd)	39630	45270
Destination Charge:		445	445

Standard Equipment

S6: 2.2 liter 227 HP 5 cylinder turbocharged 20-valve engine (incls electronic engine management system with dual knock sensors, turbocharger with separate water cooling system, boost air intercooler), hydraulic engine mounts, engine oil cooler, Quattro-Permanently engaged all-wheel drive with TORSEN center differential and automatic disengage of rear differential lock, 5-speed manual transmission, self-adjusting hydraulic clutch, long-life exhaust system, vehicle speed-sensitive rack and pinion power steering, front coil spring/shock absorber (gas charged) struts with lower control arms, fully independent rear suspension with trapezoidal lower control arms and upper links, front stabilizer bar, 8J x 16 forged 5-spoke alloy wheels, 225/50ZR16 SBR high performance tires, power assisted 4-wheel disc brakes (vented front and rear with load-sensitive pressure proportioning), anti-lock braking system (ABS), asbestos-free brake and clutch linings, 4-door sedan body style, unit body using fully galvanized sheet steel (all panels, both sides), multi-step factory rust protection, integrated body color front/rear bumpers, body color outside mirrors and door handles, body color protective bodyside moldings, flush-mounted glass and door handles, aerodynamic halogen triple headlights (halogen high beam, elliptical projector low beam, and fog lights in one unit), integrated rear fog lights, high pressure headlight washers, heated windshield washer nozzles, full-width rear reflective/light panel, fuel cap hanger feature, foldable windshield wipers, 5-mph bumpers, right outside convex mirror, flared front fenders, clearcoat metallic paint, Seiden Nappa leather seat upholstery, wraparound dash/door panel design, burled walnut wood inlays (incls instrument panel, center console, door panels), color-coordinated lower dashboard trim, reclining front sport seats with lumbar and thigh adjustments, 8-way power front seats, driver's 4-position memory seat function and outside mirror adjustments, heatable front/rear outboard seats with individual temperature controls, folding height adjustable front center armrests, hands-free operation cellular telephone with voice recognition feature (stored in front center armrest), fold-down rear center armrest with expandable ski/storage sack, full center console with storage bins and beverage holders, front/rear "Full Cushion" head restraints, driver and front passenger air bags with knee bar (supplemental restraint system), front 3-point safety belts with height adjustment and automatic tensioners, rear outboard 3-point safety belts with comfort adjustment, ratcheting mechanism for securing a child seat, leather-wrapped sport steering wheel, leather shift knob and boot, folding overhead assist handles, individual passenger reading lamps, front seatback storage pockets, red backlit instrumentation with light gray instrument faces, tachometer, 160-mph electric speedometer, coolant temperature gauge, analog clock, voltmeter, fuel/oil temperature/oil pressure gauges, trip odometer, outside temperature gauge, Active Auto Check System, low fuel warning light, driver and passenger illuminated vanity mirrors, illuminated glove box/trunk/lighter/ashtrays, lockable glove box, interior lighting with courtesy delay feature, retained accessory power for windows and sunroof, ignition key with infrared transmitter, front/rear color-coordinated carpet floor mats, fully carpeted trunk, tilt and telescopic adjustable steering column, anti-theft vehicle alarm system (incls horn and lights), CFC-free air conditioner, automatic climate control system, rear seat heat/AC vents, tinted glass, windshield with tint band, electric rear window defogger with automatic timed shut-off feature, electronic cruise control with resume and speed-up features, power windows with driver's one-touch down feature, dual power outside mirrors with defog feature, right outside mirror with reverse tilt, power central locking system (incls trunk and fuel filler door), infrared remote locking system (incls automatic driver's seat/mirror adjustments, alarm arm and disarm, interior illumination), child safety rear door locks/rear window lock-outs, 2-way tilt/slide power glass moonroof with convenience close feature (incls automatic pre-select function and sun shade), Audi/Bose music system with 4 acoustically tuned amplified speaker modules, 2 tweeters, 2 bass modules and dual diversity antenna system; electronically tuned AM/FM stereo cassette radio with anti-theft coding, 2-speed intermittent wipers, electric remote trunk lid release, gas strut supports for hood and trunk, compact disc changer prep.

Accessories

Code	Description	Invoice	MSRP
CD2	Compact Disc Changer — 10 disc	687	790
HR4	Tire/Wheel Pkg *incls 6-spoke sport alloy wheels, 215/60VR15 all-season BW tires*	NC	NC
—	Paint — metallic pearlescent	461	530

318iC CONVERTIBLE (1995)

CODE	DESCRIPTION	INVOICE	MSRP
—	2-Dr Convertible (5-spd)	26120	31050
Destination Charge:		470	470

Standard Equipment

318iC CONVERTIBLE: 1.8 liter DOHC 16-valve inline 4 cylinder engine, 5-speed manual transmission, Digital Motor Electronics engine-management system, direct ignition system with knock control, strut type front suspension, central link rear suspension, front and rear anti-roll (stabilizer) bars, twin-tube gas pressure shock absorbers, engine speed-sensitive variable assist power steering, vacuum assisted 4-wheel disc brakes, anti-lock braking system (ABS), 15 x 7J cast alloy wheels, 205/65R15 91H all-season radial tires, body color bumpers with hydraulic energy absorbers (damage control to 9 mph), halogen free-form low beam headlights, halogen free-form fog lights, 2-speed intermittent windshield wipers, dual power outside mirrors, illuminating master key, courtesy lights with fade-in/out feature, map reading lights, take-out flashlight in glove box, height adjustable steering wheel, cruise control, fully reclining front seats with height adjustable driver's seat, seatback easy-entry feature, split folding rear seats, storage nets on front seatbacks, electronic analog speedometer and tachometer, LCD main and trip odometers, Service Interval Indicator, analog fuel economy indicator, Multi-Information Display, leatherette upholstery, front center armrest, rear center armrest, power windows with one-touch lowering and raising of front windows, all-window switch with one-touch operation, positive side-window sealing system, blower-type 2-stage rear window defroster, air conditioning and heating with separate left/right temperature controls, fully lined manual convertible top, anti-theft AM/FM stereo radio/cassette audio system with 6 speakers and mast antenna, pre-wiring for CD changer, drop-down tool kit in trunk, full size spare wheel and tire (steel wheel), central locking system with friction anti-theft feature, Drive-away Protection, pre-wired for BMW remote keyless entry security system, dual air bag system.

Accessories

CODE	DESCRIPTION	INVOICE	MSRP
—	**Automatic Transmission**	740	900
—	**Metallic Paint**	390	475
—	**Limited Slip Differential**	430	530

CODE	DESCRIPTION	INVOICE	MSRP
—	**Heated Front Seats** *incls heated mirrors*	370	450
—	**Premium Pkg** *incls leather seat trim, premium audio system*	1270	1545
—	**Rollover Protection System**	1140	1390
—	**Premium Audio System**	410	500

318i SEDAN *(1995)*

—	4-Dr Sedan (5-spd)	21010	24975
Destination Charge:		470	470

Standard Equipment

318i SEDAN: 1.8 liter DOHC 16-valve inline 4 cylinder engine, 5-speed manual transmission, Digital Motor Electronics engine management system, direct ignition system with knock control, strut type front suspension, central link rear suspension, front and rear anti-roll (stabilizer) bars, twin-tube gas pressure shock absorbers, engine speed-sensitive variable assist power steering, vacuum-assisted 4-wheel disc brakes, anti-lock braking system (ABS), 15 x 6J steel wheels with wheel covers, 185/65R15 87T all-season radial tires, body color bumpers with hydraulic energy absorbers (damage control to 9 mph), halogen free-form low beam headlights, 2-speed intermittent windshield wipers, dual power outside mirrors, illuminating master key, courtesy lights with fade-in/out feature, map reading lights, take-out flashlight in glove box, cruise control, fully reclining front seats with height adjustable driver's seat, split folding rear seats, storage nets on front seatbacks, electronic analog speedometer and tachometer, LCD main and trip odometers, service interval indicator, analog fuel economy indicator, Multi Information Display, leatherette upholstery, power windows with one-touch lowering and raising of front windows, 2-stage rear window defroster, air conditioning and heating with separate left/right temperature controls, power 2-way sunroof with wind deflector, anti-theft AM/FM stereo radio/cassette audio system with 6 speakers, diversity antenna system, pre-wiring for CD changer, drop-down tool kit in trunk, full-size spare wheel and tire (steel wheel), central locking system with friction anti-theft feature, Drive-away Protection, pre-wiring for BMW remote keyless entry security system, dual air bag system.

CODE	DESCRIPTION	INVOICE	MSRP
	Accessories		
—	**Heated Front Seats** *incls heated mirrors*	370	450
—	**Folding Rear Seat**	225	275
—	**Automatic Transmission**	740	900
—	**Limited Slip Differential**	430	530
—	**Leather Seat Trim**	1070	1300
—	**Fog Lights**	200	240
—	**Alloy Wheels**	655	800
—	**Metallic Paint**	390	475
—	**Premium Pkg** *incls alloy wheels, tilt steering column, leather seat trim, fog lights, premium audio system*	2010	2445
—	**Sport Pkg** *incls alloy wheels, limited slip differential, fog lights, sport suspension, tilt steering column*	1390	1695
—	**Premium Audio System**	410	500

318is COUPE *(1995)*

CODE	DESCRIPTION	INVOICE	MSRP
—	2-Dr Coupe (5-spd)	22440	26675
Destination Charge:		470	470

Standard Equipment

318is COUPE: 1.8 liter DOHC 16-valve inline 4 cylinder engine, 5-speed manual transmission, Digital Motor Electronics engine management system, direct ignition system with knock control, strut-type front suspension, Central Link rear suspension, front and rear anti-roll (stabilizer) bars, twin-tube gas pressure shock absorbers, engine speed-sensitive variable assist power steering, 4-wheel disc brakes (vacuum-assisted), anti-lock braking system (ABS), 15 x 7J cast alloy wheels, 205/65R15 91H all-season radial tires, body color bumpers with hydraulic energy absorbers (damage control to 9 mph), halogen free-form low beam headlights, halogen free-form fog lights, 2-speed intermittent windshield wipers, dual power outside mirrors, illuminating master key, courtesy lights with fade-in/out feature, map reading lights, take-out flashlight in glove box, cruise control, fully reclining front seats with height adjustable driver's seat, seatback easy-entry feature, split folding rear seats, storage nets on front seatbacks, electronic analog speedometer and tachometer, LCD main and trip odometers, Service Interval Indicator, analog fuel economy indicator, Multi Information Display, leatherette upholstery, power windows with one-touch lowering and raising of front windows, 2-stage rear window defroster, air conditioning and heating with separate left/right temperature controls, power 2-way sunroof with wind deflector, anti-theft AM/FM stereo radio/cassette audio system with 6 speakers, diversity antenna system, pre-wiring for CD changer, drop-down tool kit in trunk, full-size spare wheel and tire (steel wheel), central locking system with friction anti-theft feature, Drive-away Protection, pre-wired for BMW remote keyless entry security system, dual air bag system.

Accessories

CODE	DESCRIPTION	INVOICE	MSRP
—	**Heated Front Seats** *incls heated mirrors*	370	450
—	**Automatic Transmission**	740	900
—	**Limited Slip Differential**	430	530
—	**Metallic Paint**	390	475
—	**Premium Audio System**	410	500
—	**Premium Pkg** *incls tilt steering column, leather seat trim, premium audio system*	1350	1645
—	**Sport Pkg** *incls limited slip differential, sport suspension, tilt steering column*	610	745

325i SEDAN *(1995)*

CODE	DESCRIPTION	INVOICE	MSRP
—	4-Dr Sedan (5-spd)	26455	31450
Destination Charge:		470	470

CODE	DESCRIPTION	INVOICE	MSRP

Standard Equipment

325i SEDAN: 2.5 liter DOHC 24-valve inline 6 cylinder engine with variable valve timing, 5-speed manual transmission, Digital Motor Electronics engine management system, direct ignition system with knock control, strut type front suspension, central link rear suspension, front and rear anti-roll (stabilizer) bars, twin-tube gas pressure shock absorbers, engine speed-sensitive variable assist power steering, vacuum-assisted 4-wheel disc brakes, anti-lock braking system (ABS), 15 x 7J cast alloy wheels, 205/65R15 91H all-season radial tires, body color bumpers with hydraulic energy absorbers (damage control to 9 mph), halogen free-form low beam headlights, halogen free-form fog lights, 2-speed intermittent windshield wipers, dual power outside mirrors, illuminating master key, courtesy lights with fade-in/out feature, rear reading lights, map reading lights, take-out flashlight in glove box, cruise control, 8-way power front seats, split folding rear seats, storage nets on front seatbacks, electronic analog speedometer and tachometer, LCD main and trip odometers, Service Interval Indicator, analog fuel economy indicator, Multi Information Display, leatherette upholstery, front center armrest, power windows with one-touch lowering and raising of front windows, 2-stage rear window defroster, air conditioning and heating with separate left/right temperature controls, power 2-way sunroof and wind deflector, anti-theft AM/FM stereo radio/cassette audio system with 10 x 20 watt amplification/10 speakers/diversity antenna system, pre-wiring for CD changer, drop-down tool kit in trunk, full-size spare wheel and tire (steel wheel), central locking system with friction anti-theft feature, Drive-away Protection, pre-wiring for BMW remote keyless entry security system, dual air bag system.

Accessories

CODE	DESCRIPTION	INVOICE	MSRP
—	**Automatic Transmission**	740	900
—	**Metallic Paint**	390	475
—	**Leather Trim**	1070	1300
—	**Heated Front Seats** *incls heated mirrors*	370	450
—	**On-Board Computer**	355	430
—	**Folding Rear Seat**	225	275
—	**Traction Control**	815	995
—	**Sport Pkg** *incls 16" alloy wheels, 225/50ZR16 tires, sport suspension, on-board computer, sport seats*	1145	1395
—	**Premium Pkg** *incls leather seat trim, on-board computer, wood trim*	1560	1895

BMW

325is COUPE *(1995)*

CODE	DESCRIPTION	INVOICE	MSRP
—	2-Dr Coupe (5-spd)	27635	32850
	Destination Charge:	470	470

Standard Equipment

325is COUPE: 2.5 liter DOHC 24-valve inline 6 cylinder engine with variable valve timing, 5-speed manual transmission, Digital Motor Electronics engine management system, direct ignition system with knock control, strut type front suspension, central link rear suspension, front and rear anti-roll (stabilizer) bars, twin-tube gas pressure shock absorbers, engine speed-sensitive variable assist power steering, vacuum-assisted 4-wheel disc brakes, anti-lock braking system (ABS), 15 x 7J cast alloy wheels, 205/65R15 91H all-season radial tires, body color bumpers with hydraulic energy absorbers (damage control to 9 mph), halogen free-form low beam headlights, halogen free-form fog lights, 2-speed intermittent windshield wipers, dual power outside mirrors, illuminating master key, courtesy lights with fade-in/out feature, rear reading lights, map reading lights, take-out flashlight in glove box, cruise control, seatback easy-entry feature, 8-way power front seats, split folding rear seats, storage nets on front seatbacks, electronic analog speedometer and tachometer, LCD main and trip odometers, Service Interval Indicator, analog fuel economy indicator, Multi Information Display, gathered-leather seating, leather manual shift knob/steering wheel/hand brake grip/boot, front center armrest, power windows with one-touch lowering and raising of front windows, 2-stage rear window defroster, air conditioning and heating with separate left/right temperature controls, power 2-way sunroof with wind deflector, anti-theft AM/FM stereo radio/cassette audio system with 10 x 20 watt amplification/10 speakers/diversity antenna system, pre-wiring for CD changer, drop-down tool kit in trunk, full-size spare wheel and tire (steel wheel), central locking system with friction anti-theft feature, Drive-away Protection, pre-wiring for BMW remote keyless entry security system, dual air bag system.

Accessories

CODE	DESCRIPTION	INVOICE	MSRP
—	**Automatic Transmission**	740	900
—	**Metallic Paint**	390	475
—	**Heated Front Seats** *incls heated mirrors*	370	450
—	**On-Board Computer**	355	430

CODE	DESCRIPTION	INVOICE	MSRP
—	**Traction Control**	815	995
—	**Sport Pkg** *incls 16" alloy wheels, 225/50ZR16 tires, on-board computer, sport seats, sport suspension*	1145	1395
—	**Premium Pkg** *incls on-board computer, wood trim*	570	695

325iC CONVERTIBLE *(1995)*

CODE	DESCRIPTION	INVOICE	MSRP
—	2-Dr Convertible (5-spd)	33310	39600
Destination Charge:		470	470

Standard Equipment

325iC CONVERTIBLE: 2.5 liter DOHC 24-valve inline 6 cylinder engine with variable valve timing, 5-speed manual transmission, Digital Motor Electronics engine-management system, direct ignition system with knock control, strut-type front suspension, central link rear suspension, front and rear anti-roll (stabilizer) bars, twin-tube gas pressure shock absorbers, engine speed-sensitive variable assist power steering, vacuum-assisted 4-wheel disc brakes, anti-lock braking system, 15 x 7 cast alloy wheels, 205/65R15 91H all-season radial tires, body color bumpers (damage control to 9 mph), halogen free-form low beam headlights, halogen free-form fog lights, 2-speed intermittent windshield wipers, dual power outside mirrors, illuminating master key, courtesy lights with fade-in/out feature, map reading lights, takeout flashlight in glove box, height adjustable steering wheel, cruise control, seatback easy entry feature, 8-way power front seats, split folding rear seats, storage nets on front seatbacks, electronic analog speedometer and tachometer, LCD main and trip odometers, service interval indicator, analog fuel economy indicator, multi-information display, check control vehicle monitor system, gathered-leather seating plus leather manual shift knob, steering wheel, hand brake grip and boot; front center armrest, rear center armrest, power windows with one-touch lowering and raising of front windows, all-window switch with one-touch operation, positive side window sealing system, blower type rear window defroster, air conditioning with separate left/right temperature controls, fully lined power convertible top, anti-theft AM/FM stereo radio/cassette audio system with 10 x 20 watt amplification and 10 speakers, mast antenna, pre-wiring for CD changer, drop-down tool kit in trunk, full-size spare wheel and tire, central locking system with friction anti-theft feature, Drive-away Protection, pre-wiring for BMW remote keyless entry security system.

CODE	DESCRIPTION	INVOICE	MSRP
	Accessories		
—	**Automatic Transmission**	740	900
—	**Metallic Paint**	390	475
—	**Heated Front Seats** *incls heated mirrors*	370	450
—	**On-Board Computer**	355	430
—	**Traction Control**	815	995
—	**Sport Pkg** *incls 16" alloy wheels, 225/50ZR16 tires, on-board computer, sport seats*	1065	1295
—	**Premium Pkg** *incls on-board computer, wood trim*	570	695
—	**Rollover Protection System**	1140	1390

525i *(1995)*

CODE	DESCRIPTION	INVOICE	MSRP
—	4-Dr Sedan (5-spd)	29585	35300
—	4-Dr Touring Wagon (auto)	31595	37700
	Destination Charge:	470	470

Standard Equipment

525i SEDAN: 2.5 liter DOHC 24-valve inline 6-cylinder engine with variable valve timing, 5-speed manual transmission, Digital Motor Electronics engine-management system, direct ignition system with knock control, double-pivot strut-type front suspension, Track Link rear suspension, front and rear anti-roll stabilizer bars, twin-tube gas-pressure shock absorbers, engine-speed-sensitive variable assist power steering, 4-wheel disc brakes (ventilated front discs, vacuum-assisted), anti-lock braking system (ABS), 15" x 7"J cast alloy wheels (short spoke design), 205/65R15 94H all-season radial tires, body color bumpers with hydraulic energy absorbers and front compressible elements (damage control to 9 mph), halogen ellipsoid low-beam headlights, halogen fog lights, 2-speed intermittent windshield wipers (incls car-speed controlled wiping speed and interval, single-wipe control, windshield washer system with heated washer jets), metallic paint (no additional charge), dual power/heated outside mirrors, pre-wiring

CODE DESCRIPTION INVOICE MSRP

for automatic-dimming inside rearview mirror, heated driver's door lock, illuminating master key, time-delay courtesy lights with actuation from driver's exterior door handle (automatic switch-on when engine is turned off), map reading lights, take-out flashlight in glove box, telescopically adjustable steering wheel, 10-way power front seats with power head restraints (incls driver's seat power lumbar support, folding front center armrests), electronic analog speedometer and tachometer, LCD main and trip odometers, Service Interval Indicator, fuel-economy indicator, check control vehicle monitor system, leatherette upholstery, leather-covered steering wheel, rear center armrest with storage compartment, seatback storage pockets, velour carpeting, power windows with key-off and operation (incls one-touch lowering of all windows, one-touch lowering and raising of driver's windows), 2-stage rear window defroster, air conditioning and heating with separate left/right temperature controls (CFC-free refrigerant, microfiltered ventilation), power 2-way sunroof with key-off and one-touch operation, anti-theft AM/FM stereo radio/cassette audio system (incls 10 x 20 watt amplification, 10 speakers), diversity antenna system, pre-wiring for BMW cellular phone (incls hands-free operation, remote functions and audio muting), pre-wiring for BMW CD changer, fully finished trunk with luggage straps and drop-down toolkit, full-size spare wheel and tire (steel wheel), central locking system with friction anti-theft feature (window and sunroof closing possible from both front door locks), drive-away protection, pre-wiring for BMW remote keyless entry security system, dual air bag SRS with differentiated deployment system, automatic height adjustment for front seatbelts, automatic front seatbelt tensioners, impact sensor (unlocks doors, switches on interior lights and hazard flashers after serious impact).

525i TOURING WAGON (in addition to or instead of 525i SEDAN equipment): 4-speed electronically controlled automatic transmission, 225/60R15 96H all-season radial tires, rear window wiper and washer, tracks for multi-function roof-rack system, 2/3-1/3 split folding rear seats, power windows include one-touch lowering and raising of both front windows, power 2-way sunroof deleted, diversity antenna system deleted, variable cargo area with velour carpeting and 4 tie-downs, cargo cover, full-use spare wheel and tire (alloy wheel), tailgate with separately openable rear window and drop-down tool kit.

Accessories

CODE	DESCRIPTION	INVOICE	MSRP
—	**Heated Front Seats**	305	370
—	**Automatic Transmission** (Sedan)	740	900
—	**Traction Control**	815	995
—	**Premium Pkg** *incls leather seat trim, leather door trim, wood trim, on-board computer, keyless remote entry system with alarm, cross-spoke cast alloy wheels*	2890	3525
—	**Dual Electric Sunroofs** (Touring Wagon)	1090	1325
—	**Luggage Net** (Touring Wagon)	215	260

BMW

530i SEDAN *(1995)*

CODE	DESCRIPTION	INVOICE	MSRP
—	530i 4-Dr Sedan (5-spd)	35825	42750
Destination Charge:		470	470
Gas Guzzler Tax: 530i w/5-spd		1300	1300

Standard Equipment

530i SEDAN: 3.0 liter DOHC 4-cam 32-valve V8 engine, 5-speed manual transmission, Digital Motor Electronics engine management system, direct ignition system with knock control, double-pivot strut-type front suspension, Track Link rear suspension, front and rear anti-roll stabilizer bars, twin-tube gas-pressure shock absorbers, engine-speed-sensitive variable assist power steering, 4-wheel disc brakes (ventilated front discs, vacuum-assisted), anti-lock braking system (ABS), 15" x 7"J cast alloy wheels (cross-spoke design), 225/60R15 96H all-season radial tires, body color bumpers with hydraulic energy absorbers and front compressible elements (damage control to 9 mph), halogen ellipsoid low-beam headlights, halogen fog lights, 2-speed intermittent windshield wipers (incls car-speed controlled wiping speed and interval, single wipe control, windshield washer system with heated washer jets), metallic paint (at no additional charge), dual power/heated outside mirrors, pre-wiring for automatic dimming inside rearview mirror, heated driver's door lock, illuminating master key, time delay courtesy lights with actuation from driver's exterior door handle (automatic switch-on when engine is turned off), map reading lights, take-out flashlight in glove box, telescopically adjustable steering wheel, 10-way power front seats with power head restraints (incls driver's seat power lumbar support, folding front center armrests), electronic analog speedometer and tachometer, LCD main and trip odometers, Service Interval Indicator, fuel-economy indicator, check control vehicle monitor system, onboard computer, leather and wood interior trim (gathered-leather seating surfaces and door trim, leather covered steering wheel/handbrake boot and grip/door armrests/door pulls/manual-transmission shift boot), rear center armrest with storage compartment, seatback storage pockets, velour carpeting, power windows with key-off and operation (incls one-touch lowering of all windows, one-touch lowering and raising of driver's window), 2-stage rear window defroster, air conditioning and heating with separate left/right temperature controls (CFC-free refrigerant, microfiltered ventilation), automatic ventilation system (can be programmed to operate interior ventilation when car is standing), power 2-way sunroof with key-off and one-touch operation, anti-theft AM/FM stereo radio/cassette audio system (incls 10 x 20 watt amplification, 10 speakers), diversity antenna system, pre-wiring for

BMW cellular phone (incls hands-free operation, remote functions and audio muting), pre-wiring for BMW CD changer, fully finished trunk with luggage straps and drop-down tool kit, full-use spare wheel and tire (alloy wheel), central locking system with friction anti-theft feature (window and sunroof closing possible from both front door locks), drive-away protection, pre-wiring for BMW remote keyless entry security system, dual air bag SRS with differentiated deployment system, automatic height adjustment for front seatbelts, automatic front seatbelt tensioners, impact sensor (unlocks doors, switches on interior lights and hazard flashers after serious impact).

Accessories

Code	Description	Invoice	MSRP
—	**All-Season Traction**	1110	1350
—	**Automatic Transmission** — 5-spd w/overdrive	900	1100
—	**Heated Front Seats**	305	370

530i TOURING WAGON *(1995)*

Code	Description	Invoice	MSRP
—	4-Dr Touring Wagon (auto)	39430	47050
Destination Charge:		470	470

Standard Equipment

530i TOURING WAGON: 3.0 liter DOHC (4-cam) 32-valve V8 engine, 5-speed electronically controlled automatic transmission, Digital Motor Electronics engine management system, direct ignition system with knock control, double-pivot strut type front suspension, track link rear suspension, front and rear anti-roll (stabilizer) bars, twin-tube gas pressure shock absorbers, engine speed-sensitive variable assist power steering, vacuum-assisted 4-wheel disc brakes, anti-lock braking system, all-season traction, 15 x 7 cross-spoke design cast alloy wheels, 225/60R15 96H all-season radial tires, body color bumpers (damage control to 9 mph), halogen ellipsoid low beam headlights, halogen fog lights, 2-speed intermittent windshield wipers with heated washer jets, rear window wiper/washer, metallic paint (no charge), dual power/heated outside mirrors, heated driver's door lock, illuminating master key, time-delay courtesy lights, map reading lights, take-out flashlight in glove box, telescopically adjustable steering wheel, 10-way power front seats with power head restraints, driver's seat power lumbar support, folding front center armrests; 2/3 - 1/3 split folding rear seats, electronic analog speedometer and tachometer, LCD main and trip odometers, service interval indicator, fuel economy indicator, check control vehicle monitor system, on-board computer, leather and wood interior trim,

CODE	DESCRIPTION	INVOICE	MSRP

rear center armrest with storage compartment, seatback storage pockets, velour carpeting, power windows with one-touch lowering and raising of both front windows, 2-stage rear window defroster, air conditioning with separate left/right temperature controls, automatic ventilation system, power twin-panel sunroof with one-touch operation, anti-theft AM/FM stereo radio/cassette audio system with 10 x 20 watt amplification and 10 speakers, variable cargo area with velour carpeting, four tie-downs, cargo cover, full-use spare wheel and tire, drop-down tool kit, central locking system, drive-away protection, remote keyless entry security system, central locking system, dual air bag supplemental restraint system.

Accessories

CODE	DESCRIPTION	INVOICE	MSRP
—	**Heated Front Seats**	305	370
—	**Luggage Net**	215	260

540i SEDAN *(1995)*

CODE	DESCRIPTION	INVOICE	MSRP
—	540i 4-Dr Sedan (6-spd)	40730	48600
—	540iA 4-Dr Sedan (auto)	40185	47950
	Destination Charge:	470	470
	Gas Guzzler Tax:	1300	1300

Standard Equipment

540i SEDAN: 4.0 liter DOHC 4-cam 32-valve V8 engine, 5-speed electronically controlled automatic transmission, Digital Motor Electronics engine management system, direct ignition system with knock control, double-pivot strut-type front suspension, track link rear suspension, front and rear anti-roll stabilizer bars, twin-tube gas-pressure shock absorbers, engine-speed-sensitive variable assist power steering, 4-wheel disc brakes (ventilated front discs, vacuum assisted; ventilated front and rear discs), anti-lock braking system (ABS), 15" x 7"J cast alloy wheels (honeycomb design), 225/60R15 96H all-season radial tires, body color bumpers with hydraulic energy absorbers and front compressible elements (damage control to 9 mph), halogen ellipsoid low-beam headlights, halogen fog lights, 2-speed intermittent windshield wipers (incls car speed controlled wiping speed and interval, single-wipe control, windshield washer system with heated washer jets), metallic paint

CODE	DESCRIPTION	INVOICE	MSRP

(no additional charge), dual power/heated outside mirrors, automatic tilt-down of right outside mirror (for visibility of curb when backing up), pre-wiring for automatic dimming inside rearview mirror, heated driver's door lock, time delay courtesy lights with actuation from driver's exterior door handle (automatic switch-on when engine is turned off), map reading lights, take-out flashlight in glove box, telescopically adjustable power steering wheel, 10-way power front seats with power head restraints (incls driver's seat power lumbar support, folding front center armrests), memory system for driver's seat and seatbelt height/steering wheel/outside mirrors (3 settings), electronic analog speedometer and tachometer, LCD main and trip odometers, service interval indicator, fuel economy indicator, check control vehicle monitor system, onboard computer, leather and wood interior trim (gathered leather seating surfaces and door trim, leather-covered steering wheel/handbrake boot and grip), rear center armrest with storage compartment, seatback storage pockets, velour carpeting, power windows with key-off and operation (incls one-touch lowering of all windows, one-touch lowering and raising of driver's window), 2-stage rear window defroster, air conditioning and heating with separate left/right temperature controls (CFC-free refrigerant, microfiltered ventilation), automatic ventilation system (can be programmed to operate interior ventilation when car is standing), power 2-way sunroof with key-off and one-touch operation, anti-theft AM/FM stereo radio/cassette audio system (incls 10 x 20 watt amplification, 10 speakers), diversity antenna system, pre-wiring for BMW cellular phone (incls hands-free operation, remote functions, audio muting), pre-wiring for BMW CD changer, fully finished trunk with luggage straps and drop-down tool kit, full-use spare wheel and tire (alloy wheel), central locking system with friction anti-theft feature (window and sunroof closing possible from both front door locks), drive-away protection, remote keyless entry security system (keyhead remote), dual air bag SRS with differentiated deployment system, automatic height adjustment for front seatbelts, automatic front seatbelt tensioners, impact sensor (unlocks doors, switches on interior lights and hazard flashers after serious impact).

Accessories

—	**All-Season Traction**	1110	1350
—	**Heated Front Seats**	305	370

What's New for *BMW* in 1995?

3-Series: The stellar M3 debuted mid-1994, and if you're in the market for a sport coupe under $40,000, check this car out. Expected shortly after New Year's, BMW's 316ti will offer a budget Bimmer for enthusiasts. It will have a 1.8L 138 hp motor under the hood, and will be the least expensive BMW in the U.S. Other 3 Series models undergo slight trim and option changes.

5-Series: The wide hood from the 540i is now standard on all models, as is body color trim. The 540i gets an optional 6-speed tranny and sport suspension.

7-Series: All-new for 1995, the 7-Series differs little visually from the car it replaces. The new car is longer, wider, heavier and lower than the previous car, and still offers the ultimate in luxury motoring.

BMW

7-Series (1995)

CODE	DESCRIPTION	INVOICE	MSRP
—	740i 4-Dr Sedan (auto)	47545	57900
—	740iL 4-Dr Sedan (auto)	49585	59900
Destination Charge:		570	570
Gas Guzzler Tax:		1000	1000

Standard Equipment

740i: 4.0 liter DOHC 4-cam 32-valve V8 engine, 5-speed electronically controlled automatic transmission with Adaptive Transmission Control (ATC), double-pivot strut-type front suspension with forged aluminum lower arms and variable diameter coil springs, 4-link integral rear suspension, front and rear anti-roll stabilizer bars, twin-tube gas-pressure shock absorbers, vehicle-speed-sensitive variable assist power steering, 4-wheel disc brakes w/anti-lock, 16" x 7.5"J cast alloy wheels (Style 6), 235/60R16 100H all-season SBR tires, body color bumpers with hydraulic energy absorbers and front compressible elements (damage control to 9 mph), halogen ellipsoid low-beam headlights, halogen free form high-beam headlights, halogen free form fog lights, 2-speed intermittent windshield wipers (with adjustable and car-speed sensitive wiping interval, single-wipe control, windshield washer system with heated washer jets), heated windshield wiper parking area, dual power/heated outside mirrors, automatic tilt-down of right-side mirror (for visibility of curb when backing up), automatic dimming inside rearview mirror, heated driver's door lock, courtesy lights with fade-in/fade-out feature (actuation from remote control; automatic switch-on when engine is turned off), map reading lights, rear reading lights, power tilt/telescopic steering wheel, 14-way power front seats w/4-way power adjustable lumbar support, memory system for driver's seat and seatback height/steering wheel/ outside mirrors (3 settings), locking glove box (with rechargeable flashlight), electronic analog speedometer and tachometer, LCD main and trip odometers, Service Interval Indicator, fuel economy indicator, check control vehicle monitor system, multi-information display (incorporates audio and telephone controls/onboard computer), gathered leather seating and door trim, leather-covered steering wheel, high-gloss walnut trim on instrument panels/doors/console, walnut shift grip, power windows with key-off operation (incls one-touch lowering and raising of all windows, anti-trapping feature), automatic climate control (incls full separate left/right controls, automatic recirculation and residual heating features), micro/active-charcoal ventilation filter, automatic ventilation system, power 2-way sunroof with key-off and one-touch operation, anti-theft AM/FM stereo cassette audio system (incls 10-channel/200-watt amplification, 10 speakers), FM diversity antenna system, pre-wiring for CD changer, pre-wiring for BMW cellular phone, steering wheel controls (incls cruise control, audio system, telephone, air recirculation), front and rear dual cup holders, dual front illuminated visor mirrors, rear center armrest with storage compartment, closeable seatback storage compartments, rear window defroster, fully finished trunk (incls luggage straps, cargo net, drop-down toolkit, power soft-close trunk lid), full-use spare wheel and tire, central locking system with double-lock anti-theft feature (2-step unlocking), window and sunroof opening and closing possible from driver's door lock (opening possible from remote), drive-away protection, remote keyless entry security system with keyhead remote/remote trunk opening/panic feature, interlocking door anchoring system for side impacts, dual air bag SRS with differentiated deployment, ergonomic seatbelt system.

740iL (in addition or instead of 740i equipment): Self-leveling rear suspension.

Accessories

CODE	DESCRIPTION	INVOICE	MSRP
—	**Comfort Seats**	805	1000
—	**All-Season Traction**	1110	1350
—	**Cold Weather Pkg** *incls heated front seats, headlamp washers, ski sack*	805	1000
—	**Premium Sound System**	1610	2000
—	**Power Rear Sunshade** - 740iL	540	675
—	**Parking Distance Control** - 740iL	660	825

840Ci Coupe *(1995)*

CODE	DESCRIPTION	INVOICE	MSRP
—	840Ci 2-Dr Coupe (auto)	58580	69900
Destination Charge:i		570	570
Gas Guzzler Tax:i		1000	1000

Standard Equipment

840Ci: 4.0 liter DOHC (4-cam) 32-valve V8 engine, Digital Motor Electronics engine management system, 5-speed electronically controlled automatic transmission, double-pivot strut type front suspension, 5-link integral rear suspension, front and rear anti-roll stabilizer bars, twin-tube gas-pressure shocks, engine speed-sensitive variable assist power steering, power 4-wheel disc brakes with anti-lock braking system, all-season traction, 16 x 7.5J cross-spoke design cast alloy wheels, 235/50ZR16 tires, body color bumpers (damage control to 9 mph), retractable halogen headlights, flasher beams/auxiliary high beams in bumper, halogen free-form fog lights, 2-speed intermittent windshield wipers with heated washer jets, metallic paint (no additional charge), dual power heated OS mirrors, automatic-dimming inside rearview mirror, heated driver's door lock, illuminated master key, time-delay courtesy lights, map reading lights, locking glove box with beverage holder, rechargeable take-out flashlight, power tilt/telescopic steering wheel with automatic tilt-away for entry and exit, power seats (driver - 10-way w/head restraints/seatbelt height as function of cushion height, power lumbar support; passenger - 8-way w/head restraint/seatbelt height as function of cushion height, power lumbar support), memory system for seat and head restraint/seatbelt height, steering wheel and OS mirrors; split fold-down rear seats, electronic analog speedometer and tachometer, LCD main and trip odometers, leather seats, leather steering wheel, leather lower instrument panel, leather door inserts, leather center console sides, leather sun visors, heated front seats, fixed rear center armrest, velour carpeting, power windows with one-touch feature, 2-state rear window defroster, automatic climate control, microfiltered ventilation, automatic ventilation system, power 2-way sunroof with one-touch operation, radio (anti-theft AM/FM stereo radio/cassette audiosystem with 10 x 20-watt amplification, 12 speakers, weather band, diversity antenna system, pre-wiring for BMW cellular phone including remote operation and audio muting, pre-wiring for CD changer), velour lined trunk with drop-down tool kit, trunk-to-interior pass-through and ski bag, full-use spare wheel and tire, central locking system, drive-away protection, remote keyless entry security system with keyhead remote, dual air bag SRS.

Accessories

CODE	DESCRIPTION	INVOICE	MSRP
298	**Forged Alloy Wheels**	880	1100

M3 *(1995)*

DESCRIPTION	INVOICE	MSRP
M3 2 Dr Coupe (5-spd)	30955	36800
Destination Charge:	450	450

CODE	DESCRIPTION	INVOICE	MSRP

Standard Equipment

M3: 3.0L DOHC 24-valve 6 cylinder engine with variable valve timing, electronic fuel injection, electronic breakerless direct ignition system, Digital Motor Electronics engine-management system with knock control and self-diagnosis capability, variable rpm limiting, 5-speed manual transmission with direct-drive 5th gear, 25% limited slip differential, exhaust system with stainless steel components, 4-wheel independent suspension (front - strut type; rear - central link), twin-tube gas pressure shock absorbers, engine-speed-sensitive variable assist/variable ratio power rack and pinion steering, front and rear anti-roll bars, vacuum-assisted 4-wheel ventilated disc brakes, anti-lock braking system (ABS), 17x7.5J cast alloy wheels (BMW M 10-spoke design), 235/40ZR17 SBR high-performance tires, undercoating and cavity seal, special BMW M paint colors, BMW M aerodynamic features (special front and lower rear spoiler, rocker panels), hydraulic impact bumpers with compressible mounting elements (damage control to 9 mph), halogen free form low-beam headlights, halogen free form fog lights, 2-speed windshield wipers with single-wipe control (car-speed-controlled intermittent operation), dual power/heated outside mirrors, heated driver's door lock and windshield washer jets, illuminating master key, central locking system with double-lock anti-theft feature (incls trunk and fuel filler door), Driveaway Protection (disables engine when double-lock feature is engaged), pre-wiring for BMW remote keyless entry security system, leather-covered height adjustable M-Technic steering wheel, front sports seats with adjustable thigh support and shoulder support/head-restraint height (driver's seat height adjustable), automatic front seat forward movement for access to rear seats, automatic front seatbelt tensioners, dual-airbag supplementary restraint system, Nappa leather seating with special M design, leather shift knob/handbrake grip/boot, velour carpeting, time-delay courtesy lights, impact sensor (unlocks doors, switches on interior lights and 4-way hazard flashers in case of accident), tinted glass with dark upper windshield band, power front windows with key-off operation (one-touch lowering and raising, automatic positioning of windows for positive sealing), openable rear side windows, electronic analog speedometer and tachometer, LCD main and trip odometers, Service Interval Indicator (recommends maintenance on basis of actual car use), multi-information display with alphanumeric LCD readout (incls outside temperature display and freeze warning, multi-function digital clock, check control vehicle monitor system), air conditioning and heating with separate electronic temperature control for left and right sides (CFC-free refrigerant), microfiltered ventilation, rear window defroster, anti-theft AM/FM stereo radio/cassette CD-ready audio system (10x25 watt amplification, 10 speakers, diversity antenna system), pre-wiring for BMW CD changer, illuminated locking glove box with rechargable flashlight, split fold-down rear seats, drop-down toolkit in trunklid, full-use spare wheel and tire.

Accessories

CODE	DESCRIPTION	INVOICE	MSRP
494	**Heated Front Seats**	305	370
401	**Power Sunroof** — incls cruise control	920	1120
540	**Cruise Control**	375	455
554	**On-Board Computer**	355	430
—	**Automatic Transmission**	900	1100
325	**Rear Spoiler**	535	650
783	**Forged Alloy Wheels**	1100	1340
228	**Luxury Pkg**	2600	2900
	incls on-board computer, cruise control, dual 8-way power seats, front spoiler, leather door trim, aluminum wheel rims, side sills and chrome door handles		

BMW

CENTURY CUSTOM SEDAN *(1995)*

CENTURY CUSTOM SEDAN 4 CYL

CODE	DESCRIPTION	INVOICE	MSRP
H69	4-Dr Sedan	16222	17350
Destination Charge:		535	535

Standard Equipment

CENTURY CUSTOM SEDAN: 3.1 liter V6 SFI engine, electronically controlled 4-speed automatic transmission, power rack and pinion steering, power front disc/rear drum anti-lock brakes, automatic power door locks with lock/unlock/relock feature, P195/75R14 SBR all-season WW tires, 14" deluxe chrome wheel covers, AM/FM ETR stereo radio with seek/scan/clock, air conditioning, driver SRS air bag, fixed-mast antenna, Delco Freedom II Plus battery, brake/transmission interlock, front and rear bumper guards, front and rear carpeting, computer-selected chassis springs, engine and transmission cooling, front/side window defogger outlets, electric rear window defogger, front wheel drive, electronic warning tones for: seat belt/ignition key/headlamps on; hydraulic-tuned engine mounts, Soft-Ray tinted glass, lockable glove box, composite tungsten-halogen headlamps, adjustable front seat head restraints, inside release hood lock, stand-up hood ornament, dual note horn, instrumentation includes: speedometer/fuel gauge/voltage/temperature/trip odometer; center high mounted stop lamp, crystalline park/turn lenses lamps, lights include: ashtray/instrument panel courtesy/dome/glove box/ trunk and engine compartment/front seat reading/map; deluxe black outside rearview mirrors (left remote, right manual), non-lighted covered visor vanity driver and passenger mirrors, moldings include: belt reveal/pillar/roof drip/black door/window frame; body color bodyside moldings, multi-function control lever includes: turn signal/headlamp high-low beam/windshield wiper-washer controls; basecoat/clearcoat paint with anti-chip lower protection, driver and passenger power seatback recliners, 55/45 seats with storage armrest, automatic front seat belts, lap/shoulder rear seat belts, dual standard-range front/extended-range rear speakers, tilt-wheel adjustable steering column, deluxe steering wheel, gas cylinder hood support struts, independent MacPherson front strut suspension, DynaRide suspension, compact spare tire, 2-speed wipers with low-speed delay feature, front seat storage armrest, door courtesy lights, bright wheel opening moldings, accent stripes.

CODE	DESCRIPTION	INVOICE	MSRP
	Accessories		
SA	**Base Pkg** *incls vehicle plus standard equipment*	NC	NC
SD	**Luxury Pkg** *incls automatic power antenna, front carpet savers, rear carpet savers, electronic cruise control, electric rearview deluxe outside mirrors (black, left and right remote), radio (cassette tape and ETR AM/FM stereo w/seek and scan, auto reverse and clock), trunk convenience net, electric remote trunk lock release*	643	748
SE	**Prestige Pkg** *incls SD Luxury Pkg plus remote keyless entry, 6-way power driver's seat, premium dual speaker system (front and rear coaxial)*	1082	1258
YF5	**California Emissions**	NC	NC
NG1	**Massachusetts Emissions**	NC	NC
—	**Leather Seats w/Storage Armrest**	430	500
AP9	**Trunk Convenience Net** — w/SA	26	30
AU0	**Remote Keyless Entry** — w/SA or SD	116	135
A90	**Trunk Lock Release** — electric remote - w/SA	52	60
B34	**Carpet Savers** — front - w/SA *B35 req'd*	22	25
B35	**Carpet Savers** — rear - w/SA *B34 req'd*	17	20
B93	**Door Edge Guards**	22	25
DG7	**Mirrors** — w/SA *incls deluxe outside, electric rearview (black, left and right remote)*	67	79
K05	**Engine Block Heater**	15	18
K34	**Cruise Control** — electronic - w/SA	194	225
N91	**Wheel Covers** — 14" custom locking wire	206	240
PG4	**Wheels** — 14" aluminum	254	295
QMW	**Tires** *incls steel belted all-season radial ply blackwall P195/75R14*	(62)	(72)
UM6	**Radio** — w/SA *incls cassette tape and ETR AM/FM stereo w/seek-scan, auto reverse and clock*	120	140
U62	**Speakers** — w/SA or SD *incls premium dual front and rear coaxial (UM6 or U1C req'd)*	60	70
U75	**Antenna** — automatic power - w/SA	73	85
VK3	**License Plate Mounting Package** — front	NC	NC
V08	**Cooling** — heavy duty engine	34	40
WG1	**Seat** — 6-way power driver side - w/SA or SD	262	305

CENTURY SPECIAL SEDAN *(1995)*

CENTURY SPECIAL SEDAN 4 CYL

CODE	DESCRIPTION	INVOICE	MSRP
G69	4-Dr Sedan	14787	15815
Destination Charge:		535	535

CODE	DESCRIPTION	INVOICE	MSRP

Standard Equipment

CENTURY SPECIAL SEDAN: 2.2 liter 2200 PFI 4-cylinder engine, 3-speed automatic transmission, power rack and pinion steering, power front disc/rear drum anti-lock brakes, automatic power door locks with lock/unlock/relock feature, P185/75R14 SBR all-season BW tires, 14" deluxe chrome wheel covers, AM/FM ETR stereo radio with seek/scan/clock; air conditioning, driver SRS air bag, fixed-mast antenna, front seat storage armrest with dual cup holders, Delco Freedom II Plus battery, brake/transmission interlock, front and rear bumper guards, front and rear carpeting, computer-selected chassis springs, engine and transmission cooling, front/side window outlet defoggers, electric rear window defogger, front wheel drive, electronic warning tone for: seatbelt/ignition key/headlamps on; hydraulic-tuned engine mounts, Soft-Ray tinted glass, lockable glove box, composite tungsten-halogen headlamps, adjustable front seat head restraints, inside release hood lock, stand-up hood ornament, dual note horn, instrumentation includes: speedometer/fuel gauge/voltage/temperature/ trip odometer, center high-mounted stop lamp, crystalline park/turn lenses lamps, lights include: ashtray/instrument panel courtesy/dome/glove box/trunk and engine compartments/front seat reading/ map; deluxe black outside rearview mirrors (left remote, right manual), non-lighted covered visor vanity driver and passenger mirrors, moldings include: belt reveal/pillar/roof drip/black door/window frame; body color bodyside moldings, multi-function control lever includes: turn signal/headlamp high-low beam/windshield wiper-washer controls; basecoat/clearcoat paint with anti-chip lower protection, driver and passenger power seatback recliners, 55/45 seats with storage armrest, automatic front seatbelts, rear seat lap/shoulder seat belts, dual standard-range front/extended-range rear speakers, tilt-wheel adjustable steering column, deluxe steering wheel, gas cylinder hood support struts, independent MacPherson front strut suspension, DynaRide suspension, compact spare tire, 2-speed wipers with low-speed delay feature.

Accessories

CODE	DESCRIPTION	INVOICE	MSRP
SA	**Base Pkg** *incls vehicle plus standard equipment*	NC	NC
SC	**Premium Pkg** *incls front seat storage armrest, electric rear window defogger, front seat reading lights, dual visor vanity mirrors (non-lighted), power windows*	514	598
SD	**Luxury Pkg** *incls SC Premium Pkg plus front carpet savers, rear carpet savers, electronic cruise control, electric remote trunk lock release, radio (cassette tape and ETR AM/FM stereo w/seek and scan, auto reverse and clock)*	918	1068
SE	**Prestige Pkg** *incls SD Luxury Pkg plus automatic power antenna, remote keyless entry, electric rearview deluxe outside mirrors (black, left and right remote), 6-way power driver's seat, trunk convenience net*	1463	1701
SJ	**SJ Pkg** *incls front seat storage armrest, front and rear carpet savers, electronic cruise control, electric rear window defogger, front seat reading lights, dual visor vanity mirrors (non-lighted), steel belted radial-ply whitewall P185/75R14 all-season tires, electric trunk lock release, power windows*	857	996
SK	**6 Cylinder Special Pkg** *incls 3.1 liter SFI V6 engine, front seat storage armrest, front and rear carpet savers, electronic cruise control, electric rear window defogger, front seat reading lights, dual visor vanity mirrors (non-lighted), steel belted radial-ply whitewall P185/75R14 all-season tires, electronically controlled 4-speed automatic transmission with overdrive, electric remote trunk lock release, power windows, radio (cassette tape and ETR AM/FM stereo with seek/scan, auto reverse and clock)*	1674	1946

CENTURY SPECIAL SEDAN

CODE	DESCRIPTION	INVOICE	MSRP
SL	**Limited Leather Pkg**	2781	3234
	incls SK Pkg plus remote keyless entry, deluxe outside electric rearview mirrors (black, left and right remote), 6-way power driver side seat (leather), trunk convenience net, 14" custom locking wire wheels		
L82	**3.1 Liter SFI V6 Engine** — w/SC, SD or SE	525	610
	MXO req'd		
YF5	**California Emissions**	NC	NC
NG1	**Massachusetts Emissions**	NC	NC
AP9	**Trunk Convenience Net** — w/SC, SD or SK	26	30
AU0	**Remote Keyless Entry** — w/SC, SD or SK	116	135
	req's A90 w/SC or SD		
A90	**Trunk Lock Release** — electric remote - w/SC	52	60
	req w/SC		
B34	**Carpet Savers** — front - w/SC	22	25
	B35 req'd)		
B35	**Carpet Savers** — rear - w/SC	17	20
	B34 req'd)		
B93	**Door Edge Guards** — w/SC, SD, SE, SK or SL	22	25
BF9	**Carpet Saver Delete** — front & rear - w/SD or SE	(39)	(45)
DG7	**Mirrors** — w/SC, SD or SK	67	78
	incls deluxe outside electric rearview (black, left and right remote)		
K05	**Engine Block Heater** — w/SC, SD, SE, SJ, SK or SL	15	18
K34	**Cruise Control** — electronic - w/SC	194	225
MX0	**Transmission** — w/SC, SD or SE	172	200
	incls electronically controlled 4-speed automatic trans w/overdrive (L82 req'd)		
N91	**Wheel Covers** — 14" custom locking wire - w/SC, SD, SE or SK	206	240
PC7	**Wheels** — 14" styled steel - w/SC, SD, SE, SJ or SK	99	115
PG4	**Wheels** — 14" aluminum - w/SC, SD, SE or SK	254	295
	w/SL	47	55
P08	**Wheels** — 14" chrome styled - w/SC, SD, SE, SJ or SK	30	35
—	**Tires**		
QFE	steel belted radial-ply - w/SJ, SK or SL	(58)	(68)
	incls blackwall P185/75R14 all-season		
QFF	steel belted radial-ply - w/SC, SD or SE	59	68
	incls whitewall P185/75R14 all-season		
QMW	steel belted radial-ply - w/SC, SD or SE	34	40
	incls blackwall P195/75R14 all-season		
QMX	steel belted radial-ply - w/SC, SD or SE	93	108
	incls whitewall P195/75R14 all-season		
-A	**Stripe** — bodyside	39	45
UM6	**Radio** — w/SC or SJ	120	140
	incls cassette tape and ETR AM/FM stereo w/seek-scan, auto reverse and clock		
U62	**Speaker System** — w/SC, SD, SE, SK or SL	60	70
	incls premium dual front and rear coaxial		
U75	**Antenna** — automatic power - w/SC, SD, SE, SK or SL	73	85
V08	**Cooling** — heavy duty engine - w/SC, SD, SE, SK or SL	34	40
VK3	**License Plate Mounting Package** — front	NC	NC

CODE	DESCRIPTION	INVOICE	MSRP
WG1	**Seat** — 6-way power driver side - w/SC, SD, SJ or SK	262	305
T61	**Daytime Running Lights** — w/SC, SD or SE	34	39
V58	**Luggage Rack** — chrome decklid - w/SK or SL	99	115

CENTURY SPECIAL WAGON *(1995)*

CENTURY SPECIAL WAGON 4 CYL

G35	4-Dr Wagon	15428	16500
Destination Charge:		535	535

Standard Equipment

CENTURY SPECIAL WAGON: 2.2 liter 2200 PFI engine, 3-speed automatic transmission, power rack and pinion steering, anti-lock power front disc/rear drum brakes, automatic power door locks with lock/unlock/relock feature, P185/75R14 SBR all-season BW tires, 14" deluxe chrome wheel covers, AM/FM ETR stereo radio with seek/scan/clock; air conditioning, driver SRS air bag, fixed-mast antenna, front seat storage armrest with dual cup holders, Delco Freedom II Plus battery, brake/transmission interlock, front and rear bumper guards, load floor carpeting, front and rear carpeting, computer-selected chassis springs, engine and transmission cooling, front and side window outlet defoggers, electric rear window defogger, front wheel drive, electronic warning tone for: seatbelt/ ignition key/headlamps on; hydraulic-tuned engine mounts, Soft-Ray tinted glass, lockable glove box, composite tungsten-halogen headlamps, adjustable front seat head restraint, inside release hood lock, stand-up hood ornament, dual note horn, instrumentation includes: speedometer/fuel gauge/voltage/temperature/trip odometer; center high-mounted stop lamp, crystalline park/turn lenses lamps, rear compartment light, lights include: ashtray/instrument panel courtesy/dome/glove box/ trunk and engine compartments/front seat reading/map; deluxe black outside rearview mirrors (left remote, right manual), non-lighted covered visor vanity driver and passenger mirrors, moldings include: belt reveal/pillar/roof drip/black door/window frame; black bodyside moldings, multi-function control lever includes: turn signal/headlamp high-low beam/windshield wiper-washer controls; basecoat/ clearcoat paint with anti-chip lower protection, driver and passenger power seatback recliners, 55/45 seats with storage armrests, split folding rear seatback, automatic front seat belts, rear seat lap/ shoulder seatbelts, dual standard-range front/extended-range rear speakers, tilt-wheel adjustable steering column, deluxe steering wheel, lockable load area/floor storage compartment, gas cylinder hood support struts, independent MacPherson front strut suspension, electric remote tailgate release, compact spare tire, 2-speed wipers with low-speed delay feature.

Accessories

SA	**Base Pkg** *incls vehicle plus standard equipment*	NC	NC
SC	**Luxury Pkg** *incls air deflector, front seat storage armrest, electric rear window defogger, front seat reading lights, dual visor vanity mirrors (non-lighted), power windows*	549	638
SD	**Luxury Pkg** *incls SC Luxury Pkg plus front carpet savers, rear carpet savers, electronic cruise control, electric rearview deluxe outside mirrors (black, left and right remote), radio (cassette tape and ETR AM/FM stereo w/seek and scan, auto reverse and clock)*	968	1126
SE	**Prestige Pkg** *incls SD Luxury Pkg plus cargo area security cover, roof luggage carrier, vinyl third seat, rear swing-out vent*	1312	1525

CODE	DESCRIPTION	INVOICE	MSRP
SJ	**4 Cylinder Special Pkg**	1183	1375
	incls air deflector, front seat storage armrest, cargo area security cover, front and rear carpet savers, electronic cruise control, electric rear window defogger front seat reading lights, dual visor vanity mirrors (non-lighted), roof luggage carrier, vinyl third seat, steel belted radial-ply whitewall P185/75R14 all-season tires, power windows		
SK	**6 Cylinder Special Pkg**	2000	2325
	incls SJ 4 Cylinder Special Pkg plus 3.1 liter SFI V6 engine, radio (cassette tape and ETR AM/FM stereo with seek/scan, auto reverse and clock), electronically controlled 4-speed automatic transmission with overdrive		
L82	**3.1 Liter SFI V6 Engine** — w/SC, SD or SE	525	610
	MX0 req'd		
YF5	**California Emissions**	NC	NC
NG1	**Massachusetts Emissions**	NC	NC
AU0	**Remote Keyless Entry** — w/SC, SD, SE or SK	116	135
BF9	**Carpet Saver Delete** — front and rear - w/SD or SE	(39)	(45)
BX3	**Woodgrain Bodyside Applique** — w/SC, SD, SE, SJ or SK	327	380
	incls B93 in woodgrain		
B93	**Door Edge Guards** — w/SC, SD, SE, SJ or SK	22	25
	incl w/BX3		
C25	**Window Washer/Wiper Tailgate** — w/SC, SD, SE, SJ or SK	73	85
	NA w/C51		
DG7	**Mirror** — w/SC, SJ or SK	67	78
	incls deluxe outside electric rearview (black, left and right remote)		
K05	**Engine Block Heater** — w/SC, SD, SE, SJ or SK	15	18
K34	**Cruise Control** — electronic - w/SC	194	225
MX0	**Transmission** — w/SC, SD or SE	172	200
	incls electronically controlled 4-speed automatic trans w/overdrive (L82 req'd)		
PC7	**Wheels** — 14" styled steel - w/SC, SD, SE, SJ or SK	99	115
PG4	**Wheels** — 14" aluminum - w/SC, SD, SE or SK	254	295
P08	**Wheels** — 14" chrome styled - w/SC, SD, SE or SJ	30	35
—	**Tires**		
QFE	steel belted radial-ply - w/SJ or SK	(58)	(68)
	incls blackwall P185/75R14 all-season		
QFF	steel belted radial-ply - w/SC, SD or SE	59	68
	incls whitewall P185/75R14 all-season		
QMW	steel belted radial-ply - w/SC, SD or SE	34	40
	w/SJ or SK	(24)	(28)
	incls blackwall P195/75R14 all-season		
QMX	steel belted radial-ply - w/SC, SD or SE	93	108
	w/SJ or SK	34	40
	incls whitewall P195/75R14 all-season		
-A	**Stripes** — bodyside	39	45
UM6	**Radio** — w/SC or SJ	120	140
	incls cassette tape and ETR AM/FM stereo w/seek-scan, auto reverse and clock		
T61	**Daytime Running Lights** — w/SC, SD or SE	34	39
U75	**Antenna** — automatic power - w/SC, SD, SE or SK	73	85
VK3	**License Plate Mounting Package** — front	NC	NC

CODE	DESCRIPTION	INVOICE	MSRP
V08	**Cooling** — heavy duty engine - w/SC, SD, SE or SK	34	40
WG1	**Seat** — 6-way power driver side - w/SC, SD, SE, SJ or SK	262	305

LE SABRE CUSTOM SEDAN *(1995)*

LE SABRE CUSTOM SEDAN 6 CYL

P69	4-Dr Sedan	18962	20724
Destination Charge:		585	585

Standard Equipment

LE SABRE CUSTOM SEDAN: 3800 V6 tuned-port injection engine, electronically controlled 4-speed automatic transmission with overdrive, power rack and pinion steering, anti-lock power front disc/rear drum brakes, power windows with driver's express-down and passenger lockout feature, power door locks, P205/70R15 SBR all-season BW tires, deluxe wheel covers, AM/FM ETR stereo radio with seek/scan/clock; air conditioning, driver and front passenger side air bag SRS, fixed-mast antenna, front seat armrest, Delco Freedom II Plus battery, push to set and release parking brake, brake/transmission interlock, front bumper guards, front and rear carpeting, front/side window outlet defoggers, front wheel drive, electronic warning tone for: seatbelt/ignition key/parking brake/headlamps on; stainless steel exhaust system, Soft-Ray tinted glass, wrap-around composite tungsten-halogen headlamps, adjustable front seat head restraints, inside release hood lock, backlit analog gauge cluster with trip odometer, center high-mounted stop lamp, lights include: front ashtray/front and rear door operated dome/trunk/engine compartment/glove box/instrument panel courtesy, deluxe body color outside rearview mirrors (left remote, right manual), black bodyside moldings, moldings include: wheel opening/belt reveal/roof drip, malfunction control lever for: turn signal/headlamp high-low beam/ windshield wiper-washer controls, basecoat/clearcoat paint with anti-chip lower protection, driver and passenger manual seatback recliners, front seat lap/shoulder seatbelts with front shoulder belt comfort adjuster, rear seat lap/shoulder seatbelts with child comfort guide, 55/45 cloth seats, rear door child security locks, dual front/extended-range rear speakers, tilt-wheel adjustable steering column, deluxe steering wheel, extendable/supplemental sunshades, independent MacPherson front strut suspension, rear independent suspension, DynaRide suspension, Pass Key II theft-deterrent system, full trunk trim, 2-speed wipers with low-speed delay.

CODE	DESCRIPTION	INVOICE	MSRP
	Accessories		
SA	**Base Pkg**	NC	NC
	incls vehicle plus standard equipment		
SD	**Luxury Pkg**	998	1161
	incls front seat storage armrest with dual cup holders, front and rear carpet savers, electronic cruise control, electric rear window defogger, radio (power-loading cassette and ETR AM/FM stereo with seek/scan and clock), bodyside stripe, steel belted radial-ply whitewall all-season P205/70R15 tires, trunk convenience net, aluminum 15" wheels		
SE	**Prestige Pkg**	1700	1977
	incls SD Luxury Pkg plus automatic power antenna, body color door edge guards, remote keyless entry, passenger side lighted visor vanity mirror, outside electric rearview mirrors (left and right remote, body color), 6-way power driver's seat, Concert Sound II speaker system, electric remote trunk lock release		
SG	**SG Pkg**	1569	1824
	incls automatic power antenna, front seat storage armrest with dual cup holders, front and rear carpet savers, electronic cruise control, electric rear window defogger, remote keyless entry, outside electric rearview mirrors (left and right remote, body color), radio (power-loading cassette and ETR AM/FM stereo with seek/scan and clock), 6-way power driver side seat, bodyside stripe, steel belted radial-ply whitewall all-season P205/70R15 tires, trunk convenience net, electric remote trunk lock release, aluminum 15" wheels (4).		
YF5	**California Emissions**	NC	NC
NG1	**Massachusetts Emissions**	NC	NC
—	**Leather Trim** — w/SD or SE	856	995
	DG7 & WG1 req'd		
A90	**Trunk Lock Release** — electric remote - w/SD	52	60
	AU0 req'd		
AG2	**Seat** — 6-way power passenger side - w/SE	262	305
AU0	**Remote Keyless Entry** — w/SD	116	135
	A90 req'd		
DG7	**Mirrors** — w/SD	67	78
	incls outside electric rearview (left and right remote, body color); WG1 req'd		
N91	**Wheel Covers** — custom locking wire - w/SD, SE or SG	NC	NC
	NA w/Y56 w/SD or SE		
P42	**Tires** — w/SA	194	226
	w/SD or SE	129	150
	incls self-sealing steel belted radial-ply whitewall all-season P205/70R15		
PH3	**Wheels** — aluminum (4) 15" - w/SA	280	325
QGY	**Tires** — w/SD or SE	(65)	(76)
	w/SG	NC	NC
	incls steel belted radial-ply blackwall all-season P205/70R15; NA w/Y56 w/SD or SE		
QGZ	**Tires** — w/SA w/o P42	65	76
	incls steel belted radial-ply whitewall all-season P205/70R15; NA w/Y56		
UL0	**Radio** — w/SE	129	150
	incls power-loading cassette and ETR AM/FM stereo with seek/scan automatic tone control and clock, steering wheel radio controls		

CODE	DESCRIPTION	INVOICE	MSRP
UN0	**Radio** — w/SE *incls power-loading CD player with next/last track selector and ETR AM/FM stereo with seek/scan, automatic tone control and clock, steering wheel radio controls*	215	250
UP0	**Radio** — w/SE *incls power-loading CD and cassette player with next/last CD track selector & ETR AM/FM stereo with seek/scan, automatic tone control and clock, steering wheel radio controls*	301	350
U75	**Antenna** — automatic power - w/SD	73	85
V92	**Trailer Towing Pkg** — w/SE & Y56	129	150
	w/o SE & Y56	280	325
WG1	**Seat** — 6-way power driver side - w/SD *DG7 req'd*	262	305
Y56	**Gran Touring Pkg** — w/SE *incls 3.06 axle ratio, gran touring suspension, blackwall P215/60R16 touring tires, aluminum wheels, automatic level control and leather-wrapped steering wheel*	360	419
K05	**Engine Block Heater** — w/SC, SD or SE	15	18

LE SABRE LIMITED SEDAN *(1995)*

LE SABRE LIMITED SEDAN 6 CYL

R69	4-Dr Sedan	22216	24280
Destination Charge:		585	585

Standard Equipment

LE SABRE LIMITED SEDAN: 3800 V6 tuned-port injection engine, electrically controlled 4-speed automatic transmission with overdrive, variable effort power rack and pinion steering, anti-lock power front disc/rear drum brakes, power windows with driver's express-down and passenger lockout feature, power door locks, P205/70R15 SBR all-season WW tires, 15" aluminum wheels, AM/FM ETR stereo radio with seek/scan/cassette/clock; air conditioning, driver and front passenger side air bag SRS, Delco Freedom II Plus battery, push-to-set and release parking brake, brake/transmission interlock/front bumper guards, front and rear carpeting, front/side window outlet defoggers, front wheel drive, electronic warning tone for: seatbelt/ignition key/parking brake/headlamps on; stainless steel exhaust system, Soft-Ray tinted glass, wrap-around composite tungsten-halogen headlamps, adjustable front seat head restraints, inside release hood lock, backlit analog gauge cluster with trip odometer, center high-mounted stop lamp, lights include: front ashtray/front and rear door operated dome/trunk/engine compartment/glove box/instrument panel courtesy; black bodyside moldings, moldings include: wheel opening/belt reveal/roof drip; multi-function control lever includes: turn signal/ headlamp high-low beam/windshield wiper-washer controls; basecoat/clearcoat paint with anti-chip lower protection, driver and passenger manual seatback recliners, front seat lap/shoulder seatbelts with front shoulder belt comfort adjuster, rear seat lap/shoulder seatbelts with child comfort guide, rear door child security locks, tilt-wheel adjustable steering column, deluxe steering wheel, extendable/ supplemental sunshades, independent MacPherson front strut suspension, rear independent suspension, DynaRide suspension, Pass Key II theft-deterrent system, full trunk trim, 2-speed wipers with low-speed delay, automatic power antenna, front seat storage armrest with dual cup holders, front and rear carpet savers, electronic cruise control, electric rear window defogger, body color door edge guards, front and rear door courtesy lights, lights include: front and rear door operated dome/ front header courtesy and reading/instrument panel courtesy/ashtray/glove box/trunk/engine compartment/rear roof rail courtesy/reading; deluxe body color power outside rearview mirrors, driver and passenger lighted visor vanity mirrors, remote keyless entry, driver 6-way power seat, Concert Sound II speakers, accent stripes, trunk convenience net, remote electric trunk lock release.

CODE	DESCRIPTION	INVOICE	MSRP
	Accessories		
SD	**Base Pkg**	NC	NC
	incls vehicle plus standard equipment		
SE	**Prestige Pkg**	624	725
	incls dual automatic comfortemp climate control air conditioning, rear seat air conditioning, cornering lamps, radio (power-loading cassette and ETR AM/FM stereo with seek/scan, automatic tone control and clock, steering wheel radio controls), 6-way power passenger side seat		
SG	**SG Pkg**	1237	1438
	incls dual automatic comfortemp climate control air conditioning, rear seat air conditioning, cornering lamps, instrumentation (analog gauge cluster incls oil pressure and temperature, volts, low fuel indicator, oil level monitor, oil life monitor & tachometer), radio (power-loading cassette and ETR AM/FM stereo with seek/scan automatic tone control, clock, steering wheel radio controls), 6-way power passenger side seat		
YF5	**California Emissions**	NC	NC
NG1	**Massachusetts Emissions**	NC	NC
—	**Leather Split Bench Seats** — w/storage armrest - w/SD or SE	473	550
AG2	**Seat** — 6-way power passenger side - w/SD	262	305
N91	**Wheel Covers** — custom locking wire - w/SD or SE	NC	NC
	NA w/Y56		
NW9	**Traction Control System** — w/SD or SE	151	175
	UB3 req'd		
K05	**Engine Block Heater**	15	18
P42	**Tires** — w/SD or SE	129	150
	incls self-sealing steel belted radial-ply whitewall all-season P205/70R15		
QGY	**Tires** — w/SD or SE	(65)	(76)
	incls steel belted radial-ply blackwall all-season P205/70R15; NA w/Y56		
UB3	**Instrumentation** — w/SD or SE	140	163
	incls analog gauge cluster (incls oil pressure and temperature, volts, low fuel indicator, oil level monitor, oil life monitor and tachometer)		
UL0	**Radio** — w/SD	129	150
	incls power-loading cassette and ETR AM/FM stereo with seek/scan automatic tone control and clock, steering wheel radio controls		
UN0	**Radio** — w/SD	215	250
	w/SE o SG	86	100
	incls power-loading CD player with next/last track selector and ETR AM/FM stereo with seek/scan, automatic tone control and clock, steering wheel radio controls		
UP0	**Radio** — w/SD	301	350
	w/SE or SG	172	200
	incls power-loading CD and cassette player with next/last CD track selector & ETR AM/FM stereo with seek/scan, automatic tone control and clock, steering wheel radio controls		
V92	**Trailer Towing Pkg** — w/SD or SE, w/o Y56	280	325
	w/SD or SE, w/Y56	129	150
Y56	**Gran Touring Pkg** — w/SD or SE	360	419
	incls 3.06 axle ratio, gran touring suspension, blackwall P215/60R16 touring tires, aluminum wheels, automatic level control and leather-wrapped steering wheel		

PARK AVENUE SEDAN *(1995)*

PARK AVENUE SEDAN 6 CYL

CODE	DESCRIPTION	INVOICE	MSRP
W69	4-Dr Sedan	24376	27236
Destination Charge:		635	635

Standard Equipment

PARK AVENUE SEDAN: 3800 Series II V6 engine, electronically-controlled 4-speed automatic transmission with overdrive, variable effort power rack and pinion steering, anti-lock power front disc/rear drum brakes, power windows with driver's express-down and passenger lockout feature, automatic power door locks, P205/70R15 SBR all-season BW tires, specific 15" aluminum wheels, AM/FM ETR stereo radio with seek/scan/cassette; air conditioning, driver and front passenger side air bag SRS, fixed-mast antenna, front-seat storage armrest with dual cup holders, passenger assist handles, Delco Freedom II Plus battery, push-to-set and release parking brake, front bumper guards, front and rear carpet savers, overhead console includes: front seat reading lights/garage door opener storage, electronic cruise control, electric rear window defogger, front/side window outlet defoggers, front wheel drive, electronic warning tone includes: seatbelt/ignition key/headlamps/parking brake on; stainless steel exhaust system, remote electric fuel filler door release, Solar-Ray solar-control glass, wrap-around composite tungsten-halogen headlamps, adjustable front seat head restraints, inside release hood lock, dual note horn, backlit analog gauge cluster with trip odometer, center high-mounted stop lamp, lights include: front ashtray/trunk/engine compartment/glove box/instrument panel courtesy, front and rear door courtesy/warning lights, front and rear seat reading and courtesy lights, lighted passenger visor vanity mirror, deluxe body color outside electric rearview mirrors (left and right remote), moldings include: wheel opening/belt reveal/bodyside; basecoat/clearcoat paint with anti-chip lower protection, driver and passenger manual seatback recliners, driver 6-way power seat, front seat lap/shoulder seatbelts with shoulder belt comfort adjuster, rear seat lap/shoulder seatbelts with child comfort guide, 55/45 cloth seats with front seat storage armrest, rear door child security locks, front/rear extended-range speakers, tilt-wheel adjustable steering column, deluxe steering wheel, accent stripes, supplemental/extendable sunshades, automatic level control suspension, DynaRide suspension, front and rear independent suspension, Pass Key II theft-deterrent system, electric remote trunk lock release with security switch, full trunk trim, 2-speed wipers with low-speed delay.

CODE	DESCRIPTION	INVOICE	MSRP
	Accessories		
SA	**Base Pkg**	NC	NC
	incls vehicle plus standard equipment		
SD	**Luxury Pkg**	1588	1846
	incls dual automatic comfortemp climate control air conditioning, automatic power antenna, trunk convenience net, cornering lamps, body color door edge guards, automatic programmable door locks, twilight sentinel headlamps control, four note horn, instrumentation (analog gauge cluster type which incls oil pressure, volts, low fuel indicator, coolant temperature, oil life monitor, oil level monitor and tachometer), remote keyless entry, front and rear lamp monitors, light control (incls illuminated driver door lock and interior, retained accessory power), automatic rearview day/night mirror, driver side lighted visor vanity mirror, passenger side electric seat back recliner, reminder pkg (incls low washer fluid, low coolant and door ajar indicators), 6-way power passenger seat, Concert Sound II speaker system, theft deterrent system with starter interrupt, steel belted radial-ply whitewall all-season P205/70R15 tires, electric trunk pull down		
SE	**Prestige Pkg**	2297	2671
	incls SD Luxury Pkg plus rear seat comfortemp air conditioning, rear seat storage armrest, automatic rearview day/night mirrors with compass, electric heated mirrors (remote, automatic day/night, body color), radio (power loading cassette and ETR AM/FM stereo with seek/scan, automatic tone control, clock, steering wheel radio controls), driver side electric seat back recliner, two-position memory 6-way power driver's seat and memory mirrors, P205/70R15 whitewall self-sealing tires, trunk mat		
SG	**SG Pkg**	1626	1891
	incls dual automatic comfortemp climate control air conditioning, rear seat air conditioning, automatic power antenna, trunk convenience net, cornering lamps, body color door edge guards, automatic programmable door locks, twilight sentinel headlamp control, four-note horn, instrumentation (analog gauge cluster including oil pressure, volts, low fuel indicator, coolant temperature, oil life monitor, oil level monitor and tachometer), remote keyless entry, front and rear lamp monitors, illuminated driver door lock and interior light control, retained accessory power, automatic day/night rearview mirror, driver side lighted visor vanity mirror, passenger side electric seatback recliner, reminder package (incls low washer fluid, low coolant and door ajar indicators), Concert Sound II speaker system, starter interrupt theft deterrent system, steel belted radial-ply whitewall all-season P205/70R15 tires, electric trunk pull-down, 6-way power passenger seat		
YF5	**California Emissions**	NC	NC
NG1	**Massachusetts Emissions**	NC	NC
—	**Leather Split Bench Seats** — w/SD	559	650
—	**Leather Split Bench Seats** — w/storage armrest - w/SE	516	600
CF5	**Astroroof** — electric sliding - w/SE	789	918
FX3	**Automatic Ride Control** — w/SE	327	380
	NW9 req'd; NA w/Y56 or V92		
AM6	**Seat** — leather 55/45 w/storage armrest - w/SG	559	650
KA1	**Seat** — electric heated driver and passenger - w/SE	103	120
K05	**Engine Block Heater**	15	18
NW9	**Traction Control System** — w/SD or SE	151	175

BUICK

CODE	DESCRIPTION	INVOICE	MSRP
N91	**Wheel Covers** — custom locking wire	NC	NC
	NA w/Y56		
P42	**Tires** — w/SA or SD	129	150
	incls self-sealing steel belted radial-ply whitewall all-season P205/70R15		
QGY	**Tires** — w/SD	(65)	(76)
	w/SE	(194)	(226)
	w/SG	NC	NC
	incls steel belted radial-ply blackwall all-season P205/70R15; NA w/Y56, SD or SE		
QGZ	**Tires** — w/SA w/o P42	65	76
	incls steel belted radial-ply whitewall all-season P205/70R15		
UL0	**Radio** — w/SD or SG	129	150
	incls power-loading cassette and ETR AM/FM stereo with seek/scan, automatic tone control, clock, steering wheel radio controls		
UN0	**Radio** — w/SD or SG	215	250
	w/SE	86	100
	incls power-loading CD player with next/last CD track selector and ETR AM/FM stereo with seek/scan, automatic tone control, clock, steering wheel radio controls		
UP0	**Radio** — w/SD or SG	301	350
	w/SE	172	200
	incls power-loading CD and cassette player with next/last CD track selector and ETR AM/FM stereo with seek/scan, automatic tone control, clock, steering wheel radio controls		
V92	**Trailer Towing Pkg** — w/o Y56 - w/SD or SE	152	177
	w/Y56 - w/SD or SE	129	150
	NW9 req'd; NA w/FX3		
Y56	**Gran Touring Pkg** — w/SD or SE	193	224
	w/SG	343	399
	incls gran touring suspension, 3.06 axle ratio, leather-wrapped steering wheel, 16" aluminum wheel and P215/60R16 touring blackwall tires (NW9 req'd w/SD or SE; FX3 NA w/SD or SE)		
VK3	**License Plate Mounting** — front	NC	NC

PARK AVENUE ULTRA SEDAN *(1995)*

PARK AVENUE ULTRA SEDAN 6 CYL

CODE	DESCRIPTION	INVOICE	MSRP
U69	4-Dr Sedan	28552	31902
Destination Charge:		635	635

Standard Equipment

PARK AVENUE ULTRA SEDAN: 3800 supercharged V6 engine, electronically-controlled 4-speed automatic transmission with overdrive, variable effort power rack and pinion steering, anti-lock power front disc/rear drum brakes, power windows with driver's express-down and passenger lockout feature, automatic programmable door locks, P215/70R15 SBR all-season BW tires, specific 15" aluminum wheels, AM/FM ETR stereo radio with seek/scan/cassette/clock; dual automatic ComforTemp climate control air conditioning, rear seat ComforTemp air conditioning, driver and front passenger side air bag SRS, front seat storage armrest with dual cup holders, passenger assist handles, push-to-set and release parking brake, front bumper guards, front and rear carpet savers,

CODE	DESCRIPTION	INVOICE	MSRP

overhead console includes: front seat reading lights/garage door opener storage; electronic cruise control, electric rear window defogger, front/side window outlet defoggers, front wheel drive, electronic warning tone for: seatbelt/ignition key/headlamps/parking brake on; stainless steel exhaust system, electric remote fuel filler door release, Solar-Ray solar control glass, wrap-around composite tungsten-halogen headlamps, adjustable front-seat head restraint, inside release hood lock, center high-mounted stop lamp, lights include: front ashtray/trunk/engine compartment/glove box/instrument panel courtesy, front and rear door courtesy/warning lights, front and rear seat reading/courtesy lights, lighted passenger visor vanity mirror, deluxe body color outside electric rearview mirrors (left/right remote), moldings include: wheel opening/belt reveal/bodyside; basecoat/clearcoat paint with anti-chip lower protection, front seat lap/shoulder seatbelts with shoulder belt comfort adjuster, rear seat lap/shoulder seatbelts with child comfort guide, rear door child security locks, tilt-wheel adjustable steering column, accent stripes, supplemental/extendable sunshades, automatic level control suspension, DynaRide suspension, front and rear independent suspension, remote electric trunk lock release with security switch, full trunk trim, 2-speed wipers with low-speed delay, automatic power antenna, rear seat storage armrest (included with leather seats), heavy duty Delco Freedom II Plus battery, body color door edge guards, twilight sentinel headlamp control, rear seat head restraints, 4-note horn, analog instrumentation gauge cluster includes: tachometer/coolant temperature/oil pressure/voltage/low fuel indicator/oil level indicator/oil life monitor/trip odometer, front and rear lamp monitors, cornering lamps, automatic dimming inside rearview mirror, driver's lighted visor vanity mirror, rear seat passenger's lighted vanity mirror, moldings include: wheel opening/belt reveal/wide bodyside/lower panel/door edge guard, specific lower accent moldings, driver and passenger electric seatback recliners, reminder package includes: low washer fluid indicator/low coolant level/door ajar and trunk ajar indicators; remote keyless entry, retained accessory power includes illuminated door locks and light control, driver and passenger 6-way power reclining seats, 55/45 leather/vinyl seats with front seat storage armrest, Concert Sound II speakers, leather-wrapped steering wheel, theft-deterrent system with starter interrupt, trunk convenience net, electric trunk pull-down.

Accessories

CODE	DESCRIPTION	INVOICE	MSRP
SC	**Base Pkg**	NC	NC
	incls vehicle plus standard equipment		
SD	**Luxury Pkg**	628	730
	incls radio (power-loading cassette and ETR AM/FM stereo with seek/scan, automatic tone control, clock, steering wheel radio controls), automatic ride control, traction control system		
SE	**Prestige Pkg**	1191	1385
	incls SD Luxury Pkg plus automatic day/night rearview mirror with compass, electric heated left and right remote mirrors (day/night, body color), electric heated driver and passenger seats, two-position memory 6-way power driver's seat and memory mirrors, P215/70R15 whitewall self-sealing tires, trunk mat		
YF5	**California Emissions**	NC	NC
NG1	**Massachusetts Emissions**	NC	NC
CF5	**Astroroof** — electric sliding - w/SD or SE	690	802
D83	**Ultra Solid Exterior Color**	NC	NC
KA1	**Seat** — electric heated driver and passenger - w/SD	103	120
K05	**Engine Block Heater**	15	18
P42	**Tires** — w/SC or SD	129	150
	incls self-sealing steel belted radial-ply whitewall all-season P215/70R15		
QPK	**Tires** — w/SC or SD	(69)	(80)
	w/SE	(198)	(230)
	incls steel belted radial-ply blackwall all-season P215/70R15		

BUICK

CODE	DESCRIPTION	INVOICE	MSRP
ULO	**Radio** — w/SC	129	150
	incls power-loading cassette and ETR AM/FM stereo with seek/scan, automatic tone control, clock, steering wheel radio controls		
UNO	**Radio** — w/SC	215	250
	w/SD or SE	86	100
	incls power-loading CD player with next/last CD track selector and ETR AM/FM stereo with seek/scan, automatic tone control, clock, steering wheel radio controls		
UPO	**Radio** — w/SC	301	350
	w/SD or SE	172	200
	incls power-loading CD and cassette player with next/last CD track selector & ETR AM/FM stereo with seek/scan, automatic tone control, clock, steering wheel radio controls		
V92	**Trailer Towing Pkg** — w/SD or SE, w/o Y56	(175)	(203)
	w/SD or SE, w/Y56	(198)	(230)
	NA w/FX3		
Y56	**Gran Touring Pkg** — w/SD or SE	(253)	(294)
	incls gran touring suspension, 16" aluminum wheels and P215/60R16 touring blackwall tires; NA w/FX3		
VK3	**License Plate Mounting** — front	NC	NC

REGAL CUSTOM COUPE *(1995)*

REGAL CUSTOM COUPE 6 CYL

		INVOICE	MSRP
B57	2-Dr Coupe	17101	18690
Destination Charge:		535	535

Standard Equipment

REGAL CUSTOM COUPE: 3.1 liter 3100 SFI V6 engine, electronically-controlled automatic transmission with overdrive, power steering, anti-lock 4-wheel power disc brakes, power windows, automatic power door locks, 15" deluxe bolt-on wheel covers, AM/FM ETR stereo radio with seek/scan/clock; dual ComforTemp air conditioning, driver and front passenger side air bag SRS, fixed-

CODE	DESCRIPTION	INVOICE	MSRP

mast antenna, front seat storage armrest with cup holders, rear seat or door armrest ashtrays, Delco Freedom II Plus battery, 2-sided galvanized body panels, push-to-set/release parking brake, brake/transmission interlock, electronic cruise control, front/side window outlet defoggers, front wheel drive, electronic warning tone for: seatbelt/ignition key/turn signal/headlamps/parking brake on; stainless steel exhaust system, Soft-Ray tinted glass, composite tungsten-halogen headlamps, adjustable front seat head restraints, rear seat heat ducts, floor-mounted release inside hood lock, illuminated driver door lock, interior illumination with theatre dimming (door handle activated), analog gauge instrumentation cluster includes: tachometer/voltage/temperature/oil pressure/fuel gauges/trip odometer; center high-mounted stop lamp, crystalline park/turn lenses lamps, door-operated dome light, lights include: front ashtray/instrument panel courtesy/trunk/engine compartment/glove box; deluxe black outside rearview mirrors (left remote, right manual), dual covered non-lighted driver and passenger visor vanity mirrors, moldings include: black windshield/back window frame/side window/belt reveal; body color protective bodyside moldings, multi-function control lever includes: turn signal/headlamp high-low beam/flash-to-pass/windshield wiper-washer controls, basecoat/clearcoat paint with anti-chip lower protection, driver and passenger manual seatback recliners, auxiliary power receptacle, driver and passenger 2-way manual seat adjusters, front and rear seat lap/shoulder safety belts, 55/45 cloth reclining seats with storage armrest, four dual extended-range front and rear speakers, tilt-wheel adjustable steering column, deluxe steering wheel, slide-out sunshade extensions, independent front and rear suspension, DynaRide suspension, Pass Key II theft-deterrent system, trunk trim, 2-speed wipers with low-speed delay feature.

Accessories

CODE	DESCRIPTION	INVOICE	MSRP
SC	**Premium Pkg**	NC	NC
	incls vehicle plus standard equipment		
SD	**Luxury Pkg**	347	403
	incls SC Premium Pkg plus automatic power antenna, front carpet savers, rear carpet savers, electric deluxe outside mirrors, radio (power-loading cassette and ETR AM/FM stereo with seek/scan and clock)		
SE	**Prestige Pkg**	798	928
	incls SD Luxury Pkg plus remote keyless entry, front overhead console courtesy reading lights, sail panel courtesy lights, 6-way power driver side seat, trunk convenience net		
SJ	**Custom Pkg**	798	928
	incls automatic power antenna, front and rear carpet savers, remote keyless entry, front overhead console courtesy reading lights, sail panel courtesy lights, electric deluxe outside rearview mirrors, radio (power-loading cassette and ETR AM/FM stereo with seek/scan and clock), 6-way power driver's seat, trunk convenience net		
SK	**Gran Sport Pkg**	1968	2288
	incls SJ Custom Pkg plus gran touring suspension, 16" aluminum wheels, P225/60R16 steel belted radial-ply blackwall tires, leather-wrapped steering wheel, Concert Cound II speaker system, steering wheel radio controls, radio (power-loading cassette and ETR AM/FM stereo with seek/scan, automatic tone control and clock), 3.8 liter 3800 SFI V6 engine, variable effort steering, cloth bucket seats		
L27	**3.8 Liter 3800 SFI V6 Engine**	340	395
	incld in SK		
YF5	**California Emissions**	NC	NC
NG1	**Massachusetts Emissions**	NC	NC
AR9	**Bucket Seats** — w/full operating console	NC	NC
B34	**Carpet Savers** — front - w/SC	22	25
	B35 req'd		

CODE	DESCRIPTION	INVOICE	MSRP
B35	**Carpet Savers** — rear - w/SC	17	20
	B34 req'd		
PH6	**Wheels** — 15" aluminum (4)	280	325
	QGY or QGZ req'd; NA w/SK		
QGZ	**Tires** — w/SC, SD, SE or SJ	65	76
	incls P205/70R15 steel belted radial-ply all-season whitewall		
UK3	**Radio Controls** — steering wheel mounted - w/SE or SJ	108	125
	UN6 NA w/SE		
UN6	**Radio** — w/SC	168	195
	incls power-loading cassette and ETR AM/FM stereo with seek/scan and clock		
UL0	**Radio** — w/SD, SE or SJ	22	25
	incls power-loading cassette and ETR AM/FM stereo with seek/scan, automatic tone control and clock		
UN0	**Radio** — w/SE or SJ	108	125
	w/SK	86	100
	incls power-loading CD player with next/last CD track selector and ETR AM/FM stereo with seek/scan, automatic tone control and clock; UW6 req'd		
UP0	**Radio** — w/SE or SJ	194	225
	w/SK	172	200
	incls power-loading CD and cassette player with next/last CD track selector and ETR AM/FM stereo with seek/scan, automatic tone control and clock; UW6 req'd		
UW6	**Speaker System** — Concert Sound II - w/SE	60	70
U75	**Antenna** — automatic power - w/SC	73	85
VK3	**License Plate Mounting Pkg** — front	NC	NC
V08	**Heavy Duty Engine Cooling**	129	150
	L27 req'd		
WG1	**Seat** — 6-way power driver side - w/SD	262	305
WG5	**Seats** — 6-way power driver & passenger side - w/SK	263	305
—	**Seats** — leather bucket w/full opening console - w/SJ or SK	473	550
	AR9 & UW6 req'd		
V56	**Luggage Rack** — black decklid - w/SJ or SK	99	115
CF5	**Astroroof** — w/SJ or SK	598	695
	electric sliding/tilting with sunshade; incls rearview mirrors w/reading lamps		
DH6	**Mirrors** — driver & passenger dual lighted visor vanity - w/SK	79	92
K05	**Engine Block Heater** — w/SJ or SK	15	18
UW6	**Speaker System** — Concert Sound II - w/SJ	60	70

REGAL CUSTOM SEDAN *(1995)*

REGAL CUSTOM SEDAN 6 CYL

		INVOICE	MSRP
B19	4-Dr Sedan	17321	18930
Destination Charge:		535	535

Standard Equipment

REGAL CUSTOM SEDAN: 3.1 liter 3100 SFI V6 engine, electronically-controlled automatic transmission with overdrive, power steering, anti-lock 4-wheel power disc brakes, power windows

BUICK

CODE	DESCRIPTION	INVOICE	MSRP

with driver's express-down and passenger lockout feature, automatic power door locks, 15" deluxe bolt-on wheel covers, AM/FM ETR stereo radio with seek/scan/clock, dual ComforTemp air conditioning, driver and front passenger side air bag SRS, fixed-mast antenna, front seat storage armrest with cup holders, rear seat or door armrest ashtrays, Delco Freedom II Plus battery, 2-sided galvanized body panels, push-to-set/release parking brake, brake/transmission interlock, electronic cruise control, front and side window outlet defoggers, front wheel drive, electronic warning tone for: seatbelt/ignition key/turn signal/headlamps/parking brake on; stainless steel exhaust system, Soft-Ray tinted glass, composite tungsten-halogen headlamps, adjustable front seat head restraints, rear seat heat ducts, floor-mounted release inside hood lock, interior illumination with theatre dimming (door handle activated), analog instrumentation gauge cluster includes: tachometer/voltage/temperature/oil pressure/fuel gauges/trip odometer; center high-mounted stop lamp, crystalline park/turn lenses lamps, door-operated dome light, lights include: front ashtray/instrument panel courtesy/trunk/engine compartment/glove box; deluxe black outside rearview mirrors (left remote, right manual), dual covered non-lighted driver and passenger visor vanity mirrors, moldings include: black windshield/back window frame/bright rear quarter window/belt reveal; front and rear wheel opening body color moldings, protective bodyside body color moldings, multi-function control lever includes: turn signal/headlamp high-low beam/flash-to-pass/windshield wiper-washer controls; basecoat/clearcoat paint with anti-chip lower protection, driver and passenger manual seatback recliners, auxiliary power receptacle, 2-way manual driver and passenger seat adjusters, front and rear seat lap/shoulder safety belts, 55/45 cloth reclining seats with storage armrest, four dual extended-range front and rear speakers, tilt-wheel adjustable steering column, deluxe steering wheel, slide-out sunshade extensions, independent front and rear suspension, DynaRide suspension, Pass Key II theft-deterrent system, trunk trim, 2-speed wipers with low-speed delay feature.

Accessories

CODE	DESCRIPTION	INVOICE	MSRP
SC	**Premium Pkg** *incls vehicle plus standard equipment*	NC	NC
SD	**Luxury Pkg** *incls SC Premium Pkg plus automatic power antenna, front carpet savers, rear carpet savers, electric deluxe outside mirrors, radio (power-loading cassette and ETR AM/FM stereo with seek/scan and clock*	347	403
SE	**Prestige Pkg** *incls SD Luxury Pkg plus remote keyless entry, front overhead console courtesy reading lights, dome lights with integral reading lights, 6-way power driver side seat, trunk convenience net*	798	928
SJ	**SJ Pkg** *incls 3.8 liter 3800 SFI V6 engine, automatic power antenna, front and rear carpet savers, remote keyless entry, front overhead console courtesy reading lights, dome lights with integral reading lights, electric deluxe outside rearview mirrors, radio (power-loading cassette and ETR AM/FM stereo with seek/scan and clock), 6-way power driver side seat, trunk convenience net*	1138	1323
YF5	**California Emissions**	NC	NC
NG1	**Massachusetts Emissions**	NC	NC
L27	**3.8 Liter 3800 SFI V6 Engine** — w/SC, SD or SE	340	395
BF9	**Carpet Savers** — delete - w/SD or SE	(39)	(45)
B34	**Carpet Savers** — front - w/SC *B35 req'd*	22	25
B35	**Carpet Savers** — rear - w/SC *B34 req'd*	17	20

CODE	DESCRIPTION	INVOICE	MSRP
CF5	**Astroroof** — electric sliding/tilting with sunshade - w/SE	598	695
DH6	**Mirrors** — dual lighted visor vanity driver and passenger - w/SE & SJ	79	92
K05	**Engine Block Heater**	15	18
PH6	**Wheels** — 15" aluminum (4)	280	325
	QGY or QGZ req'd w/SC, SD or SE		
QGZ	**Tires**	65	76
	incls P205/70R15 steel belted radial-ply all-season whitewall (NA w/Y56)		
UN6	**Radio** — w/SC	168	195
	incls power-loading cassette and ETR AM/FM stereo with seek/scan and clock		
UL0	**Radio** — w/SD, SE or SJ	22	25
	incls power-loading cassette and ETR AM/FM stereo with seek/scan, automatic tone control and clock		
UN0	**Radio** — w/SE or SJ	108	125
	incls power-loading CD player with next/last CD track selector and ETR AM/FM stereo with seek/scan, automatic tone control and clock		
UP0	**Radio** — w/SD or SE	194	225
	incls power-loading CD and cassette player with next/last CD track selector & ETR AM/FM stereo with seek/scan, automatic tone control and clock		
UK3	**Radio Controls** — steering wheel mounted - w/SE	108	125
	NA w/UN6		
UW6	**Speaker System** — Concert Sound II - w/SE or SJ	60	70
U75	**Antenna** — automatic power - w/SC	73	85
VK3	**License Plate Mounting Pkg** — front	NC	NC
V08	**Heavy Duty Engine Cooling**	129	150
	L27 req'd		
V58	**Luggage Rack** — chrome decklid - w/SE	99	115
WG1	**Seat** — 6-way power driver side - w/SD	262	305
Y56	**Gran Touring Pkg** — w/SD, SE or SJ	641	745
	incls gran touring suspension, 16" aluminum wheels with P225/60R16 blackwall radials, variable effort steering and leather-wrapped steering wheel (QGY, QGZ or PH6 ; NA w/SD or SE; L27 req'd)		
—	**Seats** — leather bucket w/full operating console - w/SJ	473	550
UV8	**Cellular Phone Pre-Wire** — w/SJ	30	35
UK3	**Radio Controls** — w/SJ	108	125
	steering wheel mounted		

REGAL LIMITED SEDAN *(1995)*

REGAL LIMITED SEDAN 6 CYL

		INVOICE	MSRP
D19	4-Dr Sedan	18526	20247
Destination Charge:		535	535

Standard Equipment

REGAL LIMITED SEDAN: 3.8 liter 3800 SFI V6 engine with tuned-port injection, electronically-controlled automatic transmission with overdrive, power steering, anti-lock 4-wheel power disc brakes, power windows with driver's express-down and passenger lockout feature, automatic power door

CODE	DESCRIPTION	INVOICE	MSRP

locks, 15" deluxe bolt-on wheel covers, AM/FM ETR stereo radio with seek/scan/cassette/clock; dual ComforTemp air conditioning, driver and front passenger side air bag SRS, fixed-mast antenna, front seat storage armrest with cup holders, rear seat or door armrest ashtray, Delco Freedom II Plus battery, 2-sided galvanized body panels, push-to-set/release parking brake, brake/transmission interlock, electronic cruise control, front and side window outlet defoggers, front wheel drive, electronic warning tone for: seatbelt/ignition key/turn signal/headlamps/parking brake on; Soft-Ray tinted glass, composite tungsten-halogen headlamps, adjustable front seat head restraints, rear seat heat ducts, floor-mounted release inside hood lock, interior illumination with theatre dimming (door handle activated), instrumentation analog gauge cluster includes: tachometer/voltage/temperature/oil pressure/fuel gauges/trip odometer; center high-mounted stop lamp, crystalline park/turn lenses lamps, lights include: front ashtray/instrument panel courtesy/trunk/engine compartment/glove box; dual covered non-lighted driver and passenger visor vanity mirrors, moldings include: black windshield/back window frame/bright rear quarter window/belt reveal; body color front and rear wheel opening moldings, multi-function control lever includes: turn signal/headlamp high-low beam/flash-to-pass/windshield wiper-washer controls; basecoat/clearcoat paint with anti-chip lower protection, driver and passenger manual seatback recliners, auxiliary power receptacle, front and rear seat lap/shoulder seatbelts, 55/45 cloth reclining seats with storage armrest, four dual extended-range front and rear speakers, tilt wheel adjustable steering column, deluxe steering wheel, slide-out sunshade extensions, independent front and rear suspension, DynaRide suspension, Pass Key II theft-deterrent system, trunk trim, 2-speed wipers with low-speed delay feature, automatic power antenna, dual outlet exhaust system, integrated dome and reading lights, overhead console courtesy/integral reading lights, front seatback map pockets, deluxe outside electric body color mirrors, wide protective bodyside body color moldings, driver's 4-way manual seat adjuster, electric remote trunk lock release.

Accessories

CODE	DESCRIPTION	INVOICE	MSRP
SD	**Luxury Pkg** *incls automatic power antenna, front carpet savers, rear carpet savers, electric deluxe outside mirrors, radio (power-loading cassette and ETR AM/FM stereo with seek/scan and clock), Concert Sound II speaker system*	407	473
SE	**Prestige Pkg** *incls SD Luxury Pkg plus remote keyless entry, dual lighted visor vanity mirrors, radio (power-loading cassette and ETR AM/FM stereo with seek/scan, automatic tone control, clock, steering wheel mounted radio controls), 6-way power driver's seat, trunk convenience net*	989	1150
YF5	**California Emissions**	NC	NC
NG1	**Massachusetts Emissions**	NC	NC
—	**Leather Split Bench Seats** — w/storage armrest *WG1 or WG5 req'd*	473	550
—	**Leather Bucket Seats** — w/full operating console - w/SE	473	550
AU0	**Remote Keyless Entry** — w/SD	116	135
CF5	**Astroroof** — electric sliding/tilting w/sunshade - w/SE	598	695
K05	**Engine Block Heater**	15	18
PH6	**Wheels** — 15" aluminum (4) *QGY or QGZ req'd; NA w/Y56*	280	325
QGZ	**Tires** *incls P205/70R15 steel belted radial-ply all-season whitewall (NA w/Y56)*	65	76
UL0	**Radio** — w/SD *incls power-loading cassette and ETR AM/FM stereo with seek/scan, automatic tone control and clock*	22	25

CODE	DESCRIPTION	INVOICE	MSRP
UN0	**Radio** — w/SD	108	125
	w/SE	86	100
	incls power-loading CD player with next/last CD track selector and ETR AM/FM stereo with seek/scan, automatic tone control and clock		
UP0	**Radio** — w/SD	194	225
	w/SE	172	200
	incls power-loading CD and cassette player with next/last CD track selector & ETR AM/FM stereo with seek/scan, automatic tone control and clock		
UK3	**Radio Controls** — steering wheel mounted - w/SD	108	125
	NA w/UN6		
VK3	**License Plate Mounting Pkg** — front	NC	NC
V08	**Heavy Duty Engine Cooling**	129	150
V58	**Luggage Rack** — chrome decklid - w/SE	99	115
WG1	**Seat** — 6-way power driver side - w/SD	232	270
WG5	**Seats** — 6-way power driver and passenger side - w/SE	262	305
Y56	**Gran Touring Pkg**	641	745
	incls gran touring suspension, 16" aluminum wheels with P225/60R16 blackwall radials, variable effort steering and leather-wrapped steering wheel (NA w/QGZ or PH6)		

BUICK

REGAL GRAN SPORT SEDAN *(1995)*

REGAL GRAN SPORT SEDAN 6 CYL

		INVOICE	MSRP
F19	4-Dr Sedan	19080	20852
Destination Charge:		535	535

Standard Equipment

REGAL GRAN SPORT SEDAN: 3.8 liter 3800 SFI V6 engine with tuned-port injection, electronically-controlled automatic transmission with overdrive, variable effort power steering, anti-lock 4-wheel power disc brakes, power windows with driver's express-down and passenger lockout feature, automatic power door locks, P225/60R16 SBR Eagle GA touring BW tires, four specific 16" aluminum wheels, AM/FM ETR stereo radio with seek/scan/cassette/clock; dual ComforTemp air conditioning, driver and front passenger side air bag SRS, front seat storage armrest with cup holders, rear seat or door armrest ashtrays, Delco Freedom II Plus battery, 2-sided galvanized body panels, push-to-set/release parking brake, brake/transmission interlock, electronic cruise control, front/side window outlet defoggers, front wheel drive, electronic warning tone for: seatbelt/ignition key/turn signal/headlamps/parking brake on; Soft-Ray tinted glass, composite tungsten-halogen headlamps, adjustable front seat head restraints, rear seat heat ducts, floor-mounted release inside hood lock, interior illumination with theatre dimming (door handle activated), analog instrumentation gauge cluster includes: tachometer/voltage/temperature/oil pressure/fuel gauges/trip odometer; center high-mounted stop lamp, crystalline park/turn lenses lamps, lights include: front ashtray/instrument panel courtesy/trunk/engine compartment/glove box; dual covered non-lighted driver and passenger visor vanity mirrors, moldings include: black windshield/back window frame/bright rear quarter window/belt reveal; body color front and rear wheel opening moldings, multi-function control lever includes: turn signal/headlamp high-low beam/flash-to-pass/windshield wiper-washer controls, driver and passenger manual seatback recliners, auxiliary power receptacle, 2-way manual driver and passenger seat adjusters, front and rear seat lap/shoulder seatbelts, four dual extended-range front and rear speakers, tilt-wheel adjustable steering column, slide-out sunshade extensions, independent front and rear suspension, Pass Key II theft-deterrent system, trunk trim, 2-speed wipers with low-speed delay

CODE	DESCRIPTION	INVOICE	MSRP

feature, automatic power antenna, integrated dome and reading lights, overhead console courtesy/integral reading lights, front seatback map pockets, deluxe outside electric body color mirrors, driver's 4-way manual seat adjusters, electric remote trunk lock release, full-length operating console includes: storage armrest with integrated cup holders, dual outlet exhaust system, body color grille, protective bodyside body color moldings with black insert, two-tone Slate Gray Metallic lower accent paint, cloth bucket seats with console, leather-wrapped steering wheel, Gran Touring suspension.

Accessories

CODE	DESCRIPTION	INVOICE	MSRP
SD	**Luxury Pkg**	407	473
	incls automatic power antenna, front carpet savers, rear carpet savers, electric deluxe outside mirrors (left and right remote), radio (power-loading cassette and ETR AM/FM stereo with seek/scan and clock), Concert Sound II speaker system		
SE	**Prestige Pkg**	989	1150
	incls SD Luxury Pkg plus remote keyless entry, dual lighted visor vanity mirrors, radio (power-loading cassette and ETR AM/FM stereo with seek/scan, automatic tone control, clock, steering wheel mounted radio controls), 6-way power driver's seat, trunk convenience net		
YF5	**California Emissions**	NC	NC
NG1	**Massachusetts Emissions**	NC	NC
—	**Leather Bucket Seat** — w/operating console	473	550
	WG1 or WG5 req'd		
AU0	**Remote Keyless Entry** — w/SD	116	135
CF5	**Astroroof** — electric sliding/tilting w/sunshade - w/SE	598	695
D83	**Monotone Paint Treatment**	NC	NC
K05	**Engine Block Heater**	15	18
QD1	**Wheels** — 16" chrome	559	650
UK3	**Radio Controls** — leather-wrapped steering wheel mounted - w/SD	108	125
	NA w/UN6		
UL0	**Radio** — w/SD	22	25
	incls power-loading cassette and ETR AM/FM stereo with seek/scan, automatic tone control and clock		
UN0	**Radio** — w/SD	108	125
	w/SE	86	100
	incls power-loading CD player with next/last CD track selector and ETR AM/FM stereo with seek/scan, automatic tone control and clock		
UP0	**Radio** — w/SD	194	225
	w/SE	172	200
	incls power-loading CD and cassette player with next/last CD track selector and ETR AM/FM stereo with seek/scan, automatic tone control and clock		
VK3	**License Plate Mounting Pkg** — front	NC	NC
V08	**Heavy Duty Engine Cooling**	129	150
V58	**Luggage Rack** — chrome decklid - w/SE	99	115
WG1	**Seat** — 6-way power driver side - w/SD	232	270
WG5	**Seats** — 6-way power driver and passenger side - w/SE	262	305

RIVIERA *(1995)*

RIVIERA 6 CYL

CODE	DESCRIPTION	INVOICE	MSRP
G07	2-Dr Coupe	25235	28195
Destination Charge:		635	635

Standard Equipment

RIVIERA: Acoustical package, driver and passenger air bags, automatic dual comfortemp climate control air conditioning with rear seat comfortemp, automatic power antenna, front seat armrest with storage and dual cupholders, two rear rail-mounted assist handles, heavy duty Delco Freedom II Plus battery, anti-lock 4-wheel power disc brakes, front and rear carpet savers, heavy duty engine and transmission cooling, electronic cruise control, front and side defogger outlets, electric rear window defogger, automatic power door locks, front wheel drive, electronic warning tone (seat belt, ignition key, headlamps on, turn signal and parking brake), 3800 "Series II" V6 engine, dual stainless steel exhaust, flash to pass signal, electric remote release fuel filler door, fuel cap holder, solar ray glass, tungsten-halogen headlamps, inside hood lock release, dual horns, instrumentation (speedometer, tachometer, coolant temperature, trip odometer, low fuel indicator, low oil, low washer fluid), electric remote keyless entry, light group, deluxe body color OS electric rearview mirrors (left and right remote), inside rearview day/night mirror, lighted visor vanity passenger mirror, moldings (protective bodyside, belt reveal, wheel opening and rocker panel), clearcoat paint with anti-chip protection, radio (ETR AM/FM stereo with seek/scan, cassette with auto reverse, search/repeat), front auxiliary power receptacle, retained accessory power, 55/45 split bench seat with driver and passenger six-way power seats and power recliners, 6-speaker Concert Sound II speakers, magnetic speed variable assist steering, tilt wheel adjustable steering column, leather-wrapped steering wheel, supplemental/extendable sun shades, 4-wheel independent suspension, automatic level control, Pass Key II theft deterrent system, electronically controlled automatic transmission with overdrive, electric remote control trunk release with security switch, full trunk trim, trunk convenience net, 16" aluminum wheels, power windows with express-down driver's side, 2-speed wipers with low speed delay, P225/60R16 SBR all-season BW tires.

CODE	DESCRIPTION	INVOICE	MSRP
	Accessories		
SD	**Luxury Pkg**	406	472
	incls convenience pkg (consists of twilight sentinel and driver lighted vanity mirror), security pkg (consists of programmable auto door locks, theft deterrent system and cornering lamps), accent paint stripe		
SE	**Prestige Pkg**	853	992
	incls SD Luxury Pkg plus traction control, automatic mirrors (incls electrochromatic inside driver and outside rearview), steering wheel remote radio controls, driver's seat lumbar support		
L67	**Supercharged 3800 V6 Engine**	946	1100
	incls 16" aluminum wheels and P225/60R16 Eagle GA touring tires		
AM6	**Leather Split Bench Seats**	516	600
AS7	**Leather Bucket Seats w/Console**	559	650
A43	**Memory/Heated Driver Seat w/Memory Mirrors**	267	310
U1R	**CD Player w/Cassette** — req's bucket seats	373	434
UM3	**CD Player** — replaces cassette	210	244
CF5	**Astroroof w/Power Sunshade**	856	995
YM5	**Paint Stripe Delete**	NC	NC
K05	**Engine Block Heater**	15	18
YF5	**California Emissions**	NC	NC
NG1	**New York Emissions**	NC	NC
VK3	**License Plate Mounting** — front	NC	NC

ROADMASTER SEDAN *(1995)*

ROADMASTER SEDAN 8 CYL

CODE	DESCRIPTION	INVOICE	MSRP
N69	4-Dr Sedan	22317	24390
Destination Charge:		585	585

CODE	DESCRIPTION	INVOICE	MSRP

Standard Equipment

ROADMASTER BASE SEDAN: 5.7 liter SFI V8 engine, electronically-controlled 4-speed automatic transmission with overdrive, power steering, anti-lock power front disc/rear drum brakes, power windows with driver's express-down and passenger lockout feature, automatic power door locks, P235/70R15 SBR all-season WW tires, 15" deluxe wheel covers, AM/FM ETR stereo radio with seek/scan/cassette/clock; air conditioning, driver and front passenger side air bag SRS, fixed-mast antenna, front seat storage armrests, rear seat armrests, front and rear assist straps, heavy duty battery, front snap-down and rear carpet savers, electronic cruise control, electric rear window defogger, front and side window outlet defoggers, delayed illuminated entry, door edge guards, electronic warning tone for: seatbelt/ignition key/headlamps/turn signal on; dual stainless steel exhaust system, Soft-Ray tinted glass, wrap-around composite tungsten-halogen headlamps, 4-note horn, indicators for: low windshield washer fluid/oil pressure/coolant level/volts/oil change/fuel; instrumentation analog gauge cluster includes: coolant temperature/trip odometer/oil level/fuel level, center high-mounted stop lamp, indirect lighting for controls and switches, lights include: front and rear door operated dome/front ashtray/glove box/instrument panel/trunk and engine compartments; front seat reading lights (integral with rearview mirror), rear roof rail lights with integral reading lights, inside day/night mirror with integral reading lights, driver and passenger cloth-covered visor vanity mirrors, body color outside foldaway rearview mirrors (left remote/right manual), deluxe wide bodyside moldings, front wheel opening moldings, hood and decklid moldings, multi-function control lever includes: turn signal/headlamp high-low beam/windshield wiper-washer controls; oil life monitor, basecoat/clearcoat paint with anti-chip lower protection, driver and passenger manual seatback recliners, front lap/shoulder safety belt system, rear seat lap/shoulder safety belts, 55/45 cloth seats with storage armrests, rear door child security locks, dual front/rear extended-range speakers, tilt-wheel adjustable steering column, deluxe steering wheel, front/rear door lower built-in storage compartments, front seatback storage pockets, DynaRide suspension, Pass Key II theft-deterrent system with starter interrupt, compact spare tire, trunk convenience net, remote electric trunk release, deluxe trunk trim, 2-speed wipers with low-speed delay.

Accessories

CODE	DESCRIPTION	INVOICE	MSRP
SA	**Base Pkg** *incls vehicle plus standard equipment*	NC	NC
SD	**Luxury Pkg** *incls electronic touch climate control air conditioning, automatic power antenna, electric outside heated mirrors (left and right remote), radio (power-loading cassette and ETR AM/FM stereo with seek/scan, automatic tone control and clock), 6-way power driver's seat, Concert Sound speaker system*	660	768
SE	**Prestige Pkg** *incls SD Luxury Pkg plus automatic programmable door locks, remote keyless entry, door courtesy and warning lamps, automatic inside rearview day/night mirror with integral reading lights, lighted visor vanity driver and passenger side mirrors, passenger side 6-way power seat*	1269	1475
SJ	**SJ Pkg** *incls electronic touch climate control air conditioning, automatic power antenna, automatic programmable door locks, remote keyless entry, door courtesy and warning lamps, electric outside heated mirrors (left and right remote), radio (power-loading cassette and ETR AM/FM stereo with seek/scan, automatic tone control and clock), 6-way power driver seat, Concert Sound speaker system*	1525	1773
YF5	**California Emissions**	86	100
NG1	**Massachusetts Emissions** (NC when SJ Pkg is ordered)	86	100

CODE	DESCRIPTION	INVOICE	MSRP
—	**Leather Split Bench Seats** — w/center armrest - w/SD or SE *incls leather-wrapped steering wheel*	667	775
C04	**Top** — landau style - w/SD or SE	598	695
AU0	**Remote Keyless Entry** — w/SD *AU4 req'd*	116	135
AU4	**Door Locks** — auto programmable - w/SD *AU0 req'd*	22	25
D84	**Paint Lower Accent** — w/SD or SE	129	150
G67	**Automatic Level Control** — w/SD or SE *incld in V92*	151	175
G80	**Limited Slip Differential** — w/SD or SE	86	100
N81	**Full Size Spare** — w/N91, w/o QUK	65	75
	w/N91 & QUK	108	125
	w/PA3, w/o QUK	108	125
	w/PA3 & QUK	151	175
	w/o N91, PA3 or QUK	65	75
	w/QUK, w/o N91 or PA3	108	125
N91	**Wheel Covers** — 15" custom locking wire	206	240
PA3	**Wheels** — 15" aluminum (4)	280	325
QUK	**Tires** *incls steel belted radial-ply whitewall self-sealing P235/70R15 (NA w/V92)*	129	150
UP0	**Radio** — w/SD or SE *incls power-loading CD and cassette player with next/last CD track selector and ETR AM/FM stereo with seek/scan, automatic tone control, clock*	172	200
VK3	**License Plate Mounting Pkg** — front - w/SA, SD or SE	NC	NC
V03	**Cooling Pkg** — w/SD or SE *incls solar control windshield, increased A/C capacity, higher output fans and engine oil cooler (NA w/V92)*	172	200
K05	**Engine Block Heater**	15	18
V92	**Gran Touring/Trailer Towing Pkg** — w/SD or SE *incls P235/70R15 whitewall tires, 2.93 axle ratio, heavy duty engine cooling, engine oil cooler, heavy duty suspension, automatic level control and solar control windshield (NA w/V03; G80 req'd)*	323	375

ROADMASTER LIMITED SEDAN *(1995)*

ROADMASTER LIMITED SEDAN 8 CYL

T69	4-Dr Sedan	24330	26590
Destination Charge:		585	585

Standard Equipment

ROADMASTER LIMITED SEDAN: 5.7 liter SFI V8 engine, electronically-controlled 4-speed automatic transmission with overdrive, variable effort power steering with steering dampener, anti-lock power front disc/rear drum brakes, power windows with driver's express-down and passenger lockout feature, programmable automatic power door locks, P235/70R15 SBR all-season WW tires, 15" deluxe wheel covers, AM/FM ETR stereo radio with seek/scan/cassette/clock; electronic touch climate control air conditioning, driver and front passenger side air bag SRS, front and rear assist

BUICK

CODE	DESCRIPTION	INVOICE	MSRP

straps, heavy duty battery, front snap-down and rear carpet savers, electronic cruise control, electric rear window defogger, front and side window outlet defoggers, delayed illuminated entry, door edge guards, electronic warning tone for: seatbelt/ignition key/headlamps/turn signal on; dual stainless steel exhaust system, Soft-Ray tinted glass, wrap-around composite tungsten-halogen headlamps, 4-note horn, indicators for: low windshield washer fluid/oil pressure/coolant level/volts/oil change/ fuel; instrumentation analog gauge cluster includes: coolant temperature/trip odometer/oil level/fuel level; center high-mounted stop lamp, indirect lighting for controls and switches, lights include: front and rear door operated dome/front ashtray/glove box/instrument panel/trunk and engine compartments; front seat reading lights (integral with rearview mirror), rear roof rail with integral reading lights, moldings include: front wheel opening/hood/decklid, deluxe wide bodyside moldings, multi-function control lever includes: turn signal/headlamp high-low beam/windshield wiper-washer controls; oil life monitor, basecoat/clearcoat paint with anti-chip lower protection, front lap/shoulder seatbelts, rear seat lap/shoulder seatbelts, rear door child security locks, tilt-wheel adjustable steering column, deluxe steering wheel, lower built-in front/rear door storage compartments, front seatback storage pockets, DynaRide suspension, Pass Key II theft-deterrent system with starter interrupt, compact spare tire, trunk convenience net, remote electric trunk release, deluxe trunk trim, 2-speed wipers with low-speed delay, automatic power antenna, front and rear seat armrest storage, 6-way front head restraints, electroluminescent coach lamps, door courtesy/warning lights, power electromechanical lumbar system, automatic dimming rearview mirror with integral reading lights, electric remote outside foldaway heated left/right rearview mirrors, driver and passenger lighted visor vanity mirrors, driver and passenger electric reclining seatbacks, remote keyless entry, driver and passenger 6-way power seat, up-level split-frame design seats with front and rear storage armrest, Concert Sound II speakers.

Accessories

CODE	DESCRIPTION	INVOICE	MSRP
SA	**Base Pkg**	NC	NC
	incls vehicle plus standard equipment		
SE	**Prestige Pkg**	593	690
	incls cornering lamps, twilight sentinel headlamp control, radio (power-loading cassette and ETR AM/FM stereo with seek/scan, automatic tone control and clock, memory driver's seat with heated driver and passenger seats, steel belted radial-ply self-sealing whitewall all-season P235/70R15 tires, electric trunk pull down		
YF5	**California Emissions**	86	100
NG1	**Massachusetts Emissions** (NC when SJ Pkg is ordered)	86	100
—	**Leather Split Bench Seats** — w/storage armrest - w/SD or SE	667	775
C04	**Top** — landau style - w/SD or SE	598	695
AG3	**Memory Driver's Seat** — w/heated driver and passenger seats - w/SD	249	290
D84	**Paint Lower Accent** — w/SD or SE	129	150
G67	**Automatic Level Control** — w/SD or SE	151	175
	incld in V92		
G80	**Limited Slip Differential** — w/SD or SE	86	100
N81	**Full Size Spare** — w/N91, w/o QUK	65	75
	w/N91 & QUK	108	125
	w/PA3, w/o QUK	108	125
	w/PA3 & QUK	151	175
	w/o N91, PA3 or QUK	65	75
	w/QUK, w/o N91 or PA3	108	125
N91	**Wheel Covers** — 15" custom locking wire	206	240
PA3	**Wheels** — 15" aluminum (4) - w/SD or SE	280	325

BUICK

CODE	DESCRIPTION	INVOICE	MSRP
QUK	**Tires** — w/SD	129	150
	incls steel belted radial-ply whitewall self-sealing P235/70R15 (NA w/V92)		
UP0	**Radio** — w/SD	215	250
	w/SE	172	200
	incls power-loading CD and cassette player with next/last CD track selector and ETR AM/FM stereo with seek/scan, automatic tone control and clock		
VK3	**License Plate Mounting Pkg** — front - w/SD or SE	NC	NC
V03	**Cooling Pkg** — w/SD or SE	172	200
	incls solar control windshield, higher output fans, increased A/C capacity and engine oil cooler (NA w/V92)		
V92	**Gran Touring/Trailer Towing Pkg**		
	w/SD	323	375
	w/SE	194	225
	incls P235/70R15 whitewall tires, 2.93 axle ratio, heavy duty engine cooling, engine oil cooler, heavy duty suspension, automatic level control and solar control windshield (NA w/V03) (G80 req'd)		
K05	**Engine Block Heater**	15	18

ROADMASTER ESTATE WAGON *(1995)*

ROADMASTER ESTATE WAGON 8 CYL

R35	4-Dr Wagon	23891	26110
Destination Charge:		585	585

Standard Equipment

ROADMASTER ESTATE WAGON: 5.7 liter SFI V8 engine, electronically-controlled 4-speed automatic transmission with overdrive, variable effort steering with steering dampener, anti-lock power front disc/rear drum brakes, power windows with driver's express-down and passenger lockout feature, automatic power door locks, P225/75R15 SBR all-season WW tires, 15" aluminum wheels, AM/FM ETR stereo radio with seek/scan/cassette/clock; air conditioning, driver and front passenger side air bag SRS, fixed-mast antenna, third seat assist handles, front and rear assist straps, heavy duty battery, front bumper guards, front/rear/load area carpeting, electric rear window defogger, front and side window outlet defoggers, delayed illuminated entry, door edge guards, electronic warning tone for seatbelt/ignition key/headlamps/turn signal on; dual stainless steel exhaust system, Soft-Ray tinted glass, Solar-Ray solar-control windshield glass; lockable glove box, composite tungsten-halogen headlamps, dual note horn, tailgate ajar indicator, indicators for: low windshield washer fluid/oil/low coolant level/volts/fuel; analog gauge cluster instrumentation includes: coolant temperature, trip odometer/oil level/fuel level; center high-mounted stop lamp, indirect lighting for controls and switches, lights include: front and rear door operated dome/front ashtray/glove box/instrument panel/load and engine compartments; front seat reading lights (integral with rearview mirror), rear roof rail with integral reading lights, integral luggage rack with vista roof, inside day/night mirror with integral reading lights, driver and passenger cloth-covered visor vanity mirrors, deluxe body color outside foldaway rearview mirrors (left remote, right manual), narrow rocker panel molding, deluxe wide bodyside moldings, multi-function control lever for: turn signal/headlamp high-low beam/windshield wiper-washer controls; oil life monitor, basecoat/clearcoat paint with anti-chip lower protection, driver and passenger manual seatback recliners, front and rear lap/shoulder seatbelts, fold-down second seat seatback, rear-facing vinyl third seat, 55/45 cloth seats with armrest, rear storage area security cover, rear door child security locks, four dual standard-range front and rear speakers, tilt-wheel adjustable steering column, deluxe steering wheel, built-in lower front and rear door storage compartments, hidden lockable storage compartments, front seatback storage pockets, instrument

CODE	DESCRIPTION	INVOICE	MSRP

panel pull-out storage tray, heavy duty suspension, two-way manual tailgate, remote tailgate lock release, Pass Key II theft-deterrent system with starter interrupt, compact spare tire, single-function convenience net, tinted vista roof glass, vista shades, 2-speed wipers with low-speed delay, rear window wiper with washer, light colonial oak woodgrain vinyl applique.

Accessories

CODE	DESCRIPTION	INVOICE	MSRP
SA	**Base Pkg**	NC	NC
	incls vehicle plus standard equipment		
SD	**Luxury Pkg**	1082	1258
	incls automatic power antenna, electronic touch climate control air conditioning, front seat storage armrest, front and rear carpet savers, electronic cruise control, door courtesy and warning lights, automatic day/night rearview mirror with integral reading lights, electric outside heated mirrors (left and right remote), 6-way power driver's seat, radio (power-loading cassette and ETR AM/FM stereo with seek/scan, automatic tone control and clock		
SE	**Prestige Pkg**	1664	1935
	incls SD Luxury Pkg plus automatic programmable door locks, twilight sentinel headlamp control, remote keyless entry, cornering lamps, passenger side lighted visor vanity mirror, driver's side lighted visor vanity mirror, 6-way power passenger side seat		
YF5	**California Emissions**	86	100
NG1	**Massachusetts Emissions**	86	100
—	**Leather Split Bench Seat** — w/center armrest - w/SD or SE	667	775
	incls leather-wrapped steering wheel		
—	**Limited Leather Split Bench Seats** — w/storage armrest	589	685
	SA & Z27 req'd; AM5 req'd		
AU0	**Remote Keyless Entry** — w/SD	116	135
	AU4 req'd		
AU4	**Door Locks** — automatic programmable - w/SD	22	25
	AU0 req'd		
G67	**Automatic Level Control** — w/SD, or SA w/Z27	151	175
	incld in V92		
G80	**Limited Slip Differential** — w/SD, or SA w/Z27	86	100
	V92 req'd		
K05	**Engine Block Heater**	15	18
N81	**Full Size Spare** — w/N91, w/o P42	65	75
	w/N91 & P42	108	125
	w/o N91 or P42	108	125
	w/P42, w/o N91	151	175
N91	**Wheel Covers** — custom locking wire - w/SA, SD or SE	NC	NC
P42	**Tires**	129	150
	incls self-sealing steel belted radial-ply whitewall P225/75R15 (QEU incld)		
VK3	**License Plate Mounting Pkg** — front - w/SA, SD or SE	NC	NC
V03	**Cooling Pkg** — w/SD, SE or SA & Z27	129	150
	incls increased A/C capacity, higher output fans and engine oil cooler (NA w/V92)		
V92	**Trailer Towing Pkg**	280	325
	incls P225/75R15 whitewall tires, 2.93 axle ratio, heavy duty engine cooling engine oil cooler, heavy duty suspension and automatic level control (NA w/V03)		

CODE	DESCRIPTION	INVOICE	MSRP
WB4	**Woodgrain Delete** *incls bodyside stripe*	NC	NC
6Y2	**Delete Third Seat** — w/SA-Z27 or SD	(185)	(215)
Z27	**Limited Wagon Pkg** *incls limited seats with power lumbar electric seatback recliners (driver and passenger), 6-way headrests, storage armrest, exterior "Limited" badging, front and rear carpet savers, leather wrapped steering wheel, cruise control, ULO radio, Concert Sound speakers, power antenna, remote keyless entry, auto door locks, power driver seat, auto electronic climate control, heated outside power mirrors, door courtesy and warning lamps, auto day/night inside mirror with reading lights, power passenger seat, passenger lighted visor vanity mirror, driver lighted visor vanity mirror, twilight sentinel, cornering lamps*	2060	2395
AG3	**Memory Driver's Seat** — w/heated driver and passenger seats *req's Z27*	249	290

SKYLARK CUSTOM COUPE/SEDAN *(1995)*

SKYLARK CUSTOM COUPE/SEDAN 4 CYL

CODE	DESCRIPTION	INVOICE	MSRP
V37	2-Dr Coupe	13561	14200
V69	4-Dr Sedan	13561	14200
V37	Custom 2-Dr Coupe (incls SJ Pkg) *incls Skylark Custom Coupe standard equipment plus SJ Pkg*	13914	14570
V69	Custom 4-Dr Sedan (incls SJ Pkg) *incls Skylark Custom Sedan standard equipment plus SJ Pkg*	13914	14570
	Destination Charge:	495	495

Standard Equipment

SKYLARK CUSTOM COUPE/SEDAN: 2.3 liter DOHC L4 MFI engine, 3-speed automatic transmission, power rack and pinion steering, anti-lock power front disc/rear drum brakes, automatic power door locks, P195/70R14 SBR low-rolling resistance all-season BW tires, 14" styled wheels,

CODE	DESCRIPTION	INVOICE	MSRP

AM/FM ETR stereo with seek/scan/clock; air conditioning, driver air bag SRS, black fixed-mast antenna, front seat storage armrest with dual cup holders (with split bench seat), Delco Freedom II battery (rundown protection system), front and rear carpeting/carpet savers, column shift (with split bench seat), front overhead storage console (with integral courtesy lights), front and side window outlet defoggers, electric rear window defogger, door map pockets and pull straps, front wheel drive, electronic warning tone for: seatbelt/ignition key/turn signal/headlamps on; stainless steel exhaust system, remote fuel filler door release, Soft-Ray tinted glass, lockable glove box, composite tungsten-halogen headlamps, headliner includes dual sunshades and front/rear courtesy lights, rear seat head restraints, backlit analog gauge cluster instrumentation with speedometer/temperature/fuel gauges/trip odometer/oil level telltale; high-mounted stop lamp, lights include: ashtray/instrument panel courtesy/dome/glove box/trunk/engine compartment; theatre dimming lights, deluxe black outside rearview mirrors (left remote, right manual), bodyside body color moldings with bright insert, basecoat/clearcoat paint, driver and passenger seatback recliners, automatic front seatbelts, rear seat lap/shoulder system with child comfort guide, 55/45 split bench cloth seats, rear door child security locks (Sedans), dual extended-range front and rear speakers, tilt-wheel adjustable steering column, deluxe steering wheel, independent MacPherson front strut suspension, rear tubular axle suspension, DynaRide suspension, compact spare tire, remote trunk lock release, full trunk trim, 2-speed wipers with low-speed delay.

Accessories

CODE	DESCRIPTION	INVOICE	MSRP
SE	**Prestige Pkg**	1079	1255
	incls air conditioning, front and rear carpet savers, electric rear window defogger, adjustable steering column/tilt wheel, two-speed windshield wiper with low speed delay feature		
SJ	**Custom Pkg** — see model listing	NC	NC
	incls air conditioning, front seat storage armrest with dual cup holders, front and rear carpet savers, electric rear window defogger, tilt wheel/adjustable steering column, two-speed windshield wiper with low-speed delay feature		
L82	**3.1 Liter 3100 SFI V6 Engine**	301	350
	MX0 req'd		
YF5	**California Emissions** — w/4 cyl engine	86	100
	w/L82 engine	NC	NC
NG1	**Massachusetts Emissions** — w/4 cyl engine	86	100
	w/L82 engine	NC	NC
	models w/SJ pkg	NC	NC
AR9	**Cloth Bucket Seats** — w/recliners & operating console	138	160
	AH3, UB3 & K34 req'd		
AH3	**Seat Adjuster** — 4-way manual driver side	30	35
A31	**Power Windows** — w/driver express-down - Coupe	237	275
	w/driver express-down and passenger lockout feature - Sedan	292	340
BF9	**Carpet Saver Delete** — models w/o SJ Pkg	(39)	(45)
CF5	**Astroroof** — electric sliding	512	595
	incls lighted visor vanity mirrors and reading lamps		
DA0	**Armrest** — front seat storage w/dual cup holder - models w/o SJ Pkg	93	108
D84	**Paint** — lower accent	168	195
K05	**Engine Block Heater**	15	18
K34	**Cruise Control** — electric	194	225
MX0	**Transmission**	172	200
	incls electronically controlled 4-speed automatic trans with overdrive		

CODE	DESCRIPTION	INVOICE	MSRP
PC4	**Wheel** — 14" styled polycast *QFB req'd*	99	115
PG1	**Wheel Cover** — 15" styled *QPD req'd*	24	28
QFC	**Tires** *incls steel belted radial-ply all-season whitewall P195/75R14 (NA w/PC4 or PG1)*	62	72
QPD	**Tires** *incls steel belted radial-ply all-season blackwall P195/65R15 (PG1 req'd)*	113	131
UB3	**Instrument Cluster** *incls backlit analog with speedometer, tachometer, voltmeter, oil pressure, oil temperature, fuel and trip odometer (AR9 & K34 req'd)*	108	126
UM6	**Radio** *incls cassette tape and ETR AM/FM stereo with seek/scan, auto reverse and clock*	142	165
U77	**Antenna** — grid, rear window *A31 req'd*	19	22
VK3	**License Plate Mounting Pkg** — front	NC	NC
Y72	**Headliner Custom** *incls dual covered vanity mirrors with map straps and front and rear courtesy lights; NA w/CF5*	21	24
WG1	**Seat** — 6-way power driver side - models w/SJ Pkg	262	305

SKYLARK LIMITED/ GRAN SPORT *(1995)*

CODE	DESCRIPTION	INVOICE	MSRP
V37	Limited 2-Dr Coupe (incls SK Pkg) *incls Coupe standard equipment plus SK Limited Pkg*	14869	15570
V69	Limited 4-Dr Sedan (incls SK Pkg) *incls Sedan standard equipment plus SK Limited Pkg*	14869	15570
V37	Gran Sport 2-Dr Coupe (incls SL Pkg) *incls Coupe standard equipment plus SL Gran Sport Pkg*	16455	17230
V69	Gran Sport 4-Dr Sedan (incls SL Pkg) *incls Sedan standard equipment plus SL Gran Sport Pkg*	16455	17230
Destination Charge:		495	495

Standard Equipment

COUPE/SEDAN: 2.3 liter DOHC L4 MFI engine, 3-speed automatic transmission, power rack and pinion steering, anti-lock power front disc/rear drum brakes, automatic power door locks, P195/70R14 SBR low-rolling resistance all-season BW tires, 14" styled wheels, AM/FM ETR stereo with seek/scan/clock; air conditioning, driver air bag SRS, black fixed-mast antenna, front seat storage armrest with dual cup holders (with split bench seat), Delco Freedom II battery (rundown protection system), front and rear carpeting/carpet savers, column shift (with split bench seat), front overhead storage console (with integral courtesy lights), front and side window outlet defoggers, electric rear window defogger, door map pockets and pull straps, front wheel drive, electronic warning tone for: seatbelt/ignition key/turn signal/headlamps on; stainless steel exhaust system, remote fuel filler door release, Soft-Ray tinted glass, lockable glove box, composite tungsten-halogen headlamps, headliner includes dual sunshades and front/rear courtesy lights, rear seat head restraints, backlit analog gauge cluster instrumentation with speedometer/temperature/fuel gauges/trip odometer/oil level telltale; high-mounted stop lamp, lights include: ashtray/instrument panel courtesy/dome/glove box/trunk/ engine compartment; theatre dimming lights, deluxe black outside rearview mirrors (left remote, right manual), bodyside body color moldings with bright insert, basecoat/clearcoat paint, driver and passenger seatback recliners, automatic front seatbelts, rear seat lap/shoulder system with child comfort guide, 55/45 split bench cloth seats, rear door child security locks (Sedans), dual extended-range front and rear speakers, tilt-wheel adjustable steering column, deluxe steering wheel, independent MacPherson front strut suspension, rear tubular axle suspension, DynaRide suspension, compact spare tire, remote trunk lock release, full trunk trim, 2-speed wipers with low-speed delay.

Accessories

Code	Description	Invoice	MSRP
SK	**Limited Pkg** — see model listing *incls air conditioning, front seat storage armrest with dual cup holders, front and rear carpet savers, electronic cruise control, electric rear window defogger, custom headliner (incls dual covered visor vanity mirrors with map straps and front and rear courtesy lamps), electric dual outside rearview mirrors, radio (cassette tape and ETR AM/FM stereo with seek/scan, auto reverse and clock), 4-way manual driver side seat adjuster, tilt wheel/adjustable steering column, trunk convenience net, 14" polycast wheels, power windows with driver's express-down, two-speed windshield wipers with low-speed delay feature*	NC	NC
SL	**Gran Sport Pkg** — see model listing *incls SK Limited Pkg plus 3.1 liter 3100 SFI V6 engine, cloth bucket seats with recliners and operating console, instrument cluster (backlit analog with speedometer, tachometer, voltmeter, oil pressure, oil temperature, fuel, trip odometer), sport suspension, 4-speed electronically controlled automatic transmission, steel belted radial-ply Eagle Touring blackwall P205/55R16 tires, 16" aluminum wheels, two-tone bodyside cladding, body color grille, black bodyside molding insert*	NC	NC
NG1	**Massachusetts Emissions**	NC	NC
—	**Leatherette Trim**— w/SL	297	345
—	**Leatherette/Cloth Trim**— w/SK *incls instrument cluster*	405	471
AR9	**Seat** — bucket w/console - w/SK	138	160
AM9	**Seat** — w/leather seats *split folding rear seat*	129	150
L82	**Engine** — 3.1 liter 3100 SFI V6 - w/SK *MX0 req'd*	301	350
AX3	**Remote Keyless Entry** *U77 req'd*	116	135
CF5	**Astroroof** — electric sliding *incls lighted visor vanity mirrors and reading lamps*	512	595
D84	**Lower Accent Paint** — w/SK	168	195
K05	**Engine Block Heater**	15	18
MX0	**Transmission** — 4-speed electronically controlled automatic - w/SK	172	200
PG1	**Wheel Cover** — 15" styled - w/SK *QPD req'd*	24	28
QPD	**Tires** — w/SK *incls steel belted radial-ply all-season blackwall P195/65R15 (PG1 req'd)*	113	131

CODE	DESCRIPTION	INVOICE	MSRP
UB3	**Instrument Cluster** — w/SK *incls backlit analog with speedometer, tachometer, voltmeter, oil pressure, oil temperature, fuel, trip odometer (AR9 req'd)*	108	126
UP3	**Radio** *incls CD player with track search/scan and ETR AM/FM stereo with seek/scan, equalizer and clock (UW6 req'd)*	220	256
UW6	**Speaker System** *incls Concert Sound II speakers (UM6 or UP3 req'd)*	39	45
U77	**Antenna** — grid, rear window	19	22
VK3	**License Plate Mounting Pkg** — front	NC	NC
WG1	**Seat** — 6-way power driver side *U77 req'd*	232	270
Y73	**Headliner** — deluxe *incls assist handles, lighted visor vanity mirrors, extendable sunshade and reading lamps; NA w/CF5*	116	135

What's New for *Buick* in 1995?

Century: New seats, chrome hubcaps, new easier-to-read gauges, taupe leather option and new colors mark changes to this value-packed sedan.

LeSabre: Platinum Gray Metallic paint is new outside, more functional climate controls with fewer buttons, new radios and a turn signal 'on' reminder round out the interior.

Park Avenue: Standard V6 engine gets big horsepower boost to 205 bhp, while minor styling tweaks and the addition of Platinum Gray Metallic paint freshen the exterior. New climate controls reduce the number of buttons on the dash, and new radios provide better sound. A turn signal 'on' reminder has been added, and a rear storage armrest with cupholders is optional, as is a heated passenger side seat.

Regal: All-new interior with dual airbags and optional dual ComforTemp controls updates the Regal for 1995. Minor styling revisions, new hubcaps and alloy wheel designs and the addition of Light Adriatic Blue Metallic and Medium Bordeaux paint colors liven up the exterior. Regal also gets the new Buick family of radios and now meets 1997 side-impact standards.

Riviera: All-new for 1995 and in showrooms since June, the Riviera sails on sans changes.

Roadmaster: Platinum Gray Metallic paint joins the roster, and the coach lamps on the Limited get 'Limited' script. New radios and improved center armrest comfort mark the changes inside the Roadmaster. Wagons get a Vista shade for the roof window and alloy wheels.

Skylark: The Quad 4 engine gets balance shafts and replaces the anemic 2.3L OHC version of the same engine. Standard power output is up to 150 bhp from 115 bhp. Rear suspension modifications round out changes to the hardware. Royal Magenta Metallic paint is new for '95, and interior revisions are limited to new carpet fabrics.

CODE	DESCRIPTION	INVOICE	MSRP

CADILLAC *(1995)*

CODE	DESCRIPTION	INVOICE	MSRP
6KD69	B De Ville Sedan	31934	34900
6KF69	P De Ville Concours	36051	39400
6EL57	H Eldorado	33060	38220
6ET57	T Eldorado Touring Coupe	35928	41535
6DW69	L Fleetwood	32569	35595
6KS69	M Seville SLS Sedan	36274	41935
6KY69	G Seville STS Sedan	39734	45935
Destination Charge:		635	635

Standard Equipment

DE VILLE SEDAN: 4.9 liter V8 SPFI engine, automatic transmission, power steering, power four-wheel disc brakes, electrically powered windows, electrically powered automatic door locks, all-season mud and snow SBR WW tires, cast aluminum wheels, AM/FM ETR stereo radio with signal seeking/scanner/digital display/cassette; air bag system, power antenna, anti-lock braking system, ignition anti-lockout feature, center front/rear seat armrests, audible reminders, body-frame integral construction, brake/transmission shift interlock, center high-mounted stop lamp, electronic climate control, digital clock display, on-board computer diagnostics, controlled cycle wiper system, cornering lights, cruise control, electric rear window defogger, front side window defoggers, rear child safety door locks, driver information center, electronic level control, engine oil life indicator, stainless steel exhaust, flash-to-pass, front and rear carpeted floor mats, front wheel drive, fuel data center, remote fuel filler door release, digital fuel gauge, Gold Key delivery system, tungsten halogen headlamps, wiper-activated headlamps, illuminated entry, digital instrument cluster, low fuel warning indicator, low windshield washer fluid level indicator, carpeted luggage compartment, electrochromatic automatic day/night inside rearview mirror, electrically powered and heated right/left outside rearview mirrors, multi-function turn signal lever, continuous outside temperature digital display, clearcoat paint, automatic parking brake release, Pass Key II anti-theft system, platinum-tipped spark plugs, driver and front passenger manual reclining seats, remote keyless entry system, retained accessory power, driver and front passenger 6-way power seat adjusters, dual comfort front seats, short/long arm rear suspension, Solar-Ray tinted glass, compact spare tire, speed-sensitive steering, speed-sensitive suspension, tilt steering wheel, leather-trimmed steering wheel rim, independent four-wheel suspension, full-range traction control, trip odometer, trunk convenience net, power trunk lid pull-down, power trunk lid release, trunk mat, trunk sill plate, twilight sentinel, rear windows with child lockout system, driver's window with express-down feature.

DE VILLE CONCOURS: 4.6 liter V8 Northstar (275 HP) DOHC engine, automatic transmission, power steering, power four-wheel disc brakes, electrically powered windows, automatic electrically powered door locks, all-season mud and snow SBR BW tires, cast aluminum wheels, AM/FM ETR stereo radio with signal seeking/scanner/digital display/cassette player; air bag system, power antenna, anti-lock braking system, ignition anti-lockout feature, center front/rear seat armrests, audible reminders, body-frame integral construction, brake/transmission shift interlock, center high-mounted stop lamp, electronic climate control, digital display clock, on-board computer diagnostics, controlled cycle wiper system, cornering lights, cruise control, electric rear window defogger, front side window defoggers, rear door child safety security locks, driver information center, electronic level control, engine oil life indicator, dual exhaust outlets, stainless steel exhaust, flash-to-pass, carpeted front and rear floor mats, front wheel drive, fuel data center, remote fuel filler door release, digital fuel gauge, 3-channel programmable garage door opener, Gold Key delivery system, tungsten halogen headlamps, wiper-activated headlamps, illuminated entry, digital instrument cluster, leather seating, low fuel warning indicator, low windshield washer fluid level indicator, carpeted luggage compartment, electrochromatic automatic day/night inside rearview mirror, electrochromatic automatic day/night outside driver side mirror, driver and passenger illuminated visor vanity mirrors, electrically powered and heated right and left outside rearview mirrors, multi-function turn signal lever, continuous outside temperature digital display, clearcoat paint, automatic parking brake release, Pass Key II anti-theft system, platinum-tipped spark plugs, driver and front passenger power reclining seats, remote keyless entry system, retained accessory power, real-time road-sensing suspension, driver and front passenger 6-way power seat adjusters, dual comfort front seats, short/long arm rear suspension, Solar-Ray tinted glass, compact spare tire, speed-sensitive steering, tilt steering wheel, leather-trimmed steering wheel rim, rear seat storage armrest, independent four-wheel suspension, full-range traction control, trip odometer, trunk convenience net, power trunk lid pull-down, power trunk lid release, trunk mat, trunk sill plate, twilight sentinel, rear window child lockout system, driver's window with express-down feature.

ELDORADO: 4.6 liter V8 Northstar (275 HP) DOHC engine, automatic transmission, power steering, power four-wheel disc brakes, electrically powered windows, electrically powered automatic door locks, all-season mud and snow SBR BW tires, cast aluminum wheels, AM/FM ETR stereo radio with signal seeking/scanner/digital display/cassette player; driver and front passenger air bags, power antenna, anti-lock braking system, ignition anti-lockout feature, center front/rear seat armrests, audible reminders, body-frame integral construction, brake/transmission shift interlock, center high-mounted stop lamp, electronic climate control, digital display clock, on-board computer diagnostics, controlled-cycle wiper system, cornering lights, cruise control, electric rear window defogger, front side window defoggers, driver information center, electronic level control, engine oil life indicator, dual exhaust outlets, stainless steel exhaust, flash-to-pass, front/rear carpeted floor mats, fog lamps, front-wheel drive, fuel data center, remote fuel filler door release, digital fuel gauge, Gold Key delivery system, tungsten halogen headlamps, wiper-activated headlamps, illuminated entry, digital instrument cluster, low fuel warning indicator, low windshield washer fluid level indicator, carpeted luggage compartment, electrochromatic automatic day/night inside rearview mirror, driver and passenger illuminated visor vanity mirrors, electrically powered and heated right/left outside rearview mirrors, multi-function turn signal lever, outside continuous digital temperature display, clearcoat paint, automatic parking brake release, Pass Key II anti-theft system, platinum-tipped spark plugs, driver/front passenger power reclining seats, remote keyless entry system, retained accessory power, real-time road-sensing suspension, 6-way power driver/front passenger seat adjuster, front bucket seats, short/long arm rear suspension, Solar-Ray tinted glass, compact spare tire, speed-sensitive steering, tilt steering wheel, leather-trimmed steering wheel rim, four-wheel independent suspension, full-range traction control, trip odometer, trunk convenience net, power pull-down trunk lid, power trunk lid release, trunk mat, trunk sill plate, twilight sentinel, driver's window with express-down feature.

ELDORADO TOURING COUPE: 4.6 liter V8 Northstar (300 HP) DOHC engine, automatic transmission, power steering, power four-wheel disc brakes, electrically powered windows, electrically powered automatic door locks, all-season mud and snow SBR BW tires, cast aluminum wheels, AM/FM ETR stereo radio with signal seeking/scanner/digital display/cassette player; driver and front passenger air bags, power antenna, anti-lock braking system, ignition anti-lockout feature, center front/rear seat armrests, audible reminders, body-frame integral construction, brake/transmission shift interlock, center high-mounted stop lamp, electronic climate control, digital display clock, on-board computer diagnostics, controlled-cycle wiper system, cornering lights, cruise control, electric rear window defogger, front side window defoggers, driver information center, electronic level control, engine oil life indicator, dual exhaust outlets, stainless steel exhaust, flash-to-pass, front/rear carpeted floor mats, fog lamps, front wheel drive, fuel data center, remote release fuel filler door, 3-channel programmable garage door opener, Gold Key delivery system, tungsten halogen headlamps, wiper-activated headlamps, illuminated entry, leather seating, low fuel warning indicator, low windshield washer fluid level indicator, carpeted luggage compartment, electrochromatic automatic day/night inside rearview mirror, driver side electrochromatic automatic day/night outside mirror, driver and passenger illuminated visor vanity mirrors, electrically powered and heated right/left outside rearview mirrors, multi-function turn signal lever, continuous outside temperature digital display, clearcoat paint, automatic parking brake release, Pass Key II anti-theft system, platinum-tipped spark plugs, driver/front passenger power reclining seats, remote keyless entry system, retained accessory power, real-time road-sensing suspension, 6-way power driver/front passenger seat adjusters, front bucket seats, short/long arm rear suspension, Solar-Ray tinted glass, compact spare tire, speed-sensitive steering, tilt steering wheel, leather-trimmed steering wheel rim, rear seat storage armrest, independent four-wheel suspension, theft-deterrent system, full-range traction control, trip odometer, trunk convenience net, power trunk lid pull-down, power trunk lid release, trunk mat, trunk sill plate, twilight sentinel, driver window with express-down feature.

FLEETWOOD: 5.7 liter V8 SPFI engine, automatic transmission, power steering, power front disc/rear drum brakes, electrically powered windows, electrically powered automatic door locks, all-season mud and snow SBR WW tires, cast aluminum wheels, AM/FM ETR stereo radio with signal seeking/scanner/digital display/cassette; driver and front passenger air bags, power antenna, anti-lock braking system, ignition anti-lockout feature, center front/rear seat armrests, audible reminders, brake/transmission shift interlock, center high-mounted stop lamp, electronic climate control, digital display clock, on-board computer diagnostics, controlled-cycle wiper, cornering lights, cruise control, electric rear window defogger, front side window defoggers, rear door child safety security locks, electronic level control, engine oil life indicator, dual exhaust outlets, stainless steel exhaust, flash-to-pass, carpeted front and rear floor mats, digital fuel gauge, Gold Key delivery system, tungsten halogen headlamps, illuminated entry, digital instrument cluster, low fuel warning indicator, low windshield washer fluid level indicator, carpeted luggage compartment, electrochromic automatic day/night inside rearview mirror, driver and passenger illuminated visor vanity mirrors, electrically powered and heated right/left outside rearview mirrors, multi-function turn signal lever, continuous outside temperature digital display, clearcoat paint, automatic parking brake release, Pass Key II anti-theft system, platinum tipped spark plugs, driver and front passenger power reclining seats, remote keyless entry, retained accessory power, driver and front passenger 6-way power seat adjusters, dual comfort front seats, Solar-Ray tinted glass, compact spare tire, variable assist steering, tilt steering wheel, leather-trimmed steering wheel rim, full-range traction control, trip odometer, trunk convenience net, power trunk lid pull-down, power trunk lid release, trunk mat, twilight sentinel, rear window child lockout system, driver's window with express-down feature.

SEVILLE SLS: 4.6 liter V8 Northstar (275 HP) DOHC engine, automatic transmission, power steering, power four-wheel disc brakes, electrically powered windows, electrically powered automatic door locks, all-season mud and snow SBR BW tires, cast aluminum wheels, AM/FM ETR stereo radio with signal seeking/scanner/digital display/cassette player; driver and front passenger air bags, power antenna, anti-lock braking system, ignition anti-lockout feature, center front/rear seat armrests, audible reminders, body-frame integral construction, brake/transmission shift interlock, center high-mounted stop lamp, electronic climate control, digital display clock, on-board computer diagnostics, controlled-

CODE	DESCRIPTION	INVOICE	MSRP

cycle wiper system, cornering lights, cruise control, electric rear window defogger, front side window defoggers, rear door child safety security locks, driver information center, electronic level control, engine oil life indicator, dual exhaust outlets, stainless steel exhaust, flash-to-pass, front and rear carpeted floor mats, front wheel drive, fuel data center, remote fuel filler door release, digital fuel gauge, Gold Key delivery system, tungsten halogen headlamps, wiper-activated headlamps, illuminated entry, digital instrument cluster, low fuel warning indicator, low windshield washer fluid level indicator, carpeted luggage compartment, electrochromatic automatic day/night inside rearview mirror, driver and passenger illuminated visor vanity mirrors, electrically powered and heated right/left outside rearview mirrors, multi-function turn signal lever, continuous outside temperature digital display, clearcoat paint, automatic parking brake release, Pass Key II anti-theft system, platinum-tipped spark plugs, driver and front passenger power reclining seats, remote keyless entry system, retained accessory power, real-time road-sensing suspension, 6-way power driver/front passenger seat adjusters, front bucket seats, short/long arm rear suspension, Solar-Ray tinted glass, compact spare tire, speed-sensitive steering, tilt steering wheel, leather-trimmed steering wheel rim, independent four-wheel suspension, full-range traction control, trip odometer, trunk convenience net, power trunk lid pull-down, power trunk lid release, trunk mat, trunk sill plate, twilight sentinel, driver's window express-down feature.

SEVILLE STS: 4.6 liter V8 Northstar (300 HP) DOHC engine, automatic transmission, power steering, power four-wheel disc brakes, electrically powered windows, electrically powered automatic door locks, all-season mud and snow SBR BW tires, cast aluminum wheels, AM/FM ETR stereo radio with signal seeking/scanner/digital display/cassette player; driver and front passenger air bags, power antenna, anti-lock braking system, ignition anti-lockout feature, center front/rear seat armrests, audible reminders, body-frame integral construction, brake/transmission shift interlock, center high-mounted stop lamp, electronic climate control, digital display clock, on-board computer diagnostics, controlled-cycle wiper system, cornering lights, cruise control, electric rear window defogger, front side window defoggers, rear door child safety security locks, driver information center, electronic level control, engine oil life indicator, dual exhaust outlets, stainless steel exhaust, flash-to-pass, carpeted front and rear floor mats, fog lamps, front wheel drive, fuel data center, remote fuel filler door release, 3-channel programmable garage door opener, Gold Key delivery system, tungsten halogen headlamps, wiper-activated headlamps, illuminated entry, leather seating, low fuel warning indicator, low windshield washer fluid level indicator, carpeted luggage compartment, electrochromatic automatic day/night inside rearview mirror, electrochromatic automatic day/night driver side outside mirror, driver and passenger illuminated visor vanity mirrors, electrically powered and heated right/left outside rearview mirrors, multi-function turn signal lever, continuous outside temperature digital display, clearcoat paint, automatic parking brake release, Pass Key II anti-theft system, platinum-tipped spark plugs, driver and front passenger power reclining seats, remote keyless entry system, retained accessory power, real-time road-sensing suspension, 6-way power driver/front passenger seat adjusters, front bucket seats, short/long arm rear suspension, Solar-Ray tinted glass, compact spare tire, speed-sensitive steering, tilt steering wheel, leather-trimmed steering wheel rim, rear seat storage armrest, independent four-wheel suspension, theft-deterrent system, full-range traction control, trip odometer, trunk convenience net, power trunk lid pull-down, power trunk lid release, trunk mat, trunk sill plate, twilight sentinel, driver's window express-down feature.

Accessories

CODE	DESCRIPTION	INVOICE	MSRP
1SB	**De Ville Option Pkg B — B** *incls automatic day/night electrochromic driver o/s rearview mirror, driver and passenger illuminated vanity mirrors, driver and passenger power recliners*	363	427
V4R	**Fleetwood Security Pkg — L (incl'd in V4U)** *incls automatic lock/unlock fuel filler door, theft deterrent system*	306	360
UY9	**Eldorado Sport Interior Pkg — H** *incls analog instrument cluster, floor console with transmission shift lever*	124	148

CODE	DESCRIPTION	INVOICE	MSRP
UY9	**Seville Sport Interior Pkg** — M	124	148
	incls analog instrument cluster, floor console with transmission shift lever		
D98	**Accent Striping** — H, M (std on B, P)	64	75
YL6	**Accent Stripe Delete** — B, P	NC	NC
CF5	**Astroroof** — P, L, H, T, M, G, B w/1SB	1318	1550
CF5	**Astroroof** — B w/o 1SB	1445	1700
	incls illuminated vanity mirrors		
GW9	**Axle, Performance** — 2.93:1 - L (incl'd in V4S, V4U, R1P)	NC	NC
V4U	**Coachbuilder Limousine Pkg** — L	642	755
DD7	**Electronic Compass** — B, P, H, T, M, G	85	100
FE9	**Federal Emissions** — B, P, L, H, T, M, G	NC	NC
YF5	**California Emissions** — B, L	85	100
	P, H, T, M, G	NC	NC
NG1	**Massachusetts Emissions** — B, L	85	100
	P, H, T, M, G	NC	NC
V4S	**Fleetwood Brougham** — cloth - L	1428	1680
V4S	**Fleetwood Brougham** — leather - L	1913	2250
UG1	**Garage Door Opener** — B, P, L, H, T, M, G	91	107
KA1	**Heated Front Seats** — B, P, H, T, M, G (incl'd in V4S on L)	102	120
C50	**Heated Windshield System** — B, P, H, T, M, G	263	309
R1P	**Heavy Duty Livery Pkg** — L (NA w/V4P or V4U)	128	150
YL1	**Leather Seating Area** — L (w/o V4S)	485	570
	B (std on P)	667	785
	H, M (std on G, T)	553	650
VK3	**License Plate Front Mount Provisions** — B, P, L, H, T, M, G	NC	NC
AQ9	**Lumbar Support** — power - H, M (std on P, G, T, L w/V4S)	248	292
DD0	**Mirror** — H, M (std on P, G, T, B w/1SB)	74	87
	incls automatic day/night electrochromic o/s driver side		
V1F	**Paint** — white diamond - B, P, H, T, M, G	425	500
YL3	**Paint** — pearl red - B, P, H, T, M, G	425	500
—	**Radios**		
	all radios (including base) are AM stereo/FM stereo, electronically tuned, digital display with signal seeking and scanner, and cassette tape player		
U1H	w/compact disc - L	337	396
—	**Radios**		
	incls 10 speaker active audio system		
U1L	cassette only - B (std on P)	233	274
U1R	cassette and compact disc - B	570	670
	P	337	396
—	**Radios**		
	incls Delco Bose sound system		
U1G	w/compact disc and cassette - H, T, M, G	826	972
CB5	**Roof** — full padded vinyl - L (incl'd w/V4S)	786	925
CA2	**Roof** — vinyl roof delete - L w/V4S	NC	NC
CB3	**Roof** — vinyl roof provisions - L w/V4U	NC	NC

CODE	DESCRIPTION	INVOICE	MSRP
UY9	**Sport Interior** — H, M	124	146
UA6	**Theft Deterrent System** — B, P, H, M (std on T, G, L w/V4R)	251	295
N81	**Tire** — full-size spare - L (incl'd w/V4U)	81	95
QPY	**Tires** — whitewall P225/60R16 - H	65	76
V4P	**Trailer Towing Pkg** — 7000# - L	183	215
V92	**Trailer Towing Pkg** — 3000# - P	94	110
PH6	**Cast Aluminum Wheels** — B	NC	NC
N83	**Chrome Wheels** — L	523	1195
N98	**Chrome Wheels** — B	523	1195
P05	**Chrome Wheels** — H, M	523	1195
QC8	**Chrome Wheels** — T, G	523	1195
QC6	**Chrome Wheels** — P	523	1195
A23	**Windshield** — Sungate automotive - L	43	50

What's New for *Cadillac* in 1995?

DeVille: Trunk lid power pull-down is now standard, and Shale, Pearl Red and Amethyst replace Platimum Gray, Academy Gray and Dark Montana Blue on the color chart. Wiper-activated headlights come on after the wipers have been on for 25 seconds. Inside, Neutral Shale replaces Light Gray cloth, while Gray and Neutral leather are dropped in favor of Cappuccino Cream and Neutral Shale. A three-channel programmable garage door opener lets you into the mansion, the summer house and executive parking with ease.

DeVille Concours: Northstar engine receives a 5 hp boost to 275, and a traction control disable switch is provided. Chrome wheels are optional, just the thing for Northern tier states. See DeVille above for other changes.

Eldorado: Freshened styling and color changes update the 1995 Eldorado nicely. Wiper-activated headlights come on 25 seconds after it starts to rain, and Charisma cloth replaces Bistro inside. Horsepower is up 5 to 275, and a new exhaust is quieter. A three-channel programmable garage door opener is optional.

Eldorado Touring Coupe: Five new colors increase the palette by 50%, and the Northstar engine now puts 300 hp onto the blacktop through the front wheels. See Eldorado above for other changes.

Fleetwood: Larger, foldaway mirrors are standard outside, and the Fleetwood can now be had in Calypso Green. The three-channel programmable garage door opener available on other Cadillac's is optional, and towing capacity is up to a whopping 7000 lbs.

Seville SLS: Wiper-activated headlights, new colors and increased horsepower sum up the changes to the 1995 Sevillle SLS. Oh yes, the trick garage door opener is optional as well.

Seville STS: Same changes as Seville SLS, but the Northstar pumps out 300 hp in this application instead of the 275 hp of its weaker sibling.

BERETTA *(1995)*

BERETTA 4 CYL

CODE	DESCRIPTION	INVOICE	MSRP
1LV37	2-Dr Coupe	11851	13095
1LW37/Z04	Z26 2-Dr Coupe	14747	16295
Destination Charge:		495	495

Standard Equipment

BERETTA: 2.2 liter MFI L4 engine, 5-speed manual transmission, power rack and pinion steering, power front disc/rear drum brakes, power automatic door locks with relock and unlock feature, P195/70R14 BW tires, 14" steel wheels with bolt-on full wheel covers, electronically tuned AM/FM stereo radio with seek-scan, digital clock and extended range front and rear speakers; air conditioning, smart run-down protection battery, 4-wheel anti-lock brake system, transmission shift interlock (auto trans only), 5-mph bumpers, stainless steel exhaust, composite halogen headlamps, dual remote black mirrors, color-keyed bodyside moldings and fascia rub strips, gloss black door moldings, quarter window moldings, base coat/clear coat paint, Level I Soft-Ride suspension, driver side air bag, center shift console with integral armrest covered storage/lighter/cup holder/ashtray; instrument panel retractable cup holder, Scotchgard fabric protector (seats, door trim, floor covering), rear seat heat ducts, dome/trunk/under dash courtesy lamps, low coolant level/low oil level lights, front door map pockets, rear Comfort Guide safety belts, front passive seat belt system, cloth reclining front bucket seats with adjustable head restraints, driver's side 4-way manual seat adjuster with easy entry, sport steering wheel, LH/RH visors with map straps, passenger side vanity mirror.

Z26 (in addition to or instead of BERETTA equipment): 3.1 liter SFI V6 engine, automatic transmission, P205/60R15 BW tires, 15" steel wheels with bolt-on wheel covers, electronically tuned AM/FM stereo radio with seek-scan, digital clock, stereo cassette tape and coaxial front/extended range rear speakers; luggage area convenience net, styled exhaust outlet, block-out body color grille, fog lamps, lower front/rear decklid spoilers, body color sport remote mirrors, Level II sport suspension, specific ground effects treatment, intermittent windshield wipers, gauge package with tachometer and trip odometer, day/night rearview mirror with reading lamps, custom cloth reclining sport bucket seats with adjustable articulating head restraints, inflatable lumbar support, driver and passenger side 4-way manual seat adjusters, easy-entry feature, 60/40 split folding rear seat, covered LH/RH visor mirrors.

CODE	DESCRIPTION	INVOICE	MSRP
	Accessories		
1SD	**Beretta Base Equipment Group**	NC	NC
UM6	w/UM6 radio, add	120	140
U1C	w/U1C radio, add	341	396
	incl'd w/model		
1SF	**Beretta Preferred Equipment Group 1**	142	165
UM6	w/UM6 radio, add	120	140
U1C	w/U1C radio, add	341	396
	incls covered LH & RH visor mirrors, luggage area convenience net, intermittent windshield wiper system, front and rear color-keyed carpeted mats, day/night rearview mirror with reading lamps		
1SG	**Beretta Preferred Equipment Group 2**	641	745
UM6	w/UM6 radio, add	120	140
U1C	w/U1C radio, add	341	396
	incls covered LH & RH visor mirrors, luggage area convenience net, split folding rear seat with armrest, power trunk opener, electronic speed control with resume speed, tilt wheel adjustable steering column, intermittent windshield wiper system, front and rear color-keyed carpeted mats, day/night rearview mirror with reading lamps		
—	**Beretta Z26 Base Equipment Group**	NC	NC
U1C	w/U1C radio, add	220	256
	incl'd w/model		
—	**Beretta Z26 Preferred Equipment Group 1**	398	463
U1C	w/U1C radio, add	220	256
	incls tilt wheel adjustable steering column, electronic speed control with resume speed, power trunk opener, front and rear color-keyed carpeted mats		
—	**Engines**		
LN2	2.2 liter MFI L4	NC	NC
L82	3.1 liter SFI V6 (reqs MX0 trans) - w/Coupe	1097	1275
	w/Z26	NC	NC
VK3	**Bracket, Front License Plate**	NC	NC
C49	**Defogger, Rear Window** — electric	146	170
R9W	**Defogger, Rear Window, Delete**	NC	NC
K05	**Heater, Engine Block**	17	20
AR9	**Bucket Seats**	NC	NC
—	**Radio Equipment** — see pkgs for specific radio pricing		
UM6	radio - see pkgs		
	incls electronically tuned AM/FM stereo radio with seek/scan, digital clock, stereo cassette tape, extended-range speakers		
U1C	radio - see pkgs		
	incls electronically tuned AM stereo/FM stereo radio with seek/scan, digital clock, compact disc player, Delco Loc II, coaxial front and extended-range rear speakers		
D52	**Spoiler, Rear** — incl'd w/Z26	95	100
AD3	**Sun Roof** — manual, removable	301	350
—	**Tires**		
QIM	P205/60R15 BW	151	175
	req's PG1 wheels; std on Z26		

CODE	DESCRIPTION	INVOICE	MSRP
QMS	P205/55R16 BW	320	372
	req's PF4 wheels		
—	**Transmissions**		
MM5	5-speed manual standard	NC	NC
MX1	3-speed automatic	477	555
MX0	4-speed automatic	NC	NC
	req's L82 engine		
—	**Wheels**		
PG1	15" steel bolt-on wheel covers	NC	NC
	req's QIM tires; std on Z26		
PF4	16" styled aluminum wheels w/locks	NC	NC
	req's QMS tires		
A31	**Windows, Power** — w/driver's express-down	237	275
UB3	**Gauge Pkg**	95	111
	incls tachometer, trip odometer, voltmeter, oil pressure & temp gauges (std on Z26)		
FE9	**Federal Emission Requirements**	NC	NC
NG1	**Massachusetts Emission Requirements** — w/L82 engine	NC	NC
	w/LN2 engine and MM5 transmission	NC	NC
	w/LN2 engine and MX1 transmission	86	100
YF5	**California Emission Requirements** — w/L82 engine	NC	NC
	w/LN2 engine and MM5 transmission	NC	NC
	w/LN2 engine and MX1 transmission	86	100

CAMARO *(1995)*

CODE	DESCRIPTION	INVOICE	MSRP
CAMARO 6 CYL			
1FP87	2-Dr Coupe	13263	14495
1FP67	2-Dr Convertible	17929	19595
CAMARO 8 CYL			
1FP87/Z28	Z28 2-Dr Coupe	16616	18160
1FP67/Z28	Z28 2-Dr Convertible	21223	23195
Destination Charge:		500	500

Standard Equipment

CAMARO - BASE COUPE: 3.4 liter V6 engine, 5-speed manual transmission, power rack and pinion steering, power front disc/rear drum brakes, P215/60R16 BW tires, 16" silver steel wheels with bolt-on wheel covers, electronically tuned AM/FM stereo radio with seek-scan, digital clock, stereo cassette tape, search, repeat and extended range speakers; single serpentine accessory drive belt, 4-wheel anti-lock brake system, transmission shift interlock (auto trans only), 5-mph energy-absorbing front and rear bumpers with body color fascias, side window defoggers, stainless steel exhaust system, Solar-Ray tinted glass, miniquad halogen headlamps, dual sport body colored mirrors (LH remote/RH manual), 2-component clear coat paint, gas charged monotube front and rear shocks, integral rear stabilizer bars, front and rear spoiler, firm ride and handling suspension, 4-wheel coil spring suspension system with computer selected springs, short-long arm de Carbon front suspension system, Pass Key II theft deterrent system, high-pressure compact spare tire, intermittent wipers, driver and front passenger air bags, full carpeting (includes cargo area), center console with cup holder and lighted storage compartment, Scotchgard fabric protector (seats/door trim/floor mats/floor carpeting), carpeted front floor mats, gauge package with tachometer, low oil level indicator, dome lamp, day/night rearview mirror with dual reading/courtesy lamps, closeout panel for cargo compartment area, headlamps on reminder, 4-way driver's side manual seat adjuster, full folding back rear seat, cloth reclining front bucket seats with integral head restraints, 115-mph speedometer, tilt-wheel steering wheel, door storage compartments, covered LH/RH visor mirrors, check gauges warning lights.

BASE CONVERTIBLE (in addition to or instead of BASE COUPE equipment): Rear window defogger, glass rear window, 3-piece hard boot with storage bag, body color mirrors, power folding top, full headliner, rear seat courtesy lamp, trunk lamp, Premium speaker system.

CAMARO - Z28 COUPE: 5.7 liter SFI V8 engine, 6-speed manual transmission, power rack and pinion steering, power front/rear disc brakes, P235/55R16 BW tires, 16" aluminum silver wheels, electronically tuned AM/FM stereo radio with seek-scan, digital clock, stereo cassette tape, search, repeat and extended range speakers; limited slip rear axle, single serpentine accessory drive belt, 4-wheel anti-lock brake system, transmission shift interlock (auto trans only), 5-mph energy-absorbing front/rear bumpers with body color fascias, side window defoggers, stainless steel exhaust system, Solar-Ray tinted glass, miniquad halogen headlamps, dual sport body color mirrors (LH remote/RH manual), 2-component clear coat paint, special black roof treatment, gas charged monotube front/ rear shocks, platinum tip spark plugs, integral rear spoiler, performance firm ride and handling suspension, 4-wheel coil spring suspension system with computer selected springs, short-long arm de Carbon front suspension, Pass Key II theft deterrent system, high pressure compact spare tire, intermittent wipers, driver and passenger air bags, full carpeting (includes cargo area), center console with cup holder and lighted storage compartment, Scotchgard fabric protector (includes seats/door trim/floor mats/floor carpeting), carpeted front floor mats, gauge package with tachometer, low oil level indicator system, dome lamp, day/night rearview mirror with dual reading/courtesy lamps, closeout panel for cargo compartment area, headlamps on reminder, 4-way manual driver's seat adjuster, full folding back rear seat, cloth reclining front bucket seats with integral head restraints, 115-mph speedometer, tilt-wheel steering wheel, door storage compartments, covered LH/RH visor mirrors, check gauges warning light.

Z28 CONVERTIBLE (in addition to or instead of Z28 COUPE equipment): Rear window defogger, glass rear window, 3-piece hard boot with storage bag, body color mirrors, folding power top, full headliner, rear seat courtesy lamp, trunk lamp, Premium speaker system.

Accessories

CODE	DESCRIPTION	INVOICE	MSRP
1SA	**Camaro Coupe Base Equipment Group**	NC	NC
	incl'd w/model		
1SB	**Camaro Coupe Preferred Equipment Group 1**	1066	1240
UU8	w/UU8 radio, add	301	350
U1T	w/U1T radio, add	521	606
	incls air conditioning, electronic speed control w/resume speed, remote hatch release, fog lamps		
1SC	**Camaro Coupe Preferred Equipment Group 2**	1751	2036
UU8	w/UU8 radio, add	301	350
U1T	w/U1T radio, add	521	606
	incls air conditioning, electronic speed control w/resume speed, remote hatch release, fog lamps, power windows with driver side express down, power door lock system, sport twin remote electric mirrors, leather-wrapped steering wheel, leather-wrapped transmission shifter and parking brake handle, remote keyless entry with illuminated interior feature		
1SH	**Z28 Coupe Base Equipment Group**	NC	NC
	incl'd w/model		
1SJ	**Z28 Coupe Preferred Equipment Group 1** — w/MN6	1191	1385
	w/MXO	1097	1275
UU8	w/UU8 radio, add	301	350
U1T	w/U1T radio, add	521	606
	incls air conditioning, electronic speed control w/resume feature, remote hatch release, engine oil cooler (w/MN6 only), fog lamps		

CODE	DESCRIPTION	INVOICE	MSRP
1SK	**Z28 Coupe Preferred Equipment Group 2 — w/MN6**	1876	2181
	w/MXO	1781	2071
UU8	w/UU8 radio, add	301	350
U1T	w/U1T radio, add	521	606
	incls air conditioning, electronic speed control with resume speed, remote hatch release, engine oil cooler (w/MN6 only), fog lamps, 4-way manual driver seat adjuster, power windows with driver side express-down, power door lock system, sport twin remote electric mirrors, remote keyless entry with illluminated interior feature, leather-wrapped steering wheel, transmission shifter and parking brake handle		
1SD	**Camaro Convertible Base Equipment Group**	NC	NC
U1C	w/U1C radio, add	194	226
1SF	**Camaro Convertible Preferred Equipment Group 1**	1161	1350
U1C	w/U1C radio, add	194	225
	incls air conditioning, electronic speed control with resume speed, remote trunk release, fog lamps		
1SG	**Camaro Convertible Preferred Equipment Group 2**	1751	2036
U1C	w/U1C radio, add	194	226
	incls air conditioning, electronic speed control with resume speed, remote trunk release, fog lamps, power windows with driver side express down, power door lock system, sport twin remote electric mirrors, leather-wrapped steering wheel, transmission shifter and parking brake handle, remote keyless entry with illuminated interior feature		
1SL	**Z28 Convertible Base Equipment Group**	NC	NC
U1C	w/U1C radio, add	194	226
1SM	**Z28 Convertible Preferred Equipment Group 1 — w/MN6**	1161	1350
	w/MXO	1066	1240
U1C	w/U1C radio, add	194	226
	incls air conditioning, electronic speed control with resume speed, remote trunk lid release, engine oil cooler (w/MN6 trans only), fog lamps		
1SN	**Z28 Convertible Preferred Equipment Group 2 — w/MN6**	1846	2146
	w/MXO	1751	2036
U1C	w/U1C radio, add	194	226
	incls air conditioning, electronic speed control with resume speed, remote trunk release, engine oil cooler (w/MN6 trans only), fog lamps, power windows with driver side express down, power door lock system, sport twin remote electric mirrors, remote keyless entry system with illuminated interior feature, leather-wrapped steering, transmission shifter and parking brake handle		
—	**Radio Equipment** — see pkgs		
U1C	Music system - Convertibles		
	incls electronically tuned AM/FM stereo radio with seek-scan, digital clock, compact disc player, extended range speakers and Delco Loc II		
UU8	Music system - Coupes		
	incls electronically tuned AM/FM stereo radio with seek-scan, stereo cassette tape and digital clock		
U1T	Delco/Bose music system - Coupes		
	incls electronically tuned AM/FM stereo radio with seek-scan, compact disc player, digital clock and Delco LOC II		

CODE	DESCRIPTION	INVOICE	MSRP
—	**Interior Trim**		
C2	cloth bucket seats	NC	NC
—	**Exterior Color** — paint, solid	NC	NC
—	**Engines**		
L32	3.4 liter SFI V6 - std on Camaro Coupe & Convertible	NC	NC
LT1	5.7 liter SFI V8 - std on Z28 Coupe & Z28 Convertible	NC	NC
B35	**Floor Covering, Rear**	13	15
B34	**Bodyside Molding**	52	60
D82	**Monochromatic Roof** — Coupes	NC	NC
DE4	**Sunshades** — removable roof panel	22	25
GU5	**Axle, Optional** — Z28	215	250
	Z28 w/o 1LE performance pkg	NA	NA
	incls engine oil cooler		
VK3	**Bracket, Front License Plate**	NC	NC
C49	**Defogger** — rear window, electric	146	170
R9W	**Defogger** — rear window, delete	NC	NC
AU3	**Door Lock System, Power** — electric	189	220
YF5	**California Emission Requirements**	86	100
FE9	**Federal Emission Requirements**	NC	NC
NG1	**Massachusetts Emission Requirements**	86	100
1LE	**Performance Package** — Z28 Coupe	267	310
	incls engine oil cooler and special handling suspension system		
CC1	**Roof Panels** — removable glass - incls locks - Coupes	834	970
AG1	**Seat, Power** — driver side only	232	270
AR9	**Cloth Bucket Seats**	NC	NC
AR9	**Leather Bucket Seats** — w/o 1SH	429	499
	w/1SH	460	534
—	**Tires**		
QPE	P215/60R16 SBR ply BW - std on Camaro Coupe & Convertible	NC	NC
QMT	P235/55R16 SBR ply BW - std on Z28 Coupe & Z28 Convertible	114	132
QLC	P245/50ZR16 SBR ply BW - Z28 Coupe	194	225
QFZ	P245/50ZR16 BW all performance - Z28	194	225
—	**Transmissions**		
MN6	6-speed manual - std on Z28 Coupe & Z28 Convertible	NC	NC
MM5	5-speed manual - std on Camaro Coupe & Convertible	NC	NC
MXO	4-speed automatic w/overdrive	645	750
N96	**Wheels** — aluminum cast 16" - std on Z28	237	275
	incls wheel locks		
NW9	**Acceleration Slip Regulation** — Z28	387	450
	QFZ tires recommended		

CAPRICE CLASSIC *(1995)*

CAPRICE CLASSIC 8 CYL

CODE	DESCRIPTION	INVOICE	MSRP
1BL19	4-Dr Sedan	17772	20310
1BL35	4-Dr Wagon	19985	22840
	Destination Charge:	585	585

Standard Equipment

CAPRICE CLASSIC - SEDAN: 4-speed electronic automatic transmission, power steering, 4-wheel anti-lock brake system, power door locks, P215/75R15 BW tires, full wheel covers, electronically tuned AM/FM stereo radio with seek-scan, digital clock and dual front/rear speakers; air conditioning, stainless steel exhaust system, tinted glass, manual outside mirrors (LH remote/RH manual), wide bodyside moldings, base coat/clear coat paint, intermittent windshield wipers, driver and front passenger air bags, cup holders, brake/transmission shift interlock, rear child security door locks, color-keyed front/rear carpeted floor mats, voltmeter/oil pressure gauges, front door courtesy lamps, RH covered visor mirror, oil change monitor, trip odometer, Pass Key theft deterrent system, door map pockets, standard custom cloth 55/45 seats with center front and rear armrests, adjustable head restraints, driver and passenger seat recliners, seat back pockets, Scotchgard fabric protector (seats/door trim/floor covering), tilt-wheel adjustable steering column, low fluid warning light.

WAGON (in addition to or instead of SEDAN equipment): Luggage rack, two-way tailgate with rear wiper/washer system, P225/75R15 WS tires, electronically tuned AM/FM stereo radio with seek-scan, stereo cassette tape with auto reverse, digital clock with coaxial front and extended range rear speakers, assist handles (3rd seat with integral lights), power tailgate window release.

Accessories

CODE	DESCRIPTION	INVOICE	MSRP
1SA	**Caprice Classic Sedan Base Equipment Group**	NC	NC
UM6	w/UM6 radio, add	172	200
UL0	w/UL0 radio, add	219	255
UN0	w/UN0 radio, add	305	355
	incls standard equipment		

CODE	DESCRIPTION	INVOICE	MSRP
1SB	**Caprice Classic Sedan Preferred Equipment Group 1**	605	703
UM6	w/UM6 radio, add	172	200
UL0	w/UL0 radio, add	219	255
UN0	w/UN0 radio, add	305	355
	incls electronic speed control with resume speed, power windows with driver's express-down, electric twin remote mirrors, power trunk opener		
1SC	**Caprice Classic Sedan Preferred Equipment Group 2**	1189	1382
UL0	w/UL0 radio, add	47	55
UN0	w/UN0 radio, add	133	155
	incls power windows with driver's express down, electronic speed control with resume speed, power trunk opener, electric twin remote mirrors, radio (electronically tuned AM/FM stereo radio with seek and scan stereo cassette tape with auto reverse, digital clock and coaxial front and extended-range rear speakers), driver's side 6-way power seat, power antenna, dual reading lamps in rearview mirror, rear compartment reading lamps, illuminated RH covered visor mirror		
1SQ	**Caprice Classic Sedan Preferred Equipment Group 3**	1734	2016
UL0	w/UL0 radio, add	47	55
UN0	w/UN0 radio, add	133	155
	incls electric twin remote mirrors, power windows with driver's express-down, electronic speed control with resume speed, power trunk opener, radio (electronically tuned AM/FM stereo radio with auto reverse, digital clock and coaxial front and extended-range rear speakers), driver's side 6-way power seat, power antenna, rear compartment lamps, rear courtesy lamps, cornering lamps, illuminated RH covered visor mirror, automatic day/night rearview mirror, remote keyless entry, passenger power seat, twilight sentinel headlamp system		
1SF	**Caprice Classic Wagon Base Equipment Group**	NC	NC
UL0	w/UL0 radio, add	47	55
UN0	w/UN0 radio, add	133	155
	incls standard equipment		
1SG	**Caprice Classic Wagon Preferred Equipment Group 1**	815	948
UL0	w/UL0 radio, add	47	55
UN0	w/UN0 radio, add	133	155
	incls electronic speed control with resume speed, electric twin remote mirrors, driver's side 6-way power seat, power windows with driver's express-down		
1SH	**Caprice Classic Wagon Preferred Equipment Group 2**	1566	1821
UL0	w/UL0 radio, add	47	55
UN0	w/UN0 radio, add	133	155
	incls power antenna, electronic speed control with resume speed, electric twin remote mirrors, driver's side 6-way power seat, power windows with driver's express-down, deluxe rear compartment decor, rear window defogger with heated outside rearview mirrors, passenger side 6-way power seat, rear security compartment cover, rear compartment reading lamps, automatic day/night rearview mirror with dual reading lamps, illuminated RH covered visor mirror		
—	**Radio Equipment** — see pkgs for specific radio pricing		
UM6	radio - see pkgs		
	incls electronically tuned AM/FM stereo radio with seek/scan, stereo cassette tape with auto reverse, digital clock and coaxial front and extended-range rear speakers		

CODE	DESCRIPTION	INVOICE	MSRP
UL0	radio - see pkgs *incls electronically tuned AM/FM stereo radio with seek/scan, digital clock with automatic tone control, cassette tape, theft lock and speed compensated volume (incls premium front and rear coaxial speakers)*		
UN0	radio - see pkgs *incls electronically tuned AM/FM stereo radio with automatic tone control, compact disc player, digital clock, theft lock and speed compensated volume (incls premium front and rear coaxial speakers)*		
G80	**Axle, Rear Limited Slip Differential** — Sedan (req's L99 engine)	215	250
	Wagon (req's V92 trailering package)	86	100
VK3	**Bracket, Front License Plate**	NC	NC
AP9	**Cargo Convenience Net**	26	30
C49	**Defogger, Rear Window** — electric		
	w/preferred equipment group (incls dual heated OS mirrors)	176	205
	w/out preferred equipment group	146	170
FE9	**Federal Emission Requirements**	NC	NC
NG1	**Massachusetts Emission Requirements**	86	100
YF5	**California Emission Requirements**	86	100
—	**Engines**		
L99	4.3 liter SFI V8 (std on Sedan)	NC	NC
LT1	5.7 liter SFI V8 (std on Wagon) *req's B4U sport suspension*	473	550
K05	**Engine Block Heater** — Sedan	17	20
B18	**Interior Package, Custom** *incls cargo net, front courtesy lamps, LH covered visor mirror and custom trim door panels; req's 1SQ or 1SH*	112	130
D84	**Custom Two-Tone Paint** *N/A on Wagon w/BX3 woodgrain*	121	141
D90	**Pinstriping, Bodyside & Rear**	52	61
F41	**Ride/Handling Suspension** — Sedan *req's QNP tires*	42	49
AG1	**Seat, Power Driver's Side** — 6-way adjuster *incld w/PEGS 1SCX & 1SQX; NA w/PEG 1SAX*	262	305
—	**Seat Type**		
AM6	55/45 custom cloth	NC	NC
AM6	55/45 custom leather — Sedan *req's PEG 1SQX*	667	775
K34	**Speed Control, Electronic** — w/resume speed	194	225
—	**Suspension**		
G67	auto leveling - Caprice Classic Wagon only *N/A w/1SG and 1SH*	151	175
B4U	sport - Caprice Classic Sedan only *incls G80 limited slip axle, QMU tires, leather wrapped steering wheel and trailering package w/HD cooling and engine oil cooler; req's LT1 engine and QMU or QMV tires*	437	508
V92	**Trailering Package** — Wagon *incls heavy duty cooling*	18	21
UV8	**Telephone, Cellular Provisions**	39	45

CODE	DESCRIPTION	INVOICE	MSRP
—	**Tires** — all-season steel belted radial-ply		
QCU	P215/75R15 blackwall (std on Sedan)	NC	NC
QCV	P215/75R15 white stripe — Sedan	69	80
QNP	P225/70R15 white stripe — Sedan *req's F41 suspension*	151	176
QEU	P225/75R15 white stripe (std on Wagon)	NC	NC
QMU	P235/70R15 blackwall (incld w/B4U) — Sedan *req's LT1 engine; N/A w/N91 wheels*	NC	NC
QMV	P235/70R15 white stripe — Sedan *req's LT1 engine*	77	90
N81	**Full Size Spare** — steel wheel		
	w/QMU tires — Sedan	52	60
	w/QCV, QMV or QNP tires — Wagon	56	65
—	**Wheels**		
PD4	aluminum - w/locks — Sedan	215	250
PB1	deluxe wheel covers	60	70
N91	wire wheel covers - w/locks	185	215
BX3	**Woodgrain Exterior** — Wagon *N/A w/D84 two-tone paint or D90 pinstriping*	512	595
A23	**Heat reflective windshield**	45	52

CAVALIER *(1995)*

CAVALIER 4 CYL

CODE	DESCRIPTION	INVOICE	MSRP
1JC37	Base 2-Dr Coupe	9507	10060
1JC69	Base 4-Dr Sedan	9700	10265
1JF69	LS 4-Dr Sedan	11530	12465
1JF37	Z24 2-Dr Coupe	12498	13810
Destination Charge:		485	485

Standard Equipment

CAVALIER - BASE: 2.2 liter MFI 4 cylinder engine, 5-speed manual transmission, power rack and pinion steering, driver and front passenger air bags, tinted glass, battery with rundown protection system, power front disc/rear drum brakes with 4-wheel anti-lock, 5-mph bumpers, stainless steel exhaust system, composite halogen headlamps, engine compartment hood insulator pad, sport LH remote and RH manual mirrors, clearcoat paint, P195/70R14 BW tires, 14" bolt-on full wheel covers, passenger compartment floor covering, console with integral armrest and storage, side window defoggers, cup holder, courtesy lighting (glove box, trunk, overhead and rear compartment), inside rearview day/night mirror, full folding rear seat, reclining front bucket seats with adjustable head restraints, deluxe trunk trim, low oil level gauge, intermittent/fixed delay windshield wipers.

LS (in addition to or instead of BASE equipment): Trunk cargo net, body color fascias, color-keyed bodyside moldings, front mud guards, 3-speed automatic transmission, P195/65R15 BW tires, air conditioning, dual reading lamps, floor mats, dual covered visor vanity mirrors with map straps, radio (electronically tuned AM/FM stereo with seek/scan, digital clock and extended-range front and rear speakers), reclining front bucket seats with adjustable head restraints and sport cloth, analog tachometer, trip odometer, remote trunk release.

Z24 (in addition to or instead of LS equipment): 2.3 liter MFI 4 cyl engine, tilt steering wheel, cast aluminum wheels, rear decklid spoiler, fog lights, 5-speed manual transmission, AM/FM ETR stereo radio w/cassette and extended range front and rear speakers, front mud guards deleted, P205/55R16 SBR BW tires.

Accessories

Code	Description	Invoice	MSRP
1SA	**Cavalier Coupe Base Equipment Group**	NC	NC
UM7	w/UM7 radio, add	295	332
UM6	w/UM6 radio, add	420	472
U1C	w/U1C radio, add	648	728
	incld with model		
1SB	**Cavalier Coupe Preferred Equipment Group 1**	187	210
UM7	w/UM7 radio, add	295	332
UM6	w/UM6 radio, add	420	472
U1C	w/U1C radio, add	648	728
	incls mechanical trunk opener, variable intermittent windshield wiper system, dual covered visor mirrors with map straps, bodyside moldings, front mud guards, easy entry passenger seat, front and rear color-keyed carpeted floor mats		
1SC	**Cavalier Coupe Preferred Equipment Group 2**	516	580
UM7	w/UM7 radio, add	295	332
UM6	w/UM6 radio, add	420	472
U1C	w/U1C radio, add	648	728
	incls tilt-wheel adjustable steering column, electronic speed control with resume speed, variable intermittent windshield wiper system, mechanical trunk opener, dual covered visor mirrors with map straps, bodyside moldings, front mud guards, easy entry passenger seat, front and rear color-keyed carpeted floor mats		
1SD	**Cavalier Sedan Base Equipment Group**	NC	NC
UM7	w/UM7 radio, add	295	332
UM6	w/UM6 radio, add	420	472

CODE	DESCRIPTION	INVOICE	MSRP
U1C	w/U1C radio, add	648	728
	incld with model		
1SF	**Cavalier Sedan Preferred Equipment Group 1**	172	193
UM7	w/UM7 radio, add	295	332
UM6	w/UM6 radio, add	420	472
U1C	w/U1C radio, add	648	728
	incls front and rear color-keyed carpeted floor mats, dual covered visor mirrors with map straps, bodyside moldings, front mud guards, mechanical trunk opener, variable intermittent windshield wiper system		
1SG	**Cavalier Sedan Preferred Equipment Group 2**	501	563
UM7	w/UM7 radio, add	295	332
UM6	w/UM6 radio, add	420	472
U1C	w/U1C radio, add	648	728
	incls front and rear color-keyed carpeted floor mats, dual covered visor mirrors with map straps, bodyside moldings, front mud guards, mechanical trunk opener, variable intermittent windshield wiper system, electronic speed control with resume speed, tilt-wheel adjustable steering column		
1SH	**Cavalier LS Sedan Base Equipment Group**	NC	NC
UM6	w/UM6 radio, add	125	140
U1C	w/U1C radio, add	352	396
	incld with model		
1SJ	**Cavalier LS Sedan Preferred Equipment Group 1**	387	435
UM6	w/UM6 radio, add	125	140
U1C	w/U1C radio, add	352	396
	incls tilt-wheel adjustable steering column, electronic speed control with resume speed, variable intermittent windshield wiper system		
1SK	**Cavalier LS Sedan Preferred Equipment Group 2**	980	1101
UM6	w/UM6 radio, add	125	140
U1C	w/U1C radio, add	352	396
	incls tilt-wheel adjustable steering column, electronic speed control with resume speed, variable intermittent windshield wiper system, twin remote electric mirrors, power door locks, power windows with driver's express-down		
1SP	**Cavalier Z24 Coupe Base Equipment Group**	NC	NC
	incld w/model		
1SQ	**Cavalier Z24 Coupe Preferred Equipment Group 1**	258	290
	incls speed control w/resume speed, intermittent variable windshield wiper system		
1SR	**Cavalier Z24 Coupe Preferred Equipment Group 2**	757	851
	incls electric twin remote mirrors, power door locks, power windows w/driver's express down		
C60	**Air Conditioning** — std on LS Sedan and Z24 Coupe	699	785
W27	**Appearance Pkg, Exterior** — w/1JC37 and PEGS 1SB or 1SC	178	200
VK3	**Bracket, Front License Plate**	NC	NC
C49	**Defogger, Rear Window** — electric	151	170
R9W	**Defogger, Rear Window; Not Desired**	NC	NC
AU3	**Door Locks, Power** — Coupe	187	210
	Sedans	223	250

CODE	DESCRIPTION	INVOICE	MSRP
K05	**Heater, Engine Block**	18	20
FE9	**Federal Emission Requirements**	NC	NC
NG1	**Massachusetts Emission Requirements**	89	100
YF5	**California Emission Requirements**	89	100
LN2	**Engine** — 2.2 liter MFI L4 — except Z24 Coupe	NC	NC
LD2	**Engine** — 2.3 liter MFI L4 — Z24 Coupe	NC	NC
AR9	**Seats** — sport cloth bucket	NC	NC
CF5	**Sunroof** — electric — Coupes	530	595
—	**Transmissions**		
MM5	5-speed manual — Base models and Z24 Coupe	NC	NC
MX1	3-speed automatic (std on LS Sedan) — Base models	441	495
MX0	4-speed automatic — Z24 Coupe	598	695
PF7	**Wheels** — 15" aluminum - w/1JF69	231	259
—	**Radio Equipment** — seek pkgs for specific radio pricing		
UM7	radio - see pkgs *incls electronically tuned AM/FM stereo radio with seek/scan, digital clock, extended range front and rear speakers*		
UM6	radio - see pkgs *incls electronically tuned AM/FM stereo radio with seek/scan, stereo cassette tape, digital clock, extended range front and rear speakers*		
U1C	radio - see pkgs *incls electronically tuned AM/FM stereo radio with seek/scan, compact disc player, Delco Loc II and digital clock, extended range front and rear speakers*		
UL5	radio delete	NC	NC

CORSICA *(1995)*

CORSICA 4 CYL

	INVOICE	MSRP
1LD69 4-Dr Sedan	12661	13990
Destination Charge:	495	495

Standard Equipment

CORSICA: Four-wheel anti-lock brake system, power front disc/rear drum brakes, brake/transmission shift interlock (auto trans only), 5-mph bumpers, 2.2 liter MFI L4 engine, stainless steel exhaust, tinted glass, black grille, composite halogen headlamps, under hood insulator blanket, dual remote body color outside rearview mirrors, black bodyside moldings and fascia rub strips with narrow black insert, door and window reveal moldings, basecoat/clearcoat paint, smart battery rundown protection, power rack and pinion steering, Level I soft ride suspension, P185/75R14 BW tires, 3-speed automatic transmission, full trunk trim, full bolt-on wheel covers, driver side air bag system, air conditioning, center shift console with integral armrest, covered storage, lighter, cupholder and ashtray; retractable cupholder in instrument panel, automatic door locks with relock and unlock feature, Scotchgard fabric protector (seats, door trim, floor covering), rear seat heat ducts, courtesy lamps (dome, under dash, trunk), delayed entry/exit lighting with theatre dimming, low coolant level light (V6 only), low oil level light, front door map pockets, electronically tuned AM/FM stereo radio with seek-scan, digital clock and extended range speakers; headlamps-on reminder, rear comfort guide safety belt, passive front seat belt system, cloth reclining bucket seats with adjustable head restraints and driver's side 4-way manual seat adjuster, LH/RH visors with map straps and passenger side vanity mirror.

Accessories

CODE	DESCRIPTION	INVOICE	MSRP
1SA	**Corsica Base Equip Group**	NC	NC
UM6	w/UM6 radio, add	120	140
U1C	w/U1C radio, add	341	396
	incld with model		
1SB	**Corsica Preferred Equipment Group 1**	142	165
UM6	w/UM6 radio, add	120	140
U1C	w/U1C radio, add	341	396
	incls reading lamps, covered LH & RH visor mirrors, luggage area convenience net, intermittent windshield wipers, front and rear color-keyed carpeted mats		
1SC	**Corsica Preferred Equipment Group 2**	641	745
UM6	w/UM6 radio, add	120	140
U1C	w/U1C radio, add	341	396
	incls electronic speed control with resume speed, reading lamps, covered LH & RH visor mirrors, luggage area convenience net, tilt wheel adjustable steering column, split folding rear seat with armrest, intermittent windshield wipers, power trunk opener, front and rear color-keyed carpeted mats		
—	**Exterior Color** — paint, solid	NC	NC
—	**Engines**		
LN2	2.2 liter MFI L4	NC	NC
L82	3.1 liter SFI V6	619	720
	req's MX0 trans		
VK3	**Bracket, Front License Plate**	NC	NC
C49	**Defogger, Rear Window** — electric	146	170
R9W	**Defogger, Rear Window, Delete**	NC	NC
K05	**Heater, Engine Block**	17	20
AR9	**Bucket Seats**	NC	NC
—	**Radio Equipment** — see pkgs for specific radio pricing		
UM6	radio - see pkgs		
	electronically tuned AM/FM stereo radio with seek/scan, digital clock & stereo cassette tape, extended-range speakers		

CODE	DESCRIPTION	INVOICE	MSRP
U1C	radio - see pkgs *electronically tuned AM/FM stereo radio with seek/scan, digital clock, compact disc player, Delco Loc II, coaxial front & extended-range speakers*		
QFC	**Tires** — P195/70R14 white stripe	58	68
—	**Transmissions**		
MX1	3-speed automatic	NC	NC
MX0	4-speed automatic *req's L82 engine*	NC	NC
PC4	**Wheels** — 14" styled steel	48	56
A31	**Windows, Power** — w/driver's express down	292	340
FE9	**Federal Emission Requirements**	NC	NC
NG1	**Massachusetts Emission Requirements** — w/L82 engine	NC	NC
	w/LN2 engine	86	100
YF5	**California Emission Requirements** — w/L82 engine	NC	NC
	w/LN2 engine	86	100

CORVETTE *(1995)*

CORVETTE 8 CYL

		INVOICE	MSRP
1YY07	2-Dr Coupe	31451	36785
1YY67	2-Dr Convertible	37334	43665
Destination Charge:		560	560

Standard Equipment

CORVETTE: 5.7 liter SFI V8 engine (includes aluminum heads, composite valve rocker covers, sequential-port fuel injection, aluminum intake manifold, roller valve lifters), power rack and pinion steering, heavy duty 4-wheel anti-lock rear disc brakes, power windows with driver side express-down feature, power door locks, P255/45ZR17 front tires, P285/40ZR17 rear tires, 17" x 8.5" aluminum front wheels, 17" x 9.5" aluminum rear wheels, electronically tuned AM/FM stereo radio with seek-scan, digital clock, stereo cassette tape, power antenna and extended range speakers; manual

CODE	DESCRIPTION	INVOICE	MSRP

control air conditioning, acceleration slip regulation, Pass Key II anti-theft system, uniframe-design body structure with corrosion-resistant coating, brake/transmission shift interlock (with auto trans only), 2.5-mph bumpers, rear window defogger, side window defoggers, passive keyless entry with remote hatch release (Coupe only), clamshell-opening front end for easy engine access, Solar-Ray glass, full-glass rear hatch with two interior remote releases/roller-shade cargo cover (Coupe only), power-operated retractable halogen headlamps, distributorless opti-spark ignition system, outside air induction system, acoustic insulation package, halogen fog lamps, front cornering/underhood courtesy lamps, outside dual electrically heated adjustable rearview mirrors, base coat/clear coat paint, 1-piece removable fiberglass roof panel (Coupe only), full folding roof (Coupe only), de Carbon shock absorbers, independent front/rear suspension with transverse fiberglass leaf springs and forged aluminum A-arms, intermittent wipers, driver and passenger air bags, locking center console includes: coin tray/cassette/CD storage/integral armrest/lighted storage compartment, Scotchgard fabric protector (floor covering), low oil level indicator, electronic liquid-crystal instrumentation with white analog and digital display/switchable English or Metric readouts; day/night rearview mirror with reading, ashtray, and courtesy lights; lighted LH/RH covered visor mirrors, headlamps on reminder, leather seating surface bucket seats with lateral support and back angle adjustment, electronic speed control with resume speed, leather-wrapped tilt-wheel sport steering wheel, integral storage compartment with door armrest.

ZR1 (in addition to or instead of CORVETTE equipment): 5.7 liter DOHC V8 engine, P275/40ZR17 front performance tires, P315/35ZR17 rear performance tires, 17" x 9.5" aluminum front wheels, 17" x 11" aluminum rear wheels, electronic control air conditioning, electronic selective ride and handling suspension package, adjustable power sport bucket seats with leather seating surfaces.

Accessories

CODE	DESCRIPTION	INVOICE	MSRP
1SA	**Corvette Coupe Base Equipment Group**	NC	NC
	incls standard equipment		
1SB	**Corvette Coupe Preferred Equipment Group 1**	1120	1333
U1F	w/U1F radio, add	333	396
	incls electronic air conditioning, Delco/Bose music system (incls electronically tuned AM/FM stereo radio with seek/scan, digital clock and stereo cassette tape), driver's side power seat		
1SC	**Corvette Convertible Base Equipment Group**	NC	NC
	incls standard equipment		
1SD	**Corvette Convertible Preferred Equipment Group 1**	1120	1333
U1F	w/U1F radio, add	333	396
	incls electronic air conditioning, Delco/Bose music system (incls electronically tuned AM/FM stereo radio with seek/scan, digital clock and stereo cassette tape), driver's power seat		
U1F	**Radio** — see pkgs for specific radio pricing		
	incls Delco/Bose music system (incls electronically tuned AM/FM stereo radio with seek/scan, digital clock, stereo cassette tape and compact disc player		
G92	**Axle, Performance Ratio**	42	50
	req's MXO transmission		
FE9	**Federal Emission Requirements**	NC	NC
NG1	**Massachusetts Emission Requirements**	84	100
YF5	**California Emission Requirements**	84	100
LT1	**Engine** — 5.7 liter SFI V8	NC	NC
CC2	**Removable Hard Top**	1676	1995
	incls rear window defogger		

CODE	DESCRIPTION	INVOICE	MSRP
Z07	**Performance Handling Package** *incls FX3 Selective Ride & Handling, Bilstein adjustable ride control system stiffer springs, stabilizer bars and bushings, 17" x 9.5" wheels and P275/40ZR17/N BL tires*	1718	2045
C2L	**Roof Package** — Coupe *incls standard solid panel and transparent panel; req's 24S or 64S*	798	950
—	**Roof Panel**		
24S	transparent, removable, blue tint — Coupe	546	650
64S	transparent, removable, bronze tint — Coupe	546	650
—	**Seats**		
AG1	6-way power, driver side	256	305
AG2	6-way power, passenger side	256	305
AR9	leather seating surface bucket	NC	NC
AQ9	adjustable sport leather seating surface bucket *req's AG1 and AG2 power seats*	525	625
FX3	**Selective Ride & Handling, Electronic** *req's AG1 and AG2 power seats*	1424	1695
AU0	**Keyless Entry** *incls auxiliary remote transmitter*	39	45
ZR1	**Special Performance Package** *incls 5.7 liter SFI DOHC 32-valve V8 engine, P275/40ZR17 front tires and P315/35ZR17 rear tires, 17" x 9.5" front and 17" x 11" rear styled aluminum wheels, electronic air conditioning, selective ride and handling, leather adjustable sport seats, 6-way passenger and driver power seats, low tire pressure warning, Delco/Bose music system with CD and cassette player*	26257	31258
WY5	**Tires** — extended mobility *incls P255/45ZR17 blackwall front, P285/40ZR17 blackwall rear*	59	70
UJ6	**Low Tire Pressure Warning Indicator**	273	325
N84	**Spare Tire Delete**	(84)	(100)
—	**Transmissions**		
MX0	4-speed automatic	NC	NC
MN6	6-speed manual	NC	NC

IMPALA SS SEDAN *(1995)*

IMPALA 8 CYL

		INVOICE	MSRP
1BL19/WX3	4-Dr Sedan	21237	23210
Destination Charge:		585	585

Standard Equipment

IMPALA SS: 5.7 liter SFI V8 engine, 4-speed electronic automatic transmission with overdrive, power rack and pinion steering, 4-wheel disc brakes with ABS, power driver's side window with express-down feature, power door locks, P255/50ZR17 BW tires, 17" aluminum wheels, electronically tuned AM/FM stereo radio with seek-scan, digital clock, stereo cassette tape with auto reverse and coaxial front/extended range rear speakers; air conditioning, 3.08 limited slip differential (rear axle), black key lock cylinder, black tail lamp moldings, black satin finish, black base antenna, body color front and rear fascias, body color wheel opening moldings/door handles/rocker moldings, bodyside and rear decklid emblems, stainless steel exhaust system, extra capacity cooling, full size spare tire, tinted glass, cornering lamps, twin electric remote mirrors, narrow bodyside moldings, base coat/ clear coat paint, rear quarter window molding, rear spoiler, de Carbon shocks, special ride and handling suspension, transmission oil cooler, intermittent windshield wipers, driver and front passenger air bags, brake/transmission shift interlock, luggage area cargo net, rear child security door locks, voltmeter/oil pressure gauges, front door courtesy lamps, color-keyed front/rear carpeted floor mats, LH/RH covered visor mirrors, oil change monitor, trip odometer, power trunk opener, Pass Key theft deterrent system, door map pockets, dual reading lamps (rearview mirror/rear compartment), door trim and floor covering Scotchgard fabric protector, driver side power seat, 45/45 leather seats, full floor console with cup holders, adjustable head restraints, driver and passenger seat recliners, seat back pockets, electronic speed control, tilt wheel adjustable steering column, low oil level warning light, low fluid warning lights.

Accessories

1SJ	**Impala SS Sedan Base Equipment Group**	NC	NC
UL0	w/UL0 radio, add	47	55
UN0	w/UN0 radio, add *incls model with standard equipment*	133	155

CODE	DESCRIPTION	INVOICE	MSRP
1SK	**Impala SS Sedan Preferred Equipment Group 1**	765	890
UL0	w/UL0 radio, add	47	55
UN0	w/UN0 radio, add	133	155
	incls automatic day/night rearview mirror, rear window defogger with heated outside rearview mirrors, power antenna, passenger side power seat with 6-way adjuster, remote keyless entry with trunk release, twilight sentinel headlamp system		
VK3	**Front License Plate Bracket**	NC	NC
C49	**Electric Rear Window Defogger**	176	205
	incls heated OS mirrors		
NG1	**Massachusetts Emission Requirement**	86	100
YF5	**California Emission Requirement**	86	100
FE9	**Federal Emission Requirements**	NC	NC
K05	**Engine Block Heater**	17	20
A23	**Heat Reflective Windshield**	45	52
—	**Radio Equipment — see pkgs for specific radio pricing**		
UL0	radio - see pkgs		
	incls electronically tuned AM/FM stereo radio with seek/scan, automatic tone control, digital clock, cassette tape, theft lock and speed compensated volume, premium front and rear coaxial speakers		
UN0	radio - see pkgs		
	incls electronically tuned AM/FM stereo radio with seek/scan, automatic tone control, compact disc player, digital clock, theft lock and speed compensated volume, premium front and rear coaxial speakers		

LUMINA SEDAN *(1995)*

LUMINA 6 CYL

Code	Description	Invoice	MSRP
1WL69/Z7H	Base 4-Dr Sedan	14263	15760
1WN69/Z7E	LS 4-Dr Sedan	15620	17260
Destination Charge:		525	525

CODE	DESCRIPTION	INVOICE	MSRP

Standard Equipment

LUMINA - BASE SEDAN: 3100 SFI V6 engine, "anti-whistle" radio antenna, power front disc/rear drum brakes, 5-mph impact-absorbing bumpers, stainless steel exhaust system, dual black sport mirrors (LH remote), bodyside molding, power rack and pinion steering, four-wheel independent "soft ride" suspension, Pass-Key II theft deterrent system, P205/70R15 BW tires, 4-speed electronic automatic transmission, 15" x 6.0" steel wheels, side window defoggers, power door locks, child-security rear door locks, Scotchgard fabric protector on all interior fabrics, front and rear color-keyed carpeted floor mats, highly readable analog gauges with trip odometer, rear seat heat ducts, horn pad (operates front anywhere on the steering wheel hub), courtesy lighting with theatre dimming, map lights, lighted driver and passenger visor vanity mirrors, dual air bags and 3-point safety belts, rear seat child comfort guide safety belts, cloth 60/40 split bench seats with storage armrest (includes cup holder), 4-way manual driver's seat adjuster, tilt-wheel adjustable steering column, storage includes extra large glove box/front door map pockets/seat-back storage pockets, variable intermittent windshield wipers, air conditioning with CFC-free refrigerant.

LS SEDAN (in addition to or instead of BASE SEDAN equipment): 4-wheel anti-lock brakes, dual body color sport mirrors (LH remote), power trunk opener, tachometer, illuminated passenger visor vanity mirror, custom cloth 60/40 split bench seats with storage armrest (includes cup holder), AM/FM stereo/cassette tape player, power windows with driver's express-down feature and power window lockout.

Accessories

CODE	DESCRIPTION	INVOICE	MSRP
1SA	**Lumina Sedan Base Equipment Group**	NC	NC
UM6	w/UM6 radio, add	120	135
ULO	w/ULO radio, add *incld with model*	184	207
UNO	w/UNO radio, add	378	425
1SB	**Lumina Sedan Preferred Equipment Group 1**	629	707
UM6	w/UM6 radio, add	120	135
ULO	w/ULO radio, add *incls luggage area cargo retaining net, electric twin remote mirrors, power trunk opener, power windows with driver's express-down and power lockout, electronic speed control with resume speed*	184	207
UNO	w/UNO radio, add	378	425
1SC	**Lumina LS Sedan Base Equipment Group**	NC	NC
ULO	w/ULO radio, add *incld with model*	64	72
UNO	w/UNO radio, add	258	290
1SD	**Lumina LS Sedan Preferred Equipment Group 1**	445	500
ULO	w/ULO radio, add *incls luggage area cargo retaining net, electric twin remote mirrors, power trunk opener, remote keyless entry, electronic speed control with resume speed*	64	72
UNO	w/UNO radio, add	258	290
—	**Interior Trim**		
AM6	cloth 60/40 seat - w/Z7H	NC	NC
	w/Z7E	NC	NC
AR9	custom cloth bucket w/console - w/Z7E	43	48
—	**Exterior Color** — paint, solid	NC	NC

CODE	DESCRIPTION	INVOICE	MSRP
—	**Engines**		
L82	3.1 liter SFI V6	NC	NC
LQ1	3.4 liter SFI DOHC - w/Z7E *req's QVG tires*	886	995
VK3	**Bracket, Front License Plate**	NC	NC
JM4	**Brakes** — 4-wheel anti-lock	512	575
C49	**Defogger, Rear Window** — electric	146	164
D83	**Accent Delete**	(33)	(37)
K05	**Engine Block Heater**	17	19
FE9	**Federal Emission Requirements**	NC	NC
NG1	**Massachusetts Emission Requirements** — w/L82	NC	NC
	w/LQ1	89	100
YF5	**California Emission Requirements** — w/L82	NC	NC
	w/LQ1	89	100
AU0	**Keyless Entry, Remote** — w/Z7H	116	130
WG1	**Seats** — power driver side	231	260
K34	**Speed Control** — electronic w/resume speed - w/1SA, 1SC	193	217
UV8	**Telephone** — cellular provision *N/A w/AR9 bucket seats on Z7E*	38	43
—	**Tires** — all-season steel belted radial ply		
QNX	P225/60R16 touring blackwall *req's NW0 wheels; req's L82 engine on Z7E*	155	175
QVG	P225/60R16 blackwall - w/Z7E *req's LQ1 engine and NW0 wheels*	169	190
MX0	**Transmission** — 4-speed automatic electronic	NC	NC
NW0	**Wheels** — 16" aluminum	267	300
—	**Wheel Covers** — w/Z7H		
PB1	15" bolt-on full chrome wheel cover	89	100
16P	15" bolt-on full white aluminum wheel cover *req's color 16UX white paint*	NC	NC
CJ3	**Air Conditioning Temperature Controls**	89	100
—	**Radio Equipment** — see pkgs for specific radio pricing		
UM6	radio - see pkgs *incls electronically tuned AM/FM stereo radio with seek/scan, digital clock, stereo cassette tape, extended-range front and rear speakers*		
UL0	radio - see pkgs *incls electronically tuned AM/FM stereo radio with seek/scan, automatic tone control, digital clock, cassette tape, theft lock and speed compensated volume, premium front and rear coaxial speakers*		
UN0	radio - see pkgs *incls electronically tuned AM/FM stereo radio, automatic tone control, digital clock, compact disc player, theft lock and speed compensated volume, premium front and rear coaxial speakers*		

MONTE CARLO (1995)

MONTE CARLO 6 CYL

Code	Description	Invoice	MSRP
1WW27/Z7F	LS 2-Dr Coupe	15177	16770
1WX27/Z7G	Z34 2-Dr Coupe	17168	18970
Destination Charge:		525	525

Standard Equipment

MONTE CARLO - LS COUPE: 3100 SFI V6, 4-speed electronic automatic transmission, P205/70R15 BW touring tires, bolt-on wheel covers, dual air bags, anti-lock brakes, 60/40 split bench cloth seats, air conditioning, power front disc/rear drum brakes, courtesy interior lights with theatre dimming, power windows with driver's express-down feature, power window lockout, Scotchgard protection, tilt steering wheel, side window defoggers, power door locks, variable intermittent windshield wipers, Pass-Key II theft deterrent system, front/rear color-keyed floor mats, AM/FM ETR stereo with seek/scan, cassette, extended-range speakers.

Z34 COUPE (in addition to or instead of LS COUPE equipment): 3.4 liter DOHC SFI V6, P225/60R16 BW Goodyear Eagle RS-A performance tires, aluminum wheels, 40/40 cloth bucket seats, remote keyless entry system, power trunk opener, luggage-area cargo net.

Accessories

Code	Description	Invoice	MSRP
1SH	**Monte Carlo LS Coupe Base Equipment Group**	NC	NC
ULO	w/ULO radio, add *incld with model*	64	72
UNO	w/UNO radio, add	258	290
1SF	**Monte Carlo LS Coupe Preferred Equipment Group 1**	525	590
ULO	w/ULO radio, add *incls luggage area cargo retaining net, electric twin remote mirrors, power trunk opener, remote keyless entry, electronic speed control with resume speed*	64	72
UNO	w/UNO radio, add	258	290
1SG	**Monte Carlo Z34 Coupe Base Equipment Group**	NC	NC

CODE	DESCRIPTION	INVOICE	MSRP
ULO	w/ULO radio, add	64	72
	incld with model		
UNO	w/UNO radio, add	258	290
—	**Interior Trim**		
AM6	custom cloth 60/40 seat - w/Z7F	NC	NC
	w/Z7G	(43)	(48)
AR9	custom cloth bucket w/console - w/Z7G	NC	NC
	w/Z7F	43	48
AR9	leather bucket w/console - w/Z7F	601	675
	w/Z7G	558	627
—	**Exterior Color** — paint, solid	NC	NC
—	**Engines**		
L82	3.1 liter SFI V6 - w/Z7F	NC	NC
LQ1	3.4 liter SFI V6 DOHC - w/Z7G	NC	NC
K05	**Engine Block Heater**	17	19
VK3	**Bracket, Front License Plate**	NC	NC
C49	**Defogger, Rear Window** — electric	151	170
FE9	**Federal Emission Requirements**	NC	NC
YF5	**California Emission Requirements** — w/L82	NC	NC
	w/LQ1	89	100
NG1	**Massachusetts Emission Requirements** — w/L82	NC	NC
	w/LQ1	89	100
WG1	**Seats** — power driver side	267	300
K34	**Speed Control** — electronic w/resume speed - w/1SH	193	217
UV8	**Telephone** — cellular provision (N/A w/AR9 bucket seats on Z7G)	38	43
—	**Tires** — all-season steel belted radial ply		
QNX	P225/60R16 touring - w/Z7F	156	175
QVG	P225/60R16 blackwall - w/Z7G	NC	NC
MX0	**Transmission** - 4-speed automatic electronic	NC	NC
CJ3	**Air Conditioning Temperature Controls**	89	100
—	**Wheels**		
PY0	16" aluminum - w/Z7F	267	300
	w/Z7G	NC	NC
16P	16" white aluminum - w/Z7G	NC	NC
	req's color 16UX white paint		
—	**Radio Equipment** — see pkgs for specific radio pricing		
UM6	radio - see pkgs		
	incls electronically tuned AM/FM stereo radio with seek/scan, digital clock, stereo cassette tape, extended-range front and rear speakers		
ULO	radio - see pkgs		
	incls electronically tuned AM/FM stereo radio with seek/scan, automatic tone control, digital clock, cassette tape, theft lock and speed compensated volume, premium front and rear coaxial speakers		
UNO	radio - see pkgs		
	incls electronically tuned AM/FM stereo radio, automatic tone control, digital clock, compact disc player, theft lock and speed compensated volume, premium front and rear coaxial speakers		
UK3	steering wheel radio controls	108	121

CHEVROLET MARKETING VEHICLES

CODE	DESCRIPTION	INVOICE	MSRP

Listed below are the "national marketing" vehicles that Chevrolet will be selling in 1995. These cars are value priced with no-haggle window stickers. Chevrolet's goal is to give customers bottom-line prices up front. These "national marketing" models are each equipped with a designated package of popular accessories and carry a lower manufacturer's suggested retail price than the traditional models from which they are derived.

BERETTA National Marketing Vehicles *(1995)*

CODE	DESCRIPTION	INVOICE	MSRP
1LV37/1SKX	**2-Dr Coupe** — *incls Beretta standard equipment plus intermittent windshield wipers, rear window defogger, floor mats, cargo area net, day/night rearview mirror, reading lamps, dual covered visor vanity mirrors*	11563	12500
1LV37/1SLX	**2-Dr Coupe** — *incls Beretta standard equipment plus 3-speed automatic transmission, rear window defogger, floor mats, cargo area net, intermittent windshield wipers, day/night rearview mirror, reading lamps, dual covered visor vanity mirrors, electronically tuned AM/FM stereo radio (incls seek/scan, digital clock, stereo cassette tape, coaxial front and extended-range rear speakers)*	12118	13100
1LV37/1SMX	**2-Dr Coupe** — *incls Beretta standard equipment plus 3.1 liter V6 engine, 4-speed automatic transmission, tilt steering wheel, rear window defogger, floor mats, cargo area net, intermittent windshield wipers, day/night rearview mirror, reading lamps, dual covered visor vanity mirrors, AM/FM stereo radio (incls seek/scan, digital clock, stereo cassette tape, coaxial front and extended-range rear speakers)*	12580	13600
1LW37/1SNX	**Z26 2-Dr Coupe** — *incls Z26 standard equipment plus 3.1 liter V6 engine, 4-speed automatic transmission, tilt steering wheel, power trunk lid opener, rear window defogger, floor mats, speed control, power windows, 16" aluminum wheels, P205/55R16 BSW tires*	15263	16500
Destination Charge:		495	495

CAPRICE CLASSIC National Marketing Vehicles *(1995)*

CODE	DESCRIPTION	INVOICE	MSRP
1BL19/1SLX	**4-Dr Sedan** — *incls Caprice Classic Sedan standard equipment plus speed control, rear window defogger, power windows, power door locks, power trunk lid release, dual remote control mirrors, full-size spare tire, 55/45 cloth seat, AM/FM stereo radio (incls seek/scan, stereo cassette tape with auto reverse, digital clock, coaxial front and extended-range rear speakers), P215/75R15 whitewall tires*	17681	18910
1BL19/1SMX	**4-Dr Sedan** — *incls Caprice Classic Sedan standard equipment plus speed control, rear window defogger, power windows, power trunk lid release, 55/45 cloth seats, full-size spare tire, power seats, P215/75R15 whitewall tires, aluminum wheels, AM/FM stereo radio (incls seek/scan, digital clock with automatic tone control, cassette tape, theft lock and speed compensated volume, premium front and rear coaxial speakers)*	18429	19710

CODE	DESCRIPTION	INVOICE	MSRP
1BL19/1SNX	**4-Dr Sedan**	19270	20610
	incls Caprice Classic Sedan standard equipment plus speed control, power windows, rear window defogger, power seats, power mirrors, power trunk lid release, 55/45 leather seats, remote keyless entry, custom interior package, cargo area net, twilight sentinel, full-size spare tire, P215/75R15 whitewall tires, aluminum wheels, AM/FM stereo radio (incls seek/scan, digital clock with automatic tone control, cassette tape, theft lock and speed compensated volume, premium front and rear coaxial speakers)		
1BL35/1SPX	**4-Dr Wagon**	20018	21410
	incls Caprice Classic Wagon standard equipment plus power windows, rear window defogger, automatic level suspension, speed control, power mirrors, custom interior package, full-size spare tire, wire wheel covers, power seats, automatic day/night rearview mirror, rear reading lamps, power antenna, AM/FM stereo radio (incls seek/scan, digital clock with automatic tone control, cassette tape, theft lock and speed compensated volume, premium front and rear coaxial speakers)		
Destination Charge:		585	585

CORSICA National Marketing Vehicles *(1995)*

CODE	DESCRIPTION	INVOICE	MSRP
1LD69/1SPX	**4-Dr Sedan**	12210	13200
	incls Corsica standard equipment plus cargo area net, intermittent windshield wipers, floor mats, day/night rearview mirror, reading lamps, rear window defogger, dual covered visor mirrors		
1LD69/1SQX	**4-Dr Sedan**	13135	14200
	incls Corsica standard equipment plus 3.1 liter V6 engine, 4-speed automatic transmission, tilt steering wheel, AM/FM stereo radio (incls seek/scan, digital clock, stereo cassette tape, coaxial front and extended-range rear speakers), cargo area net, intermittent windshield wipers, floor mats, day/night rearview mirrors, reading lamps, rear window defogger, dual covered visor mirrors		
Destination Charge:		495	495

CIRRUS (1995)

CIRRUS 6 CYL

CODE	DESCRIPTION	INVOICE	MSRP
CP41	LX 4-Dr Sedan	15987	17435
Destination Charge:		535	535

Standard Equipment

CIRRUS - LX: 2.5 liter SOHC V6 SMPI engine, variable assist speed-proportional power steering, power front disc/rear drum brakes with anti-lock, 4-speed automatic transmission, power windows, P195/65R15 all-season tires, air conditioning, side window demisters, rear heat ducts, electronic digital clock (incld w/radio), cup holders, electric rear window defroster, power door locks, child safety rear door locks, body color door handles, body color fascias with bright inserts, bright grille, gloss black window opening moldings, dual body color narrow bodyside moldings, front fog lights, driver's left footrest, solar control windshield glass, tinted rear/side windows, aerostyle halogen headlights with adjustable reflectors, inside hood release, color-keyed assist handles, color-keyed front/rear carpeting, rear coat hooks, floor console with coin holder, bright inside door handles, molded door trim panels include: map pockets, padded armrests, woodgrain accents and fabric bolsters; carpeted front rear floor mats, woodgrain instrument panel accents, carpeted shelf panel, carpeted trunk trim, interior lamps include: front courtesy/reading, forward cup holder, glove box, ignition switch with time delay, trunk, underhood, dome with 3-position switch; aero black heated dual power exterior mirrors, manual day/night rearview mirror, dual illuminated visor mirrors, Personal Security Group includes: remote keyless entry, illuminated entry, vehicle "panic" alarm, headlight time delay; electrical power outlet, AM/FM stereo ETR radio with seek/cassette with Dolby/4 speakers, "Athens" cloth and vinyl seat and bolster fabric, driver's bucket seat with lumbar and adjustable "Halo" head restraint/manual height adjuster/recliner; reclining front bucket passenger seat with "Halo" head restraint, rear folding bench seat with carpeted back/trunk and package shelf releases/valet lockout, electronic speed control with steering wheel switches, tilt low-pivot steering column, locking bin type glove compartment, instrument panel cubby bin and CD storage bin, remote trunk lid release with valet lockout, warning chimes for: key-in-ignition, headlights on, seatbelts; four "Hallmark" wheel covers, 2-speed windshield wipers and washers with vehicle speed-sensitive variable delay.

CODE	DESCRIPTION	INVOICE	MSRP
Accessories			
26K	**LXi Pkg** *incls "LX" appliques, leather seating, leather-wrapped shift knob and steering wheel, radio (premium sound AM/FM stereo with cassette, 6 speakers and clock), power antenna, 8-way power driver's seat, security alarm, sport group (incls P195/65HR15 SBR all-season touring BW tires, 15" cast aluminum wheels), sport tuned suspension*	1718	1930
NAE	**California Emissions**	91	102
NBY	**Massachusetts Emissions**	91	102
ADE	**Engine Block & Battery Heater**	27	30
RBS	**Radio** *incls premium sound AM/FM stereo with cassette, 6 speakers and clock*	328	368
RBG	**Radio** — w/o LXi pkg	437	491
	w/LXi pkg *incls premium sound AM/FM stereo with CD player, 6 speakers and clock*	109	122
LSA	**Security Alarm** *incld in LXi pkg*	133	149
TBB	**Tire** — conventional spare	85	95
—	**Paint** — extra cost	86	97
JPV	**Seat** — 8-way power driver side *incld in LXi pkg*	336	377
CFK	**Seat** — integrated child seat	89	100
—	**Seat** — w/LXi pkg *credit when cloth front low back bucket seats replace leather front low back bucket seats*	(257)	(289)

What's New for *Chrysler* in 1995?

Cirrus: Popular new compact from Chrysler takes cab-forward styling to the extreme, with a hood shorter than it is wide. Interior is large, and the Mitsubishi V6 makes decent power. Overall, not a bad value for $19,000, if you can handle the front-end design.

Concorde: Five new exterior colors and a revised hood badge are the only visual changes for the Concorde this year. Inside, a new interior color and an improved CD player sum up the revisions to this hot seller.

LeBaron Convertible: This leftover from Captain Lee's helmsmanship rolls into its final year with minor revisions, among them revised LX badging. Due to be replaced in 1996 by new convertible based on the Cirrus platform.

LHS: More powerful headlights, a power trunk pull-down and two new colors refine the LHS for 1995. The CD player is improved, and the center armrest gets leather trim.

New Yorker: Same changes as LHS, except for leather-trimmed armrest. New Yorker gets four new colors instead of two.

Sebring: Based on Mitsubishi Galant underpinnings, the Sebring is powered by a Neon-based four cylinder or Mitsubishi's 2.5L V6. Expect refined performance and pricing to compete with Monte Carlo and Thunderbird.

CONCORDE (1995)

CONCORDE 6 CYL

Code	Description	Invoice	MSRP
LP41	4-Dr Sedan	18496	20550
	Destination Charge:	535	535

Standard Equipment

CONCORDE: 3.3 liter SMPI V6 engine, 4-speed automatic transmission, power-assisted rack and pinion steering, P205/70R15 A/ST BSW tires, power-assisted 4-wheel disc brakes with ABS, power windows with driver override and one-touch open feature, power door locks, touring suspension, AM/FM ETR stereo cassette radio with 6 speakers, manual air conditioning with non-CFC refrigerant, floor console with cup holders/rear heat/AC ducts, covered storage, power decklid release, child protection rear door locks, stainless steel exhaust system with aluminized coating, two-tone fascias with bright insert, front and rear floor mats, three folding grab handles, bright grille, woodgrain instrument panel accents with unique graphics, interior lamps include: two front reading/courtesy, two rear reading/courtesy, four door with automatic dimming and time out; luggage compartment cargo net, warning lamps for: door ajar/trunk ajar/low washer fluid/traction control (when equipped)/ABS; dual illuminated visor mirrors, heated/foldaway/outside dual power mirrors, full bodyside cladding with bright insert, electric rear window defroster, front bucket seats with manual driver lumbar support and seatback map pockets, rear contoured seat with center armrest, premium cloth seat trim, speed control with cancel feature, tilt steering column, dual sun visors with sliding extension and secondary visor, compact spare tire, four "Prototec" wheel covers, speed-sensitive intermittent windshield wipers and washers with fluidic high-volume washer nozzles.

Accessories

Code	Description	Invoice	MSRP
C	**Quick Order Pkg C** *incls air conditioning with auto temp control, 8-way power driver's seat, remote/ illuminated entry group*	551	630
D	**Quick Order Pkg D** *incls quick order pkg C contents plus interior rearview mirror with automatic day/night feature, Chrysler Infinity spatial imaging cassette sound system, security alarm, speed sensitive variable assist power steering*	1536	1755

CODE	DESCRIPTION	INVOICE	MSRP
EGE	**Engine** — 3.5 liter 24-valve OHC V6	634	725
CFK	**Child Seat** — integrated	88	100
CUN	**Full Overhead Console** — w/pkg C	331	378
	incls compass/temp/trip computer, garage door opener and sunglass storage compartment, interior rearview mirror with automatic day/night feature, illuminated dual visor vanity mirrors		
NAE	**California Emissions**	89	102
NBY	**Massachusetts Emissions**	89	102
NHK	**Engine Block Heater**	18	20
GWA	**Power Moonroof** — w/pkg C	957	1094
	w/pkg D	627	716
	incls mini overhead console		
ARA	**Radio** — w/pkg C	620	708
	incls Chrysler Infinity spatial imaging cassette sound system (incls AM/FM electronically tuned stereo radio with seek/scan, cassette player with fast forward, auto reverse and DNR 5-band graphic equalizer, 120-watt 8-channel amplifier, 11 Infinity speakers, instructional tape, rear mounted power antenna)		
ARB	**Radio** — w/pkg C	767	877
	w/pkg D	148	169
	incls Chrysler Infinity spatial imaging compact disc sound system (incls AM/FM electronically tuned stereo radio with seek/scan, integral compact disc player, 5-band graphic equalizer, 120-watt 8-channel amplifier, 11 Infinity speakers, instructional CD, rear mounted power antenna)		
AJF	**Remote/Illuminated Entry Group**	193	221
	incld in pkg C and D		
JPV	**Seat** — driver side 8-way power	330	377
	incld in pkg C and D		
JPR	**Seats** — w/o pkg C or D	660	754
	w/pkg C or D	330	377
	incls driver and passenger 8-way power seats		
LSA	**Security Alarm** — w/pkg C	130	149
	incld in pkg D		
TBB	**Conventional Spare Tire**	83	95
BNM	**Traction Control** — w/pkg C or D	153	175
AGC	**16" Wheel & Handling Group** — w/Base model or pkg C	550	628
	w/pkg D	459	524
	incls P225/60R16 all-season touring BSW SBR tires, 16" aluminum "spiralcast" design wheels, variable assist speed sensitive steering		
—	**Seats**	935	1069
	incls driver and passenger 8-way power seats (leather faced front buckets, rear bench), leather steering wheel and shift knob; NA w/pkg B or CFK		
—	**Paint** — extra cost		
—	char gold	85	97
—	orchid	85	97
—	metallic red	85	97
—	spruce	85	97
—	bright platinum metallic	175	200

LEBARON GTC CONVERTIBLE *(1995)*

LEBARON GTC CONVERTIBLE 6 CYL

Code	Description	Invoice	MSRP
CH27	GTC 2-Dr Convertible	16367	17469
	Destination Charge:	530	530

Standard Equipment

LE BARON CONVERTIBLE: 3.0 liter SMPI V6 engine, 4-speed automatic transmission, power rack and pinion steering, power front vented disc brakes/rear drum brakes, power windows (door and quarter), P205/60R15 BSW Goodyear Invicta GAL tires, 15" x 6.0" JJ steel disc wheels, AM/FM stereo radio with cassette/digital clock/seek/Dolby and 4 speakers; air conditioning, soft fascia bumpers with 5-mph protection, chimes for seat belt warning/key in ignition/headlights on/turn signal cancel; center console includes transmission selector/ash receiver with light/hand brake/covered storage/ convertible top switch/armrest; power convertible top, electric rear window defroster, stainless steel exhaust system, dual exhaust tips, body color grille/fascias and bodyside moldings with body color inserts; GTC graphics, body color door handles, gloss black decklid and taillight moldings with red/ amber applique, tinted glass (all windows), aero-styled headlights with time delay, lamps include: door courtesy with time out feature/ignition with time delay/trunk/glove box/rear floor courtesy/rearview mirror/reading/courtesy; message center for low washer fluid/decklid ajar/door ajar; low back reclining cloth front bucket seats, fixed bench rear seat, road touring suspension, four accent color "Triad" wheel covers, deluxe windshield wipers and washers with intermittent wipe.

Accessories

Code	Description	Invoice	MSRP
T	**Pkg T** *incls deluxe convenience group, power convenience group, remote decklid release, 6-way power driver seat, front and rear floor mats*	946	1113
W	**Pkg W** *incls pkg T contents plus leather seating, leather-wrapped steering wheel, light group, 15" cast aluminum "cathedral" design wheels*	2068	2433
BR1	**Anti-Lock Brakes**	594	699

CODE	DESCRIPTION	INVOICE	MSRP
AJK	**Deluxe Convenience Group** *incls electronic speed control, tilt steering wheel; incld in pkg T and W*	316	372
AJW	**Power Convenience Group** *incls automatic power door locks, body color power heated outside mirrors; incld in pkg T and W*	287	338
ASW	**Bright "LX" Decor Group** *incls bright grille with bright pentastar medallion, bright nameplate, bright decklid and taillamp moldings, color-keyed bodyside moldings with bright inserts, 15" "conclave" design wheel covers*	51	60
NAE	**California Emissions**	86	102
NBY	**Massachusetts Emissions**	86	102
NHK	**Engine Block Heater**	17	20
ADA	**Light Group** — w/pkg T *incls illuminated entry, remote keyless entry with two transmitters, illuminated visor vanity mirrors; incld in pkg W*	275	324
LET	**Mini Trip Computer** — w/pkg T or W *incls trip computer, trip elapsed time, average fuel economy, instantaneous fuel economy, distance to empty*	79	93
RAY	**Radio** — w/pkg T or W *incls AM/FM stereo radio with cassette, graphic equalizer, clock and 6 Infinity speakers*	445	524
RBC	**Radio** — w/pkg T or W *incls AM/FM stereo radio with CD player, graphic equalizer, clock and 6 Infinity speakers*	590	694
LSA	**Security Alarm** — w/pkg T or W	127	149
WJF	**Wheels** — w/Base model or pkg T *incls 15" cast aluminum "cathedral" design wheels; incld in pkg W*	279	328
—	**Seats** *incls vinyl front buckets, rear bench; NA w/pkg W*	87	102
—	**Seats** — w/pkg T *incls leather front buckets (incls 6-way power driver seat), rear bench; incld w/pkg W*	568	668
—	**Paint** — extra cost		
—	driftwood	82	97
—	orchid	82	97
—	metallic red	82	97

LHS *(1995)*

LHS 6 CYL

CODE	DESCRIPTION	INVOICE	MSRP
CP41	4-Dr Sedan	26646	29595
Destination Charge:		595	595

Standard Equipment

LHS: 3.5 liter SMPI V6 engine, 4-speed automatic transmission, variable-assist power rack and pinion steering, power-assisted 4-wheel disc brakes with ABS, power windows with driver override and one-touch down, power door locks, P225/60R16 A/ST Goodyear Eagle GA tires, four aluminum "Spiralcast" wheels, Chrysler/Infinity Spatial Imaging Cassette Sound System with AM/FM stereo radio, air conditioning with automatic temperature control and non-CFC refrigerant, electronic digital clock, floor console includes: two cup holders/rear heat/AC ducts/covered storage/armrest; mini overhead console includes: compass/thermometer/trip computer/two courtesy/reading lamps; child protection rear door locks, door trim with leather bolsters and map pockets, stainless steel exhaust system with dual chrome outlets and aluminized coating, body color fascias (or two-tone with bright insert), front and rear floor mats, "Projector" style fog lights, solar control glass for windshield/side windows/rear window, three folding grab handles, body color grille, automatic on/off/delay headlights, illuminated entry system, interior lamps include: two front/reading courtesy, two rear reading/courtesy, four door with automatic dimming and time out; remote keyless entry, leather steering wheel and shift knob, luggage compartment cargo net, warning lamps include: door ajar/trunk ajar/low washer fluid/traction control/ABS; dual illuminated visor mirrors, dual power foldaway heated mirrors, automatic day/night rear view mirror, moldings include: bodyside cladding and body color with bright insert, black window opening/belt/windshield moldings, body color rear window molding, body color hood and fender leading edge, power moonroof, power antenna, electric rear window defroster, bucket seats with manual driver lumbar support, contoured rear seat with center armrest, leather seat trim, front seatback map pockets, 8-way power passenger and driver seats with power recliner, premium sound insulation, speed control, tilt steering column, dual sun visors with sliding extension and secondary visor, full trunk dress up, conventional spare tire, low speed traction control, power pull-down trunk lid release, vehicle theft security alarm, speed-sensitive intermittent windshield wipers and washers with high-volume washers, woodgrain accents on instrument panel/doors/center stack.

CODE	DESCRIPTION	INVOICE	MSRP

Accessories

CODE	DESCRIPTION	INVOICE	MSRP
NAE	**California Emissions**	89	102
NBY	**Massachusetts Emissions**	89	102
NHK	**Engine Block Heater**	18	20
GWA	**Power Moonroof**	693	792
ARB	**Radio** *incls Chrysler Infinity spacial imaging compact disc sound (incls AM/FM electronically tuned stereo radio with seek/scan, integral compact disc player, 5-band graphic equalizer, 120-watt 8- channel amplifier, 11 Infinity speakers, clock, instructional CD, rear mounted power antenna)*	148	169
—	**Paint** — extra cost		
—	char-gold	85	97
—	metallic red	85	97
—	spruce	85	97
—	bright platinum metallic	175	200

NEW YORKER *(1995)*

NEW YORKER 6 CYL

CODE	DESCRIPTION	INVOICE	MSRP
CH41	4-Dr Sedan	23067	25596
Destination Charge:		595	595

Standard Equipment

NEW YORKER: 3.5 liter SMPI V6 engine, 4-speed automatic transmission, variable assist power rack and pinion steering, power-assisted 4-wheel disc brakes with ABS, power windows with driver override and one-touch down feature, power door locks, P225/60R16 A/ST Goodyear Eagle GA tires, 16" x 7" JJ stamped disc steel wheels, AM/FM stereo cassette ETR radio with 6 speakers, manual air conditioning with non-CFC refrigerant, electronic digital clock, child protection rear door locks, door map pockets, stainless steel exhaust system (aluminized coating with dual outlets), body color fascias with bright insert, front and rear floor mats, solar control glass on windshield/side windows/

rear window; three folding grab handles, bright grille, rear heater ducts, interior lamps include: two front and two rear courtesy/reading, four door with automatic dimming and time out; luggage compartment cargo net, warning lamps for door ajar/trunk ajar/low washer fluid/ABS; dual illuminated visor mirrors, dual power foldaway heated mirrors, full-length bodyside moldings with bright insert, black window opening/belt/windshield moldings, body color rear window molding, bright hood and fender leading edge molding, electric rear window defroster, 50/50 split bench seats with dual armrests/ dual cup holders and manually adjustable driver lumbar support, front seatback map pockets, contoured rear seat with center armrest, 8-way power driver's seat, premium cloth seat trim, premium sound insulation, speed control, tilt steering column, dual sun visors with sliding extension and secondary visor, compact spare tire, full trunk dress up, power pull-down trunk lid release, four "Simplex" wheel covers, speed-sensitive intermittent windshield wipers and washers with high-volume washers, woodgrain accents on instrument panel and doors.

Accessories

CODE	DESCRIPTION	INVOICE	MSRP
B	**Quick Order Pkg B**	1171	1338
	incls air conditioning with auto temp control, mini overhead console, headlights on with automatic on/off feature, interior rearview mirror with automatic day/night feature, Chrysler Infinity spatial imaging cassette sound system, remote/illuminated entry system, security alarm		
C	**Quick Order Pkg C**	2400	2743
	incls quick order pkg B contents plus leather faced seats, leather-wrapped steering wheel, 8-way power driver and front passenger split bench seats, conventional spare tire, traction control, 16" aluminum "spiralcast" design wheels		
NAE	**California Emissions**	89	102
NBY	**Massachusetts Emissions**	89	102
NHK	**Engine Block Heater**	18	20
GWA	**Power Moonroof**	693	792
ARB	**Radio**	148	169
	incls Chrysler Infinity spatial imaging compact disc sound system (incls AM/FM electronically tuned stereo radio with seek/scan, integral compact disc player, 5-band graphic equalizer, 120-watt 8-channel amplifier, 11 Infinity speakers, clock, instructional CD, rear mounted power antenna)		
JPR	**Seats — driver & passenger 8-way power**	330	377
TBB	**Conventional Spare Tire**	83	95
BNM	**Traction Control**	153	175
WNL	**Wheels — 16" aluminum "spiralcast" design**	287	328
—	**Seat**	941	1075
	incls leather faced 50/50 split bench, rear bench; incls driver and passenger 8-way power seats and leather-wrapped steering wheel		
—	**Paint** — extra cost		
—	char gold	85	97
—	orchid	85	97
—	metallic red	85	97
—	spruce	85	97
—	bright platinum metallic	175	200

SEBRING *(1995)*

SEBRING			
CS22	LX 2-Dr Coupe	14166	15434
CP22	LXi 2-Dr Coupe	17366	19029
Destination Charge:		535	535

Standard Equipment

SEBRING - LX: 2.0 liter SMPI 16-valve 4 cylinder engine, 5-speed manual transaxle, driver and passenger air bags, air conditioning, power front disc/rear drum brakes with anti-lock, 5-mph front and rear bumpers, digital clock, rear window defroster, stainless steel single exhaust system, front fog lights, tinted glass with windshield sunshade, right assist handle, color-keyed carpeting, color-keyed trunk carpeting, cargo net hooks, floor console with armrest, color-keyed door trim panels with vinyl insert, left driver's foot rest, color-keyed headliner, cloth sunvisors with covered mirrors, locking glove compartment, dual manual remote exterior mirrors, radio (AM/FM ETR stereo with 4 speakers), fuel filler door remote release, decklid remote release, cloth low back bucket seats with adjustable head restraints (driver side with memory recliner), 2-passenger rear bench seat with split folding back, tilt steering column, warning chimes, two-speed windshield wipers and washer with variable intermittent feature, P195/70HR14 BSW AST tires, mini spare tire and wheel, full wheel covers (4).

LXi (in addition to or instead of LX equipment): 2.5 liter SMPI 24-valve V6 engine, 4-speed automatic transaxle, power 4-wheel disc brakes with anti-lock, power door locks, stainless steel dual exhaust system with chrome tips, cargo net (2), padded door trim panels with cloth insert, color-keyed carpeted front and rear floor mats, leather-wrapped steering wheel, cloth sun visors with illuminated mirrors, dual power heated exterior mirrors, power windows with driver's one-touch down feature, radio (Infinity audio system with AM/FM ETR stereo, cassette, graphic equalizer, seek/scan, 8 speakers, 150 watt amplifier), remote keyless entry/security alarm systems, leather and vinyl seat fabric, electronic speed control, 16" cast aluminum wheels (4), P205/55HR16 BSW ASP tires.

CODE	DESCRIPTION	INVOICE	MSRP
	Accessories		
21G	**Pkg 21G — LX**	NC	NC
	incls vehicle with standard equipment		
22G	**Pkg 22G — LX**	608	683
	incls pkg 21G contents plus 4-speed automatic transaxle		
21H	**Pkg 21H — LX**	876	984
	incls pkg 21G contents plus power windows, power door locks, power mirrors, electronic speed control, front and rear floor mats, trunk cargo net, illuminated dual visor vanity mirrors, radio (AM/FM stereo with cassette and clock)		
22H	**Pkg 22H — LX**	1484	1667
	incls pkg 21H contents plus 4-speed automatic transaxle		
24H	**Pkg 24H — LX**	2083	2341
	incls pkg 22H contents plus 2.5 liter V6 engine, rear disc brakes, 16" tires, battery and suspension upgrades, wheel covers		
24J	**Pkg 24J — LXi**	NC	NC
	incls vehicle with standard equipment		
24K	**Pkg 24K — LXi**	1127	1266
	incls pkg 24J contents plus power driver's seat, power sunroof and leather seats		
NAE	**California Emissions**	NC	NC
NBY	**Massachusetts Emissions**	NC	NC
JPS	**Power Driver's Seat — 6-way - LX w/H pkgs**	181	203
	LXi w/pkg 24J	181	203
GXR	**Security Alarm — LX**	242	272
	incls remote keyless entry; req's H pkgs		
NHM	**Electronic Speed Control — LX**	181	203
	incl in H pkgs		
AWS	**Smokers Group**	NC	NC
	incls ashtray and lighter		
RAS	**Radio — LX**	155	174
	incls AM/FM stereo with cassette and clock		
RAY	**Radio — LX**	490	550
	incls AM/FM stereo with cassette, equalizer, clock and 8 Infinity speakers		
RBC	**Radio — LX w/H pkgs**	629	707
	LXi	140	157
	incls AM/FM stereo with CD player, equalizer, clock and 8 Infinity speakers		

CODE	DESCRIPTION	INVOICE	MSRP

AVENGER *(1995)*

AVENGER

DH22	Base 2-Dr Coupe	12293	13341
DS22	ES 2-Dr Coupe	15720	17191
Destination Charge:		430	430

Standard Equipment

AVENGER - BASE: 2.0 liter DOHC 16-valve SMPI 4 cylinder engine, 5-speed manual transmission, power assisted rack and pinion steering, P195/70HR14 BSW AST tires, driver and passenger air bags, power front disc/rear drum brakes, 5-mph impact protection bumpers, digital clock (included w/ radio), rear window defroster with 10 minute delay, manual door locks with driver override, stainless steel single outlet exhaust system, black mirrors, black window opening moldings, body color door handles, front and rear body color fascias, body color bodyside moldings, tinted glass with windshield sunshade, right assist handle, gray molded cargo area trim, 12 oz. cut-pile color-keyed floor carpeting, trunk floor carpeting, six cargo net hooks, floor console with armrest (incls cup holders, covered storage, juice box, forward storage, covered power outlet/lighter receptacle), color-keyed padded door trim panels with vinyl insert and map pockets, driver's left footrest, color-keyed headliner, vinyl insert quarter trim panels with leather trim, molded shift knob, polyurethane steering wheel, cloth sun visors with covered mirrors, lamps include: trunk, glove box, ignition key with time delay, dual map/ dome with time delay, front courtesy, rear courtesy (in console); locking glove compartment, dual manual remote exterior mirrors, AM/FM stereo ETR radio with 4 speakers, remote release fuel filler door and decklid, front and rear 3-point safety belts, "Fresno" and "Hudson" cloth seat fabric, low back bucket driver's seat with memory recliner (incls 6-way manual cushion and adjustable head restraint), low back bucket passenger seat with recliner (incls "E-Z" entry and adjustable head restraint), 2-passenger rear bench seat with lockable split folding back and integral headrests, tilt steering column, spare mini tire and wheel, key-in-ignition/headlights on warning chime, four full wheel covers, 2-speed variable intermittent windshield wipers and washers.

ES (in addition to or instead of BASE equipment): 2.5 liter SOHC 24-valve SMPI V6 engine, 4-speed automatic transmission, P205/55HR16 BSW ASP tires, air conditioning with economy mode, power front disc/rear disc anti-lock brakes, dual outlet exhaust system with chrome tips, body color decklid-mounted spoiler, front fog lights, two cargo nets, color-keyed padded door trim panels with cloth insert and map pockets, color-keyed carpeted front and rear floor mats, cloth insert quarter trim panels and assist handles, leather-wrapped steering wheel, AM/FM stereo ETR radio with cassette and 4 speakers, "Field" and "Flint" cloth seat fabric, driver seat lumbar adjustments, electronic speed control, four 16" cast aluminum wheels.

Accessories

CODE	DESCRIPTION	INVOICE	MSRP
A	**Pkg A** — Base	NC	NC
	incls vehicle with standard equipment		
B	**Pkg B** — Base	1082	1216
	incls air conditioning, front and rear floor mats, radio (AM/FM stereo with cassette and clock), speed control		
C	**Pkg C** — Base	1558	1750
	incls pkg B contents plus trunk cargo net, power door locks, dual exterior power remote mirrors, power windows with one-touch down feature		
D	**Pkg D** — ES	NC	NC
	incls vehicle with standard equipment		
E	**Pkg E** — ES	475	534
	incls power door locks, dual exterior power remote mirrors, illuminated dual visor vanity mirrors, power windows with one-touch down feature		
F	**Pkg F** — ES	1957	2199
	incls pkg E contents plus power driver seat, radio (AM/FM stereo with cassette, equalizer, clock and 8 Infinity speakers), security alarm (incls keyless remote entry), power sunroof		
DGB	**Transmission** — 4-speed automatic - Base	608	683
BRF	**Anti-Lock Brakes** — Base	533	599
JPS	**Power Driver Seat** — Base w/pkg C	181	203
	ES w/pkg E	181	203
NAE	**California Emissions**	NC	NC
NBY	**Massachusetts Emissions**	NC	NC
RAS	**Radio** — Base w/pkg A	155	174
	incls AM/FM stereo with cassette and clock		
RAY	**Radio** — Base w/pkg B or C	490	550
	ES w/pkg D or E	490	550
	incls AM/FM stereo with cassette, equalizer, clock and 8 Infinity speakers		
RBC	**Radio** — Base w/pkg B or C	629	707
	ES	140	157
	incls AM/FM stereo with CD player, equalizer, clock and 8 Infinity speakers		
GXR	**Security Alarm** — Base w/pkg C	242	272
	ES w/pkg E	242	272
	incls remote keyless entry		
AWS	**Smokers Group**	NC	NC
	incls ashtray and lighter		
—	**Seat** — ES w/pkg E or F	376	423
	incls leather and vinyl front low back buckets and rear split folding bench; req's power driver's seat		

INTREPID *(1995)*

INTREPID 6 CYL

Code	Description	Invoice	MSRP
DH41	Base 4-Dr Sedan	16227	17974
DP41	ES 4-Dr Sedan	18739	20844
Destination Charge:		535	535

Standard Equipment

INTREPID - BASE: 3.3 liter SMPI V6 engine, 4-speed automatic transmission, power-assisted rack and pinion steering, power-assisted front disc/rear drum brakes, 15" x 6" JJ steel disc wheels, P205/70R15 A/S BSW tires, power windows with driver override and one-touch open feature, all-season tires, touring suspension, AM/FM ETR stereo radio with seek, cassette player and 6 speakers; manual air conditioning with non-CFC refrigerant, electronic digital clock (included with radio), floor console includes cup holders, rear seat heater/AC ducts, covered storage and armrest, child protection rear door locks, stainless steel exhaust system with aluminized coating, body color fascias, tinted side windows, windshield/rear window solar control glass, two front reading/courtesy lamps, two rear courtesy lamps with automatic dimming and time out, dual exterior heated power mirrors, dual covered visor mirrors, functional bodyside protection moldings, electric rear window defroster, cloth front bucket seats, rear bench seat, tilt steering column, compact spare tire, four "Flying V" wheel covers, speed-sensitive intermittent windshield wipers and washers with high-volume fluidic washer nozzles.

ES (in addition to or instead of BASE equipment): Power-assisted 4-wheel disc brakes with anti-lock, 16" x 7" JJ steel polycast wheels, P225/60R16 A/ST BSW tires, speed-proportional power steering, power door locks, touring tires, "Extender" aluminum wheels, unique two-tone or body color fascias, fog lights, front and rear floor mats, four door courtesy lamps, luggage compartment cargo net, message center warning lamps include: door ajar/trunk ajar/low washer fluid/traction control (when equipped)/ABS (when equipped), ground effect bodyside cladding, premium style and fabric front seats with manual lumbar adjustment and upgraded door trim, rear contoured bench seat with center armrest, speed control with cancel feature, power trunk lid release.

CODE	DESCRIPTION	INVOICE	MSRP
Accessories			
B	**Pkg B** — Base *incls model with standard equipment*	NC	NC
C	**Pkg C** — Base *incls power door locks, front and rear floor mats, speed control, power windows with one-touch down feature*	633	723
D	**Pkg D** — Base *incls pkg C contents plus 4-wheel disc brakes, power remote decklid release, 8-way power driver's seat, message center (incls warnings for door ajar, trunk ajar and low washer fluid, 2 traction control lights [if equipped], ABS warning [if equipped]), illuminated dual visor vanity mirrors, passenger assist grab-handles (3)*	1231	1407
K	**Pkg K** — ES *incls model with standard equipment*	NC	NC
L	**Pkg L** — ES *incls 8-way power driver's seat, illuminated dual visor vanity mirrors, passenger assist handles (3), remote/illuminated entry group, leather-wrapped steering wheel*	606	693
M	**Pkg M** — ES *incls 8-way power driver's seat, remote/illuminated entry group, leather-wrapped steering wheel, air conditioning with auto temp control, full overhead console, radio (Chrysler Infinity spatial imaging cassette sound system), security alarm, conventional spare tire, traction control*	1824	2085
HAB	**Air Conditioning w/Auto Temp Control** — ES w/pkg L	133	152
BRT	**Brakes** — 4-wheel disc w/ABS - Base w/pkg B or C	546	624
	Base w/pkg D	524	599
CUN	**Full Overhead Console** — Base w/pkg C or D	259	296
	ES w/pkg L *incls compass/temp/traveler display, interior rearview mirror with automatic day/night feature (DP41 only), front and rear reading lamps, garage door opener and sunglass storage compartment, dual illuminated visor vanity mirrors with secondary visors and sliding extensions, passenger assist handles (3), rear coat hooks*	331	378
CFK	**Child Seat** — integrated	88	100
JPB	**Power Door Locks** — Base w/pkg B	219	250
NAE	**California Emissions**	89	102
NBY	**Massachusetts Emissions**	89	102
CLE	**Floor Mats** — front and rear - Base w/pkg B	40	46
NHK	**Engine Block Heater**	18	20
GWA	**Power Moonroof** — Base w/pkg D	886	1012
	ES w/pkg L	957	1094
	w/pkg M *incls mini overhead console (incls compass/temp/traveler displays, interior rearview mirror with automatic day/night feature [DP41 only], front and rear reading lamps, dual illuminated visor vanity mirrors with secondary visors and sliding extensions, passenger assist handles, rear coat hooks)*	627	716
AJF	**Remote/Illuminated Entry Group** — Base w/pkg D *incls keyless remote entry and decklid release, two transmitters, illuminated entry*	193	221
NHM	**Speed Control** — Base w/pkg B	196	224

CODE	DESCRIPTION	INVOICE	MSRP
TBB	**Conventional Spare Tire**	83	95
AGC	**16" Wheel & Handling Group** — Base w/pkg C or D	354	404
	incls 16" polycast "Polystar" design wheels ("Extender" wheels std on ES), P225/60R16 all-season touring BSW SBR tires, variable assist speed sensitive steering		
JPR	**Seat** — driver and passenger 8-way power - ES w/pkg L or M	330	377
BNM	**Traction Control** — ES w/pkg K or L	153	175
LSA	**Security Alarm** — ES w/pkg L	130	149
AWT	**Performance Handling Group** — ES w/pkg L or M	190	217
	incls P225/60R16 all-season performance BSW SBR tires, performance suspension		
ARA	**Radio** — Base w/pkg D	620	708
	ES w/pkg L	620	708
	incls Chrysler Infinity spatial imaging cassette sound system (incls electronically tuned stereo radio with seek/scan, cassette player with fast forward/rewind and auto reverse, 5-band graphic equalizer, 120-watt 8-channel amplifier, 11 Infinity speakers, clock, instructional tape, rear mounted power antenna)		
ARB	**Radio** — ES w/pkg L	767	877
	ES w/pkg M	148	169
	incls Chrysler Infinity spatial imaging compact disc sound system (incls AM/FM electronically tuned stereo radio with seek/scan, integral compact disc player, 5 band graphic equalizer, 120-watt 8-channel amplifier, 11 Infinity speakers, clock, instructional CD, rear mounted power antenna)		
EGD	**Engine** — 3.3 liter flex fuel MPI V6 - Base w/pkg B or C	131	150
EGE	**Engine** — 3.5 liter 24-valve OHC V6 - Base w/pkg D	634	725
	ES	634	725
—	**Seats** — Base	STD	STD
	incls cloth front buckets, rear bench		
—	**Seats** — Base	NC	NC
	incls cloth front 50/50 bench, rear bench		
—	**Seats** — ES	STD	STD
	incls cloth front buckets, rear bench w/center armrest		
—	**Seats** — ES	883	1009
	incls leather faced front buckets, rear bench w/center armrest (incls driver and passenger 8-way power seats and leather shifter knob); req's pkg L or M		
—	**Paint** — special color or metallic		
	char gold	85	97
	orchid	85	97
	metallic red	85	97
	spruce	85	97
	bright platinum metallic (ES only)	175	200

CODE	DESCRIPTION	INVOICE	MSRP

NEON *(1995)*

NEON 4 CYL

CODE	DESCRIPTION	INVOICE	MSRP
DL42	Base 4-Dr Sedan	8745	9500
DH22	Highline 2-Dr Coupe	10311	11240
DH42	Highline 4-Dr Sedan	10311	11240
DS22	Sport 2-Dr Coupe	12405	13567
DS42	Sport 4-Dr Sedan	12135	13267
Destination Charge:		500	500

Standard Equipment

NEON - BASE: 85 amp alternator, 450 amp maintenance-free battery, 13" power front disc/rear drum brakes, 5-mph front and rear bumpers, child protection rear door locks, warning chimes (for key in ignition, headlights on, seat belts), console, 2.0 liter SOHC 16V SMPI 4 cylinder engine, stainless steel exhaust system, single halogen aero-style headlights, cloth covered headliner, mirrors (left exterior manual remote, black), rearview mirror with day/night feature, passenger side visor vanity mirror, driver and front passenger air bags, seats (cloth with vinyl trim, front high back buckets, rear fixed bench), manual steering, sun visors with driver side sunshade extension panel, ride tuned suspension, P165/80R13 all-season BSW SBR tires, T115/70D14 compact spare tire, 5-speed manual transaxle, carpet floor mat trunk dress-up, 13" steel painted bright silver wheels with black center cap, 2-speed windshield wipers.

HIGHLINE (in addition to or instead of BASE equipment): Front and rear body color fascias, tinted glass, mirrors (dual exterior manual remote, black), dual visor vanity mirrors (driver side covered), body color bodyside moldings, AM/FM stereo radio with clock and 4 speakers, seats (cloth with vinyl trim, front low back buckets, rear 60/40 split folding bench), premium sound insulation, 18:1 ratio power assisted steering, touring tuned suspension, P185/70R13 all-season BSW SBR tires, trunk dress-up (incls molded carpet for wheel houses, spare tire well, carpet covered spare), 13" steel wheels painted black with bright silver wheel covers, 2-speed windshield wipers with variable intermittent feature.

SPORT (in addition to or instead of HIGHLINE equipment): 14" power 4-wheel disc brakes with anti-lock, remote decklid release, rear window defroster, power door locks, 2.0 liter DOHC 16V SMPI

CODE	DESCRIPTION	INVOICE	MSRP

4 cylinder engine (Coupe), front and rear body color fascias with accent color rub strip, fog lights, "power bulge" hood design (Coupe), mirrors (dual exterior power remote, black), accent color bodyside moldings, passenger assist handles, rear decklid spoiler (Coupe), 16:1 ratio power assisted steering (Coupe), tilt steering column, performance tuned suspension (Coupe), P185/65R14 all-season touring BSW SBR tires (Sedan), P185/65R14 all-season performance BSW SBR tires (Coupe), T115/70R14 compact spare tire, 14" cast aluminum painted sparkle silver wheels (painted white with white exterior).

Accessories

CODE	DESCRIPTION	INVOICE	MSRP
—	**Quick Order Pkgs — prices include pkg discounts**		
A	**Pkg A — Base Sedan**	NC	NC
	incls model with standard equipment		
B	**Pkg B — Base Sedan**	1712	1861
	incls air conditioning, rear window defroster, manual remote dual exterior mirrors, bodyside moldings, radio (AM/FM stereo with clock and 4 speakers), power steering, tinted glass, touring tuned suspension, intermittent windshield wipers		
C	**Pkg C — Highline**	NC	NC
	incls model with standard equipment		
D	**Pkg D — Highline Coupe/Sedan**	626	703
	incls air conditioning, floor-mounted console with armrest and storage bin, remote decklid release, rear window defroster		
F	**Pkg F — Highline Coupe**	1184	1330
	Highline Sedan	1220	1371
	incls pkg D contents plus 14" front disc/rear drum brakes, power door locks, front and rear floor mats, light group, power remote dual exterior mirrors, tilt steering wheel, tachometer and low fuel light, P185/65R14 all-season touring BSW SBR tires, 14" wheel covers		
J	**Pkg J — Sport**	NC	NC
	incls model with standard equipment		
K	**Pkg K — Sport Coupe/Sedan**	557	626
	incls air conditioning, front and rear floor mats, light group, radio (AM/FM stereo with cassette, clock and 6 speakers)		
23C	**Pkg 23C "Competition" — Highline Coupe**	911	990
	incls 14" power assisted 4-wheel disc brakes, unlimited speed engine controller, front and rear body color fascias with metallic accent, bodyside moldings, heavy duty radiator, radio delete, 16:1 ratio power steering, competition suspension, tachometer with low fuel light, P185/60HR14 all-season touring BSW SBR tires, 14" bright silver cast aluminum wheels (white when ordered with white exterior)		
23D	**Pkg 23D — Highline Coupe**	1536	1693
	incls pkg 23C "Competition" contents plus air conditioning, floor-mounted console with armrest and storage bin, rear window defroster, remote decklid release		
25A	**Pkg 25A "Competition" — Base Sedan**	1449	1575
	incls 14" power assisted 4-wheel disc brakes, unlimited speed engine controller, front and rear body color fascias with metallic accent, painted body color grille bar, tinted glass, dual exterior manual remote mirrors, heavy duty radiator, 16:1 ratio power steering, competition suspension, tachometer with low fuel light, T115/70R14 compact spare tire, P175/65HR14 all-season performance BSW SBR tires, 14" bright silver cast aluminum wheels (white when ordered with white exterior)		

CODE	DESCRIPTION	INVOICE	MSRP
25B	**Pkg 25B** — Base Sedan	2687	2981
	incls pkg 25A "Competition" contents plus air conditioning, rear window defroster, dual exterior manual remote mirrors, intermittent wipers		
ECB	**Engine** — 2.0 liter SOHC 16V SMPI		
	Base Sedan	STD	STD
	Highline	STD	STD
	Sport Coupe	(89)	(100)
	Sport Sedan	STD	STD
ECC	**Engine** — 2.0 liter DOHC 16V SMPI		
	Sport Coupe	STD	STD
	Highline Coupe w/pkg 23C or 23D	138	150
DD4/DD5	**Transmission** — 5-speed manual	STD	STD
DGA	**Transmission** — 3-speed automatic	496	557
4XA	**Air Conditioning Bypass** — Base w/pkg A or 25A	NC	NC
BRH	**Anti-Lock Brakes** — 13" - Base w/pkg A or B	503	565
	Highline w/pkg C or D	503	565
	NA w/AY7 on Highline models		
BRJ	**Anti-Lock Brakes** — 14" - Highline w/pkg D or F	503	565
	req's AY7		
CFK	**Child Seat** — integrated	89	100
AJP	**Power Convenience Group** — Highline Coupe w/pkg D	228	256
	Highline Sedan w/pkg D	264	297
	incls dual exterior power remote mirrors, power door locks; incld in pkg F		
GFA	**Rear Window Defroster** — req'd in New York State		
	Base Sedan w/pkg A or 25A	154	173
	incld in pkg B or 25B		
	Highline w/pkg C or 23C	154	173
	incld in pkg D, F or 23D		
NAE	**California Emissions**	91	102
NBY	**Massachusetts Emissions**	91	102
CLE	**Floor Mats** — front and rear - Base Sedan, Highline, Sport	41	46
	incld in pkg F and K		
MWG	**Luggage Rack** — roof-mounted	89	100
GTE	**Mirrors** — dual exterior, manual remote — Base Sedan w/pkg A	62	70
	incld in pkg B and 25B		
K37	**Bodyside Moldings** — Base Sedan w/pkg A	27	30
	incld in pkg B		
RAL	**Radio** — AM/FM stereo w/clock and 4 speakers - Base Sedan	297	334
	incld in pkg B		
RAS	**Radio** — AM/FM stereo w/cassette, clock and 6 premium speakers -		
	Base Sedan w/pkg B	223	250
	Highline	223	250
	Sport w/pkg J	223	250
	incld in pkg K		
RBG	**Radio** — AM/FM stereo w/CD player, clock and 6 premium speakers -		
	Base Sedan w/pkg B	434	488

CODE	DESCRIPTION	INVOICE	MSRP
	Highline	434	488
	Sport w/pkg J	434	488
	Sport w/pkg K	212	238
SUA	**Tilt Steering Column** — Base Sedan w/pkg B	132	148
	Highline w/pkg C or D	132	148
	incld in pkg F		
NHM	**Speed Control** — Highline w/pkg D or F	199	224
	Sport w/pkg K	199	224
JHA	**Intermittent Windshield Wipers** — Base Sedan w/pkg A	59	66
	incld in pkg B and 25B		
JFH	**Tachometer & Low Fuel Warning Light** — Highline w/pkg D	83	93
	incld in pkg F		
AY7	**14" Wheel Dress-Up** — Highline w/pkg D	71	80
	incls 14" front disc/rear drum brakes, P185/65R14 all-season touring BSW SBR tires, 14" black wheels, 14" silver wheel covers (white w/quartz center when ordered w/ white exterior); incld in pkg F		
—	**Paint** — extra cost	86	97

SPIRIT *(1995)*

SPIRIT 4 CYL

DH41	4-Dr Sedan	12969	14323
Destination Charge:		505	505

Standard Equipment

SPIRIT: 2.5 liter EFI inline 4 cylinder engine, 3-speed automatic transmission, power rack and pinion steering, power front disc/rear drum brakes, P185/70R14 tires, 14" x 5.5" JJ steel disc wheels, AM/FM stereo ETR radio with digital clock, seek, cassette player, Dolby and 4 speakers; air conditioning, soft fascia bumpers with integral nerf and 5-mph protection, warning chimes for headlights on/seat belt/key in ignition, electric rear window defroster, full stainless steel exhaust system, front and rear floor mats, tinted glass (all windows), locking glove box, body color grille, single halogen aero style

CODE	DESCRIPTION	INVOICE	MSRP

headlights, counter-balanced hood (internal release), electric dual note horn, lamps include: ash receiver/glove box/trunk/dome; dual outside remote control mirrors (black), dual visor mirrors (left with cover), narrow bodyside moldings with bright stripe, "Austin" cloth seat trim, 50/50 split bench front seats with folding armrests (dual recliners), full fixed bench rear seat, electronic speed control, tilt steering column, four "Centrifuge" wheel covers, deluxe windshield wipers and washers with intermittent wipe.

Accessories

CODE	DESCRIPTION	INVOICE	MSRP
E	**Pkg E** *incls power door locks, dual exterior power remote heated mirrors, remote trunk release, power windows*	625	735
ASH	**Gold Special Equipment Decor Group** *incls gold badging and molding inserts, luggage rack, P195/70R14 all-season BSW SBR tires, 14" cast aluminum "teardrop" design wheels with gold accents*	170	200
JPS	**Power Driver Seat** — w/pkg E	260	306
JPB	**Power Door Locks** *incld in pkg E*	213	250
NAE	**California Emissions**	87	102
NBY	**Massachusetts Emissions**	87	102
NHK	**Engine Block Heater**	17	20
TBB	**Conventional Spare Tire**	81	95
—	**Seats** *incls cloth front 50/50 bench, rear fixed*	STD	STD
—	**Paint** — special color or metallic	82	97
EFA	**Engine** — 3.0 liter V6 MPI *incls P195/70R14 BSW tires*	678	798

CODE	DESCRIPTION	INVOICE	MSRP

STEALTH *(1995)*

STEALTH 6 CYL

CODE	DESCRIPTION	INVOICE	MSRP
DL24	Base 2-Dr Hatchback	21062	23236
DS24	R/T 2-Dr Hatchback	24195	26795
DX24	R/T Turbo AWD 2-Dr Hatchback	33971	37905
Destination Charge:		430	430

Standard Equipment

STEALTH - BASE: 3.0 liter SOHC SMPI V6 engine, 5-speed manual transmission, variable power-assisted rack and pinion steering, power-assisted 4-wheel disc brakes, 15" x 6" JJ polycast wheels, P205/65HR15 BSW tires, four "Sofera" polycast wheels, ultimate sound AM/FM stereo cassette radio with 6 speakers, 6 AM/FM presets, seek/scan, auto reverse, 7-band graphic equalizer and CD jack; 5-mph bumpers, center high mounted stop light (LED - mounted in spoiler), electronic digital clock (included with radio), electric rear defroster, stainless steel exhaust system, single tailpipe with dual chrome tip, front and rear base-style body color fascias, base-style black front air dam, charcoal moldings (A-pillar, roof drip, C-pillar [flush]), body color bodyside and sill molding, body color roof, rear body color spoiler, remote fuel door release, two stage opening glove compartment with lock, aero-style projector halogen headlights with automatic off, two assist handles, retractable cargo cover, storage box with cup holder and padded armrest, cloth door trim inserts, molded pillar garnish moldings, lamps include: dome with delay timer, map, door courtesy, cargo area lamp, foot well, glove box, underhood, ignition key and cigar lighter; remote liftgate release, exterior dual folding power mirrors, visor mirrors, front low back bucket seats with recliners, manual driver's lumbar and height adjustment, split back folding rear seats, full cloth front seat trim, cloth and vinyl rear seat trim, tilt steering column, leather-wrapped steering wheel, "horizontal" taillights with large applique, 2-speed intermittent windshield wipers and washers.

RT (in addition to or instead of BASE equipment): 3.0 liter DOHC SMPI V6 engine, 16" x 8" JJ polycast wheels, P225/55VR15 BSW tires, four aluminum "Sport" wheels with center cap, dual tailpipes with chrome tips, bodyside cladding, R/T style body color front and rear fascias, R/T style black front air dam, body color moldings (A-pillar, roof drip, C-pillar [flying]), projector fog lights, floor mats, electronic speed control with steering wheel mounted switches, "top-sided" taillights with small applique, rear wipers and washers.

CODE	DESCRIPTION	INVOICE	MSRP

RT TURBO (in addition to or instead of RT equipment): 3.0 liter DOHC SMPI turbo V6 engine, 6-speed manual transmission with AWD, 17" x 8.5" JJ cast aluminum wheels, P245/45ZR17 BSW tires, power windows with illuminated driver's switches, power door locks with illuminated driver's switches, four aluminum "ultimate" wheels with center cap, manual control air conditioning, gloss black roof, additional electrical accessory outlet, remote keyless entry system (radio-wave type), exterior dual folding power heated mirrors, illuminated visor mirrors, visual and audible security alarm system (door/hatch/hood sensors), anti-lock brakes.

Accessories

CODE	DESCRIPTION	INVOICE	MSRP
A	**Pkg A** — Base *incls model with standard equipment*	NC	NC
C	**Pkg C** — Base *incls power door locks, floor mats, keyless entry, speed control, rear window wiper/washer, power windows*	779	906
G	**Pkg G** — R/T *incls model with standard equipment*	NC	NC
H	**Pkg H** — R/T *incls power door locks, keyless entry, power windows*	457	531
M	**Pkg M** — R/T *incls pkg H contents plus trunk mounted compact disc changer, radio (AM/FM stereo w/cassette, graphic equalizer, clock and 8 Infinity speakers), security group (incls anti-lock brakes and security alarm)*	2059	2394
V	**Pkg V** — R/T Turbo AWD *incls model with standard equipment*	NC	NC
W	**Pkg W** — R/T Turbo AWD *incls radio (AM/FM stereo w/cassette, graphic equalizer, clock and 8 Infinity speakers), trunk mounted compact disc changer, leather-faced seating surfaces with vinyl trim*	1501	1746
Y	**Pkg Y** — R/T Turbo AWD *incls pkg W contents plus sunroof, 18" wheel group (incls 245/40ZR18 BSW SBR tires, 18" chrome cast aluminum wheels, chrome plated lug nuts*	2596	3019
DGB	**Transmission** — 4-speed automatic *NA on R/T Turbo AWD*	759	883
BRG	**Anti-Lock Brakes** — Base	687	799
	R/T w/pkg G or H	687	799
REM	**Compact Disc Changer** — Base	466	542
	R/T w/pkg G or H	466	542
	R/T Turbo AWD w/pkg V or W	466	542
NAE	**California Emissions**	NC	NC
NBY	**Massachusetts Emissions**	NC	NC
GWB	**Sunroof** — Base w/pkg C	310	361
	R/T w/pkg H or M	310	361
	R/T Turbo AWD w/pkg V or W	310	361
AEC	**18" Wheel Group** — R/T Turbo AWD w/pkg V or W *incls 245/40ZR18 BSW SBR tires, 18" chromed cast aluminum wheels, chrome plated lug nuts*	784	912
—	**Seats** — Base *incls cloth/vinyl front buckets, rear split folding bench*	NC	NC

CODE	DESCRIPTION	INVOICE	MSRP
—	**Seats** — R/T	725	843
	R/T Turbo AWD	725	843
	incls leather front buckets, rear split folding bench		
—	**Paint** — special color or metallic	176	205
	NA on Base		

STRATUS *(1995)*

CODE	DESCRIPTION	INVOICE	MSRP
STRATUS 4 CYL			
DH41	Base 4-Dr Sedan	12879	13965
STRATUS 6 CYL			
DP41	ES 4-Dr Sedan	15816	17265
Destination Charge:		535	535

Standard Equipment

STRATUS - BASE: 2.0 liter SOHC 16 valve 4 cylinder engine, 5-speed manual transmission, air conditioning, maintenance free battery, power front disc/rear drum brakes, warning chimes, floor mounted console, remote decklid release, rear window defroster, side window demisters, trunk dress up, black door handles, child-proof rear door locks, stainless steel exhaust system, 16 gallon fuel tank, tinted glass with solar control windshield, lockable glove box, rear heat ducts, dual note horn, remote hood release, front and rear floor mats, dual exterior manual remote mirrors, inside rearview day/night mirror, dual visor vanity mirrors, body color wide bodyside mirrors, power outlet socket, radio (AM/FM stereo w/cassette, 4 speakers, clock), passive driver and front passenger air bags, cloth front low back bucket seats with 2-way headrests, rear full folding bench seat, electronic speed control, tilt steering column, P195/70R14 all-season BSW SBR tires, 14" "Nitro" design wheel covers, deluxe windshield wipers with speed sensitive intermittent feature.

ES (in addition to or instead of BASE equipment): 2.5 liter SOHC 24 valve V6 engine, 4-speed automatic transmission, power front disc/rear drum brakes with 4-wheel anti-lock, body color door handles, power door locks with child-proof rear locks, fog lights, dual exterior heated power remote mirrors, illuminated dual visor vanity mirrors, premium cloth front low back buckets (incls 2-way halo headrests, driver

CODE	DESCRIPTION	INVOICE	MSRP

lumbar support and manual seat height adjusters, front seat map pockets), rear full folding bench seat, speed proportional power steering, sport tuned suspension, P195/65HR15 touring BSW SBR tires, 15" cast aluminum "Extensor" design wheels.

Accessories

CODE	DESCRIPTION	INVOICE	MSRP
A	**Quick Order Pkg A** — Base	NC	NC
	incls vehicle with standard equipment		
B	**Quick Order Pkg B** — Base	609	684
	incls power door locks, heated dual power remote mirrors, driver side seat height adjuster, power windows		
J	**Quick Order Pkg J** — ES	NC	NC
	incls vehicle with standard equipment		
K	**Quick Order Pkg K** — ES	1541	1731
	incls convenient net, leather interior group (incls leather trimmed seats, leather shift knob and steering wheel), radio (premium sound AM/FM stereo w/cassette, 6 speakers and clock), power radio antenna, personal security group (incls keyless/ remote entry, illuminated entry, panic alarm), driver side 8-way power seat, security alarm		
EDZ	**Engine** — 2.4 liter 4 cylinder - Base	388	436
ECB	**Engine** — 2.0 liter SOHC 16V 4 cylinder - ES	(863)	(970)
DGB	**Transmission** — 4-speed automatic - Base	650	730
DD5	**Transmission** — 5-speed manual - ES	(650)	(730)
BRJ	**Anti-Lock Brakes** — Base	503	565
CFK	**Integrated Child Seat**	89	100
	incls fixed rear seatback		
NAE	**California Emissions**	91	102
NBY	**Massachusetts Emissions**	91	102
ADE	**Heater** — engine block and battery	27	30
RBS	**Radio** — Base	328	368
	ES w/pkg J	328	368
	incls premium sound AM/FM stereo w/cassette, 6 speakers and clock		
RBG	**Radio** — Base	437	491
	ES w/pkg J	437	491
	ES w/pkg K	109	122
	incls premium sound AM/FM stereo w/CD player, 6 speakers and clock		
AJF	**Personal Security Group** — Base w/pkg B	150	168
	ES w/pkg J	150	168
	incls keyless remote entry, illuminated entry, panic alarm		
LSA	**Security Alarm** — ES w/pkg J	133	149
TBB	**Conventional Spare Tire**	85	95
—	**Seats** — Base	STD	STD
	ES w/pkg J	STD	STD
	ES w/pkg K	(257)	(289)
	cloth front low back buckets, rear folding bench		

CODE	DESCRIPTION	INVOICE	MSRP
—	**Paint** — extra cost		
—	light iris	86	97
—	orchid	86	97
—	light rosewood	86	97
—	light silverfern	86	97

VIPER *(1995)*

VIPER 10 CYL

CODE	DESCRIPTION	INVOICE	MSRP
DS27	2-Dr 2-Seat Open Sports Car	48725	56000
Destination Charge:		700	700
Gas Guzzler Tax:		2100	2100

Standard Equipment

VIPER: 8.0 liter SMPI V10 engine, 6-speed manual transmission, power-assisted 4-wheel disc brakes, front tires (P275/40 ZR17), rear tires (P335/35 ZR17), power-assisted rack and pinion steering, AM/FM stereo ETR Chrysler/Alpine radio includes: seek and scan/130 watt dual power amplifiers and digital time/frequency/function display/six speakers (compact disc compatible); soft fascia bumpers with high density foam energy 5-mph absorbers, Euro-look short pile carpeting, chimes for door/key/seat belt/headlamps, center horizontal color-keyed console includes: shifter/park brake lever/ash tray/fog lamp switch, 10-year anti-corrosion protection, limited slip differential (clutch-type), fog lights with covers, manual fuel filler door, tinted windshield glass, aero-polyellipsoid headlights (low beam), halogen headlights (high beam), dual latch hood release with single release located in grille opening, dual horn, instrument cluster includes: analog speedometer/tachometer/gauges for oil pressure/voltage/coolant temperature/fuel level/air outlets/glove box, map/reading lamps (in rearview mirror), inside day/night mirror, outside manual mirrors (L/R breakaway), full width roof support, premium sport style high back bucket seats (includes leather seating surfaces with leather-grain vinyl facings/adjustable lumbar supports/continuously adjustable recliner for precise back adjustment), remote control security alarm system, tilt steering column, leather-wrapped steering wheel, snap-in Tonneau cover, removable folding soft top with side curtains, removable rear window.

CODE	DESCRIPTION	INVOICE	MSRP
Accessories			
HAA	**Air Conditioning**	1020	1200
NAE	**California Emissions**	NC	NC
NBY	**Massachusetts Emissions**	NC	NC

What's New for *Dodge* in 1995?

Avenger: Daytona replacement based on Mitsubishi Galant mechanicals and built in the Diamond Star plant in Normal, Illinois. Avenger is a stylistic success, and is powered by a Neon-based four cylinder in base form, a 2.5L Mitsubishi V6 in top-of-the-line ES trim. Expect prices at or below Ford Thunderbird and Chevy Monte Carlo.

Intrepid: Best-selling family sedan gets new headlights, refined transmission, five new colors and a better CD player.

Neon: Excellent sedanlet is joined by a jaunty coupe sporting a 150 hp twin cam engine and stiff suspension. Pricing and equipment levels continue to baffle the competition, and the addition of the coupe is sure to bring buyers by the truckload. The one to get: Neon Highline Coupe with Package 23D, the twin cam motor and premium sound. Good looks, lots of equipment and blistering performance for $14,000.

Spirit: Production of this competent but unexciting sedan ended in December, as Dodge gearedup for the arrival of its replacement, the Stratus. Changes for 1995 include transmission refinements, black-on-yellow underhood identification points, and a big, fat $1,500 rebate.

Stealth: Trim and color revisions and the availablitiy of monster 18 inch chrome wheels shod with 245/40ZR18 Yokohamas are the only changes to this Japanese-built Dodge.

Stratus: Spirit replacement arrived in February, with extremely cab-forward styling and a roomy interior. Prices are in line with Ford Contour, with four and six cylinder engines available. Should be a huge hit with young families, offering some attractively-priced competition for Accord, 626, Camry and others in this crowded segment.

Viper: No changes, but last year, in case you missed it, the Viper became available in Emerald Green and Bright Yellow, and got factory air conditioning.

SUMMIT COUPE/SEDAN *(1995)*

SUMMIT COUPE/SEDAN 4 CYL

CODE	DESCRIPTION	INVOICE	MSRP
XE21	DL 2-Dr Coupe	9387	9836
XL21	ESi 2-Dr Coupe	10320	10859
XL41	LX 4-Dr Sedan	11593	12221
XH41	ESi 4-Dr Sedan	12263	13025
Destination Charge:		550	550

Standard Equipment

SUMMIT 2 DOOR - DL: 1.5 liter SMPI inline 4 cylinder engine, 5-speed manual transmission, manual rack and pinion steering, P145/80R13 A/S BSW tires, power-assisted front disc/rear drum brakes, 4 argent styled steel wheels with bright center cap, 5-mph bumper system, passenger compartment carpeting, instrument panel coin holder, center floor console with armrest and storage, side window demisters, vinyl door/quarter trim, stainless steel exhaust system, gray fascias, black side window opening molding, black outside door handles, driver side foot rest, flush aero-style halogen headlights, single note horn, flood instrument cluster illumination, dome lamps, outside left manual mirror, vinyl seat trim with cloth insert, front reclining high back bucket seats, low back rear bench seat, 4-spoke steering wheel, carpeted trunk floor, 2-speed windshield wipers, driver and passenger air bags.

ESi 2 DOOR (in addition to or instead of DL equipment): 13" x 5" steel disc wheels, P155/80R13 A/S BSW tires, 4 full wheel covers, one assist grip, cigarette lighter, dual sliding instrument panel cup holder, cloth and vinyl door trim with map pockets, body color fascias, body color bodyside moldings, body color outside door handles, rear spoiler, back lighting, remote dual manual outside mirrors, passenger side covered visor mirror, cloth and vinyl seat trim, reclining front bucket seats with adjustable head restraints, passenger side rear seat easy entry.

SUMMIT 4 DOOR - LX: 1.8 liter SMPI inline 4 cylinder engine, 5-speed manual transmission, power front disc/rear drum brakes, P175/70R13 A/S BSW tires, 4 full wheel covers, three assist grips, 5-mph bumper system, passenger compartment carpeting, instrument panel coin holder, center floor console with armrest and storage, dual sliding instrument panel cup holder, side window demisters, child protection door locks, cloth and vinyl door/quarter trim with map pockets, stainless steel exhaust system, body color fascias, black side window opening moldings, black outside door handles, driver side foot rest, rear seat heater ducts, flush aero-style halogen headlights, single note horn, back lighting, dome lamps, non-remote outside dual manual mirrors, cloth and vinyl seat trim, reclining front bucket seats with adjustable head restraints, low back rear bench seat, 4-spoke steering wheel, carpeted trunk floor, 2-speed windshield wipers, driver and passenger airbags.

ESi 4 DOOR (in addition to or instead of LX equipment): 14" x 5" steel disc wheels, P185/65R14 A/S BSW tires, rear armrests, cigarette lighter, body color bodyside moldings, body color outside door handles, rear spoiler, remote fuel filler door release, dual note horn, trunk lamp, remote outside dual manual mirrors, covered driver and passenger side visor mirrors, full cloth seat trim, rear split folding bench seat with center armrest, tilt/height control driver's seat, remote trunk release with override feature, side trunk carpet, fixed-time intermittent windshield wipers.

Accessories

CODE	DESCRIPTION	INVOICE	MSRP
21C	**Pkg 21C** — DL 2-Dr *incls rear window defroster, tinted glass, dual exterior mirrors, radio (AM/FM with clock and 4 speakers)*	371	431
21D	**Pkg 21D** — DL 2-Dr *incls pkg 21C contents plus air conditioning*	1067	1241
21E	**Pkg 21E** — DL 2-Dr *incls pkg 21D contents plus front and rear body color fascias, body color bodyside moldings, power steering, tuned touring suspension, P175/70R13 BSW tires, 13" full wheel covers*	1386	1612
K	**Pkg K** — ESi 2-Dr *incls air conditioning, convenience group #1 (incls black dual exterior power remote mirrors, dual note horn, variable speed intermittent wipers, remote fuel filler door release, remote trunk release, split folding rear seat, tilt steering column, trunk trim dress-up, trunk light), rear window defroster, ESi group (incls front vented disc brakes, dual tip exhaust, tuned touring suspension, tachometer [manual trans only], P185/65R14 tires, 14" cast aluminum wheels), tinted glass, radio (AM/FM with cassette, clock and 4 speakers), power steering*	1692	1968
23C	**Pkg 23C** — LX 4-Dr *incls convenience group #2 (incls black dual exterior manual remote mirrors, cigar lighter, fixed speed intermittent wipers, passenger side visor vanity mirror, remote fuel filler door release, remote trunk release, trunk trim dress-up, trunk light), rear window defroster, front floor mats, tinted glass, black bodyside moldings, radio (AM/FM with clock and 4 speakers)*	79	92
23D	**Pkg 23D** — LX 4-Dr *incls pkg 23C plus air conditioning*	776	902
L	**Pkg L** — ESi 4-Dr *incls air conditioning, convenience group #3 (incls tilt steering column, color-keyed dual exterior power remote mirrors, variable speed intermittent wipers, speed control), rear window defroster, power door locks, front floor mats, tinted glass, radio (AM/FM with cassette, clock and 4 speakers), power windows, 14" cast aluminum wheels*	1756	2042
EJB	**Engine** — 1.5 liter I4 MPI - DL 2-Dr	STD	STD
	ESi 2-Dr	STD	STD

CODE	DESCRIPTION	INVOICE	MSRP
EJA	**Engine** — 1.8 liter I4 MPI - LX 4-Dr	STD	STD
	ESi 4-Dr	STD	STD
	ESi 2-Dr w/pkg K	STD	STD
DDR	**Transmission** — 5-speed manual	STD	STD
DGA	**Transmission** — 3-speed automatic - DL 2-Dr	454	528
DGB	**Transmission** — 4-speed automatic - ESi 2-Dr w/pkg K	562	654
	LX 4-Dr w/pkg 23C or 23D	616	716
	ESi 4-Dr w/pkg L	562	654
GFA	**Rear Window Defroster**	57	66
	req'd in New York State		
NAE	**California Emissions**	NC	NC
NBY	**Massachusetts Emissions**	NC	NC
MJC	**Gray Bodyside Moldings** — DL 2-Dr w/pkg 21C or 21D	46	54
BGF	**Anti-Lock Brakes** — ESi 4-Dr w/pkg L	601	699
RAT	**Radio** — LX 4-Dr	243	283
	incls AM/FM with clock and 4 speakers		
RAW	**Radio** — DL 2-Dr	156	181
	LX 4-Dr	156	181
	incls AM/FM with cassette, clock and 4 speakers		
—	**Paint** — regular production colors or metallic	NC	NC

SUMMIT WAGON *(1995)*

SUMMIT WAGON 4 CYL

CODE	DESCRIPTION	INVOICE	MSRP
XM52	DL Wagon	13005	14056
XH52	LX Wagon	14102	15274
FM52	AWD Wagon	14693	15931
Destination Charge:		430	430

CODE	DESCRIPTION	INVOICE	MSRP

Standard Equipment

SUMMIT - DL WAGON: 1.8 liter SMPI 16-valve inline 4 cylinder engine, 5-speed manual transmission, driver and passenger air bags, power-assisted rack and pinion steering, power-assisted front disc brakes/rear drum brakes, P185/75R14 A/S BSW tires, side and rear quarter vented windows, four argent styled steel wheels with bright center cap, 5-mph bumpers, two instrument panel cup holders, rear window defroster, sliding side door, sliding child protection door locks, full stainless steel exhaust system, body color fascias, black side window opening moldings, gray bodyside moldings, upper black tailgate applique, remote fuel filler door, aero halogen headlights, rear seat heater ducts, remote hood release, single horn, three assist grips, floor console with center armrest, full vinyl front door trim, molded cloth covered headliner, driver's sun visor with ticket holder, inner tailgate assist handle, dome and cargo area lamps, passenger side covered visor mirror, dual manual outside mirrors, low back reclining front bucket seats with adjustable head rests and center armrest, fold and tumble removable rear seat, rear bench seat, full-face fabric seat trim, tilt steering column, flat storage (cargo floor), door map pockets, 2-speed variable intermittent wipers and washers.

LX WAGON (in addition to or instead of DL equipment): 2.4 liter SMPI 16-valve inline 4 cylinder engine, power door locks, four 7-spoke full wheel covers, body color fascias deleted, upper red and black tailgate appliques, lower gray tailgate applique, two-tone paint with accent color fascias, bodyside moldings and lower tailgate applique; tinted glass (all windows), dual horn, front door trim with cloth insert, driver side left foot rest, driver side covered visor mirror, outside dual power mirrors, split back rear bench reclining seat, premium full fabric seat trim (vinyl on back of front seats), passenger seat back pocket storage, left rear side shelf, power lock/unlock tailgate, fixed intermittent rear wiper and washer.

AWD WAGON (in addition to or instead of LX equipment): P205/70R14 A/S BSW tires, power door locks deleted, body color fascias, two-tone paint with accent color fascias, bodyside moldings and lower tailgate applique deleted; tinted glass deleted, single horn, full vinyl front door trim, driver's left foot rest deleted, front and rear mudguards, rear bench seat, full-face fabric seat trim, passenger seat back pocket storage deleted, left rear side shelf deleted, power lock/unlock tailgate deleted.

Accessories

CODE	DESCRIPTION	INVOICE	MSRP
—	**Quick Order Pkgs — prices include pkg discounts**		
C	**Pkg C — DL Wagon**	1129	1313
	incls air conditioning, power door locks, tinted glass, power remote dual exterior mirrors, radio (AM/FM with clock and 4 speakers), power remote tailgate lock, rear stabilizer bar, 9-spoke full wheel covers, rear window wiper/washer		
D	**Pkg D — DL Wagon**	1516	1763
	incls pkg C contents plus floor mats, cassette and speed control		
K	**Pkg K — LX Wagon**	1377	1601
	incls air conditioning, floor mats, radio (AM/FM with cassette, clock and 6 speakers), cargo compartment security cover, speed control, keyless entry, power windows		
W	**Pkg W — AWD Wagon**	1806	2100
	incls custom group (incls power door locks, power tailgate lock, door trim with cloth inserts, two front map pockets and storage on rear left side, driver's footrest, dual horn, full cloth front low back bucket seats with headrests, rear split folding seat), floor mats, tinted glass, keyless entry, cargo compartment security cover, air conditioning, radio (AM/FM with cassette, clock and 6 speakers), speed control, tachometer, power windows		
EJA	**Engine — 1.8 liter I4 MPI 16-valve - DL Wagon**	STD	STD
EY7	**Engine — 2.4 liter I4 MPI 16-valve - LX Wagon**	STD	STD
	AWD Wagon	STD	STD
	DL Wagon	156	181

CODE	DESCRIPTION	INVOICE	MSRP
DDR	**Transmission** — 5-speed manual	STD	STD
DGB	**Transmission** — 4-speed automatic - DL Wagon	641	745
	LX Wagon	641	745
	AWD Wagon	641	745
BGF	**4-Wheel Disc Brakes w/Anti-Lock**	601	699
NAE	**California Emissions**	NC	NC
NBY	**Massachusetts Emissions**	NC	NC
CLA	**Floor Mats**	47	55
	incld in pkg D, K and W		
MWA	**Roof Rack**	130	151
—	**Two-Tone Paint** — AWD Wagon	166	193
RAW	**Radio** — DL Wagon	156	181
	incld in pkg D		

TALON *(1995)*

TALON 4 CYL

XH24	ESi 2-Dr Hatchback	13434	14460
XP24	TSi FWD 2-Dr Hatchback	16263	17570
FS24	TSi AWD 2-Dr Hatchback	18290	19800
Destination Charge:		535	535

Standard Equipment

TALON - ESi: 2.0 liter DOHC 16-valve SMPI 4 cylinder engine, 5-speed manual transmission, power assisted rack and pinion steering, P195/70HR14 A/S BSW tires, 4-wheel disc brakes, AM/FM ETR stereo radio with 4 speakers, driver and passenger air bags, 5-mph impact protection bumpers, console-mounted cigar lighter, digital clock, two-stage door checks, stainless steel single outlet exhaust system, blackout treatment includes: roof, pillars, mirrors, window opening moldings; black door handles, front and rear body color fascias, bodyside body color moldings, black liftgate-mounted spoiler with integral center stop light, tinted glass on all windows with windshield sunshade, windshield pillar right assist handle, color-keyed molded cargo area trim, color-keyed cut-pile floor carpet needle punch cargo area, two coat hooks, floor console with armrest/cup holders, covered storage, color-

CODE	DESCRIPTION	INVOICE	MSRP

keyed molded door trim panels, driver's left foot rest, color-keyed knit headliner, molded shift knob, cloth covered sun visors with covered mirrors, lamps include: ash tray/cargo area/cigar lighter/glove box/ignition key with time delay/dual map/dome with time delay; locking glove compartment, dual manual remote exterior mirrors, remote fuel filler door and liftgate release, "Forest" cloth seat fabric, 6-way manual cushion seats, adjustable head restraint, low back bucket passenger seat with recliner, "walk-in" track and adjustable head restraint, 2-passenger rear bench seat with folding back, tilt steering column, mini spare tire and wheel, warning chime for key in ignition/headlights on/fasten seat belts, four full wheel covers, 2-speed windshield wipers and washers with variable intermittent wipe, single speed rear window wiper with intermittent wipe.

TSi (in addition to or instead of ESi equipment): Turbocharged 2.0 liter DOHC 16-valve SMPI 4 cylinder engine, P205/55VR16 A/SP BSW tires, four cast aluminum wheels (white or silver), AM/FM ETR stereo radio with cassette and 6 speakers, electric rear window defroster, dual outlet exhaust system with chrome tips, body color door handles, body color side air dams, front fog lights, cargo net, padded color-keyed door trim panels with cloth insert and map pockets, color-keyed removable shelf panel, leather-wrapped shift knob (manual transaxle only), leather-wrapped steering wheel, cloth sun visors with illuminated mirrors, footwell lamps with time delay, dual power mirrors, "Pulsar" and "Serein" cloth seat fabric, driver seat lumbar and back wing adjustments, 2-passenger rear bench seat with split folding back.

TSi AWD (in addition to or instead of TSi equipment): P215/55VR16 A/SP BSW tires, power windows with driver's one-touch down feature, central door locks, electronic speed control.

Accessories

CODE	DESCRIPTION	INVOICE	MSRP
B	**Pkg B** — ESi	1361	1601
	incls air conditioning, rear center shelf, rear window defroster, front floor mats, dual power mirrors, radio (AM/FM stereo with cassette, clock and 6 speakers), speed control		
C	**Pkg C** — ESi	1815	2135
	incls Pkg B contents plus cargo net, power door locks, soft door trim with map pockets, power windows		
P	**Pkg P** — TSi FWD	1338	1574
	incls air conditioning, power door locks, front floor mats, speed control, power windows		
S	**Pkg S** — TSi AWD	748	880
	incls air conditioning, front floor mats		
H	**Pkg H** — TSi AWD	2536	2983
	incls Pkg S contents plus radio (AM/FM stereo with cassette, equalizer, clock and 8 speakers), power driver seat, power sunroof, security alarm (incls remote keyless entry)		
ECF	**Engine** — 2.0 liter DOHC 16V I4 - ESi	STD	STD
EBG	**Engine** — 2.0 liter DOHC 16V I4 turbo - TSi FWD, TSi AWD	STD	STD
DD4	**Transmission** — 5-speed manual	STD	STD
DGL	**Transmission** — 4-speed automatic - ESi w/Pkg B or C	627	738
	TSi FWD	751	883
	TSi AWD	724	852
4XA	**Air Conditioning Bypass**	NC	NC
	req'd w/Base models w/o pkgs		
BRF	**Anti-Lock Brakes**	552	649
DSA	**Limited Slip Differential** — TSi AWD	226	266
GFA	**Rear Window Defroster** — ESi	138	162
	req'd in New York State		
JPS	**Power Driver's Seat** — TSi AWD w/Pkg S	282	332
NAE	**California Emissions**	NC	NC

CODE	DESCRIPTION	INVOICE	MSRP
NBY	**Massachusetts Emissions**	NC	NC
RAZ	**Radio** — ESi w/Pkg C	539	634
	TSi FWD w/Pkg P, TSi AWD w/Pkg S or H	539	634
	incls AM/FM stereo with CD player, cassette, clock and 6 speakers		
RAY	**Radio** — TSi FWD w/Pkg P, TSi AWD w/Pkg S	603	709
	incls AM/FM stereo with cassette, equalizer, clock and 8 speakers		
JPS	**Power Driver's Seat** — TSi FWD w/Pkg P	282	332
GXR	**Security Alarm** — ESi w/Pkg C	282	332
	TSi FWD w/Pkg P	282	332
	TSi AWD w/Pkg S	282	332
	incls remote keyless entry		
GWA	**Power Sunroof** — ESi w/Pkg C	621	730
	TSi FWD w/Pkg P	621	730
	TSi AWD w/Pkg S	621	730
—	**Paint** — regular production colors or metallic	NC	NC
ALAH	**Seats** — TSi FWD	388	457
	TSi AWD	388	457
	incls leather and vinyl front lowback buckets, rear split folding bench seat (req's JPS power driver's seat)		

VISION (1995)

VISION 6 CYL

CODE	DESCRIPTION	INVOICE	MSRP
XP41	ESi 4-Dr Sedan	17750	19697
XS41	TSi 4-Dr Sedan	20562	22871
Destination Charge:		535	535

Standard Equipment

VISION - ESi: 3.3 liter SMPI V6 engine, 4-speed automatic transmission, variable-assist power rack and pinion steering, power-assisted 4-wheel disc brakes, 15" x 6" JJ steel disc wheels, P205/70R15 A/ST BSW tires, power windows with driver override and one-touch down feature,

EAGLE

power door locks, touring tires and touring suspension, AM/FM ETR stereo radio with seek, Dolby and 6 speakers; manual control air conditioning with non-CFC refrigerant, electronic digital clock (included with radio), floor console with cup holders, rear seat heat/AC ducts, armrest and covered storage; child protection rear door locks, stainless steel exhaust system with aluminized coating, two-tone fascias, front and rear floor mats, solar control windshield and rear window glass, tinted side windows, three folding grab handles, two front reading/courtesy interior lamps, two rear reading/courtesy lamps with automatic dimming and time out, four door courtesy lamps, message center includes: door ajar/trunk ajar/low washer fluid/two traction control (when equipped)/ABS (when equipped); dual covered visor mirrors, dual foldaway heated power mirrors, functional bodyside protection moldings, full bodyside cladding, electric rear window defroster, front bucket seats with manual lumbar adjustment (premium style/fabric/upgraded door trim), contoured rear bench seat with center armrest, speed control with cancel feature, tilt steering column, compact spare tire, power trunk lid release, four "Six Spoke" wheel covers, speed sensitive intermittent windshield wipers and washers with high volume fluidic washers.

TSi (in addition to or instead of ESi equipment): 3.5 liter SMPI V6 engine, P225/60R16 A/ST BSW tires, touring tires, touring suspension, four "Caisson" aluminum wheels, air conditioning with automatic temperature control, full overhead console with compass, thermometer, trip computer, storage and two courtesy/reading lamps; fog lights, illuminated entry, remote keyless entry, leather steering wheel and shift knob, luggage compartment cargo net, dual illuminated visor mirrors, 8-way power driver's seat, dual sun visors with sliding extensions and secondary visors, anti-lock brakes.

Accessories

CODE	DESCRIPTION	INVOICE	MSRP
B	**Pkg B** — ESi	NC	NC
	incls model with standard equipment		
C	**Pkg C** — ESi	526	601
	incls 8-way power driver's seat, illuminated dual visor vanity mirrors, remote/illuminated entry group		
D	**Pkg D** — ESi	1546	1767
	incls 8-way power driver's seat, remote/illuminated entry group, air conditioning with auto temp control, full overhead console, Chrysler Infinity spatial imaging cassette sound system, interior rearview mirror with auto day/night feature, security alarm		
K	**Pkg K** — TSi	NC	NC
	incls model with standard equipment		
L	**Pkg L** — TSi	986	1127
	incls interior rearview mirror with auto day/night feature, Chrysler Infinity spatial imaging cassette sound system, 8-way power driver and passenger seats, traction control		
M	**Pkg M** — TSi	1621	1853
	incls Pkg L contents plus leather faced front buckets, rear bench, security alarm, conventional spare tire		
BRT	**Brakes** — 4-wheel anti-lock - ESi	524	599
CFK	**Child Seat** — integrated	88	100
JPV	**Driver Seat** — 8-way power - ESi	330	377
	incld in pkg C and D		
NAE	**California Emissions**	89	102
NBY	**Massachusetts Emissions**	89	102
NHK	**Engine Block Heater**	18	20
GWA	**Power Moonroof** — ESi w/pkg C	886	1012
	ESi w/pkg D	627	716
	TSi w/pkg L or M	627	716

CODE	DESCRIPTION	INVOICE	MSRP
AWT	**Performance Handling Group** — TSi w/pkg L or M	190	217
	incls P225/60VR16 all-season performance BSW SBR tires, performance suspension; req's conventional spare tire		
ARA	**Radio** — ESi w/pkg C	620	708
	TSi w/pkg K	620	708
	incls Chrysler Infinity spatial imaging cassette sound system (incls AM/FM electronically tuned stereo radio with seek/scan, cassette player with fast forward, rewind and auto reverse and DNR 5-band graphic equalizer, 120 watt 8 channel amplifier, 11 Infinity speakers, clock, instructional tape, rear mounted power antenna)		
ARB	**Radio** — ESi w/pkg D	148	169
	TSi w/pkg L or M	148	169
	incls Chrysler Infinity spatial imaging compact disc sound system (incls AM/FM electronically tuned stereo with seek/scan, integral compact disc player, 5-band graphic equalizer, 120 watt 8 channel amplifier, 11 Infinity speakers, clock, instructional CD, rear mounted power antenna)		
JPR	**Seat** — TSi w/pkg K	330	377
	incls driver and passenger 8-way power seats; incld in pkg L and M		
LSA	**Security Alarm** — TSi w/pkg L	130	149
	incld in pkg M		
TBB	**Conventional Spare Tire** — ESi	83	95
	TSi w/pkg K or L	83	95
	incld in pkg M		
AGC	**16" Wheel & Handling Group** — ESi	327	374
	incls 16" polycast "Pacifica" wheels, P225/65R16 all-season touring BSW SBR tires, variable speed proportional steering		
—	**Seats** — TSi	543	620
	incls leather faced front buckets, rear bench; NA w/pkg K or CFK		
—	**Paint** — extra cost		
—	char gold	85	97
—	orchid	85	97
—	metallic red	85	97
—	spruce	85	97
—	bright platinum metallic	175	200

What's New for *Eagle* in 1995?

Summit: This Mitsubishi-built subcompact gets a passenger-side airbag, 14 inch wheels, and revised instruments. Aggressively priced, the Summit is unfortunately overshadowed by the best-selling Neon. The wagon, a funky cross between and sedan and minivan, gets a passenger-side airbag, revised hood and grille and new colors.

Talon: All-new sport coupe plays a vital role in keeping the Eagle brand viable. Based on Mitsubishi mechanicals, Talon is much improved over the already good first generation model. Powered by a twin-cam or turbo 2.0L four with front- or all-wheel drive, Talon offers lots of bang for the buck.

Vision: Advertising dollars are expected to boost sales of the slow-selling Vision this year. New for 1995 is a refined transmission, improved CD player, and five new exterior paint colors.

ASPIRE (1995)

ASPIRE 4 CYL

CODE	DESCRIPTION	INVOICE	MSRP
T05	Base 3-Dr	7805	8440
T06	Base 5-Dr	8365	9055
T07	SE 3-Dr	8692	9415
Destination Charge:		310	310

Standard Equipment

ASPIRE: 1.3 liter EFI SOHC I4 engine, 5-speed manual overdrive transaxle, manual rack and pinion steering, power front disc/rear drum brakes, P165/70R13 BSW all-season tires, 13" x 4.5" styled steel wheels with full argent wheel covers, radio prep package with antenna cable and wiring for four speakers, body color front and rear bumpers with integral rub strip and front spoiler, body color grille, aerodynamic halogen headlamps, non-remote foldaway mirrors, color-keyed narrow bodyside protection moldings, monochromatic paint, black windshield wipers/windshield molding/door handles, black greenhouse/door/window frames, driver and right front passenger air bag supplemental restraint system, front/rear ashtrays, front/rear seat manual lap/shoulder belt, color-keyed floor and luggage compartment carpeting, cigarette lighter, dual rear coat hooks, full length console with dual cup holders, color-keyed molded door trim with integral armrests, fuel and water temperature gauges, glove box, inside hood release, courtesy lamps, color-keyed luggage compartment with molded side trim, inside day/night rearview mirror, front highback cloth and vinyl reclining bucket seats with passenger side memory seat back (3-Door), full-fold bench type rear seat, soft-feel shift knob, "B/C" pillar trim, 60 A.H. maintenance-free battery, side window demisters, front wheel drive, 10 gallon fuel tank, single note horn, safety belt warning light, shift column interlock, independent MacPherson strut front suspension, torsion beam "semi-independent" rear suspension, T115/60D13 mini spare tire, tripometer, 2-speed windshield wipers.

SE (in addition to or instead of ASPIRE equipment): Electronic AM/FM stereo/clock radio, fog lamps, dual manual remote mirrors, rear liftgate spoiler, full door trim with sport cloth inserts and map pockets, cargo area light, package tray cover, front highback sport cloth and vinyl reclining bucket seats with passenger side memory seat back, split-fold rear seat, tachometer, 2-speed interval windshield wipers.

CODE	DESCRIPTION	INVOICE	MSRP
	Accessories		
99H	**Engine** — 1.3 liter EFI	STD	STD
445	**Transmission** — 5-speed manual overdrive	STD	STD
440	**Transmission** — 3-speed automatic	516	580
422	**California Emissions System**	62	70
428	**High Altitude Principal Use Emission System**	NC	NC
T17	**Tires** — 165/70R13 BSW	STD	STD
64U	**Wheels** — 13" aluminum - Base 5-Dr, SE	316	355
—	**Seats**		
A	cloth and vinyl high back buckets - Base	STD	STD
B	premium cloth and vinyl high back buckets - Base *incld in Interior Decor & Convenience Group*		
C	sport cloth and vinyl high back buckets - SE	STD	STD
572	**Air Conditioning** — manual *incls tinted glass*	735	825
552	**Anti-Lock Braking System**	503	565
57Q	**Defroster** — rear window	143	160
414	**Interior Decor & Convenience Group** *incls interval wipers, package tray cover/cargo light, manual remote mirrors, premium cloth and vinyl seats, split fold rear seats, front door map pockets, cloth door trim inserts (NA SE model)*	236	265
52H	**Power Steering** *avail and req'd on 5-Dr w/440 auto trans*	223	250
587	**Radio** — std on SE *incls electronic AM/FM stereo/clock*	267	300
589	**Radio** — 3-Dr, 5-Dr	414	465
	SE *incls electronic AM/FM stereo/clock/cassette*	147	165
588	**Radio** — 3-Dr, 5-Dr	468	525
	SE *incls electronic AM/FM stereo/clock/cassette/premium sound*	201	225
582	**Radio** — 3-Dr, 5-Dr	557	625
	SE *incls electronic AM/FM stereo/clock/CD player/premium sound*	290	325

CONTOUR *(1995)*

CONTOUR 4 CYL

Code	Description	Invoice	MSRP
P65	GL 4-Dr Sedan	12036	13310
P66	LX 4-Dr Sedan	12646	13995

CONTOUR 6 CYL

Code	Description	Invoice	MSRP
P67	SE 4-Dr Sedan	14159	15695
	Destination Charge:	510	510

Standard Equipment

CONTOUR - GL: 2.0 liter DOHC Zetec 16-valve I4 engine, 5-speed manual transaxle with overdrive, power rack and pinion steering, power front disc/rear drum brakes, child-proof rear door locks, P185/70RX14S BSW tires, 14" full wheel covers, electronic AM/FM stereo radio, fixed rear quarter panel mounted antenna, body color "B" pillars, front and rear color-coordinated bumpers with bright insert, flush color-keyed door handles and bezels, dripless roof construction doors with water management system, semi-flush glass with solar tint, grey grille with "floating" oval, flush headlamps with replaceable halogen bulb, wraparound side marker lights, dual remote mirrors with black finish, color-keyed bodyside moldings, driver and right front passenger dual front supplemental restraint system air bags, color-keyed manual lap/shoulder safety belts for front and rear outboard seating positions, color-keyed lap belt (rear center seating position), height adjustable front outboard seating position shoulder belt, color-keyed 11 oz. carpeting, electronic digital clock, dual rear coat hooks, floor mounted console with cassette stowage/cup holder/rear ashtray; molded cloth insert door trim panels include armrest/door pull handle/front and rear speakers/front stowage bins; driver's left footrest, lockable illuminated glove box (includes integrated utility hook), grab handles, color-keyed cloth covered molded fiberglass headliner, tilt/height adjustable front headrests, rear passenger compartment heat duct, soft-feel driver oriented instrument panel with side window demisters/knee bolsters/4-positive shut-off registers, backlighted cluster includes: 130-mph speedometer/analog gauges/trip odometer/fuel gauge/high beam warning light/coolant temperature gauge; lights include: low oil pressure/RH-LH direction indicator/hand brake on/catalyst malfunction/seat belt reminder warning lamps; illuminated switches and heater control lights, illuminated rotary master light switch, glove box light, illuminated ashtray/cigarette lighter, front header-mounted interior light with door courtesy switches, courtesy light delay, side wall trim luggage compartment with floor carpet/spare wheel cover, interior cabin pollen filter Micronair filtration system, day/night rearview mirror, driver and passenger visor mirrors, individual bucket seats with full cloth trim/reclining front seat backs/front seat valance panels, soft-feel steering wheel with center horn control, cloth-covered sunvisors, 130 amp alternator, seat belt reminder chime, "driver door open" lights-on chime, remote decklid release, EEC-IV electronic engine controls, sequential multiple port electronic fuel injection, remote fuel filler door release, 14.5 gallon fuel tank with tethered cap, 4-speed blower heater/defroster, dual note horn, tilt steering column, independent MacPherson front suspension with front stabilizer bar, independent quadralink rear suspension, mini spare tire, variable intermittent windshield wipers with fluidic washers.

LX (in addition to or instead of GL equipment): 14" full luxury wheel covers, electronic AM/FM stereo radio with cassette player, fog lamps, heated dual power mirrors with body color finish, color-keyed 16 oz. carpet, full length floor-mounted console with armrest/cassette-CD stowage/pop-up cup holders/ rear ashtray, tachometer, illuminated driver/passenger mirrors, luxury cloth individual bucket seats, LH manual lumbar adjust seat, manual 4-way seat adjust, 60/40 fold-down rear seat with armrest, rear seat back carpet, valance panel stowage.

SE (in addition to or instead of LX equipment): 2.5 liter DOHC Duratec 24-valve V6 engine, power four wheel disc brakes, P205/60R15 BSW tires, 15" cast aluminum wheels, color-keyed spoiler, sport style front seat, LH/RH manual lumbar adjust seat, leather-wrapped steering wheel with center horn control, sport suspension.

Accessories

CODE	DESCRIPTION	INVOICE	MSRP
—	**Preferred Equipment Pkgs — prices include pkg discounts**		
	GL		
235A	**Pkg 235A** — GL *incls group 1 (incls AM/FM stereo radio with cassette, full console), group 2 (incls air conditioning, rear window defroster and dual heated power mirrors)*	757	850
236A	**Pkg 236A** — GL *incls group 1 (incls AM/FM stereo radio with cassette, full-length console), group 2 (incls air conditioning, rear window defroster, dual heated power mirrors), group 3 (incls light group, power door locks)*	1166	1310
240A	**Pkg 240A** — GL *incls 2.5 liter V6 engine, power windows plus group 1 (incls AM/FM stereo radio with cassette, full-length console), group 2 (incls air conditioning, rear window defroster, dual heated power mirrors), group 3 (incls light group, power door locks)*	2252	2530
	LX		
237A	**Pkg 237A** — LX *incls group 2 (incls air conditioning, rear window defroster, power windows), group 3 (incls light group, power door locks)*	1202	1350
238A	**Pkg 238A** — LX *incls 2.5 liter V6 engine plus group 2 (incls air conditioning, rear window defroster, power windows), group 3 (incls light group, power door locks)*	1998	2245
	SE		
239A	**Pkg 239A** — SE *incls group 2 (incls air conditioning, rear window defroster, power windows), group 3 (incls light group, power door locks)*	1202	1350
—	**Groups**		
—	**Group 1** — GL *incls full-length console, AM/FM stereo radio w/cassette*	196	220

FORD

CODE	DESCRIPTION	INVOICE	MSRP
—	**Group 2** — GL	917	1030
	LX, SE	846	950
	incls air conditioning, rear window defroster, power mirrors (GL), power windows (LX, SE)		
—	**Group 3**	307	345
	incls light group, power door locks		
422	**California/Massachusetts Emissions**	85	95
428	**High Altitude Emissions**	NC	NC
—	**Transmissions**		
445	5-spd manual w/overdrive	STD	STD
44T	4-spd automatic w/overdrive	725	815
—	**Engines**		
993	2.0 liter 4 cylinder - GL w/o preferred equipment pkg 240A	STD	STD
	GL w/pkg 240A	(961)	(1080)
	LX w/o pkg 238A	STD	STD
	LX w/pkg 238A	(930)	(1045)
99L	2.5 liter 24-valve V6 - GL, LX	NC	NC
	SE	STD	STD
	req's pkg 240A on GL; req's pkg 238A on LX		
572	**Air Conditioning**	694	780
13B	**Power Moonroof**	530	595
	NA w/pkg 235A		
552	**Anti-Lock Brakes**	503	565
525	**Speed Control**	191	215
57Q	**Rear Window Defroster**	143	160
	incls dual heated mirrors; req'd in New York State		
553	**Traction Control** — incls anti-lock brakes	712	800
12Y	**Floor Mats** — front and rear, carpeted	40	45
43R	**Power Windows** — GL	302	340
	req's pkg 236A, rear window defroster and door locks/light group		
—	**Power Windows Delete**	(302)	(340)
	req's pkg 240A on GL		
143	**Keyless Remote Entry System**	143	160
	req's power windows and door locks/light group; req's pkg 236A or 240A on GL		
902	**Power Door Locks/Light Group** — GL	307	345
	incls power door locks and light group (incls engine, trunk and map lights, illuminated entry system and dual illuminated visor vanity mirrors)		
41H	**Engine Block Heater**	18	20
—	**Seats**		
U	cloth, reclining bucket - GL	NC	NC
Y	cloth, reclining sport bucket - SE	NC	NC
Z	leather, reclining bucket - LX	574	645
	SE	530	595
	incls leather-wrapped steering wheel		
X	luxury cloth, reclining bucket - LX	NC	NC
21A	**Seat Adjuster** — power, driver's side - LX	294	330
	SE	258	290

CODE	DESCRIPTION	INVOICE	MSRP
—	**Audio**		
913	premium AM/FM stereo with cassette	116	130
585	premium AM/FM stereo with compact disc player - GL	240	270
	LX	240	270
	SE	240	270
—	**Tires**		
T72	P185/70R14 BSW - GL, LX	STD	STD
—	P195/65R14 BSW performance - GL, LX	NC	NC
	req's 2.5 liter V6 engine		
T35	P205/60R15 BSW - SE	STD	STD
642	**Aluminum Wheels** — GL, LX	236	265

CROWN VICTORIA *(1995)*

CROWN VICTORIA 8 CYL

P73	Crown Victoria 4-Dr Sedan	18601	20160
P74	LX 4-Dr Sedan	20248	21970
Destination Charge:		580	580

Standard Equipment

CROWN VICTORIA: 4.6 liter overhead cam SEFI V8 engine, electronically controlled automatic transmission with overdrive lockout, speed-sensitive variable assist power steering, power four wheel disc brakes, power windows with express-down driver's feature, P215/70RX15 all-season BSW tires, 15" x 6.5" HSLA wheel rims, deluxe wheel covers, electronic AM/FM stereo radio with door-mounted radio speakers, manual air conditioning with positive shut-off registers, concealed body color bumper with bright insert and one-piece full-wrap cover, low liftover design decklid with full across reflective applique, full solar-tinted glass, bright/center design grille, low profile dual aero headlamps, color-keyed heated/foldaway dual remote control power mirrors, black rocker panel moldings, black windshield/backlight moldings, blacked-out door frame/windows, side window bright surround moldings, color-keyed wide bodyside moldings with bright insert, clearcoat paint, anti-chip paint primer, black-out "B" and "C" pillar moldings, lower bodyside urethane protection, rear quarter windows, driver and front passenger dual supplemental restraint system air bags, rear seat center fold-down armrest, front seat dual fold-down armrest, 16 oz. color-keyed floor carpeting, cigar lighter, electronic digital clock with dimming feature, courtesy lamp switches (all doors), dual ashtray mounted cup holders, defroster grille with integral vertical ribs, front door trim panels with vinyl soft upper applique/armrests/courtesy lamps/lower 12 oz. carpeting/lighted door lock buttons/lighted window controls; easy-access fuse panel, gauge cluster includes: volt/oil pressure/water temperature/fuel; lockable illuminated glove box, molded headliner, two-way headrests, analog instrument cluster gauges, high gloss woodgrain instrument panel applique with side window demisters, dual instrument panel courtesy lamps with theater feature, dome/luggage compartment lights, luxury luggage compartment trim with decklid liner, integral front door map pockets, day/night inside rearview mirror, folding front/rear passenger assist handles, inside door easy-access release handles, inner/outer one-piece front/rear door color-keyed scuff plates, split bench seat with center fold-down cloth trimmed armrests, manual driver/passenger 2-way seat adjusters with 10" seat track travel, color-keyed steering wheel, cloth covered sunvisors with retention clips, tilt steering wheel with mounted stalk controls for washer/wipers, hi/low headlamp beam, turn signal and flash-to-pass; trip odometer, deep-well trunk, 130 amp alternator, radio antenna (hidden in rear window defroster), maintenance-free 58 amp battery, battery saver, body-frame construction, brake/shift interlock, rear door child safety latches, coolant recovery system, theft-resistant decklid latch, rear window defroster, driver footrest, stainless steel exhaust system, front stabilizer bar, coil spring front suspension, tethered fuel filler cap, 20 gallon fuel tank, full solar-tinted glass, automatic headlamps with on/off delay, headlamps on reminder chime, rear floor-mounted heat ducts, gas cylinder hood assists, dual note horn, distributorless ignition system, scissors jack, mini spare tire and wheel, single-stroke parking brake, 6-passenger seating capacity, automatic parking brake release with manual emergency override, plastic head ignition key (primary only), 12-volt power point, rear stabilizer bar, 4-bar link coil spring rear suspension, nitrogen pressurized hydraulic shock absorbers, luxury sound insulation package, low-friction lube-for-life upper ball joints, viscous fan, electronic voltage regulator, duel-jet fluidic windshield washers, interval windshield wipers.

LX (in addition to or instead of CROWN VICTORIA equipment): Deluxe 18 oz. color-keyed carpeting, vinyl soft upper door trim panel applique deleted, seat back map pockets, split bench seats with center fold-down armrests, driver/passenger seat power lumbar, power driver's seat with 6-way seat adjuster, 3-point active safety belts for front/rear outboard occupants.

Accessories

CODE	DESCRIPTION	INVOICE	MSRP
—	**Preferred Equipment Pkgs** — prices include pkg discounts		
111A	**Crown Victoria Pkg 111A** — Crown Victoria *incls color-keyed front and rear carpeted floor mats, group 1 (consists of power lock group, speed control, remote release fuel door, spare tire cover, illuminated entry)*	352	395
113A	**LX Pkg 113A** — LX *incls Crown Victoria Pkg 111A contents plus group 2 (consists of electronic AM/FM stereo radio with cassette, light/decor group, leather-wrapped steering wheel, cast aluminum sport wheels, cornering lamps)*	730	820
114A	**LX Pkg 114A** — LX *incls LX Pkg 113A contents plus group 3 (consists of electronic temperature control air conditioning, anti-lock braking system with electronic traction assist, high level audio system, electronic instrumentation, electronic auto dim mirror, rear air suspension, remote keyless entry, driver/passenger 6-way power seats, driver memory seat)*	3061	3440
—	**Special Value Discount** — Crown Victoria, LX *avail only w/preferred equipment pkgs 111A, 113A or 114A*	(1034)	(1140)
99W	**Engine** — 4.6 liter SEFI V8	STD	STD

FORD

CODE	DESCRIPTION	INVOICE	MSRP
44U	**Transmission** — electronic automatic overdrive	STD	STD
422	**California Emissions System**	85	95
428	**High Altitude Principal Use Emissions System**	NC	NC
T37	**Tires** — P215/70R15 BSW	STD	STD
T3P	**Tires** — P215/70R15 WSW	71	80
643	**Wheel Covers** — radial spoke - Crown Victoria		
	incld w/PEP 111A		
64S	**Wheels** — cast aluminum - LX		
	only avail w/option group 2		
K	**Seat** — cloth split bench - Crown Victoria	STD	STD
M	**Seat** — cloth split bench - LX	STD	STD
C	**Seat** — leather seating surfaces split bench - LX	472	530
	req's 21J power passenger seat		
21J	**Seat** — 6-way power passenger - LX	321	360
46A	**Seat** — driver memory - LX	156	175
21A	**Seat** — 6-way power driver	321	360
68A	**Group 1** — Crown Victoria	587	660
	incls power lock group, speed control, remote release fuel door, spare tire cover, illuminated entry		
68A	**Group 1** — LX	534	600
	incls power lock group, speed control, illuminated entry		
67A	**Group 2** — LX	877	985
	incls electronic AM/FM stereo cassette, light/decor group, leather-wrapped steering wheel, cast aluminum 12-spoke wheels, cornering lamps		
65D	**Group 3** — LX	2462	2765
	incls electronic automatic temperature control air conditioning, ABS/electronic traction assist, high level audio system, electronic instrumentation, electronic auto dim mirror, rear air suspension, remote keyless		
573	**Air Conditioning** — electronic automatic temperature control	156	175
553	**Anti-Lock Braking System/Electronic Traction Assist**	592	665
12H	**Floor Mats** — front color-keyed carpet	23	25
12Q	**Floor Mats** — rear color-keyed carpet	18	20
41G	**Handling & Performance Pkg**		
	w/PEP 114A	365	410
	w/group 2	605	680
	w/group 3	739	830
	w/all other	979	1100
144	**Remote Keyless Entry** — LX	191	215
943	**Light/Decor Group**	201	225
664	**Rear Air Suspension**	240	270
535	**Trailer Towing Pkg** — heavy duty		
	w/PEP 114A	445	500
	w/all other	708	795
58H	**Radio**	165	185
	incls electronic AM/FM stereo cassette		

CODE	DESCRIPTION	INVOICE	MSRP
586	**Radio** — LX w/group 2 or pkg 113A	321	360
	LX w/all other	485	545
	incls high level audio system		
916	**Radio** — LX w/group 2 or pkg 113A	766	860
	LX w/group 3 or pkg 114A	445	500
	incls JBL audio system		
508	**Conventional Spare Tire**		
	w/41G handling & performance pkg	232	260
	w/all other	71	80
—	**Floor Mats** — front carpet (credit w/111A, 113A or 114A)	(23)	(25)
—	**Floor Mats** — rear carpet (credit w/111A, 113A or 114A)	(18)	(20)
41H	**Engine Block Immersion Heater**	23	25
153	**License Plate Bracket**	NC	NC

ESCORT *(1995)*

ESCORT 4 CYL

P10	Escort 3-Dr	8958	9680
P11	LX 3-Dr	9737	10535
P13	LX 4-Dr	10287	11140
P14	LX 5-Dr	10133	10970
P15	LX Wagon	10638	11525
P12	GT 3-Dr	11817	12820
Destination Charge:		390	390

Standard Equipment

ESCORT 3-DOOR/5-DOOR - BASE: 1.9 liter SEFI I4 engine, 5-speed manual overdrive transaxle, manual rack and pinion steering, power front disc/rear drum brakes, P175/70RX13 BSW all-season tires, 13" x 5" semi-styled steel wheels with center cap, radio prep package includes antenna (RH front fender mount)/wiring/speaker grille; dark titanium bumpers, flush windshield and backlight glass, semi-flush side glass, flip-out quarter window (3-Door only), body color grille with Ford oval, aerodynamic single rectangular halogen headlamps, driver's side breakaway black remote control mirror, black-out door frame moldings, narrow black beltline moldings, driver/passenger side air bag SRS, motorized front shoulder belt systems with manual lap belts, manual lap/shoulder outside rear safety belts with center lap belt, removable hard-type cargo area cover, passenger compartment carpeting, cigarette lighter, center console with forward bin and cup holders, vinyl door trim with armrest and integral map pocket/speaker grille, non-locking glove box, illuminated ignition key bezel, two-tone wraparound soft instrument panel with knee bolsters, non-illuminated passenger visor mirror, low back cloth and vinyl reclining bucket seats, full-fold bench type rear seat with dual release handles, 4-spoke soft black steering wheel, heavy duty alternator, 58 amp/hour maintenance-free battery, self-adjusting linkage clutch, side window demisters, EEC-IV electronic engine controls, electronic ignition, engine malfunction indicator light, engine low coolant warning light, front wheel drive, 11.9 gallon fuel tank, tinted glass, rear seat heat ducts, 4-speed blower heater/defroster/flow-through ventilation, inside hood release, single note horn, front/rear stabilizer bar, 4-wheel independent suspension, temperature gauge, mini-spare tire, trip odometer, electronic voltage regulator, 2-speed windshield wipers, with variable interval feature.

LX 3-DOOR/5-DOOR (in addition to or instead of BASE ESCORT equipment): P175/65RX14 BSW all-season tires, 14" x 5" semi-styled steel wheels with full luxury wheel covers, electronic AM/FM stereo with digital clock (radio credit option available), unique body color bumpers, body color door handles, narrow black beltline (3-Door only), wide black beltline (5-Door only), body color bodyside protection moldings, rear reflex applique, cloth door trim with unique armrest, integral map pocket/ speaker grille and lower carpeting; upgraded low back cloth reclining bucket seats with vinyl seat backs and luxury trim, 60/40 split fold rear seat with dual release handles, child safety rear door locks (5-Door).

GT 3-DOOR (in addition to or instead of LX 3-DOOR equipment): 1.8 liter DOHC 16 valve EFI I4 engine, power rack and pinion steering, power front disc/rear disc brakes, P185/60RX15 84H BSW performance all-season tires, 15" x 5.5" styled aluminum wheels, electronic AM/FM stereo radio with cassette and digital clock (radio credit option available), body color asymmetrical grille with Ford oval, fog lamps/unique front fascia, black dual electronic remote control breakaway mirrors, narrow black beltline, rocker panel cladding, rear spoiler, deluxe passenger compartment carpeting, center console with bin and removable tray with cup holders, light group includes: dual map lights/cargo area light/engine compartment light/headlamps on warning chime/RH-LH non-illuminated visor mirrors; sport performance cloth reclining bucket seats with unique trim, integral rear seat head restraints, electronic engine controls, 13.2 gallon fuel tank, dual note horn, sport handling suspension, tachometer.

ESCORT - LX 4-DOOR: 1.9 liter SEFI I4 engine, 5-speed manual overdrive transaxle, manual rack and pinion steering, power front disc/rear drum brakes, P175/65RX14 BSW all-season tires, 14" x 5" semi-styled steel wheels with full luxury wheel covers, electronic AM/FM stereo radio with digital clock (radio credit option available), unique body color bumpers, body color door handles, flush windshield and backlight glass, semi-flush side glass, body color grille with Ford oval, aerodynamic single rectangular halogen headlamps, black remote control driver's side breakaway mirror, black-out door frame moldings, wide black beltline molding, body color bodyside protection moldings, rear reflex applique, driver/passenger side air bag SRS, motorized front shoulder safety belt system with manual lap belts, manual lap/shoulder outside rear safety belts with center lap belt, removable hard type cargo area cover, passenger compartment carpeting, cigarette lighter, center console with forward bin and cup holders, cloth door trim with unique armrest/integral map pocket/speaker grille and lower carpeting; non-locking glove box, rear seat grab handles, illuminated ignition key bezel, two-tone wrap-around instrument panel with knee bolsters, non-illuminated driver/passenger visor mirrors, upgraded low back cloth reclining bucket seats with vinyl seat back and luxury trim, 60/40 split/fold rear seat with dual release handles, integral rear seat head restraints, 4-spoke soft black steering wheel, heavy duty alternator, 58 amp/hour maintenance-free battery, self-adjusting linkage clutch, side window demisters, EEC-IV electronic engine controls, electronic ignition, engine malfunction indicator light, engine low coolant warning light, front wheel drive, 11.9 gallon fuel tank, tinted glass, rear seat heat ducts, 4-speed blower heater/defroster/flow-through ventilation, inside hood release, single note horn, child safety rear door locks, front and rear stabilizer bars, 4-wheel independent

CODE	DESCRIPTION	INVOICE	MSRP

suspension, temperature gauge, mini spare tire, trip odometer, electronic voltage regulator, 2-speed windshield wipers with variable interval feature.

ESCORT - LX WAGON: 1.9 liter SEFI I4 engine, 5-speed manual overdrive transaxle, manual rack and pinion steering, power front disc/rear drum brakes, P175/65RX14 BSW all-season tires, 14" x 5" semi-styled steel wheels with full luxury wheel covers, electronic AM/FM stereo radio with digital clock (radio credit option available), unique body color bumpers, body color door handles, flush windshield and backlight glass, semi-flush side glass, body color grille with Ford oval, aerodynamic single rectangular halogen headlamps, black remote control driver's side breakaway mirror, black-out door frame moldings, wide black beltline moldings, driver/passenger side air bag SRS, motorized front shoulder safety belt system with manual lap belts, manual lap/shoulder outside rear safety belts with center lap belt, color-keyed cargo area cover (window shade type), cigarette lighter, center console with forward bin and cup holders, cloth door trim with unique armrest, integral map pocket/speaker grille, and lower carpeting; non-locking glove box, rear seat grab handles, illuminated ignition key bezel, two-tone wrap-around soft instrument panel with knee bolsters, non-illuminated passenger visor mirrors, upgraded low back cloth reclining bucket seats with luxury trim and vinyl seat backs, 60/40 split/fold rear seat with dual release handles, 4-spoke soft black steering wheel, heavy duty alternator, 58 amp/hour maintenance-free battery, self-adjusting linkage clutch, side window demisters, EEC-IV electronic engine controls, electronic ignition, engine malfunction indicator light, engine low coolant warning light, front wheel drive, 11.9 gallon fuel tank, tinted glass, rear seat heat ducts, 4-speed blower heater/defroster/flow-through ventilation, inside hood release, single note horn, child safety rear door locks, front/rear stabilizer bars, four wheel independent suspension, temperature gauge, mini spare tire, trip odometer, electronic voltage regulator, 2-speed windshield wipers with variable interval feature, body color bodyside protection moldings.

Accessories

CODE	DESCRIPTION	INVOICE	MSRP
—	**Preferred Equipment Pkgs** — prices include pkg discounts		
320M	**LX Pkg 320M** — LX 3-Dr	170	190
	LX 4-Dr, LX 5-Dr, LX Wagon	170	190
	incls rear window defroster, light and convenience group (consists of light group/removable cup holder tray, dual electric remote control mirrors), sport appearance group, power steering		
321M	**LX Pkg 321M "One-Price 5-Speed"** — LX 3-Dr	1055	1185
	LX 4-Dr	517	580
	LX 5-Dr	669	750
	LX Wagon	174	195
	incls rear window defroster, light and convenience group, sport appearance group (LX 3-Dr only), power steering, manual air conditioning (req's power steering), 5-speed manual transmission		
322M	**LX Pkg 322M "One-Price Automatic"** — LX 3-Dr	1781	2000
	LX 4-Dr	1242	1395
	LX 5-Dr	1394	1565
	LX Wagon	899	1010
	incls rear window defroster, light and convenience group, sport appearance group (LX 3-Dr only), power steering, manual air conditioning (req's power steering), automatic transaxle, wagon group (wagon only)		
330A	**GT Pkg 330A** — GT 3-Dr	387	435
	incls rear window defroster, manual air conditioning		
99J	**Engine** — 1.9 liter SEFI - Escort, LX	STD	STD
998	**Engine** — 1.8 liter DOHC - GT	STD	STD
445	**Transmission** — 5-speed manual	STD	STD

CODE	DESCRIPTION	INVOICE	MSRP
44T	**Transmission** — 4-speed overdrive automatic	725	815
422	**California Emissions System**	62	70
428	**High Altitude Principal Use Emissions System**	NC	NC
—	**Tires**		
T15	P175/70R13 BSW - Escort	STD	STD
T75	P175/65R14 BSW - LX	STD	STD
T39	P185/60R15 BSW performance - GT	STD	STD
—	**Seats**		
Z	cloth and vinyl low back buckets - Escort Base	STD	STD
1	upgraded cloth and vinyl low back buckets - Escort LX	STD	STD
X	cloth sport performance buckets - Escort GT	STD	STD
216	child seat, integrated	120	135
572	**Air conditioning** — manual - LX, GT	699	785
552	**Anti-Lock Braking System** — GT	503	565
590	**Comfort Group** — Escort	766	860
	incls air conditioning and power steering		
57Q	**Defroster** — rear window	143	160
41H	**Engine Block Immersion Heater**	18	20
153	**License Plate Bracket** — front	NC	NC
415	**Ultra Violet Decor Group** — GT	356	400
	incls ultra violet clearcoat paint, color-keyed wheels, opal grey cloth sport performance buckets, front floor mats with GT embroidered in violet, leather wrapped steering wheel		
60A	**Light & Convenience Group** — LX	143	160
943	**Light Group/Removable Cup Holder Tray** — std on GT	58	65
54J	**Dual Electric Remote Control Mirrors** — std on GT	85	95
50A	**Luxury Convenience Group** — LX 4-Dr/5-Dr/3-Dr LX w/o 434	414	465
	LX Wagon/LX 3-Dr w/434	365	410
	GT	410	460
	incls tilt steering column, speed control, tachometer (std on GT), remote decklid release (NA on Wagon), leather-wrapped steering wheel (GT only)		
53A	**Power Equipment Group** — LX 3-Dr w/luxury convenience group, GT	410	460
	LX 3-Dr w/o luxury convenience group	458	515
	LX 4-Dr, 5-Dr/Wagon w/luxury convenience group	463	520
	LX 5-Dr/Wagon w/o luxury convenience group	512	575
	incls power locks/windows, tachometer (std on GT)		
13B	**Moonroof, Power** — LX, GT	468	525
434	**Sport Appearance Group** — 3-Dr LX	641	720
	incls aluminum wheels, liftgate spoiler, rear appliques, tachometer		
—	**Clearcoat Paint** — NC w/One-Price PEPS or 434	76	85
51W	**Wagon Group**	213	240
	incls deluxe luggage rack, rear window wiper-washer		
52H	**Power Steering** — LX	223	250
587	**Radio** — Escort	267	300
	incls electronic AM/FM stereo/clock		
589	**Radio** — Escort	414	465
	LX	147	165
	incls electronic AM/FM stereo/clock/cassette		

CODE	DESCRIPTION	INVOICE	MSRP
585	**Radio** — Escort	557	625
	LX	290	325
	GT	143	160
	incls electronic AM/FM stereo/clock/CD player		
913	**Premium Sound System**	54	60
58Y	**Radio Credit Option** — LX	(267)	(300)
	GT	(414)	(465)

MUSTANG (1995)

CODE	DESCRIPTION	INVOICE	MSRP
MUSTANG 6 CYL			
P40	Base 2-Dr Coupe	13162	14530
P44	Base 2-Dr Convertible	18916	20995
MUSTANG 8 CYL			
P42	GTS 2-Dr Coupe	15280	16910
P42	GT 2-Dr Coupe	16343	18105
P45	GT 2-Dr Convertible	20518	22795
P42	Cobra 2-Dr Coupe	19187	21300
P45	Cobra 2-Dr Convertible	23018	25605
Destination Charge:		500	500

Standard Equipment

MUSTANG - BASE: 3.8 liter V6 EFI engine, 5-speed manual transmission with overdrive, power 4-wheel disc brakes, power steering, power windows (Convertible), dual air bag restraint system, tinted glass, tilt steering wheel, dual horns, heavy duty 130-amp alternator, heavy duty 58-amp battery, tachometer, front stabilizer bar, digital clock, intermittent windshield wipers, trip odometer, carpeting, power door locks (Convertible), rocker panel moldings, center console, P205/65R15 all-season BW SBR tires, wheel covers, power trunk release (Convertible), headlights-on warning chimes, power top (Convertible), cloth reclining front bucket seats, split folding rear seat (Coupe), dual power OS mirrors, dual visor vanity mirrors (illuminated on Convertible), AM/FM ETR stereo radio with 4 speakers, 15.4 gallon fuel tank.

CODE	DESCRIPTION	INVOICE	MSRP

GTS (in addition to or instead of BASE equipment): 5.0 liter high output V8 EFI engine, traction-lok axle, dual exhaust, cast aluminum wheels with locking lug nuts, P225/55ZR16 all-season BW SBR tires, color-keyed front and rear fascias, special GT suspension.

GT (in addition to or instead of GTS equipment): Power windows, power door locks, rear spoiler, power trunk release, fog lights, leather-wrapped steering wheel, cloth reclining GT sport bucket seats, dual illuminated visor vanity mirrors.

COBRA (in addition to or instead of GT equipment): 5.0 liter SHP V8 SEFI engine, Cobra suspension, limited slip axle, anti-lock power 4-wheel disc brakes, AM/FM ETR stereo radio with cassette/ 4 speakers/80-watt amplifier, front bucket seats with power lumbar supports, power driver's seat, leather seats (Convertible), P255/45ZR17 performance BW SBR tires, 5-spoke polished aluminum wheels, dual visor vanity mirrors.

Accessories

CODE	DESCRIPTION	INVOICE	MSRP
—	**Preferred Equipment Pkgs — prices include pkg discounts**		
241A	**Base Coupe Pkg 241A** — Base Coupe	570	640
	incls air conditioning, AM/FM ETR stereo radio with cassette		
243A	**Base Coupe Pkg 243A** — Base Coupe	1807	2030
	incls air conditioning, power driver's seat, group 1 (incls power side windows, power door locks, power trunk release), group 2 (incls dual illuminated visor vanity mirrors, speed control, AM/FM ETR stereo radio with cassette and premium sound, 15" cast aluminum wheels), group 3 (incls remote keyless/illuminated entry, cargo net)		
243A	**Base Convertible Pkg 243A** — Base Convertible	1447	1625
	incls air conditioning, group 2 (incls speed control, AM/FM ETR stereo radio with cassette and premium sound, 15" cast aluminum wheels), group 3 (incls remote keyless/ illuminated entry, cargo net)		
248A	**GTS Pkg 248A** — GTS	570	640
	incls air conditioning, AM/FM ETR stereo radio with cassette		
249A	**GT Pkg 249A** — GT	1438	1615
	incls air conditioning, group 2 (incls speed control, AM/FM ETR stereo radio with cassette and premium sound), anti-lock brakes, power driver's seat		
250A	**Cobra Coupe Pkg 250A** — Cobra Coupe	1122	1260
	incls speed control, electric rear window defroster, front floor mats		
250C	**Cobra Convertible Pkg 250C** — Cobra Convertible	2454	2755
	incls air conditioning, speed control, electric rear window defroster, front floor mats, compact disc player, leather sport bucket seats, Mach 460 AM/FM ETR stereo radio with cassette, group 3 (incls remote keyless/illuminated entry)		
61A	**Group 1** — Base Coupe	449	505
	GTS Coupe	449	505
	incls power side windows, power door locks, power trunk release		
63A	**Group 2** — Base Coupe	775	870
	Base Convertible	690	775
	GT	454	510
	incls speed control, cast aluminum wheels (std on GT), dual illuminated visor vanity mirrors (std on Base Convertible & GT), AM/FM ETR stereo radio with cassette and premium sound		

CODE	DESCRIPTION	INVOICE	MSRP
60K	**Group 3** — Base, GTS	276	310
	Cobra	218	245
	incls remote keyless/illuminated entry, cargo (NA on Cobra)		
422	**California Emissions**	85	95
428	**High Altitude Emissions**	NC	NC
572	**Air Conditioning**	761	855
41H	**Engine Block Heater** — all except Cobra	18	20
552	**Anti-Lock Brakes**	503	565
	std on Cobra		
13T	**Convertible Hardtop** — Convertible	1625	1825
525	**Speed Control**	191	215
12H	**Mats** — front	27	30
18A	**Anti-Theft System**	129	145
	Base and GTS require group 1		
57Q	**Electric Rear Window Defroster**	143	160
961	**Bodyside Moldings** — Base & GT	45	50
	Base req's Base Coupe Pkg 243A		
45C	**Optional Axle Ratio** — GTS & GT	40	45
44P	**Transmission** — 4-speed automatic w/overdrive	725	815
	NA on Cobra		
217	**Power Driver's Seat** — all except Cobra	156	175
—	**Seats**		
1	leather sport bucket seats - Base Convertible	445	500
4	leather sport bucket seats - GT & Cobra	445	500
64H	**Wheels** — GT	338	380
	incls unique 17" aluminum wheels and P245/45ZR17 BW SBR tires		
64J	**Wheels** — Base	236	265
	incls 15" cast aluminum wheels		
58M	**Radio** — Base & GTS	147	165
	incls AM/FM ETR stereo radio with cassette		
586	**Radio** — Base & GT w/o group 2	596	670
	Base & GT w/group 2	334	375
	Cobra	334	375
	incls Mach 460 AM/FM ETR stereo with cassette; Base Coupe req's group 1; Cobra req's compact disc player		
585	**Radio** — Base & GT w/group 2	124	140
	Base & GT w/58M radio	240	270
	Base, GTS & GT w/std radio	387	435
	Cobra	124	140
	incls AM/FM ETR radio with compact disc and premium sound		
912	**Radio** — all models except GTS and Cobra Convertible	334	375
	incls Mach 460 sound system; req's 585M radio' Base req's group 1		
917	**Compact Disc Player** — all models except GTS	334	375
	Base, GT and Cobra require 586 radio; Base req's group 1		

FORD

CODE	DESCRIPTION	INVOICE	MSRP

PROBE *(1995)*

PROBE 4 CYL

T20	Base 3-Dr	12825	14180

PROBE 6 CYL

T22	GT 3-Dr	14930	16545
Destination Charge:		375	375

Standard Equipment

PROBE: 2.0 liter DOHC I4 4 cylinder engine, 5-speed manual transaxle, power rack and pinion steering, power front disc/rear drum brakes, wrap-around quarter windows with concealed "B/C" pillar and flush glass, P195/65R14 BSW all-season tires, wheel covers, electronic AM/FM stereo/ clock radio with 4 speakers, fixed rear quarter antenna, flush door handles, sporty integrated front/ rear fascia, concealed headlamps, sail-mounted manual adjustable RH direct activating mirror (LH remote), amber front combination lamp lens, all red taillamps lens, tinted backlight and quarter window glass, driver and right front passenger air bag supplemental restraint system, front and rear 3-point active safety belts, child rear seat tether anchor, 12 oz. color-keyed carpet, electronic digital clock (integral with radio), center console, side window demisters, door trim with integral armrest and assist handle, vinyl pad footrest (on carpet), locking glove box, instrument cluster includes: 120-mph speedometer/odometer/trip odometer/tachometer/fuel gauge/water temperature gauge/oil pressure gauge/voltmeter; lights include: dome/cargo compartment/flash-to-pass; day/night inside rearview mirror, driver and passenger seat back recline with memory, front bucket seats with dual recliners and cloth integral head restraints, 50/50 fold-down rear seat, standard cloth seat trim, floor-mounted transaxle shift, urethane shift boot and knob, urethane steering wheel, cloth covered sunvisors with covered RH vanity mirror, warning lights include: parking brake/seat belt check/brake check/air bag/ high beam/engine check; high mounted brake light, 15.5 gallon fuel tank with tethered cap, functional roof drip molding, functional "A" pillar weather strip, inside hood release, dual note horn, single ignition/door key, MacPherson strut front suspension, Quadralink rear suspension, front and rear stabilizer bars, 2-speed windshield wipers.

GT (in addition to or instead of PROBE equipment): 2.5 liter DOHC V6 engine, power 4-wheel disc brakes, P225/50VR16 BSW performance tires, 16" 5-spoke aluminum wheels, lower bodyside cladding, unique front and rear fascia with rectangular fog lamps and unique side badging, clear front combination lamp lens, cargo net, full center console with folding armrest and cup holder, 140-mph speedometer, driver side power lumbar support and seat back side bolsters, unique cloth seat trim, leather shift knob (with manual trans), leather-wrapped steering wheel, fog lamps, unique front and rear stabilizer bars, uprated/unique GT and sport suspension.

Accessories

CODE	DESCRIPTION	INVOICE	MSRP
—	Preferred Equipment Pkgs — prices include pkg discounts		
251A	**Base Pkg 251A** — Base *incls manual air conditioning, electronic AM/FM stereo/clock/cassette*	499	560
253A	**SE Pkg 253A** — Base *incls manual air conditioning, electronic AM/FM stereo/clock/cassette/premium sound, group 1 (incls rear window defroster, dual electric remote control mirrors), group 2 (incls console and storage armrest with cup holder, interval windshield wipers, tilt steering column, remote fuel door/liftgate release, speed control), group 3 (incls power side windows and power door locks), SE appearance (incls GT front fascia [w/o fog lamps], unique 15" aluminum wheels, P205/55R15 BSW tires, sport edition "SE" nomenclature), color-keyed bodyside moldings*	2267	2545
261A	**GT Pkg 261A** — GT *incls manual air conditioning, electronic AM/FM stereo/clock/cassette/premium sound, group 1 (incls rear widow defroster, dual electric remote control mirrors), group 2 (incls console and storage armrest with cup holder, interval windshield wipers, tilt steering column, remote fuel door/liftgate release, speed control), color-keyed bodyside moldings, front color-keyed floor mats*	1595	1790
263A	**GT Pkg 263A** — GT *incls GT pkg 261A contents plus group 4 (incls illuminated entry system, dual illuminated visor vanity mirrors, fade-to-off dome lamp with map lights, remote keyless entry, convenience lights), color-keyed bodyside moldings, front color-keyed floor mats, rear wiper/washer, power driver's seat, rear decklid spoiler, anti-lock braking system*	3113	3495
99A	**Engine** — 2.0 liter DOHC I4 - Base	STD	STD
99B	**Engine** — 2.5 liter DOHC V6 - GT	STD	STD
445	**Transmission** — 5-speed manual	STD	STD
44T	**Transmission** — 4-speed automatic w/overdrive	703	790
422	**California Emissions System**	85	95
428	**High Altitude Emissions System**	NC	NC
T82	**Tires** — P195/65R14 BSW - Base	STD	STD
64V	**Tires** — P205/55R15 BSW and 15" wheels - Base	383	430
T26	**Tires** — P225/50VR16 BSW performance and 16" wheels - GT	STD	STD
64X	**Tires** — P225/50VR16 BSW performance and 16" wheels - GT	347	390
—	**Seats**		
9	cloth sport buckets - Base	STD	STD
8	GT cloth buckets w/console - GT	STD	STD
7	leather seating surfaces (front buckets only) - GT	445	500
21A	power driver's seat - GT	258	290

CODE	DESCRIPTION	INVOICE	MSRP
—	**Groups**		
65B	**Group 1** — Base	232	260
	GT	255	285
	incls rear defroster, dual electric remote mirrors		
67A	**Group 2** — Base	508	570
	GT	454	510
	incls console and storage armrest (std on GT), speed control, interval wipers, tilt steering wheel, remote fuel and liftgate release		
43R	**Group 3** — Base and GT	432	485
	incls power side windows, power door locks		
97A	**Group 4** — Base and GT	432	485
	incls illuminated entry system, dual illuminated visor vanity mirrors, fade-to-off dome lamp with map lights, remote keyless entry, convenience lights, battery saver, headlamp warning chime		
572	**Manual Air Conditioning**	797	895
	incls tinted glass		
552	**Anti-Lock Braking Ssytem** — Base	654	735
	GT	503	565
	Base req's 4-wheel disc brakes and sport suspension		
12H	**Floor Mats** — front color-keyed	27	30
18A	**Anti-Theft System**	169	190
961	**Moldings** — color-keyed bodyside	45	50
173	**Rear Wiper/Washer**	116	130
416	**SE Appearance**	472	530
	incls GT front fascia (w/o fog lamps), unique 15" aluminum wheels, P205/55R15 BSW tires, sport edition "SE" nomenclature		
13B	**Power Sliding Roof**	547	615
13K	**Rear Decklid Spoiler**	209	235
—	**Audio**		
589	radio	147	165
	incls electronic AM/FM stereo/clock/cassette		
588	radio	361	405
	incls electronic AM/FM stereo/clock/cassette/premium sound, power antenna		
582	radio — w/pkg 251A	383	430
	w/pkg 253A, 261A or 263A	240	270
	incls electronic AM/FM stereo/clock/compact disc player/premium sound		

FORD

TAURUS (1995)

TAURUS 6 CYL

CODE	DESCRIPTION	INVOICE	MSRP
P52	GL 4-Dr Sedan	15887	17585
P57	GL 4-Dr Wagon	16845	18680
—	SE 4-Dr Sedan	15887	17585
P53	LX 4-Dr Sedan	17486	19400
P58	LX 4-Dr Wagon	18919	21010
P54	SHO 4-Dr Sedan	22594	25140
Destination Charge:		550	550

Standard Equipment

TAURUS - GL SEDAN: 3.0 liter sequential EFI V6 engine, 4-speed automatic overdrive transaxle (AXOD-E), power rack and pinion steering, power front disc/rear drum brakes, P205/65R15 BSW tires with mini spare, full wheel covers, electronic AM/FM stereo radio with dual access remote controls (on instrument panel), manual temperature control air conditioning, front and rear color-coordinated polycarbonate bumpers, black-out "B" pillars and door frames with bright surround, exterior accent group includes: bright door/quarter window surround moldings, body color grille with "floating" Ford oval, single aerodynamic halogen headlamps with turn signal lamps (integral to headlamp), wrap-around taillamps with integral back-up lamps and side markers, high-mount brake lamp, lower door/rocker panel urethane lower bodyside protection, sail-mounted dual electric remote control mirrors with tinted glass, color-keyed bodyside protection moldings, color-keyed rocker panel moldings, clearcoat paint, driver and right front passenger dual front supplemental restraint system air bags, front/center/dual armrests (single with bucket/console), center folding rear armrest, front illuminated ashtray, rear door ashtrays, manual front/rear seat lap/shoulder belts (outboard seating positions), lap belts (front/rear center seating positions), 14 oz. color-keyed carpet with integral sound absorber, cigarette lighter, electronic digital clock with dimming feature, cup holder/coin holder, color-keyed door handles, cloth/vinyl door trim panels with padded armrests/reflectors/front door map pockets, illuminated lockable bin-type glove box, illuminated headlamp switch, positive shut-off climate control registers, courtesy dome light switches (all doors), lights include: glove box/ashtray/ luggage compartment/front door curb, delayed dome lamp, carpeted luggage compartment with mini spare tire storage, luggage compartment light, day/night rearview mirrors, split bench seats with dual recliners and dual armrests, front seatback map pockets, cloth seat trim, tilt steering column, color-coordinated 4-spoke steering wheel with supplemental restraint system, steering wheel with center blow horn control, cloth-covered sunvisors with retention clips, 110 amp alternator, safety belt reminder chime, rear window defroster, side window demisters, child-proof rear door locks, concealed drip moldings, EEC-IV electronic engine controls, electronic ignition, 16 gallon fuel tank, tethered gas cap, tinted glass, windshield/rear solar tinted glass, heater/defroster/ventilation with positive shut-off air registers and rear seat heat ducts, instrumentation includes: temperature/fuel gauges, speedometer, low brake fluid alert light, trip odometer, low fuel indicator light, luggage compartment light, manual parking brake release, six-passenger seating capacity (with split bench seats), five-passenger seating capacity (with bucket seats), independent MacPherson front suspension with nitrogen gas-pressurized hydraulic struts and front stabilizer bar, independent MacPherson rear suspension with nitrogen gas-pressurized hydraulic struts and rear stabilizer bar, interval windshield wipers.

SE SEDAN (in addition to or instead of GL SEDAN equipment): Full wheel covers deleted, full vinyl door trim panels, split bench seats with dual recliners/dual armrests/front seatback map pockets deleted, leather bolster seat trim, five-passenger seating capacity (with bucket seats).

LX SEDAN (in addition to or instead of SE SEDAN equipment): Power rack and pinion variable assist speed-sensitive steering, power side windows with express-down driver's feature (includes lock-out switch), power door locks, bright machined cast aluminum wheels, crystalline headlamps/lens, color-keyed protective cladding, color-keyed bodyside protection moldings, paint stripe, cargo tie down net, console/floor shift (includes flip-open padded "clamshell" armrest, storage bin and depression for beverage container), cloth/vinyl door trim panels, front and rear grab handles (with power moonroof only), light group, dual illuminated visor mirrors, bucket seats with dual recliners/armrest/2-way adjustable front head restraints/front seatback map pockets/6-way power seat, luxury cloth seat trim with unique sew style, driver/passenger secondary visors for front/side coverage, remote fuel door and decklid/liftgate release, automatic on/off/delay headlamps, illuminated entry, instrumentation includes: tachometer/door ajar light/low brake fluid light/low washer fluid light/low oil level light/lamp out indicator lights, automatic parking brake release.

SHO (in addition to or instead of LX SEDAN equipment): 3.0 liter DOHC SEFI 24-valve engine (with manual 5-speed overdrive transmission), 3.2 liter DOHC SEFI 24-valve engine (with 4-speed automatic overdrive transmission), 4-wheel disc brakes, anti-lock braking system, P215/60ZR16 94V BSW high performance tires (Touring tires with automatic), sparkle unidirectional spoke cast aluminum wheels, high level audio system with dual access remote controls on instrument panel, electronic temperature control air conditioning, front/rear unique color-keyed body color A-gloss painted bumpers, black-out sport surround "B" pillars and door frames, decklid spoiler with LED stop lamp, black-out sport treatment, cornering lamps, valance panel with fog lamps, spoiler brake lamp, 18 oz. color-keyed carpeting with integral sound absorber, full vinyl door trim panels, floor mats, cloth and leather sport bucket seats with dual recliners/armrests/4-way adjustable front head restraints/front seatback map pockets, leather bolster seat trim, leather-wrapped steering wheel, 130 amp alternator (with SHO 3.0 liter/3.8 liter engine), 120 amp alternator (with SHO 3.2 liter engine), dual exhaust system, extended range fuel tank, manual parking brake release, power radio antenna, speed control, handling suspension.

TAURUS - GL WAGON: 3.0 liter sequential EFI V6 engine, 4-speed automatic overdrive transaxle (AXOD-E), power rack and pinion steering, power front disc/rear drum brakes, P205/65R15 BSW tires with mini spare, full wheel covers, electronic AM/FM stereo radio with dual access remote controls on instrument panel, manual temperature control air conditioning, front/rear color-coordinated polycarbonate bumpers, body color unique shape rear bumpers with step pad, bright door sill surround moldings, body color grille with "floating" Ford oval, single aerodynamic halogen headlamps with turn signal lamps integral to headlamp, vertical taillamps with integral back-up lamps and separate side markers, high-mount brake lamp, lower door/rocker panel urethane protection coating, luggage rack, dual electric remote control mirrors with tinted sail-mounted glass, color-keyed bodyside protection moldings, color-keyed rocker panel moldings, clearcoat paint, driver and right front passenger dual front supplemental restraint system air bags, front/center/dual armrests (single with bucket/console), front illuminated ashtray, rear door trim panel ashtrays, manual front and rear seat lap/shoulder belts for outboard seating positions, lap belts for center seating positions (front and rear), lockable cargo area (except when ordered with conventional spare tire), carpeted under floor storage compartment, 14 oz. color-keyed carpet with integral sound absorber, cigarette lighter, electronic digital clock with dimming feature, cup holder/coin holder, color-keyed door handles, cloth/vinyl door trim panels with padded armrests/reflectors/front door map pockets, locking illuminated bin-type glove box, front/rear grab handles, illuminated headlamp switch, positive shut-off climate control registers, courtesy dome light switches (all doors), lights include: glove box/ashtray/luggage compartment/front door curb, delayed dome lamp, liftgate ajar alert light, "D" pillar cargo lamps with liftgate-actuated courtesy switch, day/night rearview mirrors, split bench seats with dual recliners/dual armrests/front seatback map pockets, 60/40 split/fold-down second seat, cloth seat trim, tilt steering column, color-coordinated 4-spoke steering wheel with supplemental restraint system, steering wheel with center blow horn, cloth-covered sun visors with retention clips, 110 amp alternator, safety belt reminder chime, rear window defroster, side window demisters, child-proof rear door locks, concealed drip moldings, EEC-IV electronic engine controls, electronic ignition, 16 gallon fuel tank (includes tethered gas cap), tinted glass, solar tinted windshield glass, heater/defroster/ventilation with positive shut-off air registers and rear seat heat ducts, instrumentation includes: temperature and fuel gauges/low brake fluid alert light/trip odometer; low fuel indicator light, luggage compartment light, manual parking brake release, eight-passenger seating capacity (with split bench seats) (maximum seating with optional rear-facing third seat; rear-facing seat adds two passengers), seven-passenger seating capacity (with bucket seats) (maximum seating with optional rear-facing third seat; rear-facing seat adds two passengers), independent MacPherson front/rear suspension with nitrogen gas-pressurized hydraulic struts and front/rear stabilizer bars, interval windshield wipers.

LX WAGON (in addition to or instead of GL WAGON equipment): 3.8 liter sequential EFI V6 engine, power rack and pinion variable assist speed-sensitive steering, power side windows with express-down driver's feature and lock-out switch, power door locks, bright machined cast aluminum wheels, color-keyed protective cladding, color-keyed bodyside protection moldings, paint stripe, cargo tie down net, console/floor shift includes: flip-open padded "clamshell" armrest/storage bin/depression for beverage container; color-keyed door handles deleted, light group, dual illuminated visor mirrors, driver/passenger secondary visors for front/side coverage, remote fuel door and decklid/liftgate release, automatic on/off/delay headlamps, illuminated entry, instrumentation includes: tachometer/door ajar light/low brake fluid light/low washer fluid light/low oil level light/lamp out indicator lights, automatic parking brake release.

Accessories

CODE	DESCRIPTION	INVOICE	MSRP
—	**Preferred Equipment Pkgs** — prices include pkg discounts		
203A	**GL Pkg 203A** — GL *incls vehicle with standard equipment*	NC	NC
204A	**GL Pkg 204A** — GL *incls GL Pkg 203A contents plus group 2 (consists of decklid/liftgate/fuel door release, power door locks/side windows, light group, speed control, electronic AM/FM stereo cassette), group 3 (consists of power driver's seat, deluxe wheel covers), front and rear floor mats, GL equipment group*	1135	1275
205A	**SE Pkg 205A** — SE *incls group 2A (power door locks/side windows, electronic AM/FM stereo cassette, group 3 (driver's power seat, deluxe wheel covers), group 3A (cloth & leather sport bucket seats, floor shift/console, bright machined cast aluminum wheels, Crystaline headlampls), front and rear floor mats*	1375	1545
—	**Bonus Discount** *avail only on PEP 204A and 205A (req's 3.0 liter engine)*	(445)	(500)

CODE	DESCRIPTION	INVOICE	MSRP
208A	**LX Sedan Pkg 208A** — LX Sedan	316	355
	incls group 2 (consists of decklid/liftgate/fuel door release, power door locks/side windows, light group, speed control, electronic AM/FM stereo radio with cassette), front and rear floor mats, group 4 (consists of leather-wrapped steering wheel, power antenna, remote keyless entry)		
208A	**LX Wagon Pkg 208A** — LX Wagon	485	545
	incls LX Sedan Pkg 208A contents plus group 5 (consists of rear window washer/wiper, cargo area cover), load floor extension		
211A	**SHO Pkg 211A** — SHO	NC	NC
	incls vehicle with standard equipment		
—	**Engines**		
99U	3.0 liter - GL Sedan & Wagon, LX Sedan, SE	STD	STD
994	3.8 liter - std on LX Wagon	561	630
99Y	3.0 liter DOHC - SHO	STD	STD
99P	3.2 liter DOHC (incld w/automatic overdrive - SHO only)	STD	STD
44L	**Transmission** — automatic overdrive - SHO	703	790
	std on GL, LX and SE; incls 3.2 liter engine on SHO		
445	**Transmission** — 5-speed manual - SHO	STD	STD
422	**California Emissions System**	82	85
428	**High Altitude Principal Use Emissions System**	NC	NC
—	**Tires/Wheels**		
T32	P205/65R15 BSW - GL	STD	STD
642	wheel covers, deluxe / P205/65R15 BSW tires - GL	71	80
64R	wheels, sparkle cast aluminum / P205/65R15 touring tires - GL	205	230
508	conventional spare tire - GL, LX	62	70
T22	wheels, sparkle unidirectional cast aluminum / P215/60ZR16 BSW performance - SHO	STD	STD
T25	wheels, sparkle unidirectional cast aluminum / P215/60R16 94V BSW touring - SHO	STD	STD
—	**Seats**		
P	cloth split bench - GL	STD	STD
Q	cloth buckets/console - GL	STD	STD
B	leather seating surfaces buckets/console - GL	530	595
21A	seat, power driver only - GL	258	290
C	cloth split bench - LX	STD	STD
M	cloth buckets/console - LX	STD	STD
B	leather seating surfaces buckets/console - LX	441	495
A	leather seating surfaces split bench - LX	441	495
21J	seats, power driver/passenger - LX, SHO	258	290
9	cloth and leather sport buckets - SHO, SE	STD	STD
H	leather seating surfaces buckets - SHO, SE	441	495
214	seat, rear facing third - Wagons	134	150
77B	**Group 2** — GL w/204A	992	1115
	LX	338	380
	incls decklid/liftgate/fuel door release, power door locks/side windows, light group, speed control, AM/FM stereo/cassette		

CODE	DESCRIPTION	INVOICE	MSRP
77C	**Group 2A** — GL, SE	668	750
	incls power door locks/side windows, AM/FM stereo/cassette		
60A	**Group 2B** — GL	240	270
	incls light group, speed control		
54A	**Group 3** — GL, SE	329	370
	incls power driver seat, deluxe wheel covers		
77D	**Group 3A** — GL	921	1035
	incls cloth and leather sport buckets, console/floor shift, bright machined cast aluminum wheels, crystalline headlamps		
54B	**Group 4** — GL, SE, LX	360	405
	incls leather-wrapped steering wheel, power antenna, remote keyless entry		
96W	**Group 5** — Wagon	174	195
	incls rear window washer/wiper, cargo area cover		
573	**Air Conditioning** — electronic temperature control - std on SHO	156	175
552	**Anti-Lock Braking System** - std on SHO	503	565
12Y	**Floor Mats** — front and rear - std on SHO	40	45
414	**GL/Equipment Group**	218	245
596	**Load Floor Extension** — Wagon	76	85
902	**Power Door Locks** — GL, SE	218	245
53K	**LX Convenience Group**	917	1030
	incls power moonroof, driver and passenger power seats		
53L	**Luxury Convenience Group** — SHO	1384	1555
	incls Ford JBL Audio System, driver and passenger power seats		
516	**Cellular Telephone/Storage Armrests**	445	500
144	**Remote Keyless Entry System** — LX, SHO	191	215
	GL w/group 2 (incls illum entry)	263	295
	GL w/o group 2 (incls illum entry and remote releases)	347	390
525	**Speed Control** - std on SHO	191	215
43R	**Power Side Windows** - std on LX, SHO	302	340
13J	**Spoiler, Decklid** — w/205A only	240	270
58H	**Radio**	147	165
	incls electronic AM/FM stereo/cassette		
586	**Radio** — LX w/group 2	280	315
	LX w/o group 2	427	480
	incls high level audio system (NA on GL)		
916	**Radio**	445	500
	incls Ford JBL audio system (NA on GL or Wagons)		
917	**Compact Disc Player**	334	375
	NA on GL		
631	**Battery** — heavy duty, 72 amp	27	30
	NA on SHO		
153	**License Plate Bracket** — front	NC	NC
41H	**Engine Block Immersion Heater**	18	20
127	**Floor Covering** — heavy duty rubber	23	25
904	**Power Door Locks** — driver switch only	218	245
662	**Heavy Duty Suspension** — load carrying	23	25
	NA on SHO		

THUNDERBIRD *(1995)*

THUNDERBIRD 6 CYL

CODE	DESCRIPTION	INVOICE	MSRP
P62	LX 2-Dr Coupe	15696	17400
P64	Super Coupe 2-Dr	20600	22910
Destination Charge:		510	510

Standard Equipment

THUNDERBIRD - LX: 3.8 liter V6 EFI multiple-port sequential engine, 4-speed electronic controlled automatic overdrive transmission with overdrive lock-out, variable assist power steering, power front disc/rear drum brakes, power side windows, power lock group, P205/70R15 BSW all-season tires, Bolfon Design styled road wheel covers, electronic AM/FM stereo cassette radio, manual air conditioning with rotary controls, soft color-keyed front and rear 5-mph bumpers, solar tinted windshield/ door/quarter window glass, aerodynamic halogen headlamps/parking lamps, color-keyed dual electric remote control mirrors, black windshield/door/quarter moldings, window/backlight moldings, body color double spear-shaped bodyside protection moldings, driver and front passenger dual supplemental restraint system, 3-point active restraint system (front/rear outboard), lap belt (rear center/five seating position), safety belt reminder chimes, foot-operated parking brake, 24 oz. cut-pile carpeting, full-length console with floor-mounted shift/storage, dual console-mounted cup holders, luxury level door trim with courtesy lights and illuminated door switches, driver side footwell lights, illuminated entry system, leather shift knob, lights include: map/dome/luggage compartment/front ashtray/glove box; low liftover design carpeted luggage compartment, dual visor mirrors, luxury cloth bucket seats, driver's 6-way power seat, rear seat center armrest, side window defoggers, speed control, luxury leather-wrapped steering wheel, tilt steering wheel, 130 amp alternator, 58 amp maintenance-free battery, digital clock, EEC-IV electronic engine controls, 18 gallon fuel tank, tethered gas cap, dual note horn, performance analog instrument cluster with trip odometer, fuel gauge/temperature gauge, oil pressure gauge and voltmeter; front long spindle SLA suspension with stabilizer bar, variable rate springs, lower control arm and tension strut; rear independent suspension with stabilizer bar/variable rate springs, mini spare tire, interval windshield wipers.

SUPER COUPE (in addition to or instead of LX equipment): 3.8liter V6 EFI engine with multi-port sequential (supercharged/intercooled with dual exhaust), 5-speed manual overdrive transmission, anti-lock braking system (ABS) with 4-wheel power disc brakes, power lock group deleted,

P225/60ZR16 BSW performance tires, 16" x 7" directional cast aluminum wheels with locking lug nuts, electronic semi-automatic temperature control air conditioning, unique rear bumper treatment, lower bodyside cladding, front fascia integral fog lamps, hand-operated parking brake (mounted on console/leather-wrapped handle), driver's footrest, integrated warning lamp module, light group (RH instrument panel courtesy light and engine light), articulated bucket seats in cloth/leather/vinyl trim with power adjustable lumbar support and power adjustable seatback side bolsters, rear seat headrests, speed control deleted, 110 amp alternator, traction-lok axle, 72 amp maintenance-free battery, automatic ride control adjustable suspension.

Accessories

CODE	DESCRIPTION	INVOICE	MSRP
—	**Engines**		
994	3.8 liter EFI V6 - LX	STD	STD
99R	3.8 liter EFI super charged V6 - Super Coupe	STD	STD
99W	4.6 liter EFI V8 - LX	1006	1130
	incls speed sensitive power steering, heavy duty battery		
445	**Transmission** — manual - Super Coupe	STD	STD
44L	**Transmission** — automatic - LX	STD	STD
	Super Coupe (incls heavy duty battery)	703	790
422	**California Emissions System**	85	95
428	**High Altitude Principal Use Emissions System**	NC	NC
—	**Tires**		
T33	P205/70R15 BSW - LX	STD	STD
T37	P215/70R15 BSW - w/aluminum wheels only - LX	NC	NC
T24	P225/60ZR16 BSW performance - Super Coupe	STD	STD
T29	P225/60ZR16 BSW all-season performance - Super Coupe	62	70
—	**Seats**		
X	luxury cloth buckets - LX	STD	STD
Y	leather seating surfaces buckets - LX	436	490
Z	cloth/leather/vinyl articulated buckets - Super Coupe	STD	STD
1	leather seating surfaces articulated buckets - Super Coupe	547	615
411	**Group 1** — Super Coupe (std on LX)	712	800
	incls power lock group, speed control, 6-way power driver's seat		
432	**Group 2** — LX	280	315
	Super Coupe	143	160
	incls rear window defroster, electronic semi-automatic temperature control (LX)		
463	**Group 3** — LX	187	210
	incls cast aluminum wheels, P215/70R15 BSW		
552	**Anti-Lock Braking System** — Std. on Super Coupe	503	565
45A	**Axle, Traction Lok** — LX	85	95
153	**License Plate Bracket** — front	NC	NC
12H	**Floor Mats** — front	27	30
144	**Remote Keyless Entry** — LX; Super Coupe w/luxury/lighting group	191	215
	Super Coupe w/o luxury/lighting group	263	295
	req's group 1, 2 and 3		
545	**Luxury/Lighting Group** — LX	313	350
	Super Coupe	290	325
	req's 1, 2 and 3; incls autolamp, power antenna, dual illuminated visor mirrors, light group (LX), ILM (LX), illuminated entry (SC)		

CODE	DESCRIPTION	INVOICE	MSRP
13B	**Moonroof** — power *req's groups 1, 2 and 3 and luxury/lighting group*	658	740
21J	**Seat** — 6-way power passenger *req's group 1*	258	290
516	**Cellular Telephone** — "hands-free"	472	530
553	**Traction Assist** — LX	187	210
—	**Tri-Coat Paint**	201	225
58H	**Radio** *incls electronic AM/FM stereo/cassette*	STD	STD
586	**Radio** *incls AM/FM stereo/cassette/premium sound*	258	290
585	**Radio** *incls electronic AM/FM stereo/CD player/premium sound*	383	430
631	**Battery** — heavy duty, 72 amp *incld w/LX 4.6 liter engine and Super Coupe auto trans*	23	25
41H	**Engine Block Heater**	18	20

What's New for *Ford* in 1995?

Aspire: Korean-built minicompact receives minimal trim changes for 1995.

Contour: All new mid-size replacement for Tempo charges onto the market with bold styling and competent powertrains. Platinum tipped spark plugs mean tuneups happen every 100,000 miles. The Zetec twin cam four cylinder provides 125 hp, while an optional 2.5L V6 gives 170 ponies. Dual airbags are standard, and the top-of-the-line SE can be had for less than $18,000 loaded with options.

Crown Victoria: The Crown Vic gets an exterior freshening and a new interior for 1995. New radios, more standard equipment and an improved transmission complement the visual alterations.

Escort: A passenger-side airbag and a new wraparound dashboard mark the changes for the 1995 Escort. An integrated child seat option is now available. Sedans and wagons can be ordered with an optional sport appearance group.

Mustang: Two new colors (Bright Sapphire Blue Metallic and Silver Frost Metallic), and the addition of a GTS model (base Mustang with GT engine, suspension, wheels and fascias) are the only changes to Ford's ponycar. Look for a potent 4.6L V8 making 280 hp for the 1996 model year.

Probe: Freshened rear end styling and new wheel designs update the timeless shape of the Probe. Two new interior colors and five new exterior colors are available. Probe sales have suffered since the introduction of the new Mustang, and the Probe's days are said to be numbered. Don't expect it to be around after 1996.

Taurus: A rear defroster and air conditioning are now standard on Taurus. A new SE model includes alloy wheels, sport seats and a rear spoiler. Taurus is set to be replaced by a radically different car in the fall of 1995.

METRO *(1995)*

METRO 3 CYL

CODE	DESCRIPTION	INVOICE	MSRP
1MR08	Base 3-Dr Hatchback Coupe	7616	8085
1MR08/B4M	LSi 3-Dr Hatchback Coupe	7815	8385

METRO 4 CYL

CODE	DESCRIPTION	INVOICE	MSRP
1MR69	Base 4-Dr Sedan	8467	9085
1MR69/B4M	LSi 4-Dr Sedan	8840	9485
Destination Charge:		310	310

Standard Equipment

METRO: 1.0 liter SOHC L3 engine with EFI (Coupe only), 1.3 liter SOHC L4 engine with EFI (Sedan only), 5-speed manual transmission with 4th and 5th gear overdrive, rack and pinion steering, power front disc/rear drum brakes, rear child security door locks, P155/80R13 all-season SBR BW tires, styled steel wheels with center caps (Coupe only), 3-spoke full cover wheels (Sedan only), stainless steel exhaust system, black dual outside mirrors (LH and RH manual) (LH only on Coupe), dark gray bodyside molding (Sedan), independent 4-wheel MacPherson strut suspension with front and rear stabilizer bars, fixed intermittent wipers (Sedan only), driver and front passenger air bags, front and rear passenger assist grips (Sedan only), full carpeting (includes cargo area on Coupe), center console with cup holders and storage tray, temperature gauge, trip odometer (Sedan only), 3-position dome light, inside rearview day/ night mirror, passenger side visor vanity mirror, lap-shoulder safety belts, full-folding rear seat (with pass-through feature on Sedan), reclining high-back front bucket seats with integral head restraints, Scotchgard fabric protector on cloth seats, cloth-covered seating surface with vinyl backs and sides, driver and passenger door storage bins, reminder tones for headlamps on/key-in-ignition/safety belts.

LSi (in addition to or instead of METRO equipment):3-spoke full cover wheels (Coupe only), 7-spoke full cover wheels (Sedan only), front and rear body color bumpers (Sedan only), remote release fuel-filler door (Sedan only), tinted band glass (Sedan only), composite halogen headlamps, LH and RH dual outside remote mirrors (Sedan only), remote release trunk, front passenger assist grips (Coupe only), Scotchgard fabric protector door trim (Sedan only), cargo area light (Sedan only), split folding 50/50 rear seat with pass-through feature (Sedan only), custom cloth and vinyl seat trim (Sedan only), push-button reset trip odometer.

Accessories

CODE	DESCRIPTION	INVOICE	MSRP
1SA	**Metro Coupe Preferred Equipment Group 1 — 1MR08**	NC	NC
UL1	w/UL1 radio, add	268	301
UL0	w/UL0 radio, add	464	521
	incld with model		
1SC	**Metro LSi Hatchback Coupe Preferred Equipment Group 1 — 1MR08/B4M**	NC	NC
UL1	w/UL1 radio, add	268	301
UL0	w/UL0 radio, add	464	521
UP0	w/UP0 radio, add	642	721
	incld with model		
1SA	**Metro Sedan Preferred Equipment Group 1 — 1MR69**	NC	NC
UL1	w/UL1 radio, add	268	301
UL0	w/UL0 radio, add	464	521
UP0	w/UP0 radio, add	642	721
	incld with model		
1SB	**Metro Sedan Preferred Equipment Group 2 — 1MR69**	930	1045
UL1	w/UL1 radio, add	268	301
UL0	w/UL0 radio, add	464	521
UP0	w/UP0 radio, add	642	721
	incls air conditioning with R-134a refrigerant, power steering		
1SC	**Metro LSi Sedan Equipment Group 1 — 1MR69/B4M**	NC	NC
UL1	w/UL1 radio, add	268	301
UL0	w/UL0 radio, add	464	521
UP0	w/UP0 radio, add	642	721
	incld with model		
1SD	**Metro LSi Sedan Preferred Equipment Group 2 — 1MR69/B4M**	930	1045
UL1	w/UL1 radio, add	268	301
UL0	w/UL0 radio, add	464	521
UP0	w/UP0 radio, add	642	721
	incls air conditioning with R-134a refrigerant, power steering		
C60	**Air Conditioning** — w/R-134a refrigerant	699	785
	incld with PEGS 1SB and 1SD		
YG6	**Air Conditioning Delete**	NC	NC
JM4	**Brakes** — 4-wheel anti-lock	503	565
D42	**Cover, Cargo Security**	45	50
C49	**Defogger, Rear Window**	142	160
AU3	**Door Locks, Power**	196	220
FE9	**Federal Emission Requirements**	NC	NC
NG1	**Massachusetts Emission Requirements**	62	70
YF5	**California Emission Requirements**	62	70
—	**Engines**		
LP2	1.0 liter SOHC L3 EFI - Coupe	NC	NC
L72	1.3 liter SOHC L4 EFI - Sedan	NC	NC
	LSi Coupe	320	360

CODE	DESCRIPTION	INVOICE	MSRP
BYP	**Exterior Appearance Pkg, Metro Expressions** - LSi Coupe *incls body color bumpers, body color side moldings, 7-spoke full wheel covers*	177	199
B37	**Floor Mats** — front and rear carpeted, color-keyed	31	35
—	**Mirrors**		
DR1	dual outside LH and RH manual, black - Coupe	18	20
D68	dual outside LH and RH remote, black - Sedan	18	20
B84	**Moldings, Bodyside** - Base Coupe	45	50
N41	**Power Steering** - Sedans *incld w/PEGS 1SB and 1SD*	231	260
U16	**Tachometer w/Trip Odometer**	62	70
—	**Transmissions**		
MM5	5-speed manual w/4th and 5th gear overdrive	NC	NC
MX1	3-speed automatic - Sedans and LSi Coupe	445	500
C25	**Wiper/Washer** — rear window - LSi Coupe	111	125
—	**Radio Equipment** — see pkgs for specific radio pricing		
UL1	radio - see pkgs *incls electronically tuned AM/FM stereo radio with seek, digital clock and four speakers*		
UL0	radio - see pkgs *incls electronically tuned AM/FM stereo radio with seek/scan, tone select, stereo cassette player, digital clock, theft deterrent and four speakers*		
UP0	radio - seek pkgs *incls electronically tuned AM/FM stereo radio with seek/scan, tone select, stereo cassette player, compact disc player, digital clock, theft deterrent and four speakers*		

CODE DESCRIPTION INVOICE MSRP

PRIZM *(1995)*

PRIZM 4 CYL

CODE	DESCRIPTION	INVOICE	MSRP
1SK19	Base 4-Dr Sedan (except Calif.)	11115	11675
1SK19	Base 4-Dr Sedan (Calif.)	10896	11445
1SK19/B4M	LSi 4-Dr Sedan (except Calif.)	11377	12340
1SK19/B4M	LSi 4-Dr Sedan (Calif.)	11165	12110
Destination Charge:		375	375

Standard Equipment

PRIZM: 1.6 liter 16 valve DOHC MFI L4 engine, 5-speed manual transmission with 4th and 5th gear overdrive, manual rack and pinion steering, power vented front disc/rear drum brakes, P175/65R14 tires, 14" styled steel wheels with center caps, front and rear body color bumpers, stainless steel exhaust system, black dual outside mirrors (LH remote), black bodyside molding, 4-wheel independent MacPherson strut suspension with coil springs (rear stabilizer bar with optional 1.8 liter), mist-cycle wipers, driver and front passenger air bags, full carpeting, center console with cup holders and storage tray, child security rear door locks, Scotchgard fabric protection, temperature/trip odometer gauges, 3-position dome light, inside rearview day/night mirror, lap/shoulder safety belts, reclining front bucket seats, rear bench seat, cloth covered seating surface with vinyl backs and trim, storage includes: driver door bin/glove box/center console tray; warning tones for: headlamps-on, key in ignition, safety belts.

LSi (in addition to or instead of PRIZM equipment): 14" styled full wheel covers, blackout B-pillar, console storage box, luggage compartment light, dual map pockets, dual visor vanity mirrors, split folding 60/40 rear seat with pass-through feature, custom cloth seat and door trim, interior lid trunk trim.

Accessories

CODE	DESCRIPTION	INVOICE	MSRP
1SA	**Prizm Base Equipment Group 1 — 1SK19**	NC	NC
UL1	w/UL1 radio, add	284	330

CODE	DESCRIPTION	INVOICE	MSRP
UL0	w/UL0 radio, add	473	550
1SB	**Prizm Preferred Group 2** — 1SK19	507	590
UL0	w/UL0 radio, add	189	220
	incls standard equipment, electronically tuned AM/FM stereo radio with seek, digital clock and four speakers, power steering		
1SC	**Prizm LSi Preferred Equipment Group 1** — 1SK19/B4M	NC	NC
UL1	w/UL1 radio, add	284	330
UL0	w/UL0 radio, add	473	550
	incls LSi equipment		
1SD	**Prizm LSi Preferred Equipment Group 2** — 1SK19/B4M	1329	1545
UL0	w/UL0 radio, add	189	220
UP0	w/UP0 radio, add	488	568
	incls LSi equipment, air conditioning, electronically tuned AM/FM stereo radio with seek, digital clock and four speakers, black dual outside electric remote mirrors, power steering, trunk release remote, variable intermittent wipers		
1SF	**Prizm LSi Preferred Equipment Group 3** — 1SK19/B4M	1926	2240
UL0	w/UL0 radio, add	189	220
UP0	w/UP0 radio, add	361	420
	incls LSi equipment, air conditioning, electronically tuned AM/FM stereo radio with seek, digital clock and four speakers, black dual outside electric remote mirrors, power steering, trunk release remote, variable intermittent wipers, cruise control w/resume speed, power door locks, power windows		
—	**Radio Equipment** — see pkgs		
UL1	radio - see pkgs		
	incls electronically tuned AM/FM stereo radio with seek, digital clock and four speakers		
UL0	radio - see pkgs		
	incls electronically tuned AM/FM stereo radio with seek and scan, tone select, stereo cassette tape, digital clock, theft deterrent and four speakers		
UP0	radio - see pkgs		
	incls electronically tuned AM/FM stereo radio with seek and scan, tone select, stereo cassette tape, compact disc player, digital clock, theft deterrent and six extended range speakers		
—	**Interior Trim**		
—	cloth & vinyl bucket seats - Base	NC	NC
—	custom cloth bucket seats - LSi	NC	NC
—	**Prizm Expressions Leather Pkg** - LSi	512	595
—	**Exterior Color** — paint, solid	NC	NC
C60	**Air Conditioning** — CFC free - Base	684	795
JM4	**Brakes** — 4-wheel anti-lock brake system	512	595
K34	**Cruise Control w/Resume Speed** - LSi	151	175
C49	**Defogger** — rear window	146	170
R9W	**Defogger** — rear window, delete	NC	NC
AU3	**Door Locks** — power	189	220
YF5	**California Emission Requirements**	60	70
FE9	**Federal Emission Requirements**	NC	NC
NG1	**Massachusetts Emission Requirements**	60	70
B37	**Floor Mats** — front & rear, carpeted, color-keyed	34	40

PRIZM

CODE	DESCRIPTION		
CA1	**Sun Roof** — electric w/map light & tilt-up feature - LSi		
U16	**Tachometer**		
—	**Transmissions**		
MM5	5-speed manual w/4th & 5th gear overdrive	NC	
MX1	3-speed automatic	426	495
MS7	4-speed electronically controlled automatic w/overdrive - LSi	688	800
—	**Engines**		
LO1	1.6 liter DOHC 16-valve L4 MFI	NC	NC
LV6	1.8 liter DOHC 16-valve L4 MFI - LSi	303	352
	incls P185/65R14 all-season steel belted radial BW tires and rear stabilizer bar		
PG4	**Wheels** — 14" alloy - LSi	288	335
PB2	**Full Wheel Covers** - Base	45	52
CD4	**Wipers** — intermittent variable - Base	34	40

What's New for *Geo* in 1995?

Metro: Metro has been totally redesigned for 1995. A sedan version has been added to the roster, but at the expense of the five-door hatchback. Base or LSi trim levels are available, and for the first time, a four cylinder engine beats under the hood of the Metro. A three cylinder is still standard on the base Metro hatch. Dual airbags are standard and ABS is optional. Look for Ford Aspire sales to fall.

Prizm: Geo's excellent Prizm undergoes few changes for its third model year. The optional 1.8L engine loses 10 horsepower due to emissions restrictions, four new colors are available and the LSi gets redesigned wheelcovers.

GEO

		INVOICE	MSRP

ACCORD COUPE *(1995)*

CD713S	LX 2-Dr Coupe w/o ABS (5-spd)	15508	17550
CD723S	LX 2-Dr Coupe w/o ABS (auto)	16171	18300
CD714S	LX 2-Dr Coupe w/ABS (5-spd)	16347	18500
CD724S	LX 2-Dr Coupe w/ABS (auto)	17010	19250
CD715S	EX 2-Dr Coupe w/Cloth Interior (5-spd)	17770	20110
CD725S	EX 2-Dr Coupe w/Cloth Interior (auto)	18432	20860
CD716S	EX 2-Dr Coupe w/Leather Interior (5-spd)	18697	21160
CD726S	EX 2-Dr Coupe w/Leather Interior (auto)	19360	21910
Destination Charge:		380	380

Standard Equipment

ACCORD COUPE - LX: 2.2 liter 130 HP 16-valve engine with second-order balance system, aluminum alloy cylinder head and block with cast iron liners, electronic ignition, multi-point programmed fuel injection, dual air bags (SRS), effort-sensitive power rack and pinion steering, 5-speed manual transmission, power assisted front disc/rear drum brakes, integrated rear window antenna, body color dual power mirrors, bodyside molding, multi-reflector halogen headlights, impact-absorbing body color bumpers, air conditioning, power windows, power door locks, AM/FM high-power stereo cassette (4 x 12.5-watt), cruise control, center console armrest with storage compartment, front 3-point seatbelts, rear 3-point seatbelts with center lap belt, adjustable steering column, fold-down rear seatback with lock, quartz digital clock, beverage holder, dual illuminated vanity mirrors, trunk-open warning light, remote fuel filler door release, remote trunk release with lock, rear window defroster with timer, 2-speed intermittent windshield wipers, rear seat heater ducts, low fuel warning light, maintenance interval indicator.

EX (in addition to or instead of LX equipment): 145 HP VTEC engine, anti-lock brakes (ABS), power assisted 4-wheel disc brakes, 15" alloy wheels, power moonroof, body color bodyside molding, driver's seat with power height adjustment and adjustable lumbar support, AM/FM high-power stereo cassette with 6 speakers (4 x 20-watt).

CODE	DESCRIPTION	INVOICE	MSRP

Accessories

NOTE: Honda accessories are dealer installed. Contact a Honda dealer for accessory availability.

16347
380
16727
→ 17,150

ACCORD SEDAN *(1995)*

CODE	DESCRIPTION	INVOICE	MSRP
CD552S	DX 4-Dr Sedan (5-spd)	13078	14800
CD562S	DX 4-Dr Sedan (auto)	13741	15550
CD553S	LX 4-Dr Sedan w/o ABS (5-spd)	15685	17750
CD563S	LX 4-Dr Sedan w/o ABS (auto)	16347	18500
CD554S	LX 4-Dr Sedan w/ABS (5-spd)	16524	18700
CD564S	LX 4-Dr Sedan w/ABS (auto)	17187	19450
CE664S	LX V6 4-Dr Sedan (auto)	19705	22300
CD555S	EX 4-Dr Sedan w/Cloth Interior (5-spd)	17946	20310
CD565S	EX 4-Dr Sedan w/Cloth Interior (auto)	18609	21060
CD556S	EX 4-Dr Sedan w/Leather Interior (5-spd)	18874	21360
CD566S	EX 4-Dr Sedan w/Leather Interior (auto)	19537	22110
CE666S	EX V6 4-Dr Sedan (auto)	22047	24950
Destination Charge:		380	380

Standard Equipment

ACCORD SEDAN - DX: 2.2 liter 130 HP 16-valve engine with second-order balance system, aluminum alloy cylinder head and block with cast iron liners, electronic ignition, multi-point programmed fuel injection, dual air bags (SRS), effort-sensitive power rack and pinion steering, 5-speed manual transmission, power assisted front disc/rear drum brakes, dual manual remote operated mirrors, bodyside molding, multi-reflector halogen headlights, impact-absorbing body color bumpers, center console armrest with storage compartment, front 3-point seatbelts with adjustable shoulder anchors, rear 3-point seatbelts with center lap belt, adjustable steering column, fold-down rear seatback with lock, quartz digital clock, passenger vanity mirror, trunk-open warning light, remote fuel filler door release, remote trunk release with lock, rear window defroster with timer, 2-speed intermittent windshield wipers, rear seat heater ducts, low fuel warning light, maintenance interval indicator.

LX (in addition to or instead of DX equipment): Rear fender-mounted power antenna, body color dual power mirrors, air conditioning, power windows, power door locks, AM/FM high-power stereo cassette (4 x 12.5-watt), cruise control, fold-down rear seat center armrest, beverage holder, illuminated dual vanity mirror.

LX V6 (in addition to LX equipment): 2.7 liter V6 EFI engine, front and rear stabilizer bars, power 4-wheel disc anti-lock brakes, map lights, variable intermittent windshield wipers, Michelin MXV 205/60R15 steel belted radial tires.

EX (in addition to or instead of LX equipment): 145 HP VTEC engine, anti-lock brakes (ABS), power assisted 4-wheel disc brakes, 15" alloy wheels, power moonroof, body color bodyside molding, driver's seat with power height adjustment and adjustable lumbar support, AM/FM high-power stereo cassette with 6 speakers and anti-theft feature (4 x 20-watt).

EX V6 (in addition to EX equipment): 2.7 liter V6 EFI engine, 8-way power driver seat, variable intermittent windshield wipers, map lights, leather upholstery, Michelin MXV 205/60R15 steel belted radial tires.

Accessories

NOTE: Honda accessories are dealer installed. Contact a Honda dealer for accessory availability.

ACCORD WAGON *(1995)*

CODE	DESCRIPTION	INVOICE	MSRP
CE172S	LX 4-Dr Wagon (5-spd)	16533	18710
CE182S	LX 4-Dr Wagon (auto)	17195	19460
CE189S	EX 4-Dr Wagon (auto)	19520	22090
Destination Charge:		380	380

Standard Equipment

ACCORD WAGON - LX: 2.2 liter 130 HP 16-valve engine with second-order balance system, aluminum alloy cylinder head and block with cast iron liners, electronic ignition, multi-point programmed fuel injection, dual air bags (SRS), effort-sensitive power rack and pinion steering, 5-speed manual transmission, power assisted front disc/rear drum brakes, full wheel covers, rear fender-mounted power antenna, rear window wiper/washer, body color dual power mirrors, bodyside molding, multi-reflector halogen headlights, impact absorbing body color bumpers, full-size spare tire, air conditioning, power windows, power door locks with tailgate lock, AM/FM high-power stereo cassette (4 x 12.5-watt), cruise control, center console armrest with storage compartment, front 3-point seatbelts with adjustable shoulder anchors, rear 3-point seatbelts with center lap belt, adjustable steering column, split 60/40 fold-down rear seatback, quartz digital clock, beverage holder, dual illuminated vanity mirrors, tailgate-open warning light, remote fuel filler door release, rear window defroster with timer, 2-speed intermittent windshield wipers, rear seat heater ducts, low-fuel warning light, maintenance interval indicator, cargo cover, cargo area storage compartments.

EX (in addition to or instead of LX equipment): 145 HP VTEC engine, electronically controlled 4-speed automatic transmission with lockup torque converter and grade logic programming, anti-lock brakes (ABS), power assisted 4-wheel disc brakes, 15" alloy wheels, power moonroof, body color bodyside molding, driver's seat with power height adjustment and adjustable lumbar support, AM/FM high-power stereo cassette with 6 speakers and anti-theft feature (4 x 20-watt), fold-down rear seat center armrest, remote entry system.

Accessories

NOTE: Honda accessories are dealer installed. Contact a Honda dealer for accessory availability.

See the Automobile Dealer Directory on page 448 for a Dealer near you!

HONDA

CIVIC COUPE *(1995)*

CODE	DESCRIPTION	INVOICE	MSRP
EJ212S	DX 2-Dr Coupe (5-spd)	10399	11590
EJ222S	DX 2-Dr Coupe (auto)	11277	12570
EJ112S	EX 2-Dr Coupe (5-spd)	12588	14030
EJ113S	EX 2-Dr Coupe w/ABS (5-spd)	13351	14880
EJ122S	EX 2-Dr Coupe (auto)	13261	14780
EJ123S	EX 2-Dr Coupe w/ABS (auto)	14024	15630
Destination Charge:		380	380

Standard Equipment

CIVIC COUPE - DX: 1.5 liter 102 HP 16-valve SOHC engine, aluminum alloy cylinder head and block with cast iron cylinder liners, multi-point programmed fuel injection (PGM-FI), electronic ignition, 5-speed manual transmission, power assisted front disc/rear drum brakes, dual air bags (SRS), chin spoiler, impact-absorbing body color bumpers, bodyside molding, dual manual remote operated mirrors, tinted glass, adjustable steering column, beverage holder, 2-speed intermittent windshield wipers, front 3-point seat belts, rear 3-point seat belts with center lap belt, reclining front seatbacks, fold-down rear seatbacks with lock, remote fuel filler door release, remote trunk release with lock, trunk-open warning light, rear window defroster with timer, coin box.

EX (in addition to or instead of DX equipment): 1.6 liter 125 HP 16-valve SOHC VTEC engine, power assisted rack and pinion steering, power moonroof with tilt feature, body color dual power mirrors, full wheel covers, AM/FM high-power stereo cassette with 6 speakers, power windows, power door locks, cruise control, quartz digital clock, tachometer, cargo area light, passenger vanity mirror.

Accessories

NOTE: Honda accessories are dealer installed. Contact a Honda dealer for accessory availability.

CODE	DESCRIPTION	INVOICE	MSRP

CIVIC HATCHBACK *(1995)*

CODE	DESCRIPTION	INVOICE	MSRP
EH235S	CX 3-Dr Hatchback (5-spd)	9146	9750
EH236S	DX 3-Dr Hatchback (5-spd)	9959	11100
EH246S	DX 3-Dr Hatchback (auto)	10839	12080
EH237S	VX 3-Dr Hatchback (5-spd)	10587	11800
EH338S	Si 3-Dr Hatchback (5-spd)	12148	13540
Destination Charge:		380	380

Standard Equipment

CIVIC HATCHBACK - CX: 1.5 liter 70 HP 8-valve SOHC engine, aluminum alloy cylinder head and block with cast iron cylinder liners, multi-point programmed fuel injection (PGM-FI), electronic ignition, 5-speed manual transmission, power assisted front disc/rear drum brakes, dual air bags (SRS), impact-absorbing body color bumpers, two-piece hatch, dual manual remote operated mirrors, near-flush windshield and side windows, tinted glass, beverage holder, 3-point seat belts at all outboard seating positions, reclining front seatbacks, 50/50 split fold-down rear seatback, remote hatch and fuel filler door releases, hatch-open warning light, rear window defroster with timer, coin box, variable-diameter tubular door reinforcing beams.

DX (in addition to or instead of CX equipment): 1.5 liter 102 HP 16-valve SOHC engine, rear window wiper/washer, bodyside molding, adjustable steering column, cargo cover, 2-speed intermittent windshield wipers, rear magazine pocket.

VX (in addition to or instead of DX equipment): 1.5 liter 92 HP 16-valve SOHC VTEC-E engine, chin spoiler, bodyside molding deleted, lightweight alloy wheels, tachometer, adjustable steering column deleted, cargo cover deleted, 2-speed intermittent windshield wipers deleted, rear magazine pocket deleted, rear window wiper/washer deleted.

Si (in addition to or instead of VX equipment): 1.6 liter 125 HP 16-valve SOHC VTEC engine, power assisted rack and pinion steering, power assisted 4-wheel disc brakes, power moonroof with tilt feature, rear window wiper/washer, chin spoiler deleted, bodyside molding, body color dual power mirrors, full wheel covers, lightweight alloy wheels deleted, cruise control, quartz digital clock, adjustable steering column, cargo cover, 2-speed intermittent windshield wipers, cargo area light, passenger's vanity mirror, driver's footrest, rear magazine pocket.

Accessories

NOTE: Honda accessories are dealer installed. Contact a Honda dealer for accessory availability.

CIVIC SEDAN *(1995)*

CODE	DESCRIPTION	INVOICE	MSRP
EG854S	DX 4-Dr Sedan (5-spd)	10749	11980
EG864S	DX 4-Dr Sedan (auto)	11422	12730
EG855S	LX 4-Dr Sedan (5-spd)	11950	13320
EG865S	LX 4-Dr Sedan (auto)	12623	14070
EG856S	LX 4-Dr Sedan w/ABS (5-spd)	12713	14170
EG866S	LX 4-Dr Sedan w/ABS (auto)	13386	14920
EH959S	EX 4-Dr Sedan (5-spd)	14535	16200
EH969S	EX 4-Dr Sedan (auto)	15208	16950
Destination Charge:		380	380

Standard Equipment

CIVIC SEDAN - DX: 1.5 liter 102 HP 16-valve SOHC engine, aluminum alloy cylinder head and block with cast iron cylinder liners, multi-point programmed fuel injection (PGM-FI), electronic ignition, 5-speed manual transmission, power assisted rack and pinion steering, power assisted front disc/ rear drum brakes, dual air bags (SRS), impact-absorbing body color bumpers, bodyside molding, dual manual remote operated mirrors, tinted glass, adjustable steering column, beverage holder, 2-speed intermittent windshield wipers, 3-point seat belts (front and rear), reclining front seatbacks, adjustable front seat belt anchors, fold-down rear seatback with lock, remote trunk and fuel filler door releases, trunk-open warning light, rear window defroster with timer, child-safety seat anchors, coin box, child-proof rear door locks, driver's footrest, lined trunk with under-floor storage compartment.

CODE	DESCRIPTION	INVOICE	MSRP

LX (in addition to or instead of DX equipment): Dual power mirrors, full wheel covers, AM/FM high-power stereo cassette, power windows, power door locks, cruise control, quartz digital clock, tachometer, center console armrest with storage compartment, cargo area light, passenger's vanity mirror, rear magazine pocket.

EX (in addition to or instead of LX equipment): 1.6 liter 125 HP 16-valve SOHC VTEC engine, power assisted 4-wheel disc brakes, anti-lock braking system (ABS), power moonroof with tilt feature, body color dual power mirrors, air conditioning.

Accessories

NOTE: Honda accessories are dealer installed. Contact a Honda dealer for accessory availability.

CIVIC DEL SOL *(1995)*

CODE	DESCRIPTION	INVOICE	MSRP
EG114S	S 2-Dr Coupe (5-spd)	13261	14780
EG124S	S 2-Dr Coupe (auto)	14140	15760
EH616S	Si 2-Dr Coupe (5-spd)	15208	16950
EH626S	Si 2-Dr Coupe (auto)	15880	17700
EG217S	VTEC 2-Dr Coupe (5-spd)	17226	19200
Destination Charge:		380	380

Standard Equipment

DEL SOL - S: 1.5 liter 102 HP 16-valve SOHC engine, aluminum alloy cylinder head and block with cast iron cylinder liners, multi-point programmed fuel injection (PGM-FI), electronic ignition, 5-speed manual transmission, power assisted ventilated front disc/rear drum brakes, dual air bags (SRS), impact-absorbing body color bumpers, body color dual manual mirrors, removable roof panel, quartz halogen headlights, center armrest with storage compartment and beverage holder, centrally locking rear storage compartments, driver's footrest, fully carpeted floor/trunk, sun visors with vanity mirror on passenger side, remote fuel filler door release, remote trunk release with lock, power side windows, power rear window, 3-point seat belts, reclining seatbacks, trunk-open warning light, cigarette lighter and front ashtray, rear speakers, rear window defroster with timer, 2-speed intermittent windshield wipers with washer, adjustable steering column, tachometer, automatic transmission mode indicator, quartz digital clock, interior light, cargo area light.

Si (in addition to or instead of S equipment): 1.6 liter 125 HP 16-valve SOHC VTEC engine, power assisted rack and pinion steering, power assisted 4-wheel disc brakes, alloy wheels, body color dual power mirrors, 4 x 20-watt AM/FM high-power stereo cassette, power door locks, cruise control.

VTEC (in addition to or instead of Si equipment): 1.6 liter 160 HP 16-valve DOHC VTEC engine, anti-lock braking system (ABS), automatic transmission mode indicator deleted.

Accessories

NOTE: Honda accessories are dealer installed. Contact a Honda dealer for accessory availability.

PRELUDE *(1995)*

CODE	DESCRIPTION	INVOICE	MSRP
BA814S	S 2-Dr Coupe (5-spd)	16950	19550
BA824S	S 2-Dr Coupe (auto)	17600	20300
BB215S	Si 2-Dr Coupe (5-spd)	19247	22200
BB225S	Si 2-Dr Coupe (auto)	19898	22950
BB117S	VTEC 2-Dr Coupe (5-spd)	21978	25350
Destination Charge:		380	380

Standard Equipment

PRELUDE - S: 2.2 liter 135 hp 16-valve SOHC engine with multi-point programmed fuel injection, dual air bags, variable assist power rack and pinion steering, 5-speed manual transmission, power assisted 4-wheel disc brakes, power sunroof with tilt feature, rear fender-mounted power antenna, body color dual power mirrors, halogen headlights, impact-absorbing body color bumpers, dual outlet exhaust, air conditioning, center console armrest with storage compartment, power windows, cruise control, digital clock, tachometer, adjustable steering column, 2-speed intermittent windshield wipers, reclining front seatbacks, right-side fold-down rear seatback with lock, remote trunk and fuel filler door releases, rear window defroster with timer, cargo area light, child safety seat anchors, dual vanity mirrors, beverage holder, AM/FM high-power stereo cassette.

Si (in addition to or instead of S equipment): 2.3 liter 160 hp 16-valve DOHC engine with multi-point programmed fuel injection, electronic ignition with knock sensor, dual-stage induction system, alloy wheels, anti-lock braking system, chin spoiler, driver's seat adjustable lumbar support, ignition switch light, power door locks, 6 speakers.

VTEC (in addition to or instead of Si equipment): 2.2 liter 190 hp 16-valve DOHC VTEC engine with multi-point programmed fuel injection, rear spoiler with integral LED stop light, leather-trimmed seats and door panel inserts, leather-wrapped steering wheel, map lights.

Accessories

NOTE: Honda accessories are dealer installed. Contact a Honda dealer for accessory availability.

What's New for *Honda* in 1995?

Accord: New wheelcover styling and an optional V6 engine are the major changes to this best-selling family sedan.

Civic: Paradise Blue Green, Torino Red and Horizon Gray replace Aztec Green and Camellia Red on the color chart.

Civic del Sol: New alloy wheels and standard power door locks on the Si and VTEC, while new colors are available across the line. The VTEC gets ABS as standard, while all models get remote trunk releases.

Prelude: Base models get air conditioning standard. Four-wheel steering has been dropped from the options list.

CODE	DESCRIPTION	INVOICE	MSRP

ACCENT *(1995)*

CODE	DESCRIPTION	INVOICE	MSRP
12393A	L 3-Dr Hatchback (5-spd)	7540	8079
12303A	3-Dr Hatchback (5-spd)	7891	8455
12302A	3-Dr Hatchback (auto)	8546	9185
12403A	4-Dr Sedan (5-spd)	8380	8979
12402A	4-Dr Sedan (auto)	9035	9709
Destination Charge:		405	405

Standard Equipment

ACCENT - L HATCHBACK: Front assist grips, detachable cargo area cover, carpeting, console with cup holder, side window defoggers, electric rear window defroster, full door trim with armrests, front door map pockets, temperature and trip odometer gauges, glove box, overhead courtesy illumination, cargo area illumination, day/night rearview mirrors, front passenger visor vanity mirror, remote fuel door release, remote hood release, front 3-point seat belts with height adjustment, rear seatbelts, full-face seat trim with bolster, front reclining bucket seats with adjustable headrests, passenger side walk-in device, full-folding rear bench seat, 4-spoke soft-grip steering wheel with air bag, warning lights include: oil pressure/parking brake/brake fluid level/door ajar/battery discharge/ low fuel/hatch open/trunk open; rear swiveling windows, single piece bodyside panel, front ventilated power assisted disc brakes, rear self-adjusting drum brakes, transverse-mounted front wheel drive, electronic multi-port fuel injection (MPI), front and rear stabilizer bars, rack and pinion steering, front independent MacPherson strut suspension, rear fully independent multi-link suspension, 5-speed manual overdrive transmission, fixed mast antenna, 5-mph energy absorbing body color bumpers, aerodynamic halogen headlamps, dual remote control mirrors, back panel moldings, P155/80R13 SBR tires with styled steel wheels and center caps, intermittent wipers/washers.

ACCENT HATCHBACK (in addition to or instead of L HATCHBACK equipment): Digital quartz clock, remote trunk/hatch releases, bodyside moldings, P175/70R13 SBR tires with deluxe full wheel covers.

ACCENT SEDAN (in addition to or instead of ACCENT HATCHBACK equipment): Rear assist grip, detachable cargo area cover deleted, rear child safety door locks, passenger side walk-in device deleted, full-folding rear bench seat deleted, rear roll-down windows, body color back panel moldings.

CODE	DESCRIPTION	INVOICE	MSRP

Accessories

02/AB	**Option Pkg 2** — L *incls air conditioning, tinted glass and AM/FM stereo radio*	991	1190
03/AC	**Option Pkg 3** — NA on L *incls tinted glass, AM/FM stereo radio and power steering*	461	555
04/AD	**Option Pkg 4** — NA on L *incls option pkg 3 plus air conditioning*	1223	1450
05/AE	**Option Pkg 5** — NA on L *incls air conditioning, tinted glass, AM/FM stereo radio with cassette, power steering and sunroof*	1601	1920
06/AF	**Option Pkg 6** — NA on L *incls option pkg 5 plus anti-lock brakes*	2198	2570
07/AG	**Option Pkg 7** — NA on L *incls AM/FM stereo radio with cassette, tinted glass and power steering*	553	675
08/AH	**Option Pkg 8** — NA on L *incls option pkg 7 plus air conditioning*	1315	1570
CF	**Floor Mats** — carpeted	38	58

ELANTRA *(1995)*

40423A	Base 4-Dr Sedan (5-spd)	9207	10199
40422A	Base 4-Dr Sedan (auto)	10376	11499
40443A	GLS 4-Dr Sedan (5-spd)	10234	11599
40442A	GLS 4-Dr Sedan (auto)	10885	12324
Destination Charge:		405	405

Standard Equipment

ELANTRA: Front illuminated/dual rear ashtrays, front and rear assist grips, cargo area floor carpeting, cut-pile carpeting, illuminated cigarette lighter, rotary-type climate controls, digital quartz clock, coin

HYUNDAI

box, full center console with storage box, dual cup holders, front side window defoggers, electric rear window defroster, rear child safety door locks, full door trim with cloth inserts, temperature/trip odometer gauges, lockable glove box, rear seat heater ducts, cargo area light, overhead courtesy light, passenger visor vanity mirror, remote fuel door and hood releases, remote trunk release, color-keyed seat belts, full face cloth seat trim, front reclining bucket seats with adjustable headrests, color-keyed 4-spoke steering wheel with air bag, collapsible steering column, warning lights for: door ajar/trunk open/low fuel, maintenance-free battery, unitized body construction, front ventilated power assisted disc brakes, self-adjusting rear drum brakes, 1.6 liter DOHC 16-valve 4 cylinder dual balance shaft engine (manual trans), 1.8 liter DOHC 16-valve 4-cylinder dual balance shaft engine (auto trans), front wheel drive, electronic multi-point fuel injection (MPI), front and rear stabilizer bars, power rack and pinion steering, front independent MacPherson strut suspension, rear multi-link axle suspension, 5-speed manual overdrive transmission, fixed mast antenna, body color bumpers with charcoal accent, body color door handles, tinted glass, windshield sunshade band, body color grille, aerodynamic halogen headlamps, dual remote control black mirrors, body color bodyside molding with black accent, P175/65R14 SBR tires with full wheel covers, front variable intermittent wipers.

GLS (in addition to or instead of ELANTRA equipment): AM/FM ETR 40-watt stereo cassette audio system with 4 speakers, cargo area side trim carpeting, deluxe cut-pile carpeting, full center console with covered storage box, power door locks, carpeted door kick panels, front door courtesy lamps, front door map pockets, tachometer gauge, front map lights, deluxe full cloth seat trim, driver's 6-way adjustable seat, 60/40 split fold-down rear seat, tilt steering wheel, power windows, 1.8 liter DOHC 16-valve 4 cylinder dual balance shaft engine, gas pressure shock absorbers, body color bumpers with bright accent, dual power remote control body color mirrors, body color bodyside moldings with bright accent, bright side window accents, body color rocker panel molding, bright trim tailpipe, P185/60HR14 SBR tires with deluxe full wheel covers.

Accessories

CODE	DESCRIPTION	INVOICE	MSRP
AR	**Console** — armrest	70	108
—	**Tires**		
—	P185/60HR14 (4) - GLS	STD	STD
—	P175/65R14 (4) - Base	STD	STD
MG	**Mud Guards**	47	78
CA	**California Emissions**	NC	NC
WD	**Wind Deflector** — moonroof - GLS *req's option pkg 12, 14 or 15*	30	52
—	**Engines**		
—	4 cyl 16V MFI 1.8L - Base w/auto trans, GLS	STD	STD
—	4 cyl 16V MFI 1.8L - Base w/manual trans	STD	STD
DG	**Door Edge Guards**	23	36
CD	**Radio Equipment** — compact disc *req's option pkg 14 or 15*	290	395
CF	**Floor Mats** — carpeted	38	58
02/AB	**Option Pkg 2** — Base *incls AM/FM stereo with cassette*	268	350
03/AC	**Option Pkg 3** — Base *incls option pkg 2 plus air conditioning*	998	1245
04/AD	**Option Pkg 4** — Base *incls option pkg 3 plus speed control*	1178	1465
10/AJ	**Option Pkg 10** — GLS *incls air conditioning, speed control, AM/FM stereo with cassette*	1053	1303

CODE	DESCRIPTION	INVOICE	MSRP
11/AK	**Option Pkg 11** — GLS *incls option pkg 10 plus aluminum alloy wheels*	1330	1643
12/AL	**Option Pkg 12** — GLS *incls option pkg 10 plus power sliding glass moonroof*	1469	1813
13/AM	**Option Pkg 13** — GLS *incls option pkg 10 plus anti-lock braking system*	1764	2078
14/AN	**Option Pkg 14** — GLS *incls option pkg 15 plus anti-lock braking system*	2605	3120
15/AO	**Option Pkg 15** — GLS *incls option pkg 11 plus power sliding glass moonroof, AM/FM stereo with cassette*	1894	2345

SCOUPE *(1995)*

CODE	DESCRIPTION	INVOICE	MSRP
30223A	Base 2-Dr Coupe (5-spd)	9022	9995
30222A	Base 2-Dr Coupe (auto)	9635	10670
30243A	LS 2-Dr Coupe (5-spd)	10089	11435
30242A	LS 2-Dr Coupe (auto)	10702	12110
30253A	Turbo 2-Dr Coupe (5-spd)	10813	12255
Destination Charge:		405	405

Standard Equipment

SCOUPE: Front illuminated ashtray, front assist grip, cargo area floor carpeting, cut-pile carpeting, illuminated cigarette lighter, rotary-type climate controls, digital quartz clock, full console with coin holder, front side window defoggers, electric rear window defroster, front door map pockets, full door trim with cloth inserts, tachometer gauge, temperature and trip odometer gauges, illuminated lockable glove box, rear seat heater ducts, cargo area light, overhead courtesy light, front map lights, day/night mirrors, front passenger visor vanity mirror, remote fuel door and hood release, remote trunk release, color-keyed seat belts, full face deluxe cloth seat trim, front reclining bucket seats with adjustable headrests, passenger side walk-in device, 60/40 split fold-down rear seat, color-keyed 3-spoke steering wheel, collapsible steering column, warning lights for: door ajar/trunk ajar/low fuel,

CODE	DESCRIPTION	INVOICE	MSRP

maintenance-free battery, unitized body construction, front ventilated power assisted disc brakes, self-adjusting rear drum brakes, 1.5 liter SOHC 4 cylinder engine, transverse mounted layout front wheel drive, electronic multi-port fuel injection (MPI), front and rear stabilizer bars, rack and pinion steering, front independent MacPherson strut suspension, rear independent trailing arm suspension, 5-speed manual overdrive transmission, manual telescopic antenna, body color bumpers, black door handles, green tinted glass, windshield sunshade band, body color air inlet grille, aerodynamic halogen headlamps, dual remote control black mirrors, black rocker panel moldings, body color bodyside moldings, rear spoiler, dual tailpipe with chrome finishers, P175/65R14 SBR tires with full wheel covers, front variable intermittent wipers.

LS (in addition to or instead of SCOUPE equipment): Deluxe AM/FM stereo cassette audio system with 4 speakers, cargo area side trim carpeting, deluxe cut-pile carpeting, dual cup holder, full sporty cloth seat trim, driver's 6-way adjustable seat, passenger's 4-way adjustable seat, soft-grip type steering wheel, tilt steering column, power windows, power rack and pinion steering, body color door handles, dual power remote control body color mirrors, body color bodyside cladding molding, Michelin P185/60HR14 performance radial tires with deluxe full wheel covers.

TURBO (in addition to or instead of LS equipment): LED turbo boost meter gauge, turbo badged full sporty cloth seat trim, leather-wrapped steering wheel with leather-wrapped gear shift knob, turbocharged 1.5 liter SOHC 4 cylinder engine, sport tuned package suspension, fog lamps, Michelin P185/60HR14 performance radial tires with aluminum alloy wheels.

Accessories

CODE	DESCRIPTION	INVOICE	MSRP
—	**Floor Mats**		
CF	carpeted	38	58
TM	deluxe - LS, Turbo	45	70
CA	**California Emissions**	NC	NC
—	**Tires**		
—	P175/65R14 (4) - Base *NA LS or Turbo*	STD	STD
—	P185/60HR14 (4) - LS, Turbo *NA Base*	STD	STD
CD	**Radio Equipment** — compact disc	290	395
AR	**Console** — armrest	64	105
SH	**Sun Shade**	38	58
—	**Engines**		
—	4 cyl turbo 1.5L - Turbo	STD	STD
—	4 cyl MFI 1.5L - Base, LS	STD	STD
02/AB	**Option Pkg 2** — Base *incls AM/FM stereo with cassette, power steering*	496	610
03/AC	**Option Pkg 3** — Base *incls option pkg 2 plus air conditioning*	1235	1505
06/AF	**Option Pkg 6** — Base *incls option pkg 3 plus glass flip-up sunroof*	1479	1800
10/AJ	**Option Pkg 10** — LS *incls air conditioning*	739	895
11/AK	**Option Pkg 11** — LS *incls option pkg 10 plus glass flip-up sunroof*	983	1190
12/AL	**Option Pkg 12** — LS *incls option pkg 11 plus AM/FM stereo with cassette, alloy wheels*	1405	1715

CODE	DESCRIPTION	INVOICE	MSRP
15/A0	**Option Pkg 15** — Turbo *incls AM/FM stereo with cassette, air conditioning, glass flip-up sunroof*	1132	1385

SONATA *(1995)*

CODE	DESCRIPTION	INVOICE	MSRP
22403B	Base 4-Dr Sedan (5-spd)	12027	13399
22402B	Base 4-Dr Sedan (auto)	12820	14209
22422B	GL 4-Dr Sedan (auto)	13248	14929
22432B	GL V6 4-Dr Sedan (auto)	14016	15919
22452B	GLS V6 4-Dr Sedan (auto)	15085	17399
Destination Charge:		405	405

Standard Equipment

SONATA: Non-CFC air conditioning, front illuminated/single rear ashtrays, front and rear assist grips, AM/FM ETR stereo cassette with 4 speakers, cargo area floor carpeting, cut-pile carpeting, illuminated cigarette lighter, rotary climate controls, digital quartz clock, full center console with coin holder and storage box, dual cup holder, front side window defoggers, electric rear window defroster with timer, rear child safety door locks, front door map pockets, full door trim with cloth inserts, gauges for: tachometer/water temperature/trip odometer, illuminated lockable glove box, rear seat heater ducts, illuminated cargo area, delay-out illumination with illuminated ignition, overhead courtesy lights, dual visor vanity mirrors, remote fuel door and hood releases, remote trunk release with lock-out feature, dual air bags, color-keyed seat belts, two front passive motorized type seat belts, full cloth seat trim, driver's 4-way adjustable seat, front reclining bucket seats, rear integral headrests, color-keyed 4-spoke soft-grip steering wheel with air bag and tilt feature, warning lights for: door ajar/ trunk ajar/low fuel, full roll-down rear windows, maintenance-free battery, unitized body construction, front ventilated power assisted disc brakes, self-adjusting rear drum brakes, 2.0 liter DOHC 16-valve 4 cylinder dual balance shaft engine, front wheel drive, electronic multi-port (MPI) fuel injection, front and rear stabilizer bars, power rack and pinion steering, front independent MacPherson strut suspension, fully independent multi-link rear suspension, 5-speed manual overdrive transmission, fixed mast antenna, body color bumpers with body color inserts, body color door handles, tinted glass, body color grille, aerodynamic halogen headlamps, dual remote control black mirrors, body color bodyside moldings, bright side window accent moldings, black front/rear window moldings, P195/70R14 SBR tires with full wheel covers, front variable intermittent wipers.

CODE	DESCRIPTION	INVOICE	MSRP

GL (in addition to or instead of SONATA equipment): Power door locks, power windows, 4-speed electronically controlled automatic overdrive transmission with lock-up torque converter and dual mode selector, adaptive control (V6), dual power remote control black mirrors, P195/70R14 SBR tires with deluxe full wheel covers.

GLS (in addition to or instead of GL equipment): Deluxe AM/FM ETR stereo cassette with 6 speakers, cargo area side trim, deluxe cut-pile carpeting, push button climate controls, full center console with armrest box cover and cassette tape holder, carpeted door kick panels, front door courtesy lamps, front map lamps, front passenger visor vanity mirror, cruise control, power telescopic antenna, deluxe full cloth seat trim, driver's 6-way adjustable seat, 60/40 split fold-down seat with center armrest, front seatback storage pockets, 4-wheel power assisted disc brakes, 3.0 liter SOHC V6 engine, adaptive control transmission, power telescopic antenna, windshield sunshade band, body color grille with bright accent, dual power remote control body color mirrors, bright front/rear window moldings, P205/60HR15 high performance radial tires with aluminum alloy wheels.

Accessories

CODE	DESCRIPTION	INVOICE	MSRP
AR	**Console** — armrest	84	135
—	**Tires**		
—	P205/60HR15 high performance (4) - GLS	NC	NC
—	P195/70R14 BSW (4) - Base, GL	NC	NC
CA	**California Emissions**	154	154
MG	**Mud Guards**	43	75
—	**Engines**		
—	V6 MFI 3.0L - GL V6, GLS	STD	STD
—	4 cyl 16V MFI 2.0L - Base, GL 4 cyl	STD	STD
WD	**Wind Deflector** — sunroof - GL, GLS *req's option pkg 6 on GL; req's option pkg 10, 13, 14 or 15 on GLS*	32	55
CF	**Floor Mats** — carpeted	42	72
05/AE	**Option Pkg 5** — GL *incls speed control*	188	230
06/AF	**Option Pkg 6** — GL *incls option pkg 5 plus sunroof*	678	830
08/AH	**Option Pkg 8** — GL V6 *incls option pkg 5 plus anti-lock braking system*	1014	1110
10/AJ	**Option Pkg 10** — GLS *incls sunroof*	490	600
11/AK	**Option Pkg 11** — GLS *incls AM/FM stereo with cassette and CD, leather pkg (incls leather seat trim, simulated leather door trim panels, leather-wrapped steering wheel)*	1214	1400
13/AM	**Option Pkg 13** — GLS *incls option pkg 10 and option pkg 11 plus anti-lock braking system*	2530	2880
14/AN	**Option Pkg 14** — GLS *incls option pkg 10 and option pkg 11*	1704	2000
15/AO	**Option Pkg 15** — GLS *incls option pkg 10 plus AM/FM stereo with cassette and CD*	1102	1350

HYUNDAI

CODE	DESCRIPTION	INVOICE	MSRP

G20 *(1995)*

92055	4-Dr Sedan (5-spd)	19215	22875
92015	4-Dr Sedan (auto)	20055	23875
Destination Charge:		450	450

Standard Equipment

G20: Power heated outside mirrors, tinted glass, 3-coat/3-bake paint with clearcoat, halogen headlights, body color bumpers/moldings, bright grille and door handle accents, contoured front bucket seats, driver's seat lumbar support and seat height adjustment, leather-wrapped steering wheel and shift knob, carpeted floor mats, non-CFC R134a air conditioning, cruise control, tilt steering column, driver's and passenger's windows with one-touch down, power door locks, power trunk release, power fuel filler door release, rear window defroster with timer, driver and passenger front seatback pockets, illuminated driver and passenger vanity mirrors, fade-out interior lamp, cargo net in trunk, driver and passenger side air bags, driver and passenger side seatbelt pre-tensioners, height adjustable rear seat head restraints, child safety rear door locks, energy-absorbing front/rear bumpers, protective side door guard beams, anti-theft system, 6-speaker premium audio system with 2 A-pillar mounted tweeters, 160-watt amplifier, in-dash CD player, automatic power antenna and diversity antenna system, electronic speedometer, analog tachometer, coolant temperature and fuel gauges, trip odometer, digital quartz clock, anti-lock brakes.

Accessories

J01	**Power Sunroof** — glass	840	1000
V01	**Touring Pkg** *incls leather appointment pkg, limited slip differential axle, fog lights, power sport bucket seats with split fold-down rear seat, rear spoiler*	2604	3100
V01	**Leather Appointment Pkg** *incls leather appointed interior, leather console and armrest, power sunroof, power sport bucket seats, keyless remote entry system*	1932	2300

J30 *(1995)*

Code	Description	Invoice	MSRP
97015	4-Dr Sedan	31997	38550
	Destination Charge:	450	450

Standard Equipment

J30: 3.0 liter EFI V6 engine, 4-speed ECT automatic transmission, power 4-wheel disc brakes with anti-lock braking system, speed-sensitive power steering, dual air bags, leather seating, power windows, tinted glass, power sunroof, cruise control, clock, front and rear stabilizer bars, anti-theft alarm system, limited slip differential, tachometer, automatic air conditioning, trip odometer, cast aluminum alloy wheels, radio (AM/FM ETR stereo with Dolby, cassette, compact disc, 6 Bose speakers), rear seat center armrest, dual 8-way power front bucket seats (heated), center console, keyless remote entry, dual power OS mirrors, automatic dimming day/night rearview mirror, tilt steering column, power trunk/fuel filler door releases, power door locks, cargo convenience net, leather-wrapped steering wheel, P215/60HR15 SBR all-season tires, floor mats.

Accessories

Code	Description	Invoice	MSRP
R01	**Touring Pkg** *incls rear spoiler, performance alloy wheels, revised stabilizer bar diameters, recalibrated springs*	1660	2000

See the Automobile Dealer Directory on page 448 for a Dealer near you!

CODE	DESCRIPTION	INVOICE	MSRP

Q45 *(1995)*

CODE	DESCRIPTION	INVOICE	MSRP
94215	Q45 4-Dr Sedan (auto)	43672	52400
94615	Q45a 4-Dr Sedan w/Full Active Suspension (auto)	49639	59350
Destination Charge:		450	450
Gas guzzler tax:			
	Q45	1000	1000
	Q45a	2100	2100

Standard Equipment

Q45: 4.5 liter V8 4-cam 32-valve engine, 4-speed automatic transmission, power steering, power 4-wheel disc brakes with ABS, power sunroof, power heated outside mirrors, tinted glass, 3-coat/3-bake paint with clearcoat, halogen headlights, 10-way driver/8-way passenger power seats, driver's entry/exit system with two-position memory, leather seating surfaces/head restraints, leather-wrapped steering wheel and shift knob, front center console with storage compartment, rear center armrest, illuminated trunk, carpeted floor mats, wood appointments, automatic temperature control air conditioning with non-CFC R134a refrigerant, cruise control, tilt and telescoping steering column, power windows with one-touch down driver's window, power door locks, power trunk release, power fuel filler door release, rear window defroster with timer, illuminated entry/exit system with time delay fade-out, automatic anti-glare rearview mirror, cargo net in trunk, driver/passenger side air bags, 3-point front seatbelts with pre-tensioners, 3-point rear outboard seatbelts with 2-point center belt (A/ELR belts for outboard passengers), front/rear head restraints, child safety rear door locks, energy-absorbing body color front/rear bumpers, protective side door guard beams, anti-theft system, pick-resistant door lock cylinders, 12-cut key design, keyless remote entry system (electronic key), 5-mph energy-absorbing front/rear bumpers, 6-speaker Bose audio system with 4 amplifiers and 2 A-pillar tweeters, AM/FM stereo tuner with auto reverse and full logic cassette deck, automatic power antenna, diversity antenna system, pre-wiring for Infiniti cellular phone and CD autochanger, in-glass cellular phone antenna, analog speedometer and tachometer, dual trip odometers, fuel level/coolant/temperature gauges, analog quartz clock, 10-point diagnostic information display system.

CODE	DESCRIPTION	INVOICE	MSRP

Q45a (in addition to or instead of Q45 equipment): Full-active suspension, performance alloy wheels, traction control, rear stabilizer bar, CD auto changer, all-season tires, heated front seats.

Accessories

CODE	DESCRIPTION	INVOICE	MSRP
B01	**Traction Control** — Q45 w/o touring pkg	1619	1950
B02	Q45 w/touring pkg *incls heated front seats*	1536	1850
R02	**Touring Pkg** — Q45 *incls performance alloy wheels, rear spoiler, heated front seats, CD auto changer, rear stabilizer bar*	2864	3450

What's New for *Infiniti* in 1995?

G20: All-season tires are now standard on the G20t, otherwise, no changes.

I30: An all-new sport sedan based on the new Nissan Maxima should arrive during 1995. Slotted between the G20 and the J30, the I30 will compete with the Lexus ES 300, BMW 3-Series and the new Acura TL-Series. Expect prices starting at $30,000.

J30: A new taillight design, power lumbar support for the driver's seat and an automatic anti-glare rearview mirror define the changes to the J30 for 1995.

Q45: The Q gets new alloy wheels on the base model.

XJ-SERIES *(1995)*

CODE	DESCRIPTION	INVOICE	MSRP
—	XJ6 4.0L 4-Dr Sedan (auto)	43615	53450
—	Vanden Plas 4.0L 4-Dr Sedan (auto)	50755	62200
—	XJR 4.0L 4-Dr Sedan (auto)	53040	65000
—	XJ12 6.0L 4-Dr Sedan (auto)	63036	77250
Destination Charge:		580	580

Standard Equipment

XJ6 4.0L SEDAN: 4-speed automatic transmission, 4-wheel disc brakes with anti-lock braking system (ABS), power assisted steering, speed-sensitive steering, tilt and telescopic manually adjustable steering wheel, body color bumpers, body color door mirrors, protective body color side molding, Connolly leather-trimmed interior, walnut trim, dual illuminated sun visors and map lights, driver and passenger air bags, height adjustable upper anchorage for front seat belts, front fog lamps, rearguard fog lamps, vehicle security system with remote entry and courtesy headlamp delay, driver-only unlock/drive-away locking feature, overhead console with sunglasses storage compartment, cellular phone pre-wire, central locking doors/trunk/fuel filler door, 2-speed intermittent windshield wipers with single wipe and heated jets, heated rear window, electrochromic rearview mirror, curb illumination door lamps, multi-adjustable power front seats with power lumbar support, power adjustable heated door mirrors, power windows, one-touch down driver's window, outside temperature indicator, trip computer, automatic climate control with CFC-free air conditioning, cruise control, premium audio system, remote trunk release, retractable cup holders, child seat safety belt locking.

VANDEN PLUS 4.0L SEDAN (in addition to or instead of XJ6 4.0L SEDAN equipment): Electrical tilt and telescopic steering wheel with auto tilt-away feature, body color door mirrors deleted, chrome bodyside moldings, premium leather interior with walnut picnic trays, inlaid burl walnut trim, wood/leather steering wheel, lambswool passenger footwell rugs, his/her remote memory activation feature, integrated 4-channel garage door/entry gate opener, 3-position driver-seat/steering/door mirror memory, electrical tilt and sliding sunroof.

XJR 4.0L SEDAN (in addition to or instead of VDP 4.0L SEDAN equipment): Limited slip differential, traction control, XJR Sport Pkg (incls 17" wheels, high performance tires, sport-tuned steering and suspension), body color door mirrors, chrome bodyside moldings deleted, premium leather interior with walnut picnic trays deleted, walnut trim deleted, stained Birds Eye Maple trim and gear shift knob, inlaid burl walnut trim deleted, lambswool passenger footwell rugs deleted, All-Weather Pkg (incls traction control and heated front seats), compact disc autochanger (6-disc capacity), Harman Kardon audiophile sound system with compact disc autochanger.

XJ12 6.0L SEDAN: 4-speed automatic transmission, traction control, 4-wheel disc brakes with anti-lock braking system (ABS), power assisted steering, speed-sensitive steering, electrical tilt and telescopic steering wheel with auto tilt-away feature, body color bumpers, protective body color side moldings, chrome bodyside moldings, Connolly leather-trimmed interior, premium interior with walnut picnic trays, autolux leather/ruched seating/walnut gearshift knob/gold hood badge, walnut trim, inlaid burl walnut trim, wood/leather steering wheel, lambswool passenger footwell rugs, dual illuminated sun visors and map lights, driver and passenger air bags, height adjustable upper anchorage for front seat belts, front fog lamps, rearguard fog lamps, vehicle security system with remote entry and courtesy headlamp delay, his/her remote memory activation feature, driver-only unlock/drive-away locking feature, overhead console with sunglasses storage compartment, integrated 4-channel garage door/entry gate opener, cellular phone pre-wire, central locking doors/trunk/fuel filler door, 2-speed intermittent wipers with single wipe and heated jets, All-Weather Pkg (incls traction control and heated front seats), heated rear window, electrochromic rearview mirror, curb illumination door lamps, multi-adjustable power front seats with power lumbar support, power adjustable heated door mirrors, 3-position driver seat/steering/door mirror memory, power windows, one-touch down driver window, outside temperature indicator, trip computer, automatic climate control with CFC-free air conditioning, cruise control, premium audio system, compact disc autochanger (6-disc capacity), Harman Kardon audiophile sound system with compact disc autochanger, remote trunk release, electrical tilt and slide sunroof, retractable cup holders, child seat safety belt locking.

Accessories

CODE	DESCRIPTION	INVOICE	MSRP
—	**California Emissions Equipment**	25	30
—	**Chrome Wheels** — XJ6, Vanden Plas, XJ12	1200	1500
—	**Chrome Hood Ornament**	160	200
—	**Compact Disc Player** — XJ6, Vanden Plas	640	800
—	**Engine Block Heater**	80	100
—	**Full Size Spare Tire**	80	100
—	**All-Weather Pkg** — XJ6, Vanden Plas *incls traction control and heated front seats*	1600	2000
—	**Paint** — non-standard color	1600	2000
—	**Premium Sound System** — XJ6, Vanden Plas *incls CD player*	1440	1800
—	**Luxury Pkg** — XJ6 *incls 3-position driver seat, steering and door mirror memory with his/her remote activation feature, electrical tilt and telescopic steering wheel with auto tilt-away feature, electrical tilt and slide sunroof, and integrated 4-channel garage door/entry gate opener*	2320	2900

CODE	DESCRIPTION	INVOICE	MSRP

XJS (1995)

CODE	DESCRIPTION	INVOICE	MSRP
—	4.0L 2-Dr Coupe (auto)	43575	53400
—	6.0L 2-Dr Coupe (auto)	59038	72350
—	4.0L 2-Dr Convertible (auto)	50225	61550
—	6.0L 2-Dr Convertible (auto)	67361	82550
Destination Charge:		580	580

Standard Equipment

XJS 4.0L COUPE: 4-speed automatic transmission, limited slip differential, 4-wheel disc brakes with anti-lock braking system (ABS), power assisted steering, manually adjustable tilt steering wheel, body color bumpers, Connolly leather-trimmed interior, walnut trim, dual illuminated sun visors and map lights, driver and passenger air bags, height adjustable upper anchorage for front seat belts, rearguard fog lamps, vehicle security system with remote entry and courtesy headlamp delay, cellular phone pre-wire, central locking doors/trunk/fuel filler door, 2-speed intermittent windshield wipers with single wipe and heated jets, heated rear window, curb illumination door lamps, multi-adjustable power front seats with power lumbar support, power adjustable heated door mirrors, 2-position memory door mirrors and driver seat, power windows, automatic climate control with CFC-free air conditioning, cruise control, premium audio system, full-size spare tire.

6.0L COUPE (in addition to or instead of 4.0L COUPE equipment): Body color door mirrors, rear decklid spoiler, autolux leather/ruched seating/walnut gearshift knob/gold hood badge, inlaid burl walnut trim, All-Weather Pkg (incls headlamp power wash, engine block heater, heated seats), trip computer, compact disc autochanger (6-disc capacity), full-size spare tire deleted.

4.0L CONVERTIBLE: 4-speed automatic transmission, limited slip differential, 4-wheel disc brakes with anti-lock braking system (ABS), power assisted steering, manually adjustable tilt steering wheel, body color bumpers, power operated lined convertible top with glass rear window, Connolly leather-trimmed interior, walnut trim, dual illuminated sun visors and map lights, driver and passenger air bags, rearguard fog lamps, vehicle security system with remote entry and courtesy headlamp delay, cellular phone pre-wire, central locking doors and trunk, 2-speed intermittent windshield wipers with single wipe and heated jets, heated rear window, curb illumination door lamps, multi-adjustable power front seats with power lumbar support, power adjustable heated door mirrors, 2-position memory door mirrors and driver seat, power windows, automatic climate control with CFC-free air conditioning, cruise control, premium audio system, full-size spare tire.

6.0L CONVERTIBLE (in addition to or instead of 4.0L CONVERTIBLE equipment): Body color door mirrors, rear decklid spoiler, autolux leather/ruched seating/walnut gearshift knob/gold hood badge, inlaid burl walnut trim, All-Weather Pkg (incls headlamp power wash, engine block heater, heated seats), trip computer, compact disc autochanger (6-disc capacity), full-size spare tire deleted.

Accessories

CODE	DESCRIPTION	INVOICE	MSRP
—	**California Emissions Equipment**	25	30
—	**Chrome Wheels**	1200	1500
—	**All-Weather Pkg** — 4.0L *incls heated front seats, power headlight washers and engine block heater*	240	300
—	**Compact Disc Player** — 4.0L	640	800
—	**Paint** — non-standard color	1600	2000
—	**Sport Suspension** — 4.0L	400	500

What's New for *Jaguar* in 1995?

XJ6: Fans of the legendary Series III take note: the new Jag sedan looks very much like it. In addition to the stylistic improvements, Jaguar owner Ford Motor Company has tackled some of the ergonomic problems inside the Jag, producing a much more satisfactory car. A supercharged XJR is available in limited numbers.

XJS: Ancient personal coupe/convertible soldiers on another year, looking every bit its age despite a recent facelift. It does get the XJ6's new engine, to tide us over until the all-new XJS arrives in 1996.

CODE	DESCRIPTION	INVOICE	MSRP

SEPHIA *(1995.5)*

CODE	DESCRIPTION	INVOICE	MSRP
11101	RS 4-Dr Sedan (5-spd)	7872	8895
11102	RS 4-Dr Sedan (auto)	8562	9670
11121	LS 4-Dr Sedan (5-spd)	8504	9695
11122	LS 4-Dr Sedan (auto)	9194	10470
11141	GS 4-Dr Sedan (5-spd)	9173	10595
11142	GS 4-Dr Sedan (auto)	9863	11370
Destination Charge:		400	400

Standard Equipment

SEPHIA - RS: 1.6 liter SOHC 16-valve 4 cylinder engine, multi-port electronic fuel injection, electronic ignition, 5-speed manual transmission, 4-wheel independent suspension, front and rear anti-roll bars, power assisted front disc/rear drum brakes, black bodyside molding, gray bumpers, black dual outside mirrors, halogen headlights, gray taillight finisher, reclining front bucket seats, cloth/vinyl seat trim, front door map pockets, split folding rear seatback, floor carpeting, passenger assist grips, theft deterrent system, low-fuel warning light, tinted glass, remote fuel filler door release, remote trunk release, front and rear crush zones, rear window defogger, front side window defoggers, day/night rearview mirrors.

LS (in addition to or instead of RS equipment): Engine speed-sensitive power rack and pinion steering, full wheel covers, body color bodyside molding, body color bumpers, body color dual remote outside mirrors, translucent rear taillight finisher, B-pillar blackout, full cloth seat trim, deluxe door trim with cloth insert, digital clock, tachometer, passenger sun visor vanity mirror, trunk light, tilt steering wheel, rear seat heater ducts, two-speed intermittent windshield wipers.

GS (in addition to or instead of LS equipment): Driver's seat with lumbar support, map lights, door courtesy light, ignition key illumination, power windows, power door locks, dual power remote outside mirrors, two-speed wipers with variable intermittent setting, AM/FM electronically tuned radio with cassette and 4 speakers.

CODE	DESCRIPTION	INVOICE	MSRP
	Accessories		
AC	**Air Conditioning**	710	870
PS	**Power Steering** — RS	220	260
CF	**Carpeted Floor Mats**	40	60
AW	**Alloy Wheels** — GS	270	340
RM	**Radio** — RS, LS *incls AM/FM stereo with cassette and 4 speakers*	230	300
RP	**Radio** — GS *incls premium AM/FM stereo with cassette and 4 speakers*	100	150

What's New for *Kia* in 1995?

Sephia: Styling tweaks, dual airbags and a new twin-cam motor should be appearing in the Sephia by the time you read this. All told, the Sephia GS, when painted in dark shades, looks thousands more expensive than it is. Mazda-based mechanicals and proven durability (Kia built the Ford Festiva for years) mean the Sephia is poised to make a dent in the subcompact class.

CODE	DESCRIPTION	INVOICE	MSRP

ES 300 *(1995)*

CODE	DESCRIPTION	INVOICE	MSRP
9000	4-Dr Sport Sedan (auto)	26145	31500
Destination Charge:		480	480

Standard Equipment

ES 300: 3.0L 188HP 4-cam 24 valve V6 engine, 4-speed electronically controlled automatic transmission with intelligence (ECT-i), vehicle-speed-sensing progressive power rack and pinion steering, front-wheel drive, 4-wheel independent MacPherson strut-type suspension, MacPherson struts, front and rear stabilizer bars, 4-wheel power-assisted ventilated disc brakes, 4-wheel anti-lock braking system (ABS), 15" aluminum alloy wheels, 205/65R15 V-rated tires, halogen double projector low-beam headlamps, halogen double projector high-beam headlamps, dual power remote-controlled and color coordinated outside mirrors with defoggers, variable intermittent full-area windshield wipers with mist control, color keyed lower bodyside cladding, remote entry system, electronic analog instrumentation, driver and front passenger airbag supplemental restraint system (SRS), 3-point safety belts (front and outboard rear), rear center lap belt, automatic locking retractor (ALR)/emergency locking retractor (ELR) safety belts for all outboard positions except driver, manual tilt steering wheel with driver side airbag, driver and front passenger power seat adjustments (seat fore/aft movement, recline, front and rear vertical height, manual headrest fore/aft, driver's seat manual lumbar support), power window with driver's side "auto-down" feature, retained accessory power for windows and optional moonroof, power door locks with driver's door two-turn unlock feature, R-134a CFC-free air conditioning system, walnut wood trim, automatic climate control, automatic on/off headlamps, rear window defogger with timer, vehicle theft-deterrent system, dual illuminated visor vanity mirrors, center sun visor, remote electronic trunk lid and fuel-filler door releases, outside temperature indicator, Lexus/Pioneer AM/FM ETR with auto-reverse cassette and 8 speakers, automatic AM/FM power mast antenna with FM diversity antenna on rear window glass, pre-wired for optional Lexus cellular telephone, tool kit, first aid kit.

Accessories

CODE	DESCRIPTION	INVOICE	MSRP
HH	**Heated Front Seats** *req's leather pkg*	320	400

CODE	DESCRIPTION	INVOICE	MSRP
DC	**Remote CD Changer**	750	1000
LA	**Leather Pkg**	1040	1300
CW	**Chrome Wheels**	880	1100
WL	**Wheel Locks**	30	50
FT	**All-Season Tires** — models w/chrome wheels	NC	NC
SR	**Power Moonroof**	720	900
LM	**Trunk Mat**	38	63
CF	**Floor Mats** — carpeted	66	110

GS 300 *(1995)*

9300	4-Dr Sedan (auto)	36188	43600
Destination Charge:		480	480

Standard Equipment

GS 300: 3.0L 220HP twin-cam 24-valve in-line 6 cylinder engine, 4-speed electronically controlled automatic transmission with intelligence (ECT-i), vehicle-speed-sensing progressive power rack and pinion steering, rear-wheel drive, 4-wheel independent double-wishbone suspension, gas pressurized shock absorbers, front and rear stabilizer bars, 4-wheel power-assisted ventilated disc brakes, 4-wheel anti-lock braking system (ABS), 16" aluminum alloy wheels, 215/60R16 V-rated tires, halogen projector low beam headlamps, halogen high beam headlamps, dual power remote controlled and color coordinated outside mirrors with defoggers, variable intermittent full-area windshield wipers with mist control, monotone lower body side cladding (except white), remote entry system, electronic analog instrumentation, driver and front passenger airbag supplemental restraint system (SRS), 3-point safety belts (front and outboard rear), rear center lap belt, "easy access" front seat belts, automatic locking retractor (ALR)/emergency locking retractor (ELR), safety belts for front and rear outboard passengers, power tilt and telescoping steering column with automatic tilt-away, driver and front passenger power seat adjustments (fore/aft movement, seatback for/aft movement, cushion height, lumbar support), power windows with driver's side "auto-down" feature, retained accessory power for windows and optional moonroof, power door locks with driver's door two-turn unlock feature, R-134a CFC-free air conditioning system, walnut wood trim, automatic climate control, automatic on/off headlamps, rear window defogger with auto-off timer, vehicle and audio theft-deterrent

CODE	DESCRIPTION	INVOICE	MSRP

systems, illuminated entry system, dual illuminated visor vanity mirrors, center sun visor, remote electric trunk lid and fuel-filler door releases, outside temperature indicator, Lexus Premium Audio System with AM/FM cassette (7 speakers including 10" bi-amplified subwoofer and 225-watts maximum power), automatic 3-position AM/FM power mast antenna and FM diversity antenna system, pre-wired for Lexus cellular telephone, tool kit, first-aid kit.

Accessories

CODE	DESCRIPTION	INVOICE	MSRP
DC	**Remote CD Changer**	750	1000
LA	**Leather Pkg**	1040	1300
WL	**Wheel Locks**	30	50
FT	**All-Season Tires**	NC	NC
SR	**Power Moonroof**	720	900
LM	**Trunk Mat**	38	63
CF	**Floor Mats** — carpeted	66	110
NK	**Nakamichi Radio** *req's leather pkg and remote CD changer*	825	1100
TN	**Traction Control** *incls heated front seats; req's all-season tires and leather pkg*	1440	1800

LS 400 *(1995)*

CODE	DESCRIPTION	INVOICE	MSRP
9100	4-Dr Sedan (auto)	41984	51200
Destination Charge:		480	480

Standard Equipment

LS 400: 4.0L 250 HP 4 cam 32 valve V8 engine, 4-speed electronically controlled automatic transmission with intelligence (ECT-i), vehicle-speed-sensing progressive-power rack and pinion steering, rear-wheel drive, 4-wheel independent double-wishbone suspension, gas filled shock absorbers, front and rear stabilizer bars, 4-wheel power-assisted ventilated disc brakes, 4-wheel anti-lock braking system (ABS), 16" aluminum alloy wheels, 225/60R16 V-rated tires, halogen projector low-beam headlamps, halogen high-beam headlamps, dual power remote controlled and color coordinated outside mirrors with defoggers, monotone lower body side cladding, remote entry system, electronic analog instrumentation, driver and front passenger airbag supplemental restraint system (SRS), 3-point safety belts (front and outboard rear), rear center lap belt, automatic locking retractor (ALR)/emergency locking retractor (ELR) safety belts for front and rear outboard passengers, power tilt and manual telescopic steering column with automatic tilt-away driver and front passenger power seat adjustments (fore/aft movement, seatback fore/aft movement, cushion height, lumbar support), power windows with driver's side "auto-down" feature, retained accessory power for windows and optional moonroof, power door locks with driver's two-turn unlock feature, R-134a CFC-free air conditioning system, walnut wood trim, automatic climate control system, automatic on/off headlamps, rear window defogger with auto-off timer, vehicle and audio theft-deterrent systems, dual illuminated visor vanity mirrors, center sun visor, remote electric trunk lid and fuel-filler door releases, outside temperature indicator, Lexus premium audio system with AM/FM cassette (7 speakers including 8" bi-amplified subwoofer and 225-watts maximum power), automatic three-position AM/FM power mast antenna and FM diversity antenna system, pre-wired for Lexus cellular telephone, tool kit, first-aid kit.

Accessories

Code	Description	Invoice	MSRP
DC	**Remote CD Changer**	750	1000
CW	**Chrome Wheels**	880	1100
FT	**All-Season Tires**	NC	NC
MO	**Lexus Memory System**	600	750
NK	**Lexus/Nakamichi Premium Audio System**	825	1100
SA	**Electronic Air Suspension w/Lexus Ride Control**	1360	1700
SR	**Power Moonroof**	800	1000
TN	**Traction Control** *incls heated front seats*	1520	1900

CODE	DESCRIPTION	INVOICE	MSRP

SC 300 *(1995)*

CODE	DESCRIPTION	INVOICE	MSRP
9201	Base 2-Dr Coupe (5-spd)	34611	41700
9200	Base 2-Dr Coupe (auto)	35358	42600
Destination Charge:		480	480

Standard Equipment

SC 300: 3.0L 225HP twin-cam 24 valve in-line 6 cylinder engine, 5-speed manual transmission, vehicle speed-sensing-progressive power rack and pinion steering, rear-wheel drive, 4-wheel independent double-wishbone suspension, gas pressurized shock absorbers, front and rear stabilizer bars, 4-wheel power-assisted ventilated disc brakes, 4-wheel anti-lock braking system (ABS), 16" aluminum alloy wheels, 215/60R16 V-rated tires (choice of Goodyear Eagle GA or Bridgestone Potenza RE88), halogen projector low-beam headlamps, independent halogen high-beam headlamps, dual power remote controlled and color coordinated outside mirrors with defoggers, variable intermittent full-area windshield wipers with mist control, remote entry system, electronic analog instrumentation, driver and front passenger airbag supplemental restraint system (SRS), 3-point front safety belts for all seating positions, front passenger-slide power walk-in seat feature for easier entry/exit of rear seat passengers, automatic locking retractor (ALR)/emergency locking retractor (ELR) safety belts for front and rear passengers, front seat belt assisting arm, standard manual tilt and telescopic steering column, driver and front passenger power seat adjustments (fore/aft movement, seatback fore/aft movement, cushion height, lumbar support), power windows with driver's side "auto-down" feature, power door locks with driver's door two-turn unlock feature, R-134a CFC-free air conditioning system, maple wood trim, automatic climate control, automatic on/off headlamps, rear window defogger with auto-off timer, vehicle theft-deterrent system, illuminated entry system, dual illuminated visor vanity mirrors, center sun visor, remote electric trunk lid and fuel-filler door releases, Lexus Premium Audio System with AM/FM cassette (7 speakers including 8" bi-amplified subwoofer and 170-watts maximum power), automatic 3-position AM/FM power mast antenna and FM diversity antenna system, pre-wired for Lexus cellular telephone, toolkit, first-aid kit, passenger side cup holder, multi-adjustable power passenger seat, coat hooks, headlights on indicator, outside temperature gauge.

CODE	DESCRIPTION	INVOICE	MSRP

Accessories

CODE	DESCRIPTION	INVOICE	MSRP
DC	**Remote 12-CD Auto Changer**	750	1000
HH	**Heated Front Seats** *req's manual transmission*	320	400
LA	**Leather Trim Pkg w/Lexus Memory System**	1440	1800
NK	**Lexus/Nakamichi Premium Audio System**	825	1100
SR	**Power Tilt & Slide Moonroof w/Sunshade**	720	900
TN	**Traction Control System (TRAC) w/Heated Front Seats** *req's automatic transmission*	1440	1800
CF	**Carpeted Floor Mats**	69	115
LM	**Carpeted Trunk Mat**	41	68
WL	**Wheel Locks**	30	50

SC 400 *(1995)*

CODE	DESCRIPTION	INVOICE	MSRP
9220	Base 2-Dr Coupe (auto)	40508	49400
Destination Charge:		480	480

Standard Equipment

SC 400: 4.0L 250HP 4 cam 32 valve V8 engine, 4-speed electronically controlled automatic transmission with intelligence (ECT-i), vehicle-speed-sensing progressive power rack and pinion steering, rear-wheel drive, 4-wheel independent sport-tuned double-wishbone suspension, gas-filled shock absorbers, front and rear stabilizer bars, 4-wheel power assisted ventilated disc brakes, 4-wheel anti-lock braking system (ABS), 16" aluminum alloy wheels, 225/55R16 V-rated tires (choice of Goodyear Eagle GSD or Bridgestone Potenza RE93), halogen projector low-beam headlamps, independent halogen high-beam headlamps, dual power remote-controlled and color coordinated outside mirrors with defoggers, variable intermittent full-area windshield wipers with mist control, remote entry system, electronic analog instrumentation, driver and front passenger airbag supplemental restraint system (SRS), 3-point safety belts for all seating positions, front passenger-side power walk-in seat feature for easier entry/exit of rear seat passengers, automatic locking retractor (ALR)/ emergency locking retractor (ELR) safety belts for front and rear passengers, front seatbelt assisting

CODE	DESCRIPTION	INVOICE	MSRP

arms, power tilt and telescopic steering column with power automatic tilt-away, driver and front passenger power seat adjustments (fore/aft movement, seatback fore/aft movement, cushion height, lumbar support), power windows with driver's side "auto-down" feature, power door locks with driver's door two-turn unlock feature, R-134a CFC-free air conditioning system, maple wood trim, automatic climate control, automatic on/off headlamps, rear window defogger with auto-off timer, vehicle theft-deterrent systems, illuminated entry system, dual-illuminated visor-vanity mirrors, center sunvisor, remote electric trunk lid and fuel-filler door releases, Lexus premium audio system with AM/FM cassette (7-speakers including 8" bi-amplified subwoofer and 170-watts maximum power), automatic 3-position AM/FM power mast antenna and FM diversity antenna system, pre-wired for Lexus cellular telephone, toolkit, first-aid kit, passenger cup holder, headlights on indicator lamp, outside temperature gauge, coat hooks.

Accessories

CODE	DESCRIPTION	INVOICE	MSRP
DC	**Remote 12-CD Auto Changer**	750	1000
NK	**Lexus/Nakamichi Premium Audio System**	825	1100
RF	**Color-Keyed Rear Spoiler**	320	400
SR	**Power Tilt & Slide Moonroof w/Sunshade**	720	900
TN	**Traction Control System (TRAC) w/Heated Front Seats**	1440	1800
CF	**Carpeted Floor Mats**	69	115
LM	**Carpeted Trunk Mat**	41	68
WL	**Wheel Locks**	30	50

See the Automobile Dealer Directory on page 448 for a Dealer near you!

What's New for *Lexus* in 1995?

ES 300: Freshened styling, chrome wheels and new colors for the little Lexus.

GS 300: No changes. Is it me, or does the front styling of the GS 300 resemble the new Mustang when you look at it after having one too many?

LS 400: Lexus' flagship sedan is thoroughly reworked for 1995. More powerful styling elements grace the new LS, though you'll be hard pressed to tell it from the car it replaces. Additional power from the 4.0L V8 and a lower curb weight mean the new LS is a blast to drive. Best luxury car over $50,000? This is it.

SC 300/SC 400: New alloy wheel designs sum up the revisions to these sport coupes.

CONTINENTAL *(1995)*

CONTINENTAL 8 CYL

CODE	DESCRIPTION	INVOICE	MSRP
M97	4-Dr Sedan	35521	40760
Destination Charge:		625	625

Standard Equipment

CONTINENTAL: 4.6 liter 32 valve DOHC modular V8 engine, 4-speed automatic transaxle with non-synchronous shift, power 4-wheel disc brakes with anti-lock, front wheel drive, concealed antenna in rear backlite window, dual exhaust with bright exposed tips, solar tinted glass, high-tech complex reflector headlamps with wraparound design, cornering lamps, body color sail-mounted heated outside rearview mirrors, body color bodyside moldings, front and rear fascia moldings, 16" painted aluminum directional wheels, 18 oz. Sussex floor carpet with driver foot rest, digital clock, overhead console (incls map/ courtesy lamps, cellular phone microphone, garage door opener and sunglasses storage), full-length floor console/armrest (incls coin holder, leather armrest and internal cup holder), walnut burlwood real wood applique, dual front seat cup holders, front and rear floor mats, right front and two rear retractable grab handles, illuminated door lighting, interior theatre dimming, fully lined luggage compartment, cargo net and luggage tie-down, day/night inside rearview mirror, seating (leather seating surfaces, memory driver seat, 6-way power driver/front passenger seats, 4-way power lumbar for front seat passengers, automatic driver's seat movement for easy entry/exit, full-length integral door armrest, fold-down rear seat armrest, 4-way adjustable headrests), leather-wrapped steering wheel, cloth covered sun visors with lighted mirrors and secondary visor, electronic automatic climate control air conditioning with sunload sensor, umbrella, air filtration system, maintenance free battery, battery saver, rear window defroster, delay accessory power (provides additional time for closing windows, moonroof and radio after ignition is turned off), diagnostics system, automatic remote fuel door release, autolamp lighting, power door locks, memory profile system (settings for steering effort, ride control, radio stations, driver seat, mirror positions, autolamp delay settings, panel lighting setting, express-down window, easy entry/exit, door lock chirp, tilt-down outside mirrors), radio (high-level audio system with AM/FM stereo/cassette with electronically tuned radio, two front door and two rear door speakers, anti-theft system in trunk), driver and front passenger air bags, 24-hour roadside assistance plan, speed control, variable assist power steering, tilt steering wheel, air suspension with automatic load leveling, driver adjustable suspension (firm, normal, plush), analog gauges with tachometer, P225/60R16 97H BSW all-season tires, mini spare tire, power windows with express-down driver window, interval windshield wipers.

CODE	DESCRIPTION	INVOICE	MSRP
	Accessories		
900A	**Preferred Equipment Pkg 900A**	NC	NC
	incls vehicle with standard equipment		
99V	**Engine** — 4.6 liter 4-cam V8	STD	STD
44X	**Transaxle** — 4-speed automatic electric overdrive	STD	STD
422	**California Emissions**	86	100
428	**High Altitude Emissions**	NC	NC
T31	**Tires** — P225/60R16 BSW	STD	STD
64B	**Wheels** — directional pattern painted aluminum	STD	STD
64C	**Wheels** — chrome double window	726	845
—	**Seats**		
6	individual seats w/leather seating surface	STD	STD
7	twin comfort seats w/leather seating surface	STD	STD
467	heated seats	250	290
61A	**Mirror** — electrochromic auto dimming inside/outside w/compass	284	330
13B	**Power Moonroof**	1302	1515
516	**Cellular Telephone** — integrated voice-activated	594	690
18A	**Anti-Theft Alarm System**	250	290
18S	**Cargo Storage System**	228	265
	incls cargo net		
553	**All-Speed Electronic Traction Control**	310	360
—	**Tri-Coat Paint**	258	300
916	**JBL Audio System**	486	565
	incls digital signal processor, coaxial front speakers, dual rear speakers, subwoofer amplifier, 2 subwoofers		
919	**Compact Disc Player/Changer**	512	595
41H	**Engine Block Immersion Heater**	52	60
153	**Front License Plate Bracket**	NC	NC

What's New for *Lincoln* in 1995?

Continental: All-new Continental gains a V8, updated styling, and an ergonomically excellent interior. Three suspension settings are available, and prices have jumped into Seville and GS 300 territory.

Mark VIII: The Mark's contoversial instrument panel is slightly altered this year, and houses a new premium sound stereo. Otherwise, the VIII remains as it did in 1994. Look for a new LSC model at year's end, and lower prices.

Town Car: Front and rear styling is revised, and a new instrument panel graces the cabin. An anti-theft system has been made standard.

MARK VIII *(1995)*

MARK VIII 8 CYL

CODE	DESCRIPTION	INVOICE	MSRP
M91	2-Dr Coupe	33793	38800
Destination Charge:		640	640

Standard Equipment

MARK VIII: 4.6 liter four-cam V8 engine with aluminum block and heads, electronically controlled 4-speed automatic overdrive transmission with 3.07 rear axle ratio (includes lock-out switch), speed-sensitive variable assist rack and pinion power steering, 4-wheel disc anti-lock brake system (ABS) with self-diagnostics, power windows with driver's one-touch down feature, power door locks, P225/60R16 97V all-season BSW tires, 16" aluminum alloy lacy-spoke wheels, electronic AM/FM stereo radio with cassette player and 4-speaker premium sound system, CFC-free electronic automatic temperature control with positive shut-off registers and outside temperature, body color front/rear bumpers with bright fascia insert, bright exposed exhaust tips, decklid lock cover, flexible bright grille, body color door handles, low-profile aerodynamic halogen headlamps, cornering lamps, back-up lamps, limousine doors, body color heated remote control outside mirrors with 3-position memory, "glass-edge" type black windshield/rear window moldings, color-keyed roof-to-quarter panel moldings, body color bodyside protection moldings with bright insert, bright/black "Mark VIII" nomenclature nameplate (in rear), red illuminated rear reflex, bright-tipped tailpipe, driver and right front passenger air bag SRS, front/rear seat cigarette lighter, full length floor console includes: padded front armrest/illuminated ashtray/cigarette lighter/color-keyed leather-wrapped gearshift/rear window defrost/dual heated mirror/cup holder/storage bin; vinyl door trim panels with door map pockets/courtesy light, color-keyed door-mounted switches for: outside mirrors/illuminated window/door locks/memory seat/lockable decklid release/fuel filler door, driver's side footrest, console-mounted leather-wrapped gearshift with overdrive lockout switch, lockable illuminated glove compartment, rear seat heat registers, 4-way adjustable front head restraints, instrument panel switches for headlamp/panel dimmer, mechanical analog instrumentation includes: 140 mph speedometer/tachometer/message center/trip computer/service interval reminder; individual leather seating with shirred leather, 6-way driver and passenger power seats with Autoglide seating system, dual power recliners and dual power lumbar control, 3-position driver memory with remote recall, leather-wrapped steering wheel with center blow horn, color-keyed switches, tilt steering wheel, dual illuminated visor vanity mirrors with

CODE	DESCRIPTION	INVOICE	MSRP

cloth-wrapped secondary visors, 120 amp alternator, automatic power antenna, anti-theft alarm system, 72 amp/hour maintenance-free battery, performance camshaft, trunk-mounted cargo net, child restraint tether anchorage, door-mounted decklid/fuel filler door release, rear window defroster, delayed accessory continued power for windows/moonroof/audio/windshield wipers/message center; dual exhaust, tubular exhaust headers, 18 gallon fuel tank, universal garage door opener, solar tinted glass, automatic on/off headlamps with delay, illuminated entry system, remote keyless entry system with driver door pad/two remote key fobs, underhood/luggage compartment lights, low oil pressure warning light, speed control with tap-up/tap-down feature and switch backlighting, front/rear stabilizer bars, microprocessor-controlled air spring suspension with vehicle level control and speed-sensitive height adjustment, independent air spring/rebound springs rear suspension, depressed park/semi-concealed interval wipers.

Accessories

CODE	DESCRIPTION	INVOICE	MSRP
800A	**Preferred Equipment Pkg 800A**	NC	NC
	incls front and rear floor mats		
99V	**Engine** — 4.6 liter 4-cam V8	STD	STD
44U	**Transmission** — automatic electronic overdrive	STD	STD
422	**California Emissions System**	86	100
428	**High Altitude Principal Use Emissions System**	NC	NC
—	**Tires**		
T23	P225/60VR16 BSW	STD	STD
T21	P225/60VR16 Goodyear BSW	NC	NC
—	**Wheels**		
64J	cast aluminum directional	44	50
64U	chrome directional	726	845
—	**Audio**		
916	JBL audio system	486	565
	incls cellular telephone pre-wire		
919	compact disc changer, trunk-mounted	700	815
	req's 916 JBL audio system		
41H	**Engine Block Immersion Heater**	52	60
13B	**Power Moonroof**	1302	1515
	std w/touring pkg		
153	**Front License Plate Bracket**	NC	NC
—	**Paint** — tri-coat, ivory pearlescent	258	300
Z	**Individual Leather Seats** — reclining bucket	STD	STD
553	**Electronic Traction Assist**	184	215
516	**Cellular Telephone** — integrated voice-activated	594	690
61A	**Mirror** — electrochromic auto dimming inside/outside	184	215
60E	**Touring Pkg**	1342	1560
	incls power moonroof and chrome directional wheels; avail in Southeast Region only		

LINCOLN

TOWN CAR *(1995)*

TOWN CAR 8 CYL

CODE	DESCRIPTION	INVOICE	MSRP
M81	Executive 4-Dr Sedan	31699	36400
M82	Signature 4-Dr Sedan	33505	38500
M83	Cartier 4-Dr Sedan	35827	41200
Destination Charge:		640	640

Standard Equipment

TOWN CAR - EXECUTIVE: 4.6 liter SOHC V8 engine, electronic automatic overdrive transmission, power steering with 3-position selectable steering effort, power 4-wheel disc anti-lock brake system (ABS), power side windows with driver express-down feature, power door locks, P215/70R15 WSW SBR tires, Y-spoke aluminum wheels, 100 MM Lux electronic AM/FM stereo radio with cassette tape player and premium sound system, CFC-free automatic temperature control air conditioning with automatic blower control and sunload sensor, color-keyed bumper with bodyside moldings, pullaway door handles, bright vertical grille, crystalline-style headlamps, dual power remote control heated mirrors (RH convex), bright windshield/rear window moldings, color-keyed bodyside moldings, vertical taillamps with bright surround molding in quarter panel, driver and right front passenger air bag SRS, dual front seat fold-down armrests, rear seat center fold-down armrest, full length door armrests with front seat storage, cut-pile floor carpeting, rear window ledge carpeting, gray luggage compartment/ decklid liner/spare tire cover carpeting, lower door carpeting, electronic alert chimes, electronic digital clock, coat hooks, ashtray-mounted cup holders, cloth door inserts with cloth or leather trim, front/ rear floor mats, lockable illuminated glove box with dampened door, roof rail assist handles, cloth covered headlining, electronic instrument cluster with message center, front and rear door courtesy lights and integral reflectors, rear compartment reading lights, dual-beam dome/map lights, instrument panel courtesy lights, luggage compartment light, front seatback map pockets, day/night inside rearview mirror, dual illuminated visor mirrors, deluxe color-keyed front safety belts with adjustable D-ring, rear lap/shoulder belts (outboard passengers), front and rear center lap belts, full length door scuff plates, cloth seat trim, twin-comfort lounge seats with 6-way power and 2-way front seat head restraints, leather-wrapped two-spoke steering wheel with center blow horn, door pull straps, dual coverage sunvisors, 130 amp alternator, dual concealed diversity antenna, anti-theft deterrent system,

CODE	DESCRIPTION	INVOICE	MSRP

72 amp/hour heavy duty battery, battery saver, brake shift interlock, coolant recovery system, remote decklid release (on door trim panel), power decklid pull-down, rear window defroster, delayed accessory power, functional drip rails, EEC-IV malfunction alert light, EEC-IV electronic engine controls, sequential multi-port electronic fuel injection (EFI), electronic voltage regulator, engine temperature gauge, dual exhaust, remote fuel filler door release (on door trim panel), 20 gallon fuel tank, gas cap tether, solar tinted glass, automatic on/off headlamps with delay, dual note horn, remote keyless entry system (includes illuminated entry system), cornering lamps, lighted switches, high-mounted rear brake light, engine compartment light, low engine oil alert light, single key for door/ignition, luxury jewel key (late availability), automatic parking brake release, power point, rear seat heat ducts, nitrogen gas-pressurized hydraulic shock absorbers, soft-textured touch zones, fingertip speed control with tap-up/tap-down feature, tilt steering wheel, long/short arm coil spring front suspension, four-bar link suspension (air springs on axle), trunk cargo net, steering column control lever interval windshield wipers and fluidic washer.

SIGNATURE (in addition to or instead of EXECUTIVE equipment): Geometric spoke aluminum wheels, upper bodyside accent paint stripe, dual storage armrests, twin comfort lounge seats with 6-way/6-way power/dual power recliners/memory/power lumbar/2-way front seat head restraints; memory mirrors and seats, programmable garage door opener, steering wheel with audio/climate controls.

CARTIER (in addition to or instead of SIGNATURE equipment): P225/60R16 16" WSW SBR tires/wheels, 16" spoke aluminum wheels, JBL audio system radio with digital signal processing, supple leather seating surfaces, twin comfort lounge seats with 6-way/6-way power/dual power recliners/memory seat/power lumbar support/4-way front seat head restraints/5-temperature heated cushion and back; compass, electrochromic mirrors, traction assist.

Accessories

CODE	DESCRIPTION	INVOICE	MSRP
—	Preferred Equipment Pkgs		
751A	**Pkg 751A** — Executive	NC	NC
	incls model with standard equipment		
755A	**Pkg 755A** — Signature	NC	NC
	incls model with standard equipment		
760A	**Pkg 760A** — Cartier	NC	NC
	incls model with standard equipment		
99W	**Engine** — 4.6 liter EFI 8 cyl	STD	STD
44U	**Transmission** — 4-speed automatic overdrive	STD	STD
422	**California Emissions System**	86	100
428	**High Altitude Principal Use Emissions System**	NC	NC
—	**Audio**		
919	compact disc changer, trunk-mounted	700	815
	req's JBL audio system		
58L	JBL audio system w/digital processing	486	565
	std on Cartier and w/touring pkg		
—	**Seats**		
J/K	cloth twin comfort lounge - Executive, Signature	STD	STD
B/D	leather seating surfaces twin comfort lounge - Executive, Signature	490	570
467	driver/passenger heated seats - Signature	250	290
	req's leather seating surfaces twin comfort lounge		
M	leather twin comfort lounge - Cartier	STD	STD
153	**Front License Plate Bracket**	NC	NC

LINCOLN

LINCOLN

CODE	DESCRIPTION	INVOICE	MSRP
—	**Tires**		
508	conventional spare tire *std w/limousine builder's pkg and livery/HD trailer towing pkg*	190	220
T3P	P215/70R15 WSW tires - Executive, Signature	STD	STD
T2A	P225/60R16 all-season WSW tires - Cartier *req's ride control pkg*	STD	STD
—	**Wheels**		
64K	Y-spoke aluminum - Executive	STD	STD
64P	Geometric spoke aluminum - Signature *NA w/limousine builder's pkg*	STD	STD
64T	16" spoke aluminum - Cartier *req's ride control pkg*	STD	STD
41H	**Engine Block Immersion Heater**	52	60
516	**Cellular Telephone** — voice activated *NA on Executive*	594	690
13B	**Power Moonroof** — Signature, Cartier *NA w/limousine builder's pkg; std w/touring pkg*	1302	1515
—	**Paint** — tri-coat, ivory pearlescent	258	300
958	**Paint** — monotone - Signature *NA on Executive or Cartier*	NC	NC
60T	**Touring Pkg** *incls power moonroof, JBL audio system, ride control pkg, electronic traction assist, electrochromic automatic dimming mirror; avail in Northeast, Southeast and Southwest Regions*	2512	2920
553	**Electronic Traction Assist**	184	215
61A	**Mirror** — Executive, Signature *incls electrochromic automatic dimming rearview and compass; std on Cartier*	284	330
663	**Ride Control Pkg** — Cartier	86	100
	Signature *incls spoke aluminum wheels, HD 3.27 traction-lok axle, auxiliary power steering oil cooler, P225/60R16 WSW tires; NA w/limousine builder's pkg or livery/HD trailer towing pkg*	258	300
418	**Limousine Builder's Pkg** — Executive *NA w/livery/HD trailer towing pkg, ride control pkg, power moonroof, electronic traction assist, geometric spoke aluminum wheels or P215/70R15 WSW tires — incls 130 amp alternator, 84 amp battery, HD 3.27 ratio traction-lok axle, HD cooling pkg, auxiliary transmission and power steering oil coolers, HD front suspension and U-joint, HD frame, HD shock absorbers, unique front stabilizer bar, P225/75R15 WSW tires*	786	915
535	**Livery/HD Trailer Towing Pkg** *NA w/limousine builder's pkg or ride control pkg — incls 130 amp alternator, auxiliary wiring harness, HD 3.27 ratio traction-lok axle, aluminum wheels (5), HD shock absorbers, upgraded front stabilizer bar, HD U-joint, conventional spare tire, HD cooling, auxiliary transmission and power steering oil coolers*	494	575

CODE	DESCRIPTION	INVOICE	MSRP

626 (1995)

CODE	DESCRIPTION	INVOICE	MSRP
—	DX 4-Dr Sedan (5-spd)	13632	14795
—	ES V6 4-Dr Sedan (5-spd)	20219	22695
—	LX 4-Dr Sedan (5-spd)	15673	17395
—	LX V6 4-Dr Sedan (5-spd)	17656	19595
Destination Charge:		440	440

Standard Equipment

626 - DX: 2.0 liter 16-valve MFI 4 cylinder engine, 5-speed manual transmission with overdrive, front wheel drive, power steering, intermittent windshield wipers, rear window defroster, power front disc/ rear drum brakes, tachometer, bodyside moldings, remote fuel filler door release, remote trunk release, mud guards, front and rear stabilizer bars, wheel covers, driver and front passenger air bags, tilt steering wheel, cloth reclining front bucket seats, split folding rear seat, console, trip odometer, P195/65R14 tires, dual remote control OS mirrors, dual visor vanity mirrors, MacPherson strut front suspension.

LX (in addition to or instead of DX equipment): Power windows, air conditioning, power 4-wheel disc brakes (V6 models only), power door locks, AM/FM stereo radio with cassette, power antenna, alloy wheels (V6 models only), speed control, 2.5 liter 24-valve MFI V6 engine (V6 models only), variable intermittent windshield wipers, dual power OS mirrors, dual visor vanity mirrors with illuminated RH, P205/55R15 high performance tires.

ES (in addition to or instead of LX equipment): 2.5 liter 24-valve MFI V6 engine, alarm system, power moonroof, anti-lock brakes, leather reclining front bucket seats with 8-way power driver's seat, split folding rear seat, leather-wrapped steering wheel, keyless remote entry system, dual heated power OS mirrors, dual illuminated visor vanity mirrors, fog lights.

CODE	DESCRIPTION	INVOICE	MSRP

Accessories

CODE	DESCRIPTION	INVOICE	MSRP
ACA	**Air Conditioning** — DX	680	850
—	**Transmission** — 5-speed manual w/overdrive	STD	STD
AT1	**Transmission** — 4-speed automatic w/overdrive	696	800
AB1	**Anti-Lock Brakes** — LX w/4 cyl engine	808	950
	LX w/V6 engine	680	800
CE1	**California/New York Emission Equipment**	126	150
FLM	**Floor Mats** — carpeted	56	80
1DX	**DX Convenience Pkg** — DX *incls air conditioning, carpeted floor mats, AM/FM stereo radio with cassette*	1276	1595
1P0	**DX Fleet Pkg** — DX *incls air conditioning and AM/FM stereo radio with cassette*	1256	1495
1LX	**Luxury Pkg** — LX w/4 cyl engine *incls power moonroof, remote control entry system, alloy wheels, carpeted floor mats, dual heated mirrors, alarm system, 6 speakers*	1276	1595
2LX	**Premium Pkg** — LX w/V6 engine *incls anti-lock brakes, power moonroof, carpeted floor mats, keyless remote control entry system, alarm system, power driver's seat adjuster, dual heated mirrors, 6 speakers, illuminated LH visor vanity mirror*	1596	1995

929 *(1995)*

CODE	DESCRIPTION	INVOICE	MSRP
—	4-Dr Sedan (auto)	30802	35795
Destination Charge:		440	440

CODE	DESCRIPTION	INVOICE	MSRP

Standard Equipment

929: 3.0 liter DOHC 24-valve V6 engine, 50-state emissions certification, 4-speed electronically controlled automatic transmission with overdrive and "hold" mode, rear-wheel drive, engine rpm-sensing variable assist power rack and pinion steering, power assist 4-wheel disc brakes, anti-lock braking system (ABS), foot-operated parking brake, 4-wheel independent multi-link suspension, front and rear stabilizer bars, dual exhaust outlets with bright finishers, automatic cruise control with "fuzzy" logic, R134a CFC-free automatic climate control system (incls automatic temperature control, automatic blower control, rear compartment heater ducts, side window demisters, sunlight sensor), AM/FM ETR stereo system with full-logic auto-reverse cassette/6 speakers/rear window mounted twin-diversity antenna/steering wheel mounted controls/anti-theft coding, anti-theft alarm system, power door locks (incls 2 action unlock feature, central locking at L/R front doors), 4-function remote keyless entry system, child-safety rear door locks, illuminated entry system with fade-out delay, side-impact door beams, 15" spoke aluminum alloy wheels, alloy wheel locks, P205/65HR15 all-season SBR tires, compact spare tire, power glass moonroof with sunshade and tilt-up ventilation feature, accent color lower bumper sections and protective lower body cladding, body color door handles, dual body color power mirrors with heated mirror glass, concealed variable intermittent windshield wipers, green-tint HPR glass with dark tinted windshield sunshade band, flush-mount high efficiency halogen headlights with auto-off feature, integral fog lamps, rear window defogger with automatic shut-off, fuel cap retainer in fuel filler door, 5-passenger seating, gray or taupe leather seat trim, vinyl door trim, power driver seat with 8-way adjustment, power passenger seat with 4-way adjustment, adjustable driver seat headrest, driver seat height and fore/aft adjustments, height adjustable front passenger seat headrest, dual front seatback storage pockets, fold-down rear seat center armrest with enclosed storage compartment, leather-wrapped steering wheel, steering wheel mounted cruise control switches, leather-wrapped A/T shift control handle, power windows with driver side one-touch down feature, remote hood release, remote electric fuel door and trunk lid releases (valet lockout), analog quartz clock, 8000-rpm tachometer, resettable trip odometer, warning lamp cluster (incls parking brake/high-beam/check engine/low fuel/oil pressure/battery charge/defrost-on/door ajar/stop lamp out/seatbelts/ABS/cruise/OD off), rheostat gauge illumination control, full-logic rotary dial plus push-button HVAC controls, outside temperature display, center console with large lockable glove compartment, center console genuine wood trim, slide-out cup holder with 2-cup capacity, driver and front passenger air bag SRS, illuminated driver and passenger side visor vanity mirrors, front center sun visor, 3 roof-mounted passenger assist grips with rear coat hooks, front/rear overhead map lights, driver's footrest, full cut-pile carpeting, 3-point manual front seatbelts, 3-point outboard rear seatbelts, 2-point rear center seatbelt, adjustable front seat shoulder belt anchors, illuminated front ashtray with cigar lighter, front door map pockets, front/rear door courtesy illumination, child safety rear door locks, full cargo area trim (black woven carpet trunk mat/side trim/end trim), trunk illumination, unwoven carpet trunk lid trim.

Accessories

CODE	DESCRIPTION	INVOICE	MSRP
FLM	**Floor Mats** — carpeted	87	125
MR2	**Solar Ventilation System**	533	650
2C0	**4-Seasons Pkg** *incls all-season tires, heated front seats, larger wiper motor and washer tank, limited slip differential axle, low windshield washer fluid level warning light, 55 amp battery*	540	650

MILLENIA (1995)

CODE	DESCRIPTION	INVOICE	MSRP
—	Base 4-Dr Sedan w/Cloth Interior (auto)	23159	25995
—	Base 4-Dr Sedan w/Leather Interior (auto)	25450	28895
—	S 4-Dr Sedan (auto)	27856	31995
Destination Charge:			
	Alaska	640	640
	Other States	440	440

Standard Equipment

MILLENIA w/CLOTH INTERIOR: Front wheel drive, power steering, anti-lock power 4-wheel disc brakes, cruise control, rear window defroster, power windows, AM/FM ETR stereo radio with cassette, power antenna, anti-theft alarm system, automatic air conditioning, tachometer, power door locks, console, trip odometer, 4-speed ECT automatic transmission with overdrive, front and rear stabilizer bars, illuminated entry system, tinted glass, P205/65R15 all-season SBR tires, aluminum alloy wheels, fog lights, dual color-keyed heated power mirrors, dual illuminated visor vanity mirrors, cloth door trim panels, variable intermittent windshield wipers, remote control fuel filler door release, cloth reclining front bucket seats with 8-way power driver's seat, tilt steering wheel, driver and front passenger air bags, remote control trunk release, rear seat fold-down center armrest.

MILLENIA w/LEATHER INTERIOR (in addition to or instead of MILLENIA w/CLOTH INTERIOR equipment): Power moonroof, leather seats, 4-way power pass. seat, keyless remote entry system, leather door trim.

S (in addition to or instead of MILLENIA w/LEATHER INTERIOR equipment): P215/55R16 all-season SBR tires, 2.3L Miller Cycle V6 DOHC 24-valve engine with dual intercoolers, electronic traction control.

Accessories

CODE	DESCRIPTION	INVOICE	MSRP
RA4	**Radio** — Base w/leather interior, S *incls Bose radio w/CD player*	960	1200

CODE	DESCRIPTION	INVOICE	MSRP
RA5	**CD Player** — Base w/leather interior, S	720	900
JCS	**Paint** — Base w/leather interior, S *incls deep sea metallic paint*	147	175
JCR	**Paint** — Base w/leather interior, S *incls white pearl metallic paint*	294	350
2C0	**4-Seasons Pkg** — Base *incls electronic traction control, heated front seats, heavy-duty starter motor, heavy-duty windshield wiper motor, large capacity windshield washer tank*	504	600
3C0	**4-Seasons Pkg** — S *incls heated front seats, heavy-duty starter motor, heavy-duty windshield wiper motor, large capacity windshield washer tank*	252	300
PPA	**Protection Pkg** *incls alloy wheels and carpeted floor mats*	87	125

MX-3 (1995)

—	3-Dr Hatchback (5-spd)	13157	14440
Destination Charge:		440	440

Standard Equipment

MX-3: 1.6 liter DOHC 16-valve I4 engine with multi-port fuel injection, 5-speed manual transmission with overdrive, rack and pinion steering with engine rpm-sensing variable power assist, power assist ventilated front disc/rear drum brakes, 14" steel wheels with full wheel covers, P185/65R14 all-season tires, dual body color power mirrors, body color front and rear bumpers, body color door handles and front mud guards, variable intermittent windshield wipers, tinted glass with windshield sunshade band, dual outlet exhaust, driver and passenger side air bag SRS, reclining front bucket seats with passenger side walk-in device, cloth upholstery and door trim, fold-down rear seatback, cut-pile carpeting, full center console with covered storage compartment and cup holder, lockable glove compartment, driver's door map pocket, remote liftgate and fuel door releases, dual overhead map lights, rigid removable cargo cover, anti-static electricity system, ignition key illumination, cargo area lamp, day/night rearview mirror, dual sun visor vanity mirrors, digital clock, 8000-rpm tachometer gauge, trip odometer and engine coolant temperature gauges, warning lights for: low fuel level/low windshield washer fluid level, tilt steering column, heater/defroster with 4-speed blower, front side window demisters, rear window defogger with timer, AM/FM auto-reverse cassette stereo sound system with 4 speakers.

Accessories

Code	Description	Invoice	MSRP
1PE	**Popular Equipment Pkg** *incls power door locks, power windows, speed control*	518	595
CE1	**California/New York Emissions**	126	150
AB1	**Braking System** — anti-lock *incls front/rear disc brakes*	808	950
ACA	**Air Conditioning**	720	900
1WP	**Wheels** — locking, aluminum alloy	360	450
FLM	**Floor Mats** — carpeted	56	80
SR1	**Sunroof** — power	480	600
ARM	**Armrest Lid** — padded	80	100
AT1	**Automatic Transmission** — 4-speed w/overdrive	720	800

MAZDA

MX-5 MIATA (1995)

Code	Description	Invoice	MSRP
—	Base 2-Dr Convertible (5-spd)	15768	17500
—	M-Edition 2-Dr Convertible (5-spd)	21201	23530
Destination Charge:		440	440

Standard Equipment

MIATA-BASE: 1.8 liter DOHC 16-valve I4 engine with multi-port fuel injection, sport-tuned exhaust system with stainless steel tubular header, 5-speed manual transmission with overdrive, rack and pinion steering, front and rear stabilizer bars, 4-wheel double wishbone suspension, power assist

CODE	DESCRIPTION	INVOICE	MSRP

4-wheel disc brakes, power plant frame (PPF), 14" styled steel wheels with bright center caps, P185/60R14 tires, intermittent windshield wipers, dual body color mirrors, retractable halogen headlamps with flash-to-pass feature, reclining highback bucket seats, black cloth upholstery, full carpeting, lockable glove compartment, full center console with lockable storage compartment and removable cup holder, remote trunk and fuel door release, map pockets on driver and passenger doors and passenger seatback, one-piece sun visors, two dashboard mounted courtesy lights, gauges for 8000 RPM tachometer/trip odometer/140 MPH speedometer/oil pressure/engine coolant temperature, driver/passenger-side air bag SRS, heater/defroster with 4-speed blower and side window demisters, AM/FM auto-reverse cassette stereo sound system with 2 speakers/anti-theft coding/digital clock.

M-EDITION (in addition to or instead of Base Equipment): P195/55R15 tires, BBS wheels, air conditioning, CD player, anti-lock brakes, floor mats, leather pkg (incls tan leather interior and tan vinyl top), popular equipment pkg (incls power steering, power windows, speed control, dual power OS mirrors, limited slip differential [models w/o auto trans], leather-wrapped steering wheel, power antenna.

Accessories

CODE	DESCRIPTION	INVOICE	MSRP
ACA	**Air Conditioning** — Base	720	900
AT1	**Automatic Transmission** — 4-speed w/overdrive	739	850
	req's leather pkg or popular equipment pkg on Base		
—	**Power Steering** — Base	252	300
	incls wheel trim rings		
AB1	**Anti-Lock Brakes** — Base	765	900
	req's leather pkg or popular equipment pkg		
RA4	**Sensory Sound System**	700	875
	req's leather pkg		
1PK	**R Pkg**	1260	1500
	incls alloy wheels, limited slip differential, front and rear air dams, rear spoiler, sport suspension		
1PE	**Popular Equipment Pkg** — Base models w/o auto trans	1756	2090
	Base models w/auto trans	1428	1700
	incls power steering, power windows, speed control, dual power OS mirrors, power antenna, limited slip differential (models w/o auto trans), headrest speakers, alloy wheels, leather-wrapped steering wheel		
1LE	**Leather Pkg** — Base models w/o auto trans	2507	2985
	Base models w/auto trans	2180	2595
	incls leather seating, vinyl top, popular equipment pkg		
FLM	**Floor Mats** — carpeted - Base	56	80
HT1	**Removable Hard Top**	1215	1500
	incls rear window defroster; req's leather pkg or popular equipment pkg		

MAZDA

MX-6 *(1995)*

CODE	DESCRIPTION	INVOICE	MSRP
—	2-Dr Coupe (5-spd)	16546	18573
Destination Charge:		440	440

Standard Equipment

MX-6: 2.0 liter 16-valve DOHC 4 cylinder engine, front wheel drive, driver and front passenger air bags, 5-speed manual transmission with overdrive, rack and pinion steering with variable power assist, power front disc/rear drum brakes, 14" wheels with full wheel covers, P195/65R14 all-season radial tires, dual body color power mirrors, intermittent windshield wipers with variable control, tinted glass, tinted glass with upper windshield sunshade band, reclining bucket seats with driver's adjustable thigh support, 60/40 split fold-down rear seatback, AM/FM stereo radio with cassette, power antenna, dual visor vanity mirrors, center console, power windows with driver's side one-touch down feature, power door locks, tilt steering wheel, cruise control, rear window defroster, remote trunk release, remote fuel filler door release, front and rear stabilizer bars, tachometer.

Accessories

CODE	DESCRIPTION	INVOICE	MSRP
AC1	**Air Conditioning**	720	900
AT1	**Transmission** — 4-speed automatic w/overdrive	696	800
AB1	**Anti-Lock Brakes** — w/LS equipment group	680	800
	w/popular equipment group	808	950
FLM	**Floor Mats**	56	80
RS1	**Rear Spoiler**	300	375
CE1	**California/New York Emissions System**	126	150
1LE	**Leather Pkg**	960	1200
	incls leather seats, power driver's seat adjuster, heated power OS mirrors, keyless remote entry system; req's LS equipment group		
1LS	**LS Equipment Group**	2583	3075
	incls 2.5 liter V6 engine, power sunroof, alarm system, air conditioning, leather-wrapped		

CODE	DESCRIPTION	INVOICE	MSRP
	steering wheel, power 4-wheel disc brakes, fog lights, P205/55R15 tires, aluminum alloy wheels, variable intermittent windshield wipers, 90-amp alternator, floor mats		
10P	**Popular Equipment Group**	840	1000
	incls power sunroof, alloy wheels, alarm system, variable intermittent windshield wipers		

PROTEGE *(1995)*

—	DX 4-Dr Sedan (5-spd)	11174	11995
—	LX 4-Dr Sedan (5-spd)	12341	13395
—	ES 4-Dr Sedan (5-spd)	14710	16145
Destination Charge:		440	440

Standard Equipment

PROTEGE - DX: Front wheel drive, dual air bags, 1.5 liter DOHC 16-valve 4 cylinder engine, 5-speed manual transmission, rack and pinion steering with power assist, power assisted front disc/rear drum brakes, P175/70SR13 all-season SBR tires, tinted glass, rear window defogger, tilt steering wheel, bodyside moldings, center console with storage tray, front and rear stabilizer bars, manual remote control OS mirrors.

LX (in addition to or instead of DX equipment): Cruise control, power windows, driver's seat with 8-way adjust, power door locks, power remote control OS mirrors, AM/FM stereo radio with cassette/clock/4 speakers, trip odometer, remote trunk release, map/reading lights, courtesy lights, passenger side visor vanity mirror.

ES (in addition to or instead of LX equipment): 1.8 liter DOHC 16-valve 4 cylinder engine, power 4-wheel disc brakes with anti-lock, air conditioning, P185/65R14 all-season SBR tires, sport seats.

Accessories

AB1	**Anti-Lock Brakes** — LX	680	800
AT1	**Transmission** — 4-speed automatic w/overdrive	720	800

CODE	DESCRIPTION	INVOICE	MSRP
MR1	**Power Moonroof** — LX	560	700
FLM	**Floor Mats**	64	80
CE1	**California/New York Emissions**	126	150
DXC	**Convenience Pkg** — DX *incls air conditioning, AM/FM stereo radio w/cassette, floor mats*	1292	1575
LXC	**Luxury Pkg** — LX *incls air conditioning, floor mats, armrest spacer (models w/auto trans)*	939	1145
1ES	**Premium Pkg** — ES *incls aluminum alloy wheels, power moonroof*	956	1195
ESP	**Touring Pkg** — ES *incls floor mats and armrest spacer*	84	105

RX-7 *(1994)*

—	2-Dr Coupe (5-spd)	31493	36500
Destination Charge:		440	440

Standard Equipment

RX-7: Two-rotor inline rotary engine w/sequential twin turbochargers/air-to-air intercooler/electronic fuel injection, 5-speed manual transmission w/overdrive, engine oil cooler, power plant frame (PPF), Torsen torque-sensing limited slip differential, 4-wheel independent double-wishbone suspension, rack-and-pinion steering with engine-speed variable power assist, power assisted 4-wheel ventilated disc brakes, anti-lock braking system (ABS), 16-inch aluminum alloy wheels, 225/50VR16 radial tires, dual aerodynamic bodycolor power mirrors, tinted glass, retractable halogen headlights, light weight aluminum hood, illuminated driver's lock keyhole, intermittent windshield wipers w/variable control, driver and passenger side airbags, power windows w/driver's side one-touch down feature, power door locks, remote liftgate and fuel-door releases, seat back storage pockets, dual storage compartment behind seats, 9,000 RPM tachometer w/8,000 RPM redline, oil pressure/engine coolant temperature gauges, leather-wrapped steering wheel and shift knob, cruise control w/steering wheel

CODE	DESCRIPTION	INVOICE	MSRP

mounted controls, drilled aluminum clutch and brake pedals, anti-theft alarm system, AM/FM cassette stereo w/5 speakers and automatic power antenna, air conditioning.

Accessories

CODE	DESCRIPTION	INVOICE	MSRP
AT1	**Automatic Transmission** *NA w/Popular Equipment Group or R-2 Pkg*	783	900
1RP	**R-2 Pkg** *incls Pirelli P zero Z-rated tires, twin engine oil coolers, dedicated front brake air ducts, special RZ1 suspension, rear spoiler, front airdam, front shock tower support brace, unique cloth seat upholstery, cruise control deleted; NA w/Touring Pkg*	1640	2000
1TR	**Touring Pkg** *incls leather seating surfaces, power glass moonroof, halogen fog lights, rear window wiper/washer, Bose acoustic wave stereo music system w/compact disc player, upgraded sound insulation, rear cargo cover*	3444	4200
1PE	**Popular Equipment Pkg** *incls leather seating surfaces, power steel sunroof and rear cargo cover; NA w/R-2 Pkg*	1476	1800
FLM	**Floor Mats**	58	80
CE1	**California or New York Emissions**	126	150

What's New for *Mazda* in 1995?

626: New wheelcover designs, slightly revised interiors and minor equipment changes accompany the 626 as it rolls into its third model year.

929: Jockeying for position with the new Millenia, the 929 gets new colors, wood trim and standard leather seats.

Millenia: Introduced early in 1994 as a 1995 model, the Millenia receives no changes.

MX-3: The world's smallest V6 has been dropped due to poor sales. Base models get standard cruise control.

MX-5 Miata: Montego Blue joins the color palette, a new M-Edition with Merlot Mica paint and 15-inch BBS rims is available, and Miata has a lighter ABS system.

MX-6: New wheelcovers and the deletion of the LS trim level (it's still available as an equipment package on the base MX-6) are the only changes to this unique sport coupe for 1995.

Protege: All new for 1995, the Protege boasts the largest interior in its class, but until Mazda drops the top-of-the-line twin cam 1.8L engine into the well-equipped LX, we predict that the Neon will make this subcompact *its* protege.

RX-7: Just two versions of the RX-7 will be on sale in 1995: the base model and the R2. A lighter ABS system is on tap, and you can't get red leather seats anymore.

C-CLASS *(1995)*

CODE	DESCRIPTION	INVOICE	MSRP
—	C220 4-Dr Sedan (auto)	26330	30950
—	C280 4-Dr Sedan (auto)	30880	36300
Destination Charge:		475	475

Standard Equipment

C220 SEDAN: 2.2 liter DOHC 16-valve inline 4 cylinder engine, HFM sequential multi-port fuel injection and ignition, variable intake valve timing, Control Area Network (CAN) data management system, 4-speed automatic transmission, power assisted recirculating ball steering, independent double wishbone front suspension with shock absorbers and separate coil springs, independent multi-link rear suspension with coil springs and single-tube gas-pressurized shock absorbers, anti-roll bars, power assisted 4-wheel disc brakes, anti-lock braking system (ABS), 6.5J x 15" aluminum-alloy wheels, 195/65R15 91H steel belted radial tires, sliding electric sunroof with rear pop-up feature, dual heated electrically operated outside mirrors, heated windshield washers, halogen headlamps and front fog lamps, rear fog lamp, central locking with key-operated window and sunroof closing capability and automatic starter disable, supplemental restraint system (SRS) with an air bag, knee bolster and emergency tensioning retractor (ETR) for driver and front passenger; 3-point front seat belts attached to seat frames with adjustable shoulder belts, 3-point outboard rear seat belts with automatically adjusting shoulder belts, MB-Tex upholstery, leather-trimmed steering wheel and shift knob, 10-way electrically adjustable driver's seat, 10-way manually adjustable front passenger seat, power windows with express-down control for both front windows, electrostatic dust filter and residual heat REST mode, cruise control, delayed shut-off front courtesy light, rear compartment courtesy light, front reading lamp, illuminated visor vanity mirrors, front center armrest, folding rear center armrest, beverage holder, coin tray, Zebrano wood trim, 8-speaker sound system, automatic speed-dependent volume adjustment, anti-theft coded AM/FM stereo/weatherband radio and auto-reverse cassette player, automatic electric AM/FM/cellular antenna, prewiring for optional CD changer and cellular telephone, automatic climate control with digital temperature display.

C280 SEDAN (in addition to or instead of C220 SEDAN equipment): 2.8 liter DOHC 24-valve inline 6 cylinder engine, tuned-resonance intake manifold, 10-way electrically adjustable front seats, Bose sound system.

CODE	DESCRIPTION	INVOICE	MSRP
	Accessories		
551	**Anti-Theft Alarm System**	490	590
—	**Leather Upholstery** — C280	1349	1625
—	**Metallic Paint**	481	580
116	**C1 Pkg** — C220 *incls heated front seats, electronic traction control, headlight washer/wipers*	1332	1605
117	**C1 Pkg** — C280 *incls heated front seats, automatic slip control, headlight washer/wipers*	2353	2835
118	**C2 Pkg** *incls split fold-down rear seat and trunk pass-through with ski sack*	274	330
119	**C3 Pkg** — C280 *incls power glass sunroof with pop-up feature, retractable head restraints, leather seats*	1461	1760
441	**Telescopic Steering Column**	129	155
414	**Roof** — power glass sunroof with pop-up feature	187	225
430	**Head Restraints** — rear seats	282	340
222	**Power Passenger Seat** — C220	477	575
—	**Power Orthopedic Backrest Seats**		
404	left front	303	365
405	right front	303	365
600	**Headlight Wipers/Washers**	266	320
810	**Radio** — high performance sound system - C220 *incls 8-speaker Bose sound system*	415	500

CODE	DESCRIPTION	INVOICE	MSRP

E-CLASS (1995)

CODE	DESCRIPTION	INVOICE	MSRP
—	E300D 4-Dr Sedan (auto)	34880	41000
—	E320 2-Dr Cabriolet (auto)	65570	79000
—	E320 2-Dr Coupe (auto)	52290	63000
—	E320 4-Dr Sedan (auto)	37010	43500
—	E320 5-Dr Wagon (auto)	40410	47500
—	E420 4-Dr Sedan (auto)	43580	52500
Destination Charge:		475	475

Standard Equipment

E300D, E320 SEDAN, E320 WAGON: Cruise control, power steering, tachometer, dual air bags, automatic power antenna, trip odometer, first aid kit, power sunroof, cargo cover (Wagon), aluminum alloy wheels, Zebrano wood interior trim, anti-theft alarm, rear window intermittent wiper/washer (Wagon), outside digital temperature indicator, front/rear stabilizer bars, anti-lock power 4-wheel disc brakes, analog clock, pre-wiring for cellular telephone, tinted glass, power central door locking system includes: trunk (Sedans), tailgate (Wagon) and fuel filler door releases; leather-wrapped steering wheel, 4-speed automatic transmission, illuminated visor vanity mirrors, luggage rack (Wagon), automatic air conditioning, AM/FM ETR stereo with cassette and 6 speakers with CD compatibility, power windows with front express-down, heated power mirrors, 3.0 liter 6 cylinder 24-valve diesel engine (E300D), 3.2 liter 6 cylinder EFI 24-valve engine (E320), rear axle level control suspension (Wagon), rear seat center armrest (NA Wagon), M-B Tex upholstery (E300D, E320 Wagon), leather upholstery (E320 Sedan), front door and seatback map pockets, 195/65R15 SBR BW tires, velour carpeting, halogen fog lights, electric rear window defroster, 10-way power front bucket seats, 60/40 split fold-down rear seat (Wagon), rear-facing third seat (Wagon).

E320 COUPE & CABRIOLET (in addition to or instead of E320 SEDAN equipment): Burl walnut interior trim, pop-up roll bar (Cabriolet), rear console storage (Coupe), power convertible top (Cabriolet), 10-way power front bucket seats with driver seat 2-position memory (heated front seats on Cabriolet), air deflector (Cabriolet), tilt steering column with memory, headlight wipers/washers, AM/FM ETR stereo radio with cassette and high-performance 10-speaker sound system (Coupe).

CODE	DESCRIPTION	INVOICE	MSRP

E420 SEDAN (in addition to or instead of E320 SEDAN equipment): Headlight wipers/washers, AM/FM ETR stereo radio with cassette and high-performance 10-speaker sound system, 10-way power front bucket seats with driver seat 2-position memory, burl walnut interior trim, 4.2 liter V8 EFI 32-valve engine, tilt/telescopic steering column with 2-position memory.

Accessories

CODE	DESCRIPTION	INVOICE	MSRP
441	**Steering Column** — power, tilt - E300D, E320 Sedan & Wagon	303	365
600	**Headlight Wipers/Washers** — E300D, E320 Sedan & Wagon	266	320
—	**Upholstery** — leather - E300D, E320 Wagon	1349	1625
111	**Pkg E1** — E300D *incls heated front seats, automatic locking differential, headlight wipers/washers*	1332	1605
112	**Pkg E1** — E320 Sedan & Wagon *incls heated front seats, automatic traction control, headlight wipers/washers*	2353	2835
113	**Pkg E1** — E320 Coupe, E420 *incls heated front seats, automatic traction control*	2137	2575
114	**Pkg E2** — E300D, E320 Sedan *incls power tilt steering column, driver seat memory, high-performance sound system*	896	1080
115	**Pkg E3** — E320 Wagon *incls power tilt steering column, driver seat memory*	552	665
877	**Lights** — rear reading - E-Class Sedans	75	90
540	**Sunshade** — power rear window - E-Class Sedans, E320 Coupe	340	410
—	**Paint** — metallic - E300D, E320 Sedan & Wagon	552	665
	E320 Coupe & Cabriolet, E420	NC	NC
952	**Sportline Pkg** — E320 Sedan *incls sport steering, 4-place sport seats, sport suspension*	1581	1905
	E320 Coupe *incls sport steering, sport suspension*	905	1090
—	**Seats** — power orthopedic		
404	left front	303	365
405	right front	303	365
471	**Slip Control** — automatic - E320 Cabriolet	1785	2150
SE1	**Special Edition Pkg. SE1** - E300D *incls pkg E2, door sill trim, CD changer, metallic paint, burl walnut trim, cellular phone*	1075	1295
SE2	**Special Edition Pkg. SE2** - E320 Sedan *incls pkg E2, door sill trim, CD changer, metallic paint, burl walnut trim, cellular phone*	1075	1295
SE3	**Special Edition Pkg. SE3** - E420 Sedan *incls CD changer, door sill trim, cellular phone*	411	495

See the Automobile Dealer Directory on page 448 for a Dealer near you!

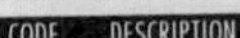

CODE	DESCRIPTION	INVOICE	MSRP

S-CLASS (1995)

CODE	DESCRIPTION	INVOICE	MSRP
—	S320 4-Dr Sedan (auto)	54700	65900
—	S350D 4-Dr Sedan (auto)	54700	65900
—	S420 4-Dr Sedan (auto)	61340	73900
—	S500 2-Dr Coupe (auto)	76280	91900
—	S500 4-Dr Sedan (auto)	72630	87500
—	S600 2-Dr Coupe (auto)	110640	133300
—	S600 4-Dr Sedan (auto)	108150	130300
Destination Charge:		475	475
Gas Guzzler Tax:			
	S420	1700	1700
	S500	1700	1700
	S600	3000	3000

Standard Equipment

S320, S350D, S420: Electric rear window defroster, analog clock, front and rear stabilizer bars, leather upholstery, heated power mirrors with 3-position memory, trip odometer, dual air bags, halogen fog lights, door map pockets, automatic power antenna, 12-way power front bucket seats with 3-position memory, electronic traction control system (NA S420), 3.5 liter 6 cylinder turbo diesel engine (S350D), 3.2 liter 6 cylinder EFI 24-valve engine (S320), 4.2 liter V8 EFI 32-valve engine (S420), tachometer, aluminum alloy wheels, rear heater ducts, power decklid release, infrared remote locking system, wipers with heated washers, automatic air conditioning with dual controls, outside temperature display, first aid kit, Zebrano wood interior trim, speed sensitive power steering, automatic dimming day/night rearview mirror with 3-position memory, automatic slip control system (S420), power decklid pull-down, tinted glass, power sunroof, 225/60HR16 SBR all-season BW tires (S350D and S320), 235/60HR16 SBR all-season BW tires (S420), power windows with express up/down, anti-theft alarm, gas pressurized shock absorbers, cruise control, headlight wiper/washers, pre-wiring for cellular telephone, front/rear center armrests, power tilt/telescopic steering column with memory, door courtesy lights, front/rear reading lights, 4-speed automatic transmission (S350D and S420), 5-speed automatic transmission (S320), anti-lock power 4-wheel disc brakes, AM/FM ETR stereo radio with cassette/anti-theft coding/Bose Beta 11-speaker sound system (CD compatible), front/rear illuminated visor vanity mirrors, power central locking door lock system (incls trunk and fuel filler door releases).

S500 (in addition to or instead of S320 equipment): 5.0 liter V8 EFI 32-valve engine, 4-speed automatic transmission, automatic slip control system, power windows with rear express-down (Coupe), automatic level control suspension, rear reading lights deleted (Coupe), active charcoal filter, 235/60HR16 SBR BW tires, electronic traction control deleted, 12-way power heated front bucket seats with 3-position memory, power heated rear seat (Sedan), automatic courtesy seat adjustment (Coupe), burl walnut interior trim, rear hydropneumatic shock absorbers, rear illuminated visor vanity mirrors deleted (Coupe).

S600 (in addition to or instead of S500 equipment): Cellular telephone, rear air conditioning (Sedan), suede headliner, adaptive damping system suspension with level control, power rear window sunshade, 6.0 liter V12 48-valve engine, special leather upholstery, trunk-mounted CD changer, 235/55ZR16 SBR performance tires, power seats with orthopedic backrests.

Accessories

CODE	DESCRIPTION	INVOICE	MSRP
—	**Paint** — metallic	NC	NC
540	**Sunshade** — rear window, power (std S600)	340	410
141	**Telephone** — portable cellular - S600	747	900
306	**Active Charcoal Filter** — S320, S350D, S420	427	515
—	**Sunroof**		
412	power sliding steel	NC	NC
414	power sliding glass	328	395
471	**Slip Control** — automatic - S320	1370	1650
582	**Air Conditioning** — rear - S320, S350D, S420, S500 Sedan	1573	1895
—	**Seats**		
873	heated front - S320, S350D, S420	490	590
404	power orthopedic, left front (std S600)	303	365
405	power orthopedic, right front (std S600)	303	365
224	four place power seating - S500 Sedan	4461	5375
	S600 Sedan	3403	4100
—	**Suspension**		
480	rear axle level control - S320, S350D, S420	735	885
214	adaptive damping - S320, S350D, S420	2353	2835
	S500	1743	2100
	incls rear axle level control		

SL-CLASS *(1995)*

CODE	DESCRIPTION	INVOICE	MSRP
—	SL320 2-Dr Coupe/Roadster (auto)	64990	78300
—	SL500 2-Dr Coupe/Roadster (auto)	74620	89900
—	SL600 2-Dr Coupe/Roadster (auto)	99680	120100
Destination Charge:		475	475
Gas Guzzler Tax:			
	SL500	1300	1300
	SL600	2600	2600

Standard Equipment

SL320: Power steering, anti-theft alarm, alloy wheels, fog lights, analog clock, storage compartments, infrared remote locking system, automatic pop-up roll bar, burl walnut trim, power central door locking system, electronic traction control system, dual air bags, wipers with heated washers, rear gas pressurized shock absorbers, leather upholstery, first aid kit, pre-wiring for cellular telephone, headlight wipers with heated washers, leather-wrapped steering wheel, front seat center armrest, cruise control, 225/55ZR16 SBR tires, trip odometer, power windows with express down, tinted glass, AM/FM ETR stereo radio with cassette/Bose Acoustimass sound system/6 speakers, automatic power antenna, front/rear stabilizer bars, tachometer, 5-speed automatic transmission, anti-lock power 4-wheel disc brakes, 3.2 liter 6 cylinder EFI 24-valve engine, automatic microfiltered ventilation system, automatic air conditioning, outside temperature display, electric rear window defroster, front courtesy lights, front reading lights, 10-way power front bucket seats with dual 3-position memory, heated power mirrors with memory, tilt steering column with memory, automatic dimming day/night rearview mirror with memory, dual illuminated visor vanity mirrors.

SL500 (in addition to or instead of SL320 equipment): Automatic slip control system, 5.0 liter V8 EFI 32-valve engine, 4-speed automatic transmission.

SL600 (in addition to or instead of SL500 equipment): 6.0 liter V12 48-valve engine, cellular telephone, trunk-mounted 6-disc CD changer, special leather upholstery, 10-way power heated front bucket seats with dual 3-position memory, adaptive damping suspension system.

CODE	DESCRIPTION	INVOICE	MSRP
	Accessories		
471	**Slip Control** — automatic - SL320	1370	1650
—	**Seats**		
404	power orthopedic, left front	303	365
405	power orthopedic, right front	303	365
873	heated front - SL320, SL500	469	565
141	**Telephone** — portable cellular - SL600	747	900
—	**Paint** — metallic	NC	NC
216	**Suspension** — adaptive damping system - SL320, SL500 *incls 4-wheel level control*	3432	4135

See the Automobile Dealer Directory on page 448 for a Dealer near you!

What's New for *Mercedes* in 1995:

C-Class: The C36 debuts, an AMG prepared C280 with 280 hp. At $50,000, only 300 copies will be produced. The line forms here.

E-Class: No changes, aside from the demise of the Porsche-built 500E hot rod. The new C36 replaces it. Next year, an all-new E-Class debuts, with round headlamps faired into the hood ala Jaguar XJ6.

S-Class: Minor styling tweaks try to slenderize the S-Class this year, but a 4500 pound car will always be a 4500 pound car, no matter what you do to the sheetmetal. Base prices have fallen as well, up to $8,000 for the S 500.

SL-Class: The Sl 320 and SL 500 drop in price dramatically, and the SL 320 gets standard traction control.

COUGAR XR7 *(1995)*

COUGAR XR7 6 CYL

	INVOICE	MSRP
M62 2-Dr Sedan	15216	16860
Destination Charge:	510	510

Standard Equipment

COUGAR XR7: 3.8 liter SEFI V6 engine, electronic automatic overdrive transmission with brake shift interlock feature, power rack and pinion steering, power front disc/rear drum brakes, power side windows with illuminated switches, P205/70R15 BSW all-season tires, luxury wheel covers, electronic AM/FM stereo cassette radio with 4 speakers, manual CFC-free air conditioning with rotary controls, front and rear color-keyed soft fascia bumpers, black door handles/lock bezels, flush side/windshield/rear window glass, bright grille with bright surround and cat head, low-profile aero halogen headlamps (integrated into parking lamp/tum signal/side marker assembly), dual power remote control body color mirrors, concealed drip moldings, black windshield/rear window moldings, bright door window/quarter window moldings, color-keyed bodyside moldings, bright antenna/black bezel (RH fender), black B-pillar moldings, black decklid lock bezel, "Mercury" nomenclature (driver side front bumper), wrap-around design taillamps, driver and right front passenger air bag SRS, luxury 24 oz. color-keyed cut-pile carpeting, chimes for: headlamps on/fasten safety belts/key in ignition reminder, full length floor console with leather-wrapped floor shift/front and rear ashtrays/armrest storage/coin holder/cup holders; color-keyed soft door trim panel with lower carpeting/cloth inserts/map pockets/courtesy lamps; quarter trim panels with courtesy lights/padded armrests/cloth inserts, locking glove box, molded color-keyed cloth headliner, rear compartment heat ducts, backlighted analog performance cluster includes: tachometer/fuel gauge/coolant temperature/120-mph speedometer/oil pressure/voltmeter gauges; stalk-mounted controls for tum signals/headlamp hi-beams/flash-to-pass/interval wiper/washer; flow-through design instrument panel with passenger air bag supplemental restraint system, side window demisters, dual beam dome/map light, carpeted lighted luggage compartment with flat load floor, day/night rearview mirror, concealed driver/unconcealed passenger visor mirrors, color-keyed 3-point active safety restraints (front/rear outboard positions), lap belt (rear center), reclining individual front bucket seats with luxury cloth and leather/inertia front seat back releases/power lumbar/2-way adjustable head restraints; rear seat center fold-down armrest, 4-spoke luxury steering wheel with tilt feature/driver air bag SRS/center blow hom; 130 amp altemator, 58 amp/hour maintenance-free battery, 3-point manual safety belt system, electric drive fan, EEC-IV

CODE	DESCRIPTION	INVOICE	MSRP

electronic engine controls, 18 gallon fuel tank, tinted glass, 4-speed heater/defroster system, counter-balanced hood, high-mounted rear brake light, plastic headed ignition key, theft-resistant decklid lock, push-push parking brake release, nitrogen gas-pressurized hydraulic shock absorbers, long spindle short/long arm front suspension with variable rate coil springs and stabilizer bar, independent rear suspension with variable rate coil springs and stabilizer bar, 2-speed electric windshield wipers with fluidic washers and interval feature.

Accessories

CODE	DESCRIPTION	INVOICE	MSRP
—	**Preferred Equipment Pkgs** — prices include pkg discounts		
260A	**Pkg 260A** *incls group 1 (incls electric rear window defroster, illuminated entry, front floor mats), group 2 (incls fingertip speed control, leather-wrapped steering wheel, cast aluminum wheels, P215/70R15 BSW tires), group 3 (incls power lock group and 6-way power driver's seat)*	882	990
—	**V8 Bonus Discount** — w/pkg 260A (w/optional 4.6L engine)	(458)	(515)
—	**Groups**		
412	**Group 1** *incls electric rear window defroster, illuminated entry, front floor mats*	241	270
433	**Group 2** *incls fingertip speed control, leather-wrapped steering wheel, cast aluminum wheels, P215/70R15 BSW tires*	458	515
466	**Group 3** *incls power lock group (incls power door locks, power decklid release and remote fuel filler door), 6-way power driver's seat*	521	585
422	**California Emissions System**	85	95
428	**High Altitude Emissions System**	NC	NC
994	**Engine** — 3.8 liter SFI 6 cyl	STD	STD
99W	**Engine** — 4.6 liter EFI 8 cyl *incls speed-sensitive power steering, heavy duty battery*	1006	1130
44L	**Transmission** — automatic w/overdrive	STD	STD
573	**Automatic Air Conditioning** *req's autolamp system*	138	155
45A	**Traction-Lok Axle** *incls 3.27 axle ratio*	85	95
13B	**Power Moonroof** — reqs groups 1, 2, 3 & luxury light group *incls dual reading lights, air deflector*	658	740
474	**Autolamp System** *incls auto headlamp on/off delay; req's air conditioning*	62	70
943	**Luxury Light Group** — reqs groups 1, 2 & 3 *incls engine compartment light, RH instrument panel courtesy lights, dual illuminated visor mirrors*	124	140
41H	**Engine Block Immersion Heater**	18	20
153	**Front License Plate Bracket**	NC	NC
631	**Heavy Duty Battery** — incl w/4.6L engine	23	25
144	**Keyless Remote Entry System** *incls automatic power door locks; reqs group 1, 2, & 3*	191	215
553	**Electronic Traction Assist** *req's anti-lock brakes*	187	210

CODE	DESCRIPTION	INVOICE	MSRP
552	**Anti-Lock Brakes**	503	565
—	**Paint** — tri-coat	201	225
53C	**Sport Appearance Group**	102	115
	incls BBS-style wheels, non-functional luggage rack		
—	**Audio**		
586	premium electronic AM/FM stereo w/cassette tape player	258	290
585	high-level audio w/electronic AM/FM stereo and CD player	383	430
91H	power antenna	71	80
	req's air conditioning		
—	**Seats**		
5	cloth and leather reclining bucket	NC	NC
6	leather reclining bucket	436	490
	req's seat adjuster		
21J	**seat adjuster, 6-way dual power**	258	290
—	**Tires**		
T33	P205/70R15 BSW (4)	STD	STD
T37	P215/70R15 BSW (4)	NC	NC

GRAND MARQUIS *(1995)*

GRAND MARQUIS 8 CYL

M74	GS 4-Dr Sedan	19626	21270
M75	LS 4-Dr Sedan	20918	22690
Destination Charge:		580	580

Standard Equipment

GRAND MARQUIS - GS: 4.6 liter SEFI OHC V8 engine, electronic automatic overdrive transmission with overdrive lockout feature, speed-sensitive variable assist power steering, power 4-wheel disc brakes, power side windows with express-down driver's window, P215/70R15 WSW (Michelin XW4) all-season SBR tires, deluxe "basket weave" full wheel covers, electronic AM/FM stereo/cassette radio with 4 speakers, manual air conditioning with positive shut-off registers, concealed front/rear bumpers with full wrap color-keyed covers, integrated rubstrip with bright insert, low liftover design decklid with liner, solar tinted glass, bright vertical bar grille, dual aerodynamic complex reflector headlamps with crystalline lens and parking, color-keyed heated fold-away dual remote control power mirrors, bright window/door frame moldings, black windshield/rear window moldings, color-keyed wide bodyside moldings with bright insert, bright taillamp, black door handles with bright housing, black "B" pillar paint, bright grille panel/rocker panel; "Mercury" nomenclature (RH side of decklid), Grand Marquis GS nomenclature (LH side of decklid), wrap-around taillamps, lower bodyside urethane protection, driver and right front passenger air bag SRS, 16 oz. color-keyed floor carpeting, luggage compartment carpeting, illuminated cigar lighter, electronic digital clock with dimming feature, ashtray mounted dual cup holders, door trim panel includes: full length armrests/woodtone applique/ front door courtesy lights/pull straps/upper vinyl/lower carpeting; lighted door lock buttons/window controls, driver footrest, lockable illuminated bin-type glove box, cloth covered color-keyed molded headliner with collapsible passenger-assist handles, instrument panel includes: woodtone applique/ knee bolsters/positive shut-off air conditioner registers/side window demisters/cup holders; backlighted analog instrumentation includes: speedometer/fuel gauge/temperature gauge/voltmeter/oil pressure/ odometer/trip odometer; warning lights for: low fuel/check engine/emissions system/air bag readiness alert/safety belts/parking brake/ABS (if equipped); lights include: luggage compartment/glove box/ ashtray/dual instrument panel courtesy/courtesy switches (all doors)/dome; inside day/night mirror, non-illuminated RH visor mirror, deluxe color-keyed lap/shoulder belts (front/rear outboard occupants), manual lap belts (front and rear center occupants), color-keyed front/rear door scuff plates, fold-down front/rear seat center armrests, front seatback map pockets, cloth twin comfort lounge seats with power recliner/2-way cloth-covered head restraints/6-way power driver's seat, spare tire cover, 1-lever multi-function steering column controls for: turn signals/flash-to-pass/high beam switch/ windshield wiper/washer; tilt steering column, color-keyed luxury 4-spoke steering wheel with twin horn buttons and driver side air bag SRS, trip odometer, deep-well design trunk with luxury carpet trim/decklid liner, driver and right front passenger air bag SRS, 130 amp alternator, radio antenna (embedded in rear window), autolamp on/off delay system, 58 amp/hour maintenance-free battery, battery saver, body/frame construction, brake/shift interlock, rear door child safety latches, reminder chimes for: key in ignition/fasten safety belt/headlamp on; coolant recovery system, electric rear window defroster, EEC-IV electronic engine controls, stainless steel exhaust system, remote fuel door release, 20 gallon fuel tank with tethered screw-in gas cap, solar tinted glass, blend-air type 4-speed blower heater/defroster with rear floor-mounted heat ducts, gas strut hood assist, inside hood release, dual note horn, distributorless electronic ignition, scissors-type jack, high-mounted rear brake light, single key for door/ignition, automatic parking brake release, 12-volt power point, nitrogen gas-pressurized hydraulic shock absorbers, luxury sound insulation package, T125/80R16 BSW mini spare tire, sunvisors, short/long arm coil spring front suspension with stabilizer bar, coil spring 4-bar link rear suspension with stabilizer bar, concealed 2-speed electric windshield wipers with fluidic washer system and interval feature.

LS (in addition to or instead of GS equipment): "LS" nomenclature (LH side of decklid), 18 oz. color-keyed floor carpeting, luxury cloth twin comfort lounge seats with power recliner/2-way cloth-covered front head restraints/fixed rear seat head restraints/6-way power driver's seat with dual power lumbar.

Accessories

Code	Description	Invoice	MSRP
—	**Preferred Equipment Pkgs** — prices include pkg discounts		
157A	**Pkg 157A** — GS *incls group 1 (front and rear carpeted floor mats, speed control, locking radial spoke wheel covers), group 2 (power lock group and illuminated entry system)*	254	285
172A	**Pkg 172A** — LS *incls group 1 (front and rear carpeted floor mats, speed control), group 2 (power lock group, illuminated entry system), group 3 (front cornering lamps, luxury light group, bodyside paint stripe, leather-wrapped steering wheel, 12-spoke aluminum wheels, keyless entry system)*	953	1070

MERCURY

CODE	DESCRIPTION	INVOICE	MSRP
172A	**Special Value Discount**	(1034)	(1140)
	avail only w/PEP 157A or 172A		
—	Groups		
68G	**Group 1** — GS	495	555
	incls front and rear carpeted floor mats, speed control, locking radial spoke wheel covers		
68G	**Group 1** — LS	232	260
	incls front and rear carpeted floor mats, speed control		
65R	**Group 2**	343	385
	incls power lock group, illuminated entry system		
67M	**Group 3** — LS	925	1040
	incls front cornering lamps, luxury light group, bodyside paint stripe, leather-wrapped steering wheel, 12-spoke aluminum wheels, keyless entry system		
99W	**Engine** — 4.6 liter SEFI V8	STD	STD
44U	**Transmission** — electronic automatic overdrive	STD	STD
422	**California Emissions System**	85	95
428	**High Altitude Principal Use Emissions System**	NC	NC
T3P	**Tires** — P215/70R15 all-season WSW	STD	STD
T21	**Tires** — P225/60R16 BSW	NC	NC
	incld in handling pkg		
508	**Tires** — conventional spare - LS only	240	270
643	**Wheel Covers** — locking wire wheel	NC	NC
	incld in group 1; avail on GS only		
64L	**Wheels** — 12" spoke aluminum	NC	NC
	incld in group 3; avail on LS only		
64P	**Wheels** — 16" BBS-style	NC	NC
	incld in handling pkg; avail on LS only		
64S	**Wheels** — dual plane cast aluminum	NC	NC
	incld in group 3; avail on LS only		
—	**Seats**		
S	cloth twin comfort - GS	STD	STD
T	cloth twin comfort - LS	STD	STD
H	leather twin comfort - LS	574	645
21J	passenger 6-way power seat - LS	321	360
553	**Anti-Lock Brakes w/Traction Assist**	592	665
155	**Electronic Group**	405	455
	incls electronic instrument cluster, tripminder computer, 72-amp/hr heavy duty maintenance-free battery		
573	**Air Conditioning** — w/auto temp control	156	175
41G	**Handling Pkg** — LS only - w/pkg 172A	534	600
	all others	908	1020
	incls 3.27 rear axle ratio, upsized front and rear stabilizer bars, P225/60R16 BSW handling tires, rear air suspension w/revised spring rates, dual exhaust system, 16" aluminum wheels, power steering cooler, unique tuned shocks, springs and steering gear		
144	**Keyless Entry System**	191	215
943	**Luxury Light Group**	169	190
	incls dual beam dome map lights, engine compartment light, dual illuminated visor mirrors, rear seat reading lamps, dual secondary sunvisors for front/side coverage		

CODE	DESCRIPTION	INVOICE	MSRP
972	**Bodyside Paint Stripe**	54	60
664	**Rear Air Suspension** — LS	240	270
586	**Radio** — LS	321	360
	incls premium electronic AM/FM stereo radio w/cassette		
535	**Trailer Towing Pkg III** — LS	801	900
41H	**Engine Block Heater**	23	25
153	**Front License Plate Bracket**	NC	NC

MYSTIQUE *(1995)*

MYSTIQUE 4 CYL

CODE	DESCRIPTION	INVOICE	MSRP
M65	GS 4-Dr Sedan	12531	13855
M66	LS 4-Dr Sedan	13755	15230
Destination Charge:		510	510

Standard Equipment

MYSTIQUE - GS SEDAN: 2.0 liter DOHC 16-valve ZETEC I4 engine with EEC-IV electronic controls, 5-speed manual transaxle with overdrive, power rack and pinion steering, power front disc/rear drum brakes, P185/70RX14 BSW radial tires, 14" deluxe wheel covers, electronic AM/FM stereo radio with 4 speakers, decklid applique with lower bright finisher, color-keyed front/rear polycarbonate 5-mph bumpers, flush color-keyed door handles/bezels, dripless water management door construction, solar tinted glass, semi-flush side glass, bright chrome grille perimeter with center black-out and chrome "Flying M," flush aerodynamic halogen headlamps, wrap-around front/rear side marker lights, body color dual remote power mirrors, body color bodyside moldings, bright front bumper sight shield, "Mystique" nomenclature (LH lower decklid shield), "Mercury" nomenclature (RH lower decklid shield); "Flying M" nomenclature (front grille center), lower bodyside and rocker panel PVC coating, rear decklid low liftover access with decklid gas-assist struts, horizontal taillamps with full-width reflex and lower bright molding, windshield water management system, driver and right front passenger air bag SRS, center console cloth covered/padded armrests, rear seat armrest, illuminated ashtray with lighter, 11 oz. color-keyed carpeting, instrument panel clock, full length console includes: armrest/CD/cassette stowage/rear ashtray/parking brake/cup holders; molded full coverage soft door trim with armrest/cloth insert/front and rear speaker provision; door trim panels include: front stowage map pockets/carpeted lower trim/door reflectors/lighted door courtesy lights/curb illumination; driver's footrest, illuminated locking glove box with dampened door and integrated purse/litter hook, grab handles, offset hand brake (center console), 4-way adjustable front contoured head restraints, illuminated headlamp switch, color-keyed cloth-covered headliner, rear floor heat ducts, backlighted analog gauges include: 130-mph speedometer/8,000-rpm tachometer/temperature and fuel gauges/ trip odometer/flash-to-pass/oil pressure/high beam warning lights; driver-oriented functional design instrument panel includes: side window demisters/driver's knee bolsters/positive shut-off registers; lights include: front footwell/courtesy switches on all doors with delay/rear dome; child-proof rear door locks, side wall trim luggage compartment with floor carpet and spare wheel cover, Micronair pollen filtration system, day/night rearview mirror, color-keyed manual lap/shoulder belts (front and rear outboard positions), lap belt (rear center position), Rubic trim individual cloth front bucket seats, seatback map storage, driver seat manual lumbar adjustment, driver seat manual tilt adjustment, 60/40 split folding rear seat with carpet backing (release knobs in trunk), infinitely variable front seat back adjustment, soft-feel 4-spoke steering wheel with center horn and air bag SRS, illuminated headlamp on/climate control switches, driver/passenger molded seat stowage bins, cloth-covered visor vanity driver and passenger mirrors, 130-amp alternator, heavy duty maintenance-free battery, brake shift interlock (automatic only), warning chimes for: key in ignition/driver's door open/lights on/ seat belt reminder, remote decklid release, diagnostic plug, front wheel drive, remote fuel filler door release, electronic sequential multi-port fuel injection, 14.5 gallon fuel tank with tethered cap, solar tinted glass, 4-speed blower heater/defroster, dual note horn, 2-key system (1 for door/ignition, 1 for trunk/glove box), mini spare wheel/tire, platinum-tipped spark plugs, front/rear stabilizer bars, tilt steering column, front MacPherson suspension, rear quadralink independent suspension, variable intermittent windshield wipers with fluidic washer jets and flip-away wiper arm blades.

LS SEDAN (in addition to or instead of GS SEDAN equipment): P205/60RX15 BSW radial tires, 15" aluminum wheels, electronic AM/FM stereo radio with cassette and 4 speakers, rear quarter panel power antenna, fog lamps (integral in front air dam), heated driver/passenger side mirrors, color-keyed 16 oz. carpeting, front/rear floor mats, pull-out fog lamp switch, Columbo trim individual cloth front bucket seats, driver seat 10-way power adjustment includes: fore/aft/recline/tilt/height/ lumbar; leather rim steering wheel with center horn and air bag SRS, electric rear defroster.

Accessories

CODE	DESCRIPTION	INVOICE	MSRP
—	**Preferred Equipment Pkgs — prices include pkg discounts**		
370A	**Pkg 370A** — GS *incls group 1 (rear defroster, heated mirrors, power antenna), group 2 (air conditioning, AM/FM stereo radio w/cassette)*	797	895
371A	**Pkg 371A** — GS *incls group 1 (rear defroster, heated mirrors, power antenna), group 2 (air conditioning, AM/FM stereo radio w/cassette), group 3 (power door locks, power windows, light group)*	1323	1485
372A	**Pkg 372A** — GS *incls pkg 371A contents plus 2.5 liter Duratec V6 engine*	2164	2430
380A	**Pkg 380A** — LS *incls group 2 (air conditioning), group 3 (power door locks, power windows, light group, remote power locking), and speed control*	1228	1380
381A	**Pkg 381A** — LS *incls group 2 (air conditioning), group 3 (power door locks, power windows, light group, remote power locking), speed control and 2.5 liter Duratec V6 engine*	1976	2220
—	**Groups**		
171	**Group 1** — GS *incls rear defroster, heated mirrors, power antenna*	223	250

CODE	DESCRIPTION	INVOICE	MSRP
462	**Group 2** — GS	841	945
	LS	694	780
	incls air conditioning, AM/FM stereo radio w/cassette; std on LS		
603	**Group 3** — GS	601	675
	LS	743	835
	incls power door locks, power windows, light group, remote power locking (LS)		
993	**Engine** — 2.0 liter 4 cyl Zetec	STD	STD
99L	**Engine** — 2.5 liter Duratec V6 - GS	930	1045
	LS	881	990
445	**Transaxle** — 5-speed manual	STD	STD
44T	**Transmission** — automatic overdrive	725	815
422	**California Emission System**	85	95
428	**High Altitude Principal Use Emission System**	NC	NC
T72	**Tires** — P185/70R14 BSW - GS	STD	STD
T35	**Tires** — P205/60R15 BSW - LS	STD	STD
642	**Wheels** — 14" cast aluminum - GS	236	265
641	**Wheels** — 15" cast aluminum - LS	STD	STD
572	**Air Conditioning**	694	780
57Q	**Rear Window Defroster**	143	160
	std on LS		
—	**Seats**		
N	cloth individual bucket - GS	STD	STD
21A	10-way power driver's - GS	294	330
	LS	STD	STD
P	cloth individual bucket - LS	STD	STD
Q	leather reclining surfaces - LS	530	595
553	**All-Speed Traction Control**	712	800
	incls anti-lock braking system		
552	**Anti-Lock Braking System**	503	565
153	**Front License Plate Bracket**	NC	NC
12Y	**Floor Mats** — carpeted front and rear	40	45
	std on LS		
13B	**Power Moonroof**	530	595
902	**Power Door Locks/Light Group** — GS w/pkg 370A	299	335
143	**Remote Locking**	143	160
41H	**Engine Block Immersion Heater**	18	20
525	**Speed Control**	191	215
—	**Audio**		
913	premium sound w/electronic AM/FM stereo/cassette	116	130
585	compact disc radio & premium sound w/electronic AM/FM stereo		
	GS w/o group 2	387	435
	GS w/group 2 or LS	240	270

MERCURY

CODE	DESCRIPTION	INVOICE	MSRP

SABLE *(1995)*

SABLE 6 CYL

CODE	DESCRIPTION	INVOICE	MSRP
M50	GS 4-Dr Sedan	16432	18210
M55	GS 4-Dr Wagon	17456	19360
M53	LS 4-Dr Sedan	18443	20470
M58	LS 4-Dr Wagon	19422	21570
Destination Charge:		550	550

Standard Equipment

SABLE - GS SEDAN: 3.0 liter SEFI V6 engine, electronic automatic 4-speed overdrive transaxle, variable assist power rack and pinion steering, power front disc/rear drum brakes, P205/65R15 BSW all-season radial tires, deluxe wheel covers, electronic AM/FM stereo radio with 4 speakers, manual CFC-free air conditioning, color-keyed front and rear polycarbonate bumpers with "Mercury" nomenclature molded in front, color-keyed door handles/bezels, wrap-around rear glass, polycarbonate "light bar" grille with full-width illumination and "Flying M" emblem, flush aerodynamic halogen headlamps, front cornering lamps, wrap-around front/rear side markers, body color dual power tinted mirrors, "glass-edge" type black windshield moldings with bright accent, black upper/lower greenhouse with bright insert, "glass edge" type black rear window/tailgate moldings with bright accent, color-keyed rocker panel, color-keyed bodyside molding with "Sable GS" molded in, black "B" and "C" pillars, black decklid/tailgate lock, "Sable" nomenclature on LH bumper sight shield, "Mercury" nomenclature on RH bumper sight shield, horizontal taillamps with full-width center reflex, lower door and rocker panel urethane coating, driver and right front passenger air bag SRS, individual front center fold-down armrest, rear seat center fold-down armrest, rear door ashtrays, color-keyed 13.5 oz. carpeting, door trim panels include: upper door cloth inserts/padded armrests/map pockets/ lighted door edge marker with curb illumination in front doors (reflectors only in rear), driver's left footrest, locking illuminated glove box, roof-mounted assist grab handles, color-keyed cloth-covered headliner, 2-way adjustable front contoured head restraints, integrated rear head restraints, rear compartment heat ducts, backlighted mechanical instrument cluster includes: tachometer/temperature and fuel gauges/trip odometer/flash-to-pass/low fuel level alert light; driver-oriented instrument panel with side window defoggers/driver's knee bolsters/positive shut-off registers; slide-out coin and cup holder trays (deleted with bucket seats or CD player), courtesy light switches on all doors, dome lamps with illumination retained (25 seconds after entry), fully trimmed luggage compartment with light, front seat back map pockets, day/night rearview mirror, covered driver vanity mirror, non-covered passenger visor mirror with secondary driver's visor, cloth 50/50 twin comfort lounge seats/ dual manual recliners, color-keyed manual lap/shoulder belts (front/rear outboard positions), lap belts (center occupant positions), 4-spoke steering wheel with center horn control and air bag SRS, recessed sun visors with document strap, driver side secondary visor for front/side coverage, 110 amp alternator, 58 amp/hour maintenance-free battery, brake shift interlock, electronic alert chimes, electronic digital clock, coolant recovery system, electric rear window defroster, EEC-IV electronic engine controls with malfunction warning light, sequential multi-port electronic fuel injection, stainless steel exhaust system, unitized body and front sub-frame front wheel drive, 16 gallon fuel tank, tinted glass, solar tinted glass (windshield/rear window), 4-speed blower heater/defroster, inside release gas cylinder assist hood, dual note horn, high-mounted rear stop light, single key for door/ignition, child-proof rear door locks, manual release parking brake, provision for child safety seat, front and rear stabilizer bar, tilt steering column, MacPherson front suspension (nitrogen gas-pressurized/ hydraulic struts with strut-mounted coil springs), independent rear suspension with 4-bar parallel arm and MacPherson nitrogen gas-pressurized hydraulic struts, T135/70D15 mini spare tire, deep well trunk, recessed 2-speed electric windshield wipers with interval feature.

GS WAGON (in addition to or instead of GS SEDAN equipment): Black bumper step pad, wrap-around rear glass deleted, stand-alone rear side markers, roof mounted aerodynamic luggage rack, bright door accent moldings (beltline), body color "B"/"C"/"D" pillars, "Sable" tailgate nomenclature, "Mercury" tailgate nomenclature, vertical taillamps with full-width center reflex, rear seat armrest deleted, integrated rear head restraints deleted, load floor tie down hooks, twin "D" pillar cargo light with on/off switch, lockable hidden under floor stowage replaces luggage compartment, 60/40 split folding second seat, independent SLA rear suspension with variable rate springs and lower shock towers, flip-up tailgate window, rear window wiper.

LS/LTS SEDAN: 3.0 liter SEFI V6 engine, electronic automatic 4-speed overdrive transaxle, variable assist rack and pinion power steering, anti-lock 4-wheel disc brakes, power side windows with express-down driver's feature and illuminated switches, P205/65R15 BSW all-season radial tires, aluminum wheels, electronic AM/FM stereo cassette radio with 4-speakers, manual CFC-free air conditioning, color-keyed front/rear polycarbonate bumpers with "Mercury" nomenclature molded in front, color-keyed door handles and bezels, wrap-around rear glass, polycarbonate "light bar" grille with full-width illumination and "Flying M" emblem, flush aerodynamic halogen headlamps, front cornering lamps, wrap-around front/rear side markers, body color dual power tinted mirrors, "glass edge" type black windshield moldings with bright accent, black upper and lower greenhouse with bright insert, "glass edge" type black rear window/tailgate moldings with bright accent, color-keyed bodyside cladding with molded "Sable LS," black "B"/"C" pillars, black decklid/tailgate lock, "Sable" nomenclature (LH bumper sight shield), "Mercury" nomenclature (RH bumper sight shield), horizontal taillamps with full-width center reflex, lower door/rocker panel urethane coating, driver and right front passenger air bag SRS, individual front center fold-down armrest (included in console), rear seat center fold-down armrest, rear door ashtrays, color-keyed 13.5 oz. carpeting (18 oz. on LTS), door trim panels include: upper cloth inserts/padded armrests/map pockets/lighted door edge markers with curb illumination in front doors (reflectors in rear), driver's left foot footrest, locking illuminated glove box, roof-mounted assist grab handles, color-keyed cloth-covered headliner, 2-way adjustable contoured front head restraints (4-way on LS), integrated rear head restraints, rear compartment heat ducts, backlighted mechanical instrument cluster includes: tachometer/temperature and fuel gauges/trip odometer/flash-to-pass/low fuel level alert light; alert lights for: low washer fluid/lamp outage/door ajar/low oil level; driver-oriented swept-away design instrument panel with side window defoggers/ driver's knee bolsters/positive shut-off registers, console-mounted cup holder, courtesy light switches (all doors), retained illumination dome lamps (25 seconds after entry), fully trimmed lighted luggage compartment, front seatback map pockets, day/night rearview mirror, dual illuminated visor mirrors with dual secondary visors for front/side coverage, cargo tie town net, cloth individual dual manual reclining bucket seats (power driver's) with center console, front seat power lumbar supports, color-keyed manual lap/shoulder belts (front and rear outboard positions), lap belts (center occupant positions), 4-spoke steering wheel with center horn and air bag SRS, recessed sun visors with document strap, driver/passenger secondary visors for front/side coverage, 110 amp alternator, 58 amp/hour maintenance-free battery, brake shift interlock, electronic alert chimes, electronic digital clock, coolant recovery system, remote decklid/liftgate release, electric rear window defroster, EEC-IV electronic engine controls with malfunction warning light, sequential multi-port electronic fuel injection, stainless steel exhaust system, unitized body and front sub-frame front wheel drive, remote release fuel filler door, 16 gallon fuel tank, tinted glass, solar-tinted windshield/rear window glass, 4-speed blower heater/defroster, gas cylinder assist inside release hood, dual note horn, high-mounted rear stop light, light group, single key for door/ignition, child-proof rear door locks, automatic release parking brake, provision for child safety seat, front/rear stabilizer bars, tilt steering column, MacPherson front suspension (nitrogen gas-pressurized, hydraulic struts with strut-mounted coil springs), MacPherson independent rear suspension (4-bar parallel arm, nitrogen gas-pressurized, hydraulic struts), T135/70D15 mini spare tire, deep well trunk, 2-speed electric recessed windshield wipers with interval feature.

LS WAGON (in addition to or instead of LS/LTS SEDAN equipment): Black bumper step pad, wrap-around rear glass deleted, stand-alone rear side marker, roof-mounted aerodynamic luggage rack, bright accent door beltline molding, body color "B"/"C"/"D" pillars, "Sable" nomenclature (LH tailgate), "Mercury" nomenclature (RH tailgate), vertical taillamps with full-width center reflex, individual front center fold-down armrest, rear seat center armrest deleted, integrated rear head restraints deleted, load floor tie down hooks, slide-out coin and cup holder trays (deleted with bucket seats or CD player), twin "D" pillar cargo light with on/off switch, lockable hidden under floor stowage replaces fully trimmed lighted trunk, cloth 50/50 twin comfort dual manual reclining seats with power driver's side seat, 60/40 split folding second seat, independent SLA rear suspension with variable rate springs and lower shock towers, flip-up tailgate window, rear window wiper.

Accessories

CODE	DESCRIPTION	INVOICE	MSRP
—	**Preferred Equipment Pkgs** — prices include pkg discounts		
450A	**Pkg 450A** — GS *incls group 1 (incls light group, front and rear carpet floor mats, bodyside accent stripe), group 2 (incls power side windows, power lock group, fingertip speed control)*	712	800
451A	**Pkg 451A** — GS *incls group 1 (incls light group, front and rear carpet floor mats, bodyside accent stripe), group 2 (incls power side windows, power lock group, fingertip speed control), group 3 (incls 6-way power driver's seat, aluminum wheels and electronic AM/FM stereo radio w/cassette tape player)*	1125	1265
—	**Bonus Discount** *avail only w/pkg 451A*	(445)	(500)
461A	**Pkg 461A** — LS *incls group 1 (incls front and rear carpet floor mats, bodyside accent stripe), group 2 (incls power lock group, fingertip speed control), group 4 (incls leather-wrapped steering wheel, power antenna, keyless entry system, high-level AM/FM stereo radio w/cassette tape player)*	397	445
462A	**Pkg 462A** — LS *incls group 1 (incls front and rear carpet floor mats, bodyside accent stripe), group 2 (incls power lock group, speed control), group 4 (incls leather-wrapped steering wheel, power radio antenna, high-level AM/FM stereo radio w/cassette tape player, keyless entry system), group 5 (incls electronic instrument cluster, electronic automatic temperature control air conditioning, autolamp on/off delay system)*	695	780

CODE	DESCRIPTION	INVOICE	MSRP
470A	**Pkg 470A "LTS"** — LS	1108	1245
	incls LTS decor group (incls leather seating surface sport bucket seats, 6-way dual power seats, leather-wrapped shift handle, luxury pile carpeting, unique floor mats, unique cast aluminum wheels, paint stripe deleted, LTS bodyside cladding), plus group 1 (incls plus front and rear carpet floor mats), group 2 (incls power door locks and fingertip speed control), group 4 (incls leather-wrapped steering wheel, power radio antenna, high-level AM/FM stereo radio w/cassette tape player, keyless entry system)		
—	**Groups**		
46A	**Group 1** — GS	143	160
	LS, LTS	93	105
	incls light group, floor mats, accent stripe		
46B	**Group 2** — GS	797	895
	LS, LTS	410	460
	incls power windows/locks, speed control		
54A	**Group 3**	632	710
	incls power driver's seat, aluminum wheels, cassette		
54B	**Group 4**	712	800
	incls leather steering wheel, high-level cassette, power antenna, keyless entry		
77A	**Group 5** — LS	476	535
	LTS 470A	298	335
	incls electronic instrument cluster, electronic air conditioning, autolamp		
99U	**Engine** — 3.0 liter EFI V6	STD	STD
994	**Engine** — 3.8 liter EFI V6	561	630
44L	**Transmission** — electronic automatic overdrive	STD	STD
422	**California Emissions System**	85	95
428	**High Altitude Principal Use Emission System**	NC	NC
T32	**Tires** — P205/65R15 BSW	STD	STD
508	**Conventional Spare Tire**	62	70
642	**Aluminum Wheels**	227	255
645	**Chrome Wheels** — LS w/pkg 470A "LTS"	516	580
—	**Seats**		
7	cloth individual - GS	STD	STD
6	cloth twin comfort - GS	STD	STD
L	cloth individual - LS	STD	STD
K	cloth twin comfort - LS	STD	STD
3	leather individual - LS	441	495
2	leather twin comfort - LS	441	495
214	seat, rear facing third - Wagons	134	150
21A	seat, 6-way power driver's	258	290
21J	seat, 6-way dual power		
	w/PEP 450A, 451A w/o group 3	516	580
	w/PEP 451A w/group 3, 461A, 462A	258	290
415	**LTS Decor Group** — LS	1024	1150
	incls leather seating surface sport bucket seats, 6-way dual power seats, leather-wrapped shift handle, luxury pile carpeting, unique floor mats, unique cast aluminum wheels, paint stripe deleted, LTS bodyside cladding		

CODE	DESCRIPTION	INVOICE	MSRP
573	**Air Conditioning** — LS *incls electronic auto temp control*	156	175
552	**Anti-Lock Braking System** *incls 4-wheel disc brakes*	503	565
631	**Heavy Duty Battery**	27	30
475	**Cargo Area Cover** — Wagons	58	65
516	**Cellular Telephone**	445	500
65Z	**Extended-Range Fuel Tank**	40	45
144	**Keyless Entry System** *req's group 2*	263	295
13B	**Power Moonroof** — LS *incls pop-up air deflector, dual outboard/dome lamps, sliding sunshade*	658	740
662	**Heavy Duty Suspension** *incls heavy duty front stabilizer bar, heavier spring rates, unique MacPherson struts*	23	25
—	**Audio**		
58H	electronic AM/FM stereo/cassette	147	165
917	compact disc player	334	375
153	**Front License Plate Bracket**	NC	NC
41H	**Engine Block Immersion Heater**	18	20

TRACER *(1995)*

TRACER 4 CYL

CODE	DESCRIPTION	INVOICE	MSRP
M10	Base 4-Dr Sedan	10515	11380
M15	Base 4-Dr Wagon	10989	11900
M14	LTS 4-Dr Sedan	12208	13240
Destination Charge:		390	390

Standard Equipment

TRACER - BASE SEDAN: 1.9 liter SEFI I4 engine, 5-speed manual overdrive transaxle, power rack and pinion steering, power front disc/rear drum brakes, P175/65R14 81S BSW tires, 14" x 5" semi-styled steel wheels with full wheel covers, electronic AM/FM stereo radio with integral clock, body color bumpers with bright insert (with "Mercury" molded in), body color door handles, flush windshield/rear window glass, semi-flush side glass, translucent grille, single halogen aerodynamic headlamps, wide bodyside body color moldings with bright insert, wide black belt line, body color "C" pillar applique, black windshield/rear window/side window moldings, blackout door frame molding, "Mercury" and "Tracer" nomenclature (on lower portion of rear finisher panel), clear turn signal/side marker lamps with amber bulbs, full width taillamps, urethane coating lower bodyside, driver and passenger air bag SRS, luxury color-keyed cut-pile passenger compartment carpeting, color-keyed load floor carpeting, console includes: bin/lift out tray/cup holder with black molded integral gearshift lever boot and knob, upper cloth/lower carpet door trim panel with map pocket and speaker grille, integral grab handles, molded cloth-covered headliner, rear floor compartment heat ducts, body color instrument panel with soft-feel knee bolsters/side window demisters/4 air registers/column-mounted wiper/light control/flash-to-pass; analog backlit instrumentation includes: speedometer/fuel and temperature gauges/trip odometer/low fuel warning light/shift indicator light (manual)/tachometer; headlamp on warning chime, dual covered visor mirrors, day/night rearview mirror, dome light (with 3-way switch), front motorized shoulder belt restraint system with manual lap belts, rear lap/shoulder belt restraint system with center manual lap belt, low back cloth reclining bucket seats with 2-way head restraints, 60/40 split fold rear seat, integral rear seat head restraints, 4-spoke sport steering wheel, cloth-covered sunvisors, heavy duty alternator, 58 amp/hour maintenance-free battery, EEC-IV electronic engine controls, distributorless electronic ignition, engine low coolant warning light, engine malfunction indicator light, fuel cap tether, 11.9 gallon fuel tank, tinted glass, single note horn, ignition/transaxle interlock, child-safety rear door locks, T115/70D14 temporary spare tire, front/rear stabilizer bars, 4-wheel independent MacPherson strut front suspension with separate engine subframe, trapezoidal four-bar with MacPherson strut, color-highlighted underhood service points, flow-through ventilation with bi-level heater/defroster and 4-speed fan, 2-speed windshield wipers with variable interval feature.

LTS SEDAN (in addition to or instead of BASE SEDAN equipment): 1.8 liter DOHC 16-valve EFI I4 engine, power 4-wheel disc brakes, P185/60R14 82H BSW tires, 14" x 5.5" 7-spoke aluminum wheels, electronic AM/FM stereo radio with cassette, front air dam, body color bumpers with red insert, dual electric remote control mirrors, wide bodyside body color moldings with red insert, black "C" pillar applique, rear decklid spoiler with integrated stop lamp, unique cloth door trim panel, shift indicator light deleted, light group includes: cargo/engine compartment/dual map lights/rear door courtesy light switch for dome lamp, 4-spoke leather-wrapped sport steering wheel, rear window defroster, EEC-IV electronic engine controls deleted, 13.2 gallon fuel tank, dual note horn, speed control, tilt steering column, sport handling suspension.

WAGON (in addition to or instead of BASE SEDAN equipment): Dual electric remote control mirrors, vertical taillamps, cargo cover, light group includes: cargo/engine compartment/dual map lights/rear door courtesy light switch for dome lamp, integral rear seat head restraints deleted, rear window defroster, rear window wiper/washer.

Accessories

CODE	DESCRIPTION	INVOICE	MSRP
—	**Preferred Equipment Pkgs** — prices include pkg discounts		
540A	**Pkg 540A** — Base Sedan	343	385
	Base Wagon	121	135
	incls air conditioning, rear window defroster, light group, dual illuminated visor vanity mirrors, remote control trunk release (Sedan)		
541A	**Pkg 541A** — Base Sedan	992	1115
	Base Wagon	765	860
	incls air conditioning, rear window defroster, light group, dual illuminated visor vanity mirrors, power group, convenience group, AM/FM stereo radio w/cassette, remote control trunk release (Sedan)		
555A	**Pkg 555A** — LTS Sedan	827	930
	incls air conditioning and power group		
99J	**Engine** — 1.9 liter SEFI 4 cyl - Base	STD	STD
998	**Engine** — 1.8 liter EFI DOHC 4 cyl - LTS	STD	STD
445	**Transmission** — 5-speed manual w/overdrive	STD	STD
44T	**Transmission** — 4-speed automatic w/overdrive	725	815
422	**California Emissions**	NC	NC
428	**High Altitude Principal Use Emissions**	NC	NC
T75	**Tires** — P175/65R14 BSW w/full wheel covers - Base	STD	STD
T83	**Tires** — P185/60R14 BSW w/aluminum wheels - LTS Sedan	STD	STD
—	**Seats**		
A	cloth low back individual seats - Base	STD	STD
B	cloth sport bucket seats - LTS Sedan	STD	STD
216	integrated child seat	120	135
572	**Air Conditioning** — manual	699	785
552	**Anti-Lock Braking System** - LTS Sedan	503	565
60B	**Convenience Group** — Base	316	355
	incls tilt steering/speed control		

CODE	DESCRIPTION	INVOICE	MSRP
940	**Light Group** — Base	58	65
	incls cargo compartment light, engine compartment light, dual map lights, rear door courtesy light switch for dome lamp		
54J	**Dual Power Mirrors** — Base	85	95
57Q	**Rear Window Defroster** — Base	143	160
613	**Remote Decklid Release**	49	55
548	**Deluxe Luggage Rack** — Wagon	98	110
13B	**Power Moonroof** — LTS	468	525
—	**Clearcoat Paint**	NC	NC
53B	**Power Group**	463	520
	incls power locks and power windows		
434	**Trio Option Pkg** — Base Sedan	276	310
	Base Wagon	187	210
	incls rear decklid spoiler (Sedan), leather-wrapped steering wheel, 7-spoke aluminum wheels, trio nomenclature		
—	**Audio**		
589	AM/FM stereo/cassette	147	165
	std on LTS		
585	electronic AM/FM stereo/compact disc player		
	Base	290	325
	LTS	143	160
913	**Premium sound system**	54	60
41H	**Engine Block Immersion Heater**	18	20
153	**Front License Plate Bracket**	NC	NC

What's New for *Mercury* in 1995?

Cougar XR7: New colors, special editions for Fall and Spring, and a Sport Appearance Group with BBS-style rims and a decklid luggage rack are the big changes to Cougar for 1995.

Grand Marquis: This distant descendant of the Turnpike Cruiser gets modified styling and sport aluminum wheels for 1995. A new instrument panel, seats and radios update the interior, and, oooh! A decklid liner is now standard!

Mystique: This is a sister vehicle to Ford's Contour. Excellent engines, a competent interior and long lists of equipment at competitive prices mean Accord, Camry and Altima have one more new model to worry about Replacing the Topaz, the Mystique will hold its own against the stiff competition in the mid-size sedan class.

Sable: Mercury's Taurus twin, the Sable, goes into 1995 with minimal changes. The sporty LTS model is available in three additional colors, and the 3.0L V6 is improved An all new Sable is going through final development and is due in showrooms at the end of 1995. We've seen photos of it. Buy a 1995.

Tracer: A passenger-side airbag and a revised dashboard update this aging subcompact. The sporty Trio trim level goes nationwide for 1995, and is available on sedan or wagon body styles. It includes alloy wheels, leather-wrapped steering wheel and a decklid spoiler. Five new colors are available, and the LTS continues as the sleeper hot rod of sedanlets.

CODE	DESCRIPTION	INVOICE	MSRP

3000GT (1995)

CODE	DESCRIPTION	INVOICE	MSRP
GT24-N	Base 2-Dr Coupe (5-spd)	23537	28718
GT24-N	Base 2-Dr Coupe (auto)	24270	29602
GT24-P	SL 2-Dr Coupe (5-spd)	27928	34072
GT24-P	SL 2-Dr Coupe (auto)	28662	34956
GT24-T	VR-4 4WD 2-Dr Coupe (6-spd)	35640	43463
Destination Charge:		470	470

Standard Equipment

3000 GT - BASE: 4-passenger seating capacity, 6-way adjustable front bucket seats with memory recline, sport knit upholstery with knit bolster, leather-wrapped steering wheel/manual transmission shift knob/parking brake lever, passenger area cut pile carpeting, cargo area carpeting, cloth insert door trim with carpeted lower section, carpeted floor mats, dual bi-level heater/defroster with rear seat heater ducts and variable speed fan, CFC-free refrigerant air conditioning with manual controls, power windows with one-touch driver's auto-down, power door locks with one-touch keyless locking, electric rear window defroster with timer, tilt steering column, full-function cruise control, courtesy lamps (incls dome, trunk, map, glove compartment), rear cargo cover, center console with storage areas/cup holders/coin holder/armrest, remote hood-latch/fuel door/trunk lid release, dual sun visors with vanity mirrors, driver and front passenger air bags, 3-point seatbelts for all passengers, side-impact door beams, 4-wheel disc brakes, full instrumentation (incls 160 MPH speedometer/ 7000 RPM redline tachometer/fuel level gauge/oil pressure gauge/coolant temperature gauge/tripmeter/ voltmeter), warning lights (include engine check, brake system, low oil pressure, low fuel door/trunk ajar, charging system, low coolant, ignition key warning chime), 4-spoke sport steering wheel, steering column mounted controls (incls headlamps, high/low beam, flash-to-pass, turn signals, windshield wipers, cruise control), rear window wiper/washer, instrument panel controls (include panel lamps dimmer, tripmeter reset, hazard flasher, heater ventilation, fog lamps, rear window defroster), digital quartz clock, Mitsubishi/ Infinity audio system (incls AM/FM cassette with graphic equalizer, 8 speakers, separate amplifier), power antenna, ETACS-IV (incls variable speed intermittent wipers, flash-to-pass, anti-theft system, fade-out dome lamp, ignition key lockout, belt warning timer, rear window defogger timer, 30-second delay power window, exterior lights auto-off), color-keyed 5-mph bumpers, color-keyed rear spoiler with high-mounted stop lamp, bright sport dual exhaust outlets, tinted glass, halogen headlamps with auto-off and flash-to-pass, projector fog lamps, power remote sideview mirrors (dual aero-type), convex right sideview mirror, upper windshield shade band, 16 x 8 aluminum alloy wheels with locks, 225/55R16 V-rated SBR performance tires, 3.0 liter DOHC V6 engine with MVIC, electronic multi-point fuel injection, automatic valve-lash adjusters, roller-type cam followers, stainless steel dual exhaust system, 5-speed manual transmission with overdrive, strut-type independent front suspension, multi-link independent rear suspension, power assisted rack and pinion steering, on-board diagnostic system, color-coded under hood service item identification.

3000 GT SL (in addition to or instead of BASE equipment): 7-way adjustable driver seat with 5-way power adjustments, leather front seating surfaces, auxiliary 12-volt power outlet, steering wheel mounted audio controls, anti-theft system with remote keyless entry, dual sun visors with vanity mirrors deleted, anti-lock braking system (ABS), Mitsubishi/Infinity audio system (incls AM/FM cassette with graphic equalizer, 8 speakers, separate amplifier, steering wheel remote audio controls), power and diversity antenna, electric sideview mirror defroster, ECS electronically controlled suspension, security system.

3000 GT VR-4 (in addition to or instead of 3000 GT SL equipment): Cloth insert door trim with lower carpeting deleted, automatic climate control with CFC-free refrigerant air conditioning and electronic pictographic controls, dual sun visors with illuminated vanity mirrors, 180 MPH speedometer, turbocharger boost gauge replaces voltmeter, Active Aero system front air dam extension and rear spoiler, 18 x 8.5 chrome plated aluminum alloy wheels with locks, 245/40R18 Z-rated SBR performance tires, 3.0 liter DOHC V6 engine with twin turbochargers and intercoolers, engine oil cooler, Getrag 6-speed manual transmission, double-wishbone type multi-link independent rear suspension, 4-wheel steering (4WS), limited slip rear differential, full-time AWD w/VCU and center differential.

Accessories

CODE	DESCRIPTION	INVOICE	MSRP
MG	**Mud Guards**	85	130
CW	**Wheels** — chrome - SL	480	600
Y99	**Paint** — yellow pearl	250	313
SR	**Sunroof** — SL	300	375
	VR-4	300	375
PR	**Sunroof** — power - SL	720	900
	VR-4	420	525
EA	**Radio Equipment** — compact disc auto changer	488	699

DIAMANTE *(1995)*

CODE	DESCRIPTION	INVOICE	MSRP
DM45-P	4-Dr Wagon (auto)	23707	28250
DM42-U	LS 4-Dr Sedan (auto)	28208	35250
Destination Charge:		470	470

Standard Equipment

DIAMANTE - WAGON: 6-way adjustable front seats, velour upholstery, high-gloss woodgrain accents (instrument panel and front armrests), cut pile carpeting, fold-down rear center armrest, cargo area carpeting, front and rear door armrests, adjustable front and rear headrests, CFC-free refrigerant air conditioning with automatic climate control, power windows, power door locks, electric rear window defroster with automatic shut-off, center console with integral armrest, instrument panel dual cup holder, rear seat heater ducts, door key illumination, courtesy lamps (include dome, trunk, front/rear map, front foot, glove compartment), ignition key with delay light, digital quartz clock, cruise control, remote fuel door and power deck lid release, height-adjustable steering column, driver and front passenger air bags, height adjustable front shoulder belts, 3-point seatbelts for outboard rear passengers, front crumple zone, side-impact door beams, four-wheel disc brakes, full instrumentation (incls 150-mph speedometer, tachometer, fuel level gauge, tripmeter, coolant temperature gauge), warning lights for engine check/brake system/low oil pressure/charging system/low fuel/door-trunk ajar/automatic transmission position indicator/economy-power overdrive, key-in-ignition warning chime, variable intermittent wipers, steering column-mounted controls (include headlamps, high/low beam, flash-to-pass, turn signals, windshield wipers, cruise control), instrument panel controls (incls panel lamp dimmer, tripmeter reset, hazard flasher), ETACS-IV (incls power window timer, variable speed intermittent wipers, washer synch wipers, power door locks with key ignition lock-out, ignition key light with timer, seat belt warning timer, exterior lights auto-off), ETR AM/FM stereo cassette with 7 speakers (incls graphic equalizer, anti-theft feature, steering wheel remote controls), diversity antenna system (power antenna and rear in-glass antenna), color-keyed 5-mph bumpers, bodyside molding, integral front air dam, flush side windows with drip channels, tinted glass, prism-type headlamps, dual power remote aero type sideview mirrors, convex right sideview mirror, upper windshield shade band, 15 x 6 5-spoke alloy wheels with locks, 205/65R15 SB performance tires (H-rated), conventional spare tire, 3.0 liter SOHC V6 engine, electronic multi-point fuel injection, automatic valve lash adjusters, roller-type rocker arms, variable induction control system, stainless steel exhaust system, 4-speed automatic transmission with power/economy modes, strut-type independent front suspension, 5-link tube axle rear suspension, front stabilizer bar, power assist

CODE	DESCRIPTION	INVOICE	MSRP

rack and pinion steering, security system, on-board diagnostic system, color-coded under hood service item identification.

DIAMANTE LS SEDAN: 3.0 liter DOHC V6 engine with twin spray fuel injectors, ELC-M engine and transmission management system, 4-speed automatic transmission with overdrive, multi-link independent rear suspension, front and rear stabilizer bars, EPS-II speed and steering wheel velocity sensitive power steering, power 4-wheel disc brakes with anti-lock braking system, V-rated 205/65R15 SB performance tires, 7-way adjustable front seats, power driver's seat adjustments with 2-position memory, leather interior trim, classic-style analog clock, remote keyless entry system, Mitsubishi/Infinity audio system (incls AM/FM stereo cassette with graphic equalizer, separate amplifier, 8 speakers, steering wheel remote controls), side sill extension, bright dual exhaust tips, dual power remote aero-type heated sideview mirrors, automatic day/night mirror, automatic air conditioning, dual air bags, tilt steering column, tachometer, tinted glass, cruise control, power door locks, power windows, electric rear window defroster, alloy wheels with locks, front air dam, bodyside moldings, variable intermittent windshield wipers, center console, power trunk release, power fuel filler door release, security system, auto-off headlights.

Accessories

CODE	DESCRIPTION	INVOICE	MSRP
PI	**Sunroof** — power w/tilt-slide	763	954
TN	**Traction Control** — LS	589	718
PE	**Seat Adjuster** — power passenger w/memory - LS	392	490
EA	**CD Auto Changer** — LS	517	739
WD	**Sunroof Air Deflector**	39	60
AB	**Anti-Lock Brakes** — Wagon	933	1166
KC	**Cargo Net** — Wagon	20	31
PL	**Leather Seat Trim** — Wagon *incls power driver's seat adjuster*	1641	1999
EC	**Radio** — Wagon *incls AM/FM stereo radio w/cassette and CD player*	245	350
KE	**Keyless Entry System** — Wagon	157	242

What's New for *Mitsubishi* for 1995?

3000GT: A new Spyder model, complete with retractable hardtop, is on line for 1995. Prices top out at $62,000 for a drop top VR4. Other 3000GT's get a power sunroof option. The base car has an upgraded stereo, the SL gets leather seats, and the VR4 gets 18 inch wheels and tires. Chrome wheels are optional on the SL and VR4.

Diamante: Just two versions of the Diamante are now available; LS sedan and wagon. New colors and a stereo upgrade for the wagon are the only changes.

Eclipse: All new sport coupe debuted in the summer of 1994. Base models are powered by a Chrysler engine, while the top-of-the-line engine is a massaged version of the previous car's turbocharged four cylinder. Dual airbags are now standard.

Galant: Interior improvements, a new hood and new colors are the changes in store for the good looking Galant. A V6 LS model will appear at the end of the year with a long list of standard equipment.

Mirage: Bye, bye sedan. The coupe remains as the sole Mirage offering, in two trim levels; bare bones basic and LS. A passenger-side airbag has been added.

ECLIPSE (1995)

CODE	DESCRIPTION	INVOICE	MSRP
EC24H	GS DOHC 3-Dr Coupe (5-spd)	14204	16329
EC24H	GS DOHC 3-Dr Coupe (auto)	14809	17019
EC24T	GS Turbo 3-Dr Coupe (5-spd)	17397	19999
EC24T	GS Turbo 3-Dr Coupe (auto)	18121	20829
EC24U	GSX Turbo AWD 3-Dr Coupe (5-spd)	19717	22929
EC24U	GSX Turbo AWD 3-Dr Coupe (auto)	20416	23739
Destination Charge:		420	420

Standard Equipment

ECLIPSE GS DOHC: 2.0 liter DOHC 16-valve 4 cylinder engine, 5-speed manual transmission with overdrive, power assisted rack and pinion steering, on-board diagnostic system, color-keyed 5-mph bumpers, hood with power bulge, tinted glass, aero-type halogen headlamps, electric rear window defroster, full wheel covers, tilt steering column, courtesy lamps, center console, remote hood latch/ fuel door/trunk lid release, driver and passenger air bags, full instrumentation, power 4-wheel disc brakes, color-keyed door handles/mirror trim, full profile color-keyed air dam, sculpted side sill cladding, color-keyed rear spoiler, dual power remote aero-type sideview mirrors, 16" x 6.0" steel wheels, 205/55HR16 tires,7-way adjustable driver's seat with dual height and reclining with memory, carpeted lower door trim, split fold-down rear seat, rear cargo cover and cargo net, ETR AM/FM stereo radio with cassette and six speakers.

GS TURBO (in addition to or instead of GS DOHC equipment): 2.0 liter DOHC 16-valve 4 cylinder turbocharged/intercooled engine, dual engine stabilizers, engine oil cooler, sport-tuned shock absorbers, power windows, power door locks, cruise control, rear window wiper/washer, integrated fog lamps, turbo boost gauges and oil pressure gauge, Mitsubishi Infinity audio system (incls AM/FM stereo radio with graphic equalizer, separate amplifier, eight speakers and CD changer controls), 16. x 6.0 aluminum alloy wheels.

GSX TURBO (in addition to or instead of GS TURBO equipment): Full-time all-wheel drive, limited slip differential, 215/55VR16 tires (size 205/55VR16 w/auto trans), leather front seating surfaces with power driver's seat, leather wrapped steering wheel and manual transmission shift knob.

CODE	DESCRIPTION	INVOICE	MSRP

Accessories

CODE	DESCRIPTION	INVOICE	MSRP
SR	**Power Sunroof**	599	731
AB	**Anti-Lock Braking System**	587	716
KE	**Keyless Entry System**	88	136
CC	**Speed Control** — GS DOHC	175	213
FM	**Floor Mats**	32	49
MG	**Mud Guards**	80	123
—	**Alarm System/Keyless Entry System**	272	332
TL	**Wheel Locks** — GS DOHC	21	32
AW	**Alloy Wheels** — GS DOHC	276	337
LS	**Leather Pkg** — GS Turbo *incls leather seat trim and power driver's seat adjuster*	647	789
—	**Audio**		
ED	compact disc - GS DOHC	399	599
EA	compact disc autochanger	598	899
EI	Infinity system - GS DOHC	541	660
PH	**Preferred Equipment Pkg** — GS DOHC *incls air conditioning, power windows, power door locks, rear window wiper/washer, AM/M stereo radio w/full logic cassette*	1298	1582

GALANT *(1995)*

CODE	DESCRIPTION	INVOICE	MSRP
GA41-N	S 4-Dr Sedan (5-spd)	12771	14349
GA41-N	S 4-Dr Sedan (auto)	13572	15249
GA41-P	ES 4-Dr Sedan (auto)	15867	18669
GA41-U	LS 4-Dr Sedan (auto)	17648	20757
Destination Charge:		420	420

Standard Equipment

GALANT - S: 2.4 liter 16-valve 4 cylinder engine, 5-speed manual transmission, front wheel drive, power front disc/rear drum brakes, power steering, color-keyed 5-mph bumpers, 185/70R14 tires,

MITSUBISHI

CODE	DESCRIPTION	INVOICE	MSRP

full wheel covers, electric rear window defroster, color-keyed bodyside moldings, black power remote control OS mirrors, driver and front passenger air bags, digital clock, front stabilizer bar, tinted glass, tilt steering wheel, intermittent windshield wipers, aero-type halogen headlamps, tachometer, 5-way adjustable driver's seat, cloth upholstery.

ES (in addition to or instead of S equipment): Air conditioning, power windows, cruise control, power door locks, floor mats, velour upholstery, color-keyed electric remote control mirrors, AM/FM ETR stereo radio with six speakers and power antenna, rear seat center armrest.

LS (in addition to or instead of ES equipment): Pwr sunroof, fog lamps, alloy whls, 195/60R15 tires, home link system, AM/FM stereo radio with cassette and graphic equalizer.

Accessories

CODE	DESCRIPTION	INVOICE	MSRP
AC	**Air Conditioning** — S	731	891
AB	**Anti-Lock Brakes** — ES, LS	781	952
KE	**Remote Keyless Entry System** — ES, LS	145	223
EC	**Radio** — AM/FM ETR stereo w/cassette - S	297	457
ED	**Compact Disc Player**— S, ES *S req's EC radio*	449	641
ED	**Compact Disc Player**— LS	488	699
CN	**Cargo Area Convenience Net**	19	23
FM	**Floor Mats** - S	47	73
MG	**Mud Guards**	76	117

MIRAGE *(1995)*

CODE	DESCRIPTION	INVOICE	MSRP
MG21-E	S 2-Dr Coupe (5-spd)	9099	9894
MG21-E	S 2-Dr Coupe (auto)	9752	10635
MG21-M	LS 2-Dr Coupe (5-spd)	11425	12721
MG21-M	LS 2-Dr Coupe (auto)	12019	13358
	Destination Charge:	420	420

CODE	DESCRIPTION	INVOICE	MSRP

Standard Equipment

MIRAGE - S COUPE: 5-passenger seating capacity, highback front bucket seats, textured vinyl upholstery with cloth inserts, soft-touch wraparound dash, passenger area carpeting, front and rear armrests, heating/ventilating system with 4-speed fan/dial-type controls/dual bi-level output, electric rear window defroster with automatic shut-off, 2-speed wipers, center console with storage bin, remote hood/latch release, keyless locking, door map pockets, driver and passenger air bags, side-impact door beams, height adjustable driver and passenger shoulder belt, ELR/ALR switchable outboard 3-point shoulder belts, child restraint anchorages, analog instrumentation (incls speedometer/ fuel level gauge/coolant temperature gauge/backglow instrument illumination), warning lights for engine check/emergency brake system/low oil pressure/door ajar/SRS light, steering column mounted controls (incls headlamps/high-low beam/flash-to-pass/turn signals/windshield washer and wipers), instrument panel controls (incls panel lamps dimmer, hazard flasher, heater/ventilation), radio accommodation package (antenna, full harness, radio bracket, 4 speakers), 5-mph bumpers, color-keyed integrated front and rear bumpers, color-keyed grille, black door sash accent, black door handles, flush mount door handles, locking fuel-filler door with cap tether, semi-concealed windshield wipers, aero-quad halogen headlamps, dual aero-type sideview mirrors, 145/80R13 all-season SBR tires, styled steel wheels with black center cap, 1.5 liter SOHC 12-valve 4 cylinder engine, electronic multi-point fuel injection, roller-type cam followers, stainless steel exhaust system, 4-wheel independent/ multi-link rear suspension, 5-speed manual transmission with overdrive, power assist front disc/rear drum brakes, rack and pinion steering.

LS COUPE (in addition to or instead of COUPE equipment): Luxury sport front bucket seats, height adjustable driver seat, adjustable front headrests, split fold-down rear seat, full cloth upholstery, cargo area carpeting, cloth insert door trim, 2-speed intermittent wipers, tilt steering column, day/ night rearview mirror, digital clock, remote fuel filler and hatch release, Convenience Pkg (incls digital clock, intermittent wipers, cloth door trim, split fold-down rear seat, full trunk trim and lamp), low fuel warning light, trip odometer, tachometer, ETR AM/FM cassette with 4 speakers, color-keyed bodyside molding, color-keyed door handles, rear spoiler, locking fuel filler door with cap tether and remote release, tinted glass, dual power remote color-keyed sideview mirrors, 185/65R14 all-season SBR tires, alloy wheels, 1.8 liter SOHC 16-valve 4 cylinder engine, power steering.

Accessories

CODE	DESCRIPTION	INVOICE	MSRP
—	**Radio**		
EC	AM/FM ETR stereo w/cassette - S	312	490
ED	compact disc *S req's AM/FM ETR stereo radio w/cassette*	407	615
VM	**Value Pkg** — LS *incls compact disc, wheel locks, air conditioning, cargo convenience net, floor mats*	853	853
CN	**Cargo Convenience Net**	25	37
TR	**Wheel Trim Rings** — S	44	68
FM	**Floor Mats**	41	64
AC	**Air Conditioning**	700	854
MG	**Mud Guards**	70	99
TL	**Wheel Locks** — LS	21	33

CODE	DESCRIPTION	INVOICE	MSRP

200SX (1995)

CODE	DESCRIPTION	INVOICE	MSRP
01155	Base 2-Dr Coupe (5-spd)	11370	11999
01115	Base 2-Dr Coupe (auto)	12129	12799
01255	SE 2-Dr Coupe (5-spd)	12786	14269
01215	SE 2-Dr Coupe (auto)	13503	15069
01455	SE-R 2-Dr Coupe (5-spd)	13683	15269
01415	SE-R 2-Dr Coupe (auto)	14400	16069
Destination Charge:		390	390

Standard Equipment

200SX - BASE: 1.6 liter DOHC 16-valve 4 cylinder engine, sequential multi-point fuel injection, 5-speed manual overdrive transmission, power rack and pinion steering, power vented front disc/ rear drum brakes, independent strut type front suspension, multi-link beam rear suspension, rear stabilizer bar, full wheel covers, flush-mounted halogen headlamps, tinted glass, dual power remote control outside mirrors with passenger side convex mirror, body color bumpers, tail pipe finisher, reclining front bucket seats, woven cloth seat trim, full vinyl door trim, passenger side walk-in device, full carpeting, front door map pockets, tilt steering column, 2-speed fixed intermittent windshield wipers/washers, electric rear window defroster, side window defoggers, dual cup holders, remote trunk/fuel filler door/hood releases, speedometer, tachometer, trip odometer, coolant temperature gauge, driver and passenger side air bags (SRS), 3-point manual front shoulder belts (passenger side is ALR/ELR), 3-point manual rear seatbelts in the outboard positions (ALR/ELR), front and rear crumple zones, bodyside reinforcement, energy-absorbing steering column.

200SX SE (in addition to or instead of 200SX BASE equipment): Front stabilizer bar, aluminum alloy wheels, fog lamps, body color side moldings, front sport bucket seats, 60/40 split fold-down rear seatbacks, sporty woven cloth seat trim, deluxe door trim with cloth insert, air conditioning with non-CFC refrigerant, power windows with driver side auto-down feature, power door locks, cruise control, front and rear assist grips, digital quartz clock, electronically tuned AM/FM cassette stereo system with auto reverse/Dolby noise reduction/4 speakers.

CODE	DESCRIPTION	INVOICE	MSRP

200SX SE-R (in addition to or instead of 200SX SE equipment): 2.0 liter DOHC 16-valve 4 cylinder engine, power-assisted 4-wheel disc brakes, viscous limited slip front differential, side sill extensions, rear spoiler, leather-wrapped steering wheel and shift knob, Vehicle Security System (incls keyless remote locking/unlocking with anti-theft, panic alarm and remote arming).

Accessories

C01	**California Emissions**	129	150
B07	**Anti-Lock Brakes** — SE & SE-R	851	995
J01	**Power Sunroof** — SE & SE-R	385	450
K01	**Rear Spoiler** — SE *std on SE-R*	129	150
F09	**Popular Equipment Pkg** *incls air conditioning, AM/FM stereo radio w/cassette and 4 speakers*	1256	1470

240SX COUPE *(1995)*

26155	Base 2-Dr Coupe (5-spd)	15722	17749
26115	Base 2-Dr Coupe (auto)	16431	18549
26255	SE 2-Dr Coupe (5-spd)	18991	21439
26215	SE 2-Dr Coupe (auto)	19700	22239
	Destination Charge:	390	390

Standard Equipment

240SX COUPE: 2.4 liter DOHC 16-valve 4-cylinder engine, 5-speed manual overdrive transmission, power assisted rack and pinion steering, power assisted 4-wheel disc brakes (front vented), power windows with driver side one-touch auto-down control, 195/60HR15 high-performance all-season tires, 15-inch steel wheels with full aerodynamic wheel covers, electronically tuned AM/FM cassette stereo audio system (50 watt) with Dolby noise reduction and 4 speakers, sequential multi-point electronic fuel injection, front-engine/rear-wheel drive, independent strut-type front suspension, front stabilizer bar, halogen headlamps, body color bumpers, semi-concealed windshield wipers, tinted glass with dark upper windshield band, dual power remote controlled body color outside mirrors, integrated high-mount stop lamp, double chrome-tipped exhaust finishers, reclining low-back front bucket seats, fold-down rear seatback (trunk through rear seat), moquette fabric seat material, cloth door trim, large front door map pockets, cut-pile carpeting, tilt steering column, 2-speed and fixed intermittent windshield wipers/twin-stream washers, electric rear window defroster with timer, side window defoggers, remote trunk/fuel-filler door/hood releases, center console with covered storage area, day/night rearview mirror, lockable glove box, covered visor vanity mirror, interior courtesy lamps, analog tachometer/trip odometer/speedometer/coolant temperature/fuel level gauges, digital quartz clock, rod antenna with diversity antenna system, driver and passenger side air bags, steel side-door guard beams, 3-point front/rear seat belts, front seat belt warning light, 5-mph energy-absorbing front and rear bumpers, energy-absorbing steering column.

240SX SE COUPE (in addition to or instead of 240SX COUPE equipment): Power door locks, 205/55VR16 high-performance all-season tires, 16-inch aluminum alloy wheels, electronically-tuned AM/FM/CD stereo audio system (160 watt) with 6 speakers, air conditioning with non-CFC refrigerant, rear stabilizer bar, sport-tuned suspension, front and rear spoilers, projector-style fog lamps, driver-adjustable lumbar support, moquette fabric seat material with sporty center insert, keyless remote entry with anti-theft security system (panic alarm, remote arming), cruise control, 2-speed and variable intermittent windshield wipers/twin-stream washers, white-meter analog gauge cluster with reverse-to-electroluminescent lighting, power antenna with diversity-type antenna system.

Accessories

CODE	DESCRIPTION	INVOICE	MSRP
A01	**Air Conditioning** — std on SE	854	999
J03	**Power Sunroof**	768	899
B10	**Anti-Lock Brakes** *incls limited slip differential*	1025	1199
C01	**California Emissions**	129	150
T04	**Alloy Wheels** *std on SE*	341	399
E07	**Pearl Glow Paint**	307	359
V04	**Convenience Pkg** *incls speed control, power door locks & AM/FM ETR stereo radio w/CD player, std on SE; req's air cond*	831	949
X03	**Leather Pkg** *incls leather seats, leather-wrapped steering wheel & dual map lights; req's alloy wheels & power sunroof on Base; req's anti-lock brakes on SE*	1025	1199

See the Automobile Dealer Directory on page 448 for a Dealer near you!

CODE	DESCRIPTION	INVOICE	MSRP

300ZX (1995)

64055	2-Dr Coupe w/o T-Bar (5-spd)	30645	35419
64155	2-Dr Coupe w/T-Bar (5-spd)	31891	36859
64115	2-Dr Coupe w/T-Bar (auto)	32669	37759
64855	2-Dr V6 Turbo Coupe w/T-Bar (5-spd)	36303	41959
64815	2-Dr V6 Turbo Coupe w/T-Bar (auto)	37082	42859
64255	2-Dr 2+2 w/T-Bar (5-spd)	33024	38169
64215	2-Dr 2+2 w/T-Bar (auto)	33802	39069
64755	2-Dr Convertible (5-spd)	36909	42659
64715	2-Dr Convertible (auto)	37688	43559
Destination Charge:		390	390

Standard Equipment

300ZX: 3.0 liter DOHC 24-valve V6 engine (all except Turbo Coupe), twin-turbocharged 3.0 liter DOHC 24-valve V6 engine with twin air-to-air intercoolers (Turbo Coupe), engine oil cooler (Turbo Coupe), Nissan valve timing control system, Nissan direct ignition system, 5-speed manual overdrive transmission, electronic speed-sensitive power rack and pinion steering, dual air bags, super HICAS 4-wheel steering system (Turbo Coupe), limited slip differential, 4-wheel independent multi-link suspension, front and rear stabilizer bars, 2-way driver-adjustable shock absorbers (Turbo Coupe), power 4-wheel vented disc brakes, anti-lock braking system, cast aluminum alloy wheels, high-performance steel belted radial tires, body color front and rear bumpers, body color front air dam, projection type low beam halogen headlamps, integrated front halogen fog lamps, dual heated power remote control outside mirrors with passenger side convex mirror, fully-tinted glass with upper shaded windshield band, removable tinted glass panels (Coupe w/T-Bar), electric rear window wiper/ washer (all except Convertible), integrated body color rear spoiler (Turbo Coupe), front air dam with twin intercooler inlets (Turbo Coupe), quad chrome-tipped exhaust finishers, reclining front bucket seats, power driver's seat (all except Coupe w/o T-Bar), fold-down rear seatback (2+2), cloth seat trim (leather seats on Convertible), center console, full cut-pile carpeting with carpeted cargo area, lockable glove box, air conditioning, automatic temperature control (all except Convertible), retractable cargo area cover (all except Convertible), power windows with driver side auto-down feature, power door locks, keyless remote entry system with anti-theft security system, cruise control, etched glass,

CODE	DESCRIPTION	INVOICE	MSRP

leather-wrapped steering wheel and gear shift knob, remote fuel filler door release, remote hatch/trunk and hood releases, passenger side-visor vanity mirror, 2-speed variable intermittent windshield wipers, electric rear window defroster with timer (all except Convertible), side window defoggers (all except Convertible), dual overhead map lamps, illuminated entry system with fade-out feature, digital quartz clock, analog style instrumentation, tachometer, turbo boost gauge (Turbo Coupe), trip odometer, gauges (coolant temperature, fuel level, oil pressure), electronically tuned AM/FM stereo radio with 2 speakers (Convertible), Bose audio system including AM/FM stereo radio with cassette (all except Convertible).

Accessories

CODE	DESCRIPTION	INVOICE	MSRP
C01	**California Emissions**	129	150
E07	**Pearl Glow Paint**	307	359
X03	**Leather Pkg** — Coupe w/T-Bar, Turbo Coupe	923	1079
	2+2	1094	1279

ALTIMA *(1995)*

CODE	DESCRIPTION	INVOICE	MSRP
15655	XE 4-Dr Sedan (5-spd)	13336	14969
15615	XE 4-Dr Sedan (auto)	14076	15799
15755	GXE 4-Dr Sedan (5-spd)	14090	15999
15715	GXE 4-Dr Sedan (auto)	14821	16829
15955	SE 4-Dr Sedan (5-spd)	16633	18999
15915	SE 4-Dr Sedan (auto)	17361	19829
15815	GLE 4-Dr Sedan (auto)	17509	19999
Destination Charge:		390	390

Standard Equipment

ALTIMA - XE: 2.4 liter 16-valve SFI 4 cylinder engine, 5-speed manual transmission, power steering, power front disc/rear drum brakes, driver and front passenger air bags, tilt steering wheel, bodyside moldings, tachometer, trip odometer, rear window defroster, intermittent windshield wipers, console, cloth reclining bucket seats, remote trunk release, remote fuel filler door release, wheel covers, power OS mirrors, visor vanity mirror.

CODE	DESCRIPTION	INVOICE	MSRP

GXE (in addition to or instead of XE equipment): Power windows, power door locks.

SE (in addition to or instead of GXE equipment): Power moonroof, air conditioning, speed control, alloy wheels, fog lights, rear spoiler, sport suspension, cornering lights, power 4-wheel disc brakes, AM/FM stereo radio with cassette, cloth reclining sport bucket seats, variable intermittent windshield wipers, leather-wrapped steering wheel, bodyside moldings deleted.

GLE (in addition to or instead of GXE equipment): Automatic air conditioning, 4-speed automatic transmission with overdrive, AM/FM stereo radio with cassette and compact disc, power antenna, alloy wheels, power moonroof, alarm system, cornering lights, speed control, variable intermittent windshield wipers, illuminated visor vanity mirrors.

Accessories

CODE	DESCRIPTION	INVOICE	MSRP
B07	**Anti-Lock Brakes** *req's F02 option pkg on XE; req's F09 option pkg on GXE*	854	999
X03	**Leather Pkg** — SE, GLE	897	1049
C01	**California Emissions System**	129	150
S07	**Speed Control** — XE w/auto trans	196	229
F02	**Option Pkg F02** — XE *incls air conditioning, speed control, AM/FM stereo radio w/cassette*	1624	1899
F09	**Option Pkg F09** — GXE *incls air conditioning, speed control, AM/FM stereo w/cassette, power antenna*	1111	1299
J01	**Power Sunroof** — GXE	742	869

MAXIMA (1995)

CODE	DESCRIPTION	INVOICE	MSRP
08455	GXE 4-Dr Sedan (5-spd)	17818	19999
08415	GXE 4-Dr Sedan (auto)	19197	21799
08255	SE 4-Dr Sedan (5-spd)	19085	21799
08215	SE 4-Dr Sedan (auto)	19961	22799
08615	GLE 4-Dr Sedan (auto)	22009	25139
	Destination Charge:	390	390

Standard Equipment

MAXIMA - GXE: DOHC 24-valve V6 engine, 5-speed manual transmission, power-assisted rack and pinion steering, power-assisted 4-wheel disc brakes (front vented), power windows with driver side auto-down feature, power door locks, steel wheels with full covers, electronically tuned AM/FM stereo audio system with auto-reverse cassette, Dolby noise reduction and 4 speakers, air conditioning with non-CFC refrigerant, sequential multi-point fuel injection, Nissan Direct Ignition System (NDIS), independent strut front suspension, front and rear stabilizer bars, flush-mounted halogen headlamps, flush-mounted halogen cornering lamps, semi-concealed windshield wipers, tinted glass with dark upper windshield band, dual power remote control outside mirrors with passenger side convex mirror, body color bodyside moldings, front bucket seats, multi-adjustable driver's seat with front and rear seat cushion tilt/seatback recline/2-way lumbar support and fore/aft adjustments, large front door map pockets, cut-pile carpeting, cruise control with steering wheel-mounted controls, tilt steering column, 2-speed windshield wipers with fixed intermittent feature, electric rear window defroster with timer, side window defoggers, cup holders, remote trunk/fuel filler door and hood releases, center console with large storage area and armrest, lockable glove box illuminated entry, overhead map lamp, interior courtesy lamps, ashtray and trunk courtesy lamps, tachometer/coolant temperature/fuel level gauges, low fuel warning light, trip odometer, digital clock, automatic power diversity antenna system, driver and passenger side air bags (SRS), 3-point manual seatbelts in outboard positions/rear center lap belts, child-safety rear door locks, energy-absorbing steering column/front and rear bumpers, side impact protection.

GLE (in addition to or instead of GXE equipment): Electronically controlled 4-speed automatic overdrive transmission, aluminum alloy wheels with bright finish, Bose electronically-tuned AM/FM cassette/CD stereo audio system with 4 amplifiers and 6 speakers, single chrome-tipped exhaust finisher, 8-way power-adjustable front driver's seat, fold-down rear seat center armrest with trunk pass-through, leather seating surfaces, leather-wrapped steering wheel and shift knob, simulated wood trim, automatic temperature control, dual illuminated visor vanity mirrors, 2-speed windshield wipers with variable intermittent feature, remote keyless entry system, theft deterrent system, automatic transmission park/lock feature.

SE (in addition to or instead of GLE equipment): 5-speed manual transmission, electronically-tuned AM/FM stereo audio system with auto-reverse cassette/Dolby noise reduction and 4 speakers, electronically controlled liquid filled front engine mount, sport-tuned suspension, halogen fog lamps, body color rear spoiler and black-out exterior trim, 8-way power adjustable front driver's seat deleted, leather seating surfaces deleted, simulated wood trim deleted, automatic temperature control deleted, dual illuminated visor vanity mirrors deleted, 2-speed windshield wipers with fixed intermittent feature, remote keyless entry system and theft deterrent feature deleted, white-faced analog-style gauges with reverse-to-electroluminescent lighting, automatic transmission park/lock feature deleted.

Accessories

CODE	DESCRIPTION	INVOICE	MSRP
B07	**Anti-Lock Brakes** *NA GXE 5-spd*	854	999
J01	**Power Sunroof** *NA GXE 5-spd*	768	899
C01	**California Emissions**	129	150
W08	**Cold Weather Pkg** *incls heated front seats, heated OS mirrors, low windshield washer fluid warning light, heavy duty battery; req's anti-lock brakes and security convenience pkg w/GXE auto and SE; NA GXE 5-spd*	174	199
H07	**Bose Audio System w/CD Player** — SE, GXE auto *incls AM/FM ETR stereo radio; req's power sunroof and security convenience pkg*	700	799

CODE	DESCRIPTION	INVOICE	MSRP
X03	**SE Leather Trim Pkg** — SE *incls leather seating surfaces, door panels with leatherette trim, automatic air conditioning controls; req's Bose audio system and security convenience pkg*	939	1099
V01	**Security Convenience Pkg** — SE, GXE auto *incls 8-way power driver's seat, keyless entry system, security system, power decklid release, variable intermittent wipers, illuminated visor vanity mirrors (GXE also incls chrome-tipped exhaust outlet and P205/60HR15 SBR all-season tires; SE req's power sunroof)*	612	699

SENTRA *(1995)*

CODE	DESCRIPTION	INVOICE	MSRP
42055	E 4-Dr Sedan (5-spd)	10422	10999
42155	XE 4-Dr Sedan (5-spd)	11818	12749
42115	XE 4-Dr Sedan (auto)	12560	13549
42255	GXE 4-Dr Sedan (5-spd)	12052	13449
42215	GXE 4-Dr Sedan (auto)	12769	14249
42555	GLE 4-Dr Sedan (5-spd)	12948	14449
42515	GLE 4-Dr Sedan (auto)	13665	15249
Destination Charge:		390	390

Standard Equipment

SENTRA - E: 1.6 liter DOHC 16-valve 4 cylinder engine, 5-speed manual overdrive transmission, power vented front disc/rear drum brakes, independent strut front suspension, multi-link beam rear suspension, styled steel wheels with center cap, flush mounted halogen headlamps, tinted glass, body color front grille, driver side outside mirror, black bumpers, 5-mph certified energy absorbing bumpers, reclining front bucket seats, woven seat trim, full molded door trim, front door map pockets, full carpeting, dual cup holders, tilt steering column, 2-speed windshield wipers/washers, rear window defroster, side window defoggers, 12-volt DC in-dash power source, foot rest, center console, front assist grip, speedometer, coolant temperature gauge, trip odometer, driver and passenger side air bags (SRS), 3-point manual front shoulder belts (passenger side is ALR/ELR), adjustable front shoulder belt anchors, 3-point manual rear seatbelts in the outboard positions (ALR/ELR), front and rear crumple zones, child-safety rear door locks, bodyside reinforcement, energy-absorbing steering column.

XE (in addition to or instead of E equipment): Power assisted rack and pinion steering, rear stabilizer bar, styled steel wheels with full covers, dual outside mirrors, body color bumpers, air conditioning with non-CFC refrigerant, 2-speed with fixed intermittent windshield wipers/washers, remote trunk/ fuel filler door releases, digital quartz clock (in radio display), electronically tuned AM/FM cassette stereo audio system with Dolby noise reduction/auto reverse/4 speakers.

GXE (in addition to or instead of XE equipment): Dual power remote control outside mirrors with passenger side convex mirror, black bodyside moldings, split fold-down rear seats with high backs, knit seat trim, deluxe door trim with cloth insert, power windows and door locks, passenger vanity mirror, trunk lamp.

GLE (in addition to or instead of GXE equipment): Aluminum alloy wheels, body color bodyside moldings, power sliding glass sunroof with privacy shade, luxury velour cloth seat trim, remote keyless entry/security system with panic alarm, fold-down center armrest (with auto trans), rear assist grips, tachometer.

Accessories

CODE	DESCRIPTION	INVOICE	MSRP
C01	**California Emissions**	129	150
B07	**Anti-Lock Brakes** — GXE, GLE	851	995

What's New for *Nissan* in 1995?

200SX: Sentra-based sport coupe replaces coupe versions of the previous Sentra. SE-R version is suave and swift, but somwhat pricey. Base models make do with a 115 horsepower 1.6L four, while the zoomy SE-R gets a 2.0L four good for 140 ponies.

240SX: All new and in showrooms since summer 1994, the 240SX is only available as a coupe. It retains rear-wheel drive and its 155 hp twin cam four, but has a much more refined and upscale character.

300ZX: Aging sports car still looks great and receives no revisions for 1995. Due to be replaced in the next two years by a more conservatively styled model. Sources say the current ZX doesn't sell well in Japan, and early reports indicate the new 300ZX will not sell well in the U.S. Buy now.

Altima: A new grille, redesigned taillights and new wheelcovers update this hot-selling sedan.

Maxima: All new for 1995, the Maxima has been on sale for a year. World-class engineering and a powerful engine make this sedan a budget alternative to pricier iron from Europe and Japan. If they could just do something about those funky tailllights.

Sentra: Have you seen it? It sure is plain Jane, huh? The spunky personality of the 1994 Sentra has been weeded out, too. What's left is a three-box sedan with Saabish rear styling, destined to clutter rental lots. Fortunately, prices didn't creep up, or the Sentra would have been a hard sell against the Neon, Prizm, and new Cavalier.

CODE	DESCRIPTION	INVOICE	MSRP

ACHIEVA S COUPE/SEDAN *(1995)*

ACHIEVA S 4 CYL

CODE	DESCRIPTION	INVOICE	MSRP
L37NS	Series I S 2-Dr Coupe (incls Pkg 1SA & Pkg R7B)	12623	13500
L69NS	Series I S 4-Dr Sedan (incls Pkg 1SA & Pkg R7B)	12814	13705
L37NS	Series II S 2-Dr Coupe (incls Pkg 1SB & Pkg R7C)	14404	15405
L69NS	Series II S 4-Dr Sedan (incls Pkg 1SB & Pkg R7C)	14404	15405
Destination Charge:		495	495

Standard Equipment

ACHIEVA S - ALL MODELS: Driver's side air bag, maintenance-free battery with automatic rundown protection, power front disc/rear drum anti-lock brakes, warning chimes for seat belts/headlamps on/ key in ignition/turn signal on; console includes: shifter/storage armrest/ashtray/lighter/coin holder/ electronic shift position display; side window/electric rear window defoggers, power programmable automatic door locks, child security rear door locks (Sedan), front and rear door-pull handles, 2.3 liter L4 DOHC quad 4 engine with MFI, transverse-mounted engine with front wheel drive, front and rear sport fascias, lower body cladding, body color rocker moldings, cut-pile wall-to-wall carpeting, "Traverse" lower door/console carpeting, luggage compartment carpeting, composite halogen headlamps, inside hood release, gas charged hood struts, illuminated entry package, analog gauge cluster instrument panel, center high-mounted stop lamp, light package includes: lamps for map/glove box/ashtray/ instrument panel lower courtesy/under hood/trunk/rear roof rail courtesy/reading; front door/seat back map pockets, inside day/night mirror, black outside mirrors (driver side remote, passenger side manual), deluxe bodyside body color moldings, rocker panel moldings (body color on Coupe, black on Sedan), Delco ETR AM/FM stereo radio with seek/scan/4-speaker sound system/digital clock/ fixed mast fender antenna; remote decklid release, remote fuel filler door release, color-keyed 3-point safety belts (for front/rear outboard positions), color-keyed rear center lap belt, contour front bucket reclining seats with Opti-Ride suspension system (driver side 4-way manual adjuster, passenger side 2-way manual adjuster), easy-entry feature (Coupe), rear bench seat, power rack and pinion steering, deluxe steering wheel with tilt-wheel adjustable column, MacPherson front strut/rear coil spring suspension system, P195/70R14 SBR all-season BW tires, 5-speed manual transmission with floor shifter, driver and passenger covered visor vanity mirrors with map straps, bolt-on wheel discs, 14" x 6" wheels, Soft-Ray tinted windows, wet-arm pulse wiper system.

SERIES I (in addition to or instead of ALL MODEL equipment): Option Pkg 1SA (LD2 quad 4 engine, 5-speed manual transmission), Pkg R7B (auxiliary front and rear carpet floor mats, four-season air conditioning, rear aero wing, dual outside power mirrors and rear window grid antenna [Coupe]).

SERIES II (in addition to or instead of ALL MODEL equipment): Option Pkg 1SB (four-season air conditioning, gauge cluster [analog speedometer, tachometer, voltmeter; gauges for coolant temperature, oil pressure, trip odometer; warning lights for parking brake/low brake fluid, low coolant level, hazard flashers, low washer fluid, check oil level; warning lights for low fuel, generator, oil pressure, hot coolant activated by "check gauges" switch], AM/FM stereo radio with cassette and 4-speaker sound system, dual outside power mirrors, auxiliary front and rear carpeted floor mats, cruise control, rear aero wing and rear window grid antenna [Coupe only]), Pkg R7C (power side windows with driver's auto-down feature, LD2 quad 4 engine, 4-speed automatic transmission).

Accessories

CODE	DESCRIPTION	INVOICE	MSRP
FE9	**Federal Emission Equipment**	NC	NC
NG1	**Massachusetts Emission Equipment**	NC	NC
YF5	**California Emission Equipment**	NC	NC
AX3	**Keyless Remote Control Pkg** — Series II	108	125
K05	**Engine Block Heater**	15	18
L82	**Engine** — 3100 SFI V6 w/variable effort steering	354	412
	Transmissions		
MM5	5-speed manual delete - Series II	(649)	(755)
MX0	4-speed automatic w/overdrive - Series I	649	755
MX1	3-speed automatic - Series I	477	555
	Series II	(172)	(200)
PF7	**Wheels** — 15" aluminum w/BW touring tires - Series II	336	391
T43	**Rear Aero Wing Pkg** — Sedan (Series I)	193	224
	Sedan (Series II)	126	147
UM6	**Radio** — Series I *incls AM/FM audio system with cassette and extended-range speakers*	142	165
U1C	**Radio** — Series II *incls AM/FM audio system with compact disc*	220	256

AURORA *(1995)*

AURORA 8 CYL

CODE	DESCRIPTION	INVOICE	MSRP
R29GS	4-Dr Sedan	30585	33065
Destination Charge:		635	635

Standard Equipment

AURORA: 4.0 liter 32-valve DOHC V8 engine, front wheel drive, 4-speed electro-shift automatic overdrive transmission, rack and pinion steering with magnetic speed variable assist, front suspension (independent strut-type with lower control arms, coil springs and stabilizer bar), rear suspension (independent semi-trailing arm with lateral links, coil springs, stabilizer bar and automatic leveling), 16" x 7" 6-spoke aluminum wheels, Goodyear Eagle GA P235/60R16 radial ply BW touring tires, Freedom battery, composite halogen headlamps with flash-to-pass feature, integrated front fascia foglamps, 5-mph bumpers, bodycolor bodyside moldings, black rocker panel moldings, cornering lamps, front seats (contour bucket with 6-way power adjustment, power recliners, power lumbar supports, manually adjustable headrests, leather seating areas and driver side memory control), rear seat (bench with integrated headrests, center folding armrest with storage and dual cupholders, center pass-through to trunk and leather seating areas), front center console including floor-mounted leather-wrapped shifter and storage compartment, E-Z Kool solar control windows, courtesy lamps, illumination package activated by remote lock control, deluxe acoustical insulation, genuine walnut burl wood trim on console and door armrests, deluxe trunk trim, front and rear floor mats, ashtrays, driver and front passenger side air bags, power 4-wheel disc anti-lock brakes, all-speed traction control system, automatic programmable door locks with remote controls, Pass-Key vehicle security system, pulse wiper system, leather-wrapped tilt steering wheel with touch controls, side window defoggers, electric rear window defogger, dual horns, chime-tone warning system, automatic dual-zone air conditioner with rear seat duct and outside temperature display, power windows with driver side auto down feature and driver-controlled lockout switch, remote lock control package, cruise control, twilight sentinel automatic headlamp control, front seatback pockets, door pockets, overhead console, retained accessory power, sunvisors with auxiliary shades, extensions and map straps, power fuel filler door release, inside hood release, gas strut hood supports, inside day/night electrochromic mirror, driver and passenger lighted visor vanity mirrors, two rear assist handles, trunk cargo net, electronic clock, power trunk lid lock release, analog instrument panel including tachometer, audio system (AM/FM stereo radio with automatic tone control, cassette, CD player, 6-speaker Dimensional Sound System, power antenna).

CODE	DESCRIPTION	INVOICE	MSRP
	Accessories		
FE9	**Federal Emission Equipment**	NC	NC
NG1	**Massachusetts Emission Equipment**	NC	NC
YF5	**California Emission Equipment**	NC	NC
CF5	**Sunroof — electric sliding, glass**	856	995
KA1	**Seats — driver/passenger heated**	254	295
K05	**Engine Block Heater**	15	18
QQX	**Autobahn Pkg** *incls Michelin P235/60VR16 SBR BW tires, 3.71 axle ratio*	340	395
UU8	**Bose Acoustimass System** *incls AM/FM ETR stereo radio with seek/scan, auto reverse cassette, speaker system with rear shelf module including woofer and 6 additional speakers*	577	671
—	**Cloth Seat Trim**	NC	NC

CUTLASS CIERA SL SEDAN *(1995)*

	INVOICE	MSRP
CUTLASS CIERA SL 4 CYL		
J69AS Series I SL 4-Dr Sedan (incls Pkg 1SA & Pkg R7B)	14047	14865
CUTLASS CIERA SL 6 CYL		
J69AS Series II SL 4-Dr Sedan (incls Pkg 1SB & Pkg R7C)	15559	16465
Destination Charge:	535	535

Standard Equipment

CIERA SL SEDAN - ALL MODELS: Driver's side air bag, four-season air conditioning, ashtray with lighter, maintenance-free Freedom battery, power front disc/rear drum anti-lock brakes, brake/ transmission shift interlock, warning chimes for seat belts/ headlamps on/key in ignition/turn signal on; side window/electric rear window defoggers, power programmable automatic door locks, front/ rear door-pull handles, 2.2 liter L4 MFI engine, transverse-mounted engine with front wheel drive, cut-pile wall-to-wall floor carpeting with carpeted lower door panels, composite halogen headlamps, interior operated hood release, illuminated entry package, analog gauge cluster instrument panel, center high-mounted stop lamp, light package includes: dome/ashtray/glove box/trunk/under hood; front door map pockets, inside day/night mirror with dual reading lamps, black outside mirrors (driver side remote, passenger side manual), body side moldings, bright roof drip/belt reveal moldings, Delco ETR AM/FM stereo radio with seek/scan/digital display clock/4-speaker sound system/fixed mast fender antenna; color-keyed 3-point safety belts (front/rear outboard positions), color-keyed center lap belts, 55/45 divided front bench seats with power reclining seat backs/dual controls/center armrest; power rack and pinion steering, deluxe steering wheel with tilt-wheel adjustable column, MacPherson front strut/rear variable-rate coil spring suspension system, P185/75R14 SBR white-stripe all-season tires, 3-speed automatic transmission with column shift, Flo-Thru ventilation, driver and passenger covered visor vanity mirrors, bolt-on wheel discs, 14" x 5.5" wheels, Soft-Ray tinted windows, pulse wiper system.

SERIES I (in addition to or instead of ALL MODEL equipment): Option Pkg 1SA (LN2 engine, 3-speed automatic transmission), Pkg R7B (auxiliary front/rear carpeted floor mats, AM/FM cassette radio with 4-speaker extended-range sound system, front-seat storage armrest with cup holders).

SERIES II (in addition to or instead of ALL MODEL equipment): Option Pkg 1SB (front seat storage armrest with cup holders, auxiliary front/rear carpeted floor mats, cruise control, dual outside power mirrors, AM/FM stereo radio with cassette and 4-speaker extended-range sound system), Pkg R7C (power side windows with driver side auto-down feature, L82 3100 SFI V6 engine, automatic overdrive transmission).

Accessories

Code	Description	Invoice	MSRP
FE9	**Federal Emission Equipment**	NC	NC
NG1	**Massachusetts Emission Equipment**	NC	NC
YF5	**California Emission Equipment**	NC	NC
AG1	**Power Driver Seat Adjuster** — Series II	262	305
AU0	**Keyless Remote Lock Control Pkg** — Series II	159	185
K05	**Engine Block Heater**	15	18
L82	**Engine/Transmission** — 3100 SFI V6 w/4-speed automatic - Series I	697	810
QMW	**Tires** — P195/75R14 BW	NC	NC

CIERA CRUISER SL WAGON *(1995)*

CIERA CRUISER SL 6 CYL

Code	Description	Invoice	MSRP
J35AS	SL 4-Dr Wagon	16504	17465
Destination Charge:		535	535

Standard Equipment

CIERA CRUISER SL WAGON: Driver side air bag, four-season air conditioning, ashtray with lighter, maintenance-free Freedom battery, power front disc/rear drum anti-lock brakes, brake/shift transmission interlock, front and rear bumper moldings, warning chimes for: seat belts/headlamps on/key in ignition/turn signal on; side window/electric rear window defoggers, power programmable automatic door locks (including tailgate lock release), front/rear door-pull handles, 3100 SFI V6 engine with sequential port fuel injection, transverse-mounted engine with front wheel drive, cut-pile wall-to-wall floor carpeting with carpeted lower door panels and cargo area, composite halogen headlamps, interior operated hood release, illuminated entry package, analog gauge cluster instrument

CODE	DESCRIPTION	INVOICE	MSRP

panel, center high-mounted stop lamp, light package includes: dome/instrument panel ashtray/glove box/cargo area/under hood; front door map pockets, inside day/night mirror with dual reading lamps, black outside mirrors (driver side remote, passenger side manual), bodyside moldings, bright roof drip/belt reveal moldings, Delco ETR AM/FM stereo radio with seek/scan/digital display clock/ 4-speaker sound system/fixed mast fender antenna; color-keyed 3-point safety belts (front/rear outboard positions), color-keyed center lap belts; 55/45 divided front bench seat with power reclining seat backs/dual controls/center armrest; split folding rear seat backs, power rack and pinion steering, deluxe steering wheel with tilt-wheel adjustable column, MacPherson front strut/rear variable rate coil spring suspension system, P185/75R14 SBR white-stripe all-season tires, electronic shift automatic overdrive transmission with column shift, Flo-Thru ventilation, driver and passenger covered visor vanity mirrors, bolt-on wheel discs, 14" x 5.5" wheels, Soft-Ray tinted windows, pulse wiper system, Option Pkg 1SB (front seat storage armrest with cup holders, auxiliary front/rear carpeted floor mats, cruise control, dual outside power mirrors, AM/FM stereo radio with cassette and extended-range rear speakers, rear window air deflector, chrome rooftop luggage carrier), Pkg R7D (power side windows with driver side auto-down feature, Wagon Pkg [rear-facing third seat, locking storage compartment, rear quarter vent windows]).

Accessories

CODE	DESCRIPTION	INVOICE	MSRP
FE9	**Federal Emission Equipment**	NC	NC
NG1	**Massachusetts Emission Equipment**	NC	NC
YF5	**California Emission Equipment**	NC	NC
AG1	**Power Driver Seat Adjuster**	262	305
AU0	**Keyless Remote Lock Control Pkg**	108	125
K05	**Engine Block Heater**	15	18
QMW	**Tires** — P195/75R15 BW	NC	NC

CUTLASS SUPREME CONVERTIBLE *(1995)*

CUTLASS SUPREME 6 CYL

CODE	DESCRIPTION	INVOICE	MSRP
T67WS	2-Dr Convertible	23041	25460
Destination Charge:		535	535

Standard Equipment

CUTLASS SUPREME CONVERTIBLE: Driver and passenger air bags, four-season air conditioning, maintenance-free Freedom battery, 4-wheel disc anti-lock brakes, brake/transmission shift interlock, body color front/rear bumper fascias, warning chimes for: safety belts/headlamps on/key in ignition/ turn signal on; full length shifting console with armrest storage and cup holder, electronic cruise control with resume and acceleration features, side window/electric rear window defoggers, pillar-mounted door handles with illuminated driver side lock, power programmable automatic door locks, interior door-pull handles, 3100 SFI V6 sequential port fuel injection engine, transverse-mounted engine with front wheel drive, dual engine cooling fans, deluxe cut-pile wall-to-wall floor carpeting, lower door panel carpeting, auxiliary front/rear carpeted floor mats, fog lamps, mini-quad headlamps with flash-to-pass provision on turn signal, interior operated hood release, gas-charged hood struts, illuminated entry package, analog gauge cluster instrument panel includes: speedometer/tachometer/ gauges for fuel level/engine temperature/indicators for oil pressure/low fuel/fasten seat belts/low coolant/"service engine soon"/anti-lock brakes/engine oil level monitor/backlit illumination; keyless remote lock control package includes: illumination package/key chain transmitter; center high-mounted stop lamp, leather trimmed seating areas, light package includes: lamps for instrument panel/glove box/roof rail/courtesy/under hood/trunk; inside day/night mirror with dual reading lamps, black outside dual power mirrors, driver and passenger covered visor vanity mirrors, color-coordinated body color wheel opening moldings, Delco ETR AM/FM stereo radio with seek/scan/auto reverse cassette/ digital display clock/4-speaker extended-range sound system/rear quarter power antenna; color-keyed 3-point deluxe safety belts (front/rear outboard positions), color-keyed rear center lap belt, reclining front bucket seats (6-way driver side power seat adjuster, 4-way passenger side manual seat adjuster), power rack and pinion steering, deluxe leather-wrapped tilt-wheel steering wheel, 4-wheel independent suspension system with touring car ride and handling components, MacPherson front strut suspension, P225/60R16 SBR BW tires, power folding vinyl top, electronic-shift automatic overdrive transmission with floor shifter, power trunk lid lock release, deluxe trunk trim Pass Key vehicle security system, Flo-Thru ventilation, 16" aluminum 5-spoke style wheels, power side windows, Soft-Ray tinted windows, wet-arm pulse wiper system.

CODE	DESCRIPTION	INVOICE	MSRP
	Accessories		
FE9	**Federal Emission Equipment**	NC	NC
NG1	**Massachusetts Emission Equipment**	NC	NC
YF5	**California Emission Equipment**	NC	NC
1SB	**Option Pkg 1SB**	186	216
	incls driver/passenger illuminated visor mirrors, variable effort steering, 6-speaker dimensional sound system		
1SC	**Option Pkg 1SC**	461	536
	incls Pkg 1SB contents plus automatic climate control with driver and passenger controls, steering wheel controls for audio system and air conditioner		
AP9	**Trunk Cargo Net**	26	30
B84	**Bodyside Moldings**	52	60
K05	**Engine Block Heater**	15	18
LQ1	**Engine Pkg** — w/o Pkg 1SB/1SC	1079	1255
	w/Pkg 1SB/1SC	1019	1185
	incls 3.4 liter DOHC V6 engine, oil level monitor, special suspension, rear aero wing, dual exhaust		
UN0	**Radio**	86	100
	incls AM/FM audio system with compact disc		
UP0	**Radio**	172	200
	incls AM/FM audio system with cassette and compact disc		

CUTLASS SUPREME S COUPE/SEDAN *(1995)*

CUTLASS SUPREME S 6 CYL

CODE	DESCRIPTION	INVOICE	MSRP
H47WS	Series I S 2-Dr Coupe (incls Pkg 1SB & Pkg R7B)	16693	17665
H69WS	Series I S 4-Dr Sedan (incls Pkg 1SB & Pkg R7B)	16693	17665
H47WS	Series II S 2-Dr Coupe (incls Pkg 1SC & Pkg R7C)	17638	18665
H69WS	Series II S 4-Dr Sedan (incls Pkg 1SC & Pkg R7C)	17638	18665
Destination Charge:		535	535

Standard Equipment

CUTLASS SUPREME S - ALL MODELS: Driver and passenger air bags, four-season air conditioning, maintenance-free Freedom battery, power 4-wheel disc anti-lock brakes, brake/transmission shift interlock, warning chimes for safety belts/headlamps on/key in ignition/turn signal on; console includes: shifter/storage armrest/cup holders, side window/electric rear window defoggers, power programmable automatic door locks, interior door-pull handles, 3100 SFI V6 sequential port fuel injection engine, transverse-mounted engine with front wheel drive, front and rear sport fascias, aero rocker moldings, cut-pile wall-to-wall floor carpeting, carpeted lower door panels, deluxe carpet trunk trim, composite halogen headlamps, interior operated hood release, gas charged hood struts, illuminated entry package, analog gauge cluster instrument panel includes: speedometer/tachometer/gauges for fuel level/engine temperature/oil level monitor; center high-mounted stop lamp, light package includes lamps for: instrument panel/glove box/roof rail courtesy/under hood/trunk; front door map pockets, inside day/night mirror with dual reading lamps, black outside mirrors (driver side remote, passenger side manual), driver and passenger covered visor vanity mirrors, black roof drip/belt reveal moldings, body color wheel opening moldings, Delco ETR AM/FM stereo radio with seek/scan/digital display clock/4-speaker extended-range sound system/rear quarter fixed mast antenna; color-keyed 3-point deluxe safety belts (front/rear outboard positions), color-keyed rear center lap belt, contour reclining front bucket seats with 4-way manual adjustment, power rack and pinion steering, deluxe steering wheel with tilt-wheel adjustable column, 4-wheel fully independent MacPherson front strut/rear transverse fiberglass leaf spring suspension system, shock struts, P205/70R15 SBR BW all-season tires, electronic-shift automatic overdrive transmission with floor shifter, Pass Key vehicle security system, Flo-Thru ventilation, bolt-on wheel discs, 15" x 6" wheels, power side windows with driver auto-down feature, Soft-Ray tinted windows, wet/arm pulse wiper system.

SERIES I (in addition to or instead of ALL MODEL equipment): Option Pkg 1SB (cruise control, auxiliary front and rear carpeted floor mats, dual outside power mirrors, AM/FM stereo radio with cassette), Pkg R7B (16" aluminum wheels, Sport Luxury Pkg).

SERIES II (in addition to or instead of ALL MODEL equipment): Option Pkg 1SC (cruise control, auxiliary front and rear carpet, dual outside power mirrors, AM/FM stereo radio with cassette, 6-speaker dimensional sound audio system, keyless remote lock control package, power antenna, lighted visor vanity mirrors, variable effort steering), Pkg R7C (16" aluminum wheels, leather trim seating areas, sport luxury package, driver side 6-way power seat adjuster, custom trim package with split-folding rear seat back).

Accessories

CODE	DESCRIPTION	INVOICE	MSRP
FE9	**Federal Emission Equipment**	NC	NC
NG1	**Massachusetts Emission Equipment**	NC	NC
YF5	**California Emission Equipment**	NC	NC
K05	**Engine Block Heater**	15	18
LQ1	**Engine Pkg** — Series II	1052	1223
	incls 3.4 liter DOHC V6 engine, oil level monitor, variable effort steering, special suspension, dual exhaust, rear aero wing (Coupe), 16" wheels with bolt-on discs, P225/60R16 black letter radial ply performance tires		
UK3	**Steering Wheel Controls** — Series II	275	320
	controls for audio system and air conditioner (incls automatic climate control with driver and passenger controls)		
UP0	**Radio** — Series I	224	260
	Series II	172	200
	incls AM/FM audio system with cassette, compact disc, 6-speaker dimensional sound system (Series I)		

EIGHTY-EIGHT LSS SEDAN *(1995)*

EIGHTY-EIGHT LSS 6 CYL

CODE	DESCRIPTION	INVOICE	MSRP
Y69HS	LSS 4-Dr Sedan	23072	24415
Destination Charge:		585	585

Standard Equipment

EIGHTY-EIGHT LSS SEDAN: Driver and passenger air bags, air conditioning with rear seat duct, maintenance-free Freedom battery, power front disc/rear drum anti-lock brakes, brake/transmission shift interlock, convenience group includes: trunk lamp/covered visor vanity mirrors/chime tones for: seat belts/headlamps on/key in ignition/turn signal on; high capacity engine cooling equipment, electronic cruise control with resume and acceleration feature, side window/electric rear window defoggers, deluxe trim luggage compartment with "jack-in-the-box" tool kit, power door locks, child security rear door locks, 3800 Series II V6 sequential fuel injection engine, transverse-mounted engine with front wheel drive, cut-pile wall-to-wall floor carpeting, carpeted lower door panels, auxiliary front/rear carpeted floor mats, composite halogen headlamps with flash-to-pass feature, interior operated hood release, instrument panel analog gauge cluster includes: fuel/coolant temperature/ low engine oil level indicator, center high-mounted stop lamp, light package includes: dome/instrument panel ashtray/glove box door/under hood/courtesy/warning/front and rear reading lamps; lighter, auxiliary 12-volt outlet (keyed through ignition), front license plate bracket, front door/seat back map pockets, inside day/night mirror, body color outside dual power mirrors, bright belt reveal/drip moldings, body color wheel opening moldings, body color wide lower bodyside moldings, Delco ETR AM/FM stereo radio with seek/scan/automatic tone control/auto reverse cassette/digital display clock/ 6-speaker Dimensional Sound system/power rear quarter antenna; color-keyed 3-point front safety belts (with height adjustment for outboard positions), color-keyed front center lap belt, color-keyed 3-point rear safety belts (with child comfort guides for outboard positions), color-keyed center rear lap belt, 55/45 divided front reclining seats with individual controls/storage armrest/dual cup holders, power rack and pinion steering, deluxe tilt-wheel vinyl rim steering wheel, four-wheel fully independent MacPherson front strut/rear coil spring suspension system, front and rear stabilizer bars, P205/ 70R15 SBR BW all-season tires, electronic-shift automatic overdrive transmission with column shift, trip odometer, power trunk lid lock release, Pass Key vehicle security system, Flo-Thru ventilation, covered visor vanity mirrors with auxiliary sunshades, deluxe wheel discs, 15" x 6" wheels, power side windows, Soft-Ray tinted windows (EZ Kool solar control windshield and rear window glass), pulse wiper system, Pkg 1SB (dual zone heat/ventilation/air conditioning system, 16" aluminum wheels, BW tires, overhead console with storage compartment and dual reading lamps, steering wheel touch controls, luxury/convenience package includes: keyless remote accessory control package/dual lighted visor vanity mirrors/front and rear reading lamps/power reclining 6-way adjustable driver's seat; reminder package includes: indicators for low fuel/low coolant/low oil pressure/high engine temperature/low washer fluid level; trunk cargo net, rear seat storage armrest with cup holders), Pkg R7C (LSS Package, leather trim seating areas, Comfort Package includes: electrochromic inside mirror with compass/6-way passenger side power seat adjuster with power recliner/cornering lamps, traction control system).

Accessories

Code	Description	Invoice	MSRP
FE9	**Federal Emission Equipment**	NC	NC
NG1	**Massachusetts Emission Equipment**	NC	NC
YF5	**California Emission Equipment**	NC	NC
K05	**Engine Block Heater**	15	18
L67	**Engine** — supercharged 3800 V6	879	1022
UP0	**Radio** *incls AM/FM audio system with cassette and compact disc*	172	200

EIGHTY-EIGHT ROYALE SEDAN *(1995)*

EIGHTY-EIGHT ROYALE 6 CYL

Code	Description	Invoice	MSRP
N69HS	Royale 4-Dr Sedan	19670	20815
Destination Charge:		585	585

Standard Equipment

EIGHTY-EIGHT ROYALE SEDAN: Driver and passenger air bags, air conditioner, maintenance-free Freedom battery, power front disc/rear drum anti-lock brakes, brake/transmission shift interlock, convenience group includes: trunk lamp/covered visor vanity mirrors/chime tones for seat belts/headlamps on/key in ignition/turn signal on; high-capacity engine cooling equipment, side window/electric rear window defoggers, deluxe trim luggage compartment with "jack-in-the-box" tool kit, power door locks, rear child security door locks, 3800 Series II V6 sequential fuel injection engine, transverse-mounted engine with front wheel drive, cut-pile wall-to-wall floor carpeting, carpeted lower door panels, composite halogen headlamps with flash-to-pass feature, interior operated hood release, instrument panel analog gauge cluster includes: fuel/coolant temperature/low engine oil level indicator; center high-mounted stop lamp, light package includes: dome/instrument panel ashtray/courtesy/glove box/under hood; lighter, auxiliary 12-volt outlet (keyed through ignition), front door map pockets, inside day/night mirror, body color outside mirrors (driver side remote, passenger side manual), bright belt reveal/drip moldings, body color wheel opening moldings, gray protective bodyside moldings, Delco ETR AM/FM stereo radio with seek/scan/digital display clock/4-speaker extended-range sound system/fixed mast rear quarter antenna; color-keyed 3-point front safety belts (height adjustment for outboard positions), color-keyed center front lap belt, color-keyed 3-point rear safety belts (child comfort guides for outboard positions), color-keyed center rear lap safety belt, 55/45 divided front reclining seats with individual controls and center armrest, power rack and pinion steering, deluxe steering wheel with tilt-wheel adjustable column, four-wheel fully independent MacPherson front strut/rear coil spring suspension system, front and rear stabilizer bars, P205/70R15 SBR BW all-season tires, electronic-shift automatic overdrive transmission with column shift, trip odometer, Pass Key vehicle security system, Flo-Thru ventilation, covered visor vanity mirrors with auxiliary sunshades, deluxe wheel discs, 15" x 6" wheels, power side windows, Soft-Ray tinted glass (EZ Kool solar control windshield and rear window glass), pulse wiper system, Pkg 1SC (15" aluminum wheels, BW tires, front seat storage armrest, cruise control, auxiliary front/rear carpeted floor mats, trunk cargo net, AM/FM stereo radio with cassette and 6-speaker Dimensional Sound system, power antenna, 6-way power seat adjuster [driver side with power recliner], dual outside power mirrors, power trunk lid lock release, dual front/rear reading lamps, lighted visor vanity mirrors), Pkg R7B (keyless remote accessory control package).

Accessories

CODE	DESCRIPTION	INVOICE	MSRP
FE9	**Federal Emission Equipment**	NC	NC
NG1	**Massachusetts Emission Equipment**	NC	NC
YF5	**California Emission Equipment**	NC	NC
K05	**Engine Block Heater**	15	18
NW9	**Traction Control System**	151	175
N91	**Wheels/Tires** — simulated wire wheel discs w/white stripe tires	NC	NC
UP0	**Radio**	172	200
	incls AM/FM audio system with cassette and compact disc		
WJ7	**Custom Leather Trim**	525	610

NINETY-EIGHT REGENCY ELITE SEDAN *(1995)*

NINETY-EIGHT REGENCY ELITE 6 CYL

CODE	DESCRIPTION	INVOICE	MSRP
X69CS	Series I 4-Dr Sedan (incls Pkg 1SB & Pkg R7B)	25104	26565
X69CS	Series II 4-Dr Sedan (incls Pkg 1SC & Pkg R7C)	26143	27665
Destination Charge:		635	635

Standard Equipment

NINETY-EIGHT REGENCY ELITE - ALL MODELS: Driver and passenger air bags, air conditioning with rear seat duct, front seat storage armrest, rear seat center armrest, instrument panel/dual rear ashtrays, front and rear assist straps, maintenance-free Freedom battery, power front disc/rear drum brakes, brake/transmission shift interlock, cut-pile wall-to-wall carpeting, carpeted lower door panels, overhead storage console, convenience group includes: trunk lamp/covered visor vanity mirrors/

chimes for seat belts/headlamps on/key in ignition/turn signal on; high capacity cooling equipment, electronic cruise control with resume and acceleration feature, dual front cup holders, side window/ electric rear window defoggers, deluxe trim luggage compartment, power door locks, child security rear door locks, front and rear door-pull handles, 3800 Series II V6 sequential fuel injection engine, transverse-mounted engine with front wheel drive, auxiliary front and rear carpeted floor mats, composite halogen headlamps with flash-to-pass feature, interior operated hood release, instrument panel analog gauge cluster includes gauges for: fuel/coolant temperature/indicators for brakes/coolant temperature/battery voltage/fuel level/low engine oil level; center high-mounted stop lamp, front license plate bracket, instrument panel lighter with auxiliary 12-volt outlet (keyed through ignition), light package includes: courtesy door warning/instrument panel ashtray/courtesy/glove box/front and rear reading lamps; front seat back map pockets, inside day/night mirror, body color outside dual power mirrors, color-coordinated bodyside/wheel opening moldings, Delco ETR AM/FM stereo radio with seek/scan/digital display clock/4-speaker extended-range sound system; power rear quarter antenna, power remote fuel filler door, color-keyed 3-point front deluxe safety belts (with height adjustment for outboard positions), color-keyed front center lap belt, color-keyed 3-point rear safety belts (with child comfort guides for outboard positions), color-keyed rear center lap belt, 55/45 divided front bench seats with 6-way power adjusters, power lumbar and power recliners for driver and passenger, storage armrest with dual cup holders, rear bench seat with center armrest, power rack and pinion steering, deluxe tilt-wheel steering wheel with vinyl rim, four-wheel fully independent MacPherson front strut/rear coil spring suspension system, automatic load leveling suspension, front and rear stabilizer bars, P205/70R15 SBR white-stripe ride tires, electronic-shift automatic overdrive transmission with column shift, power trunk lid lock release, Pass Key vehicle security system, Flo-Thru ventilation, visors with auxiliary shades, 15" aluminum wheels, EZ Kool solar control windows, power side windows, pulse wiper system.

SERIES I (in addition to or instead of ALL MODEL equipment): Pkg 1SB (reminder package, lighted visor vanity mirrors, steering wheel touch controls, trunk cargo net, keyless remote accessory control package, dual-zone heat/ventilation/air conditioning system, 8-speaker Dimensional Sound audio system, rear seat storage armrest with cup holders), Pkg R7B (leather trim seating areas).

SERIES II (in addition to or instead of ALL MODEL equipment): Pkg 1SC (reminder package, lighted visor vanity mirrors, steering wheel touch controls, trunk cargo net, keyless remote accessory control package, dual-zone heat/ventilation/air conditioning system, 8-speaker audio system with 2 woofers, rear seat storage armrest with cup holders, power trunk pull-down, twilight sentinel, heated outside electrochromic driver side mirror, inside automatic electrochromic mirror with compass, driver seat memory controls, cornering lamps), Pkg R7C (leather trim seating areas, traction control system, electronic instrument cluster).

See the Automobile Dealer Directory on page 448 for a Dealer near you!

CODE	DESCRIPTION	INVOICE	MSRP
Accessories			
FE9	**Federal Emission Equipment**	NC	NC
NG1	**Massachusetts Emission Equipment**	NC	NC
YF5	**California Emission Equipment**	NC	NC
CF5	**Sunroof** — glass, electric sliding - Series II	856	995
K05	**Engine Block Heater**	15	18
L67	**Engine Pkg** — supercharged 3800 V6 - Series II	879	1022
NW9	**Traction Control System** — Series I	151	175
N91	**Wheels** — simulated wire wheel discs - Series I	NC	NC
UP0	**Radio** *incls AM/FM audio system with cassette and compact disc*	172	200

What's New for *Oldsmobile* in 1995?

Achieva: A simplification of the options sheet results in Series I and Series II models. The SOHC Quad 4 is retired, and a refined and balance shafted DOHC version is now the standard engine. New wheelcovers and retuned suspensions are also on tap for 1995.

Aurora: The belated replacement for the Toronado, the Aurora is a world class touring sedan designed to compete with the best from Japan and Europe. A detuned version of Cadillac's excellent Northstar V8 powers the front wheels, and prices start at $32,000. The Aurora has been in showrooms since June 1994.

Ciera: What, is this thing still called a Cutlass or not? Can't tell, but it still sells well. Only available in SL trim, the Ciera gets fabric changes and a shift interlock system.

Cutlass Supreme: A redesigned instrument panel with dual airbags is the big news on the 1995 Cutlass Supreme. The seatbelts are now mounted to the floor and B-Pillar where they belong, and interior fabrics have been revised.

Eighty Eight: A big horsepower jump for the standard V6 to 205 hp and the availability of the supercharged 3.8L V6 on the LSS are the only changes to the Eighty Eight.

Ninety Eight: The base V6 now makes 205 hp, alloy wheels are standard, and a 'flash-to-pass' function has been added to the turn-signal stalk.

CODE	DESCRIPTION	INVOICE	MSRP

ACCLAIM *(1995)*

ACCLAIM 4 CYL

CODE	DESCRIPTION	INVOICE	MSRP
PH41	4-Dr Sedan	12969	14323
Destination Charge:		505	505

Standard Equipment

ACCLAIM: 2.5 liter EFI inline 4 cylinder engine, 3-speed automatic transmission, power rack and pinion steering, power front disc/rear drum brakes, 14" x 5.5" JJ steel disc wheels, P185/70R14 tires, AM/FM stereo ETR radio with digital clock, seek, cassette, Dolby and 4 speakers; air conditioning, soft fascia bumpers with integral nerf and 5-mph protection, warning chimes for: headlights on/seat belt/key in ignition, electric rear window defroster, full stainless steel exhaust system, front and rear floor mats, tinted glass (all windows), locking glove box, body color grille, single halogen aero style headlights, counter-balanced hood (internal release), electric dual note horn, lamps include: ash receiver/glove box/trunk/dome, dual outside remote control mirrors (black), dual visor mirrors (left with cover), narrow bodyside moldings with bright stripe, "Austin" cloth seat trim, 50/50 split bench front seats with folding armrests (dual recliners), full fixed bench rear seat, electronic speed control, tilt steering column, four "Centrifuge" wheel covers, deluxe windshield wipers and washers with intermittent wipe.

Accessories

CODE	DESCRIPTION	INVOICE	MSRP
D	**Pkg D** *incls model with standard equipment*	NC	NC
E	**Pkg E** *incls power door locks, heated dual exterior power remote mirrors, remote trunk release, power windows*	625	735
EFA	**Engine** — 3.0 liter V6 *incls P195/70R14 BSW tires*	678	798

CODE	DESCRIPTION	INVOICE	MSRP
ASH	**Gold Special Equipment Decor Group** *incls gold badging and molding inserts, luggage rack, P195/70R14 all-season BSW SBR tires, 14" cast aluminum "bullet" design road wheels with gold accents*	170	200
JPS	**Power Driver Seat** — w/pkg E	260	306
JPB	**Power Door Locks** — w/pkg D *incld in pkg E*	213	250
NAE	**California Emissions**	87	102
NBY	**Massachusetts Emissions**	87	102
NHK	**Engine Block Heater**	17	20
TBB	**Conventional Spare Tire**	81	95
—	**Paint** — extra cost		
—	emerald green	82	97
—	metallic red	82	97

NEON *(1995)*

NEON 4 CYL

PL42	Base 4-Dr Sedan	8745	9500
PH22	Highline 2-Dr Coupe	10311	11240
PH42	Highline 4-Dr Sedan	10311	11240
PS22	Sport 2-Dr Coupe	12405	13567
PS42	Sport 4-Dr Sedan	12135	13267
Destination Charge:		500	500

Standard Equipment

NEON - BASE: 85 amp alternator, 450 amp maintenance-free battery, 13" power front disc/rear drum brakes, 5-mph front and rear bumpers, child protection rear door locks, warning chimes (for key in ignition, headlights on, seat belts), console, 2.0 liter SOHC 16V SMPI 4 cylinder engine, stainless steel exhaust system, single halogen aero-style headlights, cloth covered headliner, mirrors

CODE	DESCRIPTION	INVOICE	MSRP

(left exterior manual remote, black), rearview mirror with day/night feature, passenger side visor vanity mirror, driver and front passenger air bags, seats (cloth with vinyl trim, front high back buckets, rear fixed bench), manual steering, sun visors with driver side sunshade extension panel, ride tuned suspension, P165/80R13 all-season BSW SBR tires, T115/70D14 compact spare tire, 5-speed manual transaxle, carpet floor mat trunk dress-up, 13" steel painted bright silver wheels with black center cap, 2-speed windshield wipers.

HIGHLINE (in addition to or instead of BASE equipment): Front and rear body color fascias, tinted glass, mirrors (dual exterior manual remote, black), dual visor vanity mirrors (driver side covered), body color bodyside moldings, AM/FM stereo radio with clock and 4 speakers, seats (cloth with vinyl trim, front low back buckets, rear 60/40 split folding bench), premium sound insulation, 18:1 ratio power assisted steering, touring tuned suspension, P185/70R13 all-season BSW SBR tires, trunk dress-up (incls molded carpet for wheel houses, spare tire well, carpet covered spare), 13" steel wheels painted black with bright silver wheel covers, 2-speed windshield wipers with variable intermittent feature.

SPORT (in addition to or instead of HIGHLINE equipment): 14" power 4-wheel disc brakes with anti-lock, remote decklid release, rear window defroster, power door locks, 2.0 liter DOHC 16V SMPI 4 cylinder engine (Coupe), front and rear body color fascias with accent color rub strip, fog lights, "power bulge" hood design (Coupe), mirrors (dual exterior power remote, black), accent color bodyside moldings, passenger assist handles, rear decklid spoiler (Coupe), 16:1 ratio power assisted steering (Coupe), tilt steering column, performance tuned suspension (Coupe), P185/65R14 all-season touring BSW SBR tires (Sedan), P185/65R14 all-season performance BSW SBR tires (Coupe), T115/70R14 compact spare tire, 14" cast aluminum painted sparkle silver wheels (painted white with white exterior).

Accessories

CODE	DESCRIPTION	INVOICE	MSRP
—	**Quick Order Pkgs — prices include pkg discounts**		
A	**Pkg A — Base Sedan** *incls model with standard equipment*	NC	NC
B	**Pkg B — Base Sedan** *incls air conditioning, rear window defroster, manual remote dual exterior mirrors, bodyside moldings, radio (AM/FM stereo with clock and 4 speakers), power steering, tinted glass, touring tuned suspension, intermittent windshield wipers*	1712	1861
C	**Pkg C — Highline** *incls model with standard equipment*	NC	NC
D	**Pkg D — Highline Coupe/Sedan** *incls air conditioning, floor-mounted console with armrest and storage bin, remote decklid release, rear window defroster*	626	703
F	**Pkg F — Highline Coupe**	1184	1330
	Highline Sedan *incls pkg D contents plus 14" front disc/rear drum brakes, power door locks, front and rear floor mats, light group, power remote dual exterior mirrors, tilt steering wheel, tachometer and low fuel light, P185/65R14 all-season touring BSW SBR tires, 14" wheel covers*	1220	1371
J	**Pkg J — Sport** *incls model with standard equipment*	NC	NC
K	**Pkg K — Sport Coupe/Sedan** *incls air conditioning, front and rear floor mats, light group, radio (AM/FM stereo with cassette, clock and 6 speakers)*	557	626

CODE	DESCRIPTION	INVOICE	MSRP
23C	**Pkg 23C "Competition"** — Highline Coupe	911	990
	incls 14" power assisted 4-wheel disc brakes, unlimited speed engine controller, front and rear body color fascias with metallic accent, bodyside moldings, heavy duty radiator, radio delete, 16:1 ratio power steering, competition suspension, tachometer with low fuel light, P185/60HR14 all-season touring BSW SBR tires, 14" bright silver cast aluminum wheels (white when ordered with white exterior)		
23D	**Pkg 23D** — Highline Coupe	1536	1693
	incls pkg 23C "Competition" contents plus air conditioning, floor-mounted console with armrest and storage bin, rear window defroster, remote decklid release		
25A	**Pkg 25A "Competition"** — Base Sedan	1449	1575
	incls 14" power assisted 4-wheel disc brakes, unlimited speed engine controller, front and rear body color fascias with metallic accent, painted body color grille bar, tinted glass, dual exterior manual remote mirrors, heavy duty radiator, 16:1 ratio power steering, competition suspension, tachometer with low fuel light, T115/70R14 compact spare tire, P175/65HR14 all-season performance BSW SBR tires, 14" bright silver cast aluminum wheels (white when ordered with white exterior)		
25B	**Pkg 25B** — Base Sedan	2687	2981
	incls pkg 25A "Competition" contents plus air conditioning, rear window defroster, dual exterior manual remote mirrors, intermittent wipers		
ECB	**Engine** — 2.0 liter SOHC 16V SMPI		
	Base Sedan	STD	STD
	Highline	STD	STD
	Sport Coupe	(89)	(100)
	Sport Sedan	STD	STD
ECC	**Engine** — 2.0 liter DOHC 16V SMPI		
	Sport Coupe	STD	STD
	Highline Coupe w/pkg 23C or 23D	138	150
DD4/5	**Transmission** — 5-speed manual	STD	STD
DGA	**Transmission** — 3-speed automatic	496	557
4XA	**Air Conditioning Bypass** — Base w/pkg A or 25A	NC	NC
BRH	**Anti-Lock Brakes** — 13" - Base w/pkg A or B	503	565
	Highline w/pkg C or D	503	565
	NA w/AY7 on Highline models		
BRJ	**Anti-Lock Brakes** — 14" - Highline w/pkg D or F	503	565
	req's AY7		
CFK	**Child Seat** — integrated	89	100
AJP	**Power Convenience Group** — Highline Coupe w/pkg D	228	256
	Highline Sedan w/pkg D	264	297
	incls dual exterior power remote mirrors, power door locks; incld in pkg F		
GFA	**Rear Window Defroster** — req'd in New York State		
	Base Sedan w/pkg A or 25A	154	173
	incld in pkg B or 25B		
	Highline w/pkg C or 23C	154	173
	incld in pkg D, F or 23D		
NAE	**California Emissions**	91	102
NBY	**Massachusetts Emissions**	91	102

CODE	DESCRIPTION	INVOICE	MSRP
CLE	**Floor Mats** — front and rear - Base Sedan, Highline, Sport	41	46
	incld in pkg F and K		
MWG	**Luggage Rack** — roof-mounted	89	100
GTE	**Mirrors** — dual exterior, manual remote — Base Sedan w/pkg A	62	70
	incld in pkg B and 25B		
K37	**Bodyside Moldings** — Base Sedan w/pkg A	27	30
	incld in pkg B		
RAL	**Radio** — AM/FM stereo w/clock and 4 speakers - Base Sedan	297	334
	incld in pkg B		
RAS	**Radio** — AM/FM stereo w/cassette, clock and 6 premium speakers -		
	Base Sedan w/pkg B	223	250
	Highline	223	250
	Sport w/pkg J	223	250
	incld in pkg K		
RBG	**Radio** — AM/FM stereo w/CD player, clock and 6 premium speakers -		
	Base Sedan w/pkg B	434	488
	Highline	434	488
	Sport w/pkg J	434	488
	Sport w/pkg K	212	238
SUA	**Tilt Steering Column** — Base Sedan w/pkg B	132	148
	Highline w/pkg C or D	132	148
	incld in pkg F		
NHM	**Speed Control** — Highline w/pkg D or F	199	224
	Sport w/pkg K	199	224
JHA	**Intermittent Windshield Wipers** — Base Sedan w/pkg A	59	66
	incld in pkg B and 25B		
JFH	**Tachometer & Low Fuel Warning Light** — Highline w/pkg D	83	93
	incld in pkg F		
AY7	**14" Wheel Dress-Up** — Highline w/pkg D	71	80
	incls 14" front disc/rear drum brakes, P185/65R14 all-season touring BSW SBR tires, 14" black wheels, 14" silver wheel covers (white w/quartz center when ordered w/white exterior); incld in pkg F		
—	**Paint** — extra cost	86	97

What's New for *Plymouth* in 1995?

Acclaim: Poor Plymouth. Down to two car lines for 1995, and the Acclaim ended production in December. Is it the end of the road for this stale brand? Acclaim gets a refined transmission and black-on-yellow service points under the hood. A $1,500 rebate is also currently offered. The Acclaim is solid value, but is about as exciting as a Chia Pet. A new version of the Chrysler Cirrus and Dodge Status is set to replace it this fall.

Neon: The hot Neon gets a sporty coupe body style for 1995. Sales are expected to really take off, like they haven't already. A new twin cam motor appears for use in Sport versions of the coupe. Hot Tip: The Neon Highline coupe with the top-of-the-line Competition Package, the twin cam engine, and a premium sound system can be had for less than $14,000 and will smoke most compacts in the performance arena.

BONNEVILLE *(1995)*

BONNEVILLE 6 CYL

Code	Description	Invoice	MSRP
X69S	4-Dr SE Sedan	18828	20804
Z69S	4-Dr SSE Sedan	23353	25804
Destination Charge:		585	585

Standard Equipment

BONNEVILLE SE: 3800 Series II SFI V6 engine, electronically-controlled 4-speed automatic transmission, power rack and pinion steering, power disc/drum brakes, 4-wheel anti-lock brake system (ABS), power windows with driver's express-down feature, power door locks, P215/65R15 SBR blackwall touring tires, 15" bolt-on wheel covers, Delco ETR AM/FM stereo radio with clock and 4-speaker sound system, manual air conditioning, soft fascia type bumpers with integral rub strips, composite polymer front fenders, fog lamps, Soft-Ray tinted glass, composite halogen headlamps, sport mirrors (LH remote/RH manual), wide bodyside molding, compact spare tire, extensive acoustical insulation, driver and passenger side air bag/safety belts, 3-point active height adjustable front safety belts, cruise control, instrumentation includes: backlit/analog speedometer/fuel and coolant temperature/oil pressure/voltage/tachometer; systems monitor includes: coolant temperature light/oil pressure indicator/battery voltage light/parking brake light; lamp group includes: engine compartment light/front overhead console/ashtray/glove box/headlamp-on warning/rear assist handles/rear rail courtesy lights/trunk light; cluster warning lights include: oil pressure/check engine/brake system/security system/inflatable restraint (air bag); front and rear floor mats, covered RH/LH visor vanity mirrors, rear seat pass-through, 45/55 split bench seats with manual recliners, 4-spoke urethane steering wheel, tilt-wheel adjustable steering column, Pass-Key II theft deterrent system, extensive anti-corrosion protection with two-side galvanized steel doors/quarters/hood/decklid/rockers; Delco Freedom II battery, brake/transmission shift interlock safety feature, stainless steel single exhaust, composite polymer front fenders, front wheel drive.

BONNEVILLE SSE (in addition to or instead of SE equipment): P225/60R16 BW Eagle GA SBR touring tires, 16" cast aluminum Torque Star wheels (white wheels with white exterior, silver wheels with all other exterior colors), Delco 2001 Series ETR AM/FM stereo radio with auto reverse cassette, 6 speakers, 7-band graphic equalizer, clock, touch control, seek up/down, search and replay, leather-wrapped steering wheel with radio controls and power antenna; heated power mirrors with blue tint, ribbed aggressive monotone bodyside applique, monotone ground effects package, rear decklid spoiler, emergency road kit, front floor console with storage and rear HVAC vents, 45/45 Doral cloth bucket seats, illuminated visor vanity mirrors, overhead console with power outlet, convenience net, deluxe floor mats, decklid release, electric rear window defogger, illuminated entry system and retained accessory power, Electronic Compass/Driver Information Center includes: check oil level/ low washer fluid/low coolant/check gauges (oil pressure, battery voltage, coolant temperature)/hood ajar/door ajar/trunk ajar/lamp monitor; Twilight Sentinel, luggage compartment cargo net, 6-way power bucket driver seat, rear center armrest with dual cup holders, electronic load leveling, stainless steel split dual rectangular exhaust.

Accessories

CODE	DESCRIPTION	INVOICE	MSRP
1SA	**SE Group 1SA**	NC	NC
	incls vehicle with standard equipment		
1SB	**SE Group 1SB**	240	270
	incls retained accessory power illuminated entry system, Delco ETR AM/FM stereo radio with auto reverse cassette, seek/scan and clock		
1SC	**SE Group 1SC**	821	923
	incls SE 1SB contents plus deck lid release, sport LH/RH power remote mirrors, 6-way power driver seat, electric rear window defogger, variable effort steering		
1SD	**SE Group 1SD**	1410	1584
	incls SE Group 1SC contents plus power antenna, RH/LH covered illuminated visor vanity mirrors, leather-wrapped steering wheel, twilight sentinel, custom trim, remote keyless entry		
1SC/H4U	**SE Value Equipment Group 1SC/H4U**	2360	2635
	incls SE Group 1SC and H4U Sport Luxury Edition (incls 16" machine faced crosslace aluminum wheels, P225/60R16 BSW STL Touring Tires, monotone appearance package, B20 leather bucket seats, 3.06 axle ratio, leather-wrapped steering wheel, rear spoiler, power antenna		
1SD/H4U	**SE Value Equipment Group 1SD/H4U**	2534	2830
	incls SE Group 1SD and H4U Sport Luxury Edition (incls 16" machine faced crosslace aluminum wheels, P225/60R16 BSW STL Touring Tires, monotone appearance .. package, B20 leather bucket seats, 3.06 axle ratio, leather-wrapped steering wheel, rear spoiler, power antenna		
1SA	**SSE Group 1SA**	NC	NC
	incls vehicle with standard equipment		
1SB	**SSE Group 1SB**	1282	1440
	incls remote keyless entry, head-up display, electrochromic inside rearview mirror, automatic air conditioning, 8-speaker performance sound system, 6-way power passenger seat, theft deterrent system, traction control		
—	**Engines**		
L36	3.8 liter 3800 Series II SFI V6	STD	STD
L67	3.8 liter 3800 SFI V6 supercharged - SE	1056	1187
	SSE	NC	NC
	req's WA6		
FE9	**Federal Emissions**	NC	NC
YF5	**California Emissions**	NC	NC
NG1	**Massachusetts Emissions**	NC	NC
—	**Tires**		

CODE	DESCRIPTION	INVOICE	MSRP
QPH	P215/65R15 BSW STL touring - SE	STD	STD
QNX	P225/60R16 BSW STL touring - SE w/o H4U & Y52	75	84
	w/H4U and/or Y52	NC	NC
QVG	P225/60HR16 BSW performance	NC	NC
	incld with L67 supercharged engine (SE)		
	req's WA6 (SSE)		
—	**Interiors**		
—	45/55 split bench w/Metrix cloth - SE	STD	STD
—	45/45 buckets w/Doral cloth - SSE	STD	STD
B20	custom interior with 45/55 split bench w/Doral cloth		
	w/o 1SD	209	235
	w/1SD	NC	NC
B20	custom interior w/bucket seats w/Doral cloth		
	w/o 1SD	449	505
	w/1SD	155	174
B20	custom interior w/bucket seats w/leather seating areas		
	w/o 1SD or H4U	1254	1409
	w/1SD and w/o H4U	915	1028
	w/H4U	NC	NC
AS7	45/45 buckets w/leather seating areas - SSE	760	854
AL7	45/45 articulating buckets w/leather seating areas - SSE		
	w/1SA	1250	1404
	w/1SB	978	1099
B57	**Monotone Appearance Pkg** — w/o H4U	178	200
	w/H4U	NC	NC
Y52	**Performance & Handling Pkg** — w/o H4U	1053	1183
	w/H4U	690	775
	incls P225/60R16 STL Touring Tires, 16" 5-blade aluminum wheels, computer command ride suspension, automatic level contol, traction control		
C68	**Air Conditioning** — electronic automatic	134	150
C49	**Defogger, Electric Rear Window** - SE	151	170
WA6	**SSEi Supercharger Pkg** - SSE	1039	1167
	incls L67 3.8 liter supercharged V6 engine, P225/60HR16 BSW performance tires, SSEi nameplates, SSEi floor mats		
FW1	**Computer Command Ride** - SSE	338	380
K05	**Engine Block Heater**	16	18
T2Z	**Enhancement Group** — w/o AS7, H4U or 1SD	183	206
	w/AS7 (cloth) and w/o 1SD or H4U	98	110
	w/AS7 (leather) or H4U and w/o 1SD	53	60
	w/1SD	NC	NC
US7	**Power Antenna** — w/o H4U, UT6, UP3 or 1SD	76	85
	w/H4U, UT6, UP3 or 1SD	NC	NC
AG1	**Power Seat** — 6-way driver - w/o 1SC or 1SD	271	305
	w/1SC or 1SD	NC	NC
AG2	**Power Seat** — 6-way passenger	271	305
	w/1SB - SSE	NC	NC

CODE	DESCRIPTION	INVOICE	MSRP
UK3	**Steering Wheel Radio Controls** — w/U1C or UN6	111	125
	w/UP3 or UT6	NC	NC
UN6	**Radio** — w/o 1SB, 1SC or 1SD	174	195
	w/1SB, 1SC or 1SD	NC	NC
	incls ETR AM/FM stereo cassette with auto reverse		
U1C	**Radio** — w/o 1SB, 1SC or 1SD	263	295
	w/1SB, 1SC or 1SD	89	100
	incls ETR AM/FM stereo with compact disc player		
UW6	**6-Speaker Performance Sound System**		
	w/UN6 or U1C	89	100
	w/UT6 or UP3	NC	NC
UT6	**Radio** — w/o H4U, AS7 (leather), T2Z or 1SD	343	385
	w/AS7 (leather) or T2Z and w/o H4U or 1SD	298	335
	w/H4U or 1SD	223	250
	incls ETR AM/FM stereo cassette with auto reverse and 7-band graphic equalizer		
UP3	**Radio** — SE - w/o H4U, AS7 (leather), T2Z or 1SD	432	485
	w/AS7 (leather) or T2Z and w/o H4U or 1SD	387	435
	w/H4U or 1SD	312	350
	SSE	89	100
	incls ETR AM/FM stereo with compact disc and 7-band graphic equalizer		
AU0	**Remote Keyless Entry** — SE - w/o 1SD, SSE - w/o 1SB	120	135
	SE - w/1SD, SSE - w/1SB	NC	NC
D58	**Spoiler, Rear Deck Delete**	(98)	(110)
T43	**Spoiler, Rear Deck** — w/o H4U	98	110
	w/H4U	NC	NC
CF5	**Sunroof, Power Glass** — SE - w/o B20 custom interior	886	995
	SE - w/B20 custom interior	873	981
	SSE	873	981
NW9	**Traction Control** — SE - w/o Y52	156	175
	SE - w/Y52	NC	NC
	SSE - w/o 1SB	156	175
	SSE - w/1SB	NC	NC
PF5	**Wheels** — 16" 5-blade aluminum - w/wheel locks, w/o Y52	303	340
	w/o wheel locks, w/o Y52	288	324
	w/Y52	NC	NC
N73	**Wheels** — 16" aluminum gold crosslace - SE w/wheel locks	303	340
	SE - w/o wheel locks	288	324
	SSE	NC	NC
PA2	**Wheels** — 16" aluminum machine faced - SE w/wheel locks	303	340
	SE w/o wheel locks	288	324
	SSE	NC	NC
PA6	**Wheels** — 16" aluminum sparkle silver torque star - SSE	NC	NC

FIREBIRD *(1995)*

FIREBIRD 6 CYL

CODE	DESCRIPTION	INVOICE	MSRP
S87S	Firebird 2-Dr Coupe	13820	15104
S67S	Firebird 2-Dr Convertible	20166	22039
	FIREBIRD 8 CYL		
V87S	Formula 2-Dr Coupe	17700	19344
V87S	Trans Am 2-Dr Coupe	19383	21184
V67S	Formula 2-Dr Convertible	23085	25229
V67S	Trans Am 2-Dr Convertible	24924	27239
	Destination Charge:	500	500

Standard Equipment

FIREBIRD COUPE: 3.4 liter V6 engine, 5-speed manual transmission, power rack and pinion steering, power front disc/rear drum brakes, 4-wheel anti-lock braking system (ABS), P215/60R16 STL BW touring tires, 16" x 7.5" cast aluminum machine faced wheels with gray ports, Delco ETR AM/FM stereo radio with auto reverse cassette, clock and Delco theft lock; right rear fixed mast black antenna, soft fascia type bumpers, composite doors/fenders/fascias/roof/rear decklid/spoiler; Solar-Ray tinted glass, electrically operated concealed quartz halogen headlamps, rear license plate bracket with lamp, sport mirrors (LH remote/RH manual), waterborne base coat/two-component clearcoat finish paint, rear decklid spoiler with integrated center high-mounted stop lamp, compact spare tire, controlled-cycle windshield wipers, extensive acoustical insulation, driver and front passenger air bags, full cut-pile floor carpeting, fully carpeted cargo area, full length front console with cup holder and storage box, side window defogger, Metrix cloth seat fabric, locking glove box, hatch release, instrumentation includes: analog speedometer/tachometer/odometer/coolant temperature/oil pressure/voltmeter/trip odometer; lights include: ashtray/dome/glove box; carpeted front mats, day/night rearview mirror with reading lamps, RH/LH covered visor vanity mirrors, rear decklid release, passive driver and front passenger seat and shoulder safety belts, 3-point active safety belts (all outboard rear positions), driver and passenger 2-way manual front seats, reclining front bucket seats, folding rear seat, 4-spoke steering wheel, tilt-wheel adjustable steering column, Pass Key II theft deterrent system, 105 amp alternator, extensive anti-corrosion protection, Delco Freedom II battery, brake/transmission shift interlock (with auto trans), Federal emissions system, stainless steel single converter exhaust system (dual converter California V8 with auto trans), GM Computer Command Control, low oil level monitor and warning, 3.23 axle ratio, rear wheel drive, gas-charged monotube de carbon shock absorbers, short and long arm front suspension, front and rear stabilizer bars, ride and handling suspension.

FIREBIRD CONVERTIBLE(in addition to or instead of FIREBIRD COUPE equipment): Power windows with driver side express-down feature, power automatic door locks, LH/RH remote power sport mirrors with blue glass, bodyside body color moldings, cruise control, electric rear window defogger, lights include: rear seat courtesy light, trunk lamp; carpeted front mats, carpeted rear mats, remote keyless entry, 4-way manual front driver/2-way manual front passenger seats.

FORMULA COUPE (in addition to or instead of FIREBIRD COUPE equipment): 5.7 liter V8 engine, 6-speed manual transmission, power 4-wheel disc brakes, P235/55R16 SBR touring tires, 16" x 8" bright silver Sport cast aluminum wheels, air conditioning, 125 amp alternator, 3.42 axle ratio, performance suspension.

FORMULA CONVERTIBLE (in addition to or instead of FIREBIRD CONVERTIBLE equipment): 5.7 liter V8 engine, 6-speed manual transmission, power 4-wheel disc brakes, P235/55R16 SBR touring tires, 16" x 8" bright silver Sport cast aluminum wheels, air conditioning, 125 amp alternator, 3.42 axle ratio, performance suspension.

TRANS AM COUPE (in addition to or instead of FORMULA COUPE equipment): Power windows with driver side express-down feature, power automatic door locks, P235/55R16 BSW touring tires, fog lamps, LH/RH power remote sport mirrors with blue glass, bodyside body color moldings, cruise control, electric rear window defogger, rear floor mats, 4-way manual front driver/2-way manual front passenger seats, leather-wrapped steering wheel with sound system controls (includes leather-wrapped shift knob and parking brake handle).

TRANS AM CONVERTIBLE (in addition to or instead of FORMULA CONVERTIBLE equipment): P245/50ZR16 BSW STL tires, Delco 2001 Series ETR AM/FM stereo radio with auto reverse cassette and 7-band graphic equalizer (includes clock/touch control/seek/search/replay/steering wheel radio controls/leather appointment group/power antenna/Delco theft lock), fog lamps, rear seat courtesy lights deleted, trunk lamp deleted, leather-wrapped steering wheel with sound system controls (includes leather-wrapped shift knob and parking brake handle).

Accessories

CODE	DESCRIPTION	INVOICE	MSRP
1SA	**Firebird Group 1SA** ... *incls vehicle with standard equipment*	NC	NC
1SB	**Firebird Group 1SB** - Coupes ... *incls air conditioning, rear mats, bodyside moldings, 4-way adjustable seat*	864	1005
	Convertibles ... *incls remote keyless entry, graphic equalizer, 6-speaker sound system, steering wheel controls, power antenna and leather appointment group*	437	508
1SC	**Firebird Group 1SC** - Coupes ... *incls Group 1SB plus power windows and locks, cruise control, power mirrors, remote keyless entry, graphic equalizer, 10 speakers, leather steering wheel, power antenna, electric rear window defogger*	2248	2614
1SA	**Formula Group 1SA** ... *incls vehicle with standard equipment*	NC	NC
1SB	**Formula Group 1SB** - Convertibles ... *incls rear mats, bodyside moldings, power windows, power door locks, cruise control, power mirrors, electric rear window defogger*	925	1076

CODE	DESCRIPTION	INVOICE	MSRP
	Coupes	437	508
	incls remote keyless entry, graphic equalizer, 6-speaker sound system, steering wheel controls, power antenna and leather appointment group		
1SC	**Formula Group 1SC** - Coupes	1448	1684
	incls Group 1SB plus remote keyless entry, graphic equalizer, 10 speakers, leather steering wheel and power antenna		
1SA	**Trans Am Group 1SA**	NC	NC
	incls vehicle with standard equipment		
UN6	**Radio** — Firebird, Formula	STD	STD
	incls ETR AM/FM stereo with auto reverse cassette		
U1C	**Radio** — Firebird, Formula	86	100
	incls ETR AM/FM stereo radio with compact disc player		
UT6	**Radio** — Firebird, Formula Coupes	407	473
	Trans Am Coupe	342	398
	incls ETR AM/FM stereo radio with auto reverse cassette, graphic equalizer and power antenna		
	Firebird, Formula Convertibles (std Trans Am Conv)	321	373
	incls ETR AM/FM stereo radio with auto reverse cassette, graphic equalizer, power antenna, steering wheel controls, leather appointment group		
UP3	**Radio** — Firebird/Formula Coupes w/o 1SC	493	573
	Firebird/Formula Coupes w/1SC	86	100
	Trans Am Coupe	428	498
	incls ETR AM/FM stereo radio with compact disc player and graphic equalizer		
	Firebird/Formula Convertibles w/o 1SB	407	473
	Firebird/Formula Convertibles w/1SB	86	100
	Trans Am Convertible	86	100
	incls ETR AM/FM stereo with compact disc player and graphic equalizer, power antenna, steering wheel and leather appointment group		
—	**Engines**		
L32	3.4 liter SFI V6 - Firebird	STD	STD
L36	3.8 liter SFI V6 - Firebird	301	350
	req's MXO auto trans and C60 air conditioning		
LT1	5.7 liter SFI V8 - Formula, Trans Am	STD	STD
FE9	**Federal Emissions**	NC	NC
YF5	**California Emissions**	86	100
NG1	**Massachusetts Emissions**	86	100
—	**Interiors**		
AR9	bucket seats w/Metrix cloth - Firebird/Formula	STD	STD
AR9	articulating bucket seats w/leather - Formula coupe	692	804
AQ9	articulating bucket seats w/leather - Formula Convertible	713	829
AR9	bucket seats w/Metrix cloth - Trans Am	STD	STD
AQ9	articulating bucket seats w/Metrix cloth - Trans Am	284	330
AQ9	articulating bucket seats w/leather - Trans Am	713	829
Y84	**Trans Am Option** — Trans Am	STD	STD
VK3	**License Plate Bracket, Front**	NC	NC

CODE	DESCRIPTION	INVOICE	MSRP
GU5	**Rear Performance Axle** — NA Firebird *req's MXO auto trans*	151	175
AU0	**Remote Keyless Entry** — std Trans Am/Convertible	116	135
NW9	**Traction Control** — std Formula, Trans Am	387	450
MM5	**Transmission** — 5-speed manual - Firebird	STD	STD
MN6	**Transmission** — 6-speed manual - Formula, Trans Am	STD	STD
MX0	**Transmission** — 4-speed automatic	667	775
C60	**Air Conditioning** — std Formula, Trans Am	770	895
C41	**Non Air Conditioning**	(770)	(895)
B84	**Body Color Side Moldings** — Coupe - std Trans Am	52	60
K34	**Cruise Control, Resume Speed** — Coupe - std Trans Am	194	225
C49	**Defogger, Rear Window** — Coupe - std Trans Am	146	170
CC1	**Hatch Roof, Removable** — Coupe w/locks, stowage	834	970
B35	**Mats, Rear Floor** — Coupe - std Trans Am	13	15
DG7	**Mirrors** — Coupe - LH/RH power, blue glass (std Trans Am)	83	96
AU3	**Power Door Locks** — Coupe - std Trans Am	189	220
A31	**Power Windows** — Coupe - std Trans Am	249	290
T43	**Uplevel Spoiler** — Trans Am Coupe	340	395
—	**Tires** — Coupes		
QEA	P215/60R16 BSW STL touring - Firebird *NA on Formula and Trans Am*	STD	STD
QCB	P235/55R16 BSW touring - Firebird *std on Formula and Trans Am*	114	132
QFZ	P245/50ZR16 BSW STL *NA Firebird; req's NW9 traction control*	194	225
QLC	P245/50ZR16 BSW STL *NA on Firebird w/NW9 traction control*	194	225
—	**Tires** — Convertibles		
QEA	P215/60R16 BSW STL touring - Firebird *NA on Formula and Trans Am*	STD	STD
QCB	P235/55R16 BSW touring - Firebird *std on Formula; NA Trans Am*	114	132
QFZ	P245/50ZR16 BSW STL *std on Trans Am; NA Firebird*	194	225
QLC	P245/50ZR16 BSW STL *NA on Firebird w/NW9 traction control*	194	225
DE4	**Hatch Roof Sunshades** — Coupe	22	25
AG1	**Seat** — power 6-way driver side - Firebird Coupe w/o 1SB & 1SC	262	305
	w/1SB & 1SC	232	270
	Formula Coupe	262	305
	Trans Am Coupe	262	305
	Convertibles *NA w/AQ9 articulating leather bucket seats*	232	270

GRAND AM *(1995)*

GRAND AM 4 CYL

CODE	DESCRIPTION	INVOICE	MSRP
E37S	SE 2-Dr Coupe	11990	13104
E69S	SE 4-Dr Sedan	12082	13204
W37S	GT 2-Dr Coupe	13774	15054
W69S	GT 4-Dr Sedan	13866	15154
Destination Charge:		495	495

Standard Equipment

GRAND AM - SE: 2.3 liter Quad 4 16-valve 4 cylinder engine, 5-speed manual transmission, power rack and pinion steering, power disc/drum brakes, 4-wheel anti-lock braking system, power automatic door locks with unlock and relock feature, P195/70R14 SBR BW tires, 14" custom bolt-on wheel covers, Delco ETR AM/FM stereo radio with seek, up/down, and clock; fixed mast antenna, soft fascia bumpers with integral rub strips, Soft-Ray tinted glass, composite wraparound headlamps, fog lamps, sport mirrors (LH remote/RH manual), wide body color bodyside moldings, compact spare tire, low liftover design trunk, "wet-arm" windshield wipers, extensive acoustic insulation, driver side air bag, front seat armrest (includes storage bin), front floor console with storage/coin holder/armrest; decklid release, child resistant rear door locks (Sedan only), analog gauges with trip odometer, lights include: headlamp-on warning, trunk illuminated entry; carpeted luggage compartment, "Valet" lock-out feature (luggage compartment), carpeted front/rear floor mats, day/night rearview mirror, RH/LH visor vanity mirrors, passive driver and front passenger seat and shoulder safety belts, rear seat shoulder and lap safety belts (all outboard positions), grid cloth seat fabric, 45/45 reclining front bucket seats, easy-entry front passenger seat (Coupe only), 3-passenger rear seat with integrated headrests, 4-spoke sport steering wheel, front center armrest storage, front door map pockets, glove compartment with cup holders, overhead compartment storage, extensive anti-corrosion protection (two-side galvanized steel body panels), Delco Freedom battery with rundown protection, brake/transmission shift interlock safety feature (with auto trans), stainless steel exhaust system, front wheel drive, GM Computer Command Control, MacPherson front strut suspension.

GT (in addition to or instead of SE equipment): P205/55R16 BW Eagle RSA SBR tires, 16" bright-

CODE	DESCRIPTION	INVOICE	MSRP

faced aluminum wheels, air conditioning, front/side/rear skirt aero extensions, rear decklid spoiler, controlled-cycle windshield wipers, analog speedometer/odometer/tachometer/coolant temperature/oil pressure indicator/voltmeter/trip odometer; 6-way power driver seat, tilt-wheel adjustable steering column.

Accessories

CODE	DESCRIPTION	INVOICE	MSRP
1SA	**SE Group 1SA**	NC	NC
	incls vehicle with standard equipment		
1SB	**SE Group 1SB**	1402	1575
	incls air conditioning, tilt wheel adjustable steering column, controlled-cycle wipers, cruise control, electric rear window defogger, Delco ETR AM/FM stereo radio with auto reverse cassette		
1SC	**SE Group 1SC** — SE Coupe	1977	2221
	SE Sedan	2035	2286
	incls SE Group 1SB contents plus split-folding rear seat, power windows with driver side express-down, black sport power mirrors (LH/RH), keyless remote entry		
1SA	**GT Group 1SA**	NC	NC
	incls vehicle with standard equipment		
1SB	**GT Group 1SB**	531	597
	incls cruise control, electric rear window defogger, Delco ETR AM/FM stereo radio with auto reverse cassette, variable effort power steering		
1SC	**GT Group 1SC** — GT Coupe	1106	1243
	GT Sedan	1164	1308
	incls GT Group 1SB contents plus split-folding rear seat, power windows with driver side express-down, black sport power mirrors (LH/RH), remote keyless entry		
—	**Engine**		
LD2	2.3 liter DOHC quad 4 16-valve 4 cyl	STD	STD
L82	3.1 liter 3100 SFI V6	312	350
FE9	**Federal Emissions**	NC	NC
YF5	**California Emissions** — NC w/L82 engine	89	100
NG1	**Massachusetts Emissions** — NC w/L82 engine	89	100
—	**Tires**		
QFB	P195/70R14 BSW STL (NA GT)	STD	STD
QPD	P195/65R15 BSW STL touring (NA GT)	117	131
QMS	P205/55R16 BSW STL touring (NA GT)	198	223
QLG	P205/55R16 BSW Eagle RSA (NA SE, std GT)	STD	STD
—	**Interiors** — Coupe		
B9	buckets w/Grid cloth	STD	STD
	buckets w/Spectra cloth		
B20	sport interior group - w/o 1SC	384	432
	w/1SC	251	282
—	buckets w/Prado leather seating areas		
B20	sport interior group - w/o 1SC	807	907
	w/1SC	674	757
—	**Interiors** — Sedan		
D9	buckets w/Grid cloth	STD	STD
	buckets w/Spectra cloth		

PONTIAC

CODE	DESCRIPTION	INVOICE	MSRP
B20	sport interior group - w/o 1SC	384	432
	w/1SC	251	282
—	buckets w/Prado leather seating areas		
B20	sport interior group - w/o 1SC	807	907
	w/1SC	674	757
C60	**Air Conditioning, Custom** — std GT	739	830
C41	**Non Air Conditioning** — NA GT	NC	NC
K34	**Cruise Control, Resume Speed**	200	225
C49	**Defogger, Electric Rear Window**	151	170
K05	**Engine Block Heater**	16	18
UB3	**Gauges, Rally & I.P. Tach** — std GT	99	111
VK3	**License Plate Bracket, Front**	NC	NC
AG1	**Power Seat** — driver 6-way - w/o B20	303	340
	w/B20	271	305
A31	**Power Windows** — express-down driver's side - Coupe	245	275
	Sedan	303	340
UM6	**Radio**	125	140
	incls ETR AM/FM stereo cassette with auto reverse		
UX1	**Radio** — w/o 1SB or 1SC	334	375
	w/1SB or 1SC	209	235
	incls ETR AM/FM stereo cassette with auto reverse and 5-band equalizer, 6-speaker sound system		
UP3	**Radio** — w/o 1SB or 1SC	516	580
	w/1SB or 1SC	392	440
	incls ETR AM/FM stereo radio with compact disc and 5-band equalizer, 6-speaker sound system		
AX3	**Remote Keyless Entry**	120	135
AM9	**Seat** — split folding rear - w/o B20 or 1SC	134	150
	w/B20 and/or 1SC	NC	NC
T43	**Spoiler, Rear Deck** — std GT	98	110
D58	**Delete Rear Deck Spoiler** — NA SE	(98)	(110)
N33	**Steering Wheel, Tilt** — std GT	129	145
CF5	**Sunroof, Power Glass**	530	595
MM5	**Transmission** — 5-speed manual	STD	STD
MX1	**Transmission** — 3-speed automatic (NA GT)	494	555
MX0	**Transmission** — 4-speed automatic	672	755
PG1	**Wheel Covers** — 15" bolt-on (NA GT)	NC	NC
PF7	**Wheels** — 15" star aluminum (NA GT)	231	259
PH7	**Wheels** — 16" sport aluminum (NA GT)	253	284
V2C	**Wheels** — aluminum machine faced (NA SE)	NC	NC
CD4	**Windshield Wipers** — controlled cycle (std GT)	58	65

What's New for *Pontiac* in 1995?

Bonneville: The standard V6 engine now has 205 hp, up from 170. The supercharged V6 can now be had on the base SE model. Revised alloy wheels spruce up the exterior, and cruise control is now standard.

GRAND PRIX SE COUPE *(1995)*

GRAND PRIX SE COUPE 6 CYL

J37S	2-Dr Coupe	15906	17384
Destination Charge:		535	535

Standard Equipment

GRAND PRIX SE COUPE: 3.1 liter 3100 SFI V6 engine, electronically-controlled 4-speed automatic transmission and second gear start feature, power rack and pinion steering, 4-wheel disc brakes, power windows with lighted switch and LH express-down feature, automatic power door locks with unlock and relock feature, P215/60R16 BW SBR touring tires, 16" x 6.5" cast aluminum 5-blade wheels, Delco 2001 Series ETR AM/FM stereo radio with seek/up-down/auto reverse cassette/ clock; steering wheel radio controls (includes leather-wrapped steering wheel), electronic push button air conditioning, fixed mast black antenna, soft fascia type bumpers with integral rub strip, Soft-Ray tinted glass (flush fitting/safety laminated), mini-quad halogen headlamps, fog lamps, body color LH/ RH power remote sport mirrors, compact spare tire, "wet-arm" controlled-cycle windshield wipers, extensive acoustical insulation package, driver and passenger side air bags, front floor storage console, cruise control, decklid release, electric rear window defogger, flush door handles, Cordae cloth interior, instrumentation includes: mechanical analog speedometer/tachometer/coolant temperature/fuel odometer/trip odometer; entry lighting, fully carpeted luggage compartment, day/ night rearview mirror, RH/LH covered visor vanity mirrors, passive driver and front passenger seat and shoulder door safety belts, rear seat shoulder and lap belts (all outboard positions), reclining sport bucket seats, 3-passenger rear seating with integrated headrests, tilt-wheel adjustable steering column, 4-spoke leather sport steering wheel with controls and air bag (NA with base radio), lockable instrument panel compartment, front door map pockets, pocketed visors, turn signal reminder, Delco Freedom II battery, brake/transmission shift interlock, stainless steel exhaust system, extensive anti-corrosion protection, front wheel drive, GM Computer Command Control, Pass Key II theft deterrent system, 4-wheel independent MacPherson strut front suspension, Tri-link design rear suspension.

CODE	DESCRIPTION	INVOICE	MSRP
	Accessories		
1SA	**Group 1SA**	NC	NC
	incls cruise control, covered dual visor vanity mirrors, sport mirrors (LH power/RH power convex), Delco 2001 Series AM/FM stereo radio with cassette, remote deck lid release, electric rear window defogger, front and rear floor mats, steering wheel radio controls (incls leather-wrapped steering wheel)		
—	**Engines**		
L82	3.1 liter 3100 SFI V6	STD	STD
LQ1	3.4 liter DOHC V6 w/split dual exhaust and sport suspension - w/B4S	NC	NC
FE9	**Federal Emissions**	NC	NC
YF5	**California Emissions** — NC w/L82 engine	89	100
NG1	**Massachusetts Emissions** — NC w/L82 engine	89	100
—	**Tires**		
QPE	P215/60R16 BSW STL touring	STD	STD
QVG	P225/60R16 BSW STL performance - w/B4U or B4S	NC	NC
AR9	**Interior** — buckets w/Cordae cloth	STD	STD
—	**Custom Interior Groups**		
B20	sport buckets w/Doral cloth	348	391
B20	sport buckets w/Prado leather seating areas	771	866
B4U	**Special Edition** — w/o B4S	553	621
	w/B4S	NC	NC
	incls 16" aluminum wheels, P225/60R16 BSW STL performance tires, sport suspension, ground effects, dual exhaust, wheel flares, specific front and rear fascias		
B4S	**GTP Performance Pkg**	2008	2256
	incls B4U special edition plus 3.4 liter V6 engine, anti-lock brakes, hood louvers, speed sensitive power steering		
UV8	**Cellular Phone Provisions**	31	35
K05	**Engine Block Heater**	16	18
B4M	**Special Edition Accent Pkg**	263	295
	incls white aluminum wheels, decklid spoiler specific pinstriping and decals		
NC5	**Exhaust, Split Dual** — w/o B4U or B4S	80	90
	w/B4U or B4S	NC	NC
UV6	**Head-Up Display**	223	250
U40	**Trip Computer**	177	199
VK3	**License Plate Bracket, Front**	NC	NC
US7	**Power Antenna**	76	85
JL9	**Power Brakes, Anti-Lock** — w/o B4S	401	450
	w/B4S	NC	NC
AG1	**Power Seat** — driver 6-way	271	305
U1C	**Radio**	111	125
	incls AM/FM stereo with compact disc player		
UT6	**Radio**	156	175
	incls ETR AM/FM stereo with auto reverse cassette, 7-band equalizer and 8-speaker performance sound system		

CODE	DESCRIPTION	INVOICE	MSRP
UP3	**Radio** *incls ETR AM/FM stereo with compact disc player, 7-band equalizer and 8-speaker performance sound system*	245	275
AU0	**Remote Keyless Entry**	120	135
D81	**Spoiler, Rear Deck**	156	175
CF5	**Sunroof, Power Glass** — w/B20	575	646
R6S	**Wheels** — aluminum 16" crosslace silver (avail w/B4U or B4S)	NC	NC
R6G	**Wheels** — aluminum 16" crosslace gold (avail w/B4U or B4S)	NC	NC
PF9	**Wheels** — aluminum 16" 5-spoke (avail w/B4U or B4S)	NC	NC
T61	**Daytime Running Lighting** — fleet only	35	39

GRAND PRIX SE SEDAN *(1995)*

GRAND PRIX SE SEDAN 6 CYL

J19S	4-Dr Sedan	15220	16634
Destination Charge:		535	535

Standard Equipment

GRAND PRIX SE SEDAN: 3.1 liter 3100 SFI V6 engine, electronically-controlled 4-speed automatic transmission and second gear feature, power rack and pinion steering, 4-wheel disc brakes, power windows with lighted switch and LH express-down feature, power automatic door locks with unlock and relock feature, P205/70R15 BW touring tires, 15" sport wheel covers with bolt-on feature, Delco ETR AM/FM stereo radio with clock and seek up/down feature, electronic push button air conditioning, black fixed mast antenna, soft fascia type bumpers with integral rub strips, Soft-Ray tinted glass (flush fitting/safety laminated), composite halogen headlamps, fog lamps, sport mirrors (LH remote/RH manual), compact spare tire, "wet-arm" controlled-cycle windshield wipers, extensive acoustical insulation package, driver and passenger side air bags, front floor console with storage (Sedan with bucket seats only), flush door handles, Cordae cloth interior, instrumentation includes: mechanical analog speedometer/tachometer/coolant temperature/fuel and trip odometer; entry lighting, fully carpeted luggage compartment, day/night rearview mirror, passive driver and front passenger B-pillar seat and shoulder safety belts, rear seat shoulder and lap belts (all outboard positions), 45/55 split front seats with folding armrest and reclining RH/LH seatbacks, 3-passenger rear seat with

CODE	DESCRIPTION	INVOICE	MSRP

integrated headrests, 4-spoke urethane sport steering wheel with air bag, tilt-wheel adjustable steering column, front center armrest storage with Custom trim, lockable instrument panel compartment, front door map pockets, turn signal reminder, Delco Freedom II battery, brake/transmission shift interlock, stainless steel exhaust system, extensive anti-corrosion protection, front wheel drive, GM Computer Command Control, Pass Key II theft deterrent system, four-wheel independent MacPherson strut front suspension, Tri-link design rear suspension.

Accessories

CODE	DESCRIPTION	INVOICE	MSRP
1SA	**Group 1SA**	NC	NC
	incls vehicle with standard equipment		
1SB	**Group 1SB**	660	742
	incls cruise control, covered dual visor vanity mirrors, sport mirrors (LH power/RH power convex), Delco 2001 Series AM/FM stereo radio with cassette, remote deck lid release, electric rear window defogger		
1SC	**Group 1SC**	1724	1937
	incls Group 1SB contents plus front and rear floor mats, steering wheel radio controls (incls leather-wrapped steering wheel), power 6-way driver seat, power anti-lock brakes, remote keyless entry, power antenna		
—	**Engines**		
L82	3.1 liter 3100 SFI V6	STD	STD
LQ1	3.4 liter DOHC V6 w/split dual exhaust and sport suspension - w/B4Q	NC	NC
FE9	**Federal Emissions**	NC	NC
YF5	**California Emissions** — NC w/L82 engine	89	100
NG1	**Massachusetts Emissions** — NC w/L82 engine	89	100
—	**Tires**		
QIN	P205/70R15 BSW STL touring	STD	STD
QPE	P215/60R16 BSW STL touring	100	112
QVG	P225/60R16 BSW STL performance - w/B4Q	NC	NC
—	**Interiors**		
—	45/55 split bench w/Cordae cloth	STD	STD
AR9	bucket seats	62	70
—	**Custom Interior Groups**		
B20	45/55 split bench w/Doral cloth - w/1SB	434	488
	w/1SC	350	393
B20	sport buckets w/Doral cloth - w/1SB	523	588
	w/1SC	439	493
	w/B4Q and 1SB	461	518
	w/B4Q and 1SC	376	423
B20	sport buckets w/Prado leather seating areas - w/1SB	946	1063
	w/1SC	862	968
	w/B4Q and 1SB	884	993
	w/B4Q and 1SC	799	898
B4Q	**GT Performance Pkg** — w/1SB	2025	2275
	w/1SC	1624	1825
	incls LQ1 3.4 liter V6 engine, anti-lock brakes, custom bucket seats, dual exhausts, sport suspension, hood louvers, GT nameplates, speed sensitive power steering, 16" 5-blade aluminum wheels, P225/60R16 BSW STL performance tires		

CODE	DESCRIPTION	INVOICE	MSRP
UV8	**Cellular Phone Provisions**	31	35
K34	**Cruise Control, Resume Speed**	200	225
A90	**Deck Lid Release**	53	60
C49	**Defogger, Electric Rear Window**	151	170
B37	**Floor Mats** — front and rear - w/o B20	40	45
	w/B20	NC	NC
K05	**Engine Block Heater**	16	18
NC5	**Exhaust, Split Dual** — w/o B4Q	80	90
	w/B4Q	NC	NC
UV6	**Head-Up Display**	223	250
U40	**Trip Computer**	177	199
VK3	**License Plate Bracket, Front**	NC	NC
DD2	**Mirrors** — dual covered visor vanity - w/o B20, 1SB or 1SC	12	14
	w/B20 and/or 1SB or 1SC	NC	NC
US7	**Power Antenna**	76	85
JL9	**Power Brakes, Anti-Lock** — w/o B4Q	401	450
	w/B4Q	NC	NC
AG1	**Power Seat** — driver 6-way	271	305
UK3	**Radio Controls, Steering Wheel**		
	w/o B20, UT6, UP3 and 1SC	156	175
	w/B20 and w/o UT6, UP3 and 1SC	111	125
	w/UT6, UP3 or 1SC	NC	NC
	incls leather-wrapped steering wheel		
UN6	**Radio**	174	195
	incls ETR AM/FM stereo radio with auto reverse cassette		
U1C	**Radio** — w/o 1SB and 1SC	263	295
	w/1SB or 1SC	89	100
	incls ETR AM stereo/FM stereo with CD player		
UT6	**Radio** — w/1SB w/o B20	289	325
	w/1SB w/B20	245	275
	w/1SC	134	150
	incls ETR AM stereo/FM stereo with auto reverse cassette, 7-band equalizer, 8-speaker performance sound system and steering wheel controls		
UP3	**Radio** — w/1SB w/o B20	378	425
	w/1SB w/B20	334	375
	w/1SC	223	250
	incls ETR AM stereo/FM stereo with compact disc player, 7-band equalizer, 8-speaker performance sound system and steering wheel controls		
AU0	**Remote Keyless Entry**	120	135
CF5	**Sunroof, Power Glass** — w/B20	575	646
NW0	**Wheels** — aluminum sport bright faced - w/o B4Q	231	259
	w/B4Q	NC	NC
PH3	**Wheels** — aluminum sport bright faced 15"	231	259
T61	**Daytime Running Lighting** — fleet only	35	39

CODE	DESCRIPTION	INVOICE	MSRP

SUNFIRE *(1995)*

SUNFIRE 4 CYL

CODE	DESCRIPTION	INVOICE	MSRP
B37S	SE 2-Dr Coupe	10243	11074
B69S	SE 4-Dr Sedan	10382	11224
B67S	SE 2-Dr Convertible	15507	16764
D37S	GT 2-Dr Coupe	11871	12834
Destination Charge:		485	485

Standard Equipment

SUNFIRE - SE: 2.2 liter OHV 4 cylinder engine, 5-speed manual transmission (3-speed automatic transmission on Convertible), power-assisted front disc/rear drum anti-lock brakes, 14" steel wheels with bolt-on cover (15" size wheels on Convertible), P195/70R14 tires (P195/65R15 on Convertible), driver and passenger air bags, red illuminated full cluster gauges with tachometer, tilt steering wheel, rear folding seat, rear seat cup holders, console with removable ashtray/cup holder and rear seat cup holder, power mirrors, trunk and glove box lamps, door map pockets, front stabilizer bar, aluminized stainless steel muffler and tailpipe, full trunk trim, 5-mph front and rear bumpers, decklid spoiler (Convertible).

GT (in addition to or instead of SE equipment): 2.3 liter DOHC 16-valve Quad 4 engine, 5-speed manual transmission, decklid spoiler, 16" cast aluminum wheels, P205/55R16 RSA performance tires, specific GT front and rear fascias, GT bodyside moldings, dual muffler with oval outlets, PASSlock anti-theft ignition system (models with auto trans).

Accessories

CODE	DESCRIPTION	INVOICE	MSRP
1SA	**SE Group 1SA** — SE *incls vehicle with standard equipment*	NC	NC
1SB	**SE Group 1SB** — SE *incls tilt steering wheel, custom air conditioning, rear defogger, radio with cassette*	1153	1295
1SC	**SE Group 1SC** — SE *incls SE Group 1SB, cycle wipers, cruise control, convenience pkg*	1482	1665

CODE	DESCRIPTION	INVOICE	MSRP
1SD	**SE Coupe Group 1SD** — SE Coupe	1981	2226
	incls SE Group 1SC, power door locks, power windows, power mirrors		
1SE	**SE Sedan Group 1SD** — SE Sedan	2075	2331
	incls SE Group 1SC, power door locks, power windows, power mirrors		
1SA	**SE Convertible Group 1SA** — SE Convertible	NC	NC
	incls vehicle with standard equipment		
1SB	**SE Convertible Group 1SB** — SE Convertible	1282	1440
	incls custom air conditioning, rear defogger, radio with cassette, cycle wipers, cruise control		
1SC	**SE Convertible Group 1SC** — SE Convertible	1781	2001
	incls SE Convertible Group 1SB, power door locks, power windows, power mirrors		
1SA	**GT Group 1SA** — GT	NC	NC
	incls vehicle with standard equipment		
1SB	**GT Group 1SB** — GT	1353	1520
	incls custom air conditioning, rear defogger, radio with cassette, cycle wipers, cruise control, convenience package		
1SC	**GT Group 1SC** — GT	1852	2081
	incls GT Group 1SB, power door locks, power windows, power mirrors		
LN2	**Engine** — 2.2 liter OHV 4 cylinder MPFI - SE	STD	STD
LD2	**Engine** — 2.3 liter DOHC Quad 4 16-valve 4 cyl - GT	STD	STD
	SE	352	395
FE9	**Federal Emissions**	NC	NC
YF5	**California Emissions**	89	100
NG1	**Massachusetts Emissions**	89	100
—	**Tires**		
QFB	P195/70R14 BSW STL - SE Coupe, SE Sedan	STD	STD
QPD	P195/65R15 BSW STL touring - SE Coupe, SE Sedan	117	131
QLG	P205/55R16 BSW STL performance - GT	STD	STD
C60	**Custom Air Conditioning**	699	785
C41	**Non Air Conditioning**	NC	NC
R6A	**Convenience Pkg** — SE Coupe, SE Sedan	71	80
	incls remote deck lid release, trunk net, reading lamps and overhead console storage		
K34	**Cruise Control** — resume speed	200	225
C49	**Electric Rear Window Defogger**	151	170
K05	**Engine Block Heater**	16	18
VK3	**Front License Plate Bracket**	NC	NC
DG7	**Mirrors** — SE Convertible & GT	77	86
	incls sport LH/RH power mirrors		
AU3	**Power Door Locks** — Coupe & SE Convertible	187	210
	SE Sedan	223	250
A31	**Power Windows** — driver side express-down - SE Sedan	294	330
	Coupe & SE Convertible	236	265
UN6	**Radio**	174	195
	incls ETR AM/FM stereo with auto reverse cassette		
UT6	**Radio** — w/o 1SB, 1SC or 1SD	205	230
	w/1SB, 1SC or 1SD	31	35
	incls ETR AM/FM stereo cassette with auto reverse and 7-band equalizer		

CODE	DESCRIPTION	INVOICE	MSRP
UP3	**Radio** — w/o 1SB, 1SC or 1SD	294	330
	w/1SB, 1SC or 1SD	120	135
	incls ETR AM/FM stereo cassette with CD and 7-band equalizer		
N33	**Tilt Steering Wheel**	129	145
	std on SE Convertible & GT		
T43	**Rear Deck Lid Spoiler** — SE Coupe	62	70
	std on SE Convertible & GT		
CF5	**Power Sunroof** — SE Coupe w/1SC or 1SD	495	556
	GT w/1SA	530	595
	GT w/1SB or 1SC	495	556
MM5	**Transmission** — 5-speed manual - SE Coupe, SE Sedan & GT	NC	NC
	SE Convertible	(441)	(495)
MX1	**Transmission** — 3-speed automatic - SE Coupe, SE Sedan	441	495
	std on SE Convertible; NA on GT		
MX0	**Transmission** — 4-speed automatic - SE Convertible	200	225
	SE Coupe, SE Sedan & GT	641	720
PG0	**Wheels** — 16" aluminum - GT	STD	STD
	NA on SE		
PG1	**Wheel Covers** — 15" bolt-on - SE Coupe, SE Sedan	NC	NC
	std on SE Convertible		
PF7	**Wheels** — 15" aluminum - SE	231	259
—	**Interiors**		
B9/D9	buckets w/Milliweave cloth	STD	STD
C9/B20	buckets w/Milliweave cloth	71	80
	incls sport interior pkg (incls leather-wrapped steering wheel, seatback pockets and side seat bolsters)		
N9/B20	buckets w/vinyl trim - SE Convertible	129	145
	incls sport interior pkg (incls vinyl trim, leather-wrapped steering wheel, driver side lumbar adjuster, seatback pockets and side seat bolsters)		

What's New for *Pontiac* in 1995?

Firebird: Traction control is now available on Firebird. New colors and wheels liven up the exterior, as if it needed it.

Grand Am: The base 115 hp powerplant is dropped in favor of a balance-shafted, 150 hp Quad 4 motor. Suspension revisions have been made, and 16-inch alloys are no longer available. New wheelcover designs improve looks.

Grand Prix: Lots of work has gone into the center console of the 1995 Grand Prix, which now features repositioned cupholders, and a center storage armrest with more cupholders and storage for change. Another storage compartment with a coinholder is available on the floor. Try your pockets, will ya? A stunning new Grand Prix sedan is slated to appear in 1996.

Sunfire: All-new Sunbird replacement comes to market with racy styling and lots of equipment for the price, but the buzzy 2.2L four cylinder from the Sunbird has been carried over in the newer and heavier Sunfire. Alas, the Neon, while buzzy as well, turns this Pontiac into a Sunember in the performance department. The Quad 4 engine in the GT (available as you read this) may turn the tables in favor of the Sunfire, if the price is right. Sunfire is equipped with standard dual airbags and ABS.

911 CARRERA *(1995)*

CODE	DESCRIPTION	INVOICE	MSRP
993630	Carrera 2-Dr Cabriolet (6-spd)	57045	68200
993630	Carrera 2-Dr Cabriolet (Tiptronic)	59680	71350
993330	Carrera 2-Dr Coupe (6-spd)	50145	59900
993330	Carrera 2-Dr Coupe (Tiptronic)	52780	63050
993530	Carrera 4 2-Dr Cabriolet (6-spd)	62070	74200
993130	Carrera 4 2-Dr Coupe (6-spd)	55165	65900
	Destination Charge:	725	725
	Gas Guzzler Tax: Carrera 4	1000	1000

Standard Equipment

911 CARRERA COUPE & CABRIOLET: 3.6 liter 270 HP aluminum alloy twin spark plug air-cooled horizontally opposed 6 cylinder engine with partial engine encapsulation, fully integrated electronic ignition and fuel injection system Digital Motor Electronics (DME) with dual knock sensor and hot film air flow sensor systems, dual-mass flywheel, 6-speed manual transmission, hydraulically activated single disc dry clutch, rack and pinion steering with force-sensitive power assist, MacPherson front strut fully independent suspension (aluminum alloy lower control arms with stabilizer bar), rear aluminum alloy fully independent multi-link LSA axle suspension (with toe correction characteristics and stabilizer bar), power assisted 4-wheel cross-drilled disc brakes with revised anti-lock braking system (ABS 5) and asbestos-free pads (aluminum alloy 4-piston caliper, internally ventilated), redesigned 5-spoke pressure-cast light alloy wheels with locks, 7J x 16 wheels with 205/55ZR16 SBR front tires, 9J x 16 wheels with 245/45ZR16 SBR rear tires, 19.4 gallon fuel tank, two door Coupe or Cabriolet with 2+2 seating, electric sliding sunroof (Coupe), full power top with automatic latching and unlatching (Cabriolet), digital electronic fog lights (integrated into front apron), modular ellipsoid headlights with variable focus and washer system, redesigned third brake light, welded unitized body construction (double-sided, zinc galvanized steel), redesigned front and rear bumpers and fenders, second generation side-impact protection, speed-dependent extendable rear spoiler, heated windshield washer nozzles, electrically adjustable and heatable outside rearview mirrors, windshield antenna with signal amplifier, two-stage rear window defroster (Coupe), tinted glass, graduated-tint windshield, redesigned outside door handles (painted to match exterior color), driver and front seat passenger air bags, front and rear 3-point inertia-reel seatbelts, redesigned interior panels, individually folding rear seat backs

(Coupe), increased luggage compartment volume, redesigned partial leather reclining bucket seats with electric height adjustment, air conditioning with automatic temperature control, new particle filters for ventilation system, redesigned leather-covered steering wheel, backlit analog instrumentation (incls tachometer, oil pressure/oil temperature/oil level/fuel level gauges, corresponding warning lights), trip odometer, power windows, analog quartz clock, brake pad wear indicator, mirrors in sun visors, interior lighting with delayed shut off, cruise control, one-key central locking and alarm system with fixed light-emitting diodes, AM/FM digital display stereo cassette radio with 6 speakers and amplifier, cassette holder.

911 CARRERA 4 COUPE & CABRIOLET: 3.6 liter 270 HP aluminum alloy twin spark plug air-cooled horizontally opposed 6 cylinder engine with partial engine encapsulation, fully integrated electronic ignition and fuel injection system Digital Motor Electronics (DME) with dual knock sensor and hot film air flow sensor systems, dual mass flywheel, 6-speed manual transmission (Porsche-designed full-time all-wheel-drive system with viscous center clutch), hydraulically activated single disc dry clutch, rack and pinion steering with force-sensitive power assist, MacPherson front strut fully independent suspension (aluminum alloy lower control arms with stabilizer bar), rear aluminum alloy fully independent suspension (multi-link LSA axle with toe correction characteristics and stabilizer bar), limited slip differential with automatic brake differential (ABD) traction system and lockup, power assisted aluminum alloy 4-piston fixed caliper internally ventilated 4-wheel cross-drilled disc brakes with revised anti-lock braking system (ABS 5) and asbestos-free pads, redesigned 5-spoke pressure-cast light alloy wheels with locks, 7J x 17 front wheels with 205/50ZR17 SBR tires, 9J x 17 rear wheels with 255/40ZR17 SBR tires, 19.4 gallon fuel tank, two door Coupe or Cabriolet with 2+2 seating, electric sliding sunroof (Coupe), full power top with automatic latching and unlatching (Cabriolet), digital electronic fog lights integrated into front apron, newly developed modular ellipsoid headlights with variable focus and washer system, redesigned third brake light, welded unitized body construction (double-sided, zinc galvanized steel), redesigned front/rear bumpers and fenders, second generation side-impact protection, larger speed-dependent extendable rear spoiler, heated windshield washer nozzles, electrically adjustable and heatable outside rearview mirrors, windshield antenna with signal amplifier, two-stage rear window defroster (Coupe), tinted glass, windshield with graduated tint, redesigned outside door handles (painted to match exterior color), driver and front seat passenger air bags, 3-point inertia-reel front/rear seatbelts, redesigned interior panels, individually folding rear seat backs (Coupe), increased luggage compartment volume, redesigned partial leather reclining bucket seats with electric height adjustment, air conditioning with automatic temperature control, new particle filters for ventilation system, redesigned leather-covered steering wheel, backlit analog instrumentation (incls tachometer, oil pressure/oil temperature/oil level/fuel level gauges, corresponding warning lights), trip odometer, power windows, analog quartz clock, brake pad wear indicator, mirrors in sun visors, interior lighting with delayed shut off, cruise control, one-key central locking and alarm system with fixed light-emitting diodes, AM/FM digital display stereo cassette radio with 6 speakers and amplifier, cassette holder.

Accessories

CODE	DESCRIPTION	INVOICE	MSRP
659	**Computer** — on-board	338	422
—	**Engine** — 6 cylinder EFI 3.6 liter	STD	STD
—	**Seat Adjuster**		
437	power driver's	431	538
P15	dual power	766	956
—	**Tires**		
—	P205/55ZR16 front tires, P245/45ZR16 rear tires - Carrera	STD	STD
—	P205/50ZR17 front tires, P255/40ZR17 rear tires - Carrera 4	STD	STD
—	P205/50ZR17 front tires, P255/40ZR17 rear tires - Carrera *req's wheels 398*	NC	NC

CODE	DESCRIPTION	INVOICE	MSRP
X65	**Steering Wheel Pkg**	971	1212
	incls leather-covered ventilating cover, leather fresh air side and center dash vents, leather fresh air side vents		
X66	**Door Panel Pkg**	1515	1891
	incls leather inside door openers, leather outside mirror adjuster frame, leather radio speaker covers, leather power window switches, leather covered caps, leather door lock pin rosettes		
X67	**Seat Pkg**	1403	1751
	incls leather front backrest lock controls, leather ring plates for switch/seat adjuster, leather seat hinges, leather heat adjust switches, leather seat adjust switches		
551	**Windstop Deflector** — Cabriolets	275	344
SPP	**Power Pack Plus**	39	45
—	**Dashboard**		
X18	dark rootwood	3490	4356
X17	light rootwood	3490	4356
X19	leather - in color to sample	716	893
—	**Radio Equipment**		
X81	CD storage - left door panel	193	241
X53	CD storage - behind hand brake lever	370	461
490	hi-fi sound	745	930
	incls amplifier system; std w/radio equipment P49		
P48	CD player - Cabriolets	239	299
P53	CD player - Coupes	239	299
692	remote control CD changer	998	1245
P49	digital sound	1663	2075
	incls hi-fi amplifier system and sound		
XR7	**Wiper/Washer** — rear window - Coupes	654	817
425	**Wiper** — rear window - Coupes	273	340
Z07	**Carpeting** — cargo compartment	551	687
Z69	**Carpeting** — interior deviating standard colors	60	75
Z35	**Kneebar** — leather - in deviating current Porsche colors	40	50
	req's all leather interior		
Z31	**Kneebar** — leather	452	564
SAC	**Air Conditioning** — rapid charger	153	177
—	**Trim**		
Z44	leather armrests	209	260
XM5	leather control knobs (4)	323	403
XN3	leather fresh air side dash vents (2)	531	662
XZ4	leather glove box lock frame	67	83
XW4	leather light switch	72	90
XW3	leather rear window wiper switch	136	169
XV9	leather B-pillar seat belt covers	93	116
XM7	leather-covered glove box	74	93
XJ5	leather ignition/door key	125	156
XF7	leather-covered tray - behind parking brake	154	193
XP6	leather seat belt lock and housing	374	466
XR3	leather seat hinges (4)	269	335

CODE	DESCRIPTION	INVOICE	MSRP
XW5	leather wiper/instrument light knob	92	115
XN8	leather sun visors	464	579
XK7	leather shift knob and cover	182	227
XW1	leather seat belt rosettes (2)	122	153
Z65	leatherette beltline in deviating standard color	84	105
XX6	leather shift lever knob in deviating colors - models w/manual trans	55	68
XM9	leather turn signal/wiper switch	225	281
XW9	leather entrance panel cover	205	256
XV3	leather air conditioner/heat adjust covers	241	300
XF5	leather-covered instrument rings	354	442
XN7	leather parking brake lever	200	249
XV5	leather seat adjuster switches (6)	485	606
XJ8	leather tiptronic selector lever - models w/Tiptronic trans	197	246
XW8	leather-covered caps (2)	20	25
Z11	leather carpet welting - in current Porsche colors	857	1069
Z09	leather carpet welting - in deviating interior colors	1490	1860
XW6	leather door lock pin rosettes	67	83
XR6	leather front backrest lock controls	379	473
XF6	leather gear box tunnel	158	198
XJ4	leather ignition lock rosette	47	58
XP9	leather radio speaker covers (6)	383	478
XV1	leather-covered ventilating cover	346	432
XN4	leather fresh air center vent	278	347
XV7	leather fuel tank pull knob	53	66
XZ7	leather outside mirror adjuster frame	88	110
XN1	leather power window switches	274	342
XV2	leather fresh air side vents (2)	17	22
XV4	leather heat adjust switches (2)	149	188
XN2	leather inside door openers (2)	136	170
XW2	leather rear seat belt lock and housing	459	573
XV6	leather ring plates for switch/seat adjuster	287	359
398	**Wheels** — 5-spoke - Carrera models *incls P205/50ZR17 front tires and P255/40ZR17 rear tires; std Carrera 4 models; std w/chassis P31*	1104	1378
—	**Battery**		
SUL	ultra-light - small	101	118
SLB	standard - large	43	50
SBE	battery eliminator	77	90
—	**Paint**		
98/99	color to sample	2002	2498
Z41	pearl white metallic	9814	12249
—	metallic	830	1036
—	**Rim Caps**		
XD4	w/Porsche Crest	172	214
X89	w/Porsche Crest on painted rims	172	214
XD9	**Rims** — painted in vehicle color	865	1079

CODE	DESCRIPTION	INVOICE	MSRP
—	**Seats**		
P14	dual heated w/adjustable heating range	460	578
513	passenger's lumbar support	442	551
586	driver's lumbar support	442	551
374	sport passenger w/power height adjuster	293	365
373	sport driver w/power height adjuster	293	365
—	**Seat Trim**		
—	leather	1181	1474
982	supple leather	306	382
Z45	inlays in deviating current Porsche colors	82	103
Z51	leather front and rear in deviating current Porsche colors	559	697
Z21	**Seat Stitching** — in alternate current Porsche colors	72	90
—	**Interior Trim**		
—	special leather - Coupes	3392	4233
	Cabriolets	2657	3317
—	leather - Coupes	3046	3800
	Cabriolets	2311	2885
98	leather in deviating colors - Coupes	3225	4025
	Cabriolets	2491	3109
99	leather in color to sample - Coupes	4682	5843
	Cabriolets	3947	4927
—	**Floor Mats**		
M6	Porsche	81	125
XX1	Embroidered Porsche front	286	357
	req's special leather interior trim		
—	**Parking Brake Lever**		
X31	light rootwood	428	535
X32	dark rootwood	428	535
498	**Model Designation Delete** — rear	NC	NC
—	**Telephone**		
S6	cellular	2195	2395
	incls exclusive console		
S88	cellular	1275	1425
	incls mounting bracket and installation kit		
—	**Headliner**		
Z27	leather in current Porsche color - Coupe	1530	1808
	incls sun visors and A & B pillars		
Z05	leather in color to sample - Coupe	2048	2556
	incls sun visors and A & B pillars		
Z28	leatherette in deviating current Porsche colors - Coupe	56	70
—	**Chassis**		
P31	sport - Carrera Coupe	1616	2017
	incls 5-spoke wheels		
030	sport - Carrera 4 Coupe	512	639
Z53	**Head Restraints** - w/stamped Porsche crest	82	103
	req's leather seat trim		

CODE	DESCRIPTION	INVOICE	MSRP
—	**Door Trim Panels**		
X86	light rootwood	1158	1445
X87	dark rootwood	1158	1445
Z43	leather	209	260
419	**Storage** — rear compartment - Coupes	525	656
	Cabriolets	NC	NC
	deletes standard rear seat		
—	**Gear Shift Knob**		
XC8	light rootwood - models w/manual trans	289	360
XC9	dark rootwood - models w/manual trans	289	360
XP3	**Boot Cover** — leather top - Cabriolets	2069	2583
—	**Shift Lever**		
X25	light rootwood - models w/Tiptronic trans	339	423
X24	dark rootwood - models w/Tiptronic trans	339	423
—	**Axle**		
224	active brake differential - Carrera w/Tiptronic trans	732	913
	std Carrera 4		
P08	active limited slip differential - Carrera	958	1195
	std Carrera 4		

928 GTS *(1995)*

CODE	DESCRIPTION	INVOICE	MSRP
928940	2-Dr Coupe (5-spd)	68030	82260
928920	2-Dr Coupe (auto)	68030	82260
Destination Charge:		725	725
Gas Guzzler Tax:			
	w/5-spd trans	3000	3000
	w/auto trans	2100	2100

Standard Equipment

928 GTS: 5.4 liter 345 HP aluminum alloy double overhead cam V8 engine, four valves per cylinder, EZK ignition with knock sensor system, LH Jetronic fuel injection with 2-stage resonance induction system, 5-speed manual or 4-speed automatic transmission with shift lock and key lock features, "PSD" electronically-variable limited slip differential, rack and pinion steering with force-sensitive power assist, sport shock absorbers, fully independent front suspension (aluminum alloy double A-arms with coil springs negative steering roll radius and stabilizer bar), fully independent rear suspension (aluminum alloy multi-link "Weissach" rear axle with self-stabilizing toe characteristics and stabilizer bar), race-developed aluminum alloy 4-piston fixed caliper power assisted internally ventilated 4-wheel disc brakes with anti-lock braking system (ABS) and asbestos-free pads, 5-spoke pressure-cast light alloy wheels with locks, 7.5J x 17 front wheels with 225/45ZR17 SBR tires, 9J x 17 rear wheels with 255/40ZR17 SBR tires, 22.7 gallon fuel tank, two-door Coupe with 2+2 seating and rear hatch, electric sunroof (closes automatically when vehicle is locked with key), fog and driving lights integrated in front bumper, retractable halogen headlights, welded unitized body construction (double-sided zinc galvanized steel with lightweight aluminum front fenders/hood/doors), rear spoiler (painted to match exterior color), environmentally-compatible water-based metallic paint, heated windshield washer nozzles, rear window wiper and defroster with two heat settings, electrically adjustable and heatable outside rearview mirrors, roof-mounted antenna, tinted glass, windshield with graduated tint, headlight washers, driver and front seat passenger air bags, 3-point inertia-reel front and rear seatbelts, full power front seats, front and rear leather seats, fold-out front armrests, individual folding rear seatbacks, 3-position Positrol memory for driver's seat and outside mirrors, adjustable-tilt steering column and instrument cluster, automatic climate control system with separate rear air conditioning, new particle filters for ventilation system, electric rear hatch release on driver and passenger sides, leather-covered steering wheel/gearshift lever boot, backlit analog instrumentation (incls tachometer, oil pressure/coolant temperature/fuel level/battery charge gauges), driver-information and diagnostic system monitoring 10 information functions and 22 separate warning functions, power windows, illuminated mirrors in front sun visors, rear sun visors, interior lighting with delayed shut-off, red warning lights and white courtesy lights in doors, cruise control, one-key central locking and alarm system with light-emitting diodes in door lock buttons (to show the alarm is engaged), AM/FM digital display stereo cassette radio with remote CD changer and 10 speakers (hi-fi sound system with 160-watt, 6-channel amplifier), cassette holder.

Accessories

CODE	DESCRIPTION	INVOICE	MSRP
—	**Interior**		
—	leather w/leather seat trim	2480	3096
—	special leather	3066	3826
—	leather w/cloth seat inlays	2480	3096
—	**Tires**		
—	P225/45ZR17 front tires and P225/40ZR17 rear tires	STD	STD
—	**Trim**		
XN4	leather center instrument panel air vent	354	442
XV3	leather air conditioner/heater adjuster covers	241	300
XV1	leather defroster panel	253	315
XY1	leather console area for switch/dials	126	158
XZ9	leather safety belt tongue frame	106	133
XZ1	leather parking brake rosette	170	212
XK7	leather shift lever - models w/manual trans	182	227
XJ8	leather shift lever - models w/auto trans	221	276
XZ5	leather interior sensor cover	35	43
Z10	leatherette welting in current colors	37	46
XY3	leather seat adjuster w/covered memory switch	93	116

PORSCHE

CODE	DESCRIPTION	INVOICE	MSRP
XY2	leather seat adjuster w/o covered memory switch	57	71
XY5	leather auto selector lever cover	198	247
XM9	leather turn signal and wiper switch	225	281
XZ2	leather rear seat belt rosettes	153	191
XZ4	leather glove box lock frame	173	216
XP7	leather rear seat belt housing cover	164	204
Z08	leather welting in current colors	911	1137
XW6	leather door lock pin rosettes (2)	113	141
XY4	leather center console frame	225	281
XP9	leather speaker covers in doors (10)	605	755
XN7	leather parking brake lever	293	365
XY8	leather frame for switches	57	71
XJ3	leather door locking knobs and rosettes (2)	233	291
XZ6	leather RH fresh air vent	44	55
XJ5	leather-covered ignition/door key	125	156
XY6	leather ashtray cover	72	90
XP6	leather front seat belt locks and housing	374	466
XV5	leather seat adjuster switches (6)	485	606
XR5	leather backrest lock controls	555	692
XZ3	leather central locking system dial area frame	122	153
XN3	leather side instrument panel air vents (2)	516	644
XY7	leather rear window wiper/windows/sunroof switches	200	249
XM6	leather door opener handle recess plates	327	408
XV4	leather heater adjuster switches (2)	149	186
XW2	leather rear seat belt lock/housing cover	459	573
XV6	leather seat adjuster switch covers (2)	287	359
XR3	leather front seat hinges (4)	269	335
XZ7	leather outside mirror frame/knob/rocker	88	110
XZ8	leather luggage compartment cover rosette	237	295
—	**Engine** — V8 32-valve EFI 5.4 liter	STD	STD
XR7	**Wiper/Washer** — rear window	1011	1262
—	**Air Conditioning**		
570	increased output	NC	NC
SAC	rapid charger	153	177
XX5	**Radio Equipment** — cassette holder in left door	1232	1537
—	**Seats**		
586	driver's lumbar support	442	551
513	passenger's lumbar support	442	551
387	sport passenger's w/power height adjustment	NC	NC
383	sport driver's w/power height adjustment	NC	NC
340	heated passenger's	231	289
139	heated driver's	231	289
—	**Seat Trim**		
980	supple leather	450	561
95	leather in color to sample w/leatherette beltline	4855	6059
—	cloth	NC	NC
94	leather in deviating colors w/leatherette beltline	2893	3610

CODE	DESCRIPTION	INVOICE	MSRP
538	passenger's memory	831	1038
Z18	stitching in current colors	76	95
X73	**Leather Seat Pkg**	1583	1975
	incls leather heater adjuster switches, leather front seat hinges, leather seat adjuster switches/switch covers, leather seat backrest lock controls		
X74	**Leather Door Pkg**	1902	2374
	incls pkg 1 plus leather side instrument panel air vents, leather outside mirror frame, leather seat adjuster (with or without covered memory switch), leather RH fresh air vent, leather outside knob/rocker, leather door lock pin rosettes		
X13	**Pkg 1**	1048	1308
	incls leather speaker covers in doors, leather door locking knobs and rosettes, leather door handle recess plates/door openers; std w/leather door pkg X74		
X14	**Pkg 2**	855	1067
	incls leather front seat belt locks and housing, leather parking brake rosette, leather parking brake lever, leather rear seat belt lock/housing cover		
X15	**Pkg 3**	1570	1960
	incls leather heater adjuster switches, leather front seat hinges, leather seat adjuster switch covers, leather seat backrest lock controls, leather seat adjuster switches		
X16	**Pkg 4**	875	1092
	incls leather auto selector lever cover, leather rear window wiper switches, leather window and sunroof switches, leather shift lever, leather frame for switches, leather ashtray cover		
—	**Telephone**		
S88	cellular w/mounting bracket and installation kit	1275	1425
S8	cellular - installed	2095	2295
	incls exclusive console		
—	**Battery**		
SLB	standard - large	43	50
SUL	ultra-light - small	101	118
—	**Shift Lever Knob**		
XC8	light rootwood - models w/manual trans	289	360
XC9	dark rootwood - models w/manual trans	289	360
XX6	leather - models w/manual trans	55	68
—	**Floor Mats**		
M8	Porsche	81	125
XX1	Embroidered Porsche front	286	357
	req's special leather interior trim		
—	**Parking Brake Handle**		
X31	light rootwood	428	535
X32	dark rootwood	428	535
474	**Sport Shock Absorbers**	274	342
—	**Console**		
XL4	light rootwood	3927	4902
	incls door trim		
XL5	dark rootwood	3927	4902
	incls door trim		
418	**Bodyside Moldings**	NC	NC
XN9	**Sun Visors** — leather w/illuminated RH visor vanity mirror	537	671

CODE	DESCRIPTION	INVOICE	MSRP
SPP	**Power Pack Plus**	39	45
SBE	**Battery Eliminator**	77	90
498	**Model Designation Delete** — rear	NC	NC
—	**Paint**		
98/99	color to sample	2135	2664
Z16	**Head Restraints** — w/stamped Porsche Crest	85	106
—	**Selector Lever**		
X23	light rootwood - models w/auto trans	366	457
X22	dark rootwood - models w/auto trans	366	457
—	**Rim Caps**		
X89	ornamental *req's rims XD9*	172	214
XD4	w/Porsche crest	172	214
XD9	**Rims** — painted in vehicle color	865	1079
Z34	**Carpet** — in deviating current color	52	65

968 *(1995)*

968310	2-Dr Cabriolet (6-spd)	42555	51900
968310	2-Dr Cabriolet (Tiptronic)	45135	55050
968110	2-Dr Coupe (6-spd)	32760	39950
968110	2-Dr Coupe (Tiptronic)	35340	43100
Destination Charge:		725	725

Standard Equipment

968 COUPE & CABRIOLET: 3.0 liter 236 HP aluminum alloy double overhead cam 4 cylinder engine with twin balance shafts, four valves per cylinder with Vario Cam control, fully integrated electronic ignition and fuel injection system Digital Motor Electronics (DME), dual knock sensor system, front engine and rear transaxle, twin pipe high flow exhaust system coupled with reduced flow loss metal-monolith catalytic converter, lightweight forced pistons (lightened, forged crankshaft and connecting rods), 911 Turbo-type dual-mass flywheel, six-speed manual transmission, hydraulically activated single-plate clutch, rack and pinion steering with force-sensitive power assist, front fully independent suspension (MacPherson struts, aluminum alloy lower control arms with stabilizer bar), rear fully independent suspension (coil springs, aluminum alloy semi-trailing arms and torsion bars with stabilizer bar), race-developed aluminum alloy 4-piston fixed caliper power assisted dual-circuit internally ventilated 4-wheel disc brakes with anti-lock braking system (ABS) and asbestos-free pads, 5-spoke pressure-cast light alloy wheels with locks, 7J x 16 front wheels with 205/55ZR16 SBR tires, 8J x 16 rear wheels with 225/50ZR16 SBR tires, 19.6 gallon fuel tank, 2-door Coupe with 2+2 seating and rear hatch or two-seat Cabriolet with trunk, electric tilt/removable sunroof (Coupe), power top (Cabriolet), projector-type fog lights integrated into front spoiler, pop-up variable focal point halogen headlights, welded unitized body construction (double-sided, zinc galvanized steel), new integrated design energy-absorbing front/rear bumper covers, rear spoiler (Coupe), heated windshield washer nozzles, rear window wiper (Coupe), electrically adjustable and heatable outside rearview mirrors, roof-mounted antenna (Coupe), windshield antenna with signal amplifier (Cabriolet), rear window defroster (Coupe), tinted glass, windshield with graduated tint, driver and front passenger air bags, front/rear 3-point inertia-reel seatbelts (Cabriolet - front only), reclining bucket seats with electric height adjustment, individual folding rear seatbacks (Coupe), leatherette interior with cloth seat inlays, air conditioning with automatic temperature control and outside temperature display, new particle filters for ventilation system, electric release for rear/hatch (Coupe), electric trunk release (Cabriolet), leather-covered steering wheel and gear shift lever boot, backlit instrumentation (incls tachometer, oil pressure/coolant temperature/fuel level/battery charge gauges, corresponding warning lights), trip odometer, power windows, analog quartz clock, brake pad wear indicator, mirrors in sun visors, interior lighting with delayed shut-off, cruise control, one-key central locking and alarm system with light-emitting diodes in door lock buttons (to show alarm is engaged), AM/FM digital display stereo cassette radio with 6 speakers and anti-theft coding, cassette holder, storage compartments (instead of rear seats on Cabriolet).

Accessories

CODE	DESCRIPTION	INVOICE	MSRP
—	**Seat Adjuster**		
438	power passenger's	431	538
437	power driver's	431	538
P15	dual power	766	956
—	**Engine** — 4 cyl 16 valve EFI 3.0 liter	STD	STD
—	**Trim**		
Z20	leather hand brake lever in current Porsche colors	19	23
XV6	leather ring plates for seat adjust switch	287	359
XM9	leather turn signal/wiper switch	225	281
XV9	leather B-pillar seat belt covers	93	116
XR6	leather front backrest lock controls	379	473
XW6	leather door lock pin rosettes	113	141
XK7	leather shift knob and cover	182	227
XV5	leather seat adjuster switches (6)	485	606
XN7	leather parking brake lever	293	365
XP6	leather seat belt locks/housing	374	466
XJ5	leather-covered ignition/door key	125	156
XW2	leather rear seat belt locks/housing	459	573
XP9	leather speaker covers	140	174
XM6	leather door openers and handle recess plates (2)	293	365
XJ8	leather selector lever - models w/Tiptronic	197	246
XR3	leather front seat hinges (4)	269	335
XV4	leather heat adjuster switches (2)	149	186
XN1	leather power window/mirror switches	160	199

CODE	DESCRIPTION	INVOICE	MSRP
X48	**Light Rootwood Pkg**	1929	2407
	incls light rootwood parking brake lever, light rootwood gear shift knob/lever, light rootwood instrument carrier		
X50	**Dark Rootwood Pkg**	1929	2407
	incls dark rootwood parking brake lever, dark rootwood gear shift knob/lever, dark rootwood instrument carrier		
X45	**Leather Door Pkg**	452	564
	incls leather speaker covers, leather door openers and handle recess plates, leather door locking pin rosettes		
X46	**Leather Seat Pkg**	1410	1760
	incls leather heat adjuster switches, leather seat adjuster switches, leather front seat hinges, leather ring plates for seat adjust switches, leather front backrest lock controls		
398	**Wheels** — 5-spoke 17"	1104	1378
—	**Telephone**		
S88	cellular w/mounting bracket and installation kit	1275	1425
S	cellular - installed	1795	1995
	incls exclusive console		
—	**Battery**		
SUL	ultra-light - small	101	118
SLB	standard - large	43	50
SBE	battery eliminator	77	90
—	**Console**		
X95	light rootwood	712	888
X96	dark rootwood	712	888
—	**Paint**		
—	metallic	660	823
98/99	color to sample	2002	2498
Z41	pearl white metallic	9814	12249
SAC	**Air Conditioning** — rapid charger	153	177
288	**Headlamp Washers**	210	262
—	**Floor Mats**		
XX1	Embroidered Porsche front	286	357
	req's special leather interior		
M4	Porsche	81	125
220	**Limited Slip Differential Axle** — models w/manual trans	732	913
Z77	**Leather-Wrapped Steering Wheel** — in deviating current colors	20	25
—	**Interior Trim**		
98	leather w/leatherette beltline in deviating standard colors - Coupe	3810	4755
	Cabriolet	3523	4397
99	leather in color to sample w/black leatherette beltline	5240	6540
—	leather w/leatherette beltline - Coupe	3631	4532
	Cabriolet	3344	4173
—	special leather - Coupe	3977	4963
	Cabriolet	3688	4603
XX6	**Shift Lever Knob** — leather in deviating standard colors - models w/manual trans	55	68

CODE	DESCRIPTION	INVOICE	MSRP
—	**Shift Lever**		
X25	light rootwood - models w/Tiptronic	339	423
X24	dark rootwood - models w/Tiptronic	339	423
—	**Sun Visors**		
XN8	leather	464	579
XN9	leather w/illuminated RH visor vanity mirror	537	671
—	**Radio Equipment**		
490	hi-fi sound system *incls amplifier system*	450	561
P45	CD player - Coupe	239	299
P46	CD player - Cabriolet	239	299
692	remote control CD changer	998	1245
XD9	**Rims** — painted in vehicle color	865	1079
595	**Spoiler** — color-keyed rear - Coupe	170	213
—	**Seats**		
P14	dual heated	460	578
513	passenger's lumbar support	442	551
586	driver's lumbar support	442	551
387	sport passenger w/power height adjuster	251	314
383	sport driver's w/power height adjuster	251	314
—	**Seat Trim**		
Z55	supple leather front	355	443
—	leather - Coupe	1807	2256
	Cabriolet	1561	1949
—	partial leather w/leatherette	547	682
418	**Bodyside Moldings**	280	350
—	**Boot Cover**		
Z57	deviating current colors - Cabriolet	78	98
XP3	leather - Cabriolet	2076	2591
Z53	**Head Restraints** — stamped w/Porsche Crest *req's leather seat trim*	82	103
498	**Model Designation Delete** — rear	NC	NC
SPP	**Power Pack Plus**	39	45
—	**Tires**		
—	P205/55ZR16 front tires and P225/50ZR16 rear tires	STD	STD
—	P225/45ZR17 front tires and P255/40ZR17 rear tires *std w/chassis P31*	NA	NA
Z36	**Cargo Cover** — leather in current Porsche colors - Coupe	770	963
—	**Door Trim Panels**		
Z81	leather in deviating current color	41	51
Z80	leather	214	267
Z82	leather in full leather interior	43	53
—	**Kneebar**		
Z31	leather	539	672
Z35	leather in deviating current colors	65	81

CODE	DESCRIPTION	INVOICE	MSRP
—	**Rim Caps**		
X89	painted w/Porsche Crest	172	214
XD4	w/Porsche Crest	172	214
—	**Parking Brake Lever**		
X31	light rootwood or leather in color to sample	428	535
X32	dark rootwood or leather in color to sample	428	535
—	**Carpet**		
Z69	deviating in std color - Coupe	60	75
Z70	deviating in std color - Cabriolet	94	118
—	**Instrument Carrier**		
XL2	light rootwood	1397	1743
XL3	dark rootwood	1397	1743
—	**Gear Shift Knob**		
XC8	light rootwood - models w/manual trans	289	360
XC9	dark rootwood - models w/manual trans	289	360
P31	**Sport Chassis** — Coupe *incls 5-spoke wheels, larger front/rear stabilizer bars, P225/45ZR17 front tires, P225/40ZR17 rear tires*	1616	2017

CODE DESCRIPTION INVOICE MSRP

900 (1995)

CODE	DESCRIPTION	INVOICE	MSRP
902MT	S 2-Dr Convertible (5-spd)	29201	32995
903M	S 3-Dr Coupe (5-spd)	20970	23695
905M	S 5-Dr Hatchback (5-spd)	20687	23375
952MT	SE Turbo 2-Dr Convertible (5-spd)	34383	39520
953MSR	SE Turbo 3-Dr Coupe (5-spd)	25656	28990
975MSR	SE 5-Dr Hatchback (5-spd)	25381	28680
Destination Charge:		470	470

Standard Equipment

900S - 5-DOOR: 2.3 liter naturally aspirated 150 HP engine, double overhead camshafts, light alloy cylinder head with 4 valves per cylinder, electronic fuel injection/knock detector, 4-wheel power assisted disc brakes with ABS, ventilated front discs, power assisted rack and pinion steering, independent front suspension with MacPherson struts, front and rear stabilizer bars, high speed SBR tires, steel wheels with wheel covers, 5-speed manual transmission, Saab Supplemental Restraint System (SRS) (incls driver and passenger side air bags, automatic belt tensioner system for front seat occupants), 3-point safety belts for all occupants, welded unit body construction and side-impact protection system designed in front and rear crumple zones, well-isolated fuel tank location, collapsible steering column, manually activated "child-proof" rear door locks, lock-out switch for rear power window switches, anti-lock braking system (ABS), mechanically-activated rear-wheel hand brake, headlamp wiper and washer, daytime running lights, rear window wiper and washer system, color-keyed "self-restoring" bumpers and black window trim, protective bodyside moldings, aerodynamic headlamps with flush lenses and replaceable halogen bulbs, side guidance reversing lights and side-mounted direction indicator lights, front/rear fog lights, front spoiler, undercoating and anti-corrosion treatment, CFC-free air conditioning with interior air filtration system, electrically heated reclining front bucket seats (with on/off control), remote central locking and anti-theft alarm, deadlock security system, telescopic steering wheel, power windows with one-touch feature on front windows, electronic speed control with "cruise on" indicator light, electrically adjustable and heated rearview mirrors, windshield wiper/washer with interval and clean sweep feature, head restraints at front and rear outboard seating positions, two-position fold-down back seat and fold-down rear center armrest, pass-through opening from trunk to back seat (behind center armrest), automatic headlamp shut-off and courtesy headlamp delay feature, illuminated visor vanity mirrors, interior courtesy light delay feature, luggage compartment light and built-in tool kit, heat absorbent tinted glass, electric rear window demister, two-tone luxury velour upholstery, adjustable front safety belt guide loops, rear side window demisters, front/rear plush carpet floor mats, AM/FM stereo cassette with CD changer controls (incls anti-theft lock-out code, front/rear fader control, electronic tuning with programmable AM/FM pre-sets, seek up and down tuning, auto-reverse cassette with Dolby noise reduction, full-logic cassette transport with head and roller release), automatic electric antenna, 6 acoustically engineered speakers (in four locations), analog speedometer, analog tachometer, digital odometer and trip meter, fuel and temperature gauges, dashboard "black panel" feature with integrated warning system, quartz analog clock, warning lights (incls traction control system [TCS, V6 only], supplemental restraint system [SRS], anti-lock braking system [ABS], low fuel, oil pressure, battery, brake fluid), indicator lamps (incls rear demister, hand brake, high beam, open door, rear fog light).

S COUPE (in addition to or instead of S 5-DOOR equipment): Manually activated "child-proof" rear door locks deleted, lock-out switch for rear power window switches deleted.

SE 5-DOOR (in addition to or instead of S COUPE equipment): 2.5 liter V6 170 HP engine, Saab Traction Control System (TCS), light alloy wheels, manually activated "child-proof" rear door locks, lock-out switch for rear power window switches, electric tilt/slide tinted glass sunroof with interior ventilated sunshade, CFC-free automatic climate control with interior air filtration system, power 8-way adjustable front seats with driver's side memory, leather seating surfaces, leather-wrapped steering wheel, 8 acoustically engineered speakers (in 6 locations), Saab Car Computer (SCC).

SE COUPE (in addition to or instead of SE 5-DOOR equipment): 2.0 liter turbocharged 185 HP engine, Saab Traction Control System (TCS) deleted, lowered sport chassis, manually activated "child-proof" rear door locks deleted, lock-out switch for rear power window switches deleted, rear spoiler.

S CONVERTIBLE: 2.3 liter naturally aspirated 150 HP engine, double overhead camshaft, light alloy cylinder head with 4 valves per cylinder, electronic fuel injection/knock detector, 4-wheel power assisted disc brakes with ABS, ventilated front discs, power assisted rack and pinion steering, independent front suspension with MacPherson struts, front and rear stabilizer bars, high speed SBR tires, light alloy wheels, 5-speed manual transmission, Saab Supplemental Restraint System (SRS) (incls driver and passenger air bags, automatic belt tensioner system for front seat occupants), 3-point safety belts for all occupants, welded unit-body construction and side-impact protection system designed in front and rear crumple zones, well-isolated fuel tank location, collapsible steering column, lock-out switch for rear power window switches, Saab anti-lock braking system (ABS), mechanically activated rear-wheel hand brake, headlamp wiper and washer, daytime running lights, electrically operated top with automatic retraction under molded boot cover, color-keyed "self-restoring" bumpers and black window trim, protective bodyside moldings, aerodynamic headlamps with flush lenses and replaceable halogen bulbs, side guidance reversing lights and side mounted direction indicator lights, front/rear fog lights, front spoiler, undercoating and anti-corrosion treatment, CFC-free air conditioning with interior air filtration system, electrically heated reclining front bucket seats (with on/off control), remote central locking and anti-theft alarm, deadlock security system, telescopic steering wheel, power windows with one-touch opening for front windows (separate switch for simultaneous operation of all side windows), electronic speed control with "cruise on" indicator light, electrically adjustable and heated rearview mirrors, windshield wiper/washer with interval and clean sweep feature, head restraints at front and rear outboard seating positions, fold-down lockable rear seat back, automatic headlamp shut-off and courtesy headlamp delay feature, illuminated visor vanity mirrors, interior courtesy light delay feature, luggage compartment light and built-in tool kit, electric rear window demister, leather seating surfaces, leather-wrapped steering wheel, front and rear plush carpet floor mats, AM/FM stereo/cassette with CD changer controls (incls anti-theft lock-out code, front/rear fader control, electronic tuning with programmable AM/FM pre-sets, seek up and down tuning, auto-reverse cassette with Dolby noise reduction, full-logic cassette transport with head and roller release), automatic electric antenna, 6 acoustically engineered speakers (in four locations), analog speedometer, analog tachometer, digital odometer and trip meter, fuel and temperature gauges, dashboard "black panel" feature with integrated warning system, quartz analog clock, warning lights (incls Traction Control system [TCS, V6 only], Supplemental Restraint System [SRS], anti-lock braking system [ABS], low fuel, oil pressure, battery, brake fluid), indicator lamps (incls rear demister, hand brake, high beam, open door, rear fog light).

SE CONVERTIBLE (in addition to or instead of S CONVERTIBLE equipment): 2.0 liter turbocharged 185 HP engine, CFC-free automatic climate control with interior air filtration system, power 8-way adjustable front seats with driver's side memory, 8 acoustically engineered speakers (in 6 locations), CD changer, Saab Car Computer (SCC).

Accessories

Code	Description	Invoice	MSRP
972	**Engine** — 2.5 liter 24-valve V6 - SE Convertible *incls traction control*	467	550
SR	**Power Sunroof** — S Coupe & Hatchback	843	995
—	**Alloy Wheels** — S Coupe & Hatchback	322	380
—	**Automatic Transmission** — S, SE Convertible & Hatchback *req's 2.5 liter V6 engine on SE Convertible*	843	995

9000 *(1995)*

Code	Description	Invoice	MSRP
065MSR	Aero Turbo 5-Dr Hatchback (5-spd)	35488	41750
065ASR	Aero Turbo 5-Dr Hatchback (auto)	35105	41300
074ASR	CDE 4-Dr Sedan (auto)	33731	38995
015M	CS 5-Dr Hatchback (5-spd)	26338	29845
055MSR	CSE Turbo 5-Dr Hatchback (5-spd)	31581	36510
075ASR	CSE 5-Dr Hatchback (auto)	33433	38650
Destination Charge:		470	470

Standard Equipment

9000 - CDE/CSE V6: 3.0 liter V6 210 HP engine, double overhead camshafts, light alloy cylinder head with 4 valves per cylinder, motronic electronic fuel injection and ignition, Saab Traction Control System (TCS), 4-wheel power assisted disc brakes with ABS (ventilated front discs), power assisted rack and pinion steering, gas-hydraulic shock absorbers, independent front suspension with MacPherson struts, front and rear stabilizer bars, light alloy wheels, high speed SBR tires, 4-speed/overdrive automatic transmission with split torque and direct drive, Saab Supplemental Restraint System (SRS) (incls driver and passenger air bags, automatic belt tensioner system for front seat occupants, padded knee bolsters for front seat occupants), 3-point safety belts at all outboard seating positions, rear center lap belt, welded unit body construction (designed in front and rear crumple zones), side-impact protection system, well-isolated fuel tank location, collapsible steering column, manually activated "child-proof" rear door locks, lock-out switch for rear door power window switches, Saab anti-lock braking system (ABS), mechanically activated rear-wheel hand brake, headlamp wiper and washer system, daytime running lights, electric tilt/slide tinted glass sunroof with interior sunshade, aerodynamic headlamps with flush lenses and replaceable halogen headlamp bulbs, color-keyed "self-restoring" bumpers and black window trim, protective bodyside moldings, side-guidance reversing lights and side-mounted direction indicator lights, front and rear fog lights, front spoiler, neutral-density dark-tinted taillight lenses, undercoating and anti-corrosion treatment, CFC-free automatic climate control with manual override and interior air filtration system, electrically heated reclining front bucket seats with temperature controls for both seat heaters, power 8-way adjustable front seats with driver's seat memory, electronic speed control with "cruise on" indicator light, remote central locking with anti-theft alarm, lockable center storage console, power windows with "one-touch" opening for front windows, electrically adjustable and heated rearview mirrors, rear side window demisters and electric rear window demister, windshield wiper/washer system with interval wipe feature, illuminated visor vanity mirrors, interior courtesy light delay feature, overhead console with swiveling map light/dual rear seat reading lamps, adjustable front safety belt guide loops, head restraints at front and rear outboard seating positions, leather seating surfaces, leather-wrapped steering wheel, leather shift boot cover (manual trans), telescopic steering wheel, walnut instrument panel, front and rear plush carpet floor mats, fold-down rear center armrest, remote trunk/hatch release button on driver's door, pass-through opening from trunk to rear seat, luggage compartment light and built-in/removable tool kit, tinted/heat-absorbent glass, "Prestige" AM/FM stereo/cassette with removable keypad controls (incls anti-theft lock-out code and warning light, 150 watt amplifier, front/rear fader control, electronic tuning with 18 programmable AM/FM pre-sets, seek and scan up and down tuning, auto-reverse cassette with Dolby noise reduction, full-logic cassette transport with key-off eject), 10 acoustically engineered speakers, automatic electric antenna, compact disc player (pre-wired for CD changer), analog speedometer with odometer and trip meter, analog tachometer/fuel and temperature gauges, Saab Car Computer (incls digital clock), electronic display (incls voltage, outside temperature, average/inst. fuel economy, miles to empty, message prompts to check coolant and oil levels), pictogram (incls bulb failure, door/trunk open, low oil pressure), warning lights (incls Supplemental Restraint System [SRS], anti-lock braking system [ABS], low fuel, battery brake fluid, washer fluid), indicator lamps (incls rear demister, hand brake, high beam).

AERO (in addition to or instead of CDE equipment): 2.3 liter turbocharged 225 HP engine, water-cooled turbocharger/air-to-air charge air intercooler/engine oil cooler, Saab Trionic engine management system (incls Saab Direct Ignition [Saab DI], electronic fuel injection, knock detection, charge-pressure control), Saab Traction Control System (TCS) deleted, 5-speed/overdrive manual transmission, rear window wiper/washer system, rear spoiler, three-position fold-down back seat, full leather sports seats, pass-through opening from trunk to rear seat deleted, turbo boost pressure gauge, "shift up" indicator.

CSE (in addition to or instead of AERO equipment): 2.3 liter turbocharged 200 HP engine, leather seating surfaces.

CODE	DESCRIPTION	INVOICE	MSRP

CS (in addition to or instead of CSE equipment): 2.3 liter light pressure turbocharged 170 HP engine, electric tilt/slide tinted glass sunroof with interior sunshade deleted, rear spoiler deleted, power 8-way adjustable front seats with driver's seat memory deleted, velour fabric upholstery, leather-wrapped steering wheel/leather shift boot cover deleted, walnut instrument panel deleted, "Premium" AM/FM stereo/cassette audio system with removable keypad controls, 8 acoustically engineered speakers, compact disc player and pre-wiring for CD changer deleted, turbo boost pressure gauge deleted, Saab Car Computer deleted, quartz analog clock.

Accessories

CODE	DESCRIPTION	INVOICE	MSRP
—	**Automatic Transmission** — CS	885	1045
	CSE Turbo	885	1045
—	**Leather Pkg** — CS	1131	1335
	incls leather seat trim, leather-wrapped steering wheel, leather-wrapped shift knob (CS w/manual trans)		
—	**Power Sunroof** — CS	945	1115

What's New for *Saab* in 1995?

900: A convertible 900 appeared in 1995, and all 900's get a new three-spoke steering wheel and an anti-theft alarm.

9000: A new 3.0L V6 is installed in the CSE and CDE trim levels, which have traction control standard. The CSE can be had with a 225 hp 2.3L turbocharged engine. The base CS gets a 2.3L turbo motor as well, but it's not nearly as powerful as the monster motor found in the CSE.

SATURN (1995)

SATURN 4 CYL

CODE	DESCRIPTION	INVOICE	MSRP
ZZF69	SL 4-Dr Sedan (5-spd)	8996	9995
ZZG69	SL1 4-Dr Sedan (5-spd)	9896	10995
ZZH69	SL1 4-Dr Sedan (auto)	10634	11815
ZZJ69	SL2 4-Dr Sedan (5 spd)	10796	11995
ZZK69	SL2 4-Dr Sedan (auto)	11534	12815
ZZE27	SC1 2-Dr Coupe (5-spd)	10706	11895
ZZF27	SC1 2-Dr Coupe (auto)	11444	12715
ZZG27	SC2 2-Dr Coupe (5-spd)	11696	12995
ZZH27	SC2 2-Dr Coupe (auto)	12434	13815
ZZG35	SW1 4-Dr Wagon (5-spd)	10526	11695
ZZH35	SW1 4-Dr Wagon (auto)	11264	12515
ZZJ35	SW2 4-Dr Wagon (5-spd)	11426	12695
ZZK35	SW2 4-Dr Wagon (auto)	12164	13515
Destination Charge:		360	360

Standard Equipment

SATURN - ALL MODELS: Front wheel drive, 5-speed manual transmission, 5-mph front and rear bumpers, dent-resistant exterior panels on fenders, doors, quarters and fascias, integral bodyside moldings, high gloss polyurethane clearcoat paint finish, flush tinted glass, adjustable driver and front passenger head restraints, cloth door trim panels, 60/40 fold-down rear seatbacks, fabric seats, rear seat heater ducts, reclining front seatbacks, fully trimmed trunk/cargo area, AM/FM stereo radio with seek/scan tuning and four 6" speakers, digital quartz clock, rear window defogger, 3-speed intermittent windshield wipers, headlamps-on chime, high mounted audio controls, interior storage features, passenger vanity mirror, adjustable steering column, remote fuel filler door release, independent 4-wheel suspension, power front disc/rear drum brakes, rack and pinion steering, driver-side air bag, automatic shoulder/manual lap belt system for driver and front passenger, manual lap/ shoulder safety belts for rear seats, flash to pass headlamps, halogen headlamps, child security rear

CODE	DESCRIPTION	INVOICE	MSRP

door locks, combined low engine oil pressure and coolant level telltale, tachometer, coolant temperature gauge, centralized electrical fuse centers, long-life engine coolant, maintenance-free suspension, maintenance-free battery, scissors jack, self-adjusting accessory drive belt, stainless steel exhaust system, steel spaceframe construction, 1.9 liter SOHC 4 cylinder PFI engine (SL, SL1, SC1, SW1), 1.9 liter DOHC 4 cylinder PFI engine (SL2, SC2, SW2), P175/70R14 radial tires (SL, SL1, SC1, SW1), P195/60R15 radial tires (SL2, SC2, SW2).

Accessories

CODE	DESCRIPTION	INVOICE	MSRP
—	**Pkg 1** — SL1	1625	1805
	SC1	1512	1680
	SW1	1625	1805
	SW2	1625	1805
	incls air conditioning, power windows, power locks, power passenger side mirror, speed control		
—	**Pkg 2** — SL2	1899	2110
	SC2	1697	1885
	incls air conditioning, power windows, power locks, power passenger side mirror, "sawtooth" alloy wheels, speed control		
—	**California Emissions**	63	70
—	**Massachusetts Emissions**	63	70
C60	**Air Conditioning**	815	905
C66	**Air Conditioning Prep** — SL, SL1, SC1, SW1	239	NC
K34	**Speed Control** — NA on SL	225	250
—	**Anti-Lock Brakes** — w/5-spd trans	653	725
	w/auto trans (incls traction control)	702	780
CF5	**Power Sunroof** — SL1, SL2, SC1, SC2	608	675
D80	**Rear Spoiler** — SL2, SC1, SC2	162	180
T96	**Fog Lights** — SL2, SW2	140	155
PG5	**Alloy Wheels** — "teardrop" - SC2	185	205
PH6	**Alloy Wheels** — "sawtooth" - SL2, SW2	275	305
	SC1	365	405
AB5	**Power Door Locks** — SL1, SW1	225	250
—	**Leather Trim** — SL2, SC2, SW2	608	675
—	**Mirror** — passenger side, outside - SL1	32	35
	incl in pkg 1 & 2		
UM6	**Radio** — AM/FM stereo w/cassette	180	200
UU6	**Radio** — AM/FM stereo w/cassette & equalizer	329	365
U79	**Coaxial Speakers** — extended range	68	75

What's New for *Saturn* in 1995?

SC: Saturn's sporty coupe receives revised front and rear styling, an all new interior and more power from the base engine. Color choices inside and out have been revised as well.

SL, SW: A new instrument panel with dual airbags is the biggest change to the 1995 Saturn SL, and it was a much needed one. The motorized mouse automatic seatbelts have thankfully been canned. The base engine gets a 15 hp boost to 100. Two new colors enhance the SL's dated bodywork. The SL is expected to be thoroughly restyled for 1996.

CODE	DESCRIPTION	INVOICE	MSRP

IMPREZA *(1995)*

IMPREZA 2WD

CODE	DESCRIPTION	INVOICE	MSRP
SMM	1.8L Base 2-Dr Coupe (5-spd)	11061	11850
SJA	1.8L Base 4-Dr Sedan (5-spd)	11061	11850
SMN	1.8L L 2-Dr Coupe (5-spd)	12565	13750
SJB	1.8L L 4-Dr Sedan (5-spd)	12565	13750
SNA	1.8L L Special Edit. 4-Dr Sedan (auto)	13294	14645

IMPREZA AWD

CODE	DESCRIPTION	INVOICE	MSRP
SLF	1.8L L 4-Dr Wagon (5-spd)	13728	15150
SOA	1.8L L Special Edit. 4-Dr Wagon (5-spd)	14306	15845
SLI	1.8L Outback Sport 4-Dr Wagon (5-spd)	14271	15750
SOA	1.8L Outback Special Edit. 4-Dr Wagon (5-spd)	14306	15845
SMV	2.2L LX 2-Dr Coupe (auto)	15658	17295
SJJ	2.2L LX 4-Dr Sedan (auto)	15385	16995
SLJ	2.2L LX Sport 4-Dr Wagon (auto)	15747	17395

Standard Equipment

IMPREZA - BASE: Aluminum SOHC 16-valve horizontally opposed 1.8 liter engine, front wheel drive, 5-speed manual transmission, 4-wheel independent suspension, power front disc/rear drum brakes, 165/80HR13 all-season radial tires, 5-mph bumpers, halogen headlamps with key-off feature, rear window defogger, tinted glass, black bodyside molding, dual air bags, speed sensitive power steering, 4-spoke tilt steering wheel, analog instrumentation, reclining front bucket seats with height adjustable headrests, center console with storage box, fuel filler/hood remote releases, front stabilizer bar, rear heater ducts, front spoiler.

L (in addition to or instead of BASE equipment): P165/80HR13 tires (Sedan), 175/70HR14 tires (Coupe, Wagon), air conditioning, tachometer, dual power assisted rearview mirrors, remote trunk release (Sedan, Coupe), AM/FM cassette stereo system, fog lights, rear window wiper/washer (Wagon), all-wheel drive (Wagon), rear spoiler (Coupe), 60/40 split fold-down rear seat (Wagon).

CODE	DESCRIPTION	INVOICE	MSRP

L SPECIAL EDITION (in addition to or instead of L equipment): Power windows, power door locks.

OUTBACK (in addition to or instead of L WAGON equipment): Two-tone paint/stripes/graphics package, luggage rack, mud guards.

LX (in addition to or instead of L equipment): 4-speed automatic transmission, power 4-wheel disc brakes with ABS, horizontally opposed 16-valve SOHC 2.2 liter 4 cylinder engine, 195/60HR15 all-season radial tires, rear stabilizer bar, power antenna, dual body color power assisted rearview mirrors, rear spoiler (Coupe, Sedan), 60/40 split folding rear seat, dual map lights.

Accessories

CODE	DESCRIPTION	INVOICE	MSRP
—	**Automatic Transmission** — 4-speed - AWD L Sedan	716	800
	L Coupe & Wagon	716	800
—	**All-Wheel Drive (AWD)** — L Coupe	859	1000
	L Sedan	831	1000
	incls P175/70HR14 tires		
—	**Engine** — 2.2 liter 16-valve 4 cylinder - L, L Special Edit, Outback	895	1000
	incls automatic transmission, power 4-wheel disc brakes, P195/60HR15 tires, rear stabilizer bar and rear spoiler		
ARB	**Air Conditioning** — Base	876	1095
LVI	**Engine Block Heater**	39	56
CP	**Cruise Control**	239	340
—	**Alloy Wheels**		
—	13"	425	575
HSA	5-spoke - NA on Base	443	590
HPA	7-spoke - NA on Base	393	510
HPB	cross-spoke - NA on Base	449	585
BP	**Floor Mats**	39	60
LPA	**Mud Guards** — std on Outback	49	75
LP	**Console w/Armrest** — L Sedan & Wagon	71	110
S54	**Convenience Pkg** — L w/5-speed trans	288	329
	L w/auto trans	288	329
	incls cruise control and cassette		
GPB	**Bicycle Rack** — Wagons	49	75
S51	**Audio Pkg** — L Coupe	262	299
	incls AM/FM stereo radio with cassette		
GNA	**Ski Rack** — Wagons	62	94
HL	**Active Safety Group** — L Coupe	892	1300
	incls all-wheel drive, power 4-wheel disc brakes, alloy wheels, anti-lock brakes and AM/FM stereo radio		
—	**Preferred Equipment Pkg** — L Coupe	376	429
	incls cruise control and compact disc player		
—	**Radio Equipment**		
DPA	AM/FM stereo radio - Base	200	295
DRA	AM/FM stereo radio & additional speakers - Base Coupes	254	339
EPA	cassette - req's DPA or DRA radio - Base	148	214
EPB	compact disc player	375	495

LEGACY *(1995)*

CODE	DESCRIPTION	INVOICE	MSRP
LEGACY FWD			
SAA	Base 4-Dr Sedan (5-spd)	13271	14364
SAC	L 4-Dr Sedan (5-spd)	15062	16620
SBC	L 5-Dr Wagon (5-spd)	15680	17320
LEGACY AWD			
SBJ	Brighton 5-Dr Wagon (5-spd)	14905	15999
SBW	Outback 5-Dr Wagon (5-spd)	17760	19820
SAP	LS 4-Dr Sedan (auto)	18907	21120
SBS	LS 5-Dr Wagon (auto)	19525	21820
SAQ	LSi 4-Dr Sedan (auto)	21130	23620
SBT	LSi 5-Dr Wagon (auto)	21748	24320
Destination Charge:		475	475

Standard Equipment

LEGACY - BASE: Horizontally opposed 16-valve 2.2 liter 4 cylinder engine with multi-point fuel injection system, 5-speed manual transmission, "hill holder," front-wheel drive, 4-wheel independent suspension, front and rear stabilizer bars, speed sensitive power assisted rack and pinion steering, power assisted dual diagonal disc/drum brakes, 185/70SR14 tires, 5.5" x 14" wheels, unit-body construction, 5-mph bumpers, low-profile halogen headlights with "key-off" feature, protective side moldings, tinted glass, rear window defogger, store-guard coating, driver and front passenger air bags, analog instrumentation, tilt adjustable steering wheel, driver's footrest, reclining front bucket seats, center console with storage box, dual cup holder.

BRIGHTON (in addition to or instead of BASE equipment): All-wheel drive, air conditioning, AM/FM/cassette audio system with 40 watts and two speakers, upgraded fabric and door trim.

CODE	DESCRIPTION	INVOICE	MSRP

L (in addition to or instead of above equipment): Front wheel drive, seven-spoke full wheel covers, dual power mirrors, remote trunk (Sedan) and fuel releases, air conditioning, power door locks, power windows with one-touch down driver's side, AM/FM/cassette audio system with 80 watts and four speakers, analog instrumentation with tachometer, digital clock, rear window wiper/washer (Wagon), 60/40 split folding rear seat (lockable trunk-through on Sedan), passenger side visor vanity mirror, cargo area cover (Wagon), multi-box storage tray (Wagon).

LS (in addition to or instead of above equipment): All-wheel drive, 4-speed electronically controlled automatic transmission, 4-wheel disc brakes with anti-lock system, 195/60HR15 tires, 6" x 15" polished alloy wheels, body color door handles, body color side moldings, dual body color power mirrors, power antenna, woodgrain trim, cruise control, power moonroof, adjustable intermittent windshield wipers, height adjustable driver's seat, folding rear center armrest, velour seat material, dual lighted vanity visor mirrors.

LSi (in addition to or instead of above equipment): Interior leather package (incls seating surfaces, steering wheel cover, shift-knob cover, hand brake lever cover), security system, compact disc player, 6 speakers.

Outback (in addition or instead of L equipment): All-wheel drive, power 4-wheel disc brakes with anti-lock, fog lights, luggage rack, two-tone paint, cruise control, P195/60HR15 tires, alloy wheels.

Accessories

CODE	DESCRIPTION	INVOICE	MSRP
—	**Engine** — 2.2 liter 4 cyl MFI	STD	STD
—	**Full Time All-Wheel Drive** — L	748	1000
—	**Transmissions**		
—	5-speed manual w/overdrive - Base, L, Brighton, Outback	STD	STD
—	4-speed automatic w/overdrive - LS, LSi	STD	STD
	L, Brighton, Outback	715	800
ASA	**Air Conditioning** — Base	876	1095
MSE	**Cigarette Lighter**	18	28
—	**Fog Lights**		
JSA	projector	181	278
JSB	standard	129	198
FSA	**Luggage Rack** — Wagons	180	277
LSC	**Rear Gate Bar** — Wagons	56	87
CSA	**Speed Control** — Base, L, Brighton	238	369
LSE	**Tail Pipe Extension**	19	30
LSF	**Mud Guards**	50	80
LSN	**Air Deflector** — L Sedan, LS, LSi	42	65
	req's RN option pkg on L Sedan		
LV1	**Engine Block Heater**	39	56
BSC	**Floor Mats** — gray	48	74
BSE	**Floor Mats** — taupe	48	74
LSD	**Bumper Cover** — Wagons	51	78
PSA	**Front Spoiler** — under	63	97
PS	**Rear Spoiler** — Sedans	282	375
PSB	**Rear Spoiler** — under - Sedans	63	97
PSC	**Rear Spoiler** — Wagons	63	97

CODE	DESCRIPTION	INVOICE	MSRP
—	**Wheels**		
HSA	5-spoke alloy	442	590
HPA	7-spoke alloy	393	510
HPB	cross-spoke alloy	449	585
LSJ	**Mirror** — RH power - Base, Brighton	77	119
MSH	**Cargo Tray** — Wagons	48	73
RN	**Option Pkg RN** — L	1872	2100
	incls power moonroof, automatic transmission, speed control, power antenna, dual map lights		
DQ	**Option Pkg DQ** — L FWD Sedan	2050	2300
	L AWD Sedan	1157	1300
	L FWD Wagon	2057	2300
	L AWD Wagon	442	500
	incls anti-lock brakes, speed control, power 4-wheel disc brakes, automatic transmission (FWD Wagon, Sedan)		
—	**Radio Equipment**		
DSA	AM/FM stereo - Base	254	339
EPB	compact disc player - Base, Brighton	375	495
ESB	compact disc player - L, LS, Outback	375	495
	incls 6 speakers		
EPA	cassette - Base	148	214
DSB	tweeter kit	66	101

SVX *(1995)*

CODE	DESCRIPTION	INVOICE	MSRP
SKA	L FWD 2-Dr Coupe (auto)	24287	26800
SKC	L AWD 2-Dr Coupe (auto)	25630	28300
SKD	LSi AWD 2-Dr Coupe (auto)	30776	34350
	Destination Charge:	475	475

Standard Equipment

SVX - L: Front wheel drive, horizontally opposed 3.3 liter aluminum 6 cylinder DOHC 24-valve 230 hp engine, 4-speed electronically controlled automatic transmission, window-in-window glass system, low-profile headlamps/fog lamp lighting system, 5-mph bumpers, power mirrors, 4-wheel independent suspension, 225/50VR16 Bridgestone Potenza radial tires, 7.5JJ x 16" 5-spoke aluminum-alloy wheels, power assisted rack and pinion steering, 2-speed windshield wipers with variable intermittent control, rear wiper with washer and intermittent setting, rear window defogger, rear fender-mounted power antenna, splash guards, no-lose gas cap with retainer strap, dual air bags, automatic climate control system, power windows with driver's side one-touch down feature, anatomically designed seats and seat coverings, adjustable driver's seat (incls cushion height and pitch, seatback rake and lumbar support adjustments, complete analog instrumentation, cruise control, 80-watt AM/FM/cassette audio system with electronic tuning and preset equalizer and four speakers, dual diversity antenna system, power door locks, digital clock, dual illuminated visor mirrors, telescope and memory tilt steering column, dual overhead sport lamps, entry/exit illumination system with timer, center console with storage compartment, folding rear seatback, simulated wood dash accents.

L AWD (in addition to or instead of L equipment): All-wheel drive, rear limited slip differential, rear spoiler, power 4-wheel disc brakes with anti-lock system.

LSi AWD (in addition to or instead of L AWD equipment): Tinted glass, tilt and retract sunroof, leather seating surfaces, leather steering wheel, leather shift and parking brake lever cover, 8-way power assisted driver seat, premium 80-watt AM/FM/cassette/compact disc audio system with 6 electronically driven speakers, heated exterior mirrors, 50/50 split folding rear seatback, carpeted floor mats, infrared remote control anti-theft system, vehicle speed-sensitive power assisted steering.

Accessories

The following SVX accessories are dealer installed.

Code	Description	Invoice	MSRP
RPA	**Alarm System** — L	238	365
BNA	**Floor Mats**	48	74
LPB	**Air Deflector** — LSi	42	65
ENB	**CD Player** — L	487	649
LV1	**Engine Block Heater**	39	56

What's New for *Subaru* for 1995?

Impreza: A coupe version joins the lineup, and an optional 2.2L engine is available. A special edition wagon called the Outback gets four-wheel disc brakes, new wheelcovers and trick paint.

Legacy: All-new for 1995, the turbo Legacy disappears this year. Traction control is available, and Subaru is concentrating on four-wheel drive models in advertising. The Legacy is good looking, but the turbocharged version will be missed. Outback wagon is neat, and will be basis for Legacy-based sport ute in 1996.

CODE	DESCRIPTION	INVOICE	MSRP

SWIFT *(1995)*

CODE	DESCRIPTION	INVOICE	MSRP
HES532S	3-Dr Hatchback (5-spd)	8003	8699
HES533S	3-Dr Hatchback w/ABS (5-spd)	8518	9259
HES552S	3-Dr Hatchback (auto)	8601	9849
HES553S	3-Dr Hatchback w/ABS (auto)	9116	9909
Destination Charge:		330	330

Standard Equipment

SWIFT: 1.3 liter SOHC 4 cylinder engine, electronic throttle-body fuel injection, 5-speed manual overdrive transmission, rack and pinion steering, 4-wheel independent suspension, power assisted front disc/rear drum brakes, full aerodynamic wheel covers, P155/80R13 SBR all-season BW tires, sport style front and rear bumpers, halogen headlamps, dual outside mirrors, side protective moldings, electric rear window defogger, tinted glass, 2-speed windshield wipers/washers with intermittent feature, dual air bags, 3-point front/rear seat belts, tripmeter, day/night rearview mirror, reclining front bucket seats, fold-down rear seat, cup holder, cloth seat trim, side window demisters, dual front map pockets, deluxe floor carpeting, carpeted luggage rack, removable rear cargo area cover/shelf, sun visor with pocket and vanity mirror, 3M Scotchgard, ABS indicator light, air bag warning lamp, center console.

Accessories

NOTE: Suzuki accessories are dealer installed. Contact a Suzuki dealer for accessory availability.

What's New for *Suzuki* in 1995?

Swift: All-new Swift is available as a hatchback only and now has dual airbags standard. ABS is optional. All Swifts get a four cylinder engine, unlike the base Geo Metro hatch, the Swift's twin, which is saddled with a wimpy three cylinder. The nickel missile GT version has been dropped. A new sedan called Esteem is due shortly, to replace last year's Swift sedan.

AVALON *(1995)*

CODE	DESCRIPTION	INVOICE	MSRP
3534	XL 4-Dr Sedan w/Bucket Seats (auto)	19730	22758
3536	XL 4-Dr Sedan w/Bench Seat (auto)	20416	23548
3544	XLS 4-Dr Sedan w/Bucket Seats (auto)	22866	26688
3546	XLS 4-Dr Sedan w/Bench Seat (auto)	22866	26688
Destination Charge:		397	397

Standard Equipment

AVALON - XL: Power 4-wheel disc brakes (ventilated front disc/rear solid), 3.0 liter V6 4-cam 24-valve EFI engine, Distributorless Toyota Direct Ignition system (TDI), engine revolution-sensing progressive power rack and pinion steering, front and rear anti-vibration sub-frames, independent front MacPherson suspension with stabilizer bar, rear dual link independent MacPherson strut suspension with stabilizer bar, 205/65HR15 SBR all-season tires, 4-speed electronically controlled automatic overdrive transmission with intelligence (ECT-i), color-keyed bumpers and door handles, tinted glass, aerodynamic halogen headlamps with auto-off feature, dual color-keyed power outside mirrors, color-keyed protective bodyside moldings, full wheel covers, washer-linked intermittent windshield wipers, CFC-free air conditioning with manual controls, full cut-pile carpeting with driver side footrest, digital quartz clock, multi-function cruise control, dual cup holder, rear window defogger, side window demisters, power door locks with anti-lockout feature, gauges for speedometer/tachometer/odometer/tripmeter/coolant temperature/fuel level, illuminated entry/exit system (automatic fade-out with illuminated inside key ring), dual illuminated visor vanity mirrors, remote hood/trunk/fuel filler door releases, seats (6-way manually adjustable driver side bucket seat, 4-way manually adjustable passenger side bucket seat) or (6-way driver and front passenger power adjustable split bench seat with fold-down armrest), full fabric front seats and door trim with dual door map pockets, contoured fabric rear seats with integrated headrests and center armrest, tilt steering wheel, center console storage area with armrest (bucket seat models), fold-down center armrest with flip-out dual cup holder (optional bench seat models), warning lights for seatbelt/air bag/low fuel level/door ajar/brake/oil pressure/battery/check engine/taillamp feature, power windows with 60-second retained power feature, deluxe ETR/cassette with 4 speakers and power antenna.

XLS (in addition to or instead of XL equipment): Anti-lock brake system (ABS), headlamps with auto-on night/auto-off day feature, aluminum alloy 7-spoke wheels, CFC-free air conditioning with soft-touch automatic climate controls, outside temperature gauge, illuminated entry/exit system includes

CODE	DESCRIPTION	INVOICE	MSRP

illuminated door key, inside key ring and rear seat personal lamp; wood-like trim interior accents, keyless entry system (incls remote power 2-stage lock/unlock feature and trunk release), 7-way power adjustable driver side bucket seat, 6-way power adjustable passenger side bucket seat, leather-wrapped tilt steering wheel, theft deterrent system (integrated with security light), premium ETR/cassette with 6 speakers, power and diversity antennas, power moonroof.

Accessories

CODE	DESCRIPTION	INVOICE	MSRP
—	**Wheel Locks**		
WZ	alloy	30	50
	req's alloy wheels		
WL	alloy	30	50
	req's aluminum wheels		
WS	steel - XL	30	50
CA	**California Emissions**	130	153
GP	**Gold Pkg**	125	499
PE	**Seat Pkg** — dual power - XL w/bucket seats	663	780
MG	**Mud Guards**	40	50
C1	**Carpeted Trunk Mat**	43	72
SA	**Wheels Upgrade** — alloy	484	650
	req's aluminum wheels		
—	**Wheels**		
AW	aluminum - XL	336	420
SS	alloy - XL	500	675
	XLS	760	950
—	**Radio Equipment**		
DC	premium AM/FM stereo with CD and cassette - XL	1069	1425
	XLS	889	1185
	incls 12-disc changer, graphic equalizer		
CE	premium AM/FM stereo with cassette - XL	180	240
	incls graphic equalizer		
P5	compact disc	325	464
	NA w/DC radio		
P3	3-disc compact disc changer	455	650
	NA w/DC radio		
P9	6-disc compact disc changer	496	709
	NA w/DC radio		
LA	**Leather Trim Pkg** — XL w/bucket seats	1487	1810
	XL w/bench seat	824	1030
	XLS	780	975
	incls leather-wrapped steering wheel, leather seat trim; req's aluminum wheels on XL		
GN	**Cargo Net**	21	35
PC	**Paint** — diamond white pearl	161	190
	incls bronze glass		
AB	**Brakes** — anti-lock - XL	779	950
CF	**Floor Mats** — front and rear	86	144
	incls carpeted trunk mat		
IS	**Alarm System** - XLS	260	695

CODE	DESCRIPTION	INVOICE	MSRP
PN	**Alarm System** — XL	170	200
RK	**Alarm System Enhancement** — XL *req's PN alarm system*	275	695
—	**Dashboard**		
DU	10-piece wood - XL w/bench seat, XLS	295	595
	12-piece wood - XL w/bucket seats	355	695
SR	**Moonroof** — power - XL	776	970

CAMRY *(1995)*

CODE	DESCRIPTION	INVOICE	MSRP
COUPE			
2501	DX 4 Cyl 2-Dr Coupe (5-spd)	14147	16128
2502	DX 4 Cyl 2-Dr Coupe (auto)	14849	16928
2504	LE 4 Cyl 2-Dr Coupe (auto)	16896	19488
2508	LE V6 2-Dr Coupe (auto)	18925	21828
2506	SE V6 2-Dr Coupe (auto)	20346	23468
SEDAN			
2521	DX 4 Cyl 4-Dr Sedan (5-spd)	14401	16418
2522	DX 4 Cyl 4-Dr Sedan (auto)	15103	17218
2532	LE 4 Cyl 4-Dr Sedan (auto)	17147	19778
2540	XLE 4 Cyl 4-Dr Sedan (auto)	18950	21858
2534	LE V6 4-Dr Sedan (auto)	19176	22118
2544	XLE V6 4-Dr Sedan (auto)	21387	24668
2546	SE V6 4-Dr Sedan (auto)	20597	23758
WAGON			
2594	LE 4 Cyl 5-Dr Wagon (auto)	18378	21198
2596	LE V6 5-Dr Wagon (auto)	20433	23568
Destination Charge:		397	397

Standard Equipment

CAMRY - DX: Power assisted ventilated front disc/rear drum brakes, front wheel drive, 2.2 liter 4 cylinder twin-cam 16-valve electronically fuel injected (EFI) engine, variable assist power rack and pinion steering, 5-speed manual overdrive transmission, tinted glass, aerodynamic halogen headlamps with auto-off feature, dual black manual remote control outside mirrors, full wheel covers, intermittent front windshield wipers, digital quartz clock, dual cup holder, gauges for speedometer/tachometer/coolant temperature/fuel level/odometer/tripmeter, remote hood/trunk/fuel filler door releases, reclining front bucket seats with adjustable headrests, fabric seats and door trim with integrated armrests/dual map pockets/cut-pile carpeting with driver side footrest, 60/40 split fold down rear seat with center armrest and security lock, 4-spoke tilt steering wheel, warning lights for air bag/seatbelts/low fuel level/door ajar/battery/check engine/oil pressure/brake/taillamp bulb failure, deluxe ETR with 4 speakers.

LE: Power assisted ventilated front disc/rear drum brakes (Sedan 4 cyl, Coupe 4 cyl, Wagon 4 cyl), power assisted ventilated front disc/rear solid disc brakes (Sedan V6, Coupe V6, Wagon V6), front wheel drive, 2.2 liter 4 cylinder twin-cam 16-valve electronically fuel injected (EFI) engine (Sedan 4 cyl, Coupe 4 cyl, Wagon 4 cyl), 3.0 liter V6 four-cam 24-valve electronically fuel injected (EFI) engine (Sedan V6, Coupe V6, Wagon V6), variable assist power rack and pinion steering, 4-speed electronically controlled automatic overdrive (ECT) transmission (Sedan 4 cyl, Coupe 4 cyl, Wagon 4 cyl), 4-speed electronically controlled automatic overdrive transmission with intelligence (ECT-i) (Sedan V6, Coupe V6, Wagon V6), tinted glass, aerodynamic halogen headlamps with auto-off feature, dual color-keyed power outside mirrors, full wheel covers, intermittent front windshield wipers, dual rear wiper system (Wagon 4 cyl, Wagon V6), CFC-free air conditioning, color-coordinated rear cargo cover (Wagon 4 cyl, Wagon V6), digital quartz clock, cruise control, dual cup holder, power door locks, gauges for speedometer/tachometer/coolant temperature/fuel level/odometer/tripmeter, remote hood/trunk/fuel filler door releases, 6-way adjustable driver seat (Sedan 4 cyl, Sedan V6, Wagon 4 cyl, Wagon V6), 7-way adjustable driver seat (Coupe 4 cyl, Coupe V6), fabric seats and door trim with integrated armrests/dual map pockets/cut-pile carpeting (with driver side footrest), 60/40 split fold-down rear seat with center armrest and security lock, 4-spoke tilt steering wheel, warning lights for air bag/seatbelts/low fuel level/door ajar/battery/check engine/oil pressure/brake/taillamp bulb failure, power windows, Power Pkg (incls power windows, door locks and outside mirrors), deluxe ETR/cassette with 4 speakers and power antenna (Wagons - 6 speakers).

SE: Power assisted ventilated front disc/rear solid disc brakes, front wheel drive, 3.0 liter V6 four-cam 24-valve electronically fuel injected (EFI) engine, variable assist power rack and pinion steering, 4 speed electronically controlled automatic overdrive transmission with intelligence (ECT-i), tinted glass, aerodynamic halogen headlamps with auto-off feature, dual color-keyed power outside mirrors, aluminum alloy wheels, intermittent front windshield wipers, CFC-free air conditioning, digital quartz clock, cruise control, dual cup holder, power door locks, gauges (include speedometer/tachometer/coolant temperature/fuel level/odometer/tripmeter), remote hood/trunk/fuel filler door releases, 6-way adjustable driver seat (Coupe), 7-way adjustable driver seat (Sedan), fabric seats and door trim with integrated armrests/dual map pockets/cut-pile carpeting with driver side footrest), 60/40 split fold-down rear seat with center armrest and security lock, 4-spoke tilt steering wheel, leather-wrapped steering wheel/parking brake handle, warning lights for: air bag/seatbelts/low fuel level/door ajar/battery/check engine/oil pressure/brake/taillamp bulb failure, power windows, Power Pkg (incls power windows, door locks and outside mirrors), deluxe ETR/cassette with 4 speakers and power antenna.

XLE: Anti-lock brake system (ABS), power assisted ventilated front disc/rear solid disc brakes, front wheel drive, 2.2 liter 4 cylinder twin-cam 16-valve electronically fuel injected (EFI) engine (4 cyl), 3.0 liter V6 four-cam 24-valve electronically fuel injected (EFI) engine (V6), variable assist power rack and pinion steering, 4-speed electronically controlled automatic overdrive (ECT) transmission (4 cyl), 4-speed electronically controlled automatic overdrive transmission with intelligence (ECT-i) (V6), tinted glass, aerodynamic halogen headlamps with auto-off feature, dual color-keyed power outside mirrors, aluminum alloy wheels, intermittent front windshield wipers, CFC-free air conditioning, digital quartz clock, cruise control, dual cup holder, power door locks, gauges (include speedometer/tachometer/

CODE	DESCRIPTION	INVOICE	MSRP

coolant temperature/fuel level/odometer/tripmeter, illuminated entry/exit system (automatic fade-out with inside/outside key ring, remote hood/trunk/fuel filler door releases, 7-way adjustable power driver seat, fabric seats and door trim with integrated armrests/dual map pockets/cut-pile carpeting (with driver side footrest), 60/40 split fold-down rear seat with center armrest and security lock, 4-spoke tilt steering wheel, warning lights (include air bag/seatbelts/low fuel level/door ajar/battery/ check engine/oil pressure/brake/taillamp bulb failure, Power Pkg (incls power windows, door locks and outside mirrors), deluxe ETR/cassette with 4 speakers and power antenna.

Accessories

CODE	DESCRIPTION	INVOICE	MSRP
AC	**Air Conditioning** — DX	780	975
CA	**California Emissions** — 4 cyl models	130	153
RF	**Rear Spoiler** — DX, LE Coupes & Sedans, XLE	299	499
SR	**Power Moonroof** — LE, SE, XLE	776	970
SD	**Moonroof Deflector** — LE, SE, XLE	30	50
AB	**Anti-Lock Brakes** — (4 cyl) DX, LE	902	1100
	(V6) DX, LE, SE	779	950
	incls power 4-wheel disc brakes		
—	**Wheel Locks**		
WL	alloy - LE, SE, XLE	30	50
	req's aluminum wheels		
WS	steel - DX, LE	30	50
—	**Wheels**		
SS	alloy - LE, SE, XLE	500	675
AW	aluminum - LE 4 cyl	320	400
	LE V6	336	420
MG	**Mud Guards** — front and rear	40	50
GN	**Cargo Net**	21	35
CL	**Cruise Control** — DX	212	265
EL	**Elite Pkg** — Coupes & Sedans w/auto trans	430	1245
	incls gold pkg, floor mats, trunk mat, wood trim dashboard		
PO	**Power Pkg** — DX Coupe	516	645
	DX Sedan	592	740
	incls power windows, door locks and outer mirrors		
IS	**Alarm System**	260	695
GP	**Gold Pkg** — DX	100	499
	(4 cyl) LE Coupe & Sedan, XLE	115	499
	(V6) LE Coupe & Sedan, XLE	130	499
	LE Wagon, SE	130	499
PE	**Power Driver Seat** — LE Coupe	184	230
CF	**Floor Mats** — carpeted, front and rear - DX, SE	46	77
	LE Coupe & Sedan	49	81
	LE Wagon	56	92
	XLE	82	138
C1	**Trunk Mat** — carpeted - Coupes & Sedans	39	65
CV	**Center Armrest** — DX, LE Sedan & Wagon, SE	37	62
DR	**Luggage Rack**	203	336
DU	**Wood Dashboard** — Coupes w/auto trans	275	595
	Sedans w/auto trans	150	595

CODE	DESCRIPTION	INVOICE	MSRP
TH	**Third Rear Seat** — 4 cyl LE Wagon	375	465
	V6 LE Wagon	252	315
	NA w/anti-lock brakes		
TB	**Third Rear Seat & ABS** — 4 cyl LE Wagon	1154	1415
	V6 LE Wagon	1031	1265
LP	**Leather Trim Pkg** — LE Coupe	1008	1260
	incls leather trimmed seat and door trim, power driver seat, leather-wrapped steering wheel, adjustable leather headrest, leather covered parking brake lever (4 cyl)		
LA	**Leather Trim Pkg** — SE Coupe	780	975
	incls leather trimmed seat and door trim, adjustable leather headrest, perforated steering wheel and parking brake lever		
LS	**Leather Trim Pkg** — SE Sedan	780	975
	incls leather trimmed seat and door trim, adjustable leather headrest, perforated steering wheel and parking brake lever		
—	**Radio Equipment**		
DC	premium 3-in-1 combo — LE Coupe, SE Coupe	866	1155
	V6 XLE Sedan, SE Sedan	866	1155
	incls premium AM/FM stereo, cassette and CD player, programmable equalization, diversity reception and 6 speakers		
EX	deluxe ETR/cassette - DX	165	220
	incls deluxe AM/FM stereo radio with cassette		
CE	premium ETR/cassette - LE Wagons	180	240
	incls premium AM/FM radio with cassette, 6 speakers, programmable equalization, diversity reception		
P5	compact disc	325	464
	NA w/DC radio		
P3	3-disc compact disc changer	455	650
	NA w/DC radio		
P9	6-disc compact disc changer	496	709
P4	cassette - DX	188	268
	NA w/EX radio		

CODE	DESCRIPTION	INVOICE	MSRP

CELICA *(1995)*

CODE	DESCRIPTION	INVOICE	MSRP
2165	ST 2-Dr Coupe (5-spd)	15024	17228
2162	ST 2-Dr Coupe (auto)	15722	18028
2167	ST 3-Dr Liftback (5-spd)	15329	17578
2166	ST 3-Dr Liftback (auto)	16027	18378
2175	GT 2-Dr Coupe (5-spd)	17060	19678
2172	GT 2-Dr Coupe (auto)	17754	20478
2183	GT 2-Dr Convertible (5-spd)	21384	24388
2184	GT 2-Dr Convertible (auto)	22077	25188
2195	GT 3-Dr Liftback (5-spd)	17494	20178
2192	GT 3-Dr Liftback (auto)	18187	20978
Destination Charge:		397	397

Standard Equipment

CELICA COUPE: Power assisted ventilated front disc/rear solid disc brakes (GT), power assisted ventilated front disc/rear drum brakes (ST), front wheel drive, 1.8 liter 4 cylinder twin-cam 16-valve electronically fuel injected (EFI) engine (ST), 2.2 liter 4 cylinder twin-cam 16-valve electronically fuel injected (EFI) engine (GT), engine oil cooler (GT), front and rear stabilizer bars, variable assist power rack and pinion steering, independent MacPherson strut front suspension, dual-link independent MacPherson strut rear suspension, 5-speed manual overdrive transmission, color-keyed bumpers and door handles, tinted glass, aerodynamic halogen headlamps with auto-off feature, dual color-keyed power outside mirrors, full wheel covers, variable intermittent front windshield wipers, full carpeting with driver side footrest, digital quartz clock, center console with cover, dual cup holder, rear window defogger (w/timer on GT), power door locks (GT), gauges for speedometer/tachometer/coolant temperature/fuel level/odometer/tripmeter, overhead map lights, dual visor vanity mirrors, remote hood, hatch/trunk and fuel filler door releases; 50/50 fold-down rear seat with security lock, fabric seats and door trim with courtesy light/reflector, 4-way adjustable driver's seat, tilt steering wheel (GT), warning lights for air bags/seatbelts/low fuel level/door ajar/battery/oil pressure, power windows with driver side auto-down feature (GT), Power Pkg (incls power windows and door locks) (GT), deluxe ETR with 4 speakers and manual antenna (ST), deluxe ETR/cassette with 6 speakers and power antenna (GT).

CELICA GT CONVERTIBLE: Power assisted ventilated front disc/rear solid disc brakes, front wheel drive, 2.2 liter 4 cylinder twin-cam 16-valve electronically fuel injected (EFI) engine, engine oil cooler, front and rear stabilizer bars, variable assist power rack and pinion steering, independent MacPherson strut front suspension, dual link independent MacPherson strut rear suspension, 5-speed manual overdrive transmission, color-keyed bumpers and door handles, Cambria cloth power convertible top, tinted glass, aerodynamic halogen headlamps with auto-off feature, dual color-keyed power outside mirrors, full wheel covers, variable intermittent front windshield wipers, full carpeting with driver side footrest, digital quartz clock, center console with cover, dual cup holder, rear window defogger with timer, power door locks, gauges for speedometer/tachometer/coolant temperature/ fuel level/odometer/tripmeter, dual visor vanity mirrors, remote hood, hatch/trunk and fuel filler door; fabric seat and door trim with courtesy light/reflector, 4-way adjustable driver's seat, tilt steering wheel, warning lights for air bags/seatbelts/low fuel level/door ajar/battery/oil pressure, power rear quarter windows, power windows with driver side auto-down feature, Power Pkg (incls power windows and door locks), deluxe ETR/cassette with 6 speakers and power antenna.

CELICA LIFTBACK: Power assisted ventilated front disc/rear solid disc brakes (GT), power assisted ventilated front disc/rear drum brakes (ST), front wheel drive, 1.8 liter 4 cylinder twin-cam 16-valve fuel injected (EFI) engine (ST), 2.2 liter 4 cylinder twin-cam 16-valve electronically fuel injected (EFI) engine (GT), engine oil cooler (GT), front and rear stabilizer bars, variable assist power rack and pinion steering, independent MacPherson strut front suspension, dual-link independent MacPherson strut rear suspension, 5-speed manual overdrive transmission, color-keyed bumpers and door handles, tinted glass, aerodynamic halogen headlamps with auto-off feature, dual color-keyed power outside mirrors, full wheel covers, intermittent rear window wiper (GT), variable intermittent front windshield wipers, rear cargo area cover, full carpeting with driver side footrest, digital quartz clock, center console with cover, dual cup holder, rear window defogger (w/timer on GT), power door locks (GT), gauges for speedometer/tachometer/coolant temperature/fuel level/odometer/tripmeter, overhead map lights, dual visor vanity mirrors, remote hood, hatch/trunk and fuel filler door releases; 50/50 fold-down rear seat with security lock, fabric seats and door trim with courtesy light/reflector, 4-way adjustable driver's seat, tilt steering wheel (GT), warning lights for air bags/seatbelts/low fuel level/ door ajar/battery/oil pressure, power windows with driver side auto-down feature (GT), Power Pkg (incls power windows and door locks) (GT), deluxe ETR with 4 speakers and manual antenna (ST), deluxe ETR/cassette with 6 speakers and power antenna (GT).

Accessories

CODE	DESCRIPTION	INVOICE	MSRP
CL	**Cruise Control**	212	265
AC	**Air Conditioning**	780	975
PO	**Power Pkg** — ST *incls power door locks, power windows with driver side express- down*	408	510
LA	**Leather Pkg** — GT Coupe & Convertible *incls leather door trim panels, leather-trimmed seats, leather-wrapped steering wheel (models with 5-speed manual trans also include leather-wrapped shift knob [reqs cruise control])*	836	1045
SX	**Fabric Sport Pkg** — GT Liftback *incls aluminum wheels, cloth sport seats, front sport suspension, leather-wrapped steering wheel and shift knob, 205/55R15 summer tires (reqs cruise control)*	724	905
SL	**Leather Sport Pkg** — GT Liftback *incls aluminum wheels, leather sport seats, front sport suspension, leather-wrapped steering wheel & shift knob, 205/55R15 summer tires (reqs cruise control)*	1252	1565
RW	**Rear Window Wiper** — intermittent - ST Liftback	127	155
SR	**Power Moonroof**	592	740
EX	**Deluxe AM/FM ETR Radio** — w/cassette - ST *incls 4 speakers*	165	220

CODE	DESCRIPTION	INVOICE	MSRP
DC	**Premium 3-In-1 Combo Radio** — GT Convertible	903	1205
	GT Coupe & Liftback	941	1255
	incls compact disc, 8 speakers, AM/FM ETR stereo radio w/cassette, power antenna with diversity system, programmable equalization		
CE	**Premium AM/FM ETR Radio** — w/cassette - GT Convertible	112	150
	GT Coupe & Liftback	149	200
	incls power antenna with diversity system, 6 speakers, programmable equalization		
P9	**Compact Disc Changer**	496	709
P5	**Compact Disc**	325	464
P4	**Cassette** — ST	188	268
CA	**California Emissions** — ST	NC	NC
	GT	130	153
TW	**Tilt Steering Column** — ST	133	155
AB	**Anti-Lock Brakes**	676	825
	incls larger temporary spare tire (ST) (reqs CL cruise control)		
AW	**Aluminum Wheels** — GT	336	420
	incls 205/55R15 all-season tires		
RF	**Rear Spoiler** — Liftback	300	375
	ST reqs RW rear intermittent wiper (std GT)		
IS	**Alarm System**	260	695
MG	**Mud Guards** — front and rear	51	85
DU	**Wood Dashboard**	220	495
GN	**Cargo Net**	21	35
CV	**Center Armrest**	41	70
CF	**Floor Mats** — carpeted, front and rear	46	75
WL	**Alloy Wheel Locks** — GT	30	50

COROLLA *(1995)*

Code	Description	Invoice	MSRP
1701	Standard 4-Dr Sedan (5-spd)	11345	12498
1700	Standard 4-Dr Sedan (auto)	11799	12998
1702	DX 4-Dr Sedan (5-spd)	11944	13618
1704	DX 4-Dr Sedan (auto)	12645	14418
1767	DX 5-Dr Wagon (5-spd)	12952	14768
1766	DX 5-Dr Wagon (auto)	13655	15568
1706	LE 4-Dr Sedan (auto)	14727	16848
Destination Charge:		397	397

Standard Equipment

COROLLA - STANDARD SEDAN: Power assisted ventilated front disc/rear drum brakes, front wheel drive, 1.6 liter 4 cylinder twin-cam 16-valve electronically fuel injected (EFI) engine, rear stabilizer bar, rack and pinion steering, 5-speed manual overdrive transmission, color-keyed bumpers, tinted glass, aerodynamic halogen headlamps with auto-off feature, dual black remote control folding outside mirrors, full wheel covers, intermittent front windshield wipers, full cut-pile carpeting, dual cup holder, side window demisters, gauges for speedometer/tachometer/odometer/tripmeter/coolant temperature/fuel level, remote hood/trunk/fuel filler door releases, reclining front bucket seats with adjustable headrests, fabric seats and door trim, warning lights for air bag/seatbelts/low fuel level/battery/door ajar/engine/oil pressure/brake.

DX SEDAN/WAGON (in addition to or instead of BASE SEDAN equipment): 1.8 liter 4 cylinder twin-cam 16-valve electronically fuel injected (EFI) engine, front and rear stabilizer bars, power assisted rack and pinion steering, black wide protective bodyside moldings, rear tonneau cargo cover (Wagon), digital quartz clock, electric rear window defogger, 60/40 split fold-down rear seat with security lock.

LE (in addition to or instead of DX SEDAN equipment): 4-speed electronically controlled automatic overdrive (ECT) transmission, dual color-keyed power folding outside mirrors, color-keyed wide protective bodyside moldings, variable intermittent front windshield wipers, CFC-free air conditioning, cruise control, power door locks, driver's 4-way adjustable seat, tilt steering wheel, All-Weather Guard Equipment Pkg (incls luggage door trim, larger windshield washer tank, heavy duty electric

CODE	DESCRIPTION	INVOICE	MSRP

rear window defogger/wiper motor/battery/heater/rear heater ducts), Convenience Pkg (incls power assisted steering and air conditioning), Power Pkg (incls power windows and door locks with two-turn unlock feature), deluxe ETR with 4 speakers.

Accessories

CODE	DESCRIPTION	INVOICE	MSRP
AB	**Anti-Lock Brakes**	676	825
CQ	**Convenience Pkg** — Standard	958	1180
	incls air conditioning, power steering		
RR	**Radio Prep Pkg** — (except LE)	75	100
	incls antenna, wiring harness, 2 speakers		
CK	**All Weather Guard Pkg**		
	Standard w/manual trans	191	235
	Standard w/auto trans	199	245
	DX	55	65
	incls 4.5L washer tank, rear heater ducts, heavy-duty battery, heavy-duty windshield wiper motor, 1.4 kilowatt starter motor, luggage door trim, heavy-duty rear window defroster with timer (std w/auto trans), heavy-duty booster ventilator and heater		
VP	**Value Pkg** — Standard	762	847
	incls power steering, air conditioning, carpeted floor mats		
VP	**Value Pkg** — DX Sedan	1500	1667
	DX Wagon	1361	1512
	incls tilt steering column (Sedan only), carpeted floor mats, air conditioning, AM/FM radio with cassette & 4 speakers, Power Pkg		
VP	**Value Pkg** — LE	1523	1692
	incls aluminum wheels, anti-lock brakes, carpeted floor mats, AM/FM stereo radio with cassette and 4 speakers, sunroof		
AC	**Air Conditioning** — (std LE)	736	920
PO	**Power Pkg** — DX	496	620
	incls power door locks, power windows with driver side express- down		
TA	**Tachometer** — DX w/manual trans	52	65
MG	**Black Mud Guards** — DX, LE	40	50
PS	**Power Steering** — Standard	222	260
CL	**Cruise Control** — DX	212	265
	incls variable intermittent wipers with timer		
RW	**Rear Window Wiper** — Wagon	143	175
CA	**California Emissions**	130	153
AW	**Aluminum Wheels** — LE	320	400
	incls P185/65R14 SBR all-season tires, alloy wheels caps		
SR	**Power Steel Sliding Sunroof** — DX & LE Sedans	464	580
DE	**Rear Window Defroster** — Standard	136	170
TW	**Tilt Steering Column** — DX	133	155
IS	**Alarm System**	260	695
CF	**Floor Mats** — carpeted, front and rear	42	69
GN	**Cargo Net** — Sedans	21	35
DU	**Wood Dashboard**	150	295
RF	**Rear Spoiler** — Sedans	299	499
DQ	**Digital Clock** — Standard	50	82

CODE	DESCRIPTION	INVOICE	MSRP
GP	**Gold Pkg** — DX Sedans, LE	115	499
—	**Wheel Locks**		
WL	alloy - LE *req's aluminum wheels*	30	50
WS	steel	30	50
DB	**Luggage Rack** — Wagons	145	242
SK	**Console**	43	72
—	**Radio Equipment**		
ER	deluxe AM/FM stereo - Standard, DX *NA w/radio prep pkg*	289	385
E1	mid-line AM/FM stereo w/cassette - Standard, DX *req's radio prep pkg*	271	387
R2	AM/FM stereo - Standard, DX *req's radio prep pkg*	135	160
EX	deluxe AM/FM stereo w/cassette - Standard, DX	454	605
	LE *NA w/radio prep pkg*	165	220
B1	AM/FM stereo w/cassette - Standard, DX *req's radio prep pkg*	178	265
P4	cassette *req's ER or R2 radio*	188	268
P3	3-disc compact disc changer *req's ER, EX, E1 or B1 radio*	455	650
P5	compact disc *req's ER, EX1, E1 or B1 radio*	325	464
P9	6-disc compact disc changer - Sedans *req's ER, EX, E1 or B1 radio*	496	709

CODE	DESCRIPTION	INVOICE	MSRP

MR2 *(1995)*

CODE	DESCRIPTION	INVOICE	MSRP
3088	Base 2-Dr Coupe (5-spd)	20718	24038
3087	Base 2-Dr Coupe (auto)	21407	24838
3098	Base 2-Dr Coupe w/T-Bar Roof (5-spd)	22261	25828
3085	Turbo 2-Dr Coupe w/T-Bar Roof (5-spd)	25200	29238
Destination Charge:		397	397

Standard Equipment

MR2 - BASE: 2.2 liter 4 cylinder EFI 16-valve engine, front and rear color-keyed bumpers, 5-speed manual transmission, color-keyed front and rear spoilers, power 4-wheel disc brakes, black cloth interior, four-way adjustable sport seats, front and rear stabilizer bars, tinted glass, manual steering, door map pockets, tilt steering column, SBR BW tires (front - 195/55R15, rear - 225/50R15), locking glove box, assist grip, dome/map light, digital clock, driver and passenger side air bags, 6 x 15 inch aluminum alloy wheels (front), 7 x 15 inch aluminum alloy wheels (rear), 140-mph speedometer, tachometer, odometer, resettable tripmeter, fuel level gauge, coolant temperature gauge, voltmeter, bodyside and rocker panel moldings, dual color-keyed power mirrors, full carpeting, lockable right rear storage, electric rear window defroster, AM/FM ETR stereo radio with cassette and 6 speakers, manually operated antenna, air conditioning, remote decklid release, remote fuel filler door release, intermittent wipers, T-Bar roof with dual removable tinted glass panels (T-Bar), power windows (T-Bar), power door locks (T-Bar), illuminated entry/exit fade-out system (T-Bar), leather-wrapped steering wheel (T-Bar).

TURBO (in addition to or instead of BASE w/T-Bar equipment): Turbocharged 2.0 liter 16-valve EFI 4 cylinder engine with intercooler, front air dam, retractable halogen headlamps, fog lights, 7-way adjustable driver's seat, passenger side seatback map pocket, cruise control, variable intermittent wipers, 3-compartment center console storage box, door courtesy lights, premium AM/FM ETR stereo radio with cassette, programmable equalization, 8 speakers, power antenna and diversity reception; leather-wrapped steering wheel, manual shift knob and parking brake handle; turbo boost gauge (replaces voltmeter), power windows, power door locks, illuminated entry/exit.

CODE	DESCRIPTION	INVOICE	MSRP

Accessories

CODE	DESCRIPTION	INVOICE	MSRP
AB	**Anti-Lock Brakes**	779	950
PS	**Power Steering**	590	690
CA	**California Emissions** — Base	130	153
CL	**Cruise Control** — Base	228	285
	incls intermittent windshield wipers		
SR	**Sunroof** — NA on models w/T-Bar roof	320	400
PN	**Anti-Theft System**	160	200
LD	**Limited Slip Differential** — Turbo	368	460
PO	**Power Pkg** — Base	444	555
	incls power door locks and power windows; std on T-Bar models		
CE	**Radio** — Base w/o T-Bar roof	330	440
	Base w/T-Bar roof	255	330
	incls premium AM/FM ETR radio w/cassette, 8 speakers and power antenna w/diversity reception		
DC	**Radio** — Base w/o T-Bar roof	1016	1355
	Base w/T-Bar roof	941	1255
	Turbo	686	915
	incls premium AM/FM ETR radio w/cassette, CD player, 8 speakers and power antenna w/diversity reception		
LA	**Leather Pkg** — Base w/T-Bar roof	964	1205
	Turbo	648	810

PASEO *(1995)*

CODE	DESCRIPTION	INVOICE	MSRP
1525	2-Dr Coupe (5-spd)	12155	13698
1526	2-Dr Coupe (auto)	12865	14498
Destination Charge:		397	397

CODE	DESCRIPTION	INVOICE	MSRP

Standard Equipment

PASEO: Power assisted front ventilated disc/rear drum brakes, front wheel drive, 1.5 liter 4 cylinder twin-cam 16-valve electronically fuel injected (EFI) engine, power assisted rack and pinion steering, 185/60R14 all-season SBR BW tires, 5-speed manual overdrive transmission, color-keyed bumpers, tinted glass, aerodynamic halogen headlamps, dual black remote control outside mirrors, black protective bodyside moldings, full wheel covers, intermittent windshield wipers, full carpeting with driver side footrest, digital quartz clock, dual cup holder, rear window defogger, gauges for speedometer/tachometer/coolant temperature/fuel level/odometer/tripmeter, trunk area courtesy light, remote hood/trunk/fuel filler door releases, reclining high back sport type front seats with integrated headrests, fold-down rear seat with security lock, sport fabric seat trim (incls door trim), front door/rear quarter area storage pockets, warning lights for air bag/seatbelts/battery/brake/oil pressure/engine/low fuel level/door ajar, head!amps on/seatbelt warning tones, ETR with 2 speakers.

Accessories

CODE	DESCRIPTION	INVOICE	MSRP
AW	**Aluminum Wheels** *incls center wheel ornament, 4 aluminum alloy wheels, four 185/60R14 SBR all-season tires*	320	400
WL	**Alloy Wheel Locks**	30	50
AC	**Air Conditioning**	720	900
EX	**Deluxe AM/FM ETR Radio** — w/cassette *incls 4 speakers*	274	365
P9	**Compact Disc Changer**	496	709
P5	**Compact Disc**	325	464
P4	**Cassette**	188	268
CL	**Cruise Control**	212	265
RF	**Rear Spoiler**	300	375
AB	**Anti-Lock Brakes**	676	825
CK	**All-Weather Guard Pkg** *incls heavy-duty rear defroster, heavy-duty battery, heavy-duty heater*	54	65
SR	**Pop-Up Moonroof** — removable	320	400
CA	**California Emissions**	130	153
MG	**Mud Guards**	53	85
GN	**Cargo Net**	21	35
SK	**Console**	41	70
IS	**Alarm System**	260	695
CF	**Floor Mats** — carpeted, front and rear	41	67

CODE	DESCRIPTION	INVOICE	MSRP

SUPRA *(1995)*

CODE	DESCRIPTION	INVOICE	MSRP
2398	Base 2-Dr Liftback (5-spd)	31448	37600
2396	Base 2-Dr Liftback (auto)	32201	38500
2393	Base 2-Dr Liftback w/Sport Roof (5-spd)	32368	38700
2394	Base 2-Dr Liftback w/Sport Roof (auto)	33121	39600
2381	Turbo 2-Dr Liftback (6-spd)	39729	47500
2383	Turbo 2-Dr Liftback w/Sport Roof (6-spd)	40732	48700
2387	Turbo 2-Dr Liftback w/Sport Roof (auto)	39729	47500
Destination Charge (approx):		400	400

Standard Equipment

SUPRA - BASE: Tachometer, front and rear stabilizer bars, aluminum alloy wheels, tinted glass, power door locks, power windows, driver and front passenger airbags, cargo area cover, front spoiler, cold kit, digital clock, front fog lights, digital trip odometer, diagnostic master warning lights, premium AM/FM ETR stereo w/cassette/6 speakers/theft deterrent system, power antenna w/diversity reception, front and rear color-keyed bumpers, leather-wrapped steering wheel, cruise control, tilt steering column, illuminated entry system w/automatic fade-out, halogen retractable headlights w/automatic-off system, dual color-keyed heated power mirrors, right visor vanity mirror, 3-way adjustable sport seats w/power slide and recline, driver's seat height adjustment, 2-way manual adjustable passenger seat, fold-down rear seat, automatic air conditioning, speed-sensitive power steering, anti-lock power 4-wheel disc brakes, heavy-duty electric rear window defroster w/timer, remote hatch release, variable intermittent wipers, 3.0L 6 cylinder EFI DOHC 24-valve engine, 5-speed manual transmission, rear window intermittent wipers, remote fuel-filler door release, 225/50ZR16 SBR high-performance front tires, 245/50ZR16 SBR high-performance rear tires, full cut-pile carpeting (including cargo area), lights include door/luggage area/glove box/ignition, cloth upholstery.

TURBO (in addition to or instead of BASE equipment): Engine oil cooler, sport-tuned suspension, Torsen limited slip differential, 235/45ZR17 SBR high-performance front tires, 255/40ZR17 SBR high-performance rear tires, 3.0L 6 cylinder EFI 24-valve twin turbocharged engine w/intercooler, traction control system w/indicator light, 6-speed manual transmission.

CODE	DESCRIPTION	INVOICE	MSRP

Accessories

CODE	DESCRIPTION	INVOICE	MSRP
LD	**Limited Slip Differential** — Base	368	460
LA	**Leather Trim Pkg** *incls leather trimmed armrests and seats*	880	1100
DC	**Premium Radio** — 3-in-1 combo *incls AM/FM ETR stereo radio w/cassette, programmable equalization and logic control, compact disc, power antenna w/diversity system, 7 speakers (includes subwoofer)*	739	985
P3	**CD Changer** *NA w/DC premium radio*	455	650
P5	**CD Player** *NA w/DC premium radio*	325	464
CF	**Floor Mats** — front and rear	31	78
MG	**Mud Guards**	59	99
RK	**Alarm Enhancement System**	310	695
WL	**Alloy Wheel Locks**	30	50
FE	**50-State Emissions** — Turbo	NC	NC
CA	**California Emissions** — Base	130	153
RF	**Rear Spoiler**	336	420

TERCEL *(1995)*

CODE	DESCRIPTION	INVOICE	MSRP
1301	Standard 2-Dr Sedan (4-spd)	9329	9998
1302	Standard 2-Dr Sedan (auto)	9983	10698
1315	DX 2-Dr Sedan (5-spd)	10123	11028
1316	DX 2-Dr Sedan (auto)	10775	11738
1325	DX 4-Dr Sedan (5-spd)	10398	11328
1326	DX 4-Dr Sedan (auto)	11050	12038
Destination Charge:		397	397

CODE	DESCRIPTION	INVOICE	MSRP

Standard Equipment

TERCEL - STANDARD: Power assisted ventilated front disc/rear drum brakes, front wheel drive, 1.5 liter 4 cylinder twin-cam 16-valve electronically fuel injected (EFI) engine, distributorless Toyota Direct Ignition (TDI) system, rack and pinion steering, 155/SR13 all-season SBR tires, 4-speed manual overdrive transmission, color-keyed grille, aerodynamic halogen headlights, driver side black outside mirror, mist-cycle windshield wipers, full carpeting, cup holders and storage pockets (rear quarter area), gauges for speedometer/coolant temperature/fuel level/odometer/tripmeter, dual front door map pockets, remote hood/trunk/fuel filler door releases, reclining front bucket seats with integrated headrests, vinyl seat material, warning lights for air bag/seatbelts/brake/oil pressure/engine/battery/door ajar.

DX (in addition to or instead of Standard equipment): 5-speed manual overdrive transmission, tinted glass, dual black outside mirrors, black protective bodyside moldings, full wheel covers, dual cup holder, rear quarter area cup holders and storage pockets deleted (4 Dr), remote hood/trunk/fuel filler door releases deleted, fabric seat material.

Accessories

CODE	DESCRIPTION	INVOICE	MSRP
AC	**Air Conditioning**	720	900
PS	**Power Steering** — DX	222	260
CA	**California Emissions**	NC	NC
DE	**Rear Window Defroster**	144	170
AB	**Anti-Lock Brakes** — including larger temporary spare tire	676	825
CQ	**Convenience Pkg** — DX	264	330
	incls split fold-down rear seat, dual manual remote mirrors, remote decklid release, digital clock, intermittent wipers, remote fuel-filler door release		
CK	**All-Weather Guard Pkg**	201	235
	incls heavy-duty heater, heavy-duty electric rear window defroster, heavy-duty battery		
PO	**Power Pkg** — DX 4-Dr	496	620
	incls power windows and door locks		
CB	Color-Keyed Bumpers — DX	68	85
FW	**Wheel Covers** — Standard	52	87
CF	**Floor Mats** — carpeted, front and rear	36	60
VE	**Value Pkg** — DX 2-Dr	1033	1260
	incls air conditioning, power steering, AM/FM radio, 2 speakers		
GN	**Cargo Net**	21	35
MG	**Mud Guards**	51	85
IS	**Alarm System**	260	695
WS	**Wheel Locks** — steel	30	50
SK	**Console**	41	70
RM	**Dual Mirrors** — Standard	38	63
DQ	**Digital Clock** — DX	50	82
—	**Radio Equipment**		
RA	AM/FM stereo	180	240
	incls 2 speakers		
R2	AM/FM stereo	180	240
	incls 2 speakers		

CODE	DESCRIPTION	INVOICE	MSRP
B1	AM/FM stereo w/cassette *incls 2 speakers*	227	335
E2	mid-line AM/FM stereo w/cassette - DX *incls 4 speakers*	376	537
E1	mid-line AM/FM stereo w/cassette *incls 2 speakers*	315	450
EX	deluxe AM/FM stereo w/cassette - DX *incls 4 speakers; NA w/Value Pkg*	454	605
ER	deluxe AM/FM stereo - DX *incls 4 speakers; NA w/Value Pkg*	289	385
P5	compact disc - DX *req's ER deluxe AM/FM stereo or E2 mid-line AM/FM stereo w/cassette or EX deluxe AM/FM stereo w/cassette*	325	464
P9	6-disc compact disc changer - DX *req's ER deluxe AM/FM stereo or EX deluxe AM/FM stereo w/cassette or E2 mid-line AM/FM stereo w/cassette*	496	709
P3	3-disc compact disc changer - DX *req's ER deluxe AM/FM stereo radio or E2 mid-line AM/FM stereo w/cassette or EX deluxe AM/FM stereo w/cassette*	455	650
P4	auto-reverse cassette *req's RA or R2 AM/FM stereo radio or ER deluxe AM/FM stereo or Value Pkg*	188	268

What's New for *Toyota* in 1995?

Avalon: New full-size entry from Toyota boasts six passenger seating and pricing in the mid-$20,000 range. A 3.0L V6 provides the motivational power to the front wheels. With the Caprice, Crown Victoria and Intrepid starting at thousands less, we're skeptical about Avalon's chances for success.

Camry: Mild styling tweaks update the already attractive Camry for 1995.

Celica: A convertible joins the lineup this year, based on the Celica GT. Fisheye headlamps continue to make this car difficult to look at.

Corolla: No changes to this outstanding sedan, except that the 1.8L engine loses 10 hp to federal emissions regulations.

MR2: The sports car that won't die. After threatening to pull the plug on this stylish two seater for two years, Toyota has evidently granted another reprieve. Power windows and locks come standard on base models equipped with the T-bar roof this year.

Paseo: Tercel-based econoscooter loses 7 hp in California. No changes for other states.

Supra: Toyota's wild-looking supercar is carried over unchanged.

Tercel: An all-new Tercel arrived this year, styled with more creases and edges than the melted bar of soap design of the 1994 model. A twin-cam 1.5L good for 93 ponies resides under the hood, and prices for a loaded DX can top $15,000. Yikes!

VOLKSWAGEN

CABRIO (1995)

CODE	DESCRIPTION	INVOICE	MSRP
1E75Q4	2-Dr Convertible (5-spd)	18161	19975
Destination Charge:		390	390

Standard Equipment

CABRIO: 2.0 liter 4 cylinder 115 HP engine, 5-speed manual transmission, front wheel drive, anti-lock brake system (ABS), power front disc/rear drum brakes, 195/60HR14 all-season tires, power steering, dual horns, space saver spare tire, anti-theft vehicle (and radio) alarm system, roll bar, 50-state certified engine, tinted glass, cruise control, instrumentation includes: speedometer with digital odometer and trip odometer, tachometer, digital clock, fuel and temperature gauges, service indicator, warning lights; central locking system with lighted key, driver and passenger dual air bag supplemental restraint system, front and rear 3-point safety belts, power front and rear windows with one-touch down feature, reclining front seats in full cloth trim, molded door trim with cloth insert, large front door storage pockets, height adjustable steering column, full carpeting, electric rear window defogger, rear folding seat with trunk access, premium stereo cassette with CD changer control capability, anti-theft coding and warning light, front console dual cup holders, leather shift boot/handbrake cover, ventilation system with 4-speed fan, passenger and driver side illuminated vanity mirrors, remote power driver and passenger side mirrors with defogging feature, body color grille, body color integrated bumpers, black bumper bottom extensions and rocker panel, interior color "boot" cover for folded top, black door handles, body color mirror housings, black narrow bodyside moldings, 2-speed wiper with variable (programmable) intermittent mode, aero-style headlamps with dual bulbs/reflectors, body color license plate surround panel, manually-operated fully-padded 6-layer convertible top.

Accessories

CODE	DESCRIPTION	INVOICE	MSRP
—	**Automatic Transmission**	856	875
—	**Leather Seats & Door Trim**	1113	1275
9AB	**Air Conditioning**	742	850
PJ1	**Alloy Wheels**	511	585
CDC	**CD Player**	412	495
—	**Clearcoat Metallic Paint**	153	175

CODE	DESCRIPTION	INVOICE	MSRP

VOLKSWAGEN

GOLF III *(1995)*

CODE	DESCRIPTION	INVOICE	MSRP
1H1LQ4	Base 4-Dr Hatchback (5-spd)	11941	12500
1H1MQ4	GL 4-Dr Hatchback (5-spd)	13096	14200
1H0MQ4	Sport 2-Dr Hatchback (5-spd)	14050	15250
Destination Charge:		435	435

Standard Equipment

GOLF III - BASE: 2.0 liter SFI 4 cylinder engine, 5-speed manual transmission, power 4-wheel disc brakes, front wheel drive, rear window defroster, power steering, driver and front passenger air bags, tachometer, console, front and rear spoilers, P185/60HR14 tires, central locking system, wheel covers, intermittent windshield wipers, intermittent rear window wiper/washer, trip odometer, bodyside moldings, alarm system, power fuel filler door release, front stabilizer bar, remote control OS rearview mirrors, power trunk release, cloth reclining bucket seats, split folding rear seat, temperature gauge, cloth door trim panels, 70-amp alternator, 63-amp battery.

GL (in addition to or instead of BASE equipment): Air conditioning, deluxe AM/FM stereo radio with cassette, 90-amp alternator.

SPORT (in addition to or instead of GL equipment): Power moonroof, P195/60HR14 tires, premium AM/FM stereo radio with cassette, spoke alloy wheels, fog lights, rocker panel moldings, cloth reclining sport bucket seats, split folding rear seat.

Accessories

CODE	DESCRIPTION	INVOICE	MSRP
—	**Transmission** — 4-speed automatic - GL, Sport *incls P195/60HR14 tires*	856	875
1AC	**Anti-Lock Brakes** — GL, Sport	727	775
3FE	**Power Moonroof** — sliding glass - GL	511	585
B0W	**California Emissions**	NC	NC
B55	**Massachusetts Emissions**	NC	NC
CDC	**Compact Disc Changer** — Sport, GL	412	495
—	**Metallic Paint** — Sport, GL	153	175

GTI VR6 *(1995)*

1H16T4	2-Dr Coupe (5-spd)	17458	18875
Destination Charge:		390	390

Standard Equipment

GTI VR6: 2.8 liter V6 engine, 5-speed manual transmission, power 4-wheel disc brakes with anti-lock braking system, power windows with express-down feature, air conditioning, driver and front passenger air bags, alarm system, front wheel drive, traction control system, power steering, leather-wrapped tilt steering wheel, center console with storage, cruise control, tinted glass, tachometer, trip computer, trip odometer, P205/50HR15 SBR high performance all-season tires, fog lights, front and rear spoilers, front and rear stabilizer bars, sport suspension, digital clock, rear window defroster, premium AM/FM stereo radio with cassette, cloth heated reclining sport bucket sets, 60/40 split fold-down rear seat, 60 amp battery, 120 amp alternator, alloy wheels, power door locks with central locking system, power trunk release, dual horns, power tilt/slide glass sunroof, variable intermittent windshield wipers, rear window wiper/washer, cloth and leatherette door trim, color-keyed bodyside moldings, black rocker panels, dual power heated mirrors, illuminated RH visor vanity mirror, courtesy lights, map pockets.

Accessories

BOW	**California Emissions System**	NC	NC
B55	**Massachusetts Emissions System**	NC	NC
—	**Clearcoat Metallic Paint**	153	175
CDC	**Compact Disc Changer**	412	495

CODE	DESCRIPTION	INVOICE	MSRP

JETTA III *(1995)*

CODE	DESCRIPTION	INVOICE	MSRP
1H29Q4	Base 4-Dr Sedan (5-spd)	12850	13475
1H24Q4	GL 4-Dr Sedan (5-spd)	14207	15675
1H28Q4	GLS 4-Dr Sedan (5-spd)	15413	17025
1H27T4	GLX 4-Dr Sedan (5-spd)	18441	19975
Destination Charge:		435	435

Standard Equipment

JETTA III - BASE: 2.0 liter 4 cylinder 115 HP engine, 5-speed manual transmission, power rack and pinion steering, power front disc/rear drum brakes, cruise control, anti-intrusion side door beams, CFC-free air conditioning, anti-theft alarm, front illuminated ashtray, electric rear window defroster, molded door trim with cloth/leatherette inserts, integrated armrests in door panels, assist handles, trip odometer, tachometer, digital clock, cigarette lighter, interior light with time delay and reading light, luggage compartment light, child safety door locks (4-Dr), power locking system including trunk/fuel filler, driver and passenger illuminated vanity mirrors, 8-speaker sound system prep, dual air bags, fully reclining front seats with adjustable headrests, storage trays at side of front seats, 60/40 split fold-down rear seat, rear seat headrests, folding rear center armrest, 4-spoke padded steering wheel, height adjustable steering column, front storage pockets with rubber liners, rear door storage pockets, front seatback magazine/storage pockets, center console, front illuminated ashtray, power remote hatch/trunk release, "Wood" velour seat fabric, 5-mph body color bumpers with black lower section, tinted glass, dual horns, daytime running lights, Eurostyle rectangular halogen headlamps, driver and passenger side power remote OS mirrors, body color side molding, black front chin spoiler, 14" all-season tires, space saver spare tire, 14" full wheel covers, 2-speed windshield wipers with intermittent feature, heated windshield washer nozzles.

GL (in addition to or instead of BASE equipment): Premium AM/FM cassette stereo, theft-deterrent warning light and coding system, input jack for portable compact disc player.

GLS (in addition to or instead of GL equipment): Power 4-wheel disc brakes , 2 additional rear reading lights, front door courtesy lights, heatable front seats, power windows with one-touch down feature, body color mirror housings, power tilt and slide sunroof with sunshade, 14" with "Orlando" 7-spoke alloy wheels.

VOLKSWAGEN

GLX (in addition to or instead of GLS equipment): 2.8 liter 6 cylinder VR6 172 HP engine, 5-speed close-ratio manual transmission, sport tuned suspension (including rear gas shocks), high performance power assisted 4-wheel disc brakes with ABS, traction control system, trip information computer, brake wear indicator, illuminated ignition key, front sport seats, leather-covered steering wheel, "Future" sport design woven cloth seat fabric, black roof-mounted whip antenna, front fog lamps, darkened taillamp lenses, black rocker panel covering, body color rear wing spoiler, 15" "BBS" lattice design without center cap alloy wheels.

Accessories

CODE	DESCRIPTION	INVOICE	MSRP
—	**Transmission** — 4-speed automatic - GL, GLS, GLX *GL incls 195/60HR14 tires*	856	875
1AC	**Anti-Lock Brakes** — GL, GLS	727	775
3FE	**Power Moonroof** — GL	511	585
—	**Metallic Paint** — GL, GLS, GLX	153	175
CDC	**Compact Disc Changer** — GL, GLS, GLX	412	495
D02	**Radio** — deluxe AM/FM stereo w/cassette - GL	(105)	(125)
B0W	**California Emissions**	NC	NC
B55	**Massachusetts Emissions**	NC	NC
—	**Seats** — leather/leatherette — GLX	698	800

PASSAT *(1995)*

CODE	DESCRIPTION	INVOICE	MSRP
3A26Q5	GLX 4-Dr Sedan (5-spd)	18801	20890
3A56Q5	GLX 4-Dr Wagon (5-spd)	19185	21320
	Destination Charge:	390	390

Standard Equipment

PASSAT GLX: 2.8 liter VR6 172 HP engine, 5-speed manual transmission, dual air bags, power 4-wheel disc brakes with ABS, power steering, halogen headlamps, front and rear stabilizer bars, alarm system with visual indicator, traction control system, 215/50HR15 all-season radial tires, space saver spare tire, air conditioning, right front and rear assist handles, center console with ashtray and lighter, lockable storage compartment and rear cup holder, electric rear window defroster, tinted glass, tachometer, digital clock, time delay courtesy lights, rear reading lights, front comfort seats with height, recline, thigh and lumbar adjustments; 2 front and 2 rear headrests, 60/40 split folding rear seat with armrest, velour upholstery and trim, illuminated vanity mirrors, luggage compartment with full carpet trim, height adjustable steering wheel, premium stereo cassette with CD change control, anti-theft features and 8 speakers; power windows with one-touch down feature, heated dual remote power mirrors, central locking system (doors, trunk lid, fuel filler door), cruise control, leather-wrapped steering wheel, leather shift knob and parking brake handle, 2-speed wipers with variable intermittent wipe, storage areas in RH/LH quarter panels (Wagon), folding luggage compartment tonneau cover (Wagon), color-keyed bumpers, black front chin spoiler, body color mirror housings, black door handles, color-keyed bodyside moldings, 15" "BBS" 8-spoke alloy wheels, roof-mounted antenna, fog lights, rear window washer with intermittent wiper (Wagon), black roof rails (Wagon).

Accessories

CODE	DESCRIPTION	INVOICE	MSRP
—	**Automatic Transmission**	777	800
—	**Metallic Paint**	NC	NC
—	**Leather Seats**	742	850
3FE	**Power Moonroof**	742	850
PW1	**All-Weather Pkg**	262	300
	incls heated front seats and windshield washer nozzles		
CDC	**Compact Disc Changer** — Sedan	412	495
BOW	**California Emissions**	NC	NC
B55	**Massachusetts Emissions**	NC	NC

What's New for *Volkswagen* for 1995?

Cabrio: Expensive new convertible based on the Golf, the Cabrio is heavier and sturdier than the original Cabriolet. The 2.0L four doesn't provide enough oomph in the Cabrio.

Golf: The GTI has finally arrived, with VW's sweet narrow-angle V6 and a $20,000 price tag. Other Golfs are unchanged.

Jetta: The GLX arrived over a year ago, and is quite a competent sport sedan powered by a 2.8L V6 producing 172 hp. Other Jettas get new wheelcovers for 1995.

Passat: A significant restyle arrives for 1995, with new sheetmetal, dual airbags and, what's this, a grille?

CODE	DESCRIPTION	INVOICE	MSRP

850 *(1995)*

CODE	DESCRIPTION	INVOICE	MSRP
854GTO	Base 4-Dr Sedan (5-spd)	22480	24680
854GTA	Base 4-Dr Sedan (auto)	23380	25580
855GTO	Base 5-Dr Wagon (5-spd)	23780	25980
855GTA	Base 5-Dr Wagon (auto)	24680	26880
854GTOS	GLT 4-Dr Sedan (5-spd)	24710	27110
854GTSA	GLT 4-Dr Sedan (auto)	25610	28010
855GTOS	GLT 5-Dr Wagon (5-spd)	26010	28410
855GTSA	GLT 5-Dr Wagon (auto)	26910	29310
854TA	Turbo 4-Dr Sedan (auto)	28095	31045
855TA	Turbo 5-Dr Wagon (auto)	29395	32345
Destination Charge:		460	460

Standard Equipment

850 BASE SEDAN/WAGON: Inline 5 cylinder engine, 5-speed manual transmission, power rack and pinion steering, power 4-wheel disc brakes with ABS, 6.5" x 15" steel wheels, 195/60VR15 GA Goodyear all-season tires, driver and passenger side SRS, side-impact protection system (SIPS), CFC-free electronic climate control, manual dual climate control, daytime running light system, rear fog light, integral child booster cushion (Wagon), cruise control, 3-point seat belts and head restraints (in all 5 seating positions), child-proof rear door locks, central locking power windows with driver's auto down feature, heated power outside mirrors, SC 710 AM/FM stereo cassette (incls 4 x 20 watt amp, CD compatibility, 6 speakers, anti-theft), power antenna (Sedan), integrated window antenna (Wagon), tilt/telescopic steering column, trip computer, front reclining bucket seats, tilt and fold front passenger seat, 8-way manually adjustable driver's seat, plush velour upholstery, solid or metallic paint.

850 GLT SEDAN/WAGON: Inline 5 cylinder engine, 5-speed manual transmission, power rack and pinion steering, power 4-wheel disc brakes with ABS, 6.5" x 15" six-spoke alloy wheels, 195/60VR15 GA Goodyear all-season tires, driver and passenger side SRS, side-impact protection system (SIPS), CFC-free air conditioner, manual dual climate control, daytime running light system, rear fog light, integral child booster cushion (Wagon), cruise control, remote keyless entry/security system, 3-point seat belts and head restraints (in all 5 seating positions), child-proof rear door locks, power glass sunroof with tilt and slide (with sunshade), central locking power windows with driver's auto-down feature, heated power outside mirrors, SC811 AM/FM stereo full-logic cassette (incls 4 x 25 watt amp, CD compatibility, anti-theft) (6 speakers - Wagon, 8 speakers - Sedan), power antenna (Sedan), integrated window antenna (Wagon), tilt/telescope steering column, front reclining bucket seats, tilt and fold front passenger seat, 8-way power adjustable driver's seat with 3-position memory, plush velour upholstery, solid or metallic paint.

850 TURBO SEDAN/WAGON: Inline 5 cylinder engine, 4-speed automatic transmission, power rack and pinion steering, power 4-wheel disc brakes with ABS, 6.5" x 16" five-spoke swept design alloy wheels, 205/50ZR16 MXM Michelin tires, driver and front passenger side SRS, driver and front passenger side impact air bags (SIPS BAG), side-impact protection system (SIPS), 3-point seat belts and head restraints (in all 5 seating positions), child-proof rear door locks, CFC-free air conditioning system, electronic climate control, daytime running light system, rear fog light, integral child booster cushion (Wagon), cruise control, remote keyless entry/security system, power glass sunroof with tilt and slide (with sunshade), central locking power windows with driver's auto-down feature, heated power outside mirrors, SC811 AM/FM stereo full-logic cassette (incls 4 x 25 watt amp, CD compatibility, anti-theft, 8 speakers), power antenna (Sedan), integrated side window antenna (Wagon), leather steering wheel with tilt/telescope steering column, front reclining bucket seats, tilt and fold front passenger seat, 8-way power adjustable driver's seat with 3-position memory, split leather upholstery, trip computer, solid or metallic paint.

Accessories

CODE	DESCRIPTION	INVOICE	MSRP
—	**Trip Computer** — GLT	220	275
—	**California Emissions**	NC	NC
—	**Automatic Air Conditioning** — Base, GLT	280	350
—	**Cold Weather Pkg**	360	450
	incls outside temperature gauge, heated front seats, headlamp washer and wipers		
—	**Seat Trim** — leather - Base, GLT	795	995
—	**Wheels** — 24-spoke alloy - Base	320	400
—	**Touring Pkg** — GLT	520	650
	incls trip computer, automatic air conditioning, leather-wrapped steering wheel		
—	**Power Seat** — driver - Base	395	495
—	**Power Seat** — passenger - GLT, Turbo	395	495
—	**Sport Suspension**	120	150
—	**Traction Control**	305	385
—	**Traction Control/Cold Weather Pkg**	600	750
	incls traction control and cold weather pkg		
—	**Trim** — wood instrument panel	480	600
—	**Grand Lux Pkg** — Base	915	1145
	incls power driver seat with memory, alarm, 24-spoke alloy wheels, remote control keyless entry system		
—	**Restraint System** — dual side impact - Base, GLT	500	500
—	**Rear Spoiler** — Sedans	260	325

CODE	DESCRIPTION	INVOICE	MSRP

940 (1995)

CODE	DESCRIPTION	INVOICE	MSRP
944	4-Dr Sedan (auto)	22160	23360
944S	4-Dr Sedan w/Sunroof (auto)	22795	24340
944T	Turbo 4-Dr Sedan (auto)	23160	24360
944TS	Turbo 4-Dr Sedan w/Sunroof (auto)	23795	25340
945	5-Dr Wagon (auto)	23460	24660
945S	5-Dr Wagon w/Sunroof (auto)	24095	25640
945T	Turbo 5-Dr Wagon (auto)	24460	25660
945TS	Turbo 5-Dr Wagon w/Sunroof (auto)	25095	26640
Destination Charge:		460	460

Standard Equipment

940 SEDAN/WAGON: Inline 4 cylinder engine, turbocharger (Turbo), 4-speed automatic transmission, power rack and pinion steering, power 4-wheel disc brakes with ABS, 6" x 15" steel wheels with full covers, 185/65R15T Goodyear GT+4 all-season tires, driver and passenger side SRS, side-impact protection system (SIPS), 3-point seat belts and head restraints (in all 5 seating positions), child-proof rear door locks, CFC-free air conditioning, daytime running light system, rear fog light, cruise control, power windows/central locking, 6-speaker CR 915 AM/FM stereo cassette (4 x 20 watt amp, CD compatible), power antenna (Sedan), integrated window antenna (Wagon), power outside mirrors, front reclining bucket seats, velour upholstery, automatic locking differential, integral child booster cushion (Wagon), solid or metallic paint.

Accessories

CODE	DESCRIPTION	INVOICE	MSRP
—	**Leather Seats**	795	1225
—	**Cold Weather Pkg** *incls heated front seats, dual heated power mirrors, outside temperature gauge*	280	435
—	**Roof Rails**	195	300
—	**Alloy Wheels — 10-spoke**	320	495
—	**Alloy Wheels — 20-spoke**	320	495
—	**Power Driver's Seat**	395	610

CODE	DESCRIPTION	INVOICE	MSRP

960 (1995)

CODE	DESCRIPTION	INVOICE	MSRP
964	4-Dr Sedan (auto)	27700	29900
965	5-Dr Wagon (auto)	29000	31200
Destination Charge:		460	460

Standard Equipment

960 SEDAN/WAGON: Inline 6 cylinder engine, 4-speed automatic transmission with 3-gear driver option, power rack and pinion steering, power 4-wheel disc brakes with ABS, 6.0" x 15" alloy wheels (Wagon), 6.5" x 16" alloy wheels (Sedan), 195/65HR15 GA Goodyear all-season tires (Wagon), 205/55VR16 MXV 4 Michelin all-season tires, driver and passenger side SRS, side-impact protection system (SIPS), CFC-free electronic climate control, daytime running light system, cruise control, central locking power windows with driver's auto-down feature, remote entry with alarm system, leather-wrapped tilt steering wheel, power glass sunroof with tilt/slide and sunshade, headlamps washer/wipers, SC 811 Premium Sound System (incls AM/FM stereo cassette, full-logic with CD compatibility, anti-theft) (Sedan - 8 speakers, Wagon - 6 speakers), power antenna (Sedan), integrated window antenna (Wagon), heated power outside mirrors, front reclining bucket seats, 8-way power driver's seat with 3-position memory, 8-way power passenger seat, leather upholstery, automatic locking differential, front fog lamps and rear fog light, integral child booster cushion (Wagon), electronic climate control, solid or metallic paint, alloy wheels.

Accessories

CODE	DESCRIPTION	INVOICE	MSRP
—	**Roof Rails**	195	300
—	**CD Changer**	485	750
—	**Cold Weather Pkg** *incls heated front seats, outside temperature gauge*	225	350

What's New for *Volvo* in 1995?

850: Wow! Side airbags appear for the first time on the 1995 850. They are standard on the 850 Turbo and optional on other 850's. The wagon is now available in base trim. A limited-edition 850 Turbo is available this year in black and a really putrid pale yellow.

Specifications and EPA Mileage Ratings

1995 New Cars

Contents

Specifications EPA Mileage Ratings

ACURA

Specifications EPA Mileage Ratings	EPA Hwy (mpg) - auto	EPA City (mpg) - auto	EPA Hwy (mpg) - manual	EPA City (mpg) - manual	Fuel Capacity	Torque @ RPM	Horsepower @ RPM	Compression Ratio	Fuel System	Displacement (liters)	Number of Cylinders	Luggage Capacity (cu ft.)	Rear Leg Room (in.)	Front Leg Room (in.)	Rear Hip Room (in.)	Front Hip Room (in.)	Rear Shoulder Room (in.)	Front Shoulder Room (in.)	Rear Head Room (in.)	Front Head Room (in.)	Rear Track (in.)	Front Track (in.)	Wheelbase (in.)	Curb Weight (lbs.)	Height (in.)	Width (in.)	Length (in.)
Integra GS-R Cpe	N/A	N/A	31	25	13.2	128@ 6200	170@ 7600	12:1	PGMFI	1.8	4	13.3	28.1	42.7	44.1	50.3	48.8	51.7	35	38.6	57.8	58.1	101	2667	52.6	67.3	172
Integra GS-R Sdn	N/A	N/A	31	25	13.2	128@ 6200	170@ 7600	12:1	PGMFI	1.8	4	11	32.7	42.2	49.9	50.7	50.3	52	36	38.9	57.8	58.1	103	2765	53.9	67.3	178
Integra LS Cpe	31	24	31	25	13.2	127@ 5200	142@ 6300	12:1	PGMFI	1.8	4	13.3	28.1	42.7	44.1	50.3	48.8	51.7	35	38.6	57.8	58.1	101	2643	52.6	67.3	172
Integra LS Sdn	31	24	31	25	13.2	127@ 5200	142@ 6300	12:1	PGMFI	1.8	4	11	32.7	42.2	49.9	50.7	50.3	52	36	38.9	57.8	58.1	103	2703	53.9	67.3	178
Integra RS Cpe	31	24	31	25	13.2	127@ 5200	142@ 6300	12:1	PGMFI	1.8	4	13.3	28.1	42.7	44.1	50.3	48.8	51.7	35	38.6	57.8	58.1	101	2529	52.6	67.3	172
Integra RS Sdn	31	24	31	25	13.2	127@ 5200	142@ 6300	12:1	PGMFI	1.8	4	11	32.7	42.2	49.9	50.7	50.3	52	36	38.9	57.8	58.1	103	2628	53.9	67.3	178
Integra Spec Edit Cpe	31	24	31	25	13.2	127@ 5200	142@ 6300	12:1	PGMFI	1.8	4	13.3	28.1	42.7	44.1	50.3	48.8	51.7	35	38.6	57.8	58.1	101	2529	52.6	67.3	172
Integra Spec Edit Sdn	31	24	31	25	13.2	127@ 5200	142@ 6300	12:1	PGMFI	1.8	4	11	32.7	42.2	49.9	50.7	50.3	52	36	38.9	57.8	58.1	103	2628	53.9	67.3	178
Legend GS Sdn	23	18	26	18	18	206@ 5000	230@ 6200	12:1	PGMFI	3.2	6	14.8	33.5	42.7	56	53.6	56.4	56.3	36.5	38.5	60.6	61	115	3571	55.1	71.3	195

Specifications EPA Mileage Ratings	EPA Hwy (mpg) - auto	EPA City (mpg) - auto	EPA Hwy (mpg) - manual	EPA City (mpg) - manual	Fuel Capacity	Torque @ RPM	Horsepower @ RPM	Compression Ratio	Fuel System	Displacement (liters)	Number of Cylinders	Luggage Capacity (cu ft.)	Rear Leg Room (in.)	Front Leg Room (in.)	Rear Hip Room (in.)	Front Hip Room (in.)	Rear Shoulder Room (in.)	Front Shoulder Room (in.)	Rear Head Room (in.)	Front Head Room (in.)	Rear Track (in.)	Front Track (in.)	Wheelbase (in.)	Curb Weight (lbs.)	Height (in.)	Width (in.)	Length (in.)
ACURA																											
Legend L Sdn	24	19	25	18	18	210@ 4500	200@ 5500	12:1	PGMFI	3.2	6	14.8	33.5	42.7	56	53.6	56.4	56.3	36.5	38.5	60.6	61	115	3516	55.1	71.3	195
Legend L Cpe	23	18	26	18	18	206@ 5000	230@ 6200	12:1	PGMFI	3.2	6	14.1	28.7	42.9	50.1	53.5	54.9	56.3	35.9	37.3	60.6	61	111	3516	53.7	71.3	193
Legend LS Cpe	23	18	26	18	18	206@ 5000	230@ 6200	12:1	PGMFI	3.2	6	14.1	28.7	42.9	50.1	53.5	54.9	56.3	35.9	37.3	60.6	61	111	3538	53.7	71.3	193
Legend LS Sdn	24	19	N/A	N/A	18	210@ 4500	200@ 5500	12:1	PGMFI	3.2	6	14.8	33.5	42.7	56	53.6	56.4	56.3	36.5	38.5	60.6	61	115	3582	55.1	71.3	195
NSX-T Cpe	23	18	24	18	18.5	210@ 5300	270@ 7100	10.2:1	PGMFI	3.0	6	5	N/A	44.3	N/A	53.8	N/A	52.5	N/A	36.3	60.2	59.4	99.6	3142	46.1	71.3	174
ALFA ROMEO																											
164 LS Sdn	22	15	24	17	17.2	198@ 5000	210@ 6300	12:1	MPFI	3.0	6	17.8	33.9	39.3	57.5	57.5	56.6	56.4	36.6	38.2	58.6	59.6	105	3413	54.7	69.3	184
164 Quadrifoglio Sdn	N/A	N/A	24	17	17.2	202@ 5000	230@ 6300	12:1	MPFI	3.0	6	17.8	33.9	39.3	57.5	57.5	56.6	56.4	36.6	38.2	58.6	59.6	105	3406	54.7	69.3	184

Specifications EPA Mileage Ratings

AUDI

Specifications EPA Mileage Ratings	EPA Hwy (mpg) - auto	EPA City (mpg) - auto	EPA Hwy (mpg) - manual	EPA City (mpg) - manual	Fuel Capacity	Torque @ RPM	Horsepower @ RPM	Compression Ratio	Fuel System	Displacement (liters)	Number of Cylinders	Luggage Capacity (cu ft.)	Rear Leg Room (in.)	Front Leg Room (in.)	Rear Hip Room (in.)	Front Hip Room (in.)	Rear Shoulder Room (in.)	Front Shoulder Room (in.)	Rear Head Room (in.)	Front Head Room (in.)	Rear Track (in.)	Front Track (in.)	Wheelbase (in.)	Curb Weight (lbs.)	Height (in.)	Width (in.)	Length (in.)
90 Sdn	26	18	26	20	17.4	184@ 3000	172@ 5500	12:1	SMPF	2.8	6	14	32.5	42.2	N/A	N/A	52.6	53.3	37.2	37.8	57.9	57.2	103	3197	54.3	66.7	180
90 Quattro Sdn	26	18	24	19	16.9	184@ 3000	172@ 5500	12:1	SMPF	2.8	6	14	32.5	42.2	N/A	N/A	52.6	53.3	37.2	37.8	58.1	57	102	3296	54.7	66.7	180
A6 Wgn	24	18	N/A	N/A	21.1	184@ 3000	172@ 5500	12:1	SMPI	2.8	6	66	34.2	42.4	N/A	N/A	56.3	56.5	39.1	38.4	60	60.1	106	3628	56.3	70.2	193
A6 Sdn	24	18	24	19	21.1	184@ 3000	172@ 5500	12:1	SMPI	2.8	6	16.8	34.8	42.4	N/A	N/A	56.2	56.5	37.6	38.3	60	60.1	106	3363	56.3	70.2	193
A6 Quattro Wgn	23	18	N/A	N/A	21.1	184@ 3000	172@ 5500	12:1	SMPI	2.8	6	66	34.2	42.4	N/A	N/A	56.3	56.5	39.1	38.4	60.1	60.1	106	3870	57	70.2	193
A6 Quattro Sdn	23	18	24	18	21.1	184@ 3000	172@ 5500	12:1	SMPI	2.8	6	16.8	34.8	42.4	N/A	N/A	56.2	56.5	37.6	38.3	60.1	60.1	106	3726	56.6	70.2	193
Cabriolet Conv	26	18	N/A	N/A	17.4	184@ 3000	172@ 5500	12:1	SMPI	2.8	6	6.6	26.5	40.7	N/A	N/A	43	51.7	36.4	38.3	57	57.2	101	3494	54.3	67.6	176
S6 Sdn	N/A	N/A	23	18	21.1	258@ 1950	227@ 5900	12:1	SFI	2.2	5	16.4	34.8	42.4	N/A	N/A	56.2	56.5	37.6	38.3	60.1	61.5	106	3825	56.5	71	193
Sport 90 Sdn	26	18	26	20	17.4	184@ 3000	172@ 5500	12:1	SMPF	2.8	6	14	32.5	42.2	N/A	N/A	52.6	53.3	37.2	37.8	57.9	57.2	103	3197	54.3	66.7	180

Specifications EPA Mileage Ratings	EPA Hwy (mpg) - auto	EPA City (mpg) - auto	EPA Hwy (mpg) - manual	EPA City (mpg) - manual	Fuel Capacity	Torque @ RPM	Horsepower @ RPM	Compression Ratio	Fuel System	Displacement (liters)	Number of Cylinders	Luggage Capacity (cu ft.)	Rear Leg Room (in.)	Front Leg Room (in.)	Rear Hip Room (in.)	Front Hip Room (in.)	Rear Shoulder Room (in.)	Front Shoulder Room (in.)	Rear Head Room (in.)	Front Head Room (in.)	Rear Track (in.)	Front Track (in.)	Wheelbase (in.)	Curb Weight (lbs.)	Height (in.)	Width (in.)	Length (in.)
AUDI																											
Sport 90 Quattro Sdn	26	18	24	19	16.9	184@ 3000	172@ 5500	12:1	SMPF	2.8	6	14	32.5	42.2	N/A	N/A	52.6	53.3	37.2	37.8	58.1	57	102	3296	54.7	66.7	180
BMW																											
318i Sdn	29	21	32	22	17.2	129@ 4500	138@ 6000	12:1	EFI	1.8	4	10.3	34	41.1	N/A	N/A	53.3	53.5	36.7	37.1	55.9	55.4	106	2933	54.8	66.8	175
318iC Conv	29	21	31	22	17.2	129@ 4500	138@ 6000	12:1	EFI	1.8	4	8.9	28.1	41.2	N/A	N/A	43.6	53.2	36.3	38.1	55.9	55.4	106	3120	53.1	67.3	175
318is Cpe	29	21	32	22	17.2	129@ 4500	138@ 6000	12:1	EFI	1.8	4	9.2	32.7	41.2	N/A	N/A	52.1	53.2	35.9	36.7	55.9	55.4	106	2933	53.8	67.3	175
325i Sdn	28	20	28	19	17.2	181@ 4200	189@ 5900	12:1	EFI	2.5	6	10.3	34	41.1	N/A	N/A	53.3	53.5	36.7	37.1	55.9	55.4	106	3087	54.8	66.8	175
325iC Conv	28	20	28	19	17.2	181@ 4200	189@ 5900	12:1	EFI	2.5	6	8.9	28.1	41.2	N/A	N/A	43.6	53.2	36.3	38.1	55.9	55.4	106	3352	53.1	67.3	175
325is Cpe	28	20	28	19	17.2	181@ 4200	189@ 5900	12:1	EFI	2.5	6	9.2	32.7	41.2	N/A	N/A	52.1	53.2	35.9	36.7	55.9	55.4	106	3087	53.8	67.3	175
525i Sdn	25	18	28	19	21.1	184@ 4200	189@ 5900	12:1	EFI	2.5	6	13	37	41.6	N/A	N/A	55.2	54.3	36.4	36.9	58.9	57.9	109	3483	55.6	68.9	186

Specifications EPA Mileage Ratings	EPA Hwy (mpg) - auto	EPA City (mpg) - auto	EPA Hwy (mpg) - manual	EPA City (mpg) - manual	Fuel Capacity	Torque @ RPM	Horsepower @ RPM	Compression Ratio	Fuel System	Displacement (liters)	Number of Cylinders	Luggage Capacity (cu ft.)	Rear Leg Room (in.)	Front Leg Room (in.)	Rear Hip Room (in.)	Front Hip Room (in.)	Rear Shoulder Room (in.)	Front Shoulder Room (in.)	Rear Head Room (in.)	Front Head Room (in.)	Rear Track (in.)	Front Track (in.)	Wheelbase (in.)	Curb Weight (lbs.)	Height (in.)	Width (in.)	Length (in.)
BMW																											
525i Touring Wgn	25	18	N/A	N/A	21.1	184@ 4200	189@ 5900	12:1	EFI	2.5	6	31.4	34.1	41.6	N/A	N/A	55.2	54.3	37.7	36.8	58.9	57.9	109	3759	55.8	68.9	186
530i Sdn	26	17	24	16	21.1	214@ 4500	215@ 5800	12:1	EFI	3.0	8	13	37	41.6	N/A	N/A	55.2	54.3	36.4	36.9	58.9	57.9	109	3627	55.6	68.9	186
530i Touring Wgn	26	17	N/A	N/A	21.1	214@ 4500	215@ 5800	12:1	EFI	3.0	8	31.4	34.1	41.6	N/A	N/A	55.2	54.3	37.7	36.8	58.9	57.9	109	3880	55.8	68.9	186
540i Sdn	25	17	23	14	21.1	295@ 4500	282@ 5800	12:1	EFI	4.0	8	13	37	41.6	N/A	N/A	55.2	54.3	36.4	36.9	58.9	57.9	109	3693	55	68.9	186
740i Sdn	24	16	N/A	N/A	22.5	295@ 4500	282@ 5800	10:1	EFI	4.0	8	12.9	N/A	N/A	N/A	N/A	58.4	58.4	37.9	37.7	61.7	61.1	115	4145	56.5	73.3	196
840Ci Cpe	24	16	N/A	N/A	23.8	295@ 4500	282@ 5800	12:1	EFI	4.0	8	9.5	26	44	N/A	N/A	55.3	57.3	34.7	35.9	61.5	61.2	106	4167	52.8	73	188
M3 Cpe	N/A	N/A	27	19	17.2	225@ 4250	240@ 6000	12:1	EFI	3.0	6	9.2	32.7	41.2	N/A	N/A	52.1	53.2	36.3	38.1	56.9	56	106	3180	52.6	67.3	175
BUICK																											
Century Custom Sdn	29	19	N/A	N/A	16.5	185@ 4000	160@ 5200	9.6:1	SPFI	3.1	6	16.2	35.9	42.1	54.3	50	56	55.9	38.3	38.6	56.7	58.7	105	2993	54.2	69.4	189

Specifications EPA Mileage Ratings

BUICK

Specifications EPA Mileage Ratings	EPA Hwy (mpg) - auto	EPA City (mpg) - auto	EPA Hwy (mpg) - manual	EPA City (mpg) - manual	Fuel Capacity	Torque @ RPM	Horsepower @ RPM	Compression Ratio	Fuel System	Displacement (liters)	Number of Cylinders	Luggage Capacity (cu ft.)	Rear Leg Room (in.)	Front Leg Room (in.)	Rear Hip Room (in.)	Front Hip Room (in.)	Rear Shoulder Room (in.)	Front Shoulder Room (in.)	Rear Head Room (in.)	Front Head Room (in.)	Rear Track (in.)	Front Track (in.)	Wheelbase (in.)	Curb Weight (lbs.)	Height (in.)	Width (in.)	Length (in.)
Century Special Sdn	31	25	N/A	N/A	16.5	130@ 4000	120@ 5200	9:1	MPFI	2.2	4	16.2	35.9	42.1	54.3	50	56	55.9	38.3	38.6	56.7	58.7	105	2986	54.2	69.4	189
Century Special Wgn	29	22	N/A	N/A	16.5	130@ 4000	120@ 5200	9:1	MPFI	2.2	4	41.6	34.8	42.1	54.3	50	56	55.9	38.9	38.6	56.7	58.7	105	3130	54.2	69.4	191
Le Sabre Custom Sdn	29	19	N/A	N/A	18	225@ 3200	170@ 4800	9:1	SPFI	3.8	6	17.1	40.4	42.5	54.4	54.6	58.9	59.1	37.8	38.8	60.4	60.4	111	3442	55.7	74.9	200
Le Sabre Limited Sdn	29	19	N/A	N/A	18	225@ 3200	170@ 4800	9:1	SPFI	3.8	6	17.1	40.4	42.5	54.4	54.6	58.9	59.1	37.8	38.8	60.4	60.4	111	3442	55.7	74.9	200
Park Avenue Sdn	29	19	N/A	N/A	18	230@ 4000	205@ 5200	9.4:1	SPFI	3.8	6	20.3	40.8	42.7	54.2	55.1	58.9	58.7	37.9	38.9	60.6	60.4	111	3532	55.1	74.1	206
Park Avenue Ultra Sdn	27	17	N/A	N/A	18	275@ 3200	225@ 5000	8.5:1	SPFI	3.8	6	20.3	40.7	42.7	54.2	55.1	58.9	58.7	37.9	38.9	60.6	60.4	111	3642	55.1	74.1	206
Regal Custom Cpe	29	19	N/A	N/A	17.1	185@ 4000	160@ 5200	9.6:1	SPFI	3.1	6	15.6	34.8	42.3	53.1	52	56.8	57.6	37	37.8	58	59.5	108	3261	53.3	72.5	194
Regal Custom Sdn	29	19	N/A	N/A	17.1	185@ 4000	160@ 5200	9.6:1	SPFI	3.1	6	15.9	36.2	42.4	55	52.7	56.6	57.8	38.3	38.6	58	59.5	108	3335	54.5	72.5	194
Regal Gran Spt Sdn	29	19	N/A	N/A	17.1	225@ 3200	170@ 4800	9:1	SPFI	3.8	6	15.9	36.2	42.4	55	52.7	56.6	57.8	38.3	38.6	58	59.5	108	3406	54.5	72.5	194

Specifications EPA Mileage Ratings

BUICK

Specifications EPA Mileage Ratings	EPA Hwy (mpg) - auto	EPA City (mpg) - auto	EPA Hwy (mpg) - manual	EPA City (mpg) - manual	Fuel Capacity	Torque @ RPM	Horsepower @ RPM	Compression Ratio	Fuel System	Displacement (liters)	Number of Cylinders	Luggage Capacity (cu ft.)	Rear Leg Room (in.)	Front Leg Room (in.)	Rear Hip Room (in.)	Front Hip Room (in.)	Rear Shoulder Room (in.)	Front Shoulder Room (in.)	Rear Head Room (in.)	Front Head Room (in.)	Rear Track (in.)	Front Track (in.)	Wheelbase (in.)	Curb Weight (lbs.)	Height (in.)	Width (in.)	Length (in.)
Regal Gran Spt Cpe	29	19	N/A	N/A	17.1	225@ 3200	170@ 4800	9:1	SPFI	3.8	6	15.6	34.8	42.3	53.1	52	56.8	57.6	37	37.8	58	59.5	108	3328	53.3	72.5	194
Regal Limited Sdn	29	19	N/A	N/A	17.1	225@ 3200	170@ 4800	9:1	SPFI	3.8	6	15.9	36.2	42.4	55	52.7	56.6	57.8	38.3	38.6	58	59.5	108	3463	54.5	72.5	194
Riviera Cpe	29	19	N/A	N/A	20	230@ 4000	205@ 5200	9.4:1	SPFI	3.8	6	17.4	37.3	42.6	52.8	53.7	57.9	57.9	36.2	38.2	62.6	62.5	114	3748	55.2	75	207
Roadmaster Sdn	25	17	N/A	N/A	23	330@ 3200	260@ 5000	10.5:1	SPFI	5.7	8	21	38.9	42.1	56.9	56.9	63.3	63.3	38.6	39.2	60.7	61.7	116	4211	55.9	78.1	216
Roadmaster Estate Wagon Wg	25	17	N/A	N/A	21	330@ 3200	260@ 5000	10.5:1	SPFI	5.7	8	92.4	37.3	42.3	57.1	56.9	63.5	63.4	39.4	39.6	64.1	62.1	116	4563	60.3	79.9	218
Skylark Custom Sdn	38	23	N/A	N/A	15.2	145@ 4800	150@ 6000	9.5:1	MPFI	2.3	4	13.3	33.5	43.2	50.3	49.2	53.7	54.1	37	37.8	55.3	55.8	103	2941	53.5	68.7	189
Skylark Custom Cpe	38	23	N/A	N/A	15.2	145@ 4800	150@ 6000	9.5:1	MPFI	2.3	4	13.3	32.6	43.1	50.3	49.1	55	53.6	36.5	37.8	55.3	55.8	103	2888	53.5	68.7	189
Skylark Gran Spt Sdn	29	20	N/A	N/A	15.2	185@ 4000	155@ 5200	9.6:1	SPFI	3.1	6	13.3	33.5	43.2	50.3	49.2	53.4	54.1	37	37.8	55.3	55.8	103	3058	53.5	68.7	189
Skylark Gran Spt Cpe	29	20	N/A	N/A	15.2	185@ 4000	155@ 5200	9.6:1	SPFI	3.1	6	13.3	32.6	43.1	50.9	49.1	55	53.6	36.5	37.8	55.3	55.8	103	3005	53.5	68.7	189

Specifications EPA Mileage Ratings	EPA Hwy (mpg) - auto	EPA City (mpg) - auto	EPA Hwy (mpg) - manual	EPA City (mpg) - manual	Fuel Capacity	Torque @ RPM	Horsepower @ RPM	Compression Ratio	Fuel System	Displacement (liters)	Number of Cylinders	Luggage Capacity (cu ft.)	Rear Leg Room (in.)	Front Leg Room (in.)	Rear Hip Room (in.)	Front Hip Room (in.)	Rear Shoulder Room (in.)	Front Shoulder Room (in.)	Rear Head Room (in.)	Front Head Room (in.)	Rear Track (in.)	Front Track (in.)	Wheelbase (in.)	Curb Weight (lbs.)	Height (in.)	Width (in.)	Length (in.)
BUICK																											
Skylark Limited Sdn	38	23	N/A	N/A	15.2	145@ 4800	150@ 6000	9.5:1	MPFI	2.3	4	13.3	33.5	43.2	50.3	49.2	53.4	54.1	37	37.8	55.3	55.8	103	2941	53.5	68.7	189
Skylark Limited Cpe	38	23	N/A	N/A	15.2	145@ 4800	150@ 6000	9.5:1	MPFI	2.3	4	13.3	32.6	43.1	50.3	49.1	55	53.6	36.5	37.8	55.3	55.8	103	2888	53.5	68.7	189
CADILLAC																											
De Ville Sdn	26	16	N/A	N/A	20	275@ 3000	200@ 4100	9.5:1	SPFI	4.9	8	20	43.3	42.6	55.9	56.1	61.3	61.1	38.4	38.5	60.9	60.9	114	3758	56.3	76.6	210
De Ville Concours Sdn	25	16	N/A	N/A	20	300@ 4000	275@ 5600	10.3:1	TPI	4.6	8	20	43.3	42.6	55.9	56.1	61.3	61.1	38.4	38.5	60.9	60.9	114	3985	56.3	76.6	210
Eldorado Cpe	25	16	N/A	N/A	20	300@ 4000	275@ 5600	10.3:1	TPI	4.6	8	15.3	36.1	42.6	55.7	57.6	57.6	58.2	38.3	37.8	60.9	60.9	108	3774	53.6	75.5	202
Eldorado Touring Cpe	25	16	N/A	N/A	20	295@ 4400	300@ 6000	10.3:1	TPI	4.6	8	15.3	36.1	42.6	55.7	57.6	57.6	58.2	38.3	37.8	60.9	60.9	108	3818	53.6	75.5	202
Fleetwood Sdn	25	17	N/A	N/A	23	335@ 2400	260@ 5000	10.5:1	SPFI	5.7	8	21.1	43.9	42.5	59.8	59.2	64	64.3	39.1	38.7	60.7	61.7	122	4478	57.1	78	225
Seville Luxury Sdn	25	16	N/A	N/A	20	300@ 4000	275@ 5600	10.3:1	TPI	4.6	8	14.4	39.1	43	57.6	55	57.5	58.9	38.3	38	60.9	60.9	111	3892	54.5	74.2	204

Specifications EPA Mileage Ratings	EPA Hwy (mpg) - auto	EPA City (mpg) - auto	EPA Hwy (mpg) - manual	EPA City (mpg) - manual	Fuel Capacity	Torque @ RPM	Horsepower @ RPM	Compression Ratio	Fuel System	Displacement (liters)	Number of Cylinders	Luggage Capacity (cu ft.)	Rear Leg Room (in.)	Front Leg Room (in.)	Rear Hip Room (in.)	Front Hip Room (in.)	Rear Shoulder Room (in.)	Front Shoulder Room (in.)	Rear Head Room (in.)	Front Head Room (in.)	Rear Track (in.)	Front Track (in.)	Wheelbase (in.)	Curb Weight (lbs.)	Height (in.)	Width (in.)	Length (in.)
CADILLAC																											
Seville Touring Sdn	25	16	N/A	N/A	20	295@ 4400	300@ 6000	10.3:1	TPI	4.6	8	14.4	39.1	43	57.6	55	57.5	58.9	38.3	38	60.9	60.9	111	3892	54.5	74.2	204
CHEVROLET																											
Beretta Cpe	31	25	34	25	15.2	130@ 4000	120@ 5200	9:1	MFI	2.2	4	13.5	32.6	43.4	50.9	49.6	55.2	53.5	36.6	37.6	55.3	55.8	103	2756	53	53.9	187
Beretta Z26 Cpe	29	21	N/A	N/A	15.2	185@ 4000	155@ 5200	9.6:1	SFI	3.1	6	13.5	32.6	43.4	50.9	49.6	55.2	53.5	36.6	37.6	55.3	55.8	103	2990	53	53.9	187
Camaro Conv	28	19	28	19	15.5	200@ 3600	160@ 4600	9:1	SFI	3.4	6	7.6	26.8	43	43.7	52.8	43.5	57.4	39	38	60.6	60.7	101	3342	52	74.1	193
Camaro Cpe	28	19	28	19	15.5	200@ 3600	160@ 4600	9:1	SFI	3.4	6	12.9	26.8	43	44.4	52.8	55.8	57.4	35.3	37.2	60.6	60.7	101	3251	51.3	74.1	193
Camaro Z28 Conv	24	17	26	17	15.5	325@ 2000	275@ 5000	10.5:1	SFI	5.7	8	7.6	26.8	43	43.7	52.8	43.5	57.4	39	38	60.6	60.7	101	3480	52	74.1	193
Camaro Z28 Cpe	24	17	26	17	15.5	325@ 2000	275@ 5000	10.5:1	SFI	5.7	8	12.9	26.8	43	44.4	52.8	55.8	57.4	35.3	37.2	60.6	60.7	101	3390	51.3	74.1	193
Caprice Wgn	25	17	N/A	N/A	21	330@ 3200	260@ 4800	10:1	SFI	5.7	8	54.7	38	42.2	57.1	56.9	63.5	63.4	39.4	39.6	64.1	62.1	116	4473	60.9	79.6	217

Specifications EPA Mileage Ratings

CHEVROLET

Specifications EPA Mileage Ratings	EPA Hwy (mpg) - auto	EPA City (mpg) - auto	EPA Hwy (mpg) - manual	EPA City (mpg) - manual	Fuel Capacity	Torque @ RPM	Horsepower @ RPM	Compression Ratio	Fuel System	Displacement (liters)	Number of Cylinders	Luggage Capacity (cu ft.)	Rear Leg Room (in.)	Front Leg Room (in.)	Rear Hip Room (in.)	Front Hip Room (in.)	Rear Shoulder Room (in.)	Front Shoulder Room (in.)	Rear Head Room (in.)	Front Head Room (in.)	Rear Track (in.)	Front Track (in.)	Wheelbase (in.)	Curb Weight (lbs.)	Height (in.)	Width (in.)	Length (in.)
Caprice Sdn	26	18	N/A	N/A	23	235@ 2400	200@ 5200	9.9:1	SFI	4.3	8	20.4	39.5	42.2	56.9	57	63.4	63.4	37.9	39.2	62.3	61.8	116	4061	55.7	77.5	214
Cavalier Cpe	33	23	36	25	15.2	130@ 4000	120@ 5200	9:1	MFI	2.2	4	13.2	33.2	42.3	49.5	50.4	54.9	53.9	36.6	37.6	56.7	57.6	104	2617	53.2	67.4	180
Cavalier Sdn	33	23	36	25	15.2	130@ 4000	120@ 5200	9:1	MFI	2.2	4	13.2	34.6	42.3	50.6	50.8	53.9	54.6	37.2	39	56.7	57.6	104	2676	54.8	67.4	180
Cavalier LS Sdn	33	23	N/A	N/A	15.2	130@ 4000	120@ 5200	9:1	MFI	2.2	4	13.2	34.6	42.3	50.6	50.8	53.9	54.6	37.2	39	56.7	57.6	104	2736	54.8	67.4	180
Cavalier Z24 Cpe	N/A	N/A	N/A	N/A	15.2	145@ 4800	150@ 6000	9.5:1	MFI	2.3	4	13.2	33.2	42.3	49.5	50.7	54.9	53.9	36.6	37.6	56.7	57.6	104	2691	53.2	67.4	180
Corsica Sdn	31	25	N/A	N/A	15.2	130@ 4000	120@ 5200	9:1	MFI	2.2	4	13.4	35.5	43.4	51.5	49.7	54.1	53.1	37.4	38.3	55.3	55.8	103	2745	54.2	68.5	183
Corvette Cpe	24	17	27	17	20	340@ 4000	300@ 5000	10.5:1	SFI	5.7	8	12.6	N/A	42	N/A	49.3	N/A	53.9	N/A	36.5	59.1	57.7	96.2	3203	46.3	70.7	179
Corvette Conv	24	17	27	17	20	340@ 4000	300@ 5000	10.5:1	SFI	5.7	8	6.6	N/A	42	N/A	49.3	N/A	53.9	N/A	37	59.1	57.7	96.2	3360	47.3	70.7	179
Corvette ZR1 Cpe	N/A	N/A	25	17	20	385@ 5200	405@ 5800	11:1	SFI	5.7	8	12.6	N/A	42	N/A	49.3	N/A	53.9	N/A	36.5	60.6	57.7	96.2	3512	46.3	73.1	179

Specifications EPA Mileage Ratings	EPA Hwy (mpg) - auto	EPA City (mpg) - auto	EPA Hwy (mpg) - manual	EPA City (mpg) - manual	Fuel Capacity	Torque @ RPM	Horsepower @ RPM	Compression Ratio	Fuel System	Displacement (liters)	Number of Cylinders	Luggage Capacity (cu ft.)	Rear Leg Room (in.)	Front Leg Room (in.)	Rear Hip Room (in.)	Front Hip Room (in.)	Rear Shoulder Room (in.)	Front Shoulder Room (in.)	Rear Head Room (in.)	Front Head Room (in.)	Rear Track (in.)	Front Track (in.)	Wheelbase (in.)	Curb Weight (lbs.)	Height (in.)	Width (in.)	Length (in.)
CHEVROLET																											
Impala SS Sdn	25	17	N/A	N/A	23	330@ 3200	260@ 4800	10.5:1	SFI	5.7	8	20.4	39.5	42.2	56.9	57	63.4	63.4	37.9	39.2	62.7	62.3	116	4036	54.7	77.5	214
Lumina Sdn	29	19	N/A	N/A	17.1	185@ 4000	160@ 5200	9.6:1	SFI	3.1	6	15.7	36.6	42.4	55.3	55.4	57.4	58.4	37.4	38.4	59	59.1	108	3330	55.2	72.5	201
Lumina LS Sdn	29	19	N/A	N/A	17.1	185@ 4000	160@ 5200	9.6:1	SFI	3.1	6	15.7	36.6	42.4	55.3	55.4	57.4	58.4	37.4	38.4	59	59.1	108	3372	55.2	72.5	201
Monte Carlo LS Cpe	29	19	N/A	N/A	17.1	185@ 4000	160@ 5200	9.6:1	SFI	3.1	6	15.7	34.9	42.4	51.6	53.4	57.6	57.5	36.9	37.9	59	59.5	108	3306	53.8	72.5	201
Monte Carlo Z34 Cpe	26	17	N/A	N/A	17.1	215@ 4000	210@ 5200	9.2:1	SFI	3.4	6	15.7	34.9	42.4	51.6	53.4	57.6	57.5	36.9	37.9	59	59.5	108	3436	53.8	72.5	201
CHRYSLER																											
Cirrus LX Sdn	28	20	N/A	N/A	16	163@ 4350	164@ 5900	12:1	SMPI	2.5	6	15.7	37.8	42.3	52.7	52.8	54.7	55.2	36.8	38.1	60.2	60.2	108	3145	54.1	71	186
Concorde Sdn	28	20	N/A	N/A	18	181@ 3200	161@ 5300	8.9:1	SMPI	3.3	6	16.6	38.8	42.4	60.9	56.4	59	59	37.5	38.4	62	62	113	3376	56.3	74.4	202
LeBaron Conv	28	20	N/A	N/A	14	171@ 2400	141@ 5000	8.9:1	SMPI	3.0	6	9.2	33	42.4	37.6	52.4	45.7	55.9	37	38.3	57.6	57.6	101	3122	52.4	69.2	185

Specifications EPA Mileage Ratings	EPA Hwy (mpg) - auto	EPA City (mpg) - auto	EPA Hwy (mpg) - manual	EPA City (mpg) - manual	Fuel Capacity	Torque @ RPM	Horsepower @ RPM	Compression Ratio	Fuel System	Displacement (liters)	Number of Cylinders	Luggage Capacity (cu ft.)	Rear Leg Room (in.)	Front Leg Room (in.)	Rear Hip Room (in.)	Front Hip Room (in.)	Rear Shoulder Room (in.)	Front Shoulder Room (in.)	Rear Head Room (in.)	Front Head Room (in.)	Rear Track (in.)	Front Track (in.)	Wheelbase (in.)	Curb Weight (lbs.)	Height (in.)	Width (in.)	Length (in.)
CHRYSLER																											
LHS Sdn	26	18	N/A	N/A	18	221@ 3100	214@ 5850	9.6:1	SMPI	3.5	6	17.9	41.7	42.4	61.1	56.4	58.2	58.8	36.7	36.9	62	62	113	3628	55.9	74.5	207
New Yorker Sdn	26	18	N/A	N/A	18	221@ 3100	214@ 5850	9.6:1	SMPI	3.5	6	17.9	41.7	42.4	61.1	56.4	58.2	58.8	37.6	38.4	62	62	113	3592	55.9	74.5	207
Sebring LX Cpe	31	22	32	22	15.9	130@ 4800	140@ 6000	9.6:1	SMPI	2.0	4	13.1	35	43.3	49.6	55.1	55.1	53.1	36.5	39.1	59.3	59.5	104	2816	53	69.7	187
Sebring LXi Cpe	28	20	N/A	N/A	15.9	161@ 4400	155@ 5500	9.4:1	SMPI	2.5	6	13.1	35	43.3	49.6	55.1	55.1	53.1	36.5	39.1	59.3	59.5	104	2980	53	69.7	187
DODGE																											
Avenger Cpe	31	22	32	22	15.8	130@ 4800	140@ 6000	12:1	SMPI	2.0	4	13	35	43.3	N/A	N/A	N/A	N/A	36.5	39.1	59.3	59.4	104	2822	53	68.5	187
Avenger ES Cpe	28	20	N/A	N/A	15.8	161@ 4400	155@ 5500	12:1	SMPI	2.5	6	13	35	43.3	N/A	N/A	N/A	N/A	36.5	39.1	59.3	59.4	104	3152	53	68.5	187
Intrepid Sdn	28	20	N/A	N/A	18	181@ 3200	161@ 5300	8.9:1	SMPI	3.3	6	16.7	38.8	42.4	60.9	56.3	58.3	59	37.5	38.4	62	62	113	3310	56.3	74.4	202
Intrepid ES Sdn	28	20	N/A	N/A	18	181@ 3200	161@ 5300	8.9:1	SMPI	3.3	6	16.7	38.8	42.4	60.9	56.3	58.3	59	37.5	38.4	62	62	113	3372	56.3	74.4	202

Specifications EPA Mileage Ratings

DODGE

Specifications EPA Mileage Ratings	EPA Hwy (mpg) - auto	EPA City (mpg) - auto	EPA Hwy (mpg) - manual	EPA City (mpg) - manual	Fuel Capacity	Torque @ RPM	Horsepower @ RPM	Compression Ratio	Fuel System	Displacement (liters)	Number of Cylinders	Luggage Capacity (cu ft.)	Rear Leg Room (in.)	Front Leg Room (in.)	Rear Hip Room (in.)	Front Hip Room (in.)	Rear Shoulder Room (in.)	Front Shoulder Room (in.)	Rear Head Room (in.)	Front Head Room (in.)	Rear Track (in.)	Front Track (in.)	Wheelbase (in.)	Curb Weight (lbs.)	Height (in.)	Width (in.)	Length (in.)
Neon Sdn	33	27	38	29	11.2	129@ 5000	132@ 6000	9.8:1	SMPI	2.0	4	11.8	33.9	42.5	50.6	50.8	52.3	52.5	36.5	39.6	57.4	57.4	104	2320	54.8	67.4	172
Neon Highline Sdn	33	27	38	29	11.2	129@ 5000	132@ 6000	12:1	SMPI	2.0	4	11.8	33.9	42.5	50.6	50.8	52.3	52.5	36.5	39.6	57.4	57.4	104	2320	54.8	67.4	172
Neon Highline Cpe	33	27	38	29	11.2	129@ 5000	132@ 6000	12:1	SMPI	2.0	4	11.8	35.1	42.5	53.9	50.3	54.7	52	36.5	39.6	57.4	57.4	104	2384	52.8	67.2	172
Neon Sport Sdn	33	27	38	29	11.2	129@ 5000	132@ 6000	12:1	SMPI	2.0	4	11.8	33.9	42.5	50.6	50.8	52.3	52.5	36.5	39.6	57.4	57.4	104	2421	54.8	67.4	172
Neon Sport 2.0L DOHC Cpe	33	27	38	29	11.2	131@ 5600	150@ 6800	12:1	SMPI	2.0	4	11.8	35.1	42.5	53.9	50.3	54.7	52	36.5	39.6	57.4	57.4	104	2485	52.8	67.2	172
Spirit Sdn	27	22	N/A	N/A	16	135@ 2800	100@ 4800	8.9:1	EFI	2.5	4	14.4	38.3	41.9	52	51.7	55	54.3	37.9	38.4	52.2	57.6	104	2863	53.5	68.1	181
Stealth Cpe	23	18	24	19	19.8	185@ 4000	164@ 5500	8.9:1	SMPI	3.0	6	11.1	28.5	44.2	46.9	56.7	52	55.9	34.1	37.1	62.2	61.4	97.2	3064	49.1	72.4	180
Stealth R/T Cpe	24	18	25	19	19.8	205@ 4500	222@ 6000	10:1	SMPI	3.0	6	11.1	28.5	44.2	46.9	56.7	52	55.9	34.1	37.1	62.2	61.4	97.2	3164	49.1	72.4	180
Stealth R/T Turbo Cpe	N/A	N/A	24	18	19.8	315@ 2500	320@ 6000	8:1	SMPI	3.0	6	11.1	28.5	44.2	46.9	56.7	52	55.9	34.1	37.1	62.2	61.4	97.2	3792	49.3	72.4	180

Specifications EPA Mileage Ratings	EPA Hwy (mpg) - auto	EPA City (mpg) - auto	EPA Hwy (mpg) - manual	EPA City (mpg) - manual	Fuel Capacity	Torque @ RPM	Horsepower @ RPM	Compression Ratio	Fuel System	Displacement (liters)	Number of Cylinders	Luggage Capacity (cu ft.)	Rear Leg Room (in.)	Front Leg Room (in.)	Rear Hip Room (in.)	Front Hip Room (in.)	Rear Shoulder Room (in.)	Front Shoulder Room (in.)	Rear Head Room (in.)	Front Head Room (in.)	Rear Track (in.)	Front Track (in.)	Wheelbase (in.)	Curb Weight (lbs.)	Height (in.)	Width (in.)	Length (in.)
DODGE																											
Stratus Sdn	N/A	N/A	31	23	16	129@ 5000	132@ 6000	9.8:1	SMPI	2.0	4	15.7	38.1	42.3	52.7	52.8	54.7	55	36.8	38.1	60	60	108	2937	54.1	71	186
Stratus ES Sdn	29	20	N/A	N/A	16	163@ 4350	164@ 5900	9.4:1	SMPI	2.5	6	15.7	38.1	42.3	52.7	52.8	54.7	55.2	36.8	38.1	60.2	60.2	108	3153	54.1	71	186
Viper Conv	N/A	N/A	22	14	22	465@ 3600	400@ 4600	9.1:1	MPI	8.0	10	11.8	N/A	42.6	N/A	N/A	N/A	53.8	N/A	N/A	60.6	59.6	96.2	3487	44	75.7	175
EAGLE																											
Summit DL Cpe	32	28	39	32	13.2	93@ 3000	92@ 6000	9.2:1	SMPI	1.5	4	10.5	31.1	42.9	53.7	54.9	54.1	53.9	36.4	38.6	57.5	57.1	96.1	2085	51.4	66.1	171
Summit DL Wgn	29	24	29	24	14.5	116@ 4500	119@ 6000	9.5:1	SMPI	1.8	4	34.6	36.1	40.8	52.6	50.2	55.1	55.1	38.6	40	57.5	57.5	99.2	2734	62.1	66.7	169
Summit ESi Cpe	32	28	39	32	13.2	93@ 3000	92@ 6000	9.2:1	SMPI	1.5	4	10.5	31.1	42.9	53.7	54.9	54.1	53.9	36.4	38.6	57.5	57.1	96.1	2085	51.4	66.1	171
Summit ESi Sdn	33	26	33	26	13.2	116@ 4500	113@ 6000	9.5:1	SMPI	1.8	4	10.5	33.5	42.9	52.1	52.5	53.5	53.9	36.2	38.4	57.5	57.1	98.4	2195	51.4	66.1	174
Summit LX Sdn	33	26	33	26	13.2	116@ 4500	113@ 6000	9.5:1	SMPI	1.8	4	10.5	33.5	42.9	52.1	52.5	53.5	53.9	36.2	38.4	57.5	57.1	98.4	2195	51.4	66.1	174

Specifications EPA Mileage Ratings	EPA Hwy (mpg) - auto	EPA City (mpg) - auto	EPA Hwy (mpg) - manual	EPA City (mpg) - manual	Fuel Capacity	Torque @ RPM	Horsepower @ RPM	Compression Ratio	Fuel System	Displacement (liters)	Number of Cylinders	Luggage Capacity (cu ft.)	Rear Leg Room (in.)	Front Leg Room (in.)	Rear Hip Room (in.)	Front Hip Room (in.)	Rear Shoulder Room (in.)	Front Shoulder Room (in.)	Rear Head Room (in.)	Front Head Room (in.)	Rear Track (in.)	Front Track (in.)	Wheelbase (in.)	Curb Weight (lbs.)	Height (in.)	Width (in.)	Length (in.)
EAGLE																											
Summit LX Wgn	26	20	27	22	14.5	145@ 4250	136@ 5500	9.5:1	SMPI	2.4	4	34.6	36.1	40.8	52.6	50.2	55.1	55.1	38.6	40	57.5	57.5	99.2	2734	62.1	66.7	169
Summit AWD Wgn	23	19	24	20	14.5	145@ 4250	136@ 5500	9.5:1	SMPI	2.4	4	34.6	36.1	40.8	52.6	50.2	55.1	55.1	38.6	40	57.5	57.5	99.2	3064	62.6	66.7	169
Talon ESi Cpe	31	22	32	22	15.8	131@ 4800	140@ 6000	9.6:1	SMPI	2.0	4	16.6	28.4	43.3	47.2	55.1	51.2	53.1	34.1	37.9	59.4	59.7	98.8	2756	51	68.3	172
Talon TSi Cpe	N/A	N/A	31	22	15.8	214@ 3000	210@ 6000	8.5:1	SMPI	2.0	4	16.6	28.4	43.3	47.2	55.1	51.2	53.1	34.1	37.9	59.4	59.7	98.8	2866	51.6	68.7	172
Talon TSi AWD Cpe	N/A	N/A	27	21	13.8	214@ 3000	210@ 6000	8.5:1	SMPI	2.0	4	13.5	28.4	43.3	47.2	55.1	51.2	53.1	34.1	37.9	59.4	59.7	98.8	3119	51.6	68.7	172
Vision ESi Sdn	28	20	N/A	N/A	18	181@ 3200	161@ 5300	8.9:1	SMPI	3.3	6	16.6	38.8	42.4	60.9	56.3	59	59	37.5	38.4	62	62	113	3408	56.3	74.4	202
Vision TSi Sdn	26	18	N/A	N/A	18	221@ 3100	214@ 5850	9.6:1	SMPI	3.5	6	16.6	38.8	42.4	60.9	56.3	59	59	37.5	38.4	62	62	113	3507	56.3	74.4	202
FORD																											
Aspire 3 Dr Hbk	34	29	42	36	10	74@ 3000	63@ 5000	9.7:1	EFI	1.3	4	14.9	33.6	41.6	44.8	47.9	49.3	50.3	35.5	37.8	55.1	55.9	90.7	2004	55.6	65.7	153

Specifications EPA Mileage Ratings

FORD

Specifications EPA Mileage Ratings	EPA Hwy (mpg) - auto	EPA City (mpg) - auto	EPA Hwy (mpg) - manual	EPA City (mpg) - manual	Fuel Capacity	Torque @ RPM	Horsepower @ RPM	Compression Ratio	Fuel System	Displacement (liters)	Number of Cylinders	Luggage Capacity (cu ft.)	Rear Leg Room (in.)	Front Leg Room (in.)	Rear Hip Room (in.)	Front Hip Room (in.)	Rear Shoulder Room (in.)	Front Shoulder Room (in.)	Rear Head Room (in.)	Front Head Room (in.)	Rear Track (in.)	Front Track (in.)	Wheelbase (in.)	Curb Weight (lbs.)	Height (in.)	Width (in.)	Length (in.)
Aspire 3 Dr SE Hbk	34	29	42	36	10	74@ 3000	63@ 5000	9.7:1	EFI	1.3	4	14.9	33.6	41.6	44.8	47.9	49.3	50.3	35.5	37.8	55.1	55.9	90.7	2004	55.6	65.7	153
Aspire 5 Dr Hbk	34	29	42	36	10	74@ 3000	63@ 5000	9.7:1	EFI	1.3	4	17	34.2	41.6	46.3	48.7	50	50.4	36.4	38.2	55.1	55.9	93.9	2053	55.6	65.7	156
Contour GL Sdn	32	24	35	24	14.5	130@ 4000	125@ 5500	9.6:1	SEFI	2.0	4	13.9	34.3	42.4	45.5	50.7	53.3	53.9	36.7	39	58.5	59.2	107	2769	54.5	69.1	184
Contour LX Sdn	32	24	35	24	14.5	130@ 4000	125@ 5500	9.6:1	SEFI	2.0	4	13.9	34.3	42.4	45.5	50.7	53.3	53.9	36.7	39	58.5	59.2	107	2769	54.5	69.1	184
Contour SE Sdn	30	22	29	21	14.5	165@ 4200	170@ 6200	9.7:1	SEFI	2.5	6	13.9	34.3	42.4	45.5	50.7	53.3	53.9	36.7	39	58.5	59.2	107	2769	54.5	69.1	184
Crown Vic Sdn	25	17	N/A	N/A	20	260@ 3250	190@ 4250	9:1	SEFI	4.6	8	20.6	39.6	42.5	58.7	57.1	60.3	60.8	38	39.4	63.3	62.8	114	3762	56.8	77.8	212
Escort 3 Dr Base Hbk	34	26	38	30	11.9	108@ 3800	88@ 4400	9:1	SEFI	1.9	4	17.3	34.6	41.7	46.6	51.3	52.6	53	37.6	38.4	56.5	56.5	98.4	2316	52.5	66.7	170
Escort 3 Dr GT Hbk	29	23	31	25	13.2	114@ 4500	127@ 6500	9:1	EFI	1.8	4	17.3	34.6	41.7	46.6	51.3	52.6	53	38.6	37.4	56.5	56.5	98.4	2459	52.5	66.7	170
Escort 3 Dr LX Hbk	34	26	38	30	11.9	108@ 3800	88@ 4400	9:1	SEFI	1.9	4	17.3	34.6	41.7	46.6	51.3	52.6	53	37.6	38.4	56.5	56.5	98.4	2355	52.5	66.7	170

Specifications EPA Mileage Ratings

FORD

Specifications EPA Mileage Ratings	EPA Hwy (mpg) - auto	EPA City (mpg) - auto	EPA Hwy (mpg) - manual	EPA City (mpg) - manual	Fuel Capacity	Torque @ RPM	Horsepower @ RPM	Compression Ratio	Fuel System	Displacement (liters)	Number of Cylinders	Luggage Capacity (cu ft.)	Rear Leg Room (in.)	Front Leg Room (in.)	Rear Hip Room (in.)	Front Hip Room (in.)	Rear Shoulder Room (in.)	Front Shoulder Room (in.)	Rear Head Room (in.)	Front Head Room (in.)	Rear Track (in.)	Front Track (in.)	Wheelbase (in.)	Curb Weight (lbs.)	Height (in.)	Width (in.)	Length (in.)
Escort 5 Dr LX Hbk	34	26	38	30	11.9	108@ 3800	88@ 4400	9:1	SEFI	1.9	4	17.6	34.6	41.7	48	50.4	53.7	53	37.6	38.4	56.5	56.5	98.4	2404	52.5	66.7	170
Escort LX Sdn	34	26	38	30	11.9	108@ 3800	88@ 4400	9:1	SEFI	1.9	4	12.1	34.6	41.7	48	50.4	53.7	53	37.4	38.4	56.5	56.5	98.4	2385	52.7	66.7	171
Escort LX Wgn	34	26	38	30	11.9	108@ 3800	88@ 4400	9:1	SEFI	1.9	4	30.6	34.6	41.7	48	50.4	53.7	53	38.5	38.4	56.5	56.5	98.4	2451	53.6	66.7	171
Mustang Cpe	29	19	30	20	15.4	215@ 2500	145@ 4000	9:1	EFI	3.8	6	10.9	30.3	42.5	48.8	52.9	52.1	53.6	35.9	38.2	59.2	60.5	101	3077	53	71.8	182
Mustang Conv	29	19	30	20	15.4	215@ 2500	145@ 4000	9:1	EFI	3.8	6	8.5	30.3	42.5	41.1	52.4	41.2	53.6	35.7	38.1	59.2	60.5	101	3257	53.2	71.8	182
Mustang Cobra 2 Dr Conv	N/A	N/A	25	17	15.4	285@ N/A	240@	9:1	SEFI	5.0	8	8.5	N/A	42.5	41.4	52.4	41.2	53.6	35.7	38.1	58.7	60	101	3524	53.3	71.8	182
Mustang Cobra 2 Dr Cpe	N/A	N/A	25	17	15.4	285@ N/A	240@	9:1	SEFI	5.0	8	10.9	30.3	42.5	48.8	52.4	52.1	53.6	35.9	38.2	58.7	60	101	3354	53.4	71.8	182
Mustang GT Conv	24	17	25	17	15.4	285@ 3400	215@ 4200	9:1	SEFI	5.0	8	8.5	30.3	42.5	41.1	52.4	41.2	53.6	35.7	38.1	58.7	60.1	101	3451	53.3	71.8	182
Mustang GT/GTS Cpe	24	17	25	17	15.4	285@ 3400	215@ 4200	9:1	SEFI	5.0	8	10.9	30.3	42.5	48.8	52.4	52.1	53.6	35.9	38.2	58.7	60.1	101	3280	53.4	71.8	182

Specifications EPA Mileage Ratings	EPA Hwy (mpg) - auto	EPA City (mpg) - auto	EPA Hwy (mpg) - manual	EPA City (mpg) - manual	Fuel Capacity	Torque @ RPM	Horsepower @ RPM	Compression Ratio	Fuel System	Displacement (liters)	Number of Cylinders	Luggage Capacity (cu ft.)	Rear Leg Room (in.)	Front Leg Room (in.)	Rear Hip Room (in.)	Front Hip Room (in.)	Rear Shoulder Room (in.)	Front Shoulder Room (in.)	Rear Head Room (in.)	Front Head Room (in.)	Rear Track (in.)	Front Track (in.)	Wheelbase (in.)	Curb Weight (lbs.)	Height (in.)	Width (in.)	Length (in.)
FORD																											
Probe Hbk	31	22	33	26	15.5	127@ 4500	118@ 5500	9:1	SEFI	2.0	4	18	28.5	43.1	48.6	53.9	53.9	52	34.8	37.8	59.8	59.8	103	2690	51.6	69.8	179
Probe GT Hbk	26	20	26	21	15.5	160@ 4000	164@ 5600	9.2:1	SEFI	2.5	6	18	28.5	43.1	48.6	53.9	53.9	52	34.8	37.8	59.4	59.4	103	2921	51.6	69.8	180
Taurus GL Sdn	30	20	N/A	N/A	16	165@ 3250	140@ 4800	9.3:1	SEFI	3.0	6	18	37.7	41.7	54.8	55.2	57.6	57.5	37.6	38.3	60.5	61.6	106	3118	54.1	71.2	192
Taurus GL Wgn	30	20	N/A	N/A	16	165@ 3250	140@ 4800	9.3:1	SEFI	3.0	6	38.2	36.9	41.7	57	55.2	57.5	57.5	38.1	38.6	59.9	61.6	106	3285	55.5	71.2	193
Taurus LX Wgn	26	18	N/A	N/A	16	215@ 2200	140@ 3800	9:1	SEFI	3.8	6	38.2	36.9	41.7	57	55.2	57.5	57.5	38.1	38.6	59.9	61.6	106	3285	55.5	71.2	193
Taurus LX Sdn	30	20	N/A	N/A	16	165@ 3250	140@ 4800	9.3:1	SEFI	3.0	6	18	37.7	41.7	54.8	55.2	57.6	57.5	37.6	38.3	60.5	61.6	106	3118	54.1	71.2	192
Taurus SE Sdn	30	20	N/A	N/A	16	165@ 3250	140@ 4800	9.3:1	SEFI	3.0	6	18	37.7	41.7	54.8	55.2	57.6	57.5	37.6	38.3	60.5	61.6	106	3118	54.1	71.2	192
Taurus SHO 5 Spd Sdn	N/A	N/A	26	18	18.4	200@ 4800	220@ 6200	9.8:1	SEFI	3.0	6	18	37.7	41.7	54.8	55.2	57.6	57.5	37.6	38.3	60.5	61.6	106	3118	54.1	71.2	192
Taurus SHO Auto Sdn	26	18	N/A	N/A	18.4	215@ 4800	220@ 6000	9.8:1	SEFI	3.2	6	18	37.7	41.7	54.8	55.2	57.6	57.5	37.6	38.3	60.5	61.6	106	3118	54.1	71.2	192

Specifications EPA Mileage Ratings	EPA Hwy (mpg) - auto	EPA City (mpg) - auto	EPA Hwy (mpg) - manual	EPA City (mpg) - manual	Fuel Capacity	Torque @ RPM	Horsepower @ RPM	Compression Ratio	Fuel System	Displacement (liters)	Number of Cylinders	Luggage Capacity (cu ft.)	Rear Leg Room (in.)	Front Leg Room (in.)	Rear Hip Room (in.)	Front Hip Room (in.)	Rear Shoulder Room (in.)	Front Shoulder Room (in.)	Rear Head Room (in.)	Front Head Room (in.)	Rear Track (in.)	Front Track (in.)	Wheelbase (in.)	Curb Weight (lbs.)	Height (in.)	Width (in.)	Length (in.)
FORD																											
Thunderbird LX Cpe	26	19	N/A	N/A	18	215@ 2400	140@ 3800	9:1	SEFI	3.8	6	15.1	35.8	42.5	56.6	55.6	58.9	59.1	37.5	38.1	60.2	61.6	113	3536	52.5	72.7	200
Thunderbird Super Cpe	24	18	26	18	18	330@ 2500	230@ 4400	8.5:1	SEFI	3.8	6	15.1	35.8	42.5	56.6	55.6	58.9	59.1	37.5	38.1	60.2	61.6	113	3536	53	72.7	200
GEO																											
Metro Sdn	33	29	43	39	10.6	74@ 3500	70@ 6000	9.5:1	EFI	1.3	4	10.3	32.8	42.5	42.9	56.9	48.3	49	37.3	39.3	53.5	54.5	93.1	1940	55.1	62.6	164
Metro Hbk	N/A	N/A	48	43	10.6	58@ 3300	55@ 5700	9.5:1	EFI	1.0	3	8.4	32.8	42.5	43.9	47.2	48.9	48.9	36	39.1	53.5	54.5	93.1	1808	54.7	62.6	149
Metro LSi Sdn	33	29	43	39	10.6	74@ 3500	70@ 6000	9.5:1	EFI	1.3	4	10.3	32.8	42.5	42.9	46.9	48.3	49	37.3	39.3	53.5	54.5	93.1	1940	55.1	62.6	164
Metro LSi Hbk	N/A	N/A	48	43	10.6	58@ 3300	55@ 5700	9.5:1	EFI	1.0	3	8.4	32.8	42.5	43.9	47.2	48.9	48.9	36	39.1	53.5	54.5	93.1	1808	54.7	62.6	149
Prizm Sdn	29	26	34	27	13.2	100@ 4800	105@ 5800	9.5:1	MFI	1.6	4	12.7	33.1	41.7	54.2	54.3	53.4	54.1	36.4	38.5	57.1	57.5	97	2359	53.3	66.3	173
Prizm LSi Sdn	29	26	34	27	13.2	100@ 4800	105@ 5800	9.5:1	MFI	1.6	4	12.7	33.1	41.7	54.2	54.3	53.4	54.1	36.4	38.5	57.1	57.5	97	2370	53.3	66.3	173

Specifications EPA Mileage Ratings

HONDA

Model	EPA Hwy (mpg) - auto	EPA City (mpg) - auto	EPA Hwy (mpg) - manual	EPA City (mpg) - manual	Fuel Capacity	Torque @ RPM	Horsepower @ RPM	Compression Ratio	Fuel System	Displacement (liters)	Number of Cylinders	Luggage Capacity (cu ft.)	Rear Leg Room (in.)	Front Leg Room (in.)	Rear Hip Room (in.)	Front Hip Room (in.)	Rear Shoulder Room (in.)	Front Shoulder Room (in.)	Rear Head Room (in.)	Front Head Room (in.)	Rear Track (in.)	Front Track (in.)	Wheelbase (in.)	Curb Weight (lbs.)	Height (in.)	Width (in.)	Length (in.)
Accord DX Sdn	29	23	31	25	17	139@ 4200	130@ 5300	8.8:1	PGMFI	2.2	4	13	34.3	42.7	51.4	52.6	54.3	55.7	37.6	39.4	59.1	59.6	107	2800	55.1	70.1	184
Accord DX Cpe	29	23	31	25	17	139@ 4200	130@ 5300	8.8:1	MPFI	2.2	4	13	31.3	42.9	47.6	51.6	53.5	56	36.4	39.4	59.1	59.6	107	2756	54.7	70.1	184
Accord EX Wgn	30	23	31	25	17	147@ 4500	145@ 5500	8.8:1	PGMFI	2.2	4	25.7	34.1	42.7	51.4	52.6	54.3	55.7	36.4	38.4	59.1	59.6	107	3197	55.9	70.1	188
Accord EX Cpe	30	23	31	25	17	147@ 4500	145@ 5500	8.8:1	PGMFI	2.2	4	13	31.3	42.9	47.6	51.6	53.5	56	36.2	38.4	59.1	59.6	107	2954	54.7	70.1	184
Accord EX Sdn	30	23	31	25	17	147@ 4500	145@ 5500	8.8:1	PGMFI	2.2	4	13	34.3	42.7	51.4	52.6	54.3	55.7	36.7	38.4	59.1	59.6	107	3009	55.1	70.1	184
Accord EX V6 Sdn	N/A	N/A	N/A	N/A	17	165@ 4500	170@ 5600	9:1	PGMFI	2.7	6	13	34.3	42.7	51.4	52.6	54.3	55.7	36.7	38.4	59.1	59.6	107	3285	55.3	70.1	187
Accord LX Sdn	29	23	31	25	17	139@ 4200	130@ 5300	8.8:1	PGMFI	2.2	4	13	34.3	42.7	51.4	52.6	54.3	55.7	37.6	39.4	59.1	59.6	107	2877	55.1	70.1	184
Accord LX Wgn	27	21	30	24	17	139@ 4200	130@ 5300	8.8:1	PGMFI	2.2	4	25.7	34.1	42.7	51.4	52.6	54.3	55.7	39	39.8	59.1	59.6	107	3076	55.9	70.1	188
Accord LX Cpe	29	23	31	25	17	139@ 4200	130@ 5300	8.8:1	PGMFI	2.2	4	13	31.3	42.9	47.6	51.6	53.5	56	36.4	39.4	59.1	59.6	107	2822	54.7	70.1	184

Specifications EPA Mileage Ratings

HONDA

Specifications EPA Mileage Ratings	EPA Hwy (mpg) - auto	EPA City (mpg) - auto	EPA Hwy (mpg) - manual	EPA City (mpg) - manual	Fuel Capacity	Torque @ RPM	Horsepower @ RPM	Compression Ratio	Fuel System	Displacement (liters)	Number of Cylinders	Luggage Capacity (cu ft.)	Rear Leg Room (in.)	Front Leg Room (in.)	Rear Hip Room (in.)	Front Hip Room (in.)	Rear Shoulder Room (in.)	Front Shoulder Room (in.)	Rear Head Room (in.)	Front Head Room (in.)	Rear Track (in.)	Front Track (in.)	Wheelbase (in.)	Curb Weight (lbs.)	Height (in.)	Width (in.)	Length (in.)
Accord LX V6 Sdn	N/A	N/A	N/A	N/A	17	165@ 4500	170@ 5600	9:1	PGMFI	2.7	6	13	34.3	42.7	51.4	52.6	54.3	55.7	37.6	39.4	59.1	59.6	107	3219	55.3	70.1	187
Civic CX Hbk	N/A	N/A	46	42	10	91@ 2000	70@ 5000	9.1:1	PGMFI	1.5	4	13.3	30.5	42.5	44.6	49.8	52	53.4	36.6	38.6	57.7	58.1	101	2108	50.7	66.9	160
Civic DX Sdn	36	29	40	34	11.9	98@ 5000	102@ 5900	9.2:1	PGMFI	1.5	4	12.4	32.8	42.5	51.3	51	53.3	53.7	37.2	39.1	57.7	58.1	103	2313	51.7	66.9	173
Civic DX Cpe	36	29	40	34	11.9	98@ 5000	102@ 5900	9.2:1	PGMFI	1.5	4	11.8	29.3	42.5	45.7	49.8	52.1	53.4	35.1	38.6	57.7	58.1	103	2231	50.9	66.9	173
Civic DX Hbk	36	29	40	34	11.9	98@ 5000	102@ 5900	9.2:1	PGMFI	1.5	4	13.3	30.5	42.5	44.6	49.8	52	53.4	36.6	38.6	57.7	58.1	101	2178	50.7	66.9	160
Civic EX Sdn	34	26	35	29	11.9	106@ 5200	125@ 6600	9.2:1	PGMFI	1.6	4	12.4	32.8	42.5	51.3	51	53.3	53.7	36.3	38.1	57.7	58.1	103	2522	51.7	66.9	173
Civic EX Cpe	34	26	35	29	11.9	106@ 5200	125@ 6600	9.2:1	PGMFI	1.5	4	11.8	29.3	42.5	45.7	49.8	52.1	53.4	35.1	38	57.7	58.1	103	2443	50.9	66.9	173
Civic LX Sdn	36	29	40	34	11.9	98@ 5000	102@ 5900	9.2:1	PGMFI	1.5	4	12.4	32.8	42.5	51.3	51	53.3	53.7	37.2	39.1	57.7	58.1	103	2376	51.7	66.9	173
Civic Si Hbk	N/A	N/A	35	29	11.9	106@ 5200	125@ 6600	9.2:1	PGMFI	1.6	4	13.3	30.5	42.5	44.6	49.8	52	53.4	36.3	38.1	57.7	58.1	101	2390	50.7	66.9	160

Specifications EPA Mileage Ratings	EPA Hwy (mpg) - auto	EPA City (mpg) - auto	EPA Hwy (mpg) - manual	EPA City (mpg) - manual	Fuel Capacity	Torque @ RPM	Horsepower @ RPM	Compression Ratio	Fuel System	Displacement (liters)	Number of Cylinders	Luggage Capacity (cu ft.)	Rear Leg Room (in.)	Front Leg Room (in.)	Rear Hip Room (in.)	Front Hip Room (in.)	Rear Shoulder Room (in.)	Front Shoulder Room (in.)	Rear Head Room (in.)	Front Head Room (in.)	Rear Track (in.)	Front Track (in.)	Wheelbase (in.)	Curb Weight (lbs.)	Height (in.)	Width (in.)	Length (in.)
HONDA																											
Civic VX Hbk	N/A	N/A	56	47	10	97@ 4500	92@ 5500	9.3:1	PGMFI	1.5	4	13.3	30.5	42.5	44.6	49.8	52	53.4	36.6	38.6	57.7	58.1	101	2094	50.7	66.9	160
Civic del Sol S Cpe	36	29	41	35	11.9	98@ 5000	102@ 5900	9.2:1	PGMFI	1.5	4	10.5	N/A	40.3	N/A	49.3	N/A	52.9	N/A	37.5	57.7	58.1	93.3	2295	49.4	66.7	157
Civic del Sol Si Cpe	35	29	35	29	11.9	106@ 5200	125@ 6600	9.2:1	PGMFI	1.6	4	10.5	N/A	40.3	N/A	49.3	N/A	52.9	N/A	37.5	57.7	58.1	93.3	2414	49	66.7	157
Civic del Sol VTEC Cpe	30	26	28	23	11.9	111@ 7000	160@ 7600	10.2:1	PGMFI	1.6	4	10.5	N/A	40.3	N/A	49.3	N/A	52.9	N/A	37.5	57.7	58.1	93.3	2491	49	66.7	157
Prelude S Cpe	28	23	29	23	15.9	142@ 4000	135@ 5200	8.8:1	PGMFI	2.2	4	7.9	28.1	44.2	41.4	52.2	50.6	54	35.1	38	59.6	60	100	2809	50.8	69.5	175
Prelude Si Cpe	27	22	26	22	15.9	156@ 4500	160@ 5800	9.8:1	PGMFI	2.3	4	7.9	28.1	44.2	41.4	52.2	50.6	54	35.1	38	59.6	60	100	2866	50.8	69.5	175
Prelude VTEC Cpe	N/A	N/A	26	22	15.9	158@ 5500	190@ 6800	10:1	PGMFI	2.2	4	7.9	28.1	44.2	41.4	52.2	50.6	54	35.1	38	59.6	60	100	2932	50.8	69.5	175
HYUNDAI																											
Accent Sdn	36	28	38	29	11.9	96@ 3000	92@ 5500	10:1	MPI	1.5	4	10.7	32.7	42.6	53.6	53.5	52.2	52.8	38	38.7	55.5	55.9	94.5	2105	54.9	63.8	162

HYUNDAI

Specifications EPA Mileage Ratings	EPA Hwy (mpg) - auto	EPA City (mpg) - auto	EPA Hwy (mpg) - manual	EPA City (mpg) - manual	Fuel Capacity	Torque @ RPM	Horsepower @ RPM	Compression Ratio	Fuel System	Displacement (liters)	Number of Cylinders	Luggage Capacity (cu ft.)	Rear Leg Room (in.)	Front Leg Room (in.)	Rear Hip Room (in.)	Front Hip Room (in.)	Rear Shoulder Room (in.)	Front Shoulder Room (in.)	Rear Head Room (in.)	Front Head Room (in.)	Rear Track (in.)	Front Track (in.)	Wheelbase (in.)	Curb Weight (lbs.)	Height (in.)	Width (in.)	Length (in.)
Accent Hbk	36	28	38	29	11.9	96@ 3000	92@ 5500	10:1	MPI	1.5	4	16.2	32.7	42.6	51.8	53.5	52.4	52.8	37.8	38.7	55.5	55.9	94.5	2101	54.9	63.8	162
Accent L Hbk	36	28	38	29	11.9	96@ 3000	92@ 5500	10:1	MPI	1.5	4	16.2	32.7	42.6	51.8	53.5	52.4	52.8	37.8	38.7	55.5	55.9	94.5	2101	54.9	63.8	162
Elantra Base Sdn	N/A	N/A	29	22	13.7	102@ 5000	113@ 6000	12.2:1	MPFI	1.6	4	11.8	33.4	42.6	54.7	50.9	53.4	54.3	37.6	38.4	56.3	56.9	98.4	2500	52	66.1	173
Elantra GLS Sdn	29	22	28	21	13.7	116@ 4500	124@ 6000	12.2:1	MPFI	1.8	4	11.8	33.4	42.6	54.7	50.9	53.4	54.3	37.6	38.4	56.3	56.9	98.4	2581	52	66.1	173
Scoupe Base Cpe	34	25	36	28	11.9	97@ 4500	92@ 5500	12:1	MPFI	1.5	4	9.3	29.4	42.8	42.8	51.4	52.1	52.4	34.3	38.1	52.8	54.7	93.8	2176	50	63.9	166
Scoupe LS Cpe	34	25	36	28	11.9	97@ 4500	92@ 5500	12:1	MPFI	1.5	4	9.3	29.4	42.8	42.8	51.4	52.1	52.4	34.3	38.1	52.8	54.7	93.8	2266	50	63.9	166
Scoupe Turbo Cpe	N/A	N/A	33	27	11.9	123@ 4000	115@ 5500	12.5:1	MPFI	1.5	4	9.3	29.4	42.8	42.8	51.4	52.1	52.4	34.3	38.1	52.8	54.7	93.8	2240	50	63.9	166
Sonata Base Sdn	28	21	29	21	17.2	129@ 4000	137@ 6000	12.1:1	MPFI	2.0	4	13.2	36.6	43.3	57.1	57.9	56.4	58.2	37.7	38.5	59.1	59.6	106	2864	55.3	69.7	185
Sonata GL Sdn	28	21	N/A	N/A	17.2	129@ 4000	137@ 6000	12.1:1	MPFI	2.0	4	13.2	36.6	43.3	57.1	57.9	56.4	58.2	37.7	38.5	59.1	59.6	106	2864	55.3	69.7	185

Specifications EPA Mileage Ratings	EPA Hwy (mpg) - auto	EPA City (mpg) - auto	EPA Hwy (mpg) - manual	EPA City (mpg) - manual	Fuel Capacity	Torque @ RPM	Horsepower @ RPM	Compression Ratio	Fuel System	Displacement (liters)	Number of Cylinders	Luggage Capacity (cu ft.)	Rear Leg Room (in.)	Front Leg Room (in.)	Rear Hip Room (in.)	Front Hip Room (in.)	Rear Shoulder Room (in.)	Front Shoulder Room (in.)	Rear Head Room (in.)	Front Head Room (in.)	Rear Track (in.)	Front Track (in.)	Wheelbase (in.)	Curb Weight (lbs.)	Height (in.)	Width (in.)	Length (in.)
HYUNDAI																											
Sonata GL V6 Sdn	24	18	N/A	N/A	17.2	168@ 2500	142@ 5000	12.9:1	MPFI	3.0	6	13.2	36.6	43.3	57.1	57.9	56.4	58.2	37.7	38.5	59.1	59.6	106	3018	55.3	69.7	185
Sonata GLS V6 Sdn	24	18	N/A	N/A	17.2	168@ 2500	142@ 5000	12.9:1	MPFI	3.0	6	13.2	36.6	43.3	57.1	57.9	56.4	58.2	37.7	38.5	59.1	59.6	106	3018	55.3	69.7	185
INFINITI																											
G20 Sdn	28	22	32	24	15.9	132@ 4800	140@ 6400	12.5:1	SMPI	2.0	4	14.2	33.2	42	54.2	52.1	54.2	54.9	37.3	38.8	57.5	57.9	100	2877	54.7	66.7	175
J30 Sdn	23	18	N/A	N/A	19	193@ 4800	210@ 6400	12.5:1	SMPI	3.0	6	10.1	30.5	41.3	54.1	54.1	56.5	55.9	36.7	37.7	59.1	59.1	109	3527	54.7	69.7	191
Q45 Sdn	22	17	N/A	N/A	22.5	292@ 4000	278@ 6000	12.2:1	SMPI	4.5	8	14.8	32	43.9	56.4	55.2	57.5	58.3	36.3	38.2	62	61.8	113	4039	56.3	71.9	200
Q45a Sdn	21	15	N/A	N/A	22.5	292@ 4000	278@ 6000	12.2:1	SMPI	4.5	8	14.8	32	43.9	56.4	55.2	57.5	58.3	36.3	38.2	62	61.8	113	4259	56.3	71.9	200
JAGUAR																											
Vanden Plas Sdn	23	17	N/A	N/A	23.1	289@ 4000	245@ 4700	12:1	EFI	4.0	6	11.1	N/A	41.2	N/A	N/A	N/A	57.3	N/A	37.2	59	59.1	113	4080	70.8	81.7	198

Specifications EPA Mileage Ratings

	Length (in.)	Width (in.)	Height (in.)	Curb Weight (lbs.)	Wheelbase (in.)	Front Track (in.)	Rear Track (in.)	Front Head Room (in.)	Rear Head Room (in.)	Front Shoulder Room (in.)	Rear Shoulder Room (in.)	Front Hip Room (in.)	Rear Hip Room (in.)	Front Leg Room (in.)	Rear Leg Room (in.)	Luggage Capacity (cu ft.)	Number of Cylinders	Displacement (liters)	Fuel System	Compression Ratio	Horsepower @ RPM	Torque @ RPM	Fuel Capacity	EPA City (mpg) - manual	EPA Hwy (mpg) - manual	EPA City (mpg) - auto	EPA Hwy (mpg) - auto
JAGUAR																											
XJ12 Sdn	198	81.7	70.8	4420	113	59.1	59	37.2	N/A	57.3	N/A	N/A	N/A	41.2	N/A	12	12	6.0	EFI	12:1	313@ 5350	353@ 3750	23.1	N/A	N/A	12	16
XJ6 Sdn	198	81.7	70.8	4080	113	59.1	59	37.2	N/A	57.3	N/A	N/A	N/A	41.2	N/A	11.1	6	4.0	EFI	12:1	245@ 4700	289@ 4000	23.1	N/A	N/A	17	23
XJR Sdn	198	81.7	70.8	4215	113	59.1	59	37.2	N/A	57.3	N/A	N/A	N/A	41.2	N/A	11.1	6	4.0	EFI	12.5:1	322@ 5000	378@ 3050	23.1	N/A	N/A	15	21
XJS 4.0 Conv	191	74.1	48.7	4022	102	58.6	59.2	35.7	N/A	56.1	N/A	N/A	N/A	43	N/A	9.4	6	4.0	EFI	12:1	237@ 4700	282@ 4000	20.7	N/A	N/A	17	24
XJS 4.0 Cpe	191	74.1	48.7	3805	102	58.6	59.2	36.1	N/A	56.1	N/A	N/A	N/A	43	N/A	9.4	6	4.0	EFI	12:1	237@ 4700	282@ 4000	24	N/A	N/A	17	24
XJS 6.0 Conv	191	74.1	48.7	4306	102	58.6	59.2	35.7	N/A	56.1	N/A	N/A	N/A	43	N/A	10.7	12	6.0	EFI	12:1	301@ 5400	351@ 2800	20.7	N/A	N/A	12	16
XJS 6.0 Cpe	191	74.1	48.7	4053	102	58.6	59.2	36.1	N/A	56.1	N/A	N/A	N/A	43	N/A	9.4	12	6.0	EFI	12:1	301@ 5400	351@ 2800	24	N/A	N/A	12	17
KIA																											
Sephia Sdn	172	66.7	54.7	2454	98.4	56.7	56.5	38.2	37	54	53.5	55.3	55.3	42.9	34.4	11	4	1.6	MPFI	9:1	88@ 5000	98@ 4000	13.2	25	33	23	31

Specifications EPA Mileage Ratings	EPA Hwy (mpg) - auto	EPA City (mpg) - auto	EPA Hwy (mpg) - manual	EPA City (mpg) - manual	Fuel Capacity	Torque @ RPM	Horsepower @ RPM	Compression Ratio	Fuel System	Displacement (liters)	Number of Cylinders	Luggage Capacity (cu ft.)	Rear Leg Room (in.)	Front Leg Room (in.)	Rear Hip Room (in.)	Front Hip Room (in.)	Rear Shoulder Room (in.)	Front Shoulder Room (in.)	Rear Head Room (in.)	Front Head Room (in.)	Rear Track (in.)	Front Track (in.)	Wheelbase (in.)	Curb Weight (lbs.)	Height (in.)	Width (in.)	Length (in.)
LEXUS																											
ES 300 Sdn	28	20	N/A	N/A	18.5	203@ 4400	188@ 5200	12.5:1	SMPF	3.0	6	14.3	33.1	43.5	N/A	N/A	55.1	56.1	36.6	37.8	59.1	61	103	3374	53.9	70	188
GS 300 Sdn	23	18	N/A	N/A	21.1	210@ 4800	220@ 5800	12:1	MPFI	3.0	6	13	33.8	44	N/A	N/A	57.3	57.3	36.8	38.3	60.2	60.6	109	3660	55.1	70.7	195
LS 400 Sdn	25	19	N/A	N/A	22.5	270@ 4500	260@ 5300	12.4:1	SMPF	4.0	8	13.9	36.9	43.7	N/A	N/A	57.1	57.9	36.9	38.9	62	62	112	3650	55.7	72	197
SC 300 Cpe	23	17	23	18	20.6	210@ 4800	225@ 6000	12:1	MPFI	3.0	6	9.3	27.2	44.1	39.2	55.1	52.7	56	36.1	38.3	59.8	59.8	106	3555	52.6	70.5	191
SC 400 Cpe	23	18	N/A	N/A	20.6	260@ 4400	250@ 5600	12:1	MPFI	4.0	8	9.3	27.2	44.1	39.2	55.1	52.7	56	36.1	38.3	60	59.8	106	3625	52.6	70.5	191
LINCOLN																											
Continental Sdn	25	17	N/A	N/A	18	265@ 4750	260@ 5750	9.9:1	SEFI	4.6	8	18.1	39.2	41.8	56.5	55.5	56.6	57.2	38	39.1	61.5	63	109	3969	55.9	73.3	206
Mark VIII Cpe	25	18	N/A	N/A	18	285@ 4500	280@ 5500	9.9:1	SEFI	4.6	8	14.4	32.5	42.6	56.7	56.7	59.5	58.9	37.5	38.1	60.2	61.6	113	3768	53.6	74.8	207
Town Car Sdn	25	17	N/A	N/A	20	270@ 3250	210@ 4250	9:1	SEFI	4.6	8	22.3	41.1	42.6	57	57.2	62.1	62.1	38	39.1	63.3	62.8	117	4031	56.9	76.7	219

Specifications EPA Mileage Ratings	EPA Hwy (mpg) - auto	EPA City (mpg) - auto	EPA Hwy (mpg) - manual	EPA City (mpg) - manual	Fuel Capacity	Torque @ RPM	Horsepower @ RPM	Compression Ratio	Fuel System	Displacement (liters)	Number of Cylinders	Luggage Capacity (cu ft.)	Rear Leg Room (in.)	Front Leg Room (in.)	Rear Hip Room (in.)	Front Hip Room (in.)	Rear Shoulder Room (in.)	Front Shoulder Room (in.)	Rear Head Room (in.)	Front Head Room (in.)	Rear Track (in.)	Front Track (in.)	Wheelbase (in.)	Curb Weight (lbs.)	Height (in.)	Width (in.)	Length (in.)
MAZDA																											
626 DX Sdn	31	23	34	26	15.9	127@ 4500	118@ 5500	12:1	MPFI	2.0	4	13.8	35.8	43.5	N/A	N/A	54.7	55.1	37.8	39.2	59.1	59.1	103	2743	55.1	68.9	184
626 ES Sdn	26	20	26	21	15.5	160@ 4800	164@ 5600	12.2:1	MPFI	2.5	6	13.8	35.8	43.5	N/A	N/A	54.7	55.1	37.8	39.2	59.1	59.1	103	2906	55.1	68.9	184
626 LX Sdn	31	23	34	26	15.9	127@ 4500	118@ 5500	12:1	MPFI	2.0	4	13.8	35.8	43.5	N/A	N/A	54.7	55.1	37.8	39.2	59.1	59.1	103	2743	55.1	68.9	184
626 LX V6 Sdn	26	20	26	21	15.9	160@ 4800	164@ 5600	12.2:1	MPFI	2.5	6	13.8	35.8	43.5	N/A	N/A	54.7	55.1	37.8	39.2	59.1	59.1	103	2906	55.1	68.9	184
929 Sdn	24	19	N/A	N/A	18.5	200@ 3500	193@ 5750	12.2:1	MPFI	3.0	6	12.4	37	43.4	55.1	55.5	55.3	56.8	37.4	37.4	59.8	59.4	112	3627	54.9	70.7	194
Millenia Sdn	27	20	N/A	N/A	18	160@ 4800	170@ 5800	12.2:1	MPFI	2.5	6	13.3	34.1	43.3	N/A	N/A	54.2	55.1	37	39.3	60.2	60.2	108	3216	54.9	69.7	190
Millenia S Sdn	28	20	N/A	N/A	18	210@ 3500	210@ 5300	12:1	MPFI	2.3	6	13.3	34.1	43.3	N/A	N/A	54.2	55.1	37	39.3	59.8	59.8	108	3391	54.9	69.7	190
MX-3 Hbk	34	25	37	29	13.2	100@ 3600	105@ 6200	12:1	MPFI	1.6	4	36.6	31.1	42.6	45.2	51.1	48.2	52.2	33.9	38.2	57.7	57.5	96.3	2443	51.6	66.7	166
MX-5 Miata Conv	28	22	29	23	12.7	110@ 5000	128@ 6500	12:1	MPFI	1.8	4	3.6	N/A	42.7	N/A	51.7	N/A	50.4	N/A	37.1	56.2	55.5	89.2	2293	48.2	65.9	155

Specifications EPA Mileage Ratings	EPA Hwy (mpg) - auto	EPA City (mpg) - auto	EPA Hwy (mpg) - manual	EPA City (mpg) - manual	Fuel Capacity	Torque @ RPM	Horsepower @ RPM	Compression Ratio	Fuel System	Displacement (liters)	Number of Cylinders	Luggage Capacity (cu ft.)	Rear Leg Room (in.)	Front Leg Room (in.)	Rear Hip Room (in.)	Front Hip Room (in.)	Rear Shoulder Room (in.)	Front Shoulder Room (in.)	Rear Head Room (in.)	Front Head Room (in.)	Rear Track (in.)	Front Track (in.)	Wheelbase (in.)	Curb Weight (lbs.)	Height (in.)	Width (in.)	Length (in.)
MAZDA																											
MX-6 Cpe	31	23	34	26	15.5	127@ 4500	118@ 5500	12:1	MPFI	2.0	4	12.4	27.7	44	N/A	N/A	50.9	53.5	34.7	38.1	59.1	59.1	103	2625	51.6	68.9	182
MX-6 LS Cpe	26	20	26	21	15.5	160@ 4800	164@ 5600	12.2:1	MPFI	2.5	4	12.4	27.7	44	N/A	N/A	50.9	53.5	34.7	38.1	59.1	59.1	103	2800	51.6	68.9	182
Protege DX Sdn	35	26	39	31	14.5	96@ 4000	92@ 5500	12.4:1	MPFI	1.5	4	13.1	35.6	42.2	N/A	N/A	53.6	54.3	37.4	39.2	57.5	57.5	103	2385	55.9	67.3	175
Protege ES Sdn	29	23	32	26	14.5	117@ 4000	122@ 6000	12:1	MPFI	1.8	4	13.1	35.6	42.2	N/A	N/A	53.6	54.3	37.4	39.2	57.5	57.5	103	2573	55.9	67.3	175
Protege LX Sdn	35	26	39	31	14.5	96@ 4000	92@ 5500	12.4:1	MPFI	1.5	4	13.1	35.6	42.2	N/A	N/A	53.6	54.3	37.4	39.2	57.5	57.5	103	2445	55.9	67.3	175
RX-7 Cpe	24	18	25	17	20	217@ 5000	255@ 6500	12:1	EFI	1.3	RTRY	17	N/A	44.1	N/A	N/A	N/A	51.8	N/A	37.6	57.5	57.5	95.5	2826	48.4	68.9	169
MERCEDES-BENZ																											
C220 Sdn	28	23	N/A	N/A	16.4	155@ 4000	148@ 5500	12.8:1	SMPF	2.2	4	11.6	32.8	41.5	53.9	52.8	53.9	54.6	37	37.2	57.6	58.8	106	3150	56.1	67.7	177
C280 Sdn	26	20	N/A	N/A	16.4	199@ 3750	194@ 5500	12:1	SMPF	2.8	6	11.6	32.8	41.5	53.9	52.8	53.9	54.6	37	37.2	57.6	58.8	106	3350	56.1	67.7	177

Specifications EPA Mileage Ratings

MERCEDES-BENZ

Model	EPA Hwy (mpg) - auto	EPA City (mpg) - auto	EPA Hwy (mpg) - manual	EPA City (mpg) - manual	Fuel Capacity	Torque @ RPM	Horsepower @ RPM	Compression Ratio	Fuel System	Displacement (liters)	Number of Cylinders	Luggage Capacity (cu ft.)	Rear Leg Room (in.)	Front Leg Room (in.)	Rear Hip Room (in.)	Front Hip Room (in.)	Rear Shoulder Room (in.)	Front Shoulder Room (in.)	Rear Head Room (in.)	Front Head Room (in.)	Rear Track (in.)	Front Track (in.)	Wheelbase (in.)	Curb Weight (lbs.)	Height (in.)	Width (in.)	Length (in.)
E300D Sdn	32	26	N/A	N/A	23.8	155@ 2600	134@ 5000	12:1	FI	3.0	6	14.6	33.5	41.7	N/A	N/A	N/A	N/A	36.9	36.9	58.7	59.1	110	3485	56.3	68.5	187
E320 Cabriolet	23	18	N/A	N/A	18.5	229@ 3750	217@ 5500	12:1	SMPF	3.2	6	8.1	24.8	41.9	51	56.8	48.7	55.7	35.5	37.6	58.7	59.1	107	4025	54.8	68.5	184
E320 Cpe	26	20	N/A	N/A	18.5	229@ 3750	217@ 5500	12:1	SMPF	3.2	6	14.4	29.6	41.9	52.4	53.4	50.5	55.7	36.8	36	58.7	59.1	107	3525	54.9	68.5	184
E320 Sdn	26	20	N/A	N/A	18.5	229@ 3750	217@ 5500	12:1	SMPF	3.2	6	14.6	33.5	41.7	55.4	53	55.7	55.9	36.9	36.9	58.7	59.1	110	3525	56.3	68.5	187
E320 Wgn	24	18	N/A	N/A	19	229@ 3750	217@ 5500	12:1	SMPF	3.2	6	76.8	33.9	41.7	55.3	53	55.6	55.9	36.8	37.4	58.6	58.9	110	3750	59.8	68.5	188
E420 Sdn	24	18	N/A	N/A	18.5	295@ 3900	275@ 5700	12:1	SMPF	4.2	8	14.6	33.5	41.7	55.4	53	55.7	55.9	36.9	36.9	58.7	59.1	110	3745	56.3	68.5	187
S320 Sdn	24	17	N/A	N/A	26.4	232@ 3750	228@ 5600	12:1	SMPF	3.2	6	15.6	39.6	41.3	N/A	N/A	N/A	N/A	38.5	38	62.2	63.2	124	4610	58.4	74.3	205
S350D Sdn	28	21	N/A	N/A	26.4	229@ 2200	148@ 4000	12:1	FI	3.5	6	15.6	36.1	41.3	N/A	N/A	N/A	N/A	37.8	38	62.2	63.2	120	4610	58.4	74.3	201
S420 Sdn	20	15	N/A	N/A	26.4	295@ 3900	275@ 5700	12:1	SMPF	4.2	8	15.6	39.6	41.3	57.6	58	61.4	61.7	38.5	38	62.2	63.2	124	4700	58.4	74.3	205

Specifications EPA Mileage Ratings	EPA Hwy (mpg) - auto	EPA City (mpg) - auto	EPA Hwy (mpg) - manual	EPA City (mpg) - manual	Fuel Capacity	Torque @ RPM	Horsepower @ RPM	Compression Ratio	Fuel System	Displacement (liters)	Number of Cylinders	Luggage Capacity (cu ft.)	Rear Leg Room (in.)	Front Leg Room (in.)	Rear Hip Room (in.)	Front Hip Room (in.)	Rear Shoulder Room (in.)	Front Shoulder Room (in.)	Rear Head Room (in.)	Front Head Room (in.)	Rear Track (in.)	Front Track (in.)	Wheelbase (in.)	Curb Weight (lbs.)	Height (in.)	Width (in.)	Length (in.)
MERCEDES-BENZ																											
S500 Cpe	20	14	N/A	N/A	26.4	347@ 3900	315@ 5600	12:1	SMPF	5.0	8	14.2	31.5	41.7	53.1	56.7	56.5	61.7	37.2	36.5	62.2	63.2	116	4695	56.7	75.3	199
S500 Sdn	19	14	N/A	N/A	26.4	347@ 3900	315@ 5600	12:1	SMPF	5.0	8	15.6	39.6	41.3	57.6	58	61.4	61.7	38.5	38	62.2	63.2	124	4760	58.3	74.3	205
S600 Cpe	17	13	N/A	N/A	26.4	420@ 3800	389@ 5200	12:1	SMPF	6.0	12	14.2	31.5	41.7	53.1	56.7	56.5	61.7	37.2	36.5	62.2	63.2	116	4960	56.7	74.6	199
S600 Sdn	16	13	N/A	N/A	26.4	420@ 3800	389@ 5200	12:1	SMPF	6.0	12	15.6	39.6	41.3	57.6	58	61.4	61.7	38.5	38	62.2	63.2	124	5030	58.3	74.3	205
SL320 Conv	24	17	N/A	N/A	21.3	232@ 3750	229@ 5600	12:1	SMPF	3.2	4	7.9	N/A	42.4	N/A	53.2	N/A	55.4	N/A	37.1	60	60.4	99	4090	51.3	71.3	176
SL500 Conv	20	16	N/A	N/A	21.3	345@ 3900	315@ 5600	12:1	SMPF	5.0	8	7.9	N/A	42.4	N/A	53.2	N/A	55.4	N/A	37.1	60	60.4	99	4165	51.3	71.3	176
SL600 V12 Conv	17	13	N/A	N/A	21.3	420@ 3800	389@ 5200	12:1	SMPF	6.0	12	7.9	N/A	42.4	N/A	53.2	N/A	55.4	N/A	37.1	60	60.4	99	4455	51.3	71.3	178
MERCURY																											
Cougar XR7 Sdn	26	19	N/A	N/A	18	215@ 2400	140@ 3800	9:1	SEFI	3.8	6	15.1	36.5	42.5	56.6	55.6	58.9	59.1	37.6	38.1	60.2	61.6	113	3533	52.5	72.7	200

Specifications EPA Mileage Ratings

MERCURY

Specifications EPA Mileage Ratings	EPA Hwy (mpg) - auto	EPA City (mpg) - auto	EPA Hwy (mpg) - manual	EPA City (mpg) - manual	Fuel Capacity	Torque @ RPM	Horsepower @ RPM	Compression Ratio	Fuel System	Displacement (liters)	Number of Cylinders	Luggage Capacity (cu ft.)	Rear Leg Room (in.)	Front Leg Room (in.)	Rear Hip Room (in.)	Front Hip Room (in.)	Rear Shoulder Room (in.)	Front Shoulder Room (in.)	Rear Head Room (in.)	Front Head Room (in.)	Rear Track (in.)	Front Track (in.)	Wheelbase (in.)	Curb Weight (lbs.)	Height (in.)	Width (in.)	Length (in.)
Grnd Marquis GS Sdn	25	17	N/A	N/A	20	260@ 3250	190@ 4250	9:1	SEFI	4.6	8	20.6	38.4	42.5	59	58	60.3	60.1	38.1	39.4	63.3	62.8	114	3761	56.8	77.8	212
Grnd Marquis LS Sdn	25	17	N/A	N/A	20	260@ 3250	190@ 4250	9:1	SEFI	4.6	8	20.6	38.4	42.5	59	58	60.3	60.1	38.1	39.4	63.3	62.8	114	3761	56.8	77.8	212
Mystique GS Sdn	32	24	35	24	14.5	130@ 4000	125@ 5500	9.6:1	SEFI	2.0	4	13.9	34.3	42.4	45.5	50.7	53.3	53.9	36.7	39	58.5	59.2	107	2824	54.5	69.1	184
Mystique LS Sdn	32	24	35	24	14.5	130@ 4000	125@ 5500	9.6:1	SEFI	2.0	4	13.9	34.3	42.4	45.5	50.7	53.3	53.9	36.7	39	58.5	59.2	107	2824	54.5	69.1	184
Sable GS Wgn	30	20	N/A	N/A	16	165@ 3250	140@ 4800	9.3:1	SEFI	3.0	6	38.2	36.9	41.7	57	54.8	57.5	57.5	38.1	38.6	59.9	61.6	106	3292	55.5	71.2	193
Sable GS Sdn	30	20	N/A	N/A	16	165@ 3250	140@ 4800	9.3:1	SEFI	3.0	6	18	37.1	41.7	55.6	54.8	57.5	57.5	37.7	38.3	60.5	61.6	106	3144	54.1	71.2	192
Sable LS Sdn	30	20	N/A	N/A	16	165@ 3250	140@ 4800	9.3:1	SEFI	3.0	6	18	37.1	41.7	55.6	54.8	57.5	57.5	37.7	38.3	60.5	61.6	106	3144	54.1	71.2	192
Sable LS Wgn	30	20	N/A	N/A	16	165@ 3250	140@ 4800	9.3:1	SEFI	3.0	6	38.2	36.9	41.7	57	54.8	57.5	57.5	38.1	38.6	59.9	61.6	106	3292	55.5	71.2	193
Sable LTS Sdn	30	20	N/A	N/A	16	165@ 3250	140@ 4800	9.3:1	SEFI	3.0	6	18	37.1	41.7	55.6	54.8	57.5	57.5	37.7	38.3	60.5	61.6	106	3144	54.1	71.2	192

Specifications EPA Mileage Ratings	EPA Hwy (mpg) - auto	EPA City (mpg) - auto	EPA Hwy (mpg) - manual	EPA City (mpg) - manual	Fuel Capacity	Torque @ RPM	Horsepower @ RPM	Compression Ratio	Fuel System	Displacement (liters)	Number of Cylinders	Luggage Capacity (cu ft.)	Rear Leg Room (in.)	Front Leg Room (in.)	Rear Hip Room (in.)	Front Hip Room (in.)	Rear Shoulder Room (in.)	Front Shoulder Room (in.)	Rear Head Room (in.)	Front Head Room (in.)	Rear Track (in.)	Front Track (in.)	Wheelbase (in.)	Curb Weight (lbs.)	Height (in.)	Width (in.)	Length (in.)
MERCURY																											
Tracer Wgn	34	26	38	30	11.9	108@ 3800	88@ 4400	9:1	SEFI	1.9	4	30.6	34.6	41.7	48	50.4	53.7	53	38.5	38.4	56.5	56.5	98.4	2498	53.6	66.7	171
Tracer Sdn	34	26	38	30	11.9	108@ 3800	88@ 4400	9:1	SEFI	1.9	4	12.1	34.6	41.7	48	50.4	53.7	53	37.4	38.4	56.5	56.5	98.4	2418	52.7	66.7	171
Tracer LTS Sdn	29	23	31	25	13.2	114@ 4500	127@ 6500	9:1	EFI	1.8	4	12.1	34.6	41.7	48	50.4	53.7	53	37.4	38.4	56.5	56.5	98.4	2472	52.7	66.7	171
MITSUBISHI																											
3000GT Base Cpe	24	18	25	19	19.8	205@ 4500	222@ 6000	12:1	MPFI	3.0	6	11.1	28.5	44.2	46.9	56.7	52	55.9	34.1	37.1	62.2	61.4	97.2	3252	49	72.4	180
3000GT SL Cpe	24	18	25	19	19.8	205@ 4500	222@ 6000	12:1	MPFI	3.0	6	11.1	28.5	44.2	46.9	56.7	52	55.9	34.1	37.1	62.2	61.4	97.2	3351	49	72.4	180
3000GT VR-4 Cpe	N/A	N/A	24	18	19.8	315@ 2500	320@ 6000	12:1	MPFI	3.0	6	11.1	28.5	44.2	46.9	56.7	52	55.9	34.1	37.1	62.2	61.4	97.2	3781	49.3	72.4	180
Diamante Wgn	24	18	N/A	N/A	18.8	185@ 3000	175@ 5500	10:1	MPFI	3.0	6	72	36	43.9	53.9	54.2	55.2	54.7	38.4	39.2	59.3	60.4	107	3638	57.9	69.9	192
Diamante LS Sdn	25	18	N/A	N/A	19	201@ 3500	202@ 6000	12:1	MPFI	3.0	6	13.6	34.2	43.9	53.5	54.2	55.4	54.7	36.9	38.6	60.2	60.4	107	3605	52.6	69.9	190

Specifications EPA Mileage Ratings

MITSUBISHI

Model	EPA Hwy (mpg) - auto	EPA City (mpg) - auto	EPA Hwy (mpg) - manual	EPA City (mpg) - manual	Fuel Capacity	Torque @ RPM	Horsepower @ RPM	Compression Ratio	Fuel System	Displacement (liters)	Number of Cylinders	Luggage Capacity (cu ft.)	Rear Leg Room (in.)	Front Leg Room (in.)	Rear Hip Room (in.)	Front Hip Room (in.)	Rear Shoulder Room (in.)	Front Shoulder Room (in.)	Rear Head Room (in.)	Front Head Room (in.)	Rear Track (in.)	Front Track (in.)	Wheelbase (in.)	Curb Weight (lbs.)	Height (in.)	Width (in.)	Length (in.)
Eclipse GS Cpe	31	22	32	22	16.9	130@ 4800	140@ 6000	12.6:1	SEFI	2.0	4	16.6	28.4	43.3	47.2	55.1	51.2	53.1	34.1	37.9	59.4	59.6	98.8	2822	49.8	68.3	172
Eclipse GS-T Cpe	27	20	31	23	15.9	214@ 3000	210@ 6000	12.5:1	SEFI	2.0	4	16.6	28.4	43.3	47.2	55.1	51.2	53.1	34.1	37.9	59.4	59.6	98.8	2877	51	68.7	172
Eclipse GSX Cpe	25	19	27	21	15.9	214@ 3000	210@ 6000	12.5:1	SEFI	2.0	4	13.5	28.4	43.3	47.2	55.1	51.2	53.1	34.1	37.9	59.4	59.6	98.8	3120	51.6	68.7	172
Eclipse RS Cpe	31	22	32	22	16.9	130@ 4800	140@ 6000	12.6:1	SEFI	2.0	4	16.6	28.4	43.3	47.2	55.1	51.2	53.1	34.1	37.9	59.4	59.6	98.8	2723	49.8	68.3	172
Galant ES Sdn	28	22	N/A	N/A	16.9	148@ 3000	141@ 5500	12.5:1	MPFI	2.4	4	12.5	35	43.3	52.6	53.5	55.7	55.7	37.5	39.4	59.3	59.4	104	2866	53.1	68.1	187
Galant LS Sdn	28	22	N/A	N/A	16.9	148@ 3000	141@ 5500	12.5:1	MPFI	2.4	4	12.5	35	43.3	52.6	53.5	55.7	55.7	37.5	37.3	59.3	59.4	104	2976	53.1	68.1	187
Galant S Sdn	28	22	30	23	16.9	148@ 3000	141@ 5500	12.5:1	MPFI	2.4	4	12.5	35	43.3	57.1	57.3	55.7	55.7	37.5	39.4	59.3	59.4	104	2755	53.1	68.1	187
Mirage LS Cpe	33	26	33	26	13.2	116@ 4500	113@ 6000	12.5:1	MPFI	1.8	4	10.5	31.1	42.9	53.7	52.7	54.1	53.9	36.4	38.6	57.5	57.1	96.1	2125	51.6	66.5	171
Mirage S Cpe	32	28	39	32	13.2	93@ 3000	92@ 6000	12.2:1	MPFI	1.5	4	10.5	31.1	42.9	53.7	54.9	54.1	53.9	36.4	38.6	57.5	57.1	96.1	2085	51.6	66.1	171

Specifications EPA Mileage Ratings

NISSAN

Specifications EPA Mileage Ratings	EPA Hwy (mpg) - auto	EPA City (mpg) - auto	EPA Hwy (mpg) - manual	EPA City (mpg) - manual	Fuel Capacity	Torque @ RPM	Horsepower @ RPM	Compression Ratio	Fuel System	Displacement (liters)	Number of Cylinders	Luggage Capacity (cu ft.)	Rear Leg Room (in.)	Front Leg Room (in.)	Rear Hip Room (in.)	Front Hip Room (in.)	Rear Shoulder Room (in.)	Front Shoulder Room (in.)	Rear Head Room (in.)	Front Head Room (in.)	Rear Track (in.)	Front Track (in.)	Wheelbase (in.)	Curb Weight (lbs.)	Height (in.)	Width (in.)	Length (in.)
200SX Cpe	37	28	40	30	13.2	108@ 4000	115@ 6000	9.9:1	SMPI	1.6	4	10.4	31.4	42.3	52.5	50.3	52.9	52.1	35.4	39.1	56.9	58.3	99.8	2320	54.2	66.6	170
200SX SE Cpe	37	28	40	30	13.2	108@ 4000	115@ 6000	9.9:1	SMPI	1.6	4	10.4	31.4	42.3	52.5	50.3	52.9	52.1	35.4	39.1	56.5	57.9	99.8	2366	54.2	66.6	170
200SX SE-R Cpe	31	24	31	24	13.2	132@ 4800	140@ 6400	9.5:1	SMPI	2.0	4	10.4	31.4	42.3	52.5	50.3	52.9	52.1	35.4	39.1	56.5	57.9	99.8	2536	54.2	66.6	170
240SX Cpe	26	21	28	22	17.2	160@ 4400	155@ 5600	12.5:1	SMPF	2.4	4	8.5	20.8	42.6	42.2	50.6	42.2	52	34.3	38.3	57.9	58.3	99.4	2753	50.8	68.1	177
240SX SE Cpe	26	21	28	22	17.2	160@ 4400	155@ 5600	12.5:1	SMPF	2.4	4	8.5	20.8	42.6	42.2	50.6	42.2	52	34.3	38.3	57.9	58.3	99.4	2760	50.8	68.1	177
300ZX Conv	23	18	24	18	18.2	198@ 4800	222@ 6400	10.5:1	MPFI	3.0	6	5.8	N/A	43	N/A	53.5	N/A	56.7	N/A	37.1	60.4	58.9	96.5	3446	49.5	70.5	170
300ZX Hbk	23	18	24	18	18.7	198@ 4800	222@ 6400	10.5:1	MPFI	3.0	6	23.7	N/A	43	N/A	53.5	N/A	56.7	N/A	36.8	60.4	58.9	96.5	3300	48.3	70.5	170
300ZX 2+2 Hbk	23	18	24	18	18.7	198@ 4800	222@ 6400	10.5:1	MPFI	3.0	6	11.5	22.7	43	41.2	53.5	55.2	56.7	34.4	37.1	60.4	58.9	101	3414	48.1	70.9	178
300ZX Turbo Hbk	23	18	24	18	18.7	283@ 3600	300@ 6400	8.5:1	MPFI	3.0	6	23.7	N/A	43	N/A	53.5	N/A	56.7	N/A	36.8	61.2	58.9	96.5	3518	48.4	70.5	170

Specifications EPA Mileage Ratings	EPA Hwy (mpg) - auto	EPA City (mpg) - auto	EPA Hwy (mpg) - manual	EPA City (mpg) - manual	Fuel Capacity	Torque @ RPM	Horsepower @ RPM	Compression Ratio	Fuel System	Displacement (liters)	Number of Cylinders	Luggage Capacity (cu ft.)	Rear Leg Room (in.)	Front Leg Room (in.)	Rear Hip Room (in.)	Front Hip Room (in.)	Rear Shoulder Room (in.)	Front Shoulder Room (in.)	Rear Head Room (in.)	Front Head Room (in.)	Rear Track (in.)	Front Track (in.)	Wheelbase (in.)	Curb Weight (lbs.)	Height (in.)	Width (in.)	Length (in.)
NISSAN																											
Altima GLE Sdn	29	21	30	24	15.9	154@ 4400	150@ 5600	12.2:1	SMPF	2.4	4	14	34.7	42.6	52.4	52.8	54	54.8	37.6	39.3	57.3	57.7	103	3032	55.9	67.1	181
Altima GXE Sdn	29	21	30	24	15.9	154@ 4400	150@ 5600	12.2:1	SMPF	2.4	4	14	34.7	42.6	52.4	52.8	54	54.8	37.6	39.3	57.3	57.7	103	2972	55.9	67.1	181
Altima SE Sdn	29	21	30	24	15.9	154@ 4400	150@ 5600	12.2:1	SMPF	2.4	4	14	34.7	42.6	52.4	52.8	54	54.8	37.6	39.3	57.3	57.7	103	2968	55.9	67.1	181
Altima XE Sdn	29	21	30	24	15.9	154@ 4400	150@ 5600	12.2:1	SMPF	2.4	4	14	34.7	42.6	52.4	52.8	54	54.8	37.6	39.3	57.3	57.7	103	2924	55.9	67.1	181
Maxima GLE Sdn	28	21	N/A	N/A	18.5	205@ 4000	190@ 5600	12:1	SMPF	3.0	6	14.5	34.3	43.9	55.9	54.3	56.2	56.8	37.4	40.1	59.1	59.8	106	3097	56	69.7	188
Maxima GXE Sdn	28	21	27	22	18.5	205@ 4000	190@ 5600	12:1	SMPF	3.0	6	14.5	34.3	43.9	55.9	54.3	56.2	56.8	37.4	40.1	59.1	60.2	106	3001	56	69.7	188
Maxima SE Sdn	28	21	27	22	18.5	205@ 4000	190@ 5600	12:1	SMPF	3.0	6	14.5	34.3	43.9	55.9	54.3	56.2	56.8	37.4	40.1	59.1	59.8	106	3010	56	69.7	188
Sentra Base Cpe	37	28	40	30	13.2	108@ 4000	115@ 6000	9.9:1	SMPI	1.6	4	10.7	32.4	42.3	52.8	50.1	53.1	53.2	36.5	39.1	56.9	58.3	99.8	2300	54.5	66.6	170
Sentra GLE Cpe	37	28	40	30	13.2	108@ 4000	115@ 6000	9.9:1	SMPI	1.6	4	10.7	32.4	42.3	52.8	50.1	53.1	53.2	36.5	39.1	56.5	57.9	99.8	2440	54.5	66.6	170

Specifications EPA Mileage Ratings	EPA Hwy (mpg) - auto	EPA City (mpg) - auto	EPA Hwy (mpg) - manual	EPA City (mpg) - manual	Fuel Capacity	Torque @ RPM	Horsepower @ RPM	Compression Ratio	Fuel System	Displacement (liters)	Number of Cylinders	Luggage Capacity (cu ft.)	Rear Leg Room (in.)	Front Leg Room (in.)	Rear Hip Room (in.)	Front Hip Room (in.)	Rear Shoulder Room (in.)	Front Shoulder Room (in.)	Rear Head Room (in.)	Front Head Room (in.)	Rear Track (in.)	Front Track (in.)	Wheelbase (in.)	Curb Weight (lbs.)	Height (in.)	Width (in.)	Length (in.)
NISSAN																											
Sentra GXE Sdn	37	28	40	30	13.2	108@ 4000	115@ 6000	9.9:1	SMPI	1.6	4	10.7	32.4	42.3	52.8	50.1	53.1	53.2	36.5	39.1	56.9	58.3	99.8	2400	54.5	66.6	170
Sentra XE Sdn	37	28	40	30	13.2	108@ 4000	115@ 6000	9.9:1	SMPI	1.6	4	10.7	32.4	42.3	52.8	50.1	53.1	53.2	36.5	39.1	56.9	58.3	99.8	2349	54.5	66.6	170
OLDSMOBILE																											
88 LSS Sdn	29	19	N/A	N/A	18	230@ 4000	205@ 5200	9.4:1	SMPI	3.8	6	17.5	38.7	42.5	54.1	55.4	58.3	59	38.3	38.7	60.4	60.4	111	3429	55.7	74.1	200
88 Royale Sdn	29	19	N/A	N/A	18	230@ 4000	205@ 5200	9.4:1	SMPI	3.8	6	17.5	38.7	42.5	54.1	55.4	58.3	59	38.3	38.7	60.4	60.4	111	3400	55.7	74.1	200
98 Elite Series I Sdn	29	19	N/A	N/A	18	230@ 4000	205@ 5200	9.4:1	SMPI	3.8	6	20.2	40.7	42.7	54.8	56.5	58.1	59	37.7	38.8	60.6	60.4	111	3515	54.8	74.6	206
98 Elite Series II Sdn	29	19	N/A	N/A	18	230@ 4000	205@ 5200	9.4:1	SMPI	3.8	6	20.2	40.7	42.7	54.8	56.5	58.1	59	37.7	38.8	60.6	60.4	111	3515	54.8	74.6	206
Achieva S Series I Sdn	30	21	33	22	15.2	145@ 4800	150@ 6000	9.5:1	MPFI	2.3	4	14	33.5	43.3	50.2	49.2	53.4	54.1	37	37.8	55.3	55.6	103	2779	53.1	67.2	188
Achieva S Series I Cpe	30	21	33	22	15.2	145@ 4800	150@ 6000	9.5:1	MPFI	2.3	4	14	32.5	43.3	50.3	49.1	55	53.6	36.5	37.8	55.3	55.6	103	2717	53.1	67.2	188

Specifications EPA Mileage Ratings	EPA Hwy (mpg) - auto	EPA City (mpg) - auto	EPA Hwy (mpg) - manual	EPA City (mpg) - manual	Fuel Capacity	Torque @ RPM	Horsepower @ RPM	Compression Ratio	Fuel System	Displacement (liters)	Number of Cylinders	Luggage Capacity (cu ft.)	Rear Leg Room (in.)	Front Leg Room (in.)	Rear Hip Room (in.)	Front Hip Room (in.)	Rear Shoulder Room (in.)	Front Shoulder Room (in.)	Rear Head Room (in.)	Front Head Room (in.)	Rear Track (in.)	Front Track (in.)	Wheelbase (in.)	Curb Weight (lbs.)	Height (in.)	Width (in.)	Length (in.)
OLDSMOBILE																											
Achieva S Series II Cpe	30	21	33	22	15.2	145@ 4800	150@ 6000	9.5:1	MPFI	2.3	4	14	32.5	43.3	50.3	49.1	55	53.6	36.5	37.8	55.3	55.6	103	2717	53.1	67.2	188
Achieva S Series II Sdn	30	21	33	22	15.2	145@ 4800	150@ 6000	9.5:1	MPFI	2.3	4	14	33.5	43.3	50.2	49.2	53.4	54.1	37	37.8	55.3	55.6	103	2779	53.1	67.2	188
Aurora Sdn	25	16	N/A	N/A	20	260@ 4400	250@ 5600	10.3:1	TPI	4.0	8	16.1	38.4	42.6	55.8	55.1	57.9	57.9	36.9	38.4	62.6	62.5	114	2779	55.4	74.4	205
Ciera SL Cruiser Wgn	32	22	N/A	N/A	16.5	185@ 4000	160@ 5200	9.6:1	SMPI	3.1	6	74.4	34.7	42.1	54.3	50.3	56	55.8	38.9	38.6	57	58.7	105	3224	54.5	69.5	194
Ciera SL Series I Sdn	31	25	N/A	N/A	16.5	130@ 4000	120@ 5200	9:1	MPFI	2.2	4	15.8	35.8	42.1	54.3	50.3	56	55.8	38.3	38.6	57	58.7	105	2931	54.1	69.5	190
Ciera SL Series II Sdn	29	19	N/A	N/A	16.5	185@ 4000	160@ 5200	9.6:1	SPFI	3.1	6	15.8	35.8	42.1	54.3	50.3	56	55.8	38.3	38.6	57	58.7	105	3058	54.1	69.5	190
Cutlass Suprm Conv	28	19	N/A	N/A	16.5	185@ 4000	160@ 5200	9.6:1	SMPI	3.1	6	12.1	34.8	42.3	51.5	51.9	57.2	57.6	38.9	38.5	58	59.5	107	3629	54.3	71	194
Cutlass Suprm Series I Sdn	28	19	N/A	N/A	16.5	185@ 4000	160@ 5200	9.6:1	SMPI	3.1	6	15.5	36.2	42.4	55	52.6	56.6	57.4	38.3	38.7	58	59.5	107	3369	54.8	71	194
Cutlass Suprm Series I S Cpe	28	19	N/A	N/A	16.5	185@ 4000	160@ 5200	9.6:1	SMPI	3.1	6	15.5	34.8	42.3	53.3	51.9	57.2	57.6	37	37.6	58	59.5	107	3286	53.3	71	194

Specifications EPA Mileage Ratings	EPA Hwy (mpg) - auto	EPA City (mpg) - auto	EPA Hwy (mpg) - manual	EPA City (mpg) - manual	Fuel Capacity	Torque @ RPM	Horsepower @ RPM	Compression Ratio	Fuel System	Displacement (liters)	Number of Cylinders	Luggage Capacity (cu ft.)	Rear Leg Room (in.)	Front Leg Room (in.)	Rear Hip Room (in.)	Front Hip Room (in.)	Rear Shoulder Room (in.)	Front Shoulder Room (in.)	Rear Head Room (in.)	Front Head Room (in.)	Rear Track (in.)	Front Track (in.)	Wheelbase (in.)	Curb Weight (lbs.)	Height (in.)	Width (in.)	Length (in.)
OLDSMOBILE																											
Cutlass Suprm Series II Sdn	28	19	N/A	N/A	16.5	185@ 4000	160@ 5200	9.6:1	SMPI	3.1	6	15.5	36.2	42.4	55	52.6	56.6	57.4	38.3	38.7	58	59.5	107	3369	54.8	71	194
Cutlass Suprm Series II S Cpe	28	19	N/A	N/A	16.5	185@ 4000	160@ 5200	9.6:1	SMPI	3.1	6	15.5	34.8	42.3	53.3	51.9	57.2	57.6	37	37.6	58	59.5	107	3286	53.3	71	194
PLYMOUTH																											
Acclaim Sdn	27	22	N/A	N/A	16	135@ 2800	100@ 4800	8.9:1	EFI	2.5	4	14.4	38.3	41.9	52	51.7	55	54.3	37.9	38.4	57.2	57.6	104	2862	53.5	68.1	181
Neon Sdn	33	27	38	29	11.2	129@ 5000	132@ 6000	9.8:1	SMPI	2.0	4	11.8	33.9	42.5	50.6	50.8	52.3	52.5	36.5	39.6	57.4	57.4	104	2320	54.8	67.4	172
Neon Highline Cpe	33	27	38	29	11.2	129@ 5000	132@ 6000	12.8:1	SMPI	2.0	4	11.8	35.1	42.5	53.9	50.3	54.7	52	36.5	39.6	57.4	57.4	104	2384	52.8	67.2	172
Neon Highline Sdn	33	27	38	29	11.2	129@ 5000	132@ 6000	12.8:1	SMPI	2.0	4	11.8	33.9	42.5	50.6	50.8	52.3	52.5	36.5	39.6	57.4	57.4	104	2320	54.8	67.4	172
Neon Sport Sdn	33	27	38	29	11.2	129@ 5000	132@ 6800	12.8:1	SMPI	2.0	4	11.8	33.9	42.5	50.6	50.8	52.3	52.5	36.5	39.6	57.4	57.4	104	2421	54.8	67.4	172
Neon Sport 2.0L DOHC Cpe	33	27	38	29	11.2	131@ 5600	150@ 6800	12.8:1	SMPI	2.0	4	11.8	35.1	42.5	53.9	50.3	54.7	52	36.5	39.6	57.4	57.4	104	2485	52.8	67.2	172

Specifications EPA Mileage Ratings

PONTIAC

Specifications EPA Mileage Ratings	EPA Hwy (mpg) - auto	EPA City (mpg) - auto	EPA Hwy (mpg) - manual	EPA City (mpg) - manual	Fuel Capacity	Torque @ RPM	Horsepower @ RPM	Compression Ratio	Fuel System	Displacement (liters)	Number of Cylinders	Luggage Capacity (cu ft.)	Rear Leg Room (in.)	Front Leg Room (in.)	Rear Hip Room (in.)	Front Hip Room (in.)	Rear Shoulder Room (in.)	Front Shoulder Room (in.)	Rear Head Room (in.)	Front Head Room (in.)	Rear Track (in.)	Front Track (in.)	Wheelbase (in.)	Curb Weight (lbs.)	Height (in.)	Width (in.)	Length (in.)
Bonneville SE Sdn	28	19	N/A	N/A	18	230@ 4000	205@ 5200	9.4:1	SPFI	3.8	6	18	38	42.6	57.1	57.2	59.4	59.8	38.3	39.2	60.3	60.4	111	3446	55.7	74.5	200
Bonneville SSE Sdn	28	19	N/A	N/A	18	230@ 4000	205@ 5200	9.4:1	SPFI	3.8	6	18	38	42.6	57.1	57.2	59.4	59.8	38.3	39.2	60.6	60.8	111	3587	55.7	74.5	201
Firebird Conv	28	19	28	19	15.5	200@ 3600	160@ 4600	9:1	SPFI	3.4	6	12.9	28.9	43	44.4	52.8	55.8	57.4	35.3	37.2	60.6	60.7	101	3346	52	74.5	196
Firebird Cpe	28	19	28	19	15.5	200@ 3600	160@ 4600	9:1	SPFI	3.4	6	12.9	28.9	43	44.4	52.8	55.8	57.4	35.3	37.2	60.6	60.7	101	3230	52	74.5	196
Firebird Formula Conv	24	17	25	17	15.5	325@ 2400	275@ 5000	10.5:1	SPFI	5.7	8	12.9	28.9	43	44.4	52.8	55.8	57.4	35.3	37.2	60.6	60.7	101	3373	52	74.5	196
Firebird Formula Cpe	24	17	25	17	15.5	325@ 2400	275@ 5000	10.5:1	SPFI	5.7	8	12.9	28.9	43	44.4	52.8	55.8	57.4	35.3	37.2	60.6	60.7	101	3373	52	74.5	196
Firebird Trans Am Conv	24	17	25	17	15.5	325@ 2400	275@ 5000	10.5:1	SPFI	5.7	8	12.9	28.9	43	44.4	52.8	55.8	57.4	35.3	37.2	60.6	60.7	101	3610	52	74.5	196
Firebird Trans Am Cpe	24	17	25	17	15.5	325@ 2400	275@ 5000	10.5:1	SPFI	5.7	8	12.9	28.9	43	44.4	52.8	55.8	57.4	35.3	37.2	60.6	60.7	101	3345	52	74.5	196
Grand Am GT Cpe	31	21	32	21	15.2	145@ 4800	150@ 6000	9.5:1	MPFI	2.3	4	13.3	33.9	43.1	48.7	49.1	55.4	53.9	36.5	37.8	55.3	55.8	103	2888	53.5	68.7	187

Specifications EPA Mileage Ratings

PONTIAC

Specifications EPA Mileage Ratings	EPA Hwy (mpg) - auto	EPA City (mpg) - auto	EPA Hwy (mpg) - manual	EPA City (mpg) - manual	Fuel Capacity	Torque @ RPM	Horsepower @ RPM	Compression Ratio	Fuel System	Displacement (liters)	Number of Cylinders	Luggage Capacity (cu ft.)	Rear Leg Room (in.)	Front Leg Room (in.)	Rear Hip Room (in.)	Front Hip Room (in.)	Rear Shoulder Room (in.)	Front Shoulder Room (in.)	Rear Head Room (in.)	Front Head Room (in.)	Rear Track (in.)	Front Track (in.)	Wheelbase (in.)	Curb Weight (lbs.)	Height (in.)	Width (in.)	Length (in.)
Grand Am GT Sdn	31	21	32	21	15.2	145@ 4800	150@ 6000	9.5:1	MPFI	2.3	4	13.3	34.9	43.1	50.2	49.1	54.2	53.9	37	37.8	55.3	55.8	103	2941	53.5	68.7	187
Grand Am SE Sdn	30	21	33	22	15.2	145@ 4800	150@ 6000	9.5:1	MPFI	2.3	4	13.3	34.9	43.1	50.2	49.1	54.2	53.9	37	37.8	55.3	55.8	103	2881	53.5	68.7	187
Grand Am SE Cpe	30	21	33	22	15.2	145@ 4800	150@ 6000	9.5:1	MPFI	2.3	4	13.3	33.9	43.1	48.7	49.1	55.4	53.9	36.5	37.8	55.3	55.8	103	2824	53.5	68.7	187
Grand Prix GT Sdn	27	17	N/A	N/A	17.1	215@ 4000	210@ 5000	9.2:1	SPFI	3.4	6	15.5	36.2	42.4	54.3	53.1	57.4	57.2	37.7	38.6	58	59.5	108	3318	54.8	71.9	195
Grand Prix GTP Cpe	27	17	N/A	N/A	17.1	215@ 4000	210@ 5000	9.2:1	SPFI	3.4	6	14.9	34.8	42.3	53	52	57.3	57.3	36.6	37.8	58	59.5	108	3243	52.8	71.9	195
Grand Prix SE Sdn	28	19	N/A	N/A	17.1	185@ 4000	160@ 5200	9.5:1	SPFI	3.1	6	15.5	36.2	42.4	54.3	53.1	57.4	57.2	37.7	38.6	58	59.5	108	3318	54.8	71.9	195
Grand Prix SE Cpe	28	19	N/A	N/A	17.1	185@ 4000	160@ 5200	9.5:1	SPFI	3.1	6	14.9	34.8	42.3	53.3	52	57.3	57.3	36.6	37.8	58	59.5	108	3243	52.8	71.9	195
Sunfire GT Cpe	31	21	32	22	15.2	145@ 4800	150@ 6000	9.5:1	SPFI	2.3	4	12.4	32	42.4	50.9	48.7	54	54.1	36.6	37.6	56.7	57.6	104	2829	53.2	67.4	182
Sunfire SE Conv	31	24	35	24	15.2	130@ 4000	120@ 5200	9:1	MPFI	2.2	4	N/A	32.7	42.4	47.8	48.7	47.1	53	38.5	38.8	56.7	57.6	104	2835	51.9	68.4	182

Specifications EPA Mileage Ratings	EPA Hwy (mpg) - auto	EPA City (mpg) - auto	EPA Hwy (mpg) - manual	EPA City (mpg) - manual	Fuel Capacity	Torque @ RPM	Horsepower @ RPM	Compression Ratio	Fuel System	Displacement (liters)	Number of Cylinders	Luggage Capacity (cu ft.)	Rear Leg Room (in.)	Front Leg Room (in.)	Rear Hip Room (in.)	Front Hip Room (in.)	Rear Shoulder Room (in.)	Front Shoulder Room (in.)	Rear Head Room (in.)	Front Head Room (in.)	Rear Track (in.)	Front Track (in.)	Wheelbase (in.)	Curb Weight (lbs.)	Height (in.)	Width (in.)	Length (in.)
PONTIAC																											
Sunfire SE Cpe	31	24	35	24	15.2	130@ 4000	120@ 5200	9:1	MPFI	2.2	4	12.4	32	42.4	50.9	48.7	54	54.1	36.6	37.6	56.7	57.6	104	2679	53.2	67.4	182
Sunfire SE Sdn	31	24	35	24	15.2	130@ 4000	120@ 5200	9:1	MPFI	2.2	4	13.1	34.4	42.4	51.1	50.9	54	54.6	37.2	38.9	56.7	57.6	104	2723	54.8	67.3	182
PORSCHE																											
911 Carrera Cabriolet	24	17	25	17	19.4	243@ 5000	270@ 6100	11.3:1	DME	3.6	6	N/A	N/A	N/A	N/A	N/A	N/A	N/A	N/A	N/A	56.9	55.3	89.4	3064	51.8	68.3	168
911 Carrera Cpe	24	17	25	17	19.4	243@ 5000	270@ 6100	11.3:1	DME	3.6	6	N/A	N/A	N/A	N/A	N/A	N/A	N/A	N/A	N/A	56.9	55.3	89.4	3064	51.8	68.3	168
911 Carrera 4 Cabrio	N/A	N/A	23	16	19.4	243@ 5000	270@ 6100	11.3:1	DME	3.6	6	N/A	N/A	N/A	N/A	N/A	N/A	N/A	N/A	N/A	58	55.3	89.4	3175	51.8	68.3	168
911 Carrera 4 Cpe	N/A	N/A	23	16	19.4	243@ 5000	270@ 6100	11.3:1	DME	3.6	6	N/A	N/A	N/A	N/A	N/A	N/A	N/A	N/A	N/A	58	55.3	89.4	3175	51	68.3	168
928 GTS Cpe	19	15	19	12	22.7	369@ 4250	345@ 5700	10.4:1	LH-J	5.4	8	N/A	N/A	N/A	N/A	N/A	N/A	N/A	N/A	N/A	63.6	61.1	98.4	3593	50.5	74.4	178
968 Cpe	25	16	26	17	19.6	225@ 4100	236@ 6200	11:1	DME	3.0	4	N/A	N/A	N/A	N/A	N/A	N/A	N/A	N/A	N/A	57.1	58.2	94.5	3086	50.2	68.3	171

Specifications EPA Mileage Ratings	EPA Hwy (mpg) - auto	EPA City (mpg) - auto	EPA Hwy (mpg) - manual	EPA City (mpg) - manual	Fuel Capacity	Torque @ RPM	Horsepower @ RPM	Compression Ratio	Fuel System	Displacement (liters)	Number of Cylinders	Luggage Capacity (cu ft.)	Rear Leg Room (in.)	Front Leg Room (in.)	Rear Hip Room (in.)	Front Hip Room (in.)	Rear Shoulder Room (in.)	Front Shoulder Room (in.)	Rear Head Room (in.)	Front Head Room (in.)	Rear Track (in.)	Front Track (in.)	Wheelbase (in.)	Curb Weight (lbs.)	Height (in.)	Width (in.)	Length (in.)
PORSCHE																											
968 Cabriolet	25	16	26	17	19.6	225@ 4100	236@ 6200	11:1	DME	3.0	4	N/A	N/A	N/A	N/A	N/A	N/A	N/A	N/A	N/A	57.1	58.2	94.5	3240	50.2	68.3	171
SAAB																											
900 S Hbk	28	20	29	20	18	155@ 4300	150@ 5700	12.5:1	FI	2.3	4	50	36	42.3	N/A	N/A	N/A	N/A	37.8	39.3	56.8	56.9	102	2940	56.5	67.4	183
900 S Cpe	28	20	29	20	18	155@ 4300	150@ 5700	12.5:1	FI	2.3	4	50	36	42.3	N/A	N/A	N/A	N/A	37.8	39.3	56.8	56.9	102	2940	56.5	67.4	183
900 S Conv	28	20	29	20	18	155@ 4300	150@ 5700	12.5:1	FI	2.3	4	12	36	42.3	N/A	N/A	N/A	N/A	37.9	39.3	56.8	56.9	102	3130	56.5	67.4	183
900 SE Hbk	27	19	25	18	18	167@ 4200	170@ 5900	12.8:1	FI	2.5	6	49.8	36	42.3	N/A	N/A	N/A	N/A	37.8	39.3	56.8	56.9	102	3120	56.5	67.4	183
900 SE Conv	27	19	25	18	18	167@ 4200	170@ 5900	12.8:1	FI	2.5	6	12.5	36	42.3	N/A	N/A	N/A	N/A	37.9	39.3	56.8	56.9	102	3190	56.5	67.4	183
900 SE Turbo Conv	N/A	N/A	27	20	18	194@ 2100	185@ 5500	12.2:1	FI	2.0	4	12.5	36	42.3	N/A	N/A	N/A	N/A	37.9	39.3	56.8	56.9	102	3160	56.5	67.4	183
900 SE Turbo Cpe	N/A	N/A	28	21	18	194@ 2100	185@ 5500	12.2:1	FI	2.0	4	49.8	36	42.3	N/A	N/A	N/A	N/A	37.8	39.3	56.8	56.9	102	3060	56.5	67.4	183

Specifications EPA Mileage Ratings	EPA Hwy (mpg) - auto	EPA City (mpg) - auto	EPA Hwy (mpg) - manual	EPA City (mpg) - manual	Fuel Capacity	Torque @ RPM	Horsepower @ RPM	Compression Ratio	Fuel System	Displacement (liters)	Number of Cylinders	Luggage Capacity (cu ft.)	Rear Leg Room (in.)	Front Leg Room (in.)	Rear Hip Room (in.)	Front Hip Room (in.)	Rear Shoulder Room (in.)	Front Shoulder Room (in.)	Rear Head Room (in.)	Front Head Room (in.)	Rear Track (in.)	Front Track (in.)	Wheelbase (in.)	Curb Weight (lbs.)	Height (in.)	Width (in.)	Length (in.)
SAAB																											
9000 Aero Hbk	27	18	29	21	17.4	252@ 1950	225@ 5500	12.2:1	FI	2.3	4	56.5	39	41.7	N/A	N/A	N/A	N/A	37.4	38.6	58.7	59.9	105	3250	55.9	69.4	187
9000 CDE Sdn	27	18	N/A	N/A	17.4	200@ 3300	210@ 6200	12.8:1	FI	3.0	6	17.8	38.8	41.5	N/A	N/A	N/A	N/A	37.4	38.6	58.7	59.9	105	3260	55.9	69.4	189
9000 CS Hbk	25	17	29	21	17.4	192@ 3200	170@ 5700	12.2:1	FI	2.3	4	56	39	41.7	N/A	N/A	N/A	N/A	37.4	38.6	58.7	59.9	105	3170	55.9	69.4	187
9000 CSE Hbk	27	18	N/A	N/A	17.4	200@ 3300	210@ 6200	12.8:1	FI	3.0	6	23.5	39	41.7	N/A	N/A	N/A	N/A	39	38.6	58.7	59.9	105	3310	55.9	69.4	187
9000 CSE Turbo Hbk	27	18	28	20	17.4	238@ 1800	200@ 5500	12.2:1	FI	2.3	4	23.5	39	41.7	N/A	N/A	N/A	N/A	39	38.6	58.7	59.9	105	3220	55.9	69.4	187
SATURN																											
Saturn SC1 Cpe	36	27	40	28	12.8	115@ 2400	100@ 5000	9.3:1	PFI	1.9	4	10.9	26.5	42.6	49.2	51.3	51.3	53.7	35	37.5	56	56.8	99.2	2625	50.6	67.6	173
Saturn SC2 Cpe	34	24	35	25	12.8	122@ 4800	124@ 5600	9.5:1	PFI	1.9	4	10.9	26.5	42.6	49.2	51.3	51.3	53.7	35	37.5	56	56.8	99.2	2750	50.6	67.6	173
Saturn SL Sdn	36	27	40	28	12.8	115@ 2400	100@ 5000	9.3:1	PFI	1.9	4	11.9	32.6	42.5	50.7	51.7	54.3	54.3	36.3	38.5	56	56.8	102	2625	52.5	67.6	176

Specifications EPA Mileage Ratings	EPA Hwy (mpg) - auto	EPA City (mpg) - auto	EPA Hwy (mpg) - manual	EPA City (mpg) - manual	Fuel Capacity	Torque @ RPM	Horsepower @ RPM	Compression Ratio	Fuel System	Displacement (liters)	Number of Cylinders	Luggage Capacity (cu ft.)	Rear Leg Room (in.)	Front Leg Room (in.)	Rear Hip Room (in.)	Front Hip Room (in.)	Rear Shoulder Room (in.)	Front Shoulder Room (in.)	Rear Head Room (in.)	Front Head Room (in.)	Rear Track (in.)	Front Track (in.)	Wheelbase (in.)	Curb Weight (lbs.)	Height (in.)	Width (in.)	Length (in.)
SATURN																											
Saturn SL1 Sdn	36	27	40	28	12.8	115@ 2400	100@ 5000	9.3:1	PFI	1.9	4	11.9	32.6	42.5	50.7	51.7	54.3	54.3	36.3	38.5	56	56.8	102	2625	52.5	67.6	176
Saturn SL2 Sdn	34	24	35	25	12.8	122@ 4800	124@ 5600	9.5:1	PFI	1.9	4	11.9	32.6	42.5	50.7	51.7	54.3	54.3	36.3	38.5	56	56.8	102	2750	52.5	67.6	176
Saturn SW1 Wgn	37	26	40	28	12.8	115@ 2400	100@ 5000	9.3:1	PFI	1.9	4	24	32.6	42.5	50.7	51.7	54.3	54.3	37.4	38.8	56	56.8	102	2625	53.7	67.6	176
Saturn SW2 Wgn	34	24	35	25	12.8	122@ 4800	124@ 5600	9.5:1	PFI	1.9	4	24	32.6	42.5	50.7	51.7	54.3	54.3	37.4	38.8	56	56.8	102	2750	53.7	67.6	176
SUBARU																											
Impreza Sdn	30	24	31	24	13.2	110@ 4400	110@ 5600	9.5:1	MPFI	1.8	4	11.1	32.5	43.1	N/A	N/A	53.3	52.5	36.7	39.2	57.1	57.7	99.2	2420	55.5	67.1	172
Impreza Cpe	30	24	31	24	13.2	110@ 4400	110@ 5600	9.5:1	MPFI	1.8	4	11.1	32.4	43.1	N/A	N/A	52.4	53	36.7	39.2	57.1	57.8	99.2	2400	55.5	67.1	172
Impreza AWD L Wgn	28	22	28	22	13.2	110@ 4400	110@ 5600	9.5:1	MPFI	1.8	4	62	32.4	43.1	N/A	N/A	53.3	52.5	37.4	39.2	57.1	57.7	99.2	2750	55.5	67.1	172
Impreza AWD LX Cpe	29	22	N/A	N/A	13.2	140@ 4400	135@ 5400	9.5:1	MPFI	2.2	4	11.1	32.4	43.1	N/A	N/A	52.4	53	36.7	39.2	57.3	57.5	99.2	2840	55.5	67.1	172

Specifications EPA Mileage Ratings	EPA Hwy (mpg) - auto	EPA City (mpg) - auto	EPA Hwy (mpg) - manual	EPA City (mpg) - manual	Fuel Capacity	Torque @ RPM	Horsepower @ RPM	Compression Ratio	Fuel System	Displacement (liters)	Number of Cylinders	Luggage Capacity (cu ft.)	Rear Leg Room (in.)	Front Leg Room (in.)	Rear Hip Room (in.)	Front Hip Room (in.)	Rear Shoulder Room (in.)	Front Shoulder Room (in.)	Rear Head Room (in.)	Front Head Room (in.)	Rear Track (in.)	Front Track (in.)	Wheelbase (in.)	Curb Weight (lbs.)	Height (in.)	Width (in.)	Length (in.)
SUBARU																											
Impreza AWD LX Sdn	29	22	N/A	N/A	13.2	140@ 4400	135@ 5400	9.5:1	MPFI	2.2	4	11.1	32.5	43.1	N/A	N/A	53.3	52.5	36.7	39.2	57.1	57.7	99.2	2835	55.5	67.1	172
Impreza AWD LX Spt Wgn	29	22	N/A	N/A	13.2	140@ 4400	135@ 5400	9.5:1	MPFI	2.2	4	62	32.4	43.1	N/A	N/A	53.3	52.5	37.4	39.2	57.1	57.7	99.2	2925	55.5	67.1	172
Legacy Base Sdn	N/A	N/A	31	24	15.9	140@ 4400	135@ 5400	9.5:1	MPFI	2.2	4	13	34.6	43.3	N/A	N/A	53.6	54.1	36.7	38.9	57.3	57.5	104	2570	55.3	67.5	181
Legacy L Wgn	31	23	31	23	15.9	140@ 4400	135@ 5400	9.5:1	MPFI	2.2	4	73	34.8	43.3	N/A	N/A	53.6	54.1	38.8	39.5	57.1	57.5	104	2750	57.1	67.5	184
Legacy L Sdn	31	23	31	24	15.9	140@ 4400	135@ 5400	9.5:1	MPFI	2.2	4	13	34.6	43.3	N/A	N/A	53.6	54.1	36.7	38.9	57.3	57.5	104	2655	55.3	67.5	181
Legacy AWD Brighton Wgn	28	22	28	21	15.9	140@ 4400	135@ 5400	9.5:1	MPFI	2.2	4	73	34.8	43.3	N/A	N/A	53.6	54.1	38.8	39.5	57.3	57.5	104	2890	57.1	67.5	184
Legacy AWD LS Wgn	28	22	N/A	N/A	15.9	140@ 4400	135@ 5400	9.5:1	MPFI	2.2	4	73	34.8	43.3	N/A	N/A	53.6	54.1	37.7	38.1	57.3	57.5	104	3120	57.1	67.5	184
Legacy AWD LS Sdn	28	22	N/A	N/A	15.9	140@ 4400	135@ 5400	9.5:1	MPFI	2.2	4	13	34.6	43.3	N/A	N/A	53.6	54.1	36.5	37.2	57.3	57.5	104	3030	55.3	67.5	181
Legacy AWD LSi Wgn	28	22	N/A	N/A	15.9	140@ 4400	135@ 5400	9.5:1	MPFI	2.2	4	73	34.8	43.3	N/A	N/A	53.6	54.1	37.7	38.1	57.3	57.5	104	3135	57.1	67.5	184

Specifications EPA Mileage Ratings

Specifications EPA Mileage Ratings	EPA Hwy (mpg) - auto	EPA City (mpg) - auto	EPA Hwy (mpg) - manual	EPA City (mpg) - manual	Fuel Capacity	Torque @ RPM	Horsepower @ RPM	Compression Ratio	Fuel System	Displacement (liters)	Number of Cylinders	Luggage Capacity (cu ft.)	Rear Leg Room (in.)	Front Leg Room (in.)	Rear Hip Room (in.)	Front Hip Room (in.)	Rear Shoulder Room (in.)	Front Shoulder Room (in.)	Rear Head Room (in.)	Front Head Room (in.)	Rear Track (in.)	Front Track (in.)	Wheelbase (in.)	Curb Weight (lbs.)	Height (in.)	Width (in.)	Length (in.)
SUBARU																											
Legacy AWD LSi Sdn	28	22	N/A	N/A	15.9	140@ 4400	135@ 5400	9.5:1	MPFI	2.2	4	13	34.6	43.3	N/A	N/A	53.6	54.1	36.5	37.2	57.3	57.5	104	3045	55.3	67.5	181
Legacy AWD Outback Wgn	28	22	28	21	15.9	140@ 4400	135@ 5400	9.5:1	MPFI	2.2	4	73	34.8	43.3	N/A	N/A	53.6	54.1	38.8	39.5	57.3	57.5	104	2990	57.1	67.5	184
SVX L Cpe	25	17	N/A	N/A	18.5	228@ 4400	230@ 5400	10:1	MPFI	3.3	6	8.2	28.5	43.5	N/A	N/A	54.5	56.1	35	38	58.3	59.1	103	3375	51.2	69.7	182
SVX LS Cpe	25	17	N/A	N/A	18.5	228@ 4400	230@ 5400	10:1	MPFI	3.3	6	8.2	28.5	43.5	N/A	N/A	54.5	56.1	35	37.4	58.3	59.1	103	3430	51.2	69.7	182
SVX LSi Cpe	25	17	N/A	N/A	18.5	228@ 4400	230@ 5400	10:1	MPFI	3.3	6	8.2	28.5	43.5	N/A	N/A	54.5	56.1	35	37.4	58.3	59.1	103	3580	51.2	69.7	182
SVX AWD L Cpe	25	17	N/A	N/A	18.5	228@ 4400	230@ 5400	10:1	MPFI	3.3	6	8.2	28.5	43.5	N/A	N/A	54.5	56.1	35	38	58.3	59.1	103	3525	51.2	69.7	182
SUZUKI																											
Swift Hbk	34	30	43	39	10.6	74@ 3000	70@ 5500	12.5:1	EFI	1.3	4	8.4	32.8	42.5	N/A	N/A	48.9	48.9	36	39.1	53.5	54.5	93.1	1856	54.7	62.6	149

Specifications EPA Mileage Ratings

TOYOTA

Specifications EPA Mileage Ratings	EPA Hwy (mpg) - auto	EPA City (mpg) - auto	EPA Hwy (mpg) - manual	EPA City (mpg) - manual	Fuel Capacity	Torque @ RPM	Horsepower @ RPM	Compression Ratio	Fuel System	Displacement (liters)	Number of Cylinders	Luggage Capacity (cu ft.)	Rear Leg Room (in.)	Front Leg Room (in.)	Rear Hip Room (in.)	Front Hip Room (in.)	Rear Shoulder Room (in.)	Front Shoulder Room (in.)	Rear Head Room (in.)	Front Head Room (in.)	Rear Track (in.)	Front Track (in.)	Wheelbase (in.)	Curb Weight (lbs.)	Height (in.)	Width (in.)	Length (in.)
Avalon XL w/Bench Sdn	28	20	N/A	N/A	18.5	210@ 4400	192@ 5200	10.5:1	EFI	3.0	6	15.4	38.3	44.1	N/A	N/A	57.3	57.7	37.8	39.1	60	61	107	3285	56.1	70.3	190
Avalon XL w/Bucket Sdn	28	20	N/A	N/A	18.5	210@ 4400	192@ 5200	10.5:1	EFI	3.0	6	15.4	38.3	44.1	N/A	N/A	57.3	57.7	37.8	39.1	60	61	107	3263	56.1	70.3	190
Avalon XLS w/Bench Sdn	28	20	N/A	N/A	18.5	210@ 4400	192@ 5200	10.5:1	EFI	3.0	6	15.4	38.3	44.1	N/A	N/A	57.3	57.7	37.8	39.1	60	61	107	3298	56.1	70.3	190
Avalon XLS w/Bucket Sdn	28	20	N/A	N/A	18.5	210@ 4400	192@ 5200	10.5:1	EFI	3.0	6	15.4	38.3	44.1	N/A	N/A	57.3	57.7	37.8	39.1	60	61	107	3287	56.1	70.3	190
Camry DX Cpe	28	21	31	23	18.5	145@ 4400	125@ 5400	9.5:1	EFI	2.2	4	14.8	33	43.5	N/A	N/A	55.2	56.5	37.4	38.4	59.1	61	103	2910	54.9	69.7	188
Camry DX Sdn	28	21	31	23	18.5	145@ 4400	125@ 5400	9.5:1	EFI	2.2	4	14.8	35	43.4	N/A	N/A	56.1	56.8	37.1	38.4	59.1	61	103	2932	55.1	69.7	188
Camry LE Wgn	28	21	N/A	N/A	18.5	145@ 4400	125@ 5400	9.5:1	EFI	2.2	4	75	35.2	43.4	N/A	N/A	56	56.8	38.8	39.2	59.1	61	103	3263	56.3	69.7	189
Camry LE Cpe	28	21	N/A	N/A	18.5	145@ 4400	125@ 5400	9.5:1	EFI	2.2	4	14.8	33	43.5	N/A	N/A	55.2	56.5	37.4	38.4	59.1	61	103	3064	54.9	69.7	188
Camry LE Sdn	28	21	N/A	N/A	18.5	145@ 4400	125@ 5400	9.5:1	EFI	2.2	4	14.8	35	43.4	N/A	N/A	56.1	56.8	37.1	38.4	59.1	61	103	3086	55.1	69.7	188

Specifications EPA Mileage Ratings

TOYOTA

Specifications EPA Mileage Ratings	EPA Hwy (mpg) - auto	EPA City (mpg) - auto	EPA Hwy (mpg) - manual	EPA City (mpg) - manual	Fuel Capacity	Torque @ RPM	Horsepower @ RPM	Compression Ratio	Fuel System	Displacement (liters)	Number of Cylinders	Luggage Capacity (cu ft.)	Rear Leg Room (in.)	Front Leg Room (in.)	Rear Hip Room (in.)	Front Hip Room (in.)	Rear Shoulder Room (in.)	Front Shoulder Room (in.)	Rear Head Room (in.)	Front Head Room (in.)	Rear Track (in.)	Front Track (in.)	Wheelbase (in.)	Curb Weight (lbs.)	Height (in.)	Width (in.)	Length (in.)
Camry XLE Sdn	28	21	N/A	N/A	18.5	145@ 4400	125@ 5400	9.5:1	EFI	2.2	4	14.8	35	43.4	N/A	N/A	56.1	56.8	37.1	38.4	59.1	61	103	3131	55.1	69.7	188
Camry V6 LE Sdn	28	20	N/A	N/A	18.5	203@ 4400	188@ 5200	10.5:1	EFI	3.0	6	14.8	35	43.5	55.4	55.9	56.1	56.8	37.1	38.4	59	61	103	3241	55.1	69.7	188
Camry V6 LE Wgn	28	20	N/A	N/A	18.5	203@ 5200	188@ 5200	10.5:1	EFI	3.0	6	74.8	34.7	43.5	54.9	55.9	56	56.8	38.8	39.2	59.1	61	103	3406	56.5	69.7	189
Camry V6 LE Cpe	28	20	N/A	N/A	18.5	203@ 4400	188@ 5200	10.5:1	EFI	3.0	6	14.8	33	43.5	53	54.2	55.2	56.5	37.4	38.4	59	61	103	3219	54.9	69.7	188
Camry V6 SE Sdn	28	20	N/A	N/A	18.5	203@ 4400	188@ 5200	10.5:1	EFI	3.0	6	14.8	35	43.5	55.4	55.9	56.1	56.8	37.1	38.4	59	61	103	3186	55.1	69.7	188
Camry V6 SE Cpe	28	20	N/A	N/A	18.5	203@ 4400	188@ 5200	10.5:1	EFI	3.0	6	14.8	33	43.5	53	54.2	55.2	56.5	37.4	38.4	59	61	103	3164	54.9	69.7	188
Camry V6 XLE Sdn	28	20	N/A	N/A	18.5	203@ 4400	188@ 5200	10.5:1	EFI	3.0	6	14.8	35	43.5	55.4	55.9	56.1	56.8	37.1	38.4	59	61	103	3274	55.1	69.7	188
Celica GT Lbk	30	23	29	22	15.9	145@ 4400	130@ 5400	9.5:1	EFI	2.2	4	16.2	26.8	44.2	47.8	52.8	49.9	52.4	30.7	34.5	58.9	59.6	99.9	2580	50.8	68.9	174
Celica GT Cpe	30	23	29	22	15.9	145@ 4400	130@ 5400	9.5:1	EFI	2.2	4	10.6	26.8	44.2	47.8	52.8	49.9	52.4	30.7	34.5	58.9	59.6	99.9	2560	51	68.9	177

Specifications EPA Mileage Ratings

TOYOTA

	EPA Hwy (mpg) - auto	EPA City (mpg) - auto	EPA Hwy (mpg) - manual	EPA City (mpg) - manual	Fuel Capacity	Torque @ RPM	Horsepower @ RPM	Compression Ratio	Fuel System	Displacement (liters)	Number of Cylinders	Luggage Capacity (cu ft.)	Rear Leg Room (in.)	Front Leg Room (in.)	Rear Hip Room (in.)	Front Hip Room (in.)	Rear Shoulder Room (in.)	Front Shoulder Room (in.)	Rear Head Room (in.)	Front Head Room (in.)	Rear Track (in.)	Front Track (in.)	Wheelbase (in.)	Curb Weight (lbs.)	Height (in.)	Width (in.)	Length (in.)
Celica GT Conv	30	23	29	22	15.9	145@ 4400	130@ 5400	9.5:1	EFI	2.2	4	6.8	18.9	44.2	41.2	52.8	44.8	52.4	34.1	38.7	58.9	59.6	99.9	2755	51.6	68.9	177
Celica ST Lbk	34	27	34	28	15.9	115@ 2800	110@ 5600	9.5:1	EFI	1.8	4	16.2	26.8	44.2	N/A	N/A	49.9	52.4	29.2	34.3	58.9	59.6	99.9	2415	50.8	68.9	174
Celica ST Cpe	34	27	34	28	15.9	115@ 2800	110@ 5600	9.5:1	EFI	1.8	4	10.6	26.8	44.2	N/A	N/A	49.9	52.4	29.2	34.3	58.9	59.6	99.9	2560	51	68.9	177
Corolla Sdn	30	26	34	28	13.2	100@ 4800	105@ 5800	9.5:1	EFI	1.6	4	12.7	33	42.4	N/A	N/A	53.5	54.1	37.1	38.7	57.1	57.5	97	2315	53.5	66.3	172
Corolla DX Wgn	34	27	34	28	13.2	117@ 2800	105@ 5200	9.5:1	EFI	1.8	4	65	53.5	54.3	N/A	N/A	53.5	54.1	39.7	38.8	57.1	57.5	97	2403	55.3	66.3	172
Corolla DX Sdn	34	27	34	28	13.2	117@ 2800	105@ 5200	9.5:1	EFI	1.8	4	12.7	33	42.4	N/A	N/A	53.5	54.1	37.1	38.7	57.1	57.5	97	2381	53.5	66.3	172
Corolla LE Sdn	34	27	34	28	13.2	117@ 2800	105@ 5200	9.5:1	EFI	1.8	4	12.7	33	42.4	N/A	N/A	53.5	54.1	37.1	38.7	57.1	57.5	97	2524	53.5	66.3	172
MR2 Cpe	30	21	29	22	14.3	145@ 4400	135@ 5400	9.5:1	EFI	2.2	4	6.5	N/A	43.4	N/A	N/A	N/A	54	N/A	37.5	57.1	57.9	94.5	2657	48.6	66.9	164
MR2 Turbo Cpe	N/A	N/A	27	20	14.3	200@ 3200	200@ 6000	8.8:1	EFI	2.0	4	6.5	N/A	43.4	N/A	N/A	N/A	54	N/A	36.8	57.1	57.9	94.5	2888	48.6	66.9	164

Specifications EPA Mileage Ratings	EPA Hwy (mpg) - auto	EPA City (mpg) - auto	EPA Hwy (mpg) - manual	EPA City (mpg) - manual	Fuel Capacity	Torque @ RPM	Horsepower @ RPM	Compression Ratio	Fuel System	Displacement (liters)	Number of Cylinders	Luggage Capacity (cu ft.)	Rear Leg Room (in.)	Front Leg Room (in.)	Rear Hip Room (in.)	Front Hip Room (in.)	Rear Shoulder Room (in.)	Front Shoulder Room (in.)	Rear Head Room (in.)	Front Head Room (in.)	Rear Track (in.)	Front Track (in.)	Wheelbase (in.)	Curb Weight (lbs.)	Height (in.)	Width (in.)	Length (in.)
TOYOTA																											
Paseo Cpe	33	26	36	29	11.9	91@ 3200	100@ 6400	9.4:1	EFI	1.5	4	7.7	30	41.1	N/A	N/A	52.4	53.6	32	37.7	54.9	55.3	93.7	2070	50.2	65.2	163
Supra Lbk	24	18	23	18	18.5	210@ 4800	220@ 5800	10:1	SEFI	3.0	6	10.1	23.8	44	N/A	N/A	43.8	54.2	32.9	37.5	60	59.8	100	3210	49.8	71.3	178
Supra Turbo Lbk	24	19	24	17	18.5	315@ 4000	320@ 5600	8.5:1	SEFI	3.0	6	10.1	23.8	44	N/A	N/A	43.8	54.2	32.9	37.5	60	59.8	100	3445	49.8	71.3	178
Tercel Cpe	35	31	39	33	11.9	100@ 4400	93@ 5400	9.4:1	EFI	1.5	4	9.3	31.9	41.2	N/A	N/A	51.6	51.3	36.5	38.6	56.3	55.1	93.7	1950	53.2	65.3	162
Tercel DX Sdn	39	30	39	31	11.9	100@ 4400	93@ 5400	9.4:1	EFI	1.5	4	9.3	31.9	41.2	N/A	N/A	50.7	51.3	36.5	38.6	56.3	55.1	93.7	2005	53.2	65.3	162
Tercel DX Cpe	39	30	39	31	11.9	100@ 4400	93@ 5400	9.4:1	EFI	1.5	4	9.3	31.9	41.2	N/A	N/A	51.6	51.3	36.5	38.6	56.3	55.1	93.7	1975	53.2	65.3	162
VOLKSWAGEN																											
Cabrio Conv	28	21	30	23	14.5	122@ 3200	115@ 5400	12:1	SMPI	2.0	4	15.8	31.1	42.3	40.5	52.7	46.5	54.1	36.6	38.7	57	57.6	97.4	2701	55.1	66.7	161
Golf III Base Hbk	N/A	N/A	32	24	14.5	122@ 3200	115@ 5400	12:1	SMPI	2.0	4	16.9	31.5	42.3	52.3	53.2	52.8	53.8	37.4	39.2	56.9	57.6	97.3	2548	56.2	66.7	160

Specifications EPA Mileage Ratings	EPA Hwy (mpg) - auto	EPA City (mpg) - auto	EPA Hwy (mpg) - manual	EPA City (mpg) - manual	Fuel Capacity	Torque @ RPM	Horsepower @ RPM	Compression Ratio	Fuel System	Displacement (liters)	Number of Cylinders	Luggage Capacity (cu ft.)	Rear Leg Room (in.)	Front Leg Room (in.)	Rear Hip Room (in.)	Front Hip Room (in.)	Rear Shoulder Room (in.)	Front Shoulder Room (in.)	Rear Head Room (in.)	Front Head Room (in.)	Rear Track (in.)	Front Track (in.)	Wheelbase (in.)	Curb Weight (lbs.)	Height (in.)	Width (in.)	Length (in.)
VOLKSWAGEN																											
Golf III GL Hbk	29	23	32	24	14.5	122@ 3200	115@ 5400	12:1	SMPI	2.0	4	16.9	31.5	42.3	52.3	53.2	52.8	53.8	37.4	39.2	56.9	57.6	97.3	2615	56.2	66.7	160
Golf III Sport Hbk	29	23	32	24	14.5	122@ 3200	115@ 5400	12:1	SMPI	2.0	4	17.5	31.5	42.3	51.9	52.8	54.6	54	37.4	39.2	56.9	57.6	97.3	2549	56.2	66.7	160
GTI-VR6 Hbk	N/A	N/A	25	18	14.5	173@ 4200	172@ 5400	12:1	SFI	2.8	6	17.5	31.5	42.3	51.9	52.8	54.6	54	37.4	37.5	56.4	57.1	97.3	2818	56	66.7	160
Jetta III Base Sdn	N/A	N/A	31	24	14.5	122@ 3200	115@ 5400	12:1	SMPI	2.0	4	15	31.5	42.3	52.3	53.2	52.8	53.8	37.3	39.2	56.9	57.6	97.3	2647	56.1	66.7	173
Jetta III GL Sdn	29	23	31	24	14.5	122@ 3200	115@ 5400	12:1	SMPI	2.0	4	15	31.5	42.3	52.3	53.2	52.8	53.8	37.3	39.2	56.9	57.6	97.3	2714	56.1	66.7	173
Jetta III GLS Sdn	29	23	31	24	14.5	122@ 3200	115@ 5400	12:1	SMPI	2.0	4	15	31.5	42.3	52.3	53.2	52.8	53.8	37.3	37.5	56.9	57.6	97.3	2714	56.1	66.7	173
Jetta III GLX Sdn	25	18	25	18	14.5	173@ 4200	172@ 5800	12:1	SMFI	2.8	6	15	31.5	42.3	52.3	53.2	52.8	53.8	37.3	39.2	56	57.1	97.3	2915	56.2	66.7	173
Passat GLX Wgn	25	18	25	18	18.5	177@ 4200	172@ 5800	12:1	SFI	2.8	6	69	37	45.1	N/A	N/A	54	55	38.3	39.9	56.2	58.4	103	3201	58.7	67.5	181
Passat GLX Sdn	25	18	25	18	18.5	177@ 4200	172@ 5800	12:1	SMPI	2.8	6	14.4	37	45.1	N/A	N/A	54	55	36.6	39.3	56.2	58.4	103	3140	56.4	67.5	182

VOLVO

Specifications EPA Mileage Ratings	EPA Hwy (mpg) - auto	EPA City (mpg) - auto	EPA Hwy (mpg) - manual	EPA City (mpg) - manual	Fuel Capacity	Torque @ RPM	Horsepower @ RPM	Compression Ratio	Fuel System	Displacement (liters)	Number of Cylinders	Luggage Capacity (cu ft.)	Rear Leg Room (in.)	Front Leg Room (in.)	Rear Hip Room (in.)	Front Hip Room (in.)	Rear Shoulder Room (in.)	Front Shoulder Room (in.)	Rear Head Room (in.)	Front Head Room (in.)	Rear Track (in.)	Front Track (in.)	Wheelbase (in.)	Curb Weight (lbs.)	Height (in.)	Width (in.)	Length (in.)
850 Base Sdn	29	20	29	20	19.3	162@ 3300	168@ 6200	12.5:1	FI	2.4	5	33	32.3	41.4	55.2	55.2	56.3	57.1	37.8	39.1	57.9	59.8	105	3232	55.7	69.3	184
850 Base Wgn	29	20	29	20	19.3	162@ 3300	168@ 6200	12.5:1	FI	2.4	5	67	35.2	41.4	55.2	55.2	56.3	57.1	37.8	39.1	57.9	59.8	105	3342	56.9	69.3	185
850 GLT Wgn	29	20	29	20	19.3	162@ 3300	168@ 6200	12.5:1	FI	2.4	5	67	35.2	41.4	55.2	55.2	56.3	57.1	37.9	38.4	57.9	59.8	105	3342	56.9	69.3	185
850 GLT Sdn	29	20	29	20	19.3	162@ 3300	168@ 6200	12.5:1	FI	2.4	5	33	32.3	41.4	55.2	55.2	56.3	57.1	37.3	38	57.9	59.8	105	3232	55.7	69.3	184
850 Turbo Wgn	26	19	N/A	N/A	19.3	221@ 2100	222@ 5200	12.5:1	FI	2.3	5	67	35.2	41.4	55.2	55.2	56.3	57.1	37.9	38.4	57.9	59.8	105	3387	56.9	69.3	185
850 Turbo Sdn	26	19	N/A	N/A	19.3	221@ 2100	222@ 5200	12.5:1	FI	2.3	5	33	32.3	41.4	55.2	55.2	56.3	57.1	37.3	38	57.9	59.8	105	3278	55.7	69.3	184
940 Wgn	26	19	N/A	N/A	19.8	136@ 2150	114@ 5400	12.8:1	FI	2.3	4	75	34.7	41	54.7	54.7	56.4	56.4	37.6	38.6	57.5	57.9	109	3283	56.5	69.3	189
940 Sdn	26	19	N/A	N/A	19.8	136@ 2150	114@ 5400	12.8:1	FI	2.3	4	16.6	34.7	41	N/A	N/A	56.4	56.4	37.1	38.6	57.5	57.9	109	3208	55.5	69.3	192
940 Turbo Sdn	24	19	N/A	N/A	19.8	195@ 3450	162@ 4800	12.7:1	FI	2.3	4	16.6	34.7	41	N/A	N/A	56.4	56.4	37.1	38.6	57.5	57.9	109	3208	55.5	69.3	192

Specifications EPA Mileage Ratings

VOLVO

Specifications EPA Mileage Ratings	EPA Hwy (mpg) - auto	EPA City (mpg) - auto	EPA Hwy (mpg) - manual	EPA City (mpg) - manual	Fuel Capacity	Torque @ RPM	Horsepower @ RPM	Compression Ratio	Fuel System	Displacement (liters)	Number of Cylinders	Luggage Capacity (cu ft.)	Rear Leg Room (in.)	Front Leg Room (in.)	Rear Hip Room (in.)	Front Hip Room (in.)	Rear Shoulder Room (in.)	Front Shoulder Room (in.)	Rear Head Room (in.)	Front Head Room (in.)	Rear Track (in.)	Front Track (in.)	Wheelbase (in.)	Curb Weight (lbs.)	Height (in.)	Width (in.)	Length (in.)
940 Turbo Wgn	24	19	N/A	N/A	19.8	195@ 3450	162@ 4800	12.7:1	FI	2.3	4	75	34.7	41	54.7	54.7	56.4	56.4	37.6	38.6	57.5	57.9	109	3283	56.5	69.3	189
960 Wgn	25	17	N/A	N/A	20.8	199@ 4100	181@ 5200	12.7:1	FI	2.9	6	75	34.7	41	54.7	54.7	54.7	54.7	36.7	38.1	59.7	59.2	109	3547	57.6	68.9	191
960 Sdn	25	17	N/A	N/A	20.8	199@ 4100	181@ 5200	12.7:1	FI	2.9	6	16.6	34.7	41	54.3	54.3	54.5	54.5	36.9	37.4	59.7	59.2	109	3461	56.6	68.9	192

How the fuel economy estimates are obtained:

The estimates of the number of miles a vehicle can travel on a gallon of fuel are based on results of the U.S. Environmental Protection Agency (E.P.A.) "Emissions Standards Test Procedure." This procedure is used to certify that cars, vans, and light trucks comply with the Clean Air Act, as amended. Each year, manufacturers submit new vehicle codes to the E.P.A. The procedure for testing simulates every day driving conditions. Each vehicle is tested under controlled laboratory conditions by a professional driver. By using a dynamometer to simulate driving conditions, the driver can test each vehicle under identical circumstances in exactly the same way each time. Therefore, the obtained results can be compared accurately. The test vehicles are broken in, properly maintained, and driven in test conditions which simulate warm weather and dry, level roads. The quality of the fuel used is also very closely controlled. The test conditions are those the E.P.A. must use to assure emissions measurements. However, no test can cover all possible combinations of actual road conditions, climate, driving and car-care habits of individual drivers.

In 1994, the National Highway and Trafic Safety Administration (NHTSA) changed the way they rate crash test performances of the cars and trucks they run into a wall at 35 mph. Instead of using the confusing numerical scale that had been in place for years, NHTSA decided to make the data more user-friendly for interested consumers by converting to a five star rating system, just like the movie reviewer in your local paper or the lucky people AAA employs to go around the world eating and sleeping in the best hotels and restaurants.

Listed below are the results for many 1995 vehicles rated according to NHTSA's new system. A five-star rating is best.

Model	Airbag System	Driver	Passenger
Acura Integra Sedan	Dual	****	***
Acura Legend	Dual	***	****
Audi A6	Dual	*****	*****
BMW 3-Series	Dual	****	***
Buick Century	Driver	****	****
Buick Le Sabre	Dual	*****	***
Buick Park Avenue	Dual	*****	***
Buick Roadmaster	Dual	****	**
Cadillac DeVille	Dual	****	****
Cadillac Eldorado	Dual	****	****
Cadillac Seville	Dual	****	No Data
Chevrolet Astro	Driver	***	*
Chevrolet Blazer	Driver	***	*
Chevrolet Camaro	Dual	*****	*****
Chevrolet Caprice	Dual	****	**
Chevrolet Corsica	Driver	***	**
Chevrolet Impala SS	Dual	****	**
Chevrolet Lumina	Dual	****	***
Chevrolet Lumina Minivan	Driver	****	***
Chevrolet S-10 Pickup	Driver	No Data	***
Chevrolet Sportvan	Driver	***	***
Chrysler Concorde	Dual	***	****
Chrysler LHS	Dual	****	****
Chrysler Town & Country	Dual	****	****
Dodge Caravan	Dual	****	****
Dodge Dakota	Driver	*****	****
Dodge Intrepid	Dual	****	****
Dodge Neon	Dual	***	***
Dodge Ram	Driver	*****	No Data
Dodge Ram Van 2500	Driver	*	***

Dodge Spirit	Driver	****	***
Dodge Stealth	Dual	*****	No Data
Eagle Vision	Dual	***	****
Ford Aerostar	Driver	****	***
Ford Bronco	Driver	*****	*****
Ford Club Wagon	Driver	****	***
Ford Crown Victoria	Dual	***	*****
Ford Econoline	Driver	****	***
Ford Escort	Dual	****	No Data
Ford F-150	Driver	***	****
Ford Mustang	Dual	****	****
Ford Probe	Dual	*****	****
Ford Taurus	Dual	****	****
Ford Thunderbird	Dual	*****	*****
Ford Windstar	Dual	****	*****
Geo Prizm	Dual	****	****
GMC Jimmy	Driver	***	**
GMC Rally Van	Driver	***	****
GMC Safari	Driver	***	*
GMC Sonoma Pickup	Driver	No Data	***
Honda Accord	Dual	****	***
Honda Civic Sedan	Dual	***	***
Honda Civic Coupe	Dual	***	****
Honda Odyssey	Dual	****	***
Honda Passport	None	**	***
Honda Prelude	Dual	****	*****
Hyundai Accent	Dual	*****	****
Hyundai Elantra	Driver	****	*
Hyundai Scoupe	None	****	****
Hyundai Sonata	Dual	***	****
Infiniti J30	Dual	****	****
Isuzu Pickup	None	***	****
Isuzu Rodeo	None	**	***
Isuzu Trooper	None	*	**
Jeep Cherokee	Driver	****	****
Jeep Grand Cherokee	Driver	****	***
Jeep Wrangler	None	**	****
Lexus GS300	Dual	***	***
Mazda 626	Dual	****	*****
Mazda Miata	Dual	***	No Data
Mazda Millenia	Dual	****	*****
Mazda MX-6	Dual	****	*****
Mazda Navajo	None	***	****
Mercedes C-Class	Dual	****	****
Mercury Cougar	Dual	*****	*****

Mercury Grand Marquis	Dual	***	****
Mercury Sable	Dual	****	****
Mercury Tracer	Dual	****	No Data
Mercury Villager	Driver	****	***
Mitsubishi 3000GT	Dual	*****	No Data
Mitsubishi Galant	Dual	No Data	****
Mitsubishi Mighty Max	None	***	***
Nissan 300ZX	Dual	***	No Data
Nissan Altima	Dual	****	***
Nissan Maxima	Dual	****	***
Nissan Pathfinder	None	*	***
Nissan Quest	Dual	****	***
Nissan Truck	None	***	****
Oldsmobile Achieva	Driver	****	***
Oldsmobile Cutlass Ciera	Driver	****	****
Oldsmobile Cutlass Supreme	Dual	****	***
Oldsmobile Eighty-Eight	Dual	*****	***
Oldsmobile Ninety-Eight	Dual	*****	***
Oldsmobile Silhouette	Driver	No Data	****
Plymouth Acclaim	Driver	****	***
Plymouth Neon	Dual	***	***
Plymouth Voyager	Dual	****	****
Pontiac Bonneville	Dual	*****	****
Pontiac Firebird	Dual	*****	*****
Pontiac Grand Am	Driver	****	***
Pontiac Grand Prix	Dual	****	***
Pontiac Sunfire	Dual	****	*****
Pontiac Trans Sport	Driver	****	***
Saab 900	Dual	****	****
Saab 9000	Dual	****	No Data
Saturn SL	Dual	****	****
Saturn SW	Dual	****	****
Subaru Legacy	Dual	****	****
Toyota 4Runner	None	*	****
Toyota Camry	Dual	****	***
Toyota Corolla	Dual	****	****
Toyota Paseo	Driver	****	*****
Toyota Pickup	None	**	****
Toyota Previa	Driver	****	***
Toyota T100	Driver	****	****
Toyota Tercel	Dual	***	****
Volkswagen Golf III	Dual	***	***
Volkswagen Jetta III	Dual	***	***
Volkswagen Passat	Dual	****	****
Volvo 850	Dual/Side	*****	****

Edmund's wants your

SUCCESS STORIES

Edmund's wants to publish your own personal accounts of how you were able to use the information in our Buyer's Guides to save money when purchasing/leasing a vehicle. Tell us what vehicle and model you acquired, how you negotiated with the dealer/seller, and how much you saved by taking advantage of Edmund's price information. Write us your story in as few words as possible.

Success stories, to be published in future editions of Edmund's books, will be selected by a panel of experts including Dr. Burke Leon, author of *The Insider's Guide to Buying a New or Used Car.* If your smart auto-buying story is selected, it will be published together with your name, city and state. No compensation will be paid for use of your story.

Please send your money-saving success story, along with your name, address, and signature to:

EDMUND PUBLICATIONS CORPORATION

300 N. Sepulveda Blvd., Suite 2050

El Segundo, CA 90245

Attn.: Success Stories

EDMUND'S "SUCCESS STORY" FORM

NAME

ADDRESS

CITY, STATE, ZIP

By submitting story, entrant consents to publication without compensation.

SIGNATURE DATE

Edmund's Success Story!

Dear **Edmund's!**

I wanted to thank you for your publication, and also, your toll-free number and 900 number.

. . . I decided to buy a new car, and do it on my own - without a man helping me. I was interested in a Honda Civic DX 2-Door Coupe. I saw your publication recommended in auto buying articles. I called your hotline, and one of your people told me to get my new car at $200 - $300 over dealer cost, and hold at $500.

I did.

Some salespeople and dealers didn't appreciate me going in with the Edmund's prices, or that I was an educated woman consumer.

And some did. I went to a Honda dealer in Georgia. We went back and forth on the numbers, and I knew I was getting a great deal. I got the car I wanted, with automatic transmission, air-conditioning, AM/FM cassette player, pin stripes, floormats, mud guards, paint and fabric protection. I paid $14,350 and that included tax, tag, and title. That was $300 over dealer invoice.

The manager told me that when a customer comes in with Edmund's prices, and has done their homework, they are happy to work with them. (And that women are 67% of their car buyers, so they wouldn't think of treating them badly.)

I drove my new car home that day, and I am thrilled with it. Even the other dealers congratulated me, and said I did very well.

So, thanks to **Edmund's Buyer's Guide** and their information hotline, I got the information I needed, and the car I wanted, at the right price.

Sincerely,

Sandra T. D.
Atlanta, GA

Automobile Manufacturers

Customer Assistance Numbers

Acura	1-800-382-2238
Alfa Romeo	1-800-255-1575
Audi	1-800-822-2834
BMW	1-800-831-1117
Buick	1-800-521-7300
Cadillac	1-800-458-8006
Chevrolet	1-800-222-1020
Chrysler	1-800-992-1997
Dodge	1-800-992-1997
Eagle	1-800-992-1997
Ford	1-800-392-3673
Geo	1-800-222-1020
GMC	1-800-462-8782
Honda	1-310-783-2000 toll free not available
Hyundai	1-800-633-5151
Infiniti	1-800-662-6200
Isuzu	1-800-255-6727

Jaguar 1-201-818-8500
toll free not available
Land Rover 1-800-637-6837
Lexus 1-800-255-3987
Lincoln 1-800-392-3673
Mazda 1-800-222-5500
Mercedes-Benz .. 1-800-222-0100
Mercury 1-800-392-3673
Mitsubishi 1-800-222-0037
Nissan 1-800-647-7261
Oldsmobile......... 1-800-442-6537
Plymouth 1-800-992-1997
Pontiac 1-800-762-2737
Porsche 1-800-545-8039
Saab 1-800-955-9007
Saturn 1-800-553-6000
Subaru 1-800-782-2783
Suzuki 1-800-934-0934
Toyota 1-800-331-4331
Volkswagen 1-800-822-8987
Volvo 1-800-458-1552

Like most consumers, you want to know how to buy or lease the car of your choice for the best possible price. Buyers are attracted to leasing by low payments and the prospect of driving a new car every two or three years. Many people figure that a car payment is an unavoidable fact of budgetary life, and they might as well drive 'new' rather than 'old'. True, leasing is an attractive alternative, but there are some things you need to understand about leasing before jumping in feet first without a paddle. Whatever. You know what I mean.

1) Low Payments. You've seen the ads: 1995 Escort LX for $199 a month. 1995 Altima GXE for $229 a month. 1995 Infiniti Q45 for $599 a month. Zowie! Visions of new golf clubs, a 32-inch television and 2 weeks in Tahiti release endorphins at twice the Surgeon General's recommended level. Hold on a sec. Read the fine print. See where it says '*Capitalized Cost Reduction*'? That's lease-speak for 'down payment'. See where it says "36,000 miles over term?" That's lease-speak for 'You're going to the supermarket and back - and that's all folks.' Want the car for zero down? That's gonna cost you. You drive someplace more than twice a month? That's gonna cost you too.

Low payments aren't a fallacy with leasing, when taken in proper context. For example, a Ford Ranger XLT V6 stickers at about $13,900, give or take. To lease for two years with no *Capitalized Cost Reduction* (down payment), the truck will cost you about $350 per month; to lease for three years; about $275 per month. Ford allows 15,000 miles per year and charges about 11 cents per mile for each mile over the term limit. To buy the Ranger, financed for 24 months at 10% APR with no money down, you will pay $690 per month including tax and tags. For three years at 10%, the payment is $485 per month. So you see, leasing is cheaper on a monthly basis when compared to financing for the same term.

There are two flaws here. First, 60-month financing is now commonplace. The Ranger will cost $320 per month for 5 years, and still be worth a good chunk of change at the end of the loan, if cared for properly. Second, ownership is far less restrictive, even if the bank holds the title until year 2000. You can drive as far as you want, paint the thing glow-in-the-dark orange with magenta stripes, and spill coffee on the seats without sweating a big wear-and-tear bill down the road. Leasing for two years costs about $8,400, and you don't own the truck at lease end. Financing for two years costs about $16,560, but you own a truck worth about $8,500 when the payment book is empty, which makes your actual cost a tad over $8,000. Is leasing cheaper? Monthly payments, when compared to financing over the same term, are lower. But leasing is actually more expensive in the long run.

2) Restrictions. Leasing severely restricts your use of a vehicle. Mileage allowances are limited, modifications to the vehicle can result in hefty fines at the end of the lease, and if the vehicle is not in top condition when it is returned, excessive wear-and-tear charges may be levied. Many dealers will be more lenient if you buy or lease another vehicle from them at the end of your term, but if you drop off the car and walk, prepare yourself for some lease-end misery. Be sure to define these limitations at the beginning of the lease so that you know what you're getting yourself into. Find out what will be considered excessive in the wear-and-tear department and try to negotiate the mileage limit upwards.

3) How to lease. Never walk into a dealership and announce that you want to lease a car. Don't talk payment either. Concentrate on finding a car you like and know before you go into the dealership what you can afford. Most two- and three-year lease payments are calculated based on a *residual value* (the predicted value of the vehicle at the end of the lease term) of about half of the *Manufacturer's Suggested Retail Price* (MSRP). Sales tax is generally calculated using the MSRP as well, and a *money factor,* which is lease-speak for 'interest rate', is also involved in the calculation of a lease payment.

Calculating an exact lease payment is nearly impossible, but you can arrive at an approximate ball-park figure by using the following formula, which we will illustrate using a 1995 Escort GT as an example:

1995 Ford Escort GT Base MSRP	**$12,820**
Destination Charge	**$390**
Estimated Residual Value after 2 years	(50% of MSRP) $12,820 / 2 = **$6,410**
Sales Tax of 6%	(MSRP + Dest.) x 6% ($12,820 + $390) x 0.06 = **$792.60**
Money Factor of 6%	(MSRP + Residual Value) x 6% ($12,820 + $6,410) x 0.06 = **$1,153.80**
Total to be paid over 2-year term	(Res. Value + Sales Tax + Money Factor) $6,410 + $792.60 + $1,153.80 = **$8,356.40**
Divide by 24 months (2-year term)	**$348.18** per month with no money down.

Ford Motor Company, for example, has developed special calculators for the sole purpose of computing lease payments because the actual method is not nearly as simplistic as the one above, but using the ball-park figure of $348, you can find out whether or not an Escort GT fits your budget without having a salesman breathing down your neck, asking where he needs to be to get you to buy a car today.

Actual lease payments are affected by negotiation of the sticker price of the vehicle, term of the lease, available incentives, residual values, and layers of financial wizardry that even sales managers can't interpret without the magic of modern technology. Once you find a car you can afford, negotiate the sticker price and then explore leasing based on the negotiated price. Ask what the residual value is and subtract any rebates or incentives from the *Capitalized Cost* , which is lease-speak for 'selling price'. Use the formula above to calculate a ball-park figure, and if the dealer balks at your conclusion, ask them to explain the error of your ways.

4) Lease-end. Studies show that consumers generally like leases, right up until they end. The reason for their apprehension is rooted in the dark days of *open-end leasing*, when Joe Lessee was dealt a sucker punch by the lessor on the day Joe returned the car to the leasing agent. Back then, residual values were established at the end of the lease, wear-and-tear charges maxxed out credit cards and dealers laughed all the way to the S & L.

Leasing has evolved, and with today's *closed-end leases* (the only type of lease you should consider), the lease-end fees are quite minimal, unless the car has 100,000 miles on it, a busted-up grille, and melted chocolate smeared into the upholstery. Dealers want you to buy or lease another car from them, and can be rather lenient regarding excess mileage and abnormal wear. After all, if they hit you with a bunch of trumped-up charges, you're not going to remain a loyal customer, are you?

Additionally, closed-end leasing establishes the value of the car in advance, at the beginning of the lease. Also, any fees or charges you may incur at the lease-end are spelled out in detail before you sign the lease. All the worry is removed by the existence of concrete figures.

Another leasing benefit is the myriad of choices you have at the end of the term. Well, maybe not a myriad, but there are four, which is more than you have after two or three years of financing. They are:

a) Return the car to the dealer and walk away from it after paying any applicable charges such as a termination fee, wear-and-tear repairs, or excessive mileage bills. Of course, if you don't plan to buy or lease another car from the dealer, you may get hit for every minor thing, but dem's da risks.

b) Buy the car from the dealer for the residual value established at the beginning of the lease. If the car is in good shape, the residual value is probably lower than the true value of the car, making it a bargain, and many leasing companies will guarantee financing at the lowest interest rate available at the time your lease ends. We recommend this option if the lease vehicle is trashed, just to avoid the lease-end charges such a vehicle would certainly incur.

c) Use any equity in the car as leverage in a new deal with the dealer. Since residual values are generally set low, the car is likely worth more than the residual value at lease end. A well-maintained, low-mileage lease car should allow the dealer to knock off up to a couple of thousand bucks off your next deal.

d) Sell the car yourself and pay off the residual value, pocketing whatever profit you make.

Closed end leasing is a win-win situation for everybody. The manufacturer sells more cars, the dealer sells more cars, and you get low payments and a new car every couple of years. However, it is important to stress that you never own the car, and leasing could be quite restrictive. If you are a low-mileage driver who maintains cars in perfect condition, don't like tying up capital in down payments and don't mind never-ending car payments, leasing is probably just right for you. However, if you're on the road all day every day, beat the stuffing out of your wheels, enjoy a customized look or drive your cars until the wheels fall off, purchase whatever it is you're considering — it's way cheaper.

CUSTOMER REBATES:

Chrysler Corporation:

(Expire June 30, 1995. In lieu of rebate, 4.9 to 7.9% financing is offered.)

1995 Models:	
Chrysler Concorde	$1,000-1,500
Dodge Spirit	$1,500
Dodge Intrepid	$1,000-1,500
Dodge Ram Wagon (N/A B-150 SWB)	$500
Dodge Ram Van (N/A B-150 SWB)	$500
Eagle Vision	$500-1,500
Plymouth Acclaim	$1,500
Dodge/Plymouth Neon Highline w/D Pkg.	$400
Dodge/Plymouth Neon Highline w/F Pkg.	$500
Dodge/Plymouth Neon Sport w/K Pkg.	$600
All Minivans	$1,000

1994 Models:	
Chrysler LeBaron Sedan	$1,500
Dodge Spirit	$1,500
Plymouth Acclaim	$1,500
Dodge Ram Wagon (N/A B-150 SWB)	$2,000
Dodge Ram Van (N/A B-150 SWB)	$2,000
Dodge Dakota 4 cyl. (buyers under 30)	$300
Eagle Talon	$750
Jeep Wrangler 4 cyl.	$300
All Minivans	$1,500-2,000

Ford Motor Company:

(Expire July 5, 1995. In lieu of rebate, financing at 6.9% is available on Ford Taurus, SHO and Mercury Sable; 8.5% on other models)

1995 Models:	
Ford Taurus SHO	$1,500
Ford Taurus GL, SE, LX	$1,000
Ford Escort	$300
Ford Econoline E-150 w/RV Pkg.	$500
Ford Ranger 4 cyl.	$300
Lincoln Town Car	$1,500
Lincoln Mark VIII (except California)	$1,000
Mercury Sable	$1,000
Mercury Tracer	$300

Ford Motor Company (continued):

1994 Models:

Ford Taurus SHO	$1,500
Ford Taurus GL, LX	$1,000
Ford Aspire	$500
Ford Tempo	$500
Ford Escort	$300
Ford Econoline E-150 w/RV Pkg.	$1,500
Ford Club Wagon	$500
Ford Ranger 4 cyl.	$300
Lincoln Continental	$3,250
Lincoln Town Car	$2,000
Lincoln Mark VIII	$1,500
Mercury Sable	$1,000
Mercury Topaz	$500
Mercury Tracer	$300

DEALER INCENTIVES:

Cadillac: (1994 models, no expiration date)

Cadillac DeVille	$1,500
Cadillac Eldorado	$1,500
Cadillac Seville	$1,500

Isuzu: (No expiration date)

1995 Models:

Isuzu Rodeo (4WD)	$1,200
Isuzu Pickup	$750
Isuzu Trooper	$750
Isuzu Rodeo (2WD)	$500

1994 Models:

Isuzu Trooper	$1,250
Isuzu Rodeo (4WD)	$1,000
Isuzu Pickup	$750
Isuzu Rodeo (2WD)	$500

Oldsmobile: (1995 models through 1995 model year)

Oldsmobile Cutlass Supreme Convertible	$500

Suzuki: (1995 models. Expire July 31, 1995)

Sidekick 4-door	$200-400
Sidekick 2-door	$300

Edmund's ENTRY FORM

$10,000 WHEEL N'DEAL GIVE-AWAY

Edmund's is giving away $1,000 a month to lucky readers selected at random—see our announcement on the back cover of this book. To enter the drawing, complete the form below or provide the same information on a piece of paper and mail to:

Edmund Publications Corporation
300 N. Sepulveda Blvd., Suite 2050
El Segundo, CA 90245

NAME ______________________________

ADDRESS ______________________________

CITY, STATE, ZIP ______________________________

TELEPHONE ______________________________

NAME AND YEAR OF DESIRED AUTOMOBILE ______________________________

NAME, ADDRESS
AND PHONE OF ANY
DEALER IN YOUR AREA
SELLING THE CAR
YOU'RE SEEKING

____
____
____
____
____
____
____

WHEEL N'DEAL GIVE-AWAY Official Rules.

1. Identify any dealer in your area that sells the automobile you're seeking. Then, simply enter by sending us the name, address and phone for this dealer. NO PURCHASE IS NECESSARY TO PARTICIPATE OR WIN.

2. $1,000 cash prize will be awarded each month to a single entrant. Prizes will be awarded through hand-drawn drawings from all eligible entry forms timely received. The drawings will be under supervision of an independent organization (Edmund Publications' promotions department) whose decisions are final, binding and conclusive on all matters. Prizes will be awarded only if prize winner complies with these official rules. Only one winner per name or household. All prizes will be awarded.

3. Drawings will be held on the 25th day of each month starting January 1995, with the last drawing on October 25, 1995. Entry forms must be received by Edmund Publications by the end of business on the (20th) day of the month to be eligible to participate in the drawing for that month and all subsequent drawings. All eligible entry forms timely received will be automatically entered into each subsequent monthly drawing. Edmund Publications is not and will not be responsible for illegible, damaged, late, lost, or misdirected entry forms.

4. Winners will be notified by First Class Mail on or before the 15th day of the month following each drawing. Prize winners will be required to sign (a) a declaration of eligibility and release form whereby winners consent to the commercial use of their name for advertising without additional compensation and (b) any forms required by tax authorities within 21 days of notification or forfeit the prize.

5. Payment of all applicable federal, state and local taxes is the sole responsibility of and must be paid by the winner.

6. Contest is open to residents of the United States who are 18 years or older. Employees and their immediate families of Edmund Publications or any dealer listed in the Automobile Dealer Directory, or any company or individual engaged in the development, production or execution of this promotion are not eligible to participate. Residents of Florida are eligible to participate and to win prizes. Void where prohibited or restricted by law.

7. For a list of prize winners, official entry forms, or a copy of these official rules, send a stamped self-addressed envelope to: Wheel N'Deal Giveaway, c/o Edmund Publications Corp., 300 N. Sepulveda Blvd., Suite 2050, El Segundo, CA 90245.

8. Odds of winning are determined by the total number of entry forms received.

Automobile Dealer Directory

BMW

CONNECTICUT

BMW SAAB OF DARIEN
140 Ledge Road
Darien
Contact: Charles or Ron 203/656-1804

NEW YORK

PACE BMW
25 E. Main
New Rochelle
Contact: Jerry Silverstein 914/636-2000

BUICK

CALIFORNIA

MAGNUSSEN PONTIAC-BUICK-GMC
550 El Camino Real
Menlo Park
Contact: Steve Bridges 415/326-4100

MICHIGAN

SUPERIOR BUICK
15101 Michigan Avenue
Dearborn
Contact: Joe 313/846-0040

OHIO

SPITZER BUICK MITSUBISHI INC.
10901 Brookpark Road
Cleveland
Contact: John Caristo 216/362-1000

CADILLAC

CALIFORNIA

McCLEAN CADILLAC OLDS GMC-TRUCK
1 Auto Center Drive Tustin Auto Center
Tustin
Contact: Doris Hayes 714/731-0990

MASSACHUSETTS

FROST CADILLAC
399 Washington Street
Newton
Contact: Mark Gablehart 617/630-3000

CHEVROLET / GEO

ARIZONA

COURTESY CHEVROLET
1233 E. Camelback Road
Phoenix
Contact: Commercial Fleet Dept 602/279-3232

CALIFORNIA

CONNELL CHEVROLET
2828 Harbour Blvd
Costa Mesa
Contact: Eddie Cuadra or Gale Dalton 714/546-1200

MASSACHUSETTS

MCLAUGHLIN CHEVROLET INC.
741 Temple St. RT 27
Whitman
Contact: Ed Valante 617/447-4401

LANNAN CHEVROLET OLDSMOBILE GEO INC.
40 Winn
Woburn
Contact: Steve Alesse 617/935-2000

MICHIGAN

MATTHEWS HARGRAVES CHEVROLET
2000 E. 12 Mile Road
Royal Oak
Contact: Walter Tutak 810/398-8800

MINNESOTA

FRIENDLY CHEVROLET/GEO INC.
7501 N.E. Hwy 65
Fridley
Contact: John Langworthy
or Howie Lee 612/786-6100

NEWJERSEY

FISHER CHEVROLET/OLDSMOBILE
210 S. Washington Ave.
Bergenfield
Contact: Pat Sabino 201/384-5800

PINE BELT CHEVROLET/GEO
1088 State HWY 88
Lakewood
Contact: Gil Casorla **908/363-2900**

NEW YORK

AMITY CHEVROLET INC.
20 Merick Road
Amityville
Contact: Chris Sadusky 516/264-0909

NORTH CAROLINA

POWERS-SWAIN CHEVROLET/GEO
4709 Bragg Boulevard
Fayetteville
Contact: Gary Brown 800/467-5135

SOUTH CAROLINA

NEWSOME CHEVY WORLD GEO IMPORTS
4013 W. Beltline Blvd
Columbia
Contact: John Guertler or Stan Godfrey 803/254-1431

TEXAS

NORMAN FREDE CHEVROLET
16801 Feather Craft
Houston
Contact: Bob Ondrias **713/486-2200**

CHRYSLER/PLYMOUTH

CALIFORNIA

CHASE CHRYSLER/ PLYMOUTH/SUZUKI
2979 Auto Center Circle
Stockton
Contact: Ted Yee .... 209/956-7600 or 209/956-7617

For a Dealer in your area, dial 1-716-633-8856

CONNECTICUT

CALLARI CHRYSLER/PLYMOUTH JEEP/EAGLE
840 E. Main Street
Stamford
Contact: Joe Palumbury 203/326-7800

MASSACHUSETTS

DEDHAM–WEST ROXBURY CHRYSLER/PLYMOUTH INC.
17 Eastern Avenue at Dedham Square
Dedham
Contact: Pat Joyce Sr. or Mike Walsh 617/326-4040

OHIO

BOB CALDWELL CHRYSLER/PLYMOUTH
1888 Morse
Columbus
Contact: Doug Berger 614/888-2331

PENNSYLVANIA

SOUTH HILLS CHRYSLER/PLYMOUTH
3344 Washington Road
McMurray
Contact: Larry Winter 412/941-4300

DODGE

ILLINOIS

ANDERSON DODGE
5711 E. State
Rockford
Contact: Ron Heinkle or Mark Hauger 815/229-2000

ED NAPLETON DODGE
6550 W. 95th Street
Oak Lawn
Contact: Scott Pflanz 708/233-1800

MASSACHUSETTS

MOTOR MART DODGE
800 Washington Street
S. Attleboro
Contact: Martin Lamoreaux 508/761-5400

MARYLAND

FITZGERALD AUTO-MALL WHITE FLINT
11411 Rockville Pike
North Bethesda
Contact: Sam Weisgal 301/881-4000

WESTMINSTER DODGE INC.
720 Morrissey Blvd.
Boston
Contact: Bob Bickford 800/274-9922

NEW JERSEY

MOTOR WORLD DODGE HYUNDAI
315 Rt 4 West
Paramus
Contact: Phil Bell 201/488-9000

PENNSYLVANIA

DEVON HILL DODGE
20 West Lancaster Avenue
Devon
Contact: Chuck O'Keefe 610/687-9350

LANCASTER DODGE
1475 Manheim Pike
Lancaster
Contact: Jerry Cutler or Russ Osborne 717/393-0625

NORWIN DODGE
13230 Rt 30
N. Huntington
Contact: Jack Butler or Scott Gutshall 412/864-0140

WASHINGTON

TACOMA DODGE
4101 S. Tacoma Way
Tacoma
Contact: Bob Ward/John R. 206/475-7300

WISCONSIN

DODGE CITY
4640 South 27th
Milwaukee
Contact: Frank Brugger 414/281-9100

FORD

ARIZONA

BELL FORD
2401 West Bell Road
Phoenix
Contact: Larry Barnes 602/866-1776

CALIFORNIA

AIRPORT MARINA FORD
5880 Centinela Avenue
Los Angeles
Contact: Bob Garcia 310/649-3673

EL CAJON FORD
1595 E. Main Street
El Cajon
Contact: Phil Smithey 619/579-8888

HANSEL FORD
3075 Corby Avenue
Santa Rosa
Contact: Joe, Ed or Paul 707/525-3688
or 800/956-5556

S & C FORD & CITY LEASING
2001 Market Street
San Francisco
Contact: Ray Scioto 415/861-6000

SUBURBAN FORD
4625 Madison Avenue
Sacramento
Contact: Barbara Morgan 916/331-7600

SUN VALLEY AUTO PLAZA
2285 Diamond Blvd.
Concord
Contact: Geoff Dettlinger
or Dan Stillman 510/686-3325

HAWAII

CUTTER FORD/ISUZU INC.
98-015 Kamehameha Highway
Aiea
Contact: Tom Nakama or Dennis Ouchi 808/487-3811

For a Dealer in your area, dial 1-716-633-8856

Automobile Dealer Directory

ILLINOIS

JOE COTTON FORD
175 West North Avenue
Carol Stream
Contact: Kimberly Schweppe 708/682-9200

MASSACHUSETTS

MAIN STREET AUTO SALES
1022 Main Street
Waltham
Contact: Justin Barrett or Julius Simon 617/894-8000

MINNESOTA

FREEWAY FORD
9700 Lyndale Avenue
Minneapolis
Contact: Dick Lewis 612/888-9481

MISSOURI

CAVALIER FORD INC.
7501 Manchester Avenue
St. Louis
Contact: Jim Danner 314/645-2780

NEW JERSEY

KEATS FORD
2865 Brunswick Park
Lawrenceville
Contact: Joseph Keats or Gary Glauser 609/883-3400

LARSON FORD INC.
1150 State HWY 88
Lakewood
Contact: Bob Taurosa or Bob Eden 908/363-8100

MULLANE FORD
241 N. Washington Avenue
Bergenfield
Contact: Pat Moran 201/385-6500

NEW YORK

ASPEN FORD INC.
855 65th Street
Brooklyn
Contact: Pat DiDomenico or Rich Willis 718/921-9100

NORTH CAROLINA

CAPITAL FORD INC.
4900 Capital Blvd.
Raleigh
Contact: Steve Williams 919/790-4653

OHIO

PEFFLEY FORD
4600 N. Main Street
Dayton
Contact: Jake Cabay 513/278-7921

OREGON

HARVEST FORD LINCOLN/MERCURY
2833 Washburn Way
Klamath Falls
Contact: Gary Creese 503/884-3121

PENNSYLVANIA

NORRISTOWN FORD
Ridge Pike & Trooper
Norristown
Contact: Joe Lutz or Andy Stratz 215/539-5400

TEXAS

LEE JARMON FORD
1635 I-35 East
Carrollton
Contact: John Prouty 214/242-0682

LONE STAR FORD INC.
8477 North Freeway
Houston
Contact: Charlie Bradt or Teddy Dikas 713/931-3300

VIRGINIA

BEACH FORD INC.
2717 Virginia Beach Blvd.
Virginia Beach
Contact: Dick Phelps or Bob Macomber 804/486-2717
or 804/766-0497

KOONS FORD INC.
1051 E. Broad Street
Falls Church
Contact: Sean Polk 703/241-7200

HONDA

CALIFORNIA

GOUDY HONDA
1400 W. Main Street
Alhambra
Contact: Terry McCarton or Mike Tognetti 818/576-1114
213/283-7336, 800/423-1114

JIM DOTEN'S HONDA
2600 Shattuck Avenue
Berkeley
Contact: Stewart Petersen, Fleet Dept 510/843-3704

SAN FRANCISCO HONDA/KIA
10 South Van Ness Ave.
San Francisco
Contact: Brent Miletich or Philip Mah 415/441-2000
Beeper 415/202-6361

CONNECTICUT

SCHALLER
HONDA OLDS MITSU SUBARU
1 Veterans Drive
New Britain
Contact: Gary Turchetta 203/223-2230

For a Dealer in your area, dial 1-716-633-8856

FLORIDA

HOLLYWOOD HONDA
1450 N. State Road 7
Hollywood
Contact: Tom Frondczak or Alberto Verne 305/989-1600

MASSACHUSETTS

DARTMOUTH HONDA/VOLVO
26 State Rd.
North Dartmouth
Contact: Jim DiCostanzo or Dominic Caledonia 508/996-6800

NEW JERSEY

HONDA OF ESSEX
1170 Bloomfield Ave.
West Caldwell
Contact: Sales Manager 201/808-9100

VIP HONDA
555 Somerset Street/Corner of Rt 22 East
North Plainfield
Contact: Ron Lombardi 908/371-3752

NEW YORK

BAY RIDGE HONDA
8801 4th Avenue
Brooklyn
Contact: Phil Donati or Hank Berntsen 718/836-4600

PACE HONDA
25 E. Main
New Rochelle
Contact: Dave Haines 914/636-2000

WISCONSIN

DAVID HOBBS HONDA
6100 North Green Bay Avenue
Milwaukee
Contact: Randy Wilson or Jeff Hansen 414/352-6100

JEEP/EAGLE

Jeep

MICHIGAN

MIKE MILLER JEEP/EAGLE
6540 South Cedar
Lansing
Contact: Mike Hornberger 517/394-2770

NEW JERSEY

SALERNO DUANE JEEP/EAGLE
267 Broad Street
Summit
Contact: Steve Memolo 908/277-6700

LEXUS

FLORIDA

LEXUS OF KENDALL
10943 South Dixie Highway
Miami
Contact: Terry Bean 305/669-0522 x450

NEW JERSEY

PRESTIGE LEXUS
955 State Hwy 17
Ramsey
Contact: Bill Berradino 201/825-5200

LINCOLN/MERCURY

CALIFORNIA

TORRANCE LINCOLN/MERCURY VOLKS/HYUNDAI
20460 Hawthorne Blvd.
Torrance
Contact: Carol Wagner 310/370-6311

ILLINOIS

SCHAUMBURG LINCOLN/MERCURY
1200 E Golf Road
Schaumberg
Contact: Val Kholudovsky 708/882-4100

MICHIGAN

MIKE MILLER LINCOLN/MERCURY
6540 South Cedar
Lansing
Contact: Mike Hornberger 517/394-2770

NEW JERSEY

WESTWOOD LINCOLN/MERCURY
55 Kinderkamack Road
Emerson
Contact: Charlie Featherstone 201/265-7700

NEW YORK

L & B LINCOLN/MERCURY
520 Montauk Highway
West Babylon
Contact: Phil Calabretta 516/669-2600

OREGON

HARVEST FORD LINCOLN/MERCURY
2833 Washburn Way
Klamath Falls
Contact: Gary Creese 503/884-3121

PENNSYLVANIA

NORTHEAST LINCOLN/MERCURY
7001 Roosevelt Blvd
Philadelphia
Contact: Lori Swenson 215/331-6600

For a Dealer in your area, dial 1-716-633-8856

SOUTH HILLS LINCOLN/MERCURY
2760 Washington Road
Pittsburgh
Contact: Dave Arbogast 412/941-1600

TEXAS

W.O. BANKSTON LINCOLN/MERCURY SAAB
4747 LBJ Freeway
Dallas
Contact: Bill Richburg or Alex Nieto 214/233-1441

MAZDA

PENNSYLVANIA

MARTY SUSSMAN MAZDA
Jenkintown & Baeder Roads
Jenkintown
Contact: Eric Weitz or Rick Loeffler 215/887-1800

MERCEDES-BENZ

GEORGIA

CARRIAGE HOUSE IMPORTS
I-85 at Exit 14 (Flat Shoals Road)
Atlanta
Contact: Bill Harton-Fleet Manager 404/964-1600
FAX: 404/969-7456

MITSUBISHI

MASSACHUSETTS

BERNARDI MITSUBISHI
671 Worcester Rd.
Natick
Contact: George Ellis 508/655-8588

NEW JERSEY

HOLMAN MITSUBISHI
State Hwys 38 & 73
Maple Shade
Contact: Scott Gallaher 609/235-5454

NISSAN

CALIFORNIA

CONCORD NISSAN INC.
1290 Concord Avenue
Concord
Contact: Jack Tarafevic, Shawn Mosley 510/676-4400

FLORIDA

PRECISION NISSAN
4600 N. Dale Mabry Hwy
Tampa
Contact: Joe Wiggins 813/870-3333

GEORGIA

BOOMERSHINE NISSAN OF DECATUR
1625 Church Street
Decatur
Contact: Jeff Slocum **404/292-3853**

ILLINOIS

CONTINENTAL NISSAN
5750 South La Grange Road
Countryside
Contact: Mike Bromer/Tim Duda 708/352-9200

MASSACHUSETTS

FROST NISSAN
1180 Washington Street
West Newton
Contact: Dan Favre 617/630-3050

NEW JERSEY

CHERRY HILL NISSAN
State Hwy 39 & Cooper Landing
Cherry Hill
Contact: Marvin, Frank,
or Freeman **609/667-8300**

MOTOR WORLD NISSAN MAZDA VOLKS
340 Sylvan Avenue Rt 9W
Englewood Cliffs
Contact: Jeff Montemuro 201/568-4400
or 201/567-9000

NEW YORK

GEIS NISSAN
Rt 6 & Westbrook Drive
Peekskill
Contact: Tom Conaty
or Steve Pinto 914/528-4347x859/878

PENNSYLVANIA

CONCORDVILLE NISSAN
RT 202 South
Concordville
Contact: Gregory Brown 215/459-8900

WISCONSIN

ROSEN NISSAN INC.
5505 South 27th
Milwaukee
Contact: Scott Levy 414/282-9300

OLDSMOBILE

NEW JERSEY

LENIHAN OLDSMOBILE JEEP/EAGLE
Rte 73 South
Marlton
Contact: Tom Lewis 609/983-3800

PONTIAC

CALIFORNIA

MAGNUSSEN PONTIAC-BUICK-GMC
550 El Camino Real
Menlo Park
Contact: Steve Bridges 415/326-4100

ILLINOIS

JOE COTTON PONTIAC/GMC TRUCK INC.
271 East North Avenue
Glendale Heights
Contact: Kimberly Schweppe 708/682-9200

For a Dealer in your area, dial 1-716-633-8856

Automobile Dealer Directory

MASSACHUSETTS

NEWTON PONTIAC GMC
1203 Washington Street
Newton
Contact: Peter Caliendo 617/969-7800

MISSOURI

ROBERTS-ALBRAIGHT PONTIAC/GMC TRUCK
9425 Holmes
Kansas City
Contact: Jerry Payne 816/361-8520

NEW YORK

GEIS PONTIAC BUICK OLDS CADILLAC
Rt 6 & Westbrook Drive
Peekskill
Contact: Ed Rice
or Jim Lockwood 914/528-4347x811/866

NEW JERSEY

SALERNO DUANE PONTIAC
267 Broad Street
Summit
Contact: Steve Memolo 908/277-6700

TOYOTA

ARIZONA

CAMELBACK TOYOTA
1500 East Camelback Road
Phoenix
Contact: Vic Schafer 602/274-9576

CALIFORNIA

KEARNEY MESA TOYOTA
5090 Kearney Mesa Road
San Diego
Contact: Mike Hunter 619/279-8151

TOYOTA OF NORTH HOLLYWOOD
4100 Lankershim
North Hollywood
Contact: Pam Morgan or Irene Samaltanos 818/508-2900

CONNECTICUT

GIRARD TOYOTA/BMW
543 Colman Street
New London
Contact: Larry Main 203/447-3141

FLORIDA

KENDALL TOYOTA
10943 South Dixie Highway
Miami
Contact: Frank Marsala 305/665-6581 x323

PRECISION TOYOTA INC.
10909 N. Florida Avenue
Tampa
Contact: Brad Savelli or Matt Coffey 813/933-6402

MASSACHUSETTS

WOBURN FOREIGN MOTORS
394 Washington Street
Woburn
Contact: Stephan Harasim 617/933-1100

MINNESOTA

RUDY LUTHER'S TOYOTA
8801 Wayzata Blvd
Minneapolis
Contact: Larry Fenton or Curt Folstad 612/544-1313

NEW JERSEY

BOB CIASULLI MONMOUTH TOYOTA
700 State Hwy 36
Eatontown
Contact: Allison Guttman 908/544-1000

NEW YORK

GEIS TOYOTA
Rt 6 & Westbrook Drive
Peekskill
Contact: Joe Trabucco
or Pat Canavan 914/528-4347x880/894

OHIO

KINGS TOYOTA/SUZUKI
9500 Kings Automall Road
Cincinnati
Contact: Greg Plowman 513/683-5440

TEXAS

STERLING McCALL TOYOTA
9400 Southwest Freeway
Houston
Contact: Tanya Tolander 713/270-3974

VOLVO

MASSACHUSETTS

DARTMOUTH HONDA/VOLVO
26 State Rd.
North Dartmouth
Contact: Jim DiCostanzo or Dominic Caledonia 508/996-6800

BUYER'S DECISION GUIDES
SCHEDULED RELEASE DATES FOR 1995/6*

VOL. 29		RELEASE DATE	COVER DATE
U2903	USED CARS: PRICES & RATINGS	JUL 95	FALL 95
U2904	USED CARS: PRICES & RATINGS	OCT 95	WINTER 96
N2903	NEW CAR PRICES [American & Import]	DEC 95	WINTER 96
S2903	NEW PICKUP, VAN & SPORT UTILITY PRICES	DEC 95	WINTER 96

VOL. 30			
U3001	USED CARS: PRICES & RATINGS	JAN 96	SPRING 96
N3001	NEW CAR PRICES [American & Import]	MAR 96	SPRING 96
S3001	NEW PICKUP, VAN & SPORT UTILITY PRICES	MAR 96	SPRING 96
U3002	USED CARS: PRICES & RATINGS	APR 96	SUMMER 96
N3002	NEW CAR PRICES [American & Import]	JUNE 96	SUMMER 96
S3002	NEW PICKUP, VAN & SPORT UTILITY PRICES	JUNE 96	SUMMER 96
U3003	USED CARS: PRICES & RATINGS	JULY 96	FALL 96
U3004	USED CARS: PRICES & RATINGS	OCT 96	WINTER 96

**Subject to Change*